ABSORBING PERFECTIONS

ABSORBING PERFECTIONS

KABBALAH AND INTERPRETATION

MOSHE IDEL

FOREWORD BY
HAROLD BLOOM

YALE UNIVERSITY PRESS / NEW HAVEN & LONDON

Published with the assistance of the Ernst Cassirer Publications Fund.

Designed by Mary Valencia and set in Quadraat type by Keystone Typesetting, Inc., Orwigsburg, Pennsylvania.

Printed in the United States of America by Vail-Ballou Press, Binghamton, New York.

Cataloging-in-Publication Data
Idel, Moshe, 1947–
Absorbing perfections : Kabbalah and interpretation / Moshe Idel.
p. cm.
Includes bibliographical references and index.
ISBN 0-300-08379-3 (alk. paper)
1. Cabala—History. 2. Bible. O.T. Pentateuch—Criticism, interpretation, etc., Jewish. I. Title.
BM526 .I295 2002
296.1′6—dc21
2001006563

A catalogue record for this book is available from the British Library.

The paper in this book meets the guidelines for permanence and durability of the Committee on Production Guidelines for Book Longevity of the Council on Library Resources.

10 9 8 7 6 5 4 3 2

The entire world is within
the Torah
and we are all of us in
the Torah
and from within it we see
and from it we do not stray.
  —ABRAHAM ABULAFIA, *SEFER SITREI TORAH,* 1280

There is nothing new
that is not found in the Torah,
neither the prophets, nor the Hagiography,
nor the sayings of the sages,
or what has been innovated
and will be innovated from now forever.
  —MOSES CORDOVERO, *SEFER 'OR YAQAR,* ca. 1555

Toute chose sacrée
et qui veut demeurer sacrée
s'enveloppe de mystère.
Les religions se retranchent à
l'abri d'arcanes devoilés
au seul prédestiné:
l'art a les siens.
  —STÉPHANE MALLARMÉ, *HÉRÉSIES ARTISTIQUES,* 1862

Decipher! Decipher! Then you will experience
the vertigo of human absolute.
         —SALVADOR DALÍ

CONTENTS

CONTENTS

FOREWORD
Harold Bloom

Moshe Idel, born in 1947, submitted his doctoral dissertation on the Kabbalah of Abraham Abulafia to the Hebrew University, Jerusalem, in 1976. In the quarter-century since, his researches and publications have reconfigured the field of Kabbalistic study, essentially founded by his majestic precursor, Gershom Scholem (1897–1982). Half-a-century younger than Scholem, Idel is both Scholem's successor and his major revisionist. It is not too much to speak of the Kabbalah of Gershom Scholem and the Kabbalah of Moshe Idel, since these great scholars are as much visionary speculators as they are historians of what can be called "Jewish mysticism," though I distrust that term and will not use it again here. Scholem—I would not say "in conversation" since one learned to listen to him—spoke with authority, and with more than a scholarly immersion in Kabbalah. One can speak of conversations with Idel, but there also one hears a Kabbalistic voice, experiential as well as historical, which speaks with authority in both realms.

I hesitate to describe the present book as Moshe Idel's masterpiece, since his is a life's work-in-progress, but *Absorbing Perfections: Kabbalah and Interpretation* is certainly his most important volume so far, fulfilling much of the project first set forth in *Kabbalah: New Perspectives* (1988). Since I myself am a literary critic and not a Kabbalistic scholar, this Foreword will address itself largely to three matters: the relationship between Scholem's and Idel's achievements; Idel's account of the arcanization of the canon of the Hebrew Bible and of the exegetical modes that emerged to decode the arcana; the significance of Idel for interpretive procedures not in themselves Kabbalistic, nor even concerned with Kabbalah.

Kabbalah, a word meaning "tradition" with the nuance of "reception," originally referred to the entire vast body of the Jewish Oral Law, but from about 1200 on it became more specific. The term was applied to the teachings of the Ravad (Rabbi Abraham ben David), the great sage of the twelfth-century Jews of Provence. His son, Isaac the Blind, composed the first texts of Kabbalah proper, as commentaries upon the *Sefer Yezirah* (Book of Creation), which exists in two tenth-century versions and which must be much older (perhaps third century). The *Book of Creation* says that God made the world with ten *Sefirot* (possibly just the numbers one through ten) and the twenty-two letters of the Hebrew alphabet.

There were many pre-Kabbalistic (a term no Kabbalist would accept) commentaries on the *Book of Creation*, all of them quite normative. The next esoteric work was the *Book Bahir*, or "Book of Brightness," which scholars date as thirteenth century. We thus have the puzzle of a thousand years of Oral Tradition between the *Book of Creation* and *Book of Brightness*. To a true Kabbalist, this is no problem at all, since Kabbalah insists it is the esoteric side of the Oral Torah that Moses received from God at Sinai. In the *Bahir*, the *Sefirot* are what they have been ever since, the ten divine attributes, principles, or powers. Isaac the Blind circulated his treatises secretly, after dictating them to favorite disciples. It is generally agreed that Isaac re-created the *Sefirot* and that he reconceptualized God as the *en-sof*, an intranslatable Infinite. Kabbalah itself has a canonical text that is postbiblical, the *Zohar* of Moses de Leon, a book-of-books written in Guadalajara, Spain, from 1280 through 1286, but attributed by its author to much more ancient sages. The *Zohar* hardly required arcanization, but as the canonical work for Kabbalists it provoked exegetical speculation that transcends even its intricate splendors. From Isaac the Blind onward, the Kabbalah as Scholem and Idel study it was essentially formed, though the *Zohar* elaborated it magnificently.

Idel's *Absorbing Perfections: Kabbalah and Interpretation* takes all this, and much more, as the given, and works on from there. His purpose is to show the Kabbalists' very varied ways of locating the central values of the Hebrew Bible, and also to illuminate their modes of interpretation for revealing those values. This purpose was Gershom Scholem's before it was Moshe Idel's: what is the difference between these two masters of Kabbalah? Idel's reverent critique of Scholem informs all his writings; in *Messianic Mystics* (1998), he speaks of "an oftentimes critical dialogue with the magisterial studies" of his precursor. In the most memorable chapter (7, "Ancient Jewish Theurgy") of *Kabbalah: New Perspectives*, Idel dissents from Scholem's great essay on "Tradition and New Creation in the Ritual of the Kabbalists." Scholem contrasts the ritual of rabbinical Judaism, which "makes nothing happen and *transforms* nothing" with rituals established by Isaac Luria (1534–1572), the innovative genius who created later Kabbalism in Safed, Palestine. In Lurianic Kabbalah, myth reenters Judaism, according to Scholem. Idel regards this as Scholem's own powerful myth, based upon "a simplistic division between a defeated mythical Gnosticism and a triumphant rabbinism." Against this, Idel argues that ancient Jewish theurgy, the augmentation of God by man, continued throughout normative rabbinism. Idel's emphasis upon the esoteric elements in ancient Jewish religion seems to me the center of his *Kabbalah: New Perspectives*, since it marks "the beginning of a return to another approach to Judaism," as he inscribed a copy of the book for me in 1988.

Judaism, like Christianity, is a belated religion: both stem from the Roman destruction of the Jerusalem Temple in 70 C.E. Judaism before that was a transitional seething of rival sects, including the followers of Jesus, among whom St. Paul won out over James the brother of Jesus. The ultimate heirs of James and his Ebionites, or "poor men," were Muhammad and Islam. The great puzzle remains: what was the archaic Jewish religion? The Kabbalistic answer always has been that Kabbalah was, which is both impossible and yet intriguing, and which is an element in the rival speculations on the origins of pre-Judaism by Scholem and by Idel.

Scholem was not a Jewish Gnostic, but accurately could be termed a Gnostic Jew on the basis of his re-creation of Kabbalah, in which such astonishing figures as Sabbatai Zevi, Nathan of Gaza, and Jacob Frank received scrutinies as sympathetic as were accorded to Moses Cordovero, Isaac Luria, and Hayym Vital. Since Kabbalah in Scholem is identified with the genius of the Jewish religion, for Scholem even its deviant spirits are not heretics (unless they turned Christian). But Idel has no deep quarrel with Scholem upon this, since his own Kabbalism is equally intense. Visionaries do not like to think of themselves as agonistic, and Idel doubtless will not welcome my suggestion that his "critical dialogue" with Scholem has its hidden model in Jacob's wrestling with a nameless one among the *elohim* in order to win the new name of Israel. Hemingway had the audacity to say he was in training in order to go fifteen rounds with Count Leo Tolstoy, but that is not a Kabbalistic trope. Still, Kabbalah always insists it came early, not late, in Jewish spiritual history, yet to come after the Hebrew Bible and the Babylonian Talmud is necessarily to be belated, and to come after Gershom Scholem as historian-exegete of Kabbalah is also to battle belatedness. Idel's relation to Scholem is like that of the Romantic poets to John Milton, and there is something distinctly Miltonic in Scholem's Kabbalistic authority. You can correct and complete Scholem, which are the wise ambitions of Idel, but you cannot displace him, as Idel is first to acknowledge.

Idel's most compelling challenge to Scholem always has been to question the master's judgment that the eruption of Kabbalah in thirteenth-century Provence and Catalonia represented an influx of a long-dormant Jewish Gnosticism back into Jewish spirituality. Shrewdly, Idel has argued that ancient Gnosticism itself derives from Jewish speculations upon the *Anthropos*, or Divine Man, Enoch, who did not die but was mutated into the startling Angel Metatron. The second-century exemplar of the *minim*, or heretics, Elisha Ben Abuyah, is reputed to have ascended to heaven, where he saw two enthroned Gods, Yahweh and Metatron, the God-Man. Reconstructing the ancient Jewish foundations of Gnosticism, Idel turned Scholem's argument on its head, but in a manner that I think would not altogether have displeased Scholem. Like Idel, Scholem credited the Kabbalistic assertion of its continuity with an esoteric Oral Tradition, and in any case Scholem told me that both Gnosticism and Neo-Platonism, in his intuitive judgment, as well as the Hermetic Corpus, all had emerged from Jewish Alexandria. Idel does not go so far (as yet), but in this regard anyway his revision of Scholem is quite Scholemian.

Idel always has been wary of Scholem's tendency to ascribe Kabbalistic transformations to the direct effect of Jewish catastrophes, such as the Spanish Expulsion. Again, this is a disagreement mostly in degree and not in kind, almost as if Idel's aim is to sharpen Scholem's focus. Idel follows Kabbalistic tradition in being reticent about his own spiritual stance; he has published no equivalent of Scholem's fascinating "Ten Unhistorical Aphorisms on Kabbalah" (1958), in which Scholem reaffirms that the authentic Kabbalah remains hidden; that Torah and God, being one, both cannot be known; that the name of God reaches us only in fragments; and that Kafka was secular Kabbalah, whose writings therefore possess "something of the strong light of the canonical, of that perfection which destroys." Against this, Idel champions the canonical, both Scriptural and Kabbalistic, as "the perfection which absorbs." Against the Kafkan emphasis upon the Negative, Idel urges the *plenitude* of Bible, Talmud, and Kabbalah, and sets himself the task of so relating Kabbalah to interpretation that we are taught the work of "absorbing perfections."

Again, Idel is not overthrowing Scholem, but treats Scholem as another canonical work, whose arcana can be revealed through positive modes of interpretation. Scholem's disciples are displeased by this, but I suspect that Scholem himself would have been delighted, since his own Jewish Gnosticism was not dualistic and constituted for him the essence of Judaism. Hans Jonas, who with his friend Scholem made a formidable exegetical pairing, disliked the idea of a Jewish Gnosticism, and several times in discussion with me said that Idel's quest to uncover "another approach to Judaism" was bound to fail, because the archaic Jewish religion, whatever it may have been, was not to be traced. Scholem, Jonas, Henry Corbin, and Idel seem to me the inescapable fourfold of Western scholarship on esotericism or gnosis, and Idel may yet find in Kabbalah a decoding instrument of interpretation that will answer Jonas's skepticism.

Absorbing Perfections is an advanced work, going beyond Idel's previous studies of Kabbalah. Its difficulties are legitimate and rewarding, not only for the understanding of Kabbalah by general readers like myself, but also for other common readers who have wearied of postmodernist negations of interpretation and are more than ready to welcome a plenitude of meaning, in the Bible and in Kabbalah and in secular canonical works as well, from Dante and Shakespeare on to Paul Celan and Samuel Beckett. What Idel calls "the absorbing quality of the Torah" is akin to the absorbing quality of Shakespeare or of Joyce. Strong authors, like sacred texts, can be defined as those with the capacity to *absorb* us. To "absorb," in American English, means several related processes: to take something in as through the pores, or to engross one's full interest or attention, or to assimilate fully. At the beginning of Chapter 5 Idel defines his "absorbing":

> I use this term in order to convey the expanding comprehensiveness of the concept of the text which, moving to the center of the Jewish society, also integrated attributes reminiscent of wider entities like the world or God. This expansion facilitated the attribution of more dynamic qualities to the text conceived of as capable of allowing various types of influences on processes taking place in the world, in God, and in the human psyche.

That is certainly an interpretative principle of plenitude, and I find it vastly preferable to our current academic modes of reading Shakespeare, in which *King Lear* is seen as being shaped by cultural and historical circumstances, rather than by William Shakespeare, strongest of all authors. I myself read, teach, and write about Shakespeare as someone who is absorbing perfections, conceiving his text as influencing what takes place in the world and in the human psyche, and even in

God, if there is God. Shakespeare, like the Bible or Dante or the *Zohar*, absorbs us even as we absorb him, or them. Historicizing Hamlet or Lear breaks down very quickly: they themselves are the perfections that absorb us all.

Moshe Idel, as I write, sits at his desk in Jerusalem, finishing a book to be called *Kabbalah and Eros*, and starting another on Kabbalah and the Great Chain of Being. He can hear gunfire as he writes, and though I regard myself as a Jewish Gnostic, unable to pray to the alienated God, I would pray for his safety if I could. Like Scholem before him, he has made Kabbalah his life's enterprise, and like Scholem his work has become essential for anyone who desires to confront Kabbalah, and find herself there, more truly and more strange.

PREFACE

The present book deals mainly with material found in a vast body of literature designated by its authors and by modern scholars as Kabbalah. Basically a medieval corpus, this literature consists of a variety of schools, trends, models, ideals, and techniques. Influenced by many intellectual and spiritual streams—Platonism and Neoplatonism, Aristotelianism and Neoaristotelianism, Muslim Sufism and Isma'iliah, Christianity, hermeticism, magic, and astrology, to enumerate only the major external influences—Kabbalistic literature nevertheless remained much more exegetical than any of these other literatures, because many of its interests centered on topics found in sacred texts. Kabbalists developed theories about the nature of the scriptures, techniques of exegesis, and the interpretive process. In so doing, they were deeply affected by the rabbinic and other earlier Jewish esoteric literatures, as well as the various spiritual alternatives that qualified their approach to their Jewish predecessors. In order to do justice to the rich Kabbalistic trends, our discussions will have to address both the Jewish antecedents and the intellectual categories accepted from the intellectual surroundings. I thereby hope to allow a much greater role to these two main sources of Kabbalistic hermeneutics than has been done previously. At the same time, I shall attempt to differentiate, much more than has been done in the dominant forms of Kabbalistic scholarship, among several types of Kabbalistic hermeneutics.

In the following chapters I examine passages and concepts found in a variety of Jewish literatures. In their arrangement I have preferred a more thematic and diachronical approach to a historical and synchronic one. As I am most interested in the development of major themes, of methods of interpretation, or even of an exegetical system, I have adopted a vision of those themes as quite continuous, all the while acknowledging the existence of deep changes over time. Skeptical as I am that an inventory of everything found in a certain period of time can exhaust the most significant processes defining the history of Jewish mystical hermeneutics—and wary, too, of who gets to decide what a meaningful period is—I strive to trace the major stages of the development of central hermeneutical concepts in Jewish mysticism: the nature of the text, the different forms of interpretation, and the experience of the mystical interpreter. The centrality and paramount importance of these topics for understanding most of the forms of Jewish mysticism places an immense amount of discussion at the disposition of scholars.

Some of the materials treated and approaches adopted here are indebted to a lengthy article published in Hebrew in the early 1980s entitled "The Concept of the Torah in the Heikhalot Literature, and Its Reverberations in Kabbalah." The great number of texts cited, and the concise style and density of their discussion, rendered the article almost inaccessible to many scholars dealing with the Heikhalot literature or with Jewish hermeneutics. Over the years more detailed analyses of some matters dealt with in that article, new material, and, I hope, a more sophisticated approach emerged in various studies I published, some of which constitute the core of the first part of the present book. Some of the chapters were written independently for this book, especially those dealing with exegetical techniques in Kabbalah, and they make up the second part of the book. All previous analyses, however, have been reconsidered, updated, and completed in the course of preparing this book. Since the manuscript was submitted for publication, three books having implications for themes treated herein have appeared: Elliot Wolfson's *Abraham Abulafia* (2000), Yehuda Liebes's *Ars Poetica* (2000), and Moshe Halbertal's *Concealment and Revelation* (2001); unfortunately, it has not been possible to adequately take their findings into account.

Thanks are due to friends who read the book and suggested improvements: Harold Bloom of Yale University, Brian Stock of the University of Toronto, and Shira Wolosky and Amira Liver of Hebrew University. The book was written over several years during which I served as senior scholar at the Shalom Hartman Institute of Advanced Judaic Studies in Jerusalem. The institute provided an encouraging and challenging intellectual ambiance that contributed to the emergence and the writing of this book. Richard Miller has graciously edited the manuscript and improved my English. In the final stage, the generosity of Jeffrey Neuman helped see this book into print.

INTRODUCTION

I. Arcanization and Exegetical Methods

Two main processes informed most of the speculative hermeneutical corpora in the postbiblical forms of Judaism. The first is the expansion of the relevance of the content of the canonical texts to increasingly more cosmological, theosophical, intellectual, and psychological realms than those ancient texts themselves claimed to engage. This expansion is often related to processes of arcanization, secretive understandings of the canonical texts understood as pointing to these realms in allusive ways: anagrammatic, numerical, allegorical, or symbolic.

The other main process is intimately intertwined with the first: it consists in the emergence of complex exegetical systems that present specific methods to decode the arcana believed to be concealed within the canonical texts. This proliferation of exegetical systems is a corollary of the expansion of the content dimensions of the classical texts. The arcanization processes, then, should be understood as having some boundaries, which means that the term *arcana* in its various Hebrew forms is used only in order to disclose it. As I understand it, arcanization does not mean the creation of a concept of text that is opaque since the arcana cannot be decoded. No special process of arcanization is related to a transformation of the text as transcendental. Secrets are commensurable to the methods that will resolve the enigma implied in the secrets. On the other hand, secrets should be imagined to exist, otherwise the resort to eccentric exegetical techniques, without the trust that something inherent in the text or in the mind of the author is available, would become a hollow game.

To a certain extent, these processes represent two sides of the same coin: to no canonical text are attributed semantic dimensions that cannot be discovered or uncovered, and their discovery necessitates reliable, namely authoritative, techniques. The expansion of the dimensions of the canon and the proliferation of exegetical methods sometimes occurred in those intellectual moments when Judaism came into contact with other forms of thought; those encounters created both tensions and enrichments, one of the latter being the ascent of new forms of hermeneutics. We shall be concerned here not with hermeneutics in Judaism in general but with a rather specific form of esoteric literature, the mystical one. The other main type of arcanization, represented by philosophical understandings of the canonical texts and the corresponding allegorical method, will involve us only tangentially, to the extent that it has been absorbed in Kabbalistic hermeneutics.

The following discussions, I should like to make clear, attempt to describe hermeneutical developments in a fairly well-defined literary corpus. They do not make any ontological claims as to the nature of text in general, as some forms of philosophy of text strive for, nor do they make claims as to the structure of exegetical methods as such, as modern hermeneutics does from time to time. My discussions should therefore be seen as part of an effort of understanding some specific hermeneutical processes whose possible relevance for general hermeneutics is to be analyzed elsewhere (if at all), perhaps by other authors. I have tried to avoid lengthy discussions about the Kabbalistic concepts of the nature of language, because I have dealt with them on other occasions and I hope to elaborate on this topic elsewhere.[1] Here, the emphasis is solely on language as it is structured within canonical books; Kabbalistic discussions of the importance of the discrete linguistic unities are ignored.

II. Judaism: From a Geographical to a Textual Center

Jewish religion has undergone substantial changes over the millennia. One of the most important was the transition from a nomad religiosity, centered around the mobile Tabernacle, as described in the Pentateuch, to a more stable one, focused on the stationary Temple, as described elsewhere in the Hebrew Bible, and finally to a religion focusing on canonical writings: the Bible and the rabbinic texts. The renomadization of postbiblical Judaism is characterized by its novel gravitation toward books and their study,[2] together with rituals that could be performed anywhere, no longer relying on a sacred building and the rituals connected to it. According to most of the rabbinic sources, God is encountered within sacred texts rather than sacred spaces. However, the text is not a mere substitute for a sanctuary or a temple; it has, and creates, a dynamic of its own. Despite the renomadization of Judaism, or its transformation into a less topocentric religion than it was in the later biblical period, we witness a radical change of the medium of the divine theophany. In the postbiblical period God is conceived of much less as penetrating reality at His free will, using the apparatus of the Tabernacle or the Temple, than as constantly present within the literal signs of a portable book.

Or, to put it in more theological terms: the speaking God of the biblical period, who became more taciturn in rabbinic literature, was believed to have been addressing His elite few, who approached Him not by means of free direct speech—neither was He using His vibrant, imposing, direct voice when addressing them—but by the medium of a canonized formulation expressing His will, which became a written book.

In rabbinic literature it is through the canonized reification of this voice in written documents that most of the rabbinic masters conceived their encounter with the divine. Also in the rabbinic documents the assumption is that there is no absolute freezing of the text's content, and the midrashic commentators were asked to capture the resonances and nuances dormant in the canonical texts. Moreover, many of the characteristics of the divine power were transferred to the entity that now embodies the presence of the divine voice in the present religious and historical state, represented by the centrality of the sacred text.

While the notion of the sacred Bible is not itself a biblical concept, the sacralization of that book in the rabbinic period created another path, which became more and more dominant, of encountering the divine by resorting to a written document and to letters as pronounced by the student, rather than through divine voices or apparitions. While the intervention of the divine will within the life of the individual, the tribe, and the nation was central for the first two phases of Jewish religion, in the third one the divine will was conceived of as being already encapsulated within and perpetuated by the biblical text. The divine voice, as captured within the text, has been verbally reactivated by the human voice via studying or praying. It is this textualization of religious life, which stamped the nature of many aspects of rabbinic and meta-rabbinic Judaism, that will occupy us here.

One of the most important consequences of this process of textualization is the emergence of an ontologically perceived zone of literary—that is, the structured and written—expression of the divine will. This zone does not merely oblige human religious behavior because it has become, in the form of a book, canonical and thus very stable; it also—and this point needs emphasizing—restricts divine free choice itself. From the religious point of view, the idealization of the canonical text shaped Jewish society but at the same time created a vision of the content of the scriptures as embracing nonhuman and nonhistorical zones as well: both the natural and the divine. So, for example, not only humans are required to fulfill certain rituals, like praying or donning tefillin, but also God is described as doing so. In other words, rabbinic literature, and some writings composed at its periphery, has created a new myth, that of the Torah, or in more general terms a myth of a canonical book that is of overwhelming relevance for both the reader and the Author, but also for the created reality that is the arena of the encounter between them.[3] This new rabbinic myth of the text, related to the phenomenon of textualization—whose details will be treated in Chapter 1—served as the basis of many developments in the various types of hermeneutics found in Jewish mysticism. In fact, the two main processes to be discussed below depend on the transition from a topocentric to a text-oriented religion. While the former attributes special powers to the sacred place, or to the building and rituals related to that place, the text-oriented religion locates them in a new center, the book. Different as the two religious mentalities are, they nevertheless share a concern with a concrete center, which can be seen, touched, and experienced firsthand.

III. Processes of Arcanization and Dearcanization

The methodological presupposition that underlies many of the following observations is that the most significant Jewish literary corpora have never been composed in a literary, terminological, and conceptual vacuum. This means that many of the authors who contributed a substantial layer to Judaism were well acquainted with a panorama—though not always the full panorama—of Jewish culture, in either written or oral form.[4] Those corpora are based on texts and traditions that preceded them and are in a constant dialogue—often multiple dialogues, which in many cases meant sharp controversies—with some of the preceding and contemporary ideas and texts. In turn these corpora become part of a web of relations with the subsequent strata of Jewish creativity, a consideration that is pertinent in the case of Jewish esotericism as well. This assumption is based on two considerations:

(a) There was a very rigorous selection of the material that has been preserved, and those types of corpora that were seen as not salient to the rabbinic elite have been efficiently censored or even eliminated from the orbit of Jewish culture.[5] The Qumran literature, Philo, Josephus Flavius, and the apocryphal literature did not leave significant traces in the rabbinic texts. The fact that non-rabbinic forms of Jewish literature, like the Heikhalot and magical literatures, have nevertheless been transmitted presupposes the awareness of the existence of a certain consonance—or at least not a stringent dissonance—between them and the rabbinic circles who made the selection. Jewish culture is a cumulative one par excellence; it assumes that the earlier is very often the better. Moreover, the curriculum of study, which started with the Bible and went through the most important stages of cultural developments, fosters this view. The peculiar propensity to preserve as culturally active numerous layers of classical literature creates the possibility of continuous dialogues, and frictions, between those layers.

(b) Most Jewish literary corpora either consist of commentaries or resort to at least some interpretive stands. Because dialogues with literatures of the past are intrinsic features of these interpretations, both deep continuities and radical changes define the dynamics of Jewish religion. Rarely, however, have total ruptures produced significant types of influential literature. It seems that moments of crises are prone to encourage turns toward more conservative stands, toward more "authentic" types of thought that will ensure, in a religious society, the continuity of a certain sort of mentality despite the historical, social, or political ruptures. Thus, the necessity to engage a variety of literary corpora seems to me to be a sine qua non of serious studies concerning the conceptual and literary structures of Jewish religious types of literature. I would like to emphasize the difference between this importance of the layered and accumulative vision in Jewish culture, which is relevant for understanding Jewish mysticism as well, and the idea of authority, or theological authority, which informs the attitude of mystics, as least as presented in the formulations of Gershom Scholem.[6] There is a variety of attitudes toward classical texts, including classical mystical texts, even among the Jewish mystics, and one of the key points is the question of the various degrees and forms of assimilation of the prior types of Jewish literature.

Therefore, both significant forms of continuities and profound changes are well represented by the recurrent processes of arcanization of the canonical texts by those who subsequently interpreted them. The discovery, in fact the projection, of a secret meaning helps the ancient text not only to survive in new situations and to enhance its influence, but also to enrich the present. A more balanced understanding of the dynamics of a certain traditional culture must take into consideration the stabilizing factors, the stasis of the system, and the ex-static elements that are instrumental in changing, diversifying, or annihilating some of the static elements. Hermeneutics is oftentimes part of these complex processes.

An interesting formulation of the young Stéphane Mallarmé asserts, "Toute chose sacrée et qui veut demeurer sacrée s'enveloppe de mystère."[7] To take Mallarmé's statement by letter, mystery is an inherent quality of the sacred, both a systemic quality and a strategy, sometimes conscious, for ensuring the preservation and the continuation of the sacred. In fact, one of the possible definitions of the special status of a text is the feeling of the necessity to adopt it in a later period and to adapt it to that period. One of the basic strategies of adaptation is interpretive arcanization, which may correspond to Mallarmé's "s'enveloppe de mystère," a phrase that may be rendered, in a more technical way, as a crisical arcanization.[8] By this phrase I refer to arcanizations that result from the pressure of external events, historical or cultural, that demand a reorganization of the order of the text as rotating around an esoteric core that answers the repercussions of that crisis. It would, however, be too simplistic to attempt to separate the two forms of arcanization, because the crisical one will always attempt to capitalize on the systemic arcanization, and even to disguise itself as such.[9] This deep affinity is very subtly implied in Mallarmé's formulation. The whole range of classical Jewish literature—the Bible, Sefer Yetzirah, the talmudic literature, Midrash, liturgy, the Heikhalot literature, R. Abraham ibn Ezra's Commentary on the Pentateuch,[10] Maimonides' Guide of the Perplexed,[11] Nahmanides' Commentary on the Pentateuch,[12] the Book of the Zohar,[13] and even some of the Lurianic texts—has been commented upon, time and again, because of the prevailing assumption that they include secrets. The question is, why had the secrets been accepted and the above books become the subject of so many commentaries? One of the many possible reasons is the need to supply new areas of significance to the ancient canonical corpora. Thus, when crises intervene, they affect the particular form of existing arcanization which did not fulfill the needs of the intellectuals and thus is to be rejected, implicitly or explicitly, in favor of another, new type of arcanization. In that manner, I assume, most of the developments took place: the existence of a systemic arcanization allowed the development of new forms of arcanization.

Thus, a move from the exoteric nature of some of those texts to an esoteric understanding of them is one of the major moves characteristic of the development of Jewish literature, especially the speculative and some of the interpretive ones. Even in those cases when some esoteric elements are found in some interpreted texts, like ibn Ezra's commentaries, the Guide of the Perplexed, Nahmanides' commentary on the Torah, or the Book of the Zohar, the subsequent commentaries have often enhanced the scope of the esoteric topics beyond what was intended by the original authors.

This move from an exoteric to an esoteric religiosity, or from the biblical weltanschauung to some of its medieval elaborations that took the various forms of Jewish philosophy and Kabbalah, is a salient description of one of the major developments of postbiblical Judaism up to the sixteenth century and is related to the arcanization of the biblical text. Most of the works mentioned above are themselves attempts to explain, allude to, or extract secrets from the Bible, or at least to hint at their existence without revealing them, as in the case of Nahmanides. Thus, two forms of arcanization may be discerned. The primary one, which created new classics, is based on the belief that the Bible hides some secrets; however, since the medieval classics that proposed the arcane understanding of the canonical texts themselves resorted to allusive literary strategies, a second move becomes necessary, one which consists in a huge series of supercommentaries attempting to decode those secrets by elaborating on the hints included in the former writings. This second move can be described as superarcanization, not only because it decodes secrets found in an already arcane sort of writing—a medieval book—but also because the supercommentaries are inclined to the uncover secrets that are not to be found even in the medieval classics of esotericism, which already started to arcanize the Jewish canons. The main direction can be described as a gradual disclosure of secrets, received orally or in writing, or invented, which is at the same time the gradual introduction of secrets within the earlier classical texts.[14] Conscious dearcanization was preceded by, or was concomitant with, unconscious deeper arcanization. Along more general lines, only after the canonization of the Bible and the assurance of its special status, namely its integrity as an ultimate text, was it possible to move toward the process of its interpretation[15] and then to resort to another aspect of its alleged nature: the existence of nonexoteric aspects, namely the arcana. I would say that if the written Torah, which served as the main object of commentary, belongs to a prior stage of human consciousness, the orality that is characteristic of the preaxial age, the commentaries on the text that has been committed to writing, is the definite representation of what Jaspers called the "axial age." The period of the transition between the two would be the committing to writing of the Torah and its canonization, a period that roughly approximates the emergence of the axial age. The process of arcanization is an elitist impulse that moves from the tribe or community to smaller groups and is therefore part of the more complex process of axialization.

The process of arcanization in Judaism reached its peak in the sixteenth century, when the last comprehensive corpus of Jewish myths and symbols, as presented in the various versions of Lurianic Kabbalah, became crystallized. By and large, the medieval types of arcanizations can be designated as hypersemantic moves, namely the imposition of sets of symbolic meanings on the already existing plain senses of the Scriptures, or of the original meanings of the medieval interpreted texts. This hypersemantic arcanization has, however, been preceded by a late antiquity magical or hyposemantic arcanization, which means that some texts, the Pentateuch and the Psalms, have been viewed as fraught with magical powers, which underlay their plain sense and the canonical sequel of letters and words.[16]

On the other hand, a move from esotericism toward exotericism is discernible since the end of the sixteenth century. Apparently unrelated to the Protestant emphasis on the literal and historical senses and the rejection of secrecy that emerged in the sixteenth century, or the rejection of the occult symbolism described in some studies of B. Vickers, or Spinoza's rejection of the medieval theories of double meanings of the Bible, the surge in propensity for exotericism in some Jewish circles was not a matter of one specific development. Rather, it sprang from a series of smaller, yet major, developments, that included the printing of numerous Kabbalistic writings that undermined the esoteric nature of this lore, the attempts of Kabbalists to spread aspects of their secrets in more popular treatises (the ethical Kabbalistic literature), and the emergence of the last significant form of mystical literature, Hasidism, which is ostensibly exoteric in its general approaches, and finally the demythization of the mystical forms of Judaism by Enlightenment approaches. These diverse processes conspire to produce a relative dearcanization of the religious life, though the classical texts themselves are imagined as pregnant with infinite meanings. To a certain extent, the hypersemantic arcanization has been attenuated, and in some instances—Hasidism, for example—the magical arcanization has become more visible. Again this is a surfacing of much earlier views, as we shall see later on.

Let me dwell on my use of the term *move*. I scarcely can believe in the possibility of pointing out the precise meaning of many passages in ancient and medieval texts, especially those dealing with such complex topics as secrecy, mystical experience, revelations, and the structure of a dynamic divine world. Given the relative indeterminacy of so many crucial passages that inspired the later discussions, it is difficult to assess the exact nature of the semantic and conceptual moves. The scholarly effort, which is naturally inclined to pinpoint meanings, is often thwarted by the fluidity of the interpreted texts, by the inner experiences that may reflect altered states of consciousness, or by descriptions of the dynamic nature of the divine, angelic, or demonic worlds. A very creative hermeneutical approach to the sacred texts, which are reinterpreted time and again by the same mystic in new ways, is not a good prescription for the belief in a stability of meanings in the mystical texts under scrutiny below. This is why, in my opinion, it is necessary to take into account the broad semantic field of a given word, notion, or conceptual structure both in the earlier literatures and in the more recent ones, which will be able to map all its usages. As is the case with terms for secrecy in ancient and medieval Jewish literatures, the move—in fact our understanding of the different forms and directions of developments of a particular term—consists in semantic oscillations and fluctuations. Such semantic mutations, as well as continuities, are necessary for a better understanding of each of the stages of a term's evolution. The cumulative mutations of individual terms provide a clue to much larger conceptual changes.

A later semantic meaning of a given term may mark a development caused by a dramatic change, a rupture with the past—a crisical arcanization—but also a gradual development of possibilities that are inherent in the earlier texts but not obvious to a modern scholar for various reasons, like the fragmentary nature of the pertinent literature or oral transmission.[17] There may, indeed, be instances of *systemic arcanizations*, namely various visions of the secret sense of the text not caused by a rupture with the historical context that informed the text, nor characterized by a stringent dissonance with the semantic fields organizing the initial discourse and the main spiritual values that constellate the original authors, because of dramatic new changes in the cultural ambiance of the interpreter. In other words, the texts themselves are sometimes prone to provide the springboard for various esoteric logics—I emphasize the plural—which evolve through the interpretive efforts of a variety of interpreters, where the difference between them may be a matter of personal idiosyncrasy. This observation can be easily confirmed by the fact that mystics of the same religion living in the same period, sometimes in the same geographical area, offer different interpretations of the same text: for example, the Zoharic theosophical-theurgical interpretations differ drastically from the allegorical-psychological interpretations of the contemporary ecstatic Kabbalist Abraham Abulafia.

On the other hand, the same interpretations may be embraced by Jewish mystics living in different historical periods and in different geographical areas, just as a particular mystical text may be understood differently by modern scholars who subscribe to the same academic methodology. Much depends, in such subtle and obscure matters, on what the mystic (or modern scholar) is able to bring to the text in order to illuminate it. In any case, I would like to emphasize that crisical arcanization, which is invoked sometimes by scholars in order to explain the emergence of the Kabbalah itself or of the Lurianic Kabbalah, is a rather doubtful assumption, for it relies less on detailed analyses of texts than on historiosophical suppositions which, interesting as they may be, represent what the scholar under-stands as external history, the scholar's views on the impact of history on individ-uals and groups, their ways of reacting to crises, and other paratextual factors.[18]

Sometimes what can be regarded as a religious, intellectual, or cultural crisis triggering a certain type of arcanization, such as Maimonides' Aristotelian read-ing of the Jewish tradition, has been resolved by resorting to traditional esoteric terms like *sitrei torah*, *ma'aseh bereshit*, and *ma'aseh merkavah*. The perplexity of Maimonides' Jewish contemporaries has been resolved not by proposing Aris-totle's thought translated in Hebrew as the real solution but by reinterpreting ancient Jewish esotericism. To what extent there is a certain sort of continuation, in addition to obvious innovations, in Maimonides' esotericism is yet a matter of further investigation.[19] In my opinion, the Maimonidean project represents crisi-cal arcanization, which is quite obvious even in the title of the work in which it has been expounded: *Guide of the Perplexed*. This is a comprehensive, though neither systematic nor systemic, arcanization. Crisical as Maimonides' own move is, how-ever, it does not easily renounce its conservative claims, namely self-presentation as a systemic development, more precisely a partial disclosure, of rabbinic eso-tericism. It seems that Kabbalistic arcanization, as well as that of the Hasidei Ashkenaz, whose writings date from the generation immediately following Mai-monides' floruit, is much more systemic than crisical. As a reaction to Maimoni-dean arcanization, some of the Kabbalistic texts betray a crisical nature, as they attempt to counteract the purportedly pernicious views of the great eagle.

However, when criticizing Maimonides' esotericism, the Kabbalists have often asserted that they do not invent an ad hoc explanation but rather continue a much longer chain of tradition.[20] Their recurrent claim is that their esotericism, and thus their arcanization, pertains to the very nature of the original texts beginning with the Bible itself. It is, according to them, not merely one dimension of the canonical texts but rather the decisive core of a text's religious mentality that determines their esoteric interpretations. In other words, significant forms of medieval Jewish speculative literature can be described as representing different, in some cases even opposing, forms of arcanization that were aware of each other and sometimes even contested the legitimacy of its competitor. What is never-theless accepted as fact by both Maimonides' disciples and the theosophical-theurgical Kabbalists is that they retrieved, though in rather different manners and by cultivating different religious ideals, the "original" esotericism inherent in the Bible as mediated by the rabbinic conceptualization of esotericism, as men-tioned in the late-antiquity talmudic, midrashic, and in some cases even Heikhalot literatures. Thus, this is a medieval arcanization of much earlier arcanizations of

Judaism. The debates of the medieval masters about the esoteric views of the ancients constitute one of the most fascinating components of Jewish speculation since the late Middle Ages. Let me therefore turn to those earlier layers of discussion which nourished the medieval battles. Without understanding some developments that are already conspicuous in the premedieval Jewish corpora concerning esoterica, it will be difficult to assess the evolution of these topics in the Middle Ages. Medieval Jewish esoteric topics should be examined from the point of view of the continuation of earlier traditions and of their changes, adoptions and adaptations of alien material, and, oftentimes, the proposal of audacious innovations. The general move can be viewed as a greater propensity for a mysterious understanding of the ancient secrets.[21]

This approach to the text as pointing to secrets that are allegedly not evident in a prima facie reading allows a much more creative role for the reader or the commentator, who is deemed to deal with the absent, the concealed, or the omitted elements.[22] By amplifying the scope of the Torah to the status of a world-absorbing entity, some medieval Jewish authors also amplified their own role as interpreters.[23] To a great degree, they added or projected the secrets, namely what they conceived of to be the most sublime aspects of the Torah, and then extracted them, as two fundamental phases of their interpretive activity. On the other hand, by portraying the Torah as God-absorbing and man-absorbing, as we shall see in Chapter 2 and Appendix 2, the perusal and interpretation of the Torah become much more than a process of fathoming the secret meanings of the most important texts: possibilities of much more emotional and extreme forms of mystical experiences emerged.

IV. THREE MAJOR FORMS OF ARCANIZATION

The assumption that will lead the following discussion is the existence of three major modes of arcanization: the magical, the philosophical, and the mystical. Each of them comprises several distinct subcategories, whose precise mapping is still an important desideratum of modern scholarship of Judaism. As the main concern of my discussions below will be Kabbalistic hermeneutics, I shall focus my analyses on the implications of different Kabbalistic trends on the ensuing hermeneutics, relegating the implications of the distinctions of the other forms of arcanization to the margin. It is quintessential, however, to be aware of the ongoing intertwining and overlapping relations between these three modes. Direct influences, open and hidden forms of antagonism, and a variety of syntheses between them account for many of the characteristics of the historical developments and the phenomenology of Jewish hermeneutics. This methodological assumption holds as much in the case of Jewish hermeneutics as it does in the development of Jewish thought, a point that is often overlooked by those who have suggested broader pictures of the different aspects of Jewish thought. This is not the place to develop this methodological observation,[24] but I shall attempt to follow it whenever pertinent. In general I would say that Maimonides' struggle with magic and ancient Jewish esoterica has not been put into relief in modern scholarship, and consequently the possibility of the articulation of worldviews that are reactions from circles who were attacked by his critiques has not been sufficiently explored. Similarly, the fact that Maimonides has been alleged to hold exactly the same type of views to which he strongly protested has been underestimated as an indication of intellectual interactions that took place in the formative period of Kabbalah.[25] The gradual strengthening of the astromagic of ultimately Hermetic origins in post-Maimonidean thought, a development that had a deep impact on Kabbalah, supports my thesis as to the dialectical role of the relationship between magic, philosophy, and Kabbalah. In fact, the last major development in Jewish mysticism, Hasidism, owes much to this still-unrecognized dialectic.[26]

The dialectic is most evident in the metamorphoses of a statement stemming from a magical vision of the Torah that describes the unique nature of the Torah as consisting, on its esoteric level, of a continuum of divine names.[27] Moreover, the relations between allegorical-philosophical hermeneutics and the combinatory one will engage us in Chapter 11, and the integration of various exegetical trends will be shown in Appendix 1. This interpenetration between the various approaches is one of the reasons for the absence of sectarian tendencies that are characteristic of purist approaches.

V. THREE MAJOR KABBALISTIC MODELS

The working hypothesis behind my approach to Jewish mysticism since the Middle Ages is that differing speculative models informed the thought, praxis, and subsequently the writings of various Kabbalists and Hasidic masters. Far from representing a unified or monochromatic line of thought that allegedly has changed throughout history, the diverse Kabbalistic sorts of literature, and to a lesser extent various Hasidic schools, have centered around at least three major models: the theosophical-theurgical one, the ecstatic one, and the talismanic one.[28] The interplay and interactions between these models characterize many important moments of Kabbalistic creativity. To paraphrase Alexander Pope, we should better observe how system into system runs. Yet, given the fact that a theory of models in Jewish mysticism still has to be carefully formulated, I will attempt to delineate only what seems to me to be the salient points relevant to one model: the talismanic one, which will be addressed in Chapter 5. I shall not elaborate on the three models but only mention very briefly their most important characteristics relating to the nature of language.

The theosophical-theurgical model, which informs many of the discussions in Spanish Kabbalah and flourished afterward in sixteenth-century Safed, assumes that language reflects the inner structure of the divine realm, the sefirotic system of divine powers. At the same time, language was thought to influence this structure by means of theurgical activities that aim to restore the harmony within the divine realm. Either in its cognitive-symbolic role or in its theurgical-operational function, language has been conceived by this type of Kabbalah as hypersemantic. This means that not only is the ordinary sense of language maintained by the Kabbalists, but its basic function as part of the Kabbalistic enterprise is due to a surplus of meaning, which adds semantic fields to that or those designated by the ordinary meaning. The two aspects, the symbolic (referential) and the theurgical (performative), different as they may be from each other, should not be viewed as totally independent. The symbolic role of language, namely the concept that it reflects the structure of the divine powers, is often only one side of the coin; the other is the use of symbolic knowledge in order to amend processes taking place within the divine realm.[29] In the following I use the term *theurgy* to designate the rituals by which God or a divine structure like the ten sefirot is affected, rather than the techniques of spiritual purification that enable someone to elevate. Both definitions are found in modern scholarship, but I prefer the first.[30]

The ecstatic approach is palpably different; it assumes that the Kabbalist can use language and the canonical texts in order to induce a mystical experience by manipulating elements of language, together with other components of the various mystical techniques. This approach is much less concerned with divine inner structures, for it focuses on the restructuring of the human psyche in order to prepare it for the encounter with the divine. The ecstatic theory of language is less mimetic, and thus less symbolic and theurgic, than the view espoused by the theosophical Kabbalah. While the theosophical-theurgical approach to language assumes the paramount importance of information that is either absorbed by the human mind or transmitted, in an energetic form, by the soul to the divine, in many cases the ecstatic view of language encourages the effacement of knowledge as part of the opening toward the divine. Language helps, according to ecstatic Kabbalah, to cleanse someone's consciousness by breaking, as part of a mystical technique, the words of the sacred scripture into nonsemantic units.[31] While the theosophical Kabbalah emphasizes the given, structured aspects of language as manifested in the canonical writings, in ecstatic Kabbalah the deconstruction of the canonical texts, and of ordinary language as well, is an important mystical tool for restructuring the human psyche.

The talismanic model, which will occupy our attention much more in the following discussions, conceives the divine text as one of the major means to attract supernal (divine or celestial) powers on the magician or the mystic, who becomes, in many cases, the portent of extraordinary forces that can be described as magical. In general, this approach can be called hyposemantic, which means that language is regarded as magically effective even when one ignores its semantic aspects. This is a strongly anthropocentric attitude, because it envisages the enhancement of the spiritual and material well-being of an individual, and often a whole religious group, as a core value of religion.[32]

The theosophical-theurgical and the talismanic models assume that, in addition to the semantic aspect of the sacred text, and of the Hebrew language in general, there is an energetic aspect that may either have some effect on the supernal world or attract it onto the low. While in ecstatic Kabbalah these two aspects are sometimes present, they nevertheless play a relatively marginal role there. This brand of Kabbalah recognizes the magical powers of language, though it sees them as exercising an influence on an inferior level of existence as compared to the cathartic role language plays in purifying the soul and the intellect in order to prepare them for receiving the supernal effluvia.

By and large, the talismanic model, as exemplified by linguistic magic, is a synthesis between the particularistic tendency characteristic of the theosophical-theurgical model, which deals basically with halakhic behavior, and the more universalistic tendency of the Hermetic sources. Focused as they are on Hebrew words as major tools, the linguistic talismanics and sometimes also the ecstatic Kabbalists assume that not only Hebrew words but also Hebrew letters, and especially what can be called, according to the Jewish authors, "Hebrew" sounds, may serve as talismanic means. At least on the level of monadic linguistic elements, a more universalistic potentiality can be assumed; I mean that given the need to deconstruct conventional language, including Hebrew, into its elementary units, on the phonetic level the notion of a resemblance between the different languages is more plausible.[33]

The theosophical-theurgical and ecstatic models are amply represented by distinct Kabbalistic schools and literary corpora, which can be described as embodying the speculative assumptions mentioned above insofar as language is concerned. Thus, the theosophical-theurgical Kabbalah and the ecstatic Kabbalah are known from rather independent Kabbalistic bodies of writings; the talismanic model, however, has been adopted by both theosophical-theurgical and ecstatic

Kabbalists, who adapted the astromagical sources to their specific spiritual purposes. This is one of the reasons why this last model has been neglected by modern scholars of Kabbalah. The concern with a more unified picture of the development of this lore has induced a rather monochromatic view of its phenomenology, which pushed the magical schemes, and to some extent the ecstatic literature, to a corner, emphasizing—in my opinion, overemphasizing—the centrality of the theosophical mode of Kabbalah.[34]

Let me formulate the three models in terms of their objectives. The ecstatic model is concerned more with the changes a certain mystical technique, based mainly on language, may induce in man; the talismanic model emphasizes the effects that someone's ritualistic linguistic acts may have on the external world; and the theosophical-theurgical model centers on inducing harmony within the divine realm. In the following exposition I shall attempt to give a more detailed linguistic description of the talismanic model and to trace the main stages of the infiltration of this model within the various forms of Kabbalistic literature. Interesting as the description of these models may be, the models have only rarely been expounded as completely separate approaches. Indeed, the ecstatic was sometimes combined with the talismanic one, so that the talismanic operator was described as achieving contact with the divine realm before he is able to draw down the supernal power. Likewise, the theurgical operation, which ensures the continuing pulsation of energy within the divine realm, has often been combined with the magical or talismanic approach, so that drawing the emanation from the higher sefirot to the lower ones was followed by causing the emanation's descent into the extradivine world. Common to all these models is the view that language, at least as represented by the canonical texts, involves a strong type of "speech acts," to use John Searle's phrase, or, to use J. L. Austin's category, the recitations of letters are performative utterances par excellence. However, the efficiency of the Kabbalistic approaches to language or text depends much more on their parasemantic qualities than on their semantic ones.

VI. REMARKS ON THE NOTION OF HERMENEUTICS

Like Kabbalah, the term *hermeneutics* covers a variety of different schools and opinions, and it has been understood differently by various scholars. Here I would like to distinguish between three main topics that constitute the field of hermeneutics as it is approached in this book.

The first topic is the nature of the author, which encompasses a variety of authors, beginning with the Author of the divine book, Whose nature was thought to inform the nature of the text He generated, as well as the task of the reader or interpreter. The author may also be an angel or any other supernal entity who inspires the human interpreter or the interpreter's unaided spiritual activity. When the subject of the discussions is an entity heterogeneous to the interpreter, like the divine author, we are in the area of theology; when an angel, we deal with angelology. Indeed, there can be no doubt, as I shall demonstrate, that without an understanding of the overall speculative structures that informed the worldviews of the interpreters, it is hard to fathom some of the aspects of their hermeneutics. The consonance between the infinite author and the infinite text, which will be discussed in Chapter 3, is a good example. The vision of the hermeneutical project as aiming to understand the nature of the author and his intentions has been not only part of literary approaches but in fact quite widespread in religious hermeneutics, where the sacred book was conceived to be the main source for understanding of the nature of God. From this perspective hermeneutics, like philosophy, is no more than a maidservant of theology. Also in modern scholarship of Judaism, and of Kabbalah in particular, texts have been investigated basically in order to extract from them a system or theology, whose precise articulation was regarded as one of the main targets of the scholar.[35]

In keeping with the call to recognize a diversity of models of thought in Kabbalah, my goal will be not to discover the system or theology of a given text but to point out the threads that lead from a particular theology to the understanding of the text and the interpreter's task. From this point of view, I shall travel a trajectory different from the theological one: systemic and abstract knowledge that informed the thought of an author will be supposed as known by me, as part of my perusal of the pertinent texts, and my task will be the disclosure of the impact that system had on the text under scrutiny. This is the reason why, in the following chapters, discussions of theological stands will be relatively rare. By and large, without addressing the issue of the existence of ontologically heterogeneous sources for religious experiences, I will assume that the external entities are to be understood as the production of different forms of the religious imaginaire. The starting point of the enterprise of many of the hermeneutes whose views will be discussed below had, in my opinion, framed the range of their attainments, just as the modern secular imaginaire, based on a propensity for elements of negativity, confines the forms of experience a modern reader may have in any given text. The extension of the range of topics allegedly included in the canonical texts, which amounts to an imaginaire of the text, allowed the hermeneute experiences that would otherwise have been impossible.

The second topic, which will concern us much more than the first, is the nature of the text or, to resort to other terminology, Hans-Georg Gadamer's "matter of the text" or Paul Ricoeur's "the world of the text." Attempting to disassociate my discussion from an organic linkage to an external being, or to human authors—

though not from a certain way of imagining such a being—I follow, broadly speaking, Ricoeur's call for a threefold distancing of the literary work from the psychology of the author, from the circumstances of its composition, and from the audience to which it has been addressed.[36] The following analyses largely deal with the nonreferential world created by the influence of the Bible in the postbiblical forms of religion. However, unlike Ricoeur's main concern with possible worlds of the text, which are related to the readers and then attracted by a certain book, thus constituting its more comprehensive world, my claim will be that many of the Jewish elites whose concepts I shall scrutinize are initially informed by a variety of books, while the sacred book they studied and interpreted was consumed as part of a much broader and variegated culture that conditioned its understanding so substantially that it is difficult to separate it from a more comprehensive and articulated spiritual structure. The world of the book is, in the contexts to be discussed below, too vague a concept. That is why, in the first part of the present book, I shall deal with various conceptions about the sacred book, many of which have as their subject matter the Bible but often differ dramatically from the concepts found in the Bible itself.

My assumption is palpably different from Ricoeur's general theory of hermeneutics—what has been called the eclipse of the reader[37]—which separates the more objective world of the text from the reader, its psychology and subjectivity. Rather, I will take the main book under discussion, the Bible, sometimes to be a *réservoire sémantique* (following Gilbert Durand) of concepts that are far away, not to say utterly different, from what I understand to be the book's intellectual horizon. Two thinkers, Ricoeur and W. C. Smith, who were influenced by a Christian view of *gratia*, regarded the Bible as the source of inspiration. Ricoeur, who to a certain extent follows Gadamer, has been discussed briefly already. Smith formulated his view thus: "The significant question is not whether the Bible is inspired, but whether it is inspiring."[38] These views presuppose a weak reader or interpreter, while I assume that in some forms of mystical exegesis we may speak of a stronger interpreter. Characteristic of those more radical interpreters is what I propose to call an *intercorporal situation*, namely the resort of many Jewish thinkers to a long series of concepts stemming from previously alien and intellectually structured literary corpora. This situation seems to me to be symptomatic of the way the sacred book has been studied in the centuries after it was written, in historical and cultural circumstances that differ from the ancient authors' main preoccupation. I consider this intercorporal situation to characterize many of the medieval and premodern attitudes toward the Bible, a stand that attributes transformative valences to cultural encounters between Jews and other peoples.[39]

In fact, I shall be more concerned with strong readers and interpreters, whose interaction with sacred books is a matter not only of fusion of horizons, in a Gadamerian sense, or the reader's self-understanding, as Ricoeur would put it, but of much more dramatic restructurings of the ancient texts. Interpretation should be understood as more of an interpenetration than a fusion. The Kabbalists resorted to radical exegetical techniques and to more comprehensive and systematic theological conceptions that are the result of an acculturation of some parts of Jewish elites to their environment. Unlike Gadamer, I assume that it is hard to point to one specific horizon informing a given period that would serve as the conceptual receptacle for understanding a particular reading of a specific book. Moreover, I would even claim that in the writings of a given author, or perhaps even in a single text, it is possible to discern a variety of theological and other concepts that conditioned the author's horizon; thus it would be better to deal not with the fusion of two horizons but with a con-fusion of numerous spiritual horizons. Moreover, unlike Ricoeur, the assumption that will inform my discussions is that sometimes readers or interpreters did not come to the sacred scriptures only in order to better understand them, or to understand themselves better, but rather in an attempt, conscious or no, to change the conceptual identity of the scriptures by infusing their sometimes already structured identity. In fact, there can be little doubt that the regular fusion of horizons between someone's prejudices and a text being met for the first time is hardly the common situation in Jewish mysticism. The Bible was never met by the Jewish mystic for the first time when he became a mystic, but it already contributed in different manners to the religious life of the hermeneute. The ongoing reading, reflection, and confrontation with the biblical text is a constant factor in the biography of Jewish mystics. It is always a renewed encounter that is the basic experience, since the Bible served as the first main topic of study in the early childhood of the future mystic. Neither should we assume, as Gadamer does, that the canonical text has an "absolute priority over the doctrine of those who interpret it." Though such a theoretical stand may be detected in principle, our assumptions regarding the strong reader and the importance of the intercorporal form of exegesis, which will be addressed in Chapter 9, allow much more aggressive forms of interaction than extraction of some form of religious truths actually found in the Bible.

Thus Jewish mysticism in most of its main forms is exegetical, as it consists in different searches for contact with God, when the Bible plays an important role as a repository of secret knowledge about the divine realm, as a source of models to be imitated or even techniques to reach the divine encounter, in addition to the more conspicuous engagement of many Jewish mystics in the more technical interpretive sense.[40]

The emphasis I propose to put on the phenomenology of strong readers is related to some of my earlier studies of Kabbalistic exegetes like Abraham Abulafia and some of the theosophical-theurgical Kabbalists,[41] to my awareness that their eccentric exegesis has sources in earlier Jewish corpora, and to the fact that their approaches were shared by some subsequent Kabbalists. I assume that the stronger and more formative that mystical experiences are, the more radical the exegetical enterprise may be. Those forms of stronger experience were attained by resorting to mystical techniques, nomian and anomian, which represent initiatives of the Jewish mystics to encounter the divine realms in the way each of them imagined them. In line with an earlier proposal to accentuate the importance of understanding mystical techniques if one is to understand the structure and nature of mystical experience,[42] I would say that the results of the interpretive enterprises are determined largely by the nature of the exegetical technique, perhaps even more than the contents of the interpreted text. Given that I shall be concerned with exegetical texts as one of the main topics of analysis, the emphasis will fall more on the concepts and practices of the late interpreters than on the nature of the interpreted texts. Though interactions indeed took place between them and the sacred scriptures, I am inclined to attribute to the later interpreters, especially those who belong to "innovative Kabbalah," a pivotal role in the emergence of mentalities that encouraged a somewhat greater freedom of interpretation which, though radical in comparison to modern hermeneutics, was nevertheless accepted as legitimate in many Jewish conservative circles.

By moving the emphasis from theological and book-oriented approaches as the main source of meaning to the centrality of the exegetical activity of interpreters—in many cases interpreters who did not play a major role in Jewish life—I hope that a more variegated and dynamic understanding of Jewish mystical hermeneutics will be achieved. The move from the academic concern with abstract messages, theological and sometimes even teleological, to concrete exegetical practices invites more detailed analyses of the different manners in which texts were approached, and those analyses are rarely prone to be formulated in broader and more "inspiring" conclusions. Thus, the accent in some of the following discussions falls on what the Jewish mystics did rather than what they believed. To a certain extent, to follow Aby Warburg's remark, "God dwells in the details," but those details belong to human exegetical activity.

The "upward" move that I propose as a methodological approach, starting with the more concrete concepts of the nature of the texts and exegetical techniques, not only strives for a less theologically oriented discourse but is based on concrete practices and their impact on lived experience and is informed by a more kataphatic attitude than that prevalent in modern scholarship concerning Kabbalistic hermeneutics. The accent dominant in many of the modern treatments of the Kabbalistic "theory" of symbols is on an apophatic theology as informing the spiritual preoccupations of the Kabbalists, and this presumption shaped the academic analysis of the nature of symbolism.[43] I find this emphasis exaggerated, for reasons I have addressed elsewhere.[44] In any case, I shall try to demonstrate throughout the following discussions that a much more kataphatic attitude is evident among the vast majority of the theological systems directly involved in the hermeneutical projects of the Kabbalists. Most especially, the theological assumption of an infinite divinity, designated in many Kabbalistic writings by the term 'Ein Sof, which was taken as defining Kabbalistic apophasis, should be understood in much more kataphatic terms, and it invited a vision of the Bible as containing an infinite number of distinct meanings.[45] The possibility of reaching the divine intention, or an encounter with the divine realm via the interpretive process, is of paramount importance for the "technical" approach that will be described below. Preoccupation with a book that is believed to be sacred was seen as a path to attaining experiences of plenitude, rather than a casuistic enterprise.

Moreover, I shall attempt to describe the practice of interpreters whose interactions with the text presuppose a certain performance of the text, which may take different forms—for example, vocalization of nonvocalized scrolls of the Bible[46] or combination of letters[47]—as part of the exegetic enterprise. I shall designate this practice ergetic exegesis[48] and call its practitioners ergetic exegetes. This ergetic impulse is to be understood as part of a more activist anthropology characteristic of the vast majority of Kabbalistic writings, as they assumed a primordial affinity between the inner core of man, described as soul in some forms of Kabbalah and as intellect in others, and the divinity. To a certain extent the process of exegesis is a recirculation of divine power as embodied in man, when striving to return to its source. From this point of view, one of the slogans of later Kabbalah shared by Hasidic writers and some of the so-called Mitnaggedim, which contends that God, the Torah, and Israel are one unit, reflects the integrative approach dominant in the relationship between author, text, and interpreter. In a way, this primordial and recurring triunity creates a situation reminiscent of the modern hermeneutical concept of belonging.[49]

Though I adopt a historical approach to the various processes to be described below, the main purpose of this book is to point out the Jewish mystics' various attempts to locate a sense of value they imagined to be inherent in the sacred scriptures, as well as their interpretive efforts to elicit those various "values" from the sacred texts. I believe that it is important to supplement a historical approach to the emergence of Kabbalistic symbols that demystifies (in a manner reminiscent of Freud's psychoanalysis) their content by elucidating the mechanics of the emergence with the phenomenological approach that strives to understand the way in which they were thought to operate. By so doing we may adopt the socio-logical attitude of Emile Durkheim or the philosophical hermeneutics of Ricoeur, who take into consideration the fullness of the symbols as already existing fac-tors.[50] Thus, there is a conflict of interpretations, to resort to Ricoeur's term, between the scholarly analytical attempt to understand the emergence of a phe-nomenon by means of a historical approach and the concern with understanding the inner logic of this phenomenon. The two approaches are indeed in conflict—in my opinion, more than Ricoeur would assume—because the moment of recog-nizing the historicity, or contingency or subjectivity, of the symbolic meaning that is attached to a certain ancient text may become the moment of its demystifica-tion, which will attenuate or even undermine its efficacy. The drama of a strong interpreter who struggles with a canonical text, of conceptual innovators who strive to appear conservative, of exegetes who apply extreme exegetical techniques but still believe that they find some historical and spiritual truths, are the param-eters that inform many of our discussions. Struggling with the ancient text takes sometimes extravagant forms, from extreme atomization of the interpreted texts into separate letters, to the vision of the text as identical with the divinity, or from dense textuality, which addresses the peculiarities of the biblical text, to onto-theology. I shall discuss some eccentric visions of textuality and interpretive prac-tices that question more harmonistically oriented views that medieval Jewish *inter-pretatio* is to be regarded as "a process of continuation of the Bible."[51]

One argument is that some medieval exegetes may be described as strong readers in comparison to the modern or postmodern hermeneutes, given their profound belief in the all-comprehensiveness or the absorptive nature of the interpreted texts, a belief that allowed exegetical approaches much more eccentric than the modern exegetical tools. This assumption is part of a more comprehen-sive view of the difference between medieval and modern attitudes, a view that, following Nietzsche, is concerned with the will-to-power of the interpreter over the text.[52] However, my emphasis will be mainly on the plenitude that emerges from this activistic approach, and much less the negativity that is sometimes attributed to it.[53] Unlike modern hermeneutics, which is inclined to suspicion, I would say that the strong Kabbalistic and Hasidic interpreters resorted to a her-meneutic of trust, to borrow a phrase from George Steiner.[54]

Nevertheless, a much more agonistic approach, emphasizing the tensions, frictions, appropriation, and clinamenic attitudes (Harold Bloom's terms), will dominate some of the following discussions. The sociological aspects will be addressed, particularly in the last chapters and some of the appendixes, in order to account for the differences between elites who elaborated hermeneutical systems, allowing a freer approach to the arcane dimension of the classical texts, and elites who were more conservative. It is not an idealistic or romantic picture of free creativity that characterizes the discussions of most of the Kabbalistic interpretations below,[55] but much more their need to maneuver between different codes, even overdetermined codes, that often dictated contradictory ways of understanding ancient literary corpora. The Bible is a text that, because of its elliptical style and its variety of topics, invites extensive interpretation more than some other ancient religious texts do.[56] In the Middle Ages it was contemplated and commented upon from cultural angles that prompted questions alien to the cultural horizon of its ancient authors. The Bible and its rabbinic interpretations served as both centripetal and centrifugal factors in Jewish culture. On the one hand, the common book with its rabbinic satellites produced spiritual universes shared by almost all the Jews throughout Jewish history. On the other hand, some of the contents of the biblico-rabbinic tradition were perceived of as inadequate for the medieval and modern sensibilities, thus creating centrifugal impulses and the need to find strong interpretations of the Bible by resorting to exegetical methods different from the rabbinic one, and meanings different from the plain sense of the Bible. Other aspects or religious vectors of the biblico-rabbinic corpora continued to develop and change in ways more consistent with their initial logic. In the following, an effort will be made to survey the two developments, though the emphasis of the discussion will be on the most common vector, the centripetal one. Fascinating as the centrifugal forms of hermeneutics are, their transgressive propensities did not facilitate their impact on larger audiences of Jews, who preferred the charitable over the uncharitable readings.[57]

VII. The Literary Corpora under Scrutiny

Most of the material that served as the springboard for the following analyses stems from various Kabbalistic schools, in the more restricted definition of the term. Thus, the Kabbalistic writings that attracted the maximum attention date from the end of the twelfth century to the end of the eighteenth century and were written in Southern, Central, and Eastern Europe and in the Middle East. Nevertheless, a significant part of the discussions below engages also rabbinic texts, most of them midrashic, and Hasidic texts, compounded since the last third of the eighteenth century. Topics relating to ancient exegesis as found in Philo or Christian and Gnostic literatures are adduced only marginally. In comparison to the latter's more peripheral status in the general economy of this book, more substantial attention has been paid to medieval philosophical allegoresis as practiced by Jewish writers.

Needless to say, owing to the huge size of these literary corpora and of the related secondary literature, it is impossible to offer anything like an exhaustive treatment of even those topics which have been selected for systematic treatment here. Given the fact that the main topic under scrutiny is a relatively new subject in the field of Jewish mysticism, the enterprise advanced in this book suffers from the subjectivity, selectivity, tentativeness, and error characteristic of any broad exposition of topics that underlie analyses of huge corpora and countless volumes. In our case, the pertinent literature amounts to some hundreds of lengthy and often complex books and innumerable shorter treatises, many still in manuscript, which constitute the core of the Kabbalistic literature, not to speak of the daunting rabbinic corpora and the vast philosophical literature. In fact, one can hardly find an important book written by a medieval Jew that is not a potential source for a better understanding of concepts or terms related to the interpretations offered to the different parts of the Bible.

Most of the material stems from and is related to formal commentaries on the Bible, though some significant quotations stem from more theoretical treatises written by Kabbalists and Hasidic masters. They deal not only with specific exegesis of a particular text but also with issues germane to our discussions, such as recitation of the sacred scriptures, which do not involve an understanding of their meaning; reading of the text envisioned as a form of interpretation; the text's study, limmud or talmud torah, which involves intense or "absorbing" forms of preoccupation with the meaning of the canonical text; as well as the more formal interpretations that constitute the literary genre of commentary.

I have attempted to take into consideration the findings of other studies devoted to Kabbalistic hermeneutics, including my book on Abraham Abulafia's hermeneutics, the preliminary analysis of general hermeneutics in Kabbalah that constitutes Chapter 9 in Kabbalah: New Perspectives, and my forthcoming analysis of R. Menahem Recanati's hermeneutics. Nevertheless, I did not repeat my analyses there, but sought to adduce new material and approaches.

An attempt has been made to offer a balanced picture of the themes under consideration as they occur in the various forms of Kabbalistic and Hasidic literature. However, the immense amount of material creates great problems in attaining an equilibrium between various Kabbalistic schools—Sefardi, Italian, North African, Safedian, or Ashkenazi—between the Cordoverian Kabbalah and the Lurianic one, or between the Hasidic and the contemporary Mitnaggedic attitudes. Determining the weight of influence of the earlier rabbinic hermeneutics on Jewish mystical hermeneutics is a major issue that demands much more research, as does the spiritualistic hermeneutics of the Jewish Sufi in the Near East during the thirteenth and fourteenth centuries and their spiritualistic counterparts in Europe. Immensely problematic is the need to take into account the rich manuscript material that should have its place by the side of the printed literature, and thus more influential Kabbalistic material. I have tried to give special attention to unknown material extant only in manuscripts, but at the same time not to fall in the trap of conferring too great a role to idiosyncratic views just because they are extreme.

Indeed it is difficult to strike a reasonable balance between what I conceive of being representative and what seem to be the more interesting aspects of mystical hermeneutics in Judaism. I have striven to resist succumbing to the common scholarly overemphasis on the transgressive and anarchistic elements by highlighting what seem to be the more recurring and influential themes. This means that although the great figures were indeed those who formulated the most interesting ideas, we should pay equal attention to the manner of their reception and distribution. Thus, important as R. Abraham Abulafia's or R. Moses Cordovero's thought was for the articulation of some of the most influential conceptualizations of Torah, their impact was facilitated by means of other authors, such as R. Elijah da Vidas's *Reshit Hokhmah* or R. Isaiah Horowitz's *Ha-Shelah*. Nevertheless, the central question of the precise boundaries of the relevant material for the following discussions remains: Are R. Yohanan Alemanno, R. Isaac Abravanel, R. Yehudah Loewe of Prague, or even R. Moses Alshekh, all commentators on a variety of Jewish canonical writings, the most representative of some trends of Kabbalah or of Jewish mysticism? Or, one might ask: What are the hermeneutical Kabbalistic aspects of such an influential commentary on the Pentateuch as R. Hayyim ben 'Atar's *'Or ha-Hayyim*, which is venerated by the Polish Hasidim, beyond his resort to themes stemming from Lurianic Kabbalah? Those and other quandaries are inextricable both from the problem of the boundaries of the Jewish mystical literature and from the vagaries of the definition of hermeneutics.

Despite the huge number of commentaries produced by Kabbalists and Hasidic masters, very few mystical treatises had been devoted solely to the nature of the Torah. While in the rabbinic literature the central role of the discussions dedicated to the Torah had to do with the minutiae of the writing of the scroll, we find a medieval *Sermon on the Appraisal of the Torah*, based on talmudic and midrashic sources.[58] However, it is only the late-sixteenth-century Maharal who composed a treatise dealing with the nature of the Torah,[59] and it took more than a century and a half before short Kabbalistic treatises by R. Abraham ben Shlomo of Vilnius and R. Isaac Aizik Haver appeared.[60] Thus, despite the numerous short statements that define the nature and importance of the Torah, this topic was not treated to an elaborate exposition. The situation is better insofar as the methods of interpretation are concerned, as we learn from discussions of this topic by R. Eleazar of Worms and Abraham Abulafia.[61]

Given the absence of extensive treatments of the majority of the main terms and concepts that informed Jewish mystical hermeneutics,[62] the inherent quandaries related to mystical hermeneutics in general, and the initial phase of the study of Jewish mystical literature in particular, many of the findings presented in this book are preliminary and thus tentative, even more tentative than the findings in humanistic studies typically are. As to the research already done in the field, I would like to highlight the importance of Scholem's treatment of one of the foremost topics to be addressed below, his seminal study "The Meaning of the Torah in Jewish Mysticism," available in English in a major collection of his studies entitled *On the Kabbalah and Its Symbolism*. This is a supremely mature, insightful, and comprehensive contribution to Jewish mystical hermeneutics, and any further treatment of concepts in this field is indebted to Scholem's groundbreaking essay. Likewise, Scholem's various treatments of the nature of tradition and mysticism, tradition and revelation, and revelation and interpretation have shed light on many crucial aspects of these concepts.[63] Helpful in many ways for the writing of this book was the Hebrew monograph of A. Y. Heschel, *Theology of the Ancient Judaism*, a very learned three-volume work that collected and arranged an enormous number of rabbinic, medieval, and even Hasidic passages and analyzed them succinctly. Treatments of the views of the Torah in some important types of Kabbalistic literature, like Isadore Tishby's and Yehuda Liebes's analyses of this topic in the *Zohar* or B. Sack's discussions of R. Moses Cordovero's views, significantly facilitated my work. Some more recent studies, such as those of Yehuda Liebes, Elliot R. Wolfson, and Barbara Holdrege, have introduced new vistas, which I have attempted to integrate in the following pages. Recent research in related areas of Jewish studies, like the hermeneutics of halakhah, by David Weiss Halivni, Moshe Halbertal, and Yochanan Silman have contributed their share to some aspects of the following discussions. Needless to say, the present study hardly strives to address the immense area of Jewish hermeneutics even in general terms. It would even be difficult to mention the most important studies in this area, necessary though the understanding of their findings and concepts is for the description of Kabbalistic hermeneutics.[64]

I

THE WORLD-ABSORBING TEXT

The entire Torah is not [embodied] in the world
But the entire world is Torah.
—R. MOSES CORDOVERO, *Shiʿur Qomah*

I. CULTURAL CHOICES

Although most of the following discussion will rotate around the Hebrew Bible, its various perceptions and multiple modes of interpretations, it is hard to delineate a systematic textology, namely a unified approach to the status and nature of the biblical text, or of the ways of its interpretation in the biblical literature. Those concerns arise gradually in the Jewish postbiblical literatures. In this chapter I shall address succinctly the expansion of the status of the biblical text in ancient Jewish sources and one of their later major reverberations.

The nature of midrashic exegesis is determined by two main components of the interpretive experience: the text and the interpreter. The text is the canonized Hebrew Bible, whose precise borders are delimited and whose sacrosanct status is sealed. The situation of the interpreter is altogether different. As the text became fixed, the terms of the interpreter's task altered. The divine spirit, which was conceived of as instrumental in the formation of the canon, was then excluded from the interpretive process. The rabbinic interpreter, no more than a simple human being before divine revelation, had now to function without the divine help so necessary to fathoming the messages inherent in the text. In penetrating the intricacies of the Bible, he had only two tools: the tradition he inherited and his own intellectual abilities and capacity to apply the authorized rules of inter-pretation. The Godhead was now conceived of as expecting that man, on his own, would articulate His intentions as instilled for eternity within the revealed book, and He Himself was portrayed as an arduous student of the Torah.

Man faced, then, a silent Godhead and a text conceived of for centuries as the single authoritative source of divine guidance. No wonder that close scrutiny of the Bible, motivated by and combined with an overwhelming conviction that everything is hinted at or solved by the biblical verses, became the main intellec-tual activity of Jewish spiritual leadership. The whole of its literary output in the Tannaitic and Amoraic periods was aimed at elucidating the legal part of the Bible and explaining its narrative portions. The authoritative rabbinic Jewish texts were regarded as but pleiades of stars rotating around the Bible, while the other kinds of texts (philosophical, historical, apocalyptic, magical, mystical, or literary) were successfully excluded from the rabbinic universe and condemned to total obliv-ion. Some remnants of the nonrabbinic Jewish literary creations that did survive became planets in Christian literatures; only seldom did they penetrate the rab-binic firmaments. Other texts were simply suppressed, though they continued to be esoterically transmitted among select groups. Such was the case with various types of mystical treatise (the greatest of these coming to comprise the so-called Heikhalot literature) as well as with certain magical texts that remained in usage in more popular circles.

This "purification" of Jewish literature contributed to the emergence of a rela-tively uniform attitude toward the biblical text. But the apocalyptical, magical, mythical, and mystical perceptions of this text, which, naturally, could not be totally eradicated, continued to survive as vague hints or fragments incorporated into classical rabbinic literature. This literature, which was intended as a vast interpretation of the canon for the benefit of the large Jewish public, was con-sumed by a community who sought in it the guidance and instruction that it was once the role of the prophet or priest to supply.

Let us delve briefly into the main components of the midrashic literature exam-ined from the point of view of its hermeneutics. (Some of the more technical issues will be addressed later, in Chapter 6.) First and foremost, it seems that its disseminators were leading figures in Jewish communities or academies, speakers who delivered their homilies before an open audience without any restrictions regarding the age or the competence of the participants. The language of their discourses was generally perspicuous and aimed at explaining relatively simple items related to the biblical texts. Such explanation was usually achieved without resort to complex or systematic theological concepts. Further, these homilies took the form, it seems, of primarily oral speeches, delivered as part of or in connection with the oral religious service. The language of these homilies served a highly social function, its central feature being its public or collective communication. Indeed, there is a strong affinity that links the ancient Jewish interpreter, using authorized hermeneutic devices and perceiving the text as speaking mainly to the Jewish community, and the plain, public language he used in order to deliver his message. In effect, one implies the other.

As long as Jewish culture was given the chance to develop more or less autonomously, without a close encounter with or pressure from other theological systems, it generated mostly self-interpretative literature of this type. However, when attacked or criticized by sectarians, like the Karaites, or by outsiders, like the Islamic theologians, some Jewish masters reacted by absorbing some of the theological positions of their opponents, trying thereby to evidence the complete compatibility of Jewish texts with the intellectual standards of other traditions, such as Islamic Kalam or Aristotelianism. One of the most dramatic consequences of this apologetic reinterpretation of Judaism was the further suppression of some of the apocalyptic, magical, mythical, and mystical elements that survived in a diluted fashion in rabbinic sources, or in their primary form in Hebrew texts existing outside the authoritative Jewish literature. But just as the purification of Jewish literature caused a relocation of the mysterious, mystical, or magical elements in Midrash, so the rationalistic reconstructions of Judaism prompted a powerful reaction from a variety of circles, wherein an amalgam of older traditions, including the same mystical, mythical, and magical elements, came to the surface in more overt and more crystallized forms.[1]

II. AN ACCENT ON TEXTUALITY: RABBINIC CONCEPTS

Let me list what I understand as the four major characteristics of the postbiblical rabbinic conceptualization of the Torah, which apparently are new in this literature. They constitute the rabbinic imaginaire that redefined the boundaries of the Torah. As some of these features have been dealt with elsewhere in scholarship, and as the present framework strives to portray the Jewish mystical literatures, I cannot offer in this chapter a detailed analysis of all these characteristics but will elaborate on the first two alone. Naturally, they do not exhaust the rich gamut of understandings of the Torah in these literatures.

1. Torah is conceived of as a preexistent entity, which not only precedes the creation of the world but also serves as the paradigm of its creation.[2]
2. Torah encompasses the whole range of supernal and mundane knowledge, serving thereby as the depository of the perfect and complete gnosis and as an indispensable bridge between man and the divine.
3. Torah study is a religious imperative, as it embodies the will of God, which has to be further explicated by the intense devotion to the perusal and analysis of the contents inherent in the biblical text. Even God was not exempted from this religious obligation, and His study of the Torah became a leitmotif in rabbinic thought.
4. Torah is regarded, in some rabbinic texts and in a plethora of Kabbalistic ones, as the "daughter" of God.[3]

Such a special status of the text is different from that of the myths prevalent among the ancients and medieval Gnostics, or the various forms of pagan myths in the Near East, or those types of myths that were preferred in the regular scholarly expositions of the nature of mythology. First and foremost, in rabbinic sources there is an hypostatical understanding of the Torah, but not, insofar as ancient texts are concerned, a full personification. The sacred book does not possess a changing will of itself but rather embodies the dynamic will of its author. It has a feminine gender but only very marginally is it described in an erotic or sexual manner or characterized as playing the role of the divine wife or a goddess, though a more erotic role may be detected in the context of the relationship between the Torah and the people of Israel.[4] This last role was already "occupied" in Jewish thought by other hypostases, like those that represent the collective Jewish nation (knesset yisra'el) or the iconic representation of Jacob engraved on the divine throne.[5]

However, even these obvious differences between the more common Near Eastern myths and the above descriptions of the Torah cannot attenuate the mythological nature of the conception of this literary entity in some important trends of rabbinism. Its conceptualization proposes a canonization of events (some of them primordial) and of ritual by telescoping them into a mythical zone; I propose to call this literary zone a *mesocosmos*, an ontological universe that is the prototype of both cosmogonic processes and human behavior. According to some rabbinic texts, the Torah includes even directives concerning how to influence the status of the divine power.[6] This radical ontologization of the Torah in rabbinism is of paramount importance for understanding some later basic developments in Kabbalistic ontology in general and Kabbalistic textology in particular.[7] The ontological approach to the sacred text, which sometimes may presuppose a unique status for Hebrew, serves as one of the most powerful nexuses between the rabbinic literature, interested mostly in the ritual and legendary aspects of the Bible, and the theosophical Kabbalah, which projected the primordial Torah into the bosom of the divine.

III. TORAH: THE HIDDEN DIMENSION

In this section I would like to point out the existence of the concept of a hidden layer of the Torah in writings that predate both Kabbalistic literature and the masters of Hasidei Ashkenaz. The existence of such an understanding means that the dynamics of the development of the processes of arcanization will have to be analyzed as starting much earlier and to take into consideration presymbolic secret layers. It seems that without allowing magical arcanization a role in subsequent hermeneutical developments, the picture of Jewish hermeneutics will remain fragmentary.

The reception of the Torah by Moses in heaven has been described in several rabbinic and Jewish magical sources as preceded by a contest between him and the angels. After Moses' victory, the angels, which previously had opposed God's revealing the Torah to him, gave him the secret divine names.[8] Thus, the reception of the Torah was accompanied, according to several early medieval sources, by the disclosure of divine names—secret formulas, many of them unknown in classical Jewish texts and conceived as reflecting divine powers or attributes.[9] The most important discussion of this issue, found in the preface of a magical book entitled Ma'ayan ha-Hokhmah, will be translated and discussed later.[10] The assumption that potent names emerge out of the verses of the Torah has been expressed in Ma'ayan ha-Hokhmah by the verb yotze'im,[11] which means "go out." In that context it appears that a certain linguistic exegetical technique is able to extract from a regular verse something that is found in it. Interestingly enough, an early medieval midrash, called Midrash Konen, explains an operation performed by God himself on the text of the Torah: "He took the Torah and opened it and took out from her one name, which has not been transmitted to any creature, as it is written,[12] 'This is my name forever'[13] . . . He opened the Torah and took out a second name . . . He opened the Torah and took out a third name."[14]

The opening of the Torah and the taking out of names seem to reflect a certain understanding of the "emergence" of the names from the text, conceived of now as a box where the names are deposited and, presumably, kept in secret. This implies another type of imaginary, in comparison to that of Ma'ayan ha-Hokhmah, where the secrets, though also closely related to the text of the Torah, are disclosed by an external agent, angels, which teach Moses where precisely in the Bible to find the verse that generates the name pertinent to the cure of a malady or offering a remedy for a certain problem. In *Midrash Konen*, however, the Torah is conceived of as preexisting creation and as the source of the creative processes, by means of three divine names found in it. Let me designate this approach as *intratextual*. It means that the additional layer of understanding of some parts of the Torah is generated by a rearrangement of the linguistic units that constitute the interpreted text, an approach I propose to call *intracorporal*, not by the introduction of an elaborate nomenclature whose conceptualization is extraneous to the interpreted text—what may be referred to as the *extratextual* or *intercorporal* approach.[15] This approach is closer to a use of the Torah than an interpretation of it,[16] though the rearrangement of the linguistic material is presented as disclosing a dimension within the canonical text.

IV. THE COSMOLOGICAL TORAH

In the vast talmudic-midrashic literature several different ways of understanding the biblical account of creation are present. One of them, possibly influenced by Platonic thought, portrays God as consulting or contemplating the Torah as an architectonic model and creating the world according to its pattern.[17] The universe of language, as it was preestablished in the sacrosanct structure of the canon, is, according to such a view, the blueprint of the material cosmos. The peculiar arrangement of the linguistic material in the Torah is apparently regarded as compelling God Himself. He is now conceived of not as a totally free agent, a creator who may shape the nature of the world according to His unpredictable will, but as a power that enacts, on another plane and using other material, the content of a preexistent Torah. The act of creation is, in this view, an act of imposing the inner structure of the Torah on an undefined material. What seems to be absent from this description is the conception that letters are the raw material out of which the world is going to be created. Its primary material, its *hyle*, is not specified, but its "form," to speak in Aristotelian terms, is language as embodied in the Torah.

Interestingly, this presentation of creation did not specify whether God's contemplation of the Torah was accompanied by a pronunciation of its content as part of creation. This way of describing the creational process envisions Torah as the paradigm and is especially important for understanding the paramount centrality of Torah in Judaism, more specifically its commandments, whose performance is regarded as safeguarding the existence of heaven and earth.[18]

Another version of creation connected to language is expressed, tangentially, in a well-known statement according to which Bezalel created the tabernacle using his knowledge of the way heaven and earth were created by combination of letters.[19] According to this interpretation of the talmudic statement, Bezalel was cognizant of this peculiar method of creation, namely the technique of combining letters rather than using letters as raw material, as implied in the interpretation proposed by Scholem.[20] Depicted as the paragon of Jewish artisans, Bezalel was described as uniquely wise, his name being understood to mean "[being] in the shade of God." His knowledge of the combinatory device used by God, based on linguistic technique, enabled him to accomplish a creation that is second only to the creation of God—the creation of the tabernacle. The peculiar wisdom of the builder of the temple, Solomon, is well known; however, even he is not described as being in the possession of the combinatory practice that served God. In this description of creation, it is not clear whether God or Bezalel pronounced the peculiar combination of letters involved in the creational process.

The third midrashic theory regarding linguistic creation depicts God as using divine names. According to one version, He used letters that constitute His name in order to create heaven but other letters in order to create earth.[21] Again, it would be unreasonable to assume that these letters entered in the physical constitution of the creation; they are, apparently, the creative forces that served God rather than the basic elements of the universe. Also, in this description the pronunciation of the divine name is not implied.

The next important theory of linguistic creation, and seemingly the most influential one, argues that the actual pronunciation of the creational words, mentioned in the first chapter of Genesis, is the basic explanation of the account of creation.[22] God is sometimes referred as "He who spoke and the world came into being." The authors of this view identify ten creative words in Genesis 1, called ma'amarot, and interesting mystical speculations stemming from this assumption were to emerge in a long series of later Jewish mystical sources.[23]

V. THE BOOK AS THE PARADIGM OF CREATION IN RABBINIC LITERATURE

An interesting claim in rabbinic literature, reiterated later by Kabbalists, is the view of God as looking into the preexistent book of the Torah and creating the world. In this case, an extradivine pattern is contemplated by God acting as a demiurge, which follows a certain preexisting plan. The book seems to contain the universe, at least virtually, while God actualizes it just as an architect follows the preliminary plan. Preexistence, perhaps even primordiality, already confers on the Torah the aura of a cosmic book, which is corroborated by the divine gazing at it in order to create the world.[24]

Before examining the medieval treatments of the midrashic views, let me address a text whose precise date and origins are obscure but must have been composed earlier than the twelfth century[25] that assumes that God, when creating the world, had been contemplating *Sefer Yetzirah*, itself a book describing the creation of the world by letter combinations. Indubitably, this book serves as the paradigm for the world, just as the Torah did in *Genesis Rabba'*. I assume that this short treatise was composed by a more mystically and magically oriented author.[26] Indeed, whereas the midrashic source about the Torah as contemplated by God is presumably concerned with the semantic and graphic aspects of the canonical book, when *Sefer Yetzirah* is mentioned the plausible assumption is that God was conceived of as contemplating all the combinations of two letters, exposed in this book as the technique of creating the world.[27] The paramount mathematical nature of the combination of two letters implies the obliteration of the semantic aspects of language, and in fact of any significant message; therefore the divine intention, as manifested either in history or in commandments, is absent in this book. As we shall see in Chapter 12, the transition between the structured Torah as represented by verses and the status of its unconjugated letters before creation become an ongoing topic in Jewish mystical literatures.

What do the two instances of contemplating books in order to create the world mean? In my opinion, both texts subsumed the creator to their preexisting linguistic structures which, though authored by God, are nevertheless so definitive that even God is compelled to act in accordance with their order. The creating author, powerful as he may be, is therefore construed as obedient to the written articulation of his own will. Or, to put it in a different way, in some late ancient Jewish texts both God and man should contemplate and implement the structure of the primordial book, which was revealed in the present form as part of the Sinaitic revelation. In the contest between the author and his book, as represented by pre-Kabbalistic statements, in the first round the book won. In fact, this awareness is well formulated in a remarkable statement attributed to God Himself: "Rabbi Jeremy in the name of R. Hiyya bar Abba said: it is written,[28] 'They had deserted Me, and did not keep My Torah.' May they desert me but keep my Torah, because out of their studying Torah, the light within it will cause them to repent."[29]

If the choice must be made between the author and the book, a preference for the book is explicitly recommended by the author himself. The book did not yet absorb the author but it would become the most important type of preoccupation that would ultimately cause the return of the student to God. It is reasonable to assume that God is not conceived of as the "meaning" of the Torah, as Jesus was imagined to be in the Greek Bible. The Hebrew Bible was conceived of as having an independent message, teaching a way of life that will ultimately bring someone to God. Thus, it is not the presence, the passion, or the fate of God that gives meaning to the Bible, but a modus vivendi that can be extracted from a study of the biblical text. However, the ideal of attaining an experience of meeting God is not obliterated by the immersion in an enterprise that is profoundly text-oriented.

Let me address now another concept of the Torah that is recurrent in rabbinic literature and influential in Kabbalistic literature: the Torah as an entity upon which the world depends long after its creation. The assumption that the world stands, or exists—in Hebrew 'omed—upon the Torah, namely the study of the book, recurs in rabbinic literature.[30] I assume that a variety of understandings of these statements is possible, ranging from a more metaphorical one, which would assume that the world is none other than human society, to a more literal one, which would assume an ontological dependence of the created universe on the ongoing study and observance of the Torah. While the more metaphorical stands were preferred in some forms of Jewish thought, in some of the main schools of Kabbalah the more literal and thus ontological understanding becomes prevalent. We shall survey some instances of the creational and sustaining aspects of the Torah later, especially in Chapter 4.

VI. SEFER YETZIRAH AND LINGUISTIC CREATIONAL PROCESSES

The crucial formulation of the creation by means of language, which served as the cornerstone of medieval linguistic mysticism in Judaism, is to be found in a short treatise that is not part of the classical talmudic-midrashic literature. It is *Sefer Yetzirah*, the Book of Creation,[31] that contributed the theory that the letters of the Hebrew alphabet entered the process of creation not only as the creative force but also as the elements of its material structure.[32] Given the great importance of this book for many of the discussions below, especially in Chapters 11 and 12, it is appropriate here to describe briefly some of its main statements. What is unique to its linguistic theory, in comparison to the views expressed in the two other bodies of Jewish literature surveyed above, seems to be the very discussion of the emergence of language. In the Bible and in the midrashic-talmudic literature the implicit assumption is that language was not created but used, that language is coexistent with God. The very question of the production of its elements or the processes of the interaction between them was not addressed at all. Therefore, the little treatise under consideration addresses questions of the origin and organization of language but, unlike the two other corpora mentioned above, is less interested in the way ordinary language organizes reality. The search for origin often represents a certain nostalgia that reflects an uneasiness with the prevalent forms of established culture, and this seems to be the case with the linguistic thought of *Sefer Yetzirah*.

It is not the accepted formulations of language that inspired the discourse of this booklet but the ontology of the elements that precede their coalescence into language. If the later dating of this book from sometime after the fifth century is accepted, an uneasiness with the rabbinic formulation of the canonic Bible and its emphasis on commandments may underlie the discussions in *Sefer Yetzirah*. However, even if a much earlier dating is proven, we may assume that this treatise articulates a spiritual trend different from the one that is to become the more dominant form of discourse in the rabbinic sources, a fact widely recognized by scholars. Here language in its consonant form, and mainly less semantic status, is considered the archetype of the world, having a transcendental existence, and also the stuff of the cosmos, thus expressing a much more immanentist approach. Another cardinal topic that occurs only in this version of linguistic creation is the description of the extraction of the letters of the alphabet from the second sefirah, the *pneuma*, out of which God has carved the alphabet. After the completion of the emergence of the twenty-two Hebrew letters, God combined them in all possible permutations of two letters as part of the cosmogonic processes. Given the impact of this book, let me succinctly address some of the magical-linguistic elements found therein. In the second chapter God is portrayed as creating the Hebrew letters that served as the tools, and perhaps also the prime matter, for the creation of the world: "Twenty-two letters, He engraved them and He extracted them and weighted them and permuted them and combined them, and He created by them 'the soul of all the formation,' and 'the soul of all the speech,' which will be formed in the future."[33]

The Hebrew verbs expressing the divine creation of the letters are, respectively, *haqaq, hatzav, shaqal, hemir, tzeref,* and *tzar*. Three of these verbs, *haqaq, hatzav,* and *tzeref,* also occur elsewhere, in connection with the creation of the world.[34] Two of them, *haqaq* and *hatzav,* recur more than once in similar contexts.[35] Four of these verbs expressing divine acts are also among the verbs that describe, at the end of the treatise, an act of the patriarch Abraham, who is portrayed as contemplating and looking, seeing and investigating and understanding. It is then written that he "engraved, extracted and combined and formed, and he was successful."[36] The Hebrew verbs related to the creation and manipulation of letters are *haqaq, hatzav, tzeref,* and *tzar*. The recurrence of these verbs in the first and last chapters of the same book suggests that Abraham's deeds are understood as a case of *imitatio dei*. Man, or an elitist figure represented here by Abraham, may manipulate letters in a manner patently similar to God's primordial operation. Thus the correspondences between the two agents are quite explicit. This conclusion raises a question: What is the meaning of Abraham's "success"? I assume that, by dint of the parallelism between the two discussions, God's creation of the "soul of all the formation" (*nefesh kol yetzur*) and the "soul of all the speech" (*nefesh kol dibbur*) implies that Abraham also has been able to replicate these creations. As I have suggested elsewhere, the formation in late-antiquity Hebrew designated by the term *yetzur* is to be understood as standing for an anthropoid.[37] Thus, by imitating the divine acts, some of them including operations related to language like permutation and combination of letters, man is able to create here in the lower sphere. In other words, *Sefer Yetzirah* offers a special kind of *imitatio dei*, not by means of an act of intellection, as in Jewish Neoaristotelianism, nor by performance of commandments, as in talmudic thought, nor by love or suffering, as in Christianity. It is by exploiting the creative power of language that the *perfecti* are able to imitate God.

It should be emphasized, however, that it is not by delivering a semantic message, as in ritual behavior, or transmitting a certain kind of information to others that man is able to imitate God. Rather, this mimesis is attained by a combinatory practice that does not copy any preexisting pattern nor reproduce any preexisting message. God and man are conceived of as exhausting all the potential inherent in the linguistic units, as actualizing the nonsemantic parts of all the possible combinations of letters in the Hebrew alphabet. It is more the seriousness of *homo ludens* than the understanding of *homo sapiens* that is able to imitate God. Indeed, recourse to the idea of God as playing occurs sometimes in medieval interpretations of the combinatory technique of *Sefer Yetzirah*; the term used was *sha'ashu'a*, as we shall see in the next section. However, *homo faber* is also present in the parallels between God and man: both were presented as creating, formatting, by means of language. To a great extent, the *sapiens* part of man, and of God, has been minimized by the conspicuous stress placed on the importance of the meaningless combinations of two letters.

This parallelism based on the activation of language is not exclusive to *Sefer Yetzirah*; it also occurs in a well-known talmudic passage found in the Babylonian Talmud, *Berakhot*, where Bezalel, the biblical builder of the tabernacle, is described as having been acquainted with the combination of letters that served in the process of the creation of heaven and earth.[38] Again, man imitates God by permuting letters in a context that conspicuously deals with a certain form of creation. This affinity between the talmudic statement and that found in *Sefer Yetzirah* has a definite significance: it shows, unlike an opinion expressed more recently,[39] that a central aspect of *Sefer Yetzirah*, namely its linguistic magic, which includes an *imitatio dei*, is shared at least by two different layers of ancient Jewish literature. We should also mention in this context that a rather magical view of the creation of the world by means of linguistic material—the various letters of the divine names—was also expressed in rabbinic literature.[40] Thus, the magician using the divine names, or some of their letters, not only relies on the inherent power of those letters but at the same time imitates divine creative acts. Yet unlike the more clear-cut medieval parallelism between the lower and supernal languages, in *Sefer Yetzirah* and the passage from *Berakhot* it seems that the same type of linguistic unit is used by both God and the perfect religious persons. The letters were indeed created by God, but they entered the constitution of the world, and the mystic is able to use them. Thus, when imitating God's acts, the mystic is, according to these two texts, also resorting to His same tools.

According to this version of creation, there is no mention of the Torah as the archetype. Neither are the divine names crucial for understanding the process of creation in the Book of Creation; they occur only as seals securing the extremities of the world. It is noteworthy that this theory, which focuses on letters and their combinations rather than the Torah and the divine names, occurs in a work that was composed outside the literary genres characteristic of the halakhic-midrashic writings. The emphasis on the combinatory theory that, as we saw in the preceding section, is only hinted at in the talmudic passage about Bezalel assumes a degree of freedom in the usage of the letters, which are no longer conceived of as forming the fixed and powerful combinations of the letters in the canonic Torah. Now God is not copying the content of the Torah, transposing it on another plane, but is creating freely by resorting to a mathematical combination of letters. No wonder that this treatise does not even touch on the topic of commandments; the common Jewish religious concepts are rather marginal in comparison to the cosmogonic elements that permeate the entire book.[41]

Let me address now the absorbing element in *Sefer Yetzirah*. The combinations of letters to which God resorted are described in detail in this book; they consist of all the combinations of two letters of the Hebrew alphabet. However, if the combinatory technique is accepted as valid, all the other combinations, which are ostensibly much more numerous, may reflect the creative aspects of the alphabet in respect to other realms. Plausibly, the created world is one incident, or result, of the cosmogonic aspects of language, which are to be conceived as more comprehensive. Combinations of more letters, or other types of combinations that are not even mentioned in *Sefer Yetzirah*, could have been conceived of as culminating in the emergence of other universes.

The above rabbinic sources and *Sefer Yetzirah* represent cases of absorption of the material realm and sometimes also spiritual existence, within an entity conceptualized as the sacred book. The belief in a world-absorbing book[42] did not leave too much room for the book of nature, just as the emphasis found in Greek philosophical texts on what has been designated as the book of nature and the kinds of thought influenced by Greek philosophy did not allow the ascent of the textuality of the sacred book.[43]

VII. TORAH: A SUPERNAL GARMENT AND A SMALL BLACKBOARD

God as creator has been described as contemplating the Torah, according to the midrashic text, and as combining letters in *Sefer Yetzirah*. As seen above, in an anonymous early medieval text God was depicted in a manner that brings together the two divergent descriptions. (I shall have more to say about this issue in Chapter 12.) Another development in Kabbalah, however, produced the most articulated version of the world-absorbing text: the version of Lurianism commonly called the theory of the *malbush* and ascribed to R. Israel Saruq, an influential Kabbalist who disseminated his lore in Europe at the end of the sixteenth century. The details of this development have been addressed elsewhere; here I would like to restrict my discussion to the elevation of both Torah and the combinations of letters, following the pattern found in *Sefer Yetzirah*, to a pretheogonic and precosmogonic stage, which implies a moment of divine delight, *sha'ashu'a*.[44]

According to this version of Lurianism, Sarug interposed an important phase in the theogonic process, which consists in the theory of the malbush, the divine garment, which is woven of the combinations of the letters as combined in *Sefer Yetzirah*. This texture of letters, also named Torah, plays a role similar to that of the *tehiru* in Luria, being the space from which God withdrew and where the creation will take place. In order to enable this process, however, the lower half of the combinations of letters was folded up and evacuated the place that would serve as the locus of the emanative process. Only then did the supernal anthropomorphic configuration called *'Adam Qadmon* emerge. Obviously, it is an important change in comparison to other versions of Lurianism; in Sarug's and its sixteenth-century sources the combinatory technique of *Sefer Yetzirah* was placed above the emanative process concerning the ten *sefirot* or the various Lurianic configurations named *partzufim*. The Kabbalists who generated this new status of the combinations of letters as higher than the emanations of anthropomorphic entity returned to the more comprehensive perception of the process of creating an anthropoid according to the technique of *Sefer Yetzirah*.

A survey of all the main schemes related to the malbush shows that it consists of combinations of letters that are based on *Sefer Yetzirah* and are identical to the 231 two-letter combinations that are to be pronounced in order to create the golem—the 231 gates—and of the 231 that serve to undo it. The evacuation of the lower 231 gates can be explained as the evacuation of those combinations that may counteract the creation of the divine anthropos, and the Sarugian texts specify that the infolding combinations of letters represent the attribute of judgment, whereas those combinations that remained in place correspond to the attribute of grace. The appearance of the figure of the 'Adam Qadmon, after mention of the combinations of letters, is a close parallel to the technique of creating a golem, which was transposed on the theosophical level.

The primordial Torah, *torah qedumah*, has been identified with the garment and was described as "woven from the letters forward and backward, upward and downward, and was read from all the sides and from the two parts. On the higher half of the malbush the letters are in the form of seals, [as a] vessel, there are fifteen alphabets which the serving angels are using."[45]

From the perspective of this discussion, in principle the predication of the Torah as preexisting the world is nothing new. However, the insertion of the emergence of the Torah as a texture of letters, like those expounded in *Sefer Yetzirah* and its numerous reverberations in the Middle Ages, within an emanational process generates a more sophisticated theory that is worthy of elaboration. This synthesis is already found in the emerging Kabbalah, as we shall see in the next chapter, and it reverberated in the middle of the sixteenth century in the works of the Jerusalem Kabbalist R. Joseph ibn Tzayyah.[46] Yet it seems that only Sarug explicitly combined this view with that of the divine withdrawal, known as the theory of *tzimtzum*, which assumes that the space of the world was occupied in its entirety by the malbush. Thus, this texture, which is identical to the Torah, occupies both the place where all the worlds will later emerge, namely the emanated and the created worlds, but also the higher part, where it still exists after the evacuation of the lower part. The primordial Torah is therefore much more comprehensive and sublime than all the known subsequent worlds. This Torah, however, is described as folded, in order to allow the several stages of emanation and creation. In other words, though amorphous from the semantic point of view, the texture designated as Torah comprises the two main divine attributes: the creative one, grace, and the destructive one, judgment. But the two cannot remain separated; they should and must be reconnected by the ascent of the lower 231 gates to the 231 higher ones.

Creation, in this version, occurs in locus vacuus of the Torah but formerly was imprinted with its negativity. Creation is therefore dependent on a double negativity: one aspect stems from the view that half of the combinations of letters conceived of as Torah have been evacuated and elevated on high, thus overlapping with the higher part and leaving an empty space where the theogonic and cosmogonic processes will take place; the other has to do with the negative nature of this half of the Torah, whose combinations of letters are conceived of as destructive. This potential tension between the textological and the cosmogonic aspects of reality is quite interesting, for it assumes that the highest, though semantically amorphous, text is not found in our world but dramatically transcends it.

Let me turn our attention to a particular aspect of the Torah/malbush: its shape. Though its form is a square, already described in many medieval texts, it is inscribed within a circle, which is the evacuated place resulting from the divine withdrawal. This bringing together of letter combinations with a circle is reminiscent of a theme in some of Abraham Abulafia's discussions, where he contends that ma'aseh merkavah, the account of the chariot, is numerically tantamount to galgal ha-torah, the sphere or circle of the Torah that is to be understood as the combinatory circles that were related to permuting the letters of the Torah.

The divine chariot, understood here by Abulafia as a complexity of divine names, is the blueprint of the whole Torah, which was conceived by Kabbalists to contain an esoteric level that emerges from reading it as a continuum of divine names.[47] Again, as we shall see in more detail below, in the same book Abulafia subordinated creation to the combination of letters of the divine names described as found within the divine realm.[48]

A younger contemporary of Sarug, R. Joseph Shlomo of Kandia, offers a vision of the Torah as a microcosmos that includes all the worlds. In his Matzref ha-Hokhmah, one of the most perplexing surveys of Kabbalah, he writes: "Our Torah is a small board where there are the inscriptions of all the worlds. And this Torah given by Moses is found also in the [worlds of] 'A[tzilut]B[eri'ah]Y[etzirah] according to the way it is studied by Kabbalists, since all the worlds have a root on high, but the difference between them is great."[49]

The Kabbalist resorts to the topos of the small or concise blackboard, ha-luah ha-qatzar, well known in medieval Jewish literature.[50] Moses' Torah, apparently that found in the world of 'asiyah, is a reflection of the macrocosmos but introduces the three supernal Kabbalistic worlds, in a manner that assumes that the mundane Torah is both dependent on the higher worlds and different from the Torah found there, apparently a theory reminiscent of the theory of accommodation. The author, who was well acquainted with Sarug's Kabbalistic theory of malbush as a text that comprises everything before its emergence, adopts the philosophical stand that the mundane Torah, too, comprises everything.[51]

VIII. INTERPRETATION AND COSMOLOGICAL REPERCUSSIONS

Another interesting instance of a world-absorbing understanding of the text is found in a book of R. Moses Hayyim Ephrayyim of Sudylkov. A grandson of the founder of Hasidism, R. Israel Ba'al Shem Tov, he adduces his grandfather's opinion within the framework of his own homily, which deals with affinities between study of the Torah, including innovations that emerge during study, and cosmic daily changes. Elaborating on the traditional view of God as creating the world anew every day and on the assumption that God created the Torah by contemplating it, the Hasidic master contends that the innovation of the deed of creation is [tantamount to] the innovation of the world that [the people of] Israel are innovating each and every day by their innovations of the Torah, as I heard from my grandfather, blessed be his memory, that the book of the *Zohar* has each and every day another interpretation,[52] as it is written in the *Gemara*,[53] "I have put my words in your mouth"[54] "to fix the heavens in place and form the earth, and say to Zion: You are my people."[55] Do not read ʿami [my people] but ʿimi [with me] with a hiriq, which means by cooperation: Just as I create heavens and earth by speech, you also [can do] so. And the meaning of the verse "I have put my words in your mouth" in order to "fix heavens in place and form the earth" by the innovation that Israel are innovating in the Torah of Truth, and all the things that are emerging in the world, emerge by the innovation of the Torah that Israel are innovating by their looking into [the Torah] in accordance to their innovation in the Torah, so is the innovation in the world . . . In accordance with the innovations that they innovate while they learn and study, so does the Holy One, Blessed be He, innovate the deed of creation.[56]

The interpretation of the inverse order of the phrases from Isaiah 51:16 is associated with a pun. The verb *le-haddesh* is used in two ways in rabbinic Hebrew: to point to the continual creation and to the innovation emerging during learning. Combined with the two other rabbinic views that God created by contemplating the Torah and the continual creation, the Hasidic master concludes that innovations by study affect in one way or another the very nature of the cosmically existing Torah, which is the source of all the changes that took place in the lower world, the continuous creation. Therefore, by productive and original learning, a person is able to cooperate with God in the process of continuous creation. According to the Hasidic view, the Torah regulates the postcreational processes, which imitate the latest developments in the domain of Torah studies. The nature of Torah innovations is variegated: it apparently consists in mental innovation, emerging from the intellect, by oral study of the Torah and by the very contemplation of the Torah, as we learn later on the same page in the name of the author's brother, R. Barukh of Medzibezh.[57] This Hasidic passage is an interesting example of what I have called ergetic exegesis. Representative as this passage is of Hasidic views, it continues much earlier views that had also been adopted by one of the opponents of Hasidism, R. Hayyim of Volozhin.[58]

XI. CONCLUDING REMARKS

I have attempted to describe the various versions of the ancient Jewish views of linguistic creation, and now it is in order to attempt a phenomenology of the role of text and language, which will take us beyond the details of the analyzed texts. When fixed in the specific linguistic structures—Torah and the divine name—the archetypal role of the text is central, and a certain axiology, mostly a religious one, is involved: either the commandments as the most important value or the omnipotence of God or the usages of the divine name. However, when the disparate letters are mentioned as basic entities, as is the case in the Book of Creation, the focus becomes a type of anomian—though not antinomian—knowledge, namely a form of gnosis of the primordial processes that is not connected to issues regarding sacred history, classical rituals, or religious commandments. In the first way of using language, a drastic difference between the creator and the created is implicit; He transcends the material world, which emerges as a cosmos (an organized entity), by an act that is essentially different from the nature of the nascent creature. Not so in the type of creation as proposed in *Sefer Yetzirah*. There the Hebrew letters enter the constitution of the world and became part of its fabric; God Himself is portrayed as immersed in the process of creating, as arranging the letters in the specific permutations that are the source of each and every created entity, though not pronouncing them as in the Midrash. The interest in the specific relationship between each letter and the peculiar astronomical, temporal, and human domain on which it is appointed, so characteristic of the Book of Creation,[59] contributed greatly to the atomization of language that become even more manifest in the later stages of Jewish mysticism. Regression—or, as some prefer to say, return—from the informative to the magical and mythic nature of language is triggered by focusing on the singular letter as a topic in itself.

The monadization of language, which is one of the main Kabbalistic modes of perception, means the reduction, and in some cases even the obliteration, of ordinary semantics. Semantic sense, the major channel of linguistic communication effects, retreated from its role as the main function of the word within a text in order to allow an even greater role to power effects. Even in this case, however, meaning does not disappear. It is sometimes found either in the nature of the source of this power or in the specific orientation of the letters as magical tools. The first sort of meaning is exemplified by the astrological and sefirotic lexicons, where each of the letters is described as presided over by a certain supernal power. This is a far more esoteric type of sense, known by the astrologers or Kabbalists, who are in the possession of the linguistic gnosis that is not the patrimony of the common people. In lieu of an agreed language, or a symbolic one, that implies the connection between a whole word and its higher correspondent, the natural and primordial nexus between the higher entity and the isolated linguistic unit becomes the dominant factor. The intrinsic quality of the presiding power, the signified, now supplies the "meaning" of the letter. The higher superstructures, astrological or theosophical, are now the sources that engender the dismembered language with an elitist meaning. The dissipation of the ordinary structure of Torah letters as they are linked in words opens the gate for the entrance of the extraordinary; the evacuation of the visible enables the invasion of the invisible.[60]

On the other hand, the precise correspondences between the various letters and mundane entities, which may point to the influence that those letters can exercise on the lower entities, also infuses letters with a noncommunicative charge. The most conspicuous example in Jewish sources is already present in some discussions in the last parts of *Sefer Yetzirah*, where a complete list of correspondences between the Hebrew letters and human limbs is supplied. Indeed, this correspondence might have influenced the magical creation of the various limbs of the golem, the anthropoidic creature that is vivified by means of the recitation of the combinations of letters.[61]

These two different directions of infusing meaning are, to be sure, not mutually exclusive. Indeed, both the astrological and the anthropomorphic structures are explicitly mentioned in *Sefer Yetzirah*. In this case the separate letters play the role of a mesocosmos that mediates between the astronomical macrocosmos and the human microcosmos. By mediating the transition of power from above to the mundane world, as is the case in the astrological superstructures, or of the human force to the higher entities, as in some of the sefirotic Kabbalists' views of the letters,[62] the linguistic mesocosmos is therefore not only a static picture but also an agent that is part of a much more active enterprise, be it magical or theurgical. In the astrological superstructure, the talismanic conception—which is not to be found in all the cases—represents the descent of the supernal power on the corresponding character below. In a "theosophical" correspondence, the affinity is still between the higher, divine attribute or entity and the letter; however, the force that is active in this instance is not generated by the astral bodies but by a human pronunciation of sounds.

On the other hand, we may envision the hypothetical existence of a much more unified, though not always clear, system that included a more comprehensive view of language preceding the Heikhalot literature, which apparently consisted of two levels of language. This hypothesis assumes a prior development, whose articulated steps seem to elude our knowledge. The only significant and influential text that reflects a more comprehensive theory of language, *Sefer Yetzirah*, stems from circles different from those which generated the Heikhalot literature.[63] If a greater weight is allotted to the influence of certain elements in *Sefer Yetzirah*, and if those elements can be dated to an earlier period than the Heikhalot and most of the Midrashic literatures, then another historical and phenomenological picture emerges, which depends much on the interpretation one offers to some parts of this treatise. If a more magical reading of the text is preferred—one that implies the antiquity of the tradition regarding the creation of an entity that will later be called golem—to *Sefer Yetzirah* itself, a much more complex theory of magical language will better serve the understanding of the ancient Jewish theories of magical language.[64]

In any case, these discussions demonstrate not only the strong nexus between the book of God and the book of nature but also the subordination of the latter to the former. In my opinion, attempts to observe the book of nature have been minimal in Jewish mystical sources, which presuppose that the simplest and most efficient way to understand reality is to contemplate the book of God, as we shall see in Appendix 6. The paradigmatic and instrumental understandings of the Torah or *Sefer Yetzirah* conspired to bestow on language a preeminent status in comparison to natural objects. The canonical texts absorbed the attention of the Jewish masters, especially those who had mystical inclinations, who preferred to learn about what they conceived to be the lower effect by contemplating the nature of its alleged supernal cause. By absorbing the cosmological and, as we shall see in the next chapters, divine dimensions, the Torah as understood by rabbinic and many other Jewish authors becomes an absorbing being that imposed a discipline of study demanding total dedication. In a form of mysticism that contended that God looked into the Torah, saw the word 'or, "light," and created light, it is more economical to immerse oneself in study of the linguistic paradigm than its material counterpart.[65] Or, to cite a formulation found in the so-called camp of the Mitnaggedim, "the Torah encompasses all the worlds, the supernal and the lower ones, the spiritual and the corporeal, because it was the instrument of techne of the Creator of the Beginning. And the essence of the Torah letters is the principle of the mixture of all the powers of the creatures, supernal and lower."[66]

To invert Stéphane Mallarmé's famous statement that "tout, au monde, existe pour aboutir à un livre,"[67] one may assert that letters and the biblical text exist in order to culminate in a world. Unlike the poet's assumption that the book is to be in the future, and thus the world strives for its emergence, the rabbinic and Kabbalistic authors lived within a conceptual framework in which the book preceded the emergence of the world, which may be no more than one small aspect of the comprehensive book.

Or, to resort to the felicitous question that Umberto Eco put in the mouth of the quasi-Kabbalist Diotalevi, "Is there a writing that founds the world and is not the Book?"[68]

2

THE GOD-ABSORBING TEXT
Black Fire on White Fire

I. The Torah as a Transcendental Inscription

Ancient Jewish monotheism was generally uncomfortable with the idea of the preexistence of any entity to the creation of the world, a premise that would imperil the uniqueness of God as the single creator. The coexistence of an additional entity would produce a theological dynamics that would question the most singular religious achievement of ancient Judaism. Implicitly, allowing any role to such a founding and formative entity would reintroduce a type of myth that could recall the pagan mythology, where once again the relationship between the preexistent deities as a crucial condition for the cosmogonic process would be thrown into relief.

Even in the biblical account of the creation, however, there is an implicit assumption regarding the preexistence of the tool of the creation: the Hebrew language. God created—or, according to another possible interpretation of the first chapter of the Bible, organized—the chaotic matter. The language that served as a crucial instrument in the cosmogonic process is presented as naturally existent and effective, and in any case there is no hint of any need to create language itself. Its existence is taken for granted. A preexistent tool, whose mythical features are minimized, enabled the transition from the chaotic matter, which cannot be considered as a creative entity, to the structured natural world. The Hebrew language was implicitly interposed between the accomplished creation and the preexistent chaos. This language plays, in the biblical view, solely an instrumental role, and it lacks an independent organization that could transform it into a text. Language appears only in those circumstances when the emergence of a certain entity or its denomination is referred to; in itself, it seems that language was not an object of discussion in the ancient Jewish reports of cosmogony. Thus the inner structure of language did not serve as an object of contemplation in order to understand the details of the cosmogonic processes.

No metaphysics or ontology of Hebrew is manifest in the biblical sources. Even the distinction between Hebrew as the divine language and other, "lower" languages does not explicitly occur in the Bible. Although we may assume that such a distinction is inherent in biblical thought, it is conspicuous that the self-perception of the Jews as inheritors of this special language was not presented in a polemical context.

Partially it seems that this lack of metaphysics regarding language is the result of its basically oral nature. The creative processes were accomplished by means of speech; the written form of language was confined only to the legal part of the Bible, namely the Ten Commandments, and not to those sections concerning the cosmogony. In rabbinic thought the vocal form of the creative process still prevails. The creative *logoi* were articulated by the invention of a new term to denote the spoken formulas in the first chapter of Genesis. The so-called *ma'amarot* are discussed in some detail, and there are even various versions of their precise identity.[1] God is described as "He Who spoke and created the world." However, at the same time as the oral status of the creative language was articulated and preserved, rabbinic literature expressed the written dimension of the creative language. God was not conceived as creating by writing but, according to a highly influential midrash, as contemplating the Torah as the paradigm of the world. Thus the written manifestation of the Torah, and implicitly of the Hebrew language, becomes crucial for the transition from the chaotic to the cosmic state. The intermediary status of the written Torah now shares with the divine the status of preexistence, and it cooperates in the process of creation. Meanwhile it seems that the importance of the written form of the Torah in the process of creation was expanded to the letters of the Hebrew alphabet. Although we cannot establish the exact historical sequence of this expansion, I assume that the concept of the creative letters emerged somewhat later. According to a midrash, of which there are several versions, each and every letter competed with the others so that God would create the world by its means. From the various discussions in this midrash, it transpires that the written shapes of the letters were alluded to by the midrashist.[2]

Even more conspicuous is the status of the written language in the cosmogony of *Sefer Yetzirah*. For the first time in a systematic way, the creation of the world was described as preceded by the creation of the letters. They were hewn from a primordial air, or ether, and after their emergence God combined them in order to create the world. I shall have much more to say on the crucial turn introduced by the combinatory technique of *Sefer Yetzirah* in the conception of language and the hermeneutics of Jewish mysticism in the following chapters, especially Chapter 12. Here it will suffice to stress again that this basic treatise envisioned the creation of the language as preceding that of the world and as instrumental for the mystical cosmogony. From these observations we can affirm that the written form of the Torah, and of the Hebrew letters in general, antedated the cosmogonic process or are part of the initial stages of that process. Thus, the "logical" question was asked as to the status of a written document before the creation of the material cosmos. In a long series of midrashic passages, the primordial Torah is described as having been written on a white fire with the letters of a black fire.[3] More specifically, however, some midrashic sources became aware that if the Torah antedates the world, a quandary arises as to the material involved in the visible manifestation of the written. This question was explicitly posed in at least two different midrashim, using similar structural formulations, though the details differ substantially. A late midrash, 'Aseret ha-Dibberot, formulates the question as follows: "Before the creation of the world, skins for parchments were not in existence, that the Torah might be written on them, because the animals did not yet exist. So, on what was the Torah written? On the arm of the Holy One, blessed be He, by a black fire on [the surface of] a white fire."[4]

It is obvious that the quandary of the midrash is related to the written form of the Torah; only this version can raise the question of the substratum for the letters. Here the preexistence of the Torah is envisioned in purely written form, and the graphical component of the text is of paramount importance. The basic assumption is that the material for the written Torah is a skin or parchment prepared from the hides of animals. Provided the primordial status of the Torah, no such material was yet in existence. The solution proposed by the midrash seems to be adumbrated by the phrase used in the question: If skins of animals were not in existence, was there another skin upon which the Torah was written down? The answer is positive; the Torah was written on the arm of God and implicitly on the skin of God's arm. This skin, though not mentioned explicitly, is hinted at by the term "white fire," on which the black letters of the Torah were engraved. The description of God as fire is not new; it is already found in the Bible, where God is designated as 'esh 'okhelah, a "devouring fire."[5] The fact that the divine arm is envisioned as a substitute for the animal skin forcibly invites the concept that the divine skin is the locus of the primordial Torah. The above midrash is one of the rare instances of an anthropomorphic understanding of the Torah. It is not, however, a unique text. According to the view of midrash Tanhuma', the very question asked by midrash 'Aseret ha-Dibberot is answered using a biblical locus probans, which had important resonances in other discussions: "On what was the Torah written? On the white fire with the black fire, as it is said:[6] 'His locks are wavy, and black as a raven.' What is the meaning [of the phrase] 'His locks are wavy'?[7] On each and every tittle[8] there are heaps and heaps[9] of halakhot."[10]

The midrashic exegesis is based on a rather peculiar reading of the biblical verse: the locks, taltalim, are divided into two words, which are understood as tilei tilim, literally "heaps of heaps"; qevuzotav, "wavy," is understood as referring to an imaginary plural of qotz, a tittle.[11] So, the meaning of the text is that depending on the tittles of the divine locks there are heaps of implicit halakhic issues. Obviously there is an anthropomorphic overtone of the description of the Torah as written on the white fire; here the effect is achieved by mentioning the biblical verse where the description of the Beloved in the Song of Songs is included. The first part of the verse, "The locks of the Beloved," depicted here as black, is an interpretation of the black fire and implicitly the letters of the Torah and the halakhic decisions emerging from the biblical text. Thus, another text, using a different approach, alludes too to the anthropomorphic nature of the primordial Torah.

What are the theological implications of these attempts to identify the preexistent Torah with the divine skin? Such an identification may be viewed as bridging the gap between God and the primordial Torah so that the monotheistic attitude of ancient Judaism will not be imperiled. This is achieved, however, within the framework of an anthropomorphic theology. It seems that the above texts do not worry too much about the "danger" of an anthropomorphic reading. Rather, they appear to have simply accepted an anthropomorphic theology of the Heikhalot literature, which includes discussions of the huge dimension of the divine manifestation on the throne. Provided such an anthropomorphic theology operates beyond the above texts, the riddle of the material on which the Torah was written before its disclosure at Mount Sinai can be elegantly solved. These identifications of God and Torah are, however, only part of a more comprehensive view of their relationship, which asserts that the Torah was written on the limbs of God. I should like to forgo elaborating on that view here; however, we have already seen that the Torah was written on the arm and head of God, as the mention of the locks apparently implies. The Torah is viewed as an inscription on the divine body, to be compared with the inscriptions in ancient Jewish and non-Jewish magic. This mythical Torah is, at the same time, an inscription on a divine limb and a sacred canon, a perception that emphasizes the visual dimension of the text. It is a divine manifestation, to the extent that the Torah is the black fire, and we may assume that the contemplation of our Torah is reminiscent of its status *in illo tempore*, before the creation, or possibly even its status today. Contemplating the Torah will, accordingly, involve more than a study of certain sacred contents, more than the disclosure of an ideal *modus vivendi*; it will include, at least partially, a divine self-revelation. Thus the white fire will stand for the divine substance of the Torah, the black one for the letters.

Semiotically, only the black dimension operates as a meaningful signifier because it alone imparts content to the readers. Mystically, however, the white fire involves a higher status which, though semantically meaningless, directly reflects the divine body rather than God's intention as articulated in the Torah. I assume that the split in the two aspects of the written Torah, the black and the white, reflects a much deeper axiology than the common preference for white, as a positive color, over black. The implicit preference for the white and amorphous fire may represent a tendency to be immersed into a more contemplative and direct approach to the divine, which will regard the letters, namely the limited contents of the revealed religion, as a lower and mediated relation to the beyond. Such a religious phenomenology is, in my opinion, not representative of rabbinic Judaism, which was centered on the semantic facets of the text more than on its formal ones. However, it seems to be in full consonance with the theology of the Heikhalot literature, where not only is the anthropomorphic aspect central but also the importance of the semantic aspects of the Torah is attenuated. In this type of literature, and in writings related to it, the magical aspects and the measurable dimensions of the Torah are addressed much more than in the classical rabbinic tradition. A religiosity based on a theology that emphasizes the formal and dimensional aspects of the divine, and the attempt of the mystic to experience them, supports the conception of the white fire as the substratum of the Torah, as identical with the divine skin. The higher status of the white fire in the constitution of the Torah is, I would like to repeat, only implicitly found in midrashic texts. In other words, the above discussions of white and black do not invite a distinction between a transcendental deity, identified with the white fire, and a revealed one. There is no concept similar to negative theology that is involved in the whiteness of the divine skin, but perhaps some concept of purity or sublimity.

Before moving to the later reverberations of the two fires, let me record what seems to me to be a reaction to the anthropomorphic solution to the quandary of the preexistence of the Torah. In Rashi's commentary on the treatise 'Avot 5:6, it is said that the body of the letters had been created only during the six days of creation, while the preexistent Torah was standing orally, be-'al peh.[12] This stand is indeed exceptional given the midrashic view that God contemplated the Torah and created the world. I see here an attempt to neutralize the already existing understanding of the preexistence of the Torah on the divine body by assuming this oral status. I would summarize the few midrashim adduced above as describing the close relation between God and the Torah with the intention of solving a quandary produced by the previous midrashic elevation of the Torah to the status of a preexistent entity by supplying a substratum for it, rather than as consciously attempting to confer divine status on the text.[13] The passages under scrutiny above can be understood as narrowing the gap between God and Torah, but they apparently are characteristic of a later development and hardly represent the main thrust of the more classical midrash.

II. R. JACOB BEN JACOB HA-KOHEN AND R. ISAAC THE ELDER

In the medieval Kabbalistic treatments of the nature of the two fires, however, the symbolic interpretations manifestly present the white part of the letters and the Torah as symbols of the higher aspects of the Torah, in comparison to the black parts of letters. The details of the symbolic interpretations will be adduced in a moment. First, though, I would like to note the major difference between the ancient theological stand on the white/black dichotomy and the medieval position as evidenced in the following passages. The Heikhalot literature is based on a theology that emphasizes the huge dimension of God, but it is also a static theology. In comparison to rabbinic theology, which includes views of God as being influenced by human activity (essentially the commandments), the quintessence of Heikhalot theology is the knowledge of the dimensions, whose immutability endows them with the special status of an important religious gnosis.[14]

Later on, in medieval Kabbalah, the two types of theology became obsolete in the eyes of some Jewish elites. The Kabbalists among them, who held to the theosophical trend of Kabbalah, expressed their theology by resorting to a complex system of divine powers, the sefirot, whose reflections here in the world below were perceptible by means of symbols or, as I shall explain later in this study, by imposing a code on the Jewish canonical writings.[15] Though substantially different from the rabbinic and Heikhalot theologies, the Kabbalistic theosophies combine major elements of both of them; from the Heikhalot literature, or similar theologies that are only hinted at in a few texts, the Kabbalistic theosophies accepted the anthropomorphic description of the revealed divinity. From some aspects of rabbinic theology dealing with the divine attributes the Kabbalists accepted the dynamic nature of the divine realm. This synthesis was conceived as expressing ongoing processes, which are rather difficult to represent because they are ever changing. Everything in the canonical writings was taken by those Kabbalists as symbolic, either of the divine powers or of the sinister part, the side of evil. In this symbolic frame the whole biblical imagery became a tissue of symbols, as did the most significant segments of the midrashic and talmudic literatures. This process of symbolization—one major aspect of the more comprehensive process of arcanization that will be discussed below—became vital for the expression of important parts of the Kabbalistic literature.[16]

In the course of this expanding process of symbolization, the above discussions of the white and black fires underwent a profound semantic metamorphosis. They were now understood not only as describing the primordial Torah, in accordance with the literal meaning of the sources, but also as symbolically expressing the relationship between the divine, spiritual powers. Although those powers may or may not have anything in common with attributes of the Torah, the very identification of the fires with specific sefirot had some resonances in the Kabbalistic conception of the Torah. The nature of the supernal powers involved in this symbolic process was transposed by the Kabbalist to the nature of the mundane Torah.

Thus, an interesting development in Kabbalistic thought, which stems from ancient midrashic traditions, generated a special theosophical understanding of the nature of written language and, implicitly, of the biblical text. At the middle of the thirteenth century, in Castile, R. Isaac ha-Kohen, the son of R. Jacob ha-Kohen, expounded an interesting theory concerning the relation between the white and black configurations of the Hebrew letters. Regarding the letter 'aleph he wrote:

The inner [form] stands for the Holy One, blessed be He, as He is hidden from the eye of any creature and His innerness cannot be reached. The external form stands for the [external] world, which depends on the arm of the Holy One, blessed be He, as an amulet does on the arm of a powerful man.[17] And just as the inner form is the locus of the external form, so [also] is God the locus of the world, and the world is not the locus of God.[18] What I have mentioned to you [is] that the white form in the 'aleph stands for the level of

Holy One, blessed be He, but not the black one, [which is] external. I did tell you this by way of a [great] principle, and as a great secret because the white form stands for the white garment, and our sages, blessed be their memory, said:[19] Whence was the light created? It teaches that the Holy One, blessed be He, clothed Himself in a white garment, and the splendor of it shone from one end of the world to another, as it is said:[20] "Who covers himself with light as with a garment" and[21] "and the light dwells with him."[22]

The inner form is the white space that is the locus of the black configuration of the letter. It is the inner form that is the most important, as it is the soul that sustains the body. This last type of image is expressly used in the context of our passage, and it reflects the Neoplatonic view of the soul as sustaining the body by the very act of surrounding it. Moreover, the white light is conspicuously identified with the divine light, which was described as the divine garment. All this is related to the divine arm, albeit the anthropomorphic aspect was somewhat attenuated in this passage. Crucial for our discussion is the fact that the amorphous component of the letter, the white space, is conceived as the paramount element, identical with a divine manifestation. Obviously, the above discussion does not refer, as in the earlier literature, to the Torah in its entirety and to its role in the creative process. The white spaces are now described in terms reminiscent of the negative theology. Intertwined as the white and black letters are, they point to theosophical layers that sharply differ from one another.

The above passage seems to include, however, an even more striking factor: not only is the primordial written version of the Torah pregnant with a divine dimension, but so are the individual Hebrew letters in general, independent of their role in the cosmogonic process. To a certain extent the separate letters are fraught with their own meaning, independent of their context in the biblical text. Two hermeneutical processes can be discerned here: the one Rojtman described in other contexts as autonomization,[23] and the one that she identified as plenitude of the form.[24]

Consequently, not only the primordial Torah has divine status but, in principle, any Hebrew text does. The present passage conclusively demonstrates that Kabbalists have moved from a theory of the Hebrew letters as part of the divine text to the special status of Hebrew letters in general, thus opening the way for a much more comprehensive hermeneutics of Hebrew texts, though the opportunity has been hardly exploited de facto. The nature of the white light, the space surrounding the letter, is compared to an emanation of the light stemming from the divine garment. This light is comparable to the white fire, corresponding to God's skin in some midrashic texts. In both cases the external appearance of God is involved in the constitution of the written text. In the above Kabbalistic passage, however, the light is preferred because it better serves Kabbalistic theosophy, which is interested in the emanative process. As can be shown in other Kabbalistic passages as well, the emergence of the text—or, according to other Kabbalistic discussions, of the articulated verbal aspect of language[25]—is a metaphor for the emanation;[26] the white fire of the midrash, with its anthropomorphic connotations, would be less appropriate as an image of a pure spiritual emanation.

Let me examine a Kabbalistic text, whose precise dating is unclear, which combines the beginning of the emanative process with the imagery of the two fires. R. Shem Tov ben Shem Tov, an early-fifteenth-century Castilian Kabbalist, quotes from an unidentified Kabbalistic book where it was written:

> The Name, our Lord, blessed be He, who is One, Unique and Special,[27] because all needs Him, and He does not need them, His knowledge is united to Him and there is nothing outside Him.[28] And He is called 'Aleph, the head of all the letters, corresponding to the fact that He is One . . . and how did He innovate and create the world? Like a man who comprises his spirit and concentrates his spirit, and the world remains in darkness, and within this darkness He chopped rocks and chiseled cliffs in order to extract from there the paths called "Wonders of Wisdom,"[29] and this is the meaning of the verse[30] "He took out light from the hiddenness," and this is the secret of "a dark fire on the white fire," and this is the secret of "face and back."[31,32]

The anonymous Kabbalist quoted here, who apparently thrived early in the thirteenth century, combines *Sefer Yetzirah*'s emphasis on the creation of the letters as the first divine activity with the concept of divine withdrawal from the space that will serve as the locus of the cosmological processes. I assume that the black fire is hinted at by the dark elements that are the material from which or within which the letters were excavated. These raw and resistant materials emerged after, or as the result of, the withdrawal of the divine light from a certain space. On the basis of another passage very close to the one under scrutiny,[33] I propose to identify the white fire with the divine light that remained in the evacuated space. Thus, the primordial processes that are imagined to precede the process of emanation of the world are described in terms that were commonly used by midrashic sources to designate the inscription of the Torah onto the divine organism. Similar views of the two fires are combined in a text written by the above-mentioned R. Shem Tov, with the contention that the white fire is identical with the special shapes of the five letters *mem, nun, tzade, peh,* and *kaf* when they appear at the end of a word.[34] This contention is important because it assumes that the white fire entered into the very constitution of the present Torah. According to R. Shem Tov, those letters are also identical to the hidden light, stored for the righteous, the *tzaddiqim*.[35] I shall come back to this theme later on in the chapter, when dealing with Hasidism.

One of the most extensive discussions of the theme of white and black fires is found in a late-thirteenth- or early-fourteenth-century commentary on midrash *Konen*. In the unique manuscript in which this commentary is extant, it is attributed to R. Isaac the Elder (ha-Zaqen). Gershom Scholem, who was the first to call scholars' attention to this text, surmised that the author is none other than the famous R. Isaac the Blind, the Provençal sage whom the Kabbalists consider to be one of the founders of Kabbalah. The cautious attribution of the commentary to R. Isaac the Blind changed, however, in the same article of Scholem, into an explicit assignment of authorship.[36] Let me address some of the pertinent points related to our topic which play a central role in the commentary on the midrash. R. Isaac the Elder starts his commentary as follows:

> On the right hand[37] of the Holy One, blessed be He, all the engravings which are expected to be actualized are engraved. They were engraved, inscribed, and depicted out of the emanation of all the crowns,[38] in the level of Hesed, as an inner, subtle, impenetrable [entity] and it was called from the [very] beginning the Thought of the Integrated Torah[39] [and] the Torah of Hesed. And as part of the totality of all the engravings, two engravings were engraved in it [in the Sefirah of Hesed]: one [engraving] which is the depiction of the Written Torah, the other one which is the Oral Torah. The depiction of the Written Torah, is [formed out of] depictions of colors of white fire, and the depiction of the oral Torah is a depiction of likeness of colors of black fire.[40]

Here we can see how the ancient anthropomorphism was translated into theosophical terminology. The right hand of God is identical with the sefirah of Hesed, upon which the two fires are formed. The anthropomorphic tone is also explicit in the reference to the colors and their manifestations as depiction, *tziyyur*. The two kinds of Torah are only some of the engravings found in the sefirah of Hesed in an attempt not to identify the two Torahs with the divine power or hand. The specific form of existence of the two types of Torah on the divine hand, or within the sefirah of Hesed, is designated by the phrase *mahashevet torah kelulah*, which Scholem did not translate verbatim. He suggested—actually, his English translator suggested—the term "the not yet unfolded" for *kelulah*, which in my opinion is not only clumsy but to a certain extent incorrect. In my view, the two forms of Torah were found together, perhaps in an integrated manner, before the next stage of emanation, which separated the written Torah from the oral one, the former being identified with the sefirah of Tiferet (Beauty) or Rahamim (Compassion), while the latter was identified with the last sefirah, Malkhut. So far, we have a rather understandable Kabbalistic discussion describing the processes of emanation in terms related to the canonical books.

The separation between the two types of Torah corresponding to the hierarchy of the two sefirot has been known in Kabbalah since the *Book of Bahir*.[41] What is new with this author is the fact that the oral Torah is the black fire, a view that seems to be an innovation of this text. Semantically speaking, however, the novel imagery does not dramatically alter the relationship between the content of the white and the black. In the former cases the black fire reflects the limited, formed, written manifestation, whereas in this treatise the oral Torah seems to function as the limited aspect of the entity conceived of as the written, but amorphous, Torah.

III. Other Kabbalists on Black and White Letters

More precise elaborations on the significance of the blank spaces are found in some Kabbalistic fragments that discuss the nature of the letter *yod*.[42] The numerical equivalent of this letter, according to the Hebrew system of counting, is ten. In those texts, the Kabbalists assume that there is a black yod, which is sustained by a white yod. The white one, which is also hidden, is conceived of as symbolic of the ten supernal sefirot, the ten *tzahtzahot*, or divine lights, which serve as the static and hidden paradigms of the lower and dynamic sefirot.[43] According to at least one of the fragments, however, the white yod and black yod are related to each other, so that from the lower, black yod one can perceive the higher, white yod. Thus, no negative theology is involved here, but a hierarchy that allows access to the higher by means of the linguistic material.[44]

The higher sefirot are arranged, according to an esoteric teaching in the circle of the Kabbalists who wrote the above texts, in an anthropomorphic structure. Thus, the white fire is again emblematic of a divine anthropomorphic view. The late-thirteenth- or early-fourteenth-century Kabbalists returned, to a certain extent, to the ancient view of the Torah as written on the divine skin—an interesting parallel to Derrida's "transcendental space of inscription"[45]—while employing a much more sophisticated theosophy than their ancient predecessors.

Let me address the hermeneutical significance of attributing such great importance to the white parts of the text. We may distinguish between two different approaches to this matter. The ancient one, basically an anthropomorphic theology, integrates the view that the white fire points to the divine skin, thereby ensuring the divinity of the peculiar writing of the Torah scroll. On the other hand, the symbolic interpretation of the white fire has something to do with the assumption that the higher or inner level in the divine realm is made much richer by its very ambiguity. The written, namely the limited, aspects of the text are the lower ones, whereas the higher ones, which reflect the divine essence, are less definite. In the period when the Kabbalists elaborated the theory that there are infinite meanings hinted at in the biblical text, it seems strange, *prima facia*, that the external, static aspect of the biblical text became so important. Since it was possible to confer on the written aspect of the Bible such an unlimited range of interpretations (as we shall see in Chapter 3), why bother about the minutia of its manifestation? Historically speaking, it seems that the theory concerning the infinite meanings of the biblical text was emphasized by Kabbalists who were also anxious to stress the importance of the external facet of the Bible. I assume that the drastic relativization of the semantic aspect of the words by the assumption of infinite semiosis required an absolutization of their manifest side. It is precisely an attempt to postulate the absolute gestalt underlying the ongoing flow of the meaning that contributed to the ascent of the importance of the substratum of the words. That is to say, when it became obvious that the authoritative significance of the Bible depended on subjective interpretations, the need for a balance to stabilize and thus create a center of gravity contributed to the emergence of an emphasis on the other aspects of the text. The limited aspect, the black fire, became unlimited as far as the number of the senses of the text is concerned. The authority installed by the identification of the white with the divine permitted Kabbalists to relate to the Bible as the absolute text. However, this "new" authority was consonant with that mystical authority which may be amorphous, that is, which may express amorphous experiences. The view of the Torah manifest in some late-thirteenth-century Kabbalistic texts may suggest that the ultimate source and substratum of the Torah is amorphous, just as the highest aspect of the divine is conceived to be in some descriptions of the encounter between God and man, whereas the limited, black part of the text, namely the letters, is the communal, public manifestation of the divine in the external world. The retreat to the semantically indeterminate aspects of the Bible, the white "forms" of the letters, is probably the answer to the need to emphasize the uniqueness of the Hebrew formulation of the Bible, much beyond the necessity to relate to its grammatological gestalt. The elevation of the external form of the biblical text, which includes the white parts, to such an exalted rank secured among the theosophical Kabbalists a special significance for the punctilious Jewish observance of the minutiae in the copying of the biblical scroll. It is not sufficient, so the implied argument may go, to study Hebrew in order to be in contact with the innermost aspect of the Bible; the semantics of the scriptures are not sufficient for decoding the ultimate, divine message; one must accept the formal facets of its written transmission, as formulated by the rabbinic regulations, to be able to fathom the subtle, almost imponderable finesse of the scroll, which points to the indeterminate Godhead. To a certain extent, the Kabbalists attempted to validate not only the biblical text but also the importance of the rabbinical manner of writing the Torah scroll.

Let me call attention now to an additional text, written by a very influential Kabbalist, R. Joseph ben Shalom Ashkenazi.[46] R. Joseph angrily protests against the view of the characters of the Hebrew alphabet as conventional and argues for the existence of numerous secrets in each of the aspects of these letters: "God forbids that our holy Torah, namely its letters, [for it] to be said that they are signs invented by the hearts of men. How may it be in relation to characters which were engraved by the finger of God, that they are invented letters? Indeed the trace[47] of the letters consists in the ink and the blank,[48] and each and every part possesses heaps and heaps of secrets of the account of the chariot and the account of the creation."[49]

Interestingly enough, the Kabbalist resorts to the phrase that was discussed above dealing with the heaps of halakhah, which depends on each and every tittle, namely the black aspects of the letters, in order to designate the dependence of the secret aspects of the oral law, the two accounts, on the blank and black parts of the letters. Here the process of arcanization is evident: secrets are a matter of topics concerning a double or multiple message related not only to the semantic structure of the text, but also to the very layout of the text.

It is quite reasonable to assume that this emphasis on the ideogrammatic aspects of the Hebrew letters, and implicitly the Hebrew Bible, constitutes a reaction to Maimonides' view of Hebrew as a conventional language.[50] R. Joseph responds to Maimonides twice in his writings;[51] this is a revealing example of how the Kabbalistic fundamentalist attitude toward language was provoked by the introduction in Jewish circles of Greek philosophical stands, including the emergence of a symbolic interpretation of aspects of the Bible.[52]

A fundamental question should be asked about the more precise content of the above argument. Is the claim that the blank spaces contain supernal secrets more than a blank statement? Indeed, that may be the case, but it is not necessary. As we have seen, the attempt to discover the possible meaning of the blank spaces was already part of the Kabbalistic literature. Moreover, for R. Joseph the secrets of the accounts of creation and the chariot were not abstract topics; according to his own testimony he had composed commentaries on these issues, although it is not so clear whether they are extant.[53] In his own commentary on the Hebrew letters, which immediately follows the above passage, there is no attempt to address the white spaces; neither did I find any trace of such an enterprise in the other commentaries on the same topic from his circle.[54]

Exalted as the two types of account may be in the eyes of a Kabbalist, they do not point to the Infinite. Thus the white parts may be understood as more sublime than the black ones, but still not as pointing to the highest layer in the divine world. Such a stand is found, however, in the writings of a famous sixteenth-century Kabbalist, R. David ibn Avi Zimra. In the introduction to his *Magen David*, a welter of Kabbalistic traditions related to the Hebrew alphabet, R. David wrote: "Because of His outmost occultation, there is nothing that points to Him as a particular sign. But the whiteness of the parchment that encompasses all the letters from within and without includes a certain allusion that He, blessed be He, encompasses all the worlds, the supernal and the lower, from within and without . . . On this issue our sages said[55] that any letter that is not encompassed by the parchment is disqualified. Because just as the parchment supports all the letters . . . so He, blessed be He, supports all the worlds."[56]

R. David attempts to resolve a Kabbalistic quandary known since the end of the thirteenth century: Is there a term for 'Ein Sof in the Bible? Since this very phrase does not occur in classical Jewish texts, some Kabbalists assumed that its absence has to do with the sublime status of this layer of divinity, which is not even hinted at by the biblical material.[57] His answer is indeed fascinating: nothing in the black letters of the written Torah alludes to the Infinite, but the nature of the Infinite, which both encompasses and penetrates the worlds is intimated by the nature of the writing of the Torah on a scroll. Here, the white aspects of the Torah scroll are quite explicitly pointing to the Infinite.

Interestingly, the stress on the importance of the white surface safeguards, in the eyes of the Kabbalists, the unique status of the Hebrew Bible as embodied by an halakhically performed scroll, even in an age when the study of Hebrew by some Christians had been an achievement of Christian exegesis since the twelfth century. The proper study of the Torah would, a Kabbalist could claim, depend not on acquaintance with the semantics of the biblical Hebrew but on the punctilious act of copying the text according to the rabbinic instructions. In a curious manner, the hermeneutic freedom that Kabbalistic exegesis achieved by cultivating the polysemic, dynamic symbolical approach to the biblical text culminated in the apotheosis of the static, parasemantic, or hieroglyphic facets of this text. To be sure, also in talmudic-midrashic thought, there was a conspicuous concern with the precise writing of the Torah scroll; the major interest of the ancient Jewish sages, however, was limited to the possible semantic mutations that may occur as the result of changes introduced by the copyists.[58] Kabbalists added to this concern the metaphor of the Bible as the picture of God, namely the iconic-ideogrammatic facet, an issue to be addressed in more detail later in this chapter.

Let me adduce a passage from a book written by an early-eighteenth-century Lurianic Kabbalist, R. Joseph Ergas:

On the parchment that is under the [letters of] the Tetragrammaton there is a likeness of an image possessing the form of the Tetragrammaton, because under the yod of ink there is one white yod of the parchment which sustains the yod of ink, and so also underneath the he' and the other letters, in a manner that the Tetragrammaton of ink limits the whiteness of the parchment in a form similar to the form of the Tetragrammaton and so is the case in other names written on a parchment. This is so long as the letters of ink are on the parchment. But if the letters fly and disappear from there, the parchment will remain white without any letter and likeness [of letter] at all. Now, remove the shell of corporeality from the above parable and imagine that 'Ein Sof together with the sublime instrument, Keter of 'Adam Qadmon, is the simile of the parchment that does not have any name, letter or vowel, because the Keter of 'Adam Qadmon is His simple act, as mentioned above.[59] And since 'Ein Sof had emanated all the names and the sefirot by means of Keter of 'Adam Qadmon, and they are sustained and maintained within Him, like the letters on the parchment, we can attribute the names and the attributes written in the Torah to 'Ein Sof and read Him in them . . . because there is not, as we had already said, word and speech worthy to be pronounced on 'Ein Sof . . . and there is no word in prayer that points to 'Ein Sof, but the [mental] intention.[60]

The manner in which the biblical semiosis functions here is quite interesting. The names that are understood as referring to God do not do so by a regular direct reference to something outside the sign, to an ontological presence that exists independently of the signifier. According to the parable, the inked letters create their signifier, the white letters of the parchment, which point to the divine infinity. Likewise, the emanation of the divine names and of the sefirot does not take place without the absolute source, the 'Ein Sof. They constitute, so to speak, a transcendental inscription on the very substance of the Infinite. The structure of the Torah scroll, namely the forms of its letters, is therefore the aspect that points to the structures and processes taking place within the Infinite, not by means of a symbolic mode based on understanding of the semantics of the text but as structural and functional similitudes. In this case, which reflects the Lurianic theosophy that includes the concept of withdrawal, the Infinite is the substratum of all reality, and thus it constitutes an eminently positive vision of divinity.[61]

IV. R. LEVI ISAAC OF BERDITCHEV'S VIEWS OF THE WHITE LETTERS

Hasidic interest in the status of the biblical text has attracted little attention in modern scholarship. Though offering a view that was not consonant with the more intellectualistic approaches found in rabbinic circles of the eighteenth century, Hasidic masters were more inclined toward the nonsemantic aspects of the Bible, especially its oral performance as part of study.[62] The concern with the visual aspects of the text is secondary in Hasidism. Nevertheless, one of the few discussions dealing with the white letters has drawn attention from scholars. It deals with an apotheosis of the white aspects of the Torah found in a tradition connected to R. Levi Isaac of Berditchev, to which Gershom Scholem called attention; following him, it was also mentioned by Jacques Derrida and Umberto Eco. In the following I would like to deal in some detail with this Hasidic treatment, for two reasons: First, this Hasidic master apparently paid more attention to this topic than any other Jewish thinker. Second, his view has been interpreted in a manner that conflicts with our own suggestion concerning how the white aspect of the Torah functioned. In lieu of playing a conservative role, as I believe it did, it was interpreted as revolutionary.

The eighteenth-century Hasidic master was reported to have interpreted Isaiah 51:4, "A Torah will go forth from me," as follows:

> We can see by the eye of our intellect why in the Torah handed down to us one letter should not touch the other. The matter is that also the whiteness constitutes letters, but we do not know how to read them as [we know] the blackness of the letters. But in the future God, blessed be He, will reveal to us even the whiteness of the Torah. Namely we will [then] understand the white letter in our Torah, and this is the meaning of "A new Torah will go forth from me," that it stands for the whiteness of the Torah, that all the sons of Israel will understand also the letters that are white in our Torah, which was delivered to Moses. But nowadays the letters of whiteness are obscured from us. But in the Song on the Sea, when it has been said, "This is my Lord, I shall praise Him,"[63] it is written in [the writings of] Isaac Luria that "their soul flied when they heard the song of the angels" and God had opened their ear to hear etc., and this is the reason why the maidservant had seen on the sea [more Ezekiel][64]—the whiteness of the letters [she saw] what has not been seen etc., because the matter has been occulted until the advent of the Messiah.[65]

Scholem emphasized the novelty of the Torah that will be revealed in the messianic future; he understood this passage as part of a series of Kabbalistic discussions, in fact a tradition, dealing with future revelations of yet-unknown parts of the Torah.[66] Relating this passage to views found in the Talmud about the existence of seven books of the Pentateuch, and more substantially with the stand of *Sefer ha-Temunah*, which claims that one of the books of the Torah has been lost,[67] the above passage has been interpreted as concerning the revelation of another hidden religious document, or a least a part of it. This insertion of the Hasidic passage in a longer earlier tradition that has some antinomian features is characteristic of Scholem's flirtation with antinomianism in his phenomenology of Jewish mysticism, which remained part and parcel of many of Scholem's followers. Or, to use David Biale's terminology, this is part of Scholem's "counterhistory." R. Levi Isaac mentions *Sefer ha-Temunah* explicitly in the context of the shape of the letters.[68] Did, however, R. Levi Isaac of Berditchev, an icon of traditionalism in Hasidic circles, indeed subscribe to the radical view of the earlier Kabbalistic book?

It is plausible, in my opinion, to propose a much less revolutionary understanding of this passage. God is emanating a new Torah from Himself, me-'itti, and because this new Torah is the revelation of the meaning of the white letters, it is in fact a revelation not of a new document but of the divine as the background of the white letters, in the vein of the above discussions. Such an understanding is less innovative than Scholem's, but it is corroborated by at least three discussions, one stemming from R. Levi Isaac's main teacher, another by R. Levi Isaac himself, and a third adduced in his name by his disciple R. Aharon of Zhitomir. Let me therefore attempt to elucidate the meaning of the passage by resorting to the texts dealing with this topic, which should inform any analysis of R. Levi Isaac's views.

R. Dov Baer of Mezeritch, known as the Great Maggid and the master of R. Levi Isaac, interprets Isaiah 51:4 as follows:

> Behold that the Torah in its entirety is collected from [the deeds of] righteous men, from Adam, and the forefathers, and Moses, who caused the dwelling of the Shekhinah on their deeds, and this is the complete Torah. However, the luminosity of the essence[69] has not been revealed yet, until the Messiah will come and they will understand the luminosity of His essence.[70] And this is the new Torah that goes forth from me, whose meaning is "from My essence."[71,72]

The Great Maggid argues that the revealed Torah deals with human deeds and their interaction with the divine. The forefather had been able to cause the descent of the divine presence here below. However, the divine essence in itself is not expounded in the Torah that counts their deeds, perfect as it is. Thus, according to this passage, the luminosity, the new Torah, and the divine essence are explicitly related to each other. It is not a new text that is revealed but the depths of the canonical document already in the possession of the Jews. R. Levi Isaac, too, commented on this verse from Isaiah, in the context of the apprehension of God and the Torah, yet without mentioning the white letters.[73] Elsewhere, however, R. Levi Isaac writes:

> It is known that the letters of the Torah have the aspect of inner lights[74] which are revealed according to the order of the emanation of the worlds. And the boundary of the white that encompasses the letters possesses the aspect of the encompassing lights, which are not revealed but are found in a hiddenness, in the aspect of the encompassing light. From this we may understand that the white boundaries possess also the aspect of letters, but they are hidden letters, higher than the revealed letters . . . because the aspect of the whiteness which is [identical with] the hidden letters is derived from the revelation of the aspect of the revealed letters, and that is the meaning of what has been written,[75] "The maidservant had seen on the [Red] Sea [more than what Ezekiel has seen]," because the revelation of the divinity was so great that even the maidservant was capable of understanding. This is the meaning of the verse "A new Torah will go forth from me": that in the future, when the revelation of the divinity and the glory of God will be disclosed, and all men will see etc., it means that the revelation of the aspect of the encompassing[76] and the revelation of the aspect of the whiteness, namely the white letters which encompass the revealed letters of the Torah, [will take place,] this being the meaning of "A new Torah will go forth from me."[77]

This text draws upon a distinction already found in the passage from R. David ibn Avi Zimra: the white stands for the highest and hidden aspects of the divinity, although according to the Kabbalist God encompasses both the external and the internal aspects of the world. R. Levi Isaac, however, resorts to a distinction found in the thought of two of ibn Avi Zimra's contemporaries, R. Moses Cordovero and R. Isaac Luria, one between the "encompassing" divinity or transcendental light—a view already found in the thirteenth-century Kabbalah—and the inner or immanent light. In the Lurianic systems the transcendental light is totally beyond human perception. For the Hasidic master, the white is the transcendental aspect alone. But what seems to be interesting in R. Levi Isaac's last passage is the assumption that the revelation of the maidservant was higher than the highest revelation according to the Kabbalists: that of the prophet Ezekiel. I take this view as assuming that the maidservant had in fact seen the divinity, which in this context is the white aspect of the letters. Thus, it is not only a messianic experience of the text that is implied in the knowledge of the structure of the white letters, but also one that has taken place in the past. Moreover, according to some statements it is in principle available also in the present, because the white and the black letters are intertwined. Let me attempt to explicate the views of the Hasidic master from another standpoint. The text is not used in order to reach an experience of the *signifié* of the text by means of a symbolic decoding of the newly revealed letters. The Torah is not instrumental in transcending a certain common or ordinary experience in order to attain a divinity totally divorced from the text by leaving the text behind or experiencing the author without the text. The two are conceived of as profoundly intertwined. God's revelation depends on one's ability to see Him within parts of the texts that before the revelation were opaque. Therefore, the Hasidic discussions adduced above do not follow a theory of the lost text, or of a portion of it, but the approach that the divinity actually stands beyond the revealed aspects of the written Torah. In theosophical terminology, the revealed Torah is identical to the third sefirah, Binah, and the Torah to be revealed in the future is identical to the second sefirah, Hokhmah.[78]

Is there any significant difference between Scholem's interpretation and the one suggested above? In my opinion there is, and it consists in the status of the text. Scholem's interpretation stems from his framing the passage within the antinomian tradition of *Sefer ha-Temunah*,[79] mentioned immediately before and after the above quote, a strategy that construes the feeling that the Hasidic master assumes that the perfect Torah will be revealed in the messianic future. Scholem makes it quite clear that "unquestionably this doctrine left room for all manner of heretical variants and developments. Once it was supposed that a revelation of new letters or books could change the whole outward manifestation of the Torah without touching its true essence, almost everything was possible."[80]

The excitement of a modern reader to learn about the heretical variants is, however, not satisfied by Scholem's note, where only the name of Cagliostro is mentioned,[81] and I would not put too great an emphasis on the representativeness of this figure for the concept of Torah in Jewish mysticism. Yet the Hasidic master does not speak about a change in the "whole outward manifestation of the Torah," namely an ontic change of the founding document, but about an epistemological change that opens the eyes, or hearts, of the people. Is such a change something to be deferred to another eon or restricted to the advent of the Messiah? Is the life of a Hasidic mystic one that is lived in deferment, as Scholem would say?[82] Had the mystic to pay a price, as Scholem put it, when he venerates the given form of the canonical text or of the tradition? Or is there a way to attain, from the perspective of the mystic, even nowadays an epistemological transformation that will enable one to contemplate the luminosity of God without smelting down the sacred text?[83] Is his capacity to read between the lines as the ultimate space of meaning, as Walter Benjamin put it, not to be adopted as a better interpretation than the assumption that the very structure will be changed in the messianic future?[84]

The answer to these questions insofar as the above passage is concerned should be sought first and foremost in the thought of R. Levi Isaac, a Hasidic thinker whose direct attachment to God was considered to be famous. An inspection of the references to the expression *behirut ha-bore'*, namely the luminosity of the Creator, will detect instances where the ancient mystics are described as being able to transcend the limited luminosity found in this world, after the act of divine contraction, and to reach the unlimited luminosity that precedes the moment of contraction.[85] Even more important is the fact that elsewhere in the same book R. Levi Isaac identifies the white letters of the Torah and the parchment with *'ayin*, a term that literally means "nothingness" but serves in the Kabbalistic and the Hasidic theosophical literatures for a very high, even the highest, divine realm.[86] For this Hasidic master, however, as for other Hasidic masters, the righteous already have access to this divine realm.[87]

Therefore, I would suggest reading the passage adduced in the name of R. Levi Isaac of Berditchev not as a statement about a definitive deferment but as an invitation for the elite to attain now what all other Jews will attain in the eschaton. This reading is, in my opinion, consonant with other statements in early Hasidism, where the messianic experience may be attained even in the present.[88] If understood so, R. Levi Isaac's statement quoted at the beginning of this section does not exactly open the gate to "all manner of heretical statements," nor does it involve a change in the "outward manifestation of the Torah." I wonder also if, as Scholem put it elsewhere, "the sacred text loses its shape and takes a new one for the mystic."[89] Instead I would opt for an epistemic change, one that invites much more intense contemplation of the depth of the text of the Torah as it is. The reading of the Torah mystically is conceived of as an experience reminiscent of Martin Buber's *gegenwartiges Urphänomenon*. Shifting Scholem's emphasis on the ontic and messianic transformation of the canonical text to the assumption that the gist of the Hasidic text is the spiritual transformation of the recipient of the revelation contends that the Torah still retains its shape but opens its blank parts to a process of more sublime decoding. By putting the accent on this issue, I believe that we come closer to the main concern of Hasidism, namely the deepening of the spiritual life of the devotee, than if we adopt the explanation referring to an ontic transformation of the text. In Hasidism in general, and in R. Levi Isaac's generation in particular, we know about the basic indistinctness between the encompassing and the inner lights, a fact that can be perceived by the transformation of the mystic's inner capacities.[90] A long discussion that buttresses this emphasis on both the centrality of an epistemic change and the availability of such a change in the present is found in a book, which will be quoted several times in the following pages, written by R. Aharon of Zhitomir, the disciple of R. Levi Isaac: *Toledot 'Aharon*. The assumption is that there are two manners of studying the Torah: with an intellect (or "great intellect") and without intellect. Study with an intellect is related to causing the return of the letters to the primordiality of the intellect,[91] on the one hand, and on the other to causing the return of the combinations of the letters of the studied Torah to their primordial state, where they were white.[92] There is nothing specifically messianic in this discussion, but rather a contention that perfect study will retrace the primordial Torah described as consisting of white letters. Perfect study is "to bring the letters of the Torah to the primordial whiteness."[93] Thus, it is not a transcending of the black in order to meet another, more sublime entity, but the elevation of the black to its supernal source, in the vein of a more general mystical demand widespread in Hasidism. Or, to put it in more semiotic terms: the written Torah, with its semantic aspects, stems from another realm, which includes a surplus of meaning, the white letters, the knowledge of whose language adds to the written—black—document without subtracting anything from it.

Even when this master invokes the messianic nature of the revelation of the white letters, he immediately writes that "even now, when the righteous pronounces the letters in a state of devotion . . . he unites the letters to the light of the Infinite . . . and ascends higher than all the worlds to the place where the letters are white and are not combined and then he can perform there whatever combination he wants."[94] Also, the emphasis on the possibility of attaining an experience of a direct encounter with the divine, pointed out by the luminosity, does greater justice to R. Levi Isaac's thought. R. Levi Isaac asked, for example, "How is it possible to attain the supernal luminosity which has not yet been limited within the worlds? [The answer is:] By means of enthusiasm[95] man is capable of cleaving to the Creator, blessed be His name, [and] by means of that enthusiasm he will reach the supernal luminosity which has not yet limited itself within the [lower] worlds."[96]

The last two quotes allow a plausible solution to the quandary concerning the role of messianism in the revelation of the white letters: mystics are capable of attaining even nowadays the kind of experience that will be achieved by all in the eschaton. Even now there are spiritual means to anticipate the "sublime" understanding of the Torah, by a sort of study that implies a resort to a "great intellect." This answer is relevant for a theory of reading in Hasidism, but also for the importance of the reader's role. The self-transformation, in this case the resort to enthusiasm, is the clue for the ascent to a contact with the highest level of the divinity. If we may infer from this instance a possible understanding of the ideal reading of the Torah—in both cases the concept of divine luminosity is involved—the disclosure of the hidden dimension entails an experience of self-transformation that culminates in a cleaving to God. The clue for reading the invisible Torah is not lost, nor is it necessarily waiting for the advent of the Messiah. Mystics are often stubborn persons who invest all their energy in discovering clues. Moreover, I would say that the doors of spiritual understanding and contemplation were, at least in Jewish mysticism, basically open, for the clues were created using, from the very beginning, the mold of the lock.[97]

Let us reflect for a moment on the additional implications of the above Hasidic passages, which follow the way opened by the sixteenth-century Kabbalist R. David ibn Avi Zimra: the white spaces are either identical to or point to the highest realm within the divine world, the 'Ein Sof. Just as the white parts of the text are statistically more extensive than the black ones, so is the Infinite more extensive than the revealed divinity.

What, then, is the relation between the white and the black aspects according to R. Levi Isaac and his student? In one of his discussions R. Levi Isaac claims that "the letters point to the influx of 'Elohim within the world of nature."[98] Elsewhere he writes that "the shape of the letters [points to] the manner in which the intellectual [entities] and the influx [descending from] the Lord of Lords operate within corporeality and nature."[99] The black letters function, therefore, as pipes or channels for the descent of the divinity within this world. According to another text, however, these letters serve, in the case of the righteous, as the starting point for the ascent to the spiritual realms.[100] There two movements are mentioned together in the context of the righteous within the discussion of the letters.[101] Thus, the two aspects of the text reflect the two basic motions that constitute what I propose to call the mystical-magical model, which combines the mystical ascent to God with the descent of the mystic's soul that brings down the divine influence.[102] So, for example, we read:

> There are those who serve God with their human intellect, and others whose gaze is fixed as if on Nought,[103] and this is impossible without divine help . . . He who is granted this supreme degree, with divine help, to contemplate the Nought, then his intellect is effaced and he is like a dumb man, because his intellect is obliterated . . . but when he returns from such a contemplation to the essence of [his] intellect, he finds it full of influx.[104]

An interesting parallel to some of the ideas in the above quotes is found in the writing of a disciple of R. Levi Isaac, R. Aharon of Zhitomir, who cites his master as follows:

There are two kinds of righteous: there is a righteous who receives luminosity from the letters of Torah and prayer;[105] and there is another righteous, who is greater, who brings the luminosity to the letters from above, despite the fact that the letters are in the supernal world, when the great righteous brings new luminosity to the world, this luminosity cannot come to the world but by its being clothed in the letters . . . and when the luminosity comes down the letters fly upwards[106] whereas the luminosity remains here below. And the [great] degree of this righteous is connected to recitation of the speeches with all his power and with dedication and with all the 248 limbs he comes to each and every word that he recites, he brings [down] luminosity . . . and performs a unification of the Holy One, blessed be He, and the Shekhinah and by means of this he brings luminosity to the letters and from the letters to the entire world, this only when there are recipients capable of receiving the luminosity. However, if there is no recipient below, the righteous himself has to receive the luminosity arriving at the letters of the [pronounced] word.[107]

What is fascinating in this passage is the fact that the vocal actualization of the written Torah induces, rather explicitly, the descent of the luminosity of the supernal Torah. Thus the ideal and the real forms of the Torah are not in conflict but in concert. The ideal man, the righteous, causes the descent of the ideal by performing the actual. The divine luminosity is transformed into a sort of energy that is brought down and distributed by the righteous to the recipients. In fact, if my reading of R. Levi Isaac's approach to the white letters is correct, they should not be understood as betraying a sense of absolute transcendence of the mystical experience available in the present but rather as a possible promise for an active mystic. It is not the expectation of a future change that will be induced by the Messiah alone that is to be understood from the wider context of this Hasidic thought, but rather an urge to ascent to the whiteness in order to transform it into a power from which this world will benefit now.

To close this analysis of the white letters, let me adduce another passage attributed to R. Levi Isaac by R. Aharon:

Sometimes the letters are ruling over man, and sometimes man is ruling over the letters. This means that when man speaks speeches with power and devotion, the speeches are then ruling over him, because the light within the letters[108] confers to him vitality and delight so that he may speak speeches to the Creator, but this man cannot abolish anything bad by performing other combinations [of letters]. But when someone speaks speeches with devotion and brings all his power within the letters and cleaves to the light of the Infinite, blessed be He, that dwells within the letters, this person is higher than the letters and he combines letters as he likes . . . and he will be capable of drawing down the influx, the blessing, and the good things.[109]

In Hasidism the light of the infinite is not conceived of as an absolutely transcendental realm, as it is in the Cordoverian and Lurianic types of Kabbalah, but as a level of reality that is open to human experience. This light is found within letters, and the mystic can approach it and utilize it. Thus, according to the last passage, the light of the Infinite is not contemplated but rather exploited in order to bring down supernal power. In another passage, attributed to R. Levi Isaac, the process of interpretation of the Bible is described as bringing down the influx.[110] To return to the last quote: according to the Hasidic text, there are righteous whose study and prayer are done in a routine manner, and thus they are dominated by the canonical texts. The latter include the power of the Infinite, which has an impact on some form of experience—speaking to the Creator—but this is not a creative activity. The speaker is found within the net of language and is defined by it. It is possible, however, to avoid this net by intense linguistic activity, which consists in mystical devotion and magical acts, referred to here by combinations of letters. Escaping language is related to escaping, for a while, ordinary experience and even dominating it.

Yet this downward move involving a certain use of the power in order to bring even more influx here below is not the single result of the cleaving to the infinite light within letters. According to another passage by the same author, dealing expressly with the writing of the Torah black on white fire, which is even more pertinent for our discussion, devotion enables the mystic to break the external cover of the letters in order to reach the internal light, an attainment that is described as getting away with the state of tzimtzum.[111] This transcendence of the state of limitation is related there to contemplation of supernal lights: "When someone cleaves to the light of the Infinite, blessed be He, that dwells within the letters, out of his devotion, each and every moment he looks[112] to bigger lights and to the luminosity [stemming from] the light of the Infinite, and this is the essence of delight."[113]

In another context in this book, mentioned already above, the act of tracing the letters to the primordial state enables the mystic to combine them differently and thus to perform miracles.[114] Like R. Levi Isaac's "enthusiasm," his disciple's "devotion" opens the way to direct contact with the supernal worlds or, as we had seen above, with the combinations of white letters of the primordial Torah. Unlike some modern literary critics, who would emphasize the importance of the absent or the omitted aspects of the text in order to understand it,[115] R. Levi Isaac would say that the divine text does not omit anything, and the sole problem is the capacity to read what is found within the plenitude of the text.

This plenitude, however, is rather vague, white, and is not translated in particular secrets, as we had seen in the theosophical Kabbalah in the case of the ten *tzahtzahot*. Not that the concept of the secret is totally absent in the context of the lights or luminosity that are related to the white letters.[116] It seems, however, that no specific code was offered for deciphering the specific meaning of the white letters. Manifestation remained compact with proclamation. The medieval process of arcanization has been neutralized in those Hasidic texts in favor of a more emotional and devotional experience. Or, to formulate this hermeneutical move in Buber's terms, Hasidism has deschematized what he called the Kabbalistic mystery.[117] It is paramount to emphasize that the blank letters were not decoded but were left, as in the ancient mystical texts, as the divine background of the revealed Torah. Reaching them amounts to transcending the details of the written Torah and even of the Kabbalistic secrets. It is a more unified vision which is far from Maimonides' philosophical-political esotericism or from oral pieces of information that were passed down secretly at the beginning of Kabbalah. Neither are they related to the numerous technical treatments of Luria's Kabbalah. The sacred text is conceived of as understood only if experienced. Those who did experience it are anticipating the messianic revelation, but they are scarcely prone to transmit this experience. Indeed, this experiential dimension is well expressed by passages from R. Menahem Mendel of Premiszlany and R. Qalonimus Qalman Epstein, who deny the importance of the secrecy of the Kabbalistic tradition, arguing that this lore is based on an experiential attitude.[118] Understanding a text presupposes an experience of encountering a certain aspect of the author, in a manner reminiscent of more historicistic literary critical theories.

V. Iconic Visions of the Torah

The emphasis in the above texts on the importance of the white parts of the Torah scroll invites reflection on the Kabbalistic texts as embodying an iconic conception of the Torah. An iconic understanding of the human body we have encountered already in rabbinic thought.[119]

Already in early Kabbalah and the writings of the Hasidei Ashkenaz there are a few statements suggesting the identity of the Torah with a body, presumably a divine one.[120] A straightforward identity between Torah and God is found in the classic of Kabbalah, the *Zohar*, which declares, "The Torah is no other than the Holy One, blessed be He."[121]

Let us turn to some late-thirteenth-century Kabbalistic descriptions of the

Torah. The first occurs in a long-forgotten Kabbalistic work entitled *The Book of [Divine] Unity*:

> God gave us the entire perfect Torah from the [word] *bereshit* to the [words] *le-ʿeinei kol yisraʾel*.[122] Behold, how all the letters of the Torah, by their shapes, combined and separated, swaddled letters, curved ones and crooked ones, superfluous and elliptic ones, minute and large ones, and inverted, the calligraphy of the letters, the open and closed pericopes and the ordered ones, all of them are the shape of God, blessed be He. It is similar to, though incomparable with, the thing someone paints using [several] kinds of colors, likewise the Torah, beginning with the first pericope until the last one is the shape of God, the Great and Formidable, blessed be He, since if one letter be missing from the scroll of Torah, or one is superfluous, or a [closed] pericope was [written] in an open fashion or an [open] pericope was [written] in a closed fashion, that scroll of Torah is disqualified, since it has not in itself the shape of God, blessed be He the Great and Formidable, because of the change the shape caused. And you should understand it! And because it is incumbent on each and every one of Israel to say that the world has been created for him,[123] God obliged each and every one of them to write a scroll of the Torah for himself, and the concealed secret is [that he] made God, blessed be He.[124]

According to this passage, the exact form of the authorized writing of the Bible is equivalent to the shape of God. The Bible, therefore, in its ideal form, constitutes an absolute book, including in itself the supreme revelation of God, which is offered anthropomorphically and symbolically, limb by limb, within the various parts of the text. What is more important, however, for understanding the status of the canonical text is the identification between the scroll of the Torah, which was incumbent to be written for or by each and every Jew, and the concept of making or reproducing the image of God. There is no doubt that the scroll is conceived in iconic terms as a faithful representation of the divine shape.

Apparently part of the same Kabbalistic circle was a Kabbalist who was very concerned with anthropomorphic descriptions of the ten sefirot, much more than the conventional views of the other theosophical Kabbalists. R. Joseph of Hamadan, a Kabbalist whose views have been identified and analyzed recently by many scholars,[125] contends in his *Commentary on the Rationales of the Commandments*:

> Why is it called the Torah and it has an open and a closed pericope, referring[126] to the image of the building and the form of man, who is like the supernal, holy, and pure form. And just as there are in man joints connected

to each other, so in the Torah there are closed pericopes as in the case of the structure of the pericope *va-yehi be-shalah pharaoh*[127] and the secret of the song *'az yashir moshe*[128] are the secret of the joints of the Holy One, blessed be His hands. And the song of *ha-'azinu*[129] is the secret of the ear of the Holy One, blessed be He, and the secret of *'az yashir yisra'el*[130] is the secret of the divine circumcision[131] . . . and the positive commandments correspond to the secret of the male and the negative commandments correspond to the secret of the female and to the secret of the Shekhinah and to the secret of Malkhut. This is the reason why the Torah is called so, because it refers to the likeness of the Holy One, blessed be He.[132]

R. Joseph of Hamadan offers an interesting interpretation of the word *torah*. While the noun points to instruction, the medieval Kabbalist interprets it as meaning "refer," *morah*. Yet while the ancient use points to the instruction as stemming from the supernal realm to man here below, the Kabbalist assumes the inverse direction: the lower entity, the Torah, reflects a higher one, and thus it opens the way for understanding the divine by fathoming the structure of the text. This understanding is based on a type of isomorphism shared by certain portions of the Torah and the limbs of the divine anthropos. This symbolic function does not, however, work on the narrative level, by introduction of a divine myth as paralleled by and reflected in mundane events, as is the case in many types of theosophical Kabbalah. According to R. Joseph of Hamadan, it is the shape of the portion of the canonical text that counts, not its content. As in *Sefer ha-Yihud*, a book very close to this Kabbalist, the assumption is that God and the Bible are identical or at least isomorphic. What I find fascinating in the last quote, though, is not the confession about this isomorphism, an issue to which we shall return in a moment, but the attempt to flesh it out in some detail by correlating specific sections of the biblical text to specific limbs of the supernal anthropos. What may be the significance of this relation? Is it that the contemplator of the specific manner in which the letters, words, or verses were copied sees a divine form that reflects visually the divine limb? If so, how does this transformation of the text into an anthropomorphic structure take place? I have no precise answer to this quandary, but before attempting to investigate additional texts on this point, I would like to put forward a conjecture.

The Kabbalist resorts to the term *pereq*, translated above as "joint," in order to convey the human limbs at the points they are related to each other. The corresponding textual parts are described as *parshiyyot*, a term translated here as "pericope." The similarity between the Greek *pericope* and the anatomic *pereq* is rather surprising. Even more interesting is the fact that the Hebrew term adopted for expressing the Latin division of the Hebrew Bible into chapters, which do not correspond to the Jewish pericopes, is *pereq*. The history of this transition is not clear, and I assume that it is already reflected in some Kabbalistic discussions contemporary to R. Joseph of Hamadan. Given the absence of a study dealing with this adoption—a real desideratum for the understanding of the reception of the Bible among Jews—it is difficult to assess the role played by the linguistic similarity between *pereq* and *pericope* and the double meaning of the term *pereq*.[133] If this similarity can be proved, then the Kabbalistic isomorphism between the Torah and the human body, found already in the Geronese Kabbalah, will be enriched by the linguistic speculation.

Let me introduce an additional passage from another book of R. Joseph of Hamadan, dealing again with a complex isomorphism:

> This is the red attribute of judgment,[134] and from those five fingers were created five lower sefirot and corresponding to them David, blessed be his memory, has composed the five books of Psalms, and corresponding to the three joints of each and every finger there are three topics in each of the [five] books. Genesis corresponds to the thumb, is divided into three topics: the creation of heaven and earth, the events related to the forefathers, and the matter of exile. And the second finger corresponds to Exodus, and just as there are three joints in a finger, so is the book divided into three topics. The book of Exodus reports events related to Moses, our master, blessed be his memory, who brought the people of Israel from Egypt as a mission of God, blessed be He, and tells the laws and rules, and tells the matter of the Tabernacle. Behold they are three things. And the book of Leviticus, which corresponds to the third finger, so is this book the middle of the Pentateuch, and it is divided into three topics corresponding to the three joints of the middle finger. They are the law of the sacrifices, and the law of the leprosy, and the blessings and curses. The book of Numbers corresponds to the fourth finger and is divided into three topics: the numbers (census), the issue of the priesthood, and the issue of the spies. The fifth book corresponds to the fifth finger and is called Deuteronomy, which explicates the issue of the wonders and the miracles done by God to Israel, and the issue of the commandments, and Moses' death. Behold the five fingers of the right hand corresponding to the five books of the Pentateuch. But the five books in the book of Psalms correspond to the five fingers of the left hand, and each of these books too is divided into three topics corresponding to the three joints of the finger.[135]

Although there is a certain correlation between the anthropomorphic details related to the correspondences found in the two last quotes, the main intention of the Kabbalist is rather clear: the shape of the human body is the common denominator for both the Torah and the divine realm. In order to understand these topics and the correspondences between them, the Kabbalist must resort to his anatomical knowledge in offering a detailed account of the literary and divine structures:

Happy is the man who knows how to relate a limb[136] to another and a form to another, which are found in the Holy and Pure Chain, blessed be His name, because the Torah is His form, blessed be He. He commanded us to study Torah in order to know the likeness of the supernal form, as some few Kabbalists said,[137] "Cursed be he who will not keep this Torah up." Can the Torah fall? This [verse should be understood as] a warning for the cantor to show the written form of the Torah scroll to the community in order that they will see the likeness of the supernal form. Moreover, the study of the Torah brings someone about to see supernal secrets and to see the glory of the Holy One, blessed be He, indeed.[138]

The gist of this passage is the knowledge of the structural affinity between the human limbs and forms and the divine ones. The cognitive movement is expressly upward. The form of the letters in the Torah is assumed to play the same role as the human body: the latter is an icon enabling the contemplation of the supernal form. This quality explains, according to the last quote, the custom of showing the open scroll of the Torah to the members of the community after the reading of the weekly portion. Yet it seems that the formal correspondences between the lower and higher limbs should be understood more broadly. The Hebrew expression 'ever ke-neged 'ever, "a limb for a limb," is reminiscent of another recurrent phrase in R. Joseph of Hamadan's nomenclature, 'ever mahaziq 'ever, which means that the lower limb is maintaining the supernal one. This Kabbalist contends that the performance of the commandments by a certain limb strengthens the corresponding limb found on high, which is a sefirah.[139] Thus the contemplation of the higher starting from the lower is not the single, and may not even be the most important, sort of relationship between the privileged shapes here below, the human body and the Torah on the one side and the supernal sefirotic structure on high on the other. The lower not only knows the higher but also contributes to its making, as in the above quote from Sefer ha-Yihud, or maintains it, as in R. Joseph of Hamadan's books. This theurgical influence is possible only because of the affinities existing between three isomorphic structures: the Torah, the human body, and the ten sefirot conceived of as divine. Indeed, the relation between contemplation and theurgy was made explicit by R. Menahem Recanati, a Kabbalist inspired by the views found in the circle of *Sefer ha-Yihud:* "It is incumbent upon man to contemplate the commandments of the Torah, [to see] how many worlds he maintains by their performance and how many worlds he destroys by their neglect."[140]

Thus contemplation is a starting point, an invitation for another and apparently more important act, that of maintaining the supernal isomorphic structure. The Torah is, to a certain extent, the libretto for the ritual to be performed by the human body, and the result is the impact on the supernal structure. This view has had a long career in the history of Jewish mysticism, whose details have been addressed elsewhere.[141] Thus if contemplation of the Torah in order to see the isomorphic picture of God assumes the transcendence and superiority of the metaphysical over the literary, the theurgical dimensions of the significance of the instructions for action invites another form of relation between the two realms. The processes taking place within the divine structure depend on the actions of the human body. If the text does not absorb the divine within it, at least it shapes it according to its content. Both man and God depend therefore on the activating aspects of the Torah, not only its static iconic perfection.

Perhaps also under the influence of these books, another important Kabbalistic book, *Sefer ha-Temunah*, composed somewhere in the Byzantine empire at the middle of the fourteenth century, claims that the forms of the Hebrew letters constitute the image of God.[142] Another classic of Kabbalah that assumes an iconic vision of the Torah is R. Meir ibn Gabbai's *'Avodat ha-Qodesh*, composed around 1530 in the Ottoman empire. R. Meir writes: "The Torah is, therefore, the wholeness[143] of the grand and supernal Anthropos, and this is the reason it comprises the 248 positive commandments and 365 negative commandments, which are tantamount to the number of the limbs and sinews of lower and supernal man . . . and since the Torah has the shape of man it is fitting to be given to man, and man is man by its virtue, and at the end he will cleave to Man."[144] This iconization of the Torah enacts its transformation into an intermediary man, a mesoanthropos,[145] as it is "the intermediary which stirs the supernal image toward the lower [one]"[146] or, according to another statement by the same Kabbalist, "the Torah and the commandments are the intermediary which links the lower image with the supernal one, by the affinity they have with both."[147] In other words, to invoke Mallarmé, the Torah is "Le Livre, Instrument Spirituel."[148] The above quotes do not exhaust the Kabbalistic treatments of the Torah as the image or icon of God. More can be found in later Kabbalistic sources, some of which have been analyzed elsewhere.[149]

VI. FROM INTIMACY TO ALIENATION

I have described a phenomenon that can be envisioned as scroll fascination, which emerged in the same short period when the free symbolic interpretations of Kabbalists reached its apex, late in the thirteenth century, as we shall see in more detail in the next chapter. Overemphasizing the stable and static aspects of the text, Kabbalists and, later, the Hasidic masters strove, in my opinion, to balance the great freedom that emerged from the relativization of the symbolic interpretation which resulted from the ascendance of the concept of the Bible as an open text. The equilibrium between extreme semantic fluidity and extreme structural stability, namely the gestalt of the external features of the text, allowed innovative developments without endangering the authority of the canonical text.[150] It may well be that the eccentric exegetical devices that prevailed in the Kabbalistic and Hasidic literatures, like discussions of the white aspects of the letters, could flourish precisely because of the extreme canonization of all the details of the Torah scroll. The theosophical Kabbalists attempted to resolve the problem of authority of the text versus a drastic increase in exegetical creativity on the level of Kabbalistic hermeneutics; they did not rely on the three "lower" types of non-mystical interpretation in order to safeguard the authority of the text.[151] They invoked the mystical relevance of the white aspects of the text, found already in earlier sources, in order to establish a stronger authoritative anchor for their symbolic-narrative interpretations, in the case of the Kabbalists, or an anchor for a direct contemplation of the divinity, in Hasidism.

To formulate these topics in a different manner: in some forms of Kabbalah and sometimes in Hasidism, much more than in ancient Jewish literature, the Torah becomes the manifestation of the divine shape, not only the expression of the divine will. Interpretations, especially the secret one, that "retrieve" the divine significance of some parasemantic elements of the book can be understood as acts of proclamation which are part of the process of exhausting the infinity of the manifestation.[152] Here the text is conceived of as a visible and anthropomorphic manifestation; it plays a role similar to that of the concept of Jesus Christ's identity with nomos,[153] or the view found in Islam, where the early-eighth-century Shi'ite heterodox author Mughira ibn Sa'id, a magician and visionary, claimed to have had a vision of God in the form of a man of light whose body is constituted by the letters of the alphabet.[154] It is possible that these views reflect a more magical praxis of stamping the human body with special letters and seals.[155]

I would like to mention that recently some scholars of religion have proposed to regard the different reports of the mystics as reflecting experiences of different aspects of the divine: the impersonal versus the personal.[156] The affinity of the two aspects of the Torah to the two aspects of God in theosophical Kabbalah invites a comparison to the assumption of these scholars as to the various types of experience of the mystics.

According to the mystical texts analyzed above, God is not only the author of the written Torah: He is also the substratum of the written letters. The intimacy between the text and the author is therefore maximal: the text can be read only against the background of its author. It is not only conveying a certain specific authorial intention but expressing the very being of the author, sometimes in an iconic manner.[157] Yet this iconic trend, which conceives of the contemplation of the Torah as a technique for seeing God,[158] should be understood as a less influential tradition in the general economy of Jewish mystical literatures, as I understand them, than the recurrent resort to the recitation of the Torah as another technique to induce a mystical experience.[159]

According to some modern literary theories, however, the text can become meaningful only when it is understood in itself and solely from itself. Its dissociation from the author and the interplay between the different elements that constitute the text are considered part of its semiosis. In this context the material substratum, the white page, has also been introduced as part of the signification. The resort to the important status of the white page has been known in the West since Stéphane Mallarmé's discussions,[160] and they were taken over also in Derrida's thought.[161] This move was conceived of as a secularization,[162] which indeed it may be: the question, however, is whether a complete secularization is possible in speculative systems speaking about infinities and all-comprehensiveness,[163] or about mysteries of letters, as is the case with Mallarmé. This is not to say that Derrida and Mallarmé were in any way Kabbalists, or even that they derived their vision solely from Kabbalistic sources. Yet it seems to me undeniable that both were acquainted with Kabbalistic attitudes toward letters,[164] and although they were critical toward this lore, their resort to ideas that are hardly found outside Kabbalistic literature testifies to a certain contribution of Jewish mysticism to a modern philosophy of the text. The shared assumption of the two French thinkers who do not resort to a referent outside the text may be conceived of a total secularized attitude. Their claims to secularization notwithstanding, we still may encounter descriptions of their thought that are less clear-cut. So, for example, Bertrand Marchal, the author of a voluminous analysis of Mallarmé's religion, entitles his chapter dealing with the poet's conception of letters quite cogently "une théologie des lettres."[165] His view of the poem as a hierophany may also be relevant in our context.[166] Though the ontotheology is rejected, the cult of the book and the letters remains, as well as the claims of mysteries and revelations. It is an attitude rather than a faith that characterizes Mallarmé's approach, for the poet speaks of "une attitude de Mystère."[167] This may be a rebellion against a certain rather specific vision, proposed by Western theologians, of deity as transcendental, but such reverence for the book does not deviate too much from other theological attitudes centered on a spirituality gravitating around a book.[168] After all, according to both Mallarmé and Derrida, the transcendental role of the book and its cosmological status invite reflections whose intrinsic logic is not far removed from the theological one. Indeed, Derrida, apparently influenced by Scholem's approach to the status of the text as he understood R. Levi Isaac's passage, described Kabbalah as evincing "a kind of atheism" because of the emphasis on textuality and plurivocality characteristic of this lore.[169] Why atheism is characterized by a strong textuality or plurivocality is a point that was not explicated by Derrida, at least not in this context. Ignorant as I am of any other clarifications of this topic anywhere in Derrida's vast opus, I indulge in speculation that religiosity, or theology, is implicitly interpreted here as subscribing to a monosemic reading or to a tendency to speak about an abstract deity that may not be intrinsically or organically connected to a text. Such a contention, however, decides a priori what forms of theology and textuality are conceived of as religious or atheistic, without allowing the exponents of those concepts to define themselves as religious or atheistic. I would say, for example, that a text-centered community may be more religiously oriented than one that is not. Or that a polysemic text fits the belief in an infinite author, as we shall see in the next chapter, as well as a modern atheistic theory of dissemination.

Moreover, if the Kabbalists or the Hasidic masters may be thought to exhibit "a kind of atheism," then it seems to me that deconstruction may indeed contain a certain residue of Kabbalistic thought in its cult of the book or textuality or, as Eco called this phenomenon, "atheistic mystics."[170] (I shall have more to say on this issue in Chapters 5 and 9.) Or, to put it in Maurice Blanchot's terms, "The book is in essence theological."[171]

From this point of view we may describe some modern preoccupations with the text as encompassing everything (a topic to which we shall return in Chapter 4), as an almost complete absorption of the concept of divinity, by negating its independent existence while accepting some of its major attributes as pertinent for understanding the nature of the text. If the Hebrew Bible introduces a speaking God whose will is formulated in documents that constitute, inter alia, its reflection, the rabbinic sources canonized these texts while preserving the stark distinction between them and the divinity. Some trends found in mystical forms of literature gradually closed this gap, at times producing strong forms of identifications. In some cases the structure of the divine realm was conceived in terms of a written document, a strong case of a God-absorbing kind of textuality.

In modern philosophy of text, however, the author was formally excluded, but in fact some attributes of divine authorship have been transferred to the nature of the text qua text. Yet while Derrida formulated the concept of infinity by resorting to intertextuality, by contending that other texts will enrich the readings of any given text—in fact an extratextual approach insofar as any specific text is concerned—some of the Kabbalistic views discussed above extract concepts of infinity by referring to what they conceived to be an intratextual aspect, the white aspect. That is to say, for some Kabbalists the text means much more than its all-embracing textuality. The sacred text is, after all, understood to be a telescope, able to bring the divine closer, whether it be transcendent to the text or immanent in it. Even in those rare cases where Kabbalists acknowledged the difficulty in reflecting in the Torah the divine configuration in a language understandable by the common people, such a reflection is nevertheless presupposed. So, for example, the anonymous author of *Sefer ha-Temunah* claims that "the wondrous Torah," *ha-Torah ha-Nora'ah* (a recurrent term in the book)

> comprises the ten sefirot, their paths and revolution,[172] in each and every one of them all is inscribed in a supernal and hidden language, one which is very sublime, and supernal wondrous, and hidden letters, which are not understood [even] by an angel or a supernal archangel, but by God, blessed be His noble and wondrous name. He interpreted them to Moses our master and announced to him all their secret and matter and Moses wrote them in his language in the book, in a supernal manner that is hinted at in the Torah in the crowns, and in tittles, in big and small letters, in broken and crooked ones . . . all being supernal, wondrous, and hidden hints because he was unable to find a language to write them down, neither a way to relate them in detail. Sometimes [Moses resorted to] bizarre words because there is no language to catch them, all being wondrous paths and hidden allusions.[173]

The idiosyncrasy of the writing of the text is conceived of as reflecting a meaning higher than what is commonly expressed in an ordinary understanding of language. The text of the Bible text is written in a bizarre manner because only the eccentric is able to express the supernal secret. Nevertheless, such a secret may be understood by the few who are able to fathom the peculiar forms of writing the letters of the Torah.[174] Ultimately, those hints found in the ideogrammatic aspects of the Torah point to the divine shape or image, which is indeed the title of the book, *Sefer ha-Temunah*. This is one of the few passages in Kabbalah where the

Hebrew language, even in its biblical form, is not connected to an exhaustive expression of the signifié. It is the brokenness of some Torah letters, or the parasemantic aspect of the hieroglyphic language, rather than its perfection that plays a crucial role in the process of representation. The anonymous Kabbalist is resorting to a very moderate version of negative theology, which means that language as it is commonly used is not capable of reproducing a type of order that is more graphical than semantic.

For a modern thinker like Derrida, however, the text is more a kaleidoscope, whose internal changes do not reflect anything transcending its dense literacy. Given his kaleidoscopic view of the nature of the text, Derrida rejects the importance, or even the existence, of extratextual factors as conferring meaning. Most of the Kabbalists, however, positing an infinite ontology, could subsequently assume the textual infinity to be a derivative result of the authorial infinity. Both Kabbalists and Derrida did search for some forms of the infinite, although the latter was more inclined to deal with textual indeterminacy. This quest, which was sometimes conducted as interpretations of the canonical texts, will be explored in the next chapter.

3

TEXT AND INTERPRETATION
INFINITIES IN KABBALAH

I. PURGING AND HOMOGENEITY

The suppression of some conceptual elements and forms of discourse already found in ancient Jewish circles is characteristic of the rather homogeneous type of rabbinic discourse. Though allowing divergences of opinion and, one may even claim, encouraging, preserving, and studying them for generations, the ancient rabbis nevertheless controlled the nature of the topics on which divergences are allowed. No allegorical or symbolic interpretations of the Bible, abundant as they were in Alexandrian Judaism (especially Philo), were given access to the exegetical methods characteristic of rabbinic literature. Alchemy, astrology, philosophy, and physical sciences remained at the margin of rabbinic discourse. A full-fledged magical interpretation of tradition was rarely allowed, though some polemical attitude toward it is sometimes discernible, as we shall see in the next chapter. A personal divinity, whose characteristics are power and will, was addressed by people who were required to perform the divine will, the commandments, with all their power. This interaction between the human and the divine power become more prominent in some instances in rabbinic literature—an interaction I call theurgy—though it never reached the center of rabbinic literature. The more ordered reality, the independent cosmos of many of the Greek philosophers, was less attractive to the voluntaristic worldview of rabbinic literature.

The second wave of the repression of magical, theurgical, and theosophical speculations came much later, in the Middle Ages. It is characteristic of philosophical Jewish literature in general and of Maimonidean thought in particular, and this time it invited several forms of reaction. Not only was there a reaction against the philosophical readings of the canonical texts in new lights inspired by a variety of Greek philosophies, as in the case of the controversies against Maimonides, but also a resort to a more "constructive" strategy that proposed more structured alternatives. The nascent Kabbalah offers evidence of this reaction.[1] The emergence of this literature was not only a decisive development for Jewish theology; it also had the utmost influence on the subsequent unfolding of Jewish hermeneutics.[2] Underground myths and symbols surfaced in plain view, and hermeneutic methods that were rarely used by rabbinic authorities,[3] as well as entirely new perceptions about the biblical text, came to the forefront.[4] With this theological shift came also powerful new exegetical devices enabling Jewish mystics to revolutionize the conventional understanding of the biblical message. I should like to describe the nature of the components of the truly new hermeneutics.

Under the impact of ancient kinds of magic and mysticism, and in the polemical atmosphere of medieval periods, different forms of Kabbalah were able to generate a relatively unique theory of Hebrew language that applied to the Bible and its interpretation. The Hebrew language was no longer considered the exclusive instrument of divine revelation of sacred history and the Jewish way of life.[5] It was conceived also as a powerful tool which, used by God in order to create the world, could also be used by the Kabbalist masters in imitation of God in an effort to achieve their own marvelous creations or attain mystical experiences or sometimes even *unio mystica*.[6]

Another decisive change in medieval Jewish hermeneutics was the rise of a far-reaching assumption, expressed almost exclusively in Kabbalistic texts,[7] regarding the nature of the interpreter. As already mentioned, the divine spirit was categorically excluded from the interpretive process as viewed by the rabbis.[8]

Ecstatic states, prophetic inspirations, angelic revelations, and oneiric messages were unacceptable as exegetical techniques or reliable testimonies. It is true that such experiences never ceased to attract some rabbinic masters, and accounts of sporadic occurrences of altered states of consciousness in connection with particularly knotty interpretative quandaries certainly exist. Nevertheless, it was the Kabbalists alone who went so far as to condition the attainment of the sublime secrets of Torah on paranormal spiritual experiences. In certain Kabbalistic commentaries on the Bible we find indications that a prophetic state of mind is believed necessary to the proper decoding of the Bible. (I shall have more to say about this issue in Chapter 6.) And in a more general way the Kabbalists' reaching for a transcendent interpretative dimension even assumed categorical significance. Indeed, we come now to an issue of central importance in Kabbalistic interpretation: the direct relationship between the notion of the transported interpreter and the growing perception of the Torah as infinity. The Kabbalistic blurring of the distinction between God and man during prophetic experiences is coextensive, I believe, with the blurring of the difference between infinite God and infinite Torah.

In the rabbinic sources the primordial Torah is of course given a unique ontological status, unparalleled by all but the divine throne. As we saw in Chapter 1, the Torah was widely thought to predate the creation of the world; it was considered God's daughter and constituted the single way to contemplate the Godhead. However, whereas in the nonmystical texts there is a clear reticence to identify Torah with God Himself, in the Heikhalot literature there is a tendency to conceive Torah as inscribed on God's "limbs," thereby minimizing the difference between it and God.[9] The rabbinic opinion that after its revelation Torah is not to be found in heaven, as it was delivered to Moses in its entirety and is thus completely and finally in our possession, seems to be rejected by earlier Jewish mystical groups. Nevertheless, it fell to the Kabbalists to take the decisive step toward the explicit identification of Torah with God.

Thus, identification of Torah and God took place as the result of resorting to earlier anthropomorphic mythical themes, but when the divine was conceived of in terms of infinity, the possibility emerged that the Torah itself would assume qualities related to infinity. I shall attempt to describe instances of explicit awareness of the possible existence of infinite interpretations in the Bible and also (though rarely) other texts, an enterprise that has nothing to do with the rather limited range of mystical interpretations offered by the Kabbalists de facto. I strive not to make a statement about the nature of text as infinitely open but to survey the conceptualization of a sacred text as comprising, or including, infinite meanings.

II. Linguistic Infinities of the Biblical Text in Early Kabbalah

One of the interesting developments in the theosophical speculations in some early Kabbalistic circles is the resort to the term 'Ein Sof, the Infinite, in order to refer to the highest level within the divine realm.[10] Though certainly not the single term used for this purpose, it became slightly more prominent toward the end of the thirteenth century and reached its dominant status only much later, by the mid-sixteenth century.[11] Influenced as some of the uses of this term are by the negative theology that avers the impossibility of knowing this divine realm, it also has more positive meanings, which emphasize the infinity of the divinity rather than its unknown or inexpressible aspects.[12] According to some Kabbalistic statements, within the Infinite there are inner structures consisting in ten supernal sefirot.[13] This more positive aspect of the Infinite is reflected in the positive vision of the infinite interpretations implied within the special structures of the text of the Torah. In my opinion, the following discussions should be understood as pointing not always to an indeterminacy of the meaning of the text, a negation of the possibility of finding the one ultimate sense of a text, as in modern hermeneutics, but rather to the assertion by many Kabbalists of a richness intrinsic to this particular text. Many of the Kabbalists would opt for the existence of infinite specific and understandable interpretations. In contrast to Hegel's claim that Jews cannot see the infinite within the finite, Kabbalists were eager to do so, and the following discussions represent attempts to see the reflection of the absolute knowledge with a finite object, the Torah scroll. Interestingly enough, Hegel's view has been combatted by Derrida, a thinker who has been influenced by Kabbalistic views of the nature of the text, though he too was reluctant to allow that a positive infinite may be harbored by a finite object.[14]

Thus, aside from the kinds of identification of Torah with God or divine manifestations described in the previous chapter, some Kabbalists viewed the Bible as encompassing an infinity of meanings.[15] The Bible therefore is regarded by Kabbalists as akin to, and in several texts identical with, aspects of the Godhead itself. I should now like to survey three significant kinds of infinity of the Torah,[16] which are, in my opinion, consonant with various modern literary theories of writing, reading, and interpretation. Indeed, some of the Kabbalistic views of Torah discussed below were known to Christian theologians and could, at least theoretically, have influenced the subsequent unfolding of European culture. One of them is explicitly cited by Jacques Derrida, as we shall see.

(i) The characteristic of Hebrew (and Arabic) orthography that words may be written with only the consonants is the starting point of an important hermeneutical comment made by many theosophical Kabbalists. The Hebrew Bible, especially the Pentateuch, is traditionally written without vowels. Only rarely do some forms of mater lectionis indicate the vowel sounds that link the consonants. Thus, the common reading of the biblical text becomes a vocal performance that requires the application of the vowels to otherwise unpronounceable series of consonants, and then the pronunciation of the vocalized consonants. From this point of view the following discussions are reminiscent of the Qur'an, a sacred nonvocalized book to be recited as part of a religious performance. Thus, by dint of pronouncing the text the reader is an interpreter. This situation may be described as an ergetic exegesis, because understanding and interpretation involve an operation that shapes the text.

According to R. Jacob ben Sheshet of Gerona, a mid-thirteenth-century Kabbalist, "it is a well-known thing that each and every word of the Torah will change [its significance] in accordance with the change of its vocalization though its consonants will not be changed . . . and see: its significance changed . . . the word [i.e., the consonants constituting it] will not change its order. Likewise we may state that the Tetragrammaton will be used [during the prayer] with [Kabbalistic] intentions, in accordance with its vocalization. If someone who knows how to construct its construction will direct [his attention] to the construction which that [peculiar] vocalization points out, his prayer will be heard and his request will be announced by God."[17] The Torah scroll, written without vowels, is therefore pregnant with a variety of vocalizations, all of them possible without any change in the canonical form of the sacred text. The fluctuation of the vocalization, as it causes shifts in the meaning of a given combination of the consonants, alters the meaning of the sentence and of the Torah itself. Interestingly enough, the Kabbalist indicates that this process is his own discovery, or one that stems directly from the Sinaitic revelation itself.[18]

A long line of Kabbalists copied this text and expanded on it. I should like to cite and analyze only two of them, in which the implications inherent in R. Jacob ben Sheshet's observation are framed more explicitly. An anonymous Kabbalist, writing (scholars surmise) at the end of the thirteenth century, asserts:

Since the vowel [system] is the form of, and is soul to, the consonants, the scroll of Torah is written without vowels, since it [the scroll] includes all facets [i.e., aspects] and all the profound senses and all of them interpreted in relation to each and every letter, one facet out of other facets, one secret out of other secrets, and there is no limit known to us and we said: 'The depth said: It is not in me' [Job 28:14]. And if we should vocalize the scroll of Torah, it would receive a limit and measure, like the hyle that receives a peculiar form, and it [the scroll] would not be interpreted but according to the specific vocalization of a certain word.[19]

Freedom of interpretation is presented here not as a sheer accident arising from the special nature of Hebrew; rather, this freedom is implied, according to this Kabbalist, in the very prohibition against vocalizing the Torah scroll, a prohibition that permits an unlimited range of possible understandings for the divine text. The biblical text is, in this view, the touchstone of man's capacities. Its potential infinity, however, is not wholly dependent on our capacity to actualize it, but is inherent in the peculiar structure of the biblical text itself. All perfections are conceived of as being encompassed within the Torah, as each and every word of the Torah is pregnant with an immensity of meanings.[20] The various vocalizations are explicitly connected with secrets, presumably Kabbalistic secrets. Moreover, this Kabbalist notes the unlimited nature of the nonvocalized Torah scroll. According to the same source, the relationship between vocalization and consonants is like that between soul (or form) and matter; a certain vocalization is seen as tantamount to giving form to the hyle. Therefore, reading the Torah is equivalent to limiting the infinity of the Torah, and the embodiment of any meaning is potentially inherent in the consonants of the Torah. The Kabbalistic reading is an act of cooperation with God, or a co-creation of the Torah. The occurrence of the relationship between soul and body in the above passage has much to do with the metaphor of the vowels as causing, like the soul, the motion of the consonants. Thus, the vocal performance of the Torah transforms it into what Umberto Eco calls "a work in movement," as a quality of the open work.

Very close to this anonymous passage is a formulation found in one of the earlier writings of R. Joseph Gikatilla's *Commentary on Matters in the Guide of the Perplexed*:

According to this path you should know that Moses, our master, had been given a way of reading the Torah in many fashions, which are infinite, and each and every way points to the inner wisdom. This is the reason why the scroll of the Torah is not vocalized so that it may bear all the sorts of science found in the divine will. Because would it be vocalized, it would be like a matter to which a form had arrived, because the vowels are, for the words, like the form for the matter, as if you would say 'Adam, 'Odem, 'Edom. If it was not vocalized, it could bear each of the three, but if it were, it would bear only the limited one. This is the reason that the Torah has not been vocalized so that it will become as a hill in which all the intelligible sciences are found . . . All the sciences are connected to one word and no one understands the purpose of [even] one word but God, blessed be He . . . Because there is no one science in the world or wisdom or any other matter that is not hinted at in the Torah either in a letter, or a word or in a vowel or otherwise.[21]

The Castilian Kabbalist made a double claim: as in the other instances discussed in the paragraph, it is solely the divine text, and not texts compounded in Hebrew, that should be understood as inherently infinite. This infinity compresses, according to this passage, all the sciences, including the philosophical, and thus it is a more universalistic approach to the Bible as absorbing all available knowledge, regardless of source. On the other hand, Gikatilla contends that the Torah comprises only the sciences that are found in the divine will, a statement that has a much more particularistic tone.

Let me introduce another, quite similar expression of the same contention, found in a book of wide influence, R. Bahya ben Asher's *Commentary on the Pentateuch*:

The scroll of the Torah is [written] without vowels, in order to enable man to interpret it however he wishes . . . as the consonants without the vowels bear several interpretations, and [may be] divided into several sparks. This is the reason why we do not write the vowels of the scroll of the Torah, for the significance of each word is in accordance with its vocalization, but when it is vocalized it has but one single significance; but without vowels man may interpret it [extrapolating from it] several [different] things, many, marvelous and sublime.[22]

A comparison of this passage with R. Jacob ben Sheshet's discussions on this subject evinces what seems to me a major departure from older Kabbalistic views. Ben Sheshet assumes that the variation in vowels enables one to offer many interpretations of a given phrase; for him, however, there is Kabbalistic significance to this variation only in the case of the divine name, which refers to various sefirot according to the particular vowels by which it is vocalized; free Kabbalistic exegesis of the Bible is not implied. By contrast, R. Bahya explicitly refers to "several things . . . marvelous and sublime" which may be derived by interpretation of the text *ad placidum*; what is implied here is not simply a one-to-one relationship of the vocalized divine names to specific sefirot but a new tenet of Kabbalistic hermeneutics. What is described is not a magical-theurgical operation performed by the divine name when used correctly during prayer, as is the case in ben Sheshet, but a novel way of exegesis.

Another formulation of this mystical explanation of the nonvocalized form of the Torah should be noted here since it serves as a conduit between Jewish Kabbalah and Christian culture. According to the Italian Kabbalist R. Menahem ben Benjamin Recanati (early fourteenth century), in his influential *Commentary on the Torah*, "it is well known that the consonants have many aspects when nonvocalized. However, when they are vocalized they have only one significance, in accordance with the vocalization, and therefore the scroll of Torah, which has all the aspects, is nonvocalized."[23] Recanati's *Commentary* was translated into Latin by Flavius Mithridates for the use of Pico della Mirandola. The translation is apparently no longer extant, but its impact is registered in one of Pico's Kabbalistic theses: "We are shown, by the way of reading the Law without vowels, the way divine issues are written."[24]

I would like to conclude my brief survey of this aspect of the infinity of Torah with one more point. Despite the fact that these Kabbalists maintained the traditional order or *morphe* of the Torah, they still conceived its meaning as amorphous, allowing each and every interpreter an opportunity to display the range of his exegetical capacities. This initial amorphousness is not, however, identical to indeterminacy, a concept that would assume that the meaning of a given text cannot be decided in principle. A Kabbalist would say that all the meanings that are created by the different forms of vocalization are inherent in the text because they had been inserted, premeditatedly, by the Author, each of them in a rather transparent manner. It is not human feebleness to enchain language in a certain determined discourse that opens the text to many interpretations, but the infinite divine wisdom, as we shall see immediately below, that allows a powerful author to permit the existence of different vocalizations that coexist in the same consonantal gestalt. In the vein of modern literary critics like Georges Poulet, Roman Ingarden, and Wolfgang Iser, the theosophical Kabbalists would conceive the nonvocalized scroll of the Torah as the text to be recited in order to become a work; or, to adopt Roland Barthes's terminology, the work named Torah becomes a text by its production.[25] The "concretization of the text," to resort to Ingarden's term, by the ritual of reading the Torah is, according to the above Kabbalistic texts, an interpretation. However, the different, in fact infinite possibilities implicit in the nonvocalized text are to be understood as one possibility out of many distinct readings, a view that differs from Derrida's dissemination, based on *différance*, indecidability, and semantic ambiguity. There a basic instability, or to resort again to Ingarden's terminology "the places of instability," is assumed by the understanding of an unstable language and of all the texts as changing and enriching each other, in a manner that the theosophical Kabbalists would not admit. For them, to judge by the examples adduced above, each vocalized reading/interpretation constitutes a specific concretization that has its own stable meaning. These Kabbalistic passages are closer to Iser's theory of diverse concretization than to Ingarden's more static approach, which assumes some implicit idealism of meaning. It should be noted, however, that in practice the vocalization of the scroll during the ritual reading of the Torah was quite stable, and no one could imagine a free process that would depend on the reader. Nonetheless, the factual vocalization, though regulated by tradition, varies from one Jewish community to another insofar as the Sefardi and Ashkenazi pronunciation of the same vowels differs.

(ii) While the infinity mentioned above is related to the special nature of the text, which should be "animated" or performed by the act of pronunciation, some Kabbalists grounded their view of infinity on an extratextual factor, divine infinite wisdom. This is a nonergetic approach, which consists basically in exhausting the conceptual infinite cargo of the text generated by an infinite mind. The sources of this vision of Torah infinity precede Kabbalah; Charles Mopsik had kindly drawn my attention to the fact that in a late Midrash, R. Moses ha-Darshan's *Bereshit Rabbati* (p. 20), David is reported not to have known anything insofar as the Torah is concerned, because "its wisdom is infinite." In the same text the medieval Midrashist contends that David had seen the "principles of the Torah and knew that there are therein midrashim and minutiae, heaps upon heaps, to infinity." What seems to be interesting here, however, is that no divine infinity is assumed to constellate the textual one. This correlation characterizes many of the Kabbalistic treatments.

According to R. Moses de Leon, an influential late-thirteenth-century Kabbalist active in Castile, "God has bequeathed to Israel this holy Torah from above in order to bequeath to them the secret of this name and in order to [enable Israel to] cleave to Him [or to His name] . . . in order to evince that as this name [or He] is infinite and limitless, so is this Torah infinite and limitless . . . since the Torah being 'longer than the earth and broader than the sea' we must be spiritually aware and know that the essence of this existence is infinite and limitless."[26] This Kabbalist operated with the image found in Job 11:9 in the context of wisdom. Thus, not only does the infinity of the Torah reflect God's infinite wisdom, but apprehension of this infinity offers a way to cleave to Him. The Torah is here conceived in a quite instrumental manner, as a path for a uniting experience avoiding any specific reasoning that addresses its specific textuality. Moreover, we do not know precisely how this union happens. De Leon assumes that, unlike infinities related to features of the biblical text, it is the presence of God as author that ensures the text's infinity. This reading shows the deep difference between this Kabbalistic type of claim for infinity and deconstruction, which denies any form of metaphysical presence.

From a different starting point, another Kabbalist reached a similar conclusion: "Since God has neither beginning nor end, no limit at all, so also His perfect Torah, which was transmitted to us, has, from our perspective, neither limit nor end, and David therefore said,[27] 'I have seen an end of all perfection, but thy commandment is exceeding broad.'"[28] This Kabbalist learns about the infinite Torah through God's infinity. Another Kabbalist, a younger contemporary of the authors quoted above, specifically identifies Torah with God's infinite wisdom. Treating God's "unchangeability," R. David ben Abraham ha-Lavan, a fourteenth-century Neoplatonically oriented thinker, maintains that as all measure is a result of boundaries or limits, so is the wisdom of a man limited by the peculiar science he knows; and yet "the science which has no measure [i.e., is infinite] has no measure for its power; this is why the Torah has no limit since its power has no measure, because it is the primordial wisdom . . . the wisdom has no limit since this wisdom[29] and His essence are one entity."[30] Here the essential identity between God and Torah is explicit. So, too, wisdom, power, and will—as we have seen in Gikatilla's passage quoted in subsection (i)—are positive attributes of the divine which are reflected on the textual plane.

(iii) Torah is infinite, again, because the number of combinations of its letters—according to the complex Kabbalistic techniques of permutation—is infinite.[31] This is one of the most ergetic forms of interpretation, since the order of the letters of the interpreted text are changed as part of the interpretive process in order to infuse them with meanings that are not supported by the ordinary sequence of letters. These techniques of combination, developed in medieval treatises written under the impact of Ashkenazi Hasidism and in the prophetic Kabbalah,[32] are described by R. Joseph Gikatilla, a student of R. Abraham Abulafia:

> By the mixture ['eiruv] of these six letters [the consonants of the word bereshit[33]] with each other, and the profound understanding of their permutation and combination, the prophets and visionaries penetrated the mysteries of the Torah, and . . . no one is capable of comprehending the end of these things but God alone . . . it is incumbent on man to meditate upon the structures of the Torah, which depend upon the wisdom of God, and no one is able to [understand] one [parcel] of the thousands of thousands of immense [secrets] which depend upon the part of one letter[34] of the letters of the Torah.[35]

The ars combinatoria is perceived here as the path toward the partial comprehension of the secrets of the Torah. Its affinity to Abulafia's sixth path of interpretation of Torah is clear. Abulafia describes this advanced form of interpretation as the "wisdom of letter combinations," a term that recurs later in other Kabbalistic and Hasidic texts apparently influenced by him.[36] Still, we can discern here two different, though possibly complementary, views of infinity. The first is a mathematical infinity resulting from the application of complicated exegetical methods to letters of each of the separate words of the Torah and from the attempt to understand the significance of each combination. I assume that Gikatilla attributes to the combinations of the letters of a certain word a semantic function; he presumably contended that the semantic field of a given word, in this case *bereshit*, is constituted by all the meanings related to all the other combinations of the same consonants. If each word's meaning is an accumulation of all the meanings related to its letters' combinations, the aura of each word is so wide that an attempt to understand even one sentence by this technique is seen as impossible for a finite mind.

On the other hand, the monadic infinity inherent in each and every letter adds a further dimension to the mathematical infinity. The former is achieved by the deconstruction[37] of the order of the letters of the Torah by the combinatory process.[38] The latter, however, is quite independent of such permutations and, indeed, meditation upon the infinite significance depending on each letter is recommended when the "structures" of the Torah—ostensibly including also the order of the letters—remain unchanged. Yet the very concentration on one individual letter is said to have a destructive effect on the plain meaning of the text (or sentence) as a whole. Gikatilla seems to have combined Abulafia's last two paths of interpretation of the Torah into a single way. Permutation and monadization both lead away from the significant text toward an incommunicable or asocial perception achieved in a paranormal state of consciousness. The monadization is instrumental, according to Abulafia, in bringing on the Kabbalist's experience of *unio mystica*. The path of permutations, the sixth one in his exegetical system, is intended for those who attempt the *imitatio intellecti agentes*, persons who practice solitary concentration exercises and are presumed to invent novel "forms"—namely, meanings—for the combinations of letters.[39]

This effort of imitation of the *intellectus agens* is apparently to be understood as a transition from a limited state of consciousness to a larger one.[40] Interestingly, according to Abulafia, each higher path of interpretation is described as a larger sphere or circle;[41] the expansion of the intellect is therefore tantamount to the use of ever-more-complicated hermeneutic methods bent on achieving ever-more-comprehensive understandings of the Torah.[42] Indeed, Abulafia is interested here in transcending the natural understanding of reality, which in medieval philosophy was closely connected with Aristotle's logic. While Aristotelian logic is based on coherent sentences that generate conclusions significant in the natural world, Kabbalah—specifically prophetic Kabbalah—has a special logic that is the only suitable exegesis of the biblical text. To decipher the message of the Torah, this

Kabbalah relies on what it calls an "inner higher logic," which employs separate letters in lieu of concepts, as well as the combination of these letters. This method is deemed superior to Greek logic inasmuch as it returns the canonical text to its original state, when it was but a continuum of letters, all viewed as names of God.[43]

In this context it is worth noting that Jacques Derrida has combined Abulafia's view of Kabbalistic logic with Stéphane Mallarmé's definition of the role of poetry. In *La Dissémination* he writes, in explicit reference to Kabbalah, "La science de la combinaison des lettres est la science de la logique intérieure supérieure, elle coopére à une explication orphique de la terre."[44] Umberto Eco, too, refers to Lullian techniques of combination of letters in describing Mallarmé's method of combining pages.[45] As we have learned from Pico della Mirandola,[46] the Kabbalistic *ars combinatoria* is closely related to Lull's practice. Not without interest, then, is the fact that in Pico's *Theses*[47] Orphic issues were compared to and connected with Kabbalistic discussions, particularly those of Abulafia's school. Thus the concept of infinity of meaning transforms the Torah from a socially motivated document into a tool employed by mystics for the sake of their own self-perfection. Moreover, the Torah is perceived by certain Kabbalists as a divine and cosmic entity, what I have called the world-absorbing Torah, variously interpreted in the infinite series of universes. According to Gikatilla's *Sefer Sha'arei Tzedeq*:

> The scroll [i.e., the Torah] is not vocalized and has neither cantillation marks nor [indication where] the verse ends; since the scroll of the Torah includes all the sciences,[48] the exoteric and esoteric ones, [it] is interpreted in several ways, since man turns the verse up and down,[49] and therefore our sages said:[50] "Are not my words like as a fire? saith the Lord," like the forms of the flame of fire that has neither a peculiar measure nor peculiar form,[51] so the scroll of Torah has no peculiar form for [its] verses, but sometimes it [the verse] is interpreted so and sometimes it is interpreted otherwise, namely in the world of the angels it is read [as referring to] one issue and in the world of the spheres it is read [as referring to] another issue and in the lower world it is read [as referring to] another issue, and so in the thousands and thousands of worlds which are included in these three worlds,[52] each one according to its capacity and comprehension,[53] is his reading [i.e., interpretation] of the Torah.[54]

Therefore, in Gikatilla's view, there is another infinity in addition to the combinatory one, an infinity stemming from the fluctuation of the vocalizations. In my opinion, the importance of some concepts of infinity is that they are part of a polemical stand that attempts to deny the exclusivity of philosophical sciences by integrating everything within the structure of the Torah. Here, just as in the passage quoted earlier from this Kabbalists, Torah is conceived also as a sciences-absorbing text. What seems to be interesting in Gikatilla's text is that he expounded one of the first and most explicit models of Torah accommodation, what I shall designate the Neoplatonic model, on which I shall have more to say in Chapter 12.

(iv) A fourth aspect of infinite meanings of Torah is expressed in the flexible nature of Kabbalistic symbolism. The broad question of Kabbalistic symbolism has been discussed time and again in modern scholarship, and we shall have the opportunity to elaborate on this topic in a later chapter.[55] Here only a succinct description of symbolism is offered. According to some important Kabbalists,[56] an infradivine dynamic is reflected by biblical verses, wherein each word serves as a symbol for a divine manifestation[57] or sefirah.[58] The relationship between a given word and its supernal counterpart is relatively stable in earlier Kabbalah. Toward the end of the thirteenth century, however, greater fluctuation in this relationship is perceptible. In the very same treatise a word may symbolize more than one sefirah. The theoretical possibility thus emerges of decoding the same verse in several symbolic directions. Indeed, this possibility is fully exploited in the central mystical work of Kabbalah, the Zohar.[59] Therefore, the supernal dynamic is reflected not only in a symbolic rendering of the theosophical content of a particular verse but also in the very fact that the same verse can be interpreted again and again, all interpretations bearing equal authority. According to this perception, discovery of new significances in the biblical text is yet another way of testifying to the infinite workings of the sefirotic world.

The Kabbalistic transformation of words and whole sentences into symbols has a deep impact on the perception of language itself. For even as the individual word retains its original forms, even as its place in the sentence or its grammatical function remains stable, its status as a lower projection of an aspect of the Godhead renders it an absolute entity. The result is a mystical linguistics forged into a skeletal grammar. Rather than being understood as mundane and conventional units of communication or representation, the words of the Bible, grasped as moments of God's enacted autobiography, become instruments for His self-revelation in the lower realms of being.

The primary unit, then, remains the biblical word to be interpreted, which, in contrast to Abulafia's text-destroying exegesis that annihilates the "interpreted" material in order to reconstruct it in a new way, is viewed as a monadic symbol.[60] Nevertheless, as we shall see in Chapter 10, a proper understanding of Kabbalistic symbolism must take into consideration the more comprehensive symbolic system that informs each and every individual symbol.

III. NONLINGUISTIC INFINITIES AND INTERPRETATION
IN LATER JEWISH MYSTICISM

The assumption of the existence of one faithful interpretation of a text is especially conspicuous in cosmic and spiritual systems that are closed. A closed universe will tend to emphasize the uniqueness of a faithful interpretation stemming from a certain idealism of meaning, to resort to Ricoeur's expression, much more than an open one will. The basic correlation that is significant for a proper understanding of the contribution of many forms of Kabbalah to interpretation is the correspondence between the nature of the text and that of the divine realm that emanated and presides over the text. To put it in literary terms, the nature of the infinite author radiates on the conception of an infinite textual composition. Specifically in the type of Kabbalistic theosophy that explicitly emphasizes the infinity of the divine realm, and within this framework of Kabbalistic thought, are the canonical texts regarded as infinite. In contradistinction to the assumption found in many texts in Jewish philosophy that God is an intellectual entity—an assumption that is often, though not always,[61] related to the view that there is one correct meaning of the text—Kabbalists of different schools explicitly operate with the concept of infinity as relevant both for the divinity and for the text and its interpretations.

I would like to address another aspect of infinite interpretations, found in later Kabbalistic and in Hasidic texts. In addition to the view of intrinsic indeterminacy, or infinity, of the text, because of its imitating the divine infinity or because of the special nature of the canonized text, I shall deal here with reasons for the possibility of infinite interpretations as related to factors that are independent of the text. There are four main reasons offered by Jewish mystics for assuming the infinity of possible interpretations, which do not depend on the special nature of the Hebrew language and the canonical text itself: (i) the dynamic quasi-astrological structure of the metaphysical system that informs the meaning of the interpreted text; (ii) the existence of infinite and different universes that are sources of the souls of the various interpreters; (iii) the view of the constitutive Sinaitic revelation, intended differently, to each of the children of Israel; and (iv) the charismatic authority of the spiritual leader who is able instantaneously to create potentially infinite oral texts, to be discussed in Appendix 5.

1. Dynamic Theosophy and Interpretive Infinity

One of the main interpretive practices in Kabbalah is the explanation of the canonical texts as reflecting relations between divine powers. The articulation and crystallization of the theosophical systems have created strong interpretive schemes whose components and processes have been imposed on the commented texts. The understanding of the theosophical systems as quintessentially dynamic, much more than transcendental or unknown or unknowable, will open the possibility that scholars will better understand one of the basic principles of Kabbalistic hermeneutics. So, according to a Lurianic text that will be quoted and discussed below, the specific interpretations depend on the specific moment in time which is presided over by a special sefirotic constellation.[62] In principle there are no two identical interpretations, as the multiple supernal system is continuously changing. In a manner reminiscent of Gadamer's view it is time, though not history, that is an important factor in shaping the nature of the interpretations, because each moment is constellated in a different manner by the changing relations between the various divine attributes.

2. Infinity of Worlds and Infinity of Meanings

As Eco has pointed out, there are affinities between ways in which science and culture understand reality, and the structures of the artistic forms.[63] This statement is also true insofar as some of the Kabbalistic views of the Torah are concerned. The great importance of divine infinity in early Kabbalah may be related to the emergence of the existence of infinite worlds later on. The view that presupposes an infinity of coexisting worlds is relatively rare in Kabbalistic literature before the sixteenth century, but nevertheless it exists. Early Kabbalah operated with much simpler forms of universes, and only at the end of the thirteenth century or the beginning of the fourteenth a vision of four levels of existence emerged, suggesting a much greater complexity of the divine world than in the thirteenth-century Kabbalah.[64] In Lurianic Kabbalah, however, which continued some of the developments of that Kabbalah, the existence of infinite worlds between 'Adam Qadmon, the primordial cosmic man, and the totally transcendental 'Ein Sof is explicit.[65] The insertion of those infinite worlds was intended to create an even more transcendental status for 'Ein Sof, as they are unknown universes. However, R. Hayyim Vital, R. Isaac Luria's main disciple, claims that every soul has a root above, and this root reverberates in all the worlds, as a result of which "there is no soul which has no endless roots."[66] Therefore, there is an infinity of coexisting worlds, which are related to every soul in this world. From a Lurianic text, written in the second third of the seventeenth century, we learn about another form of infinity of worlds:

> The issue is that the Torah, "its measure is longer than the earth, and broader than the sea,"[67] and just as there is an infinite number of worlds, so there is the depth of the Torah infinite. Because in each and every world, the

Torah is read in accordance to its [the respective world's] subtlety and spirituality, namely that there is no end to the degrees of its interpretations. And each and every one of the Tannaites and the Amoraites in this world understands and interprets the Torah in accordance with the world his soul is emanated from it. This is why those say [so] and the other say [otherwise] and the saying of these and these are the words of the living God. This is why R. Meir apprehended in the Torah something that was not apprehended by someone else, and it was appropriate to him [to interpret this] more than to another sage, because his name was Meir, which means light, and the stored light is good.[68]

Two different approaches are combined in this passage. One assumes a process of accommodation of the meaning of the Torah to the different worlds, a view already found in Judaism and in some Kabbalistic texts.[69] A younger contemporary of Giordano Bruno and apparently a reader of one of his books,[70] R. Jacob Hayyim Tzemah, also operates with another concept, that of the infinite worlds. Indeed, the infinity of the worlds—an idea that became more compelling when thinkers like Giordano Bruno, who believed in an infinite universe, started to emphasize the existence of an infinite universe—is this Kabbalist's rationale for the existence of an infinity of souls, each of them capable of producing an interpretation corresponding to its special constitution. The Kabbalists active in the latter part of the sixteenth century acted in a spiritual and scientific ambiance different from that of the thirteenth-century Kabbalists, and the explanations of their thought should be more open to parallels, osmotic processes, and influences that were not available earlier. Thus, I suppose that the theory of infinity is not superseded by that of accommodation, although the latter is indeed mentioned in the text.

3. Primordial Spiritual Roots and Corresponding Interpretations

Already in the rabbinic literature there is a correspondence between the particular nature of the recipients of the Torah and their perception of the revelation. In *Yalqut Shim'oni* there is a hologrammatic description of God when revealing Himself: "Rabbi Levi said: The Holy One, blessed be He, has shown Himself to them as this icon[71] that is showing its faces in all the directions. A thousand people are looking at it and it looks at each of them. So does the Holy One, blessed be He, when He was speaking each and every one of Israel was saying, 'The speech was with me'. I am God is not written, but I am God, your Lord.[72] Rabbi Yossei bar Hanina said, 'According to the strength[73] of each and every one, the [divine] speech was speaking.' "[74] The aural revelation at Sinai, like the visual one related to the *eikon* that serves as an illustration to its polymorphism, presupposes an individual rather than a group that is submitted to one compact revelation. Differentiation between the recipients is quite evident in this passage. Here it is the divine voice, not the written text, that is the basic subject matter of the rabbinic passage, and thus multiplicity of meanings is the result of the divine accommodation.

The view that each and every Jew is in the possession of a special revelation and of a unique interpretation disclosed only to him is found in R. Meir ibn Gabbai, R. Shlomo Alqabetz, and R. Moses Cordovero's writings, in several Lurianic sources, and in R. Isaiah Horovitz's influential book *Ha-Shelah*, though the Kabbalistic sources implying it may be much earlier.[75] This vast topic cannot be exhausted here and deserves a much more detailed analysis. Let me adduce only a few sources, starting with a book composed at the middle of the seventeenth century, R. Naftali Bakharakh's well-known *'Emeq ha-Melekh*; I have selected this text, which in many ways paraphrases prior Lurianic texts, because it offers a more comprehensive discussion of the various Lurianic motifs.[76] In Bakharakh's version, R. Isaac Luria—who is described as someone knowing whatever exists in heaven and earth—resorted to a special mystical technique: he resorted to the souls of the dead Tannaites and Amoraites in order to learn from them the secrets of the Torah. This fact was prima facie surprising, since Luria was thought to be someone who possessed the holy spirit and a very creative master, described as *ke-ma'ayan ha-mitgabber* in the treatise *'Avot*. This quandary was resolved by the assumption, found in earlier Lurianic texts, that all the souls of the children of Israel were present at Sinai and "it was decreed that this one will innovate this issue and that one [will innovate] that issue, [and they] ought to be disclosed precisely by each of them and not by any other person, because this is the particular spark of his soul."[77]

This principle is exemplified with the help of a legend regarding Moses, who was unable to understand R. 'Aqivah's homiletic interpretations on the Torah.[78] Thus, according to the Kabbalist, even Moses was unable to fathom the interpretation of the book he wrote, an interpretation that was unique to R. 'Aqivah.[79] Likewise, Bakharakh contends, following earlier Kabbalistic sources, that all the souls of the Israelites comprise all the interpretations.

Another interesting discussion of the multiple significance of the Torah, related to the concept of particular interpretations revealed to each of the Jews present at Mount Sinai, is found in R. Moses Hayyim Luzzatto, known as Ramhal, a seminal thinker who flowered in the 1730s and was deeply influenced by Cordoverian and Lurianic themes. In his book *Qelah Pithei Hokhmah* he offers one of the most ergetic understandings of the theory of infinite meanings:

God spoke: "Are not my words like fire?"[80] . . . because just as the coal that is not enflamed, the flame within it is hidden and closed, but when you blow on it, it expands and broadens like a flame and many sorts of nuances[81] are seen which were not visible prior to it in the coal, but everything emerged from the coal. So too is the case of the Torah that is before us, whose words and letters are like a coal . . . and whoever is preoccupied and busy with it enflames the coals, and from each and every letter a great flame emerges, replete with many nuances, which are the information encoded in this letter . . . All the letters we see in the Torah point to the twenty-two lights found on high and those supernal lights are illuminating the letters, and the holiness of the Torah and the holiness of the scroll of the Torah and of tefillin and mezuzot and all the holy scriptures, and in accordance with the holiness of its writing the dwelling and the illumination of those [supernal] lights on the letters are enhanced . . . and those nuances are numerous and the ancient masters received [a tradition] that all the roots of the souls of Israel are all within the Torah and there are six hundred thousand inter-pretations to all the Torah, divided between the souls of the six hundred thousand [children of] Israel . . . This is the reason why though the Torah [as a whole] is infinite, even one of its letters is also infinite, but it is necessary to enflame it and then it will be enflamed, and so too the intellect of man.[82]

Here the reasoning is tautological: the souls of the recipients of the Torah are already within it—a Kabbalistic version of the reader in the text—and this is why there are so many meanings in the Torah, and the study of the Torah by each of them enflames it and discloses the potential colors and nuances in it. An individ-ual is tantamount to all the others, and he can actualize the significance of the Torah by his enthusiastic study of the book. In any case, the interpretation is not only an actualization of the linguistic and eideic treasuries of the text, but in fact an activation of a primordial spiritual affinity between the Torah and the souls of Israel. The act of blowing in itself contributes a substance to the flame and causes its expansion.[83] Thus, at least on the metaphorical level, the nature and spiritual effort of the interpreter contribute to the further expansion of the Torah. The importance of the metaphysical dimension of Luzzatto's discussion should be emphasized: the mundane Torah is dependent on the supernal twenty-two letters, which infuse their lower representations and permutations with light or holiness. The infinity is therefore dependent on the linkage with a higher universe, which transcends the linguistic formulations and stresses the basic units, the letters, in a manner reminiscent of *Sefer Yetzirah*. Holiness and meaning do not emerge by virtue of an intratextual relation (like permutations of letters), as part of an horizontal interaction, but by dint of a vertical interaction between the twenty-two fundamental letters on high and the multiplicity of their reflections in the scriptures. I assume that Luzzatto adopted a rather talismanic understanding of the study of the Torah, and perhaps of its interpretation, as part of the talismanic model that will be examined in more detail in the next chapter. If this proposal is correct, the intense preoccupation with the Torah, which implies vocal activity, may be understood as drawing the divine lights on the corresponding letters below. "Illumination" of the lower letters by the higher would be connected to the enflaming, and the nonmetaphorical illumination could be connected to the metaphorical one, which would be related to interpretation.

Let me return to the schematic figure of the number of children of Israel. Since there were six hundred thousand souls at Mount Sinai, six hundred thousand interpretations are available. Yet this figure, which occurs in the earlier Lurianic writings, did not satisfy the Kabbalists; according to some sources,[84] given the fact that the Torah is interpreted in accordance with the fourfold exegetical technique known as *pardes*, each of the four ways of interpretation includes six hundred thousand different interpretations.[85] According to this view, the interpretive singularity of the voice of every Jew is ensured by his very essence as a Jew, meaning his presence at the constitutive moment of Sinaitic revelation. In fact, according to some formulations of Lurianic passages, including that of R. Naftali Bakharakh, the soul is not only the depository of a certain singular interpretation; its very essence is the expression of that interpretation. Indeed, let me adduce the voice of the Kabbalist himself: "Out of each interpretation, the root of a certain soul of Israel emerged, and in the future each and every one [of Israel] will read and know the Torah in accordance with the interpretation that reaches to his root, by which he was created . . . Behold that at night, after the departure of the soul during sleep, whoever merits ascending reads there the interpretation that reaches his root."[86] Therefore, interpretation is not only a function of the peculiar quality of the soul, or of the particular universe from which the soul emerged into this world; the identity of the soul is created by the interpretation itself. Indeed, the soul not only proclaims its unique vision of the Torah but is itself the very manifestation of that unique interpretation. Faithful interpretation, therefore, is conceived not so much as the projection of the values of the religious society onto an antiquated canon but as faithfulness to the inner nature of one's soul.

The Kabbalist's emphasis on the "singularity of the voice"[87] should not, however, be overemphasized. There is nothing modern here, no special veneration of the uniqueness of the individual; the soul is conceived of as but part of the greater spiritual reservoir of primordial souls, which are no more and no less than sparks of the divine essence which descended into the mundane world and will return to their supernal source at the end of time. Thus interpretation is not the expression of the separation of the individual from the group or community, or an idiosyncratic vision that sets him apart, an act of creativity or originality particular to him, in the way the romantics would understand it. On the contrary: his interpretation is a minuscule particle of the larger and already existing tradition, which is a huge puzzle composed of six hundred thousand pieces, and without his contribution the puzzle will never be completed. Hence the theory of the singularity of the voice does not imply an insularity of the discourse, or of the soul of the interpreter; far from creating a centrifugal moment intended to facilitate personal uniqueness, this theory advocates a centripetal move, which presupposes cooperation. According to explicit statements of Lurianic Kabbalists, each and every soul includes in itself all the other souls[88]—a Kabbalistic version of a Leibnitzian monadic theory—and implicitly also the interpretations of all the others. Thus, though being unique, an interpreter reflects in himself the whole range of his community, just as his own interpretation, unique as it is, comprises in some mysterious way the whole spectrum of interpretations preserved within his community. Only by maintaining and transmitting the unique message of the text inherited by him is the individual interpreter capable of completing all the others, and of completing the proclamation of the manifold senses of the Torah. This point, which was not articulated in any of the pertinent texts, seems nevertheless to be implied in the whole Lurianic discourse. Still, the existence of a net of affinities between one's soul and the interpretation one offers is part of a new emphasis on the individual emerging in Safedian Kabbalah, an issue that deserves a separate study. However, it would be salient to see authenticity as a value that reflects the gist of the above passages rather than as a search for originality.

The above theory seems to be the hermeneutical counterpart of the tiqqun theory, so crucial for the Lurianic Kabbalah. Just as the Kabbalistic interpretation and performance of the ritual allow the restoration of the primordial unity of the 'Adam Qadmon out of the dispersed sparks, designated as tiqqun, so also the restoration of all the dispersed interpretations has an eschatological meaning. Three major entities tell the same story, or myth, of Lurianic Kabbalah in a parallel manner: the Torah, the souls of Israel, and 'Adam Qadmon.[89] All three were scattered into particles, and all are supposed to return to their source.[90] Interpretation, therefore, may become not only an ergetic involvement with the text but also an individual eschatological activity.

This eschatological move is only partially expressed in the sources. Most of them contain two possibilities, which prima facie seem to be exclusive. One is the assumption that unless the imperative of studying the Torah in accordance with the fourfold way of interpretation is fulfilled, the individual will return to this world, by means of metempsychosis, up to the moment that the imperative is to be fulfilled. Indeed, personal redemption depends on the completion of study. Thus, actualizing one's special understanding of the whole Torah means also the cessation of mundane existence, which is the arena of the actualization of one's peculiar interpretation.[91] Such a reading would necessitate human initiative, which is indispensable for acquiring perfection, an experience of plenitude that is deemed to be attainable in this world independent of the eschaton. The individual's understanding of the Torah, being a personal soteriology, is able to save him from metempsychosis.

On the other hand, statements can be found, in the same contexts as the above theory, to the effect that only in the future each and every one of the children of Israel will know the whole Torah in accordance with the interpretation that corresponds to the root of his soul.[92] Such a conception would mean that a complete awareness and manifestation of all the meanings of the Torah is a matter of the eschatological future. It seems, however, that the two views, which appear to be antithetical, can be reconciled. The retrieval of all the interpretations may be understood as an accumulative process to be completed in the collective eschaton, but its stages consist in the personal attainments of those who are able to anticipate the historical eschaton and achieve their own redemption. This is why I believe that each interpretation is part of the general complex of the eschaton, just as every performance of the commandments is part of the general tiqqun. Several Lurianic sources describe the study of the Torah in general in terms of tiqqun.

This survey of the history of the infinity of meanings as developed in Kabbalah yields a significant development: early Kabbalah is much more concerned with infinities of interpretations, without emphasizing the different types of souls or their various sources on high, than are the Kabbalistic sources after the middle of the sixteenth century. In my opinion, the shift from a more objective approach to Kabbalah to a more subjective one seems to transpire in many cases in late Kabbalah, an issue corroborated by other topics, such as the emergence of mystical diaries in the sixteenth-century Safed. The accent is not only on the fullness of the Torah and its being pregnant with infinite meanings, but much more on the contribution of the individual to this fullness.

Let me now introduce another type of infinity, which also depends on the infinite nature of the substance of God rather than on processes that constellate the meanings of the Torah. A nineteenth-century Hasidic master claims that "out of your union [with God][93] you will be able to pass from the word 'anokhi alone to the entire Torah, because just as God, blessed be He, is infinite, so too His word is infinite, and likewise you, if you will be united to God, blessed be He, will comprehend by an infinite understanding."[94] Here the infinity of the Torah depends not on an inherent quality of the text but on the infinite nature of the divine author, which is reflected in the nature of the interpreter who cleaves to God. The achievement of adherence or mystical union of the Hasidic master opens the gate to an infinity in the textual entity because of the acquired infinity of the interpreter. From this achievement, and from a primordial affinity between God and the Torah, a common denominator is created: God, Torah, and Man are one and infinite at the same time.[95] When this is achieved, the mystical interpreter will be able to discover the infinity of the divine word within the divine pronoun 'anokhi.[96]

IV. INFINITIES OF THE *ZOHAR*

The concept of infinity of the Torah was, as we have seen, well established prior to the emergence of Lurianic Kabbalah. With the ascent of the centrality of a new book for the Kabbalists, the *Zohar*, Kabbalists and Hasidic masters applied this concept to the now-canonical text.[97] One passage preserved by Luria's main disciple, R. Hayyim Vital, may appropriately illustrate Luria's influential attitude toward the *Zohar*:

> The worlds change each and every hour, and there is no hour which is similar to another. And whoever contemplates the movement of the planets and stars, and the changes of their position and constellation and how their stand changes in a moment, and whoever is born in this moment will undergo different things from those which happen to one who was born in the preceding moment; hence, one can look and contemplate what is [going on] in the supernal infinite, and numberless worlds . . . and so you will understand the changes of the constellation and the position of the worlds, which are the garments of 'Ein Sof; these changes are taking place at each and every moment, and in accordance with these changes are the aspects of the sayings of the book of the *Zohar* changing [too], and all are words of the Living God.[98]

The *Zohar* as a inexhaustible text was conceived, therefore, to reflect the nature of its ever-living Author, the living God, who composed, according to some Kabbalists, a continuously changing composition, in a manner reminiscent of Mallarmé's *Livre*. The organic vision of the Zoharic text as a body that changes, just as its Author did, is reminiscent of the rabbinic vision of the Torah, whose dialectical nature has been described in similar terms: words of the living God.

Elsewhere, Luria asserts that "in each and every moment the [meanings of the] passages of the holy *Zohar* are changing."[99] Hence, for a Kabbalist the Zoharic text has reached a status very similar to that of the Bible itself.

Another important Jewish mystic, R. Israel Ba'al Shem Tov, the founder of Polish Hasidism, also envisioned this Kabbalistic book as changing its meaning every day. He was reported by his grandson to have asserted, consonant with Luria's view, that "the book of the *Zohar* has, each and every day, a different meaning."[100] R. Eliezer Tzevi Safrin, a late-nineteenth-century Hasidic commentator on the *Zohar*, quoted his father, R. Isaac Aiziq Yehudah Yehiel Safrin of Komarno—himself a renowned commentator on this book—as saying that "each and every day, the *Zohar* is studied in the celestial academy, according to a novel interpretation."[101] In addition to the literary activity of interpreting the *Zohar*, which generated a rich literature that has yet to be explored as a special literary genre, parts of this book have been recited ritualistically, especially in the Jewish communities in Morocco and the Middle East, even by persons who were not familiar with its precise content.[102]

V. SOME CONCLUSIONS

The forms of infinity of interpretations discussed above in section III do not assume the possibility of concomitantly faithful mystical interpretations stemming from the same person. The potential anarchism inherent in the assumption that the number of mystical interpretations is not limited has been attenuated by various restricting circumstances. According to the first theory presented above, the divine constellation imposes the assumption of a proper interpretation characteristic of a given moment. As in the case of astrology, there is a certain deterministic moment that regulates the nature of the understanding of the text. According to the second view, there is only one single interpretation that characterizes the approach of each master, namely one representative of his primordial source in a specific world. In the case of the third view, the nature of the interpretation is predetermined by the primordial spiritual constitution one inherited at the time of the Sinaitic revelation. Therefore, while the Torah is still conceived of as possessing an infinite or quasi-infinite number of meanings, a much more conservative attitude toward the interpreter is expressed in the above texts.[103] If the earlier Kabbalah was much more text-oriented, in time it became more theosophically oriented. With the elaboration on the theosophical structure since the end of the thirteenth century, the symbolic meaning of the scriptures became quite determined and is imposed mechanically onto the canonical texts. From this point of view it is obvious that those texts were conceived of as pointing to supernal realms whose meaning was known to the "soul" of the interpreter. This is just one of the examples that invalidated the theory that Kabbalistic symbols are significands that have no signifieds. The signified is part and parcel of one's very identity. At least theoretically some of the Kabbalists were confident that the symbols reveal an esoteric dimension that expresses their particular identity. I would like now to compare this emphasis on the identity of the interpreter, who is also a reader and an author, to modern trends in critical theory.

Modern literary theory has turned its attention to the nature of the text in a rather intense manner by gradually marginalizing logocentric attitudes. Following the cultural crises involved in the Nietzschean and Freudian revolutions, the instability of meaning secured by factors external to the text has become a big issue, which betrays not only the fluid semantics of the interpreted texts but also the flexible attitudes of readers. A destabilization of philological certainty in the possibility of ascertaining authorial intention (intentio auctoris) facilitated the emergence of more subtle, intricate, sometimes even oversophisticated discourses over the possibilities implied in the earlier discourses. I attribute this move to the discovery of the discrepancy between the poverty of the author and the richness of language. Unstructured language, which is enchained by creative processes, is never subservient to the author's capacities and transcends his intentions by displaying a much greater spectrum of meanings than the author intended; that is to say, the work contains its own intention (intentio operis).[104] It is a weak mind, genial though it may be, that attempts to enslave the variety of possibilities inherent in language as constituted by a long series of semantic shifts. This view of the secular text entails a crisis in the former focus on the author and proposes a much greater interest in the contribution of the reader or, even more, the sophisticated interpreter. Readers and interpreters complete the meaning by bringing their own riches to the interpreted texts. The secular attitude toward texts is a fundamentally democratic discourse.

Sacred texts, however, almost always imply strong authors. Either God or His prophets or the Hasidic tzaddiq, or at least the authority of the ancients, supply an authorship that provides a much firmer basis for the belief that the canonical texts by themselves represent higher forms of intelligence, if not absolute wisdom. This faith in the distinct superiority of the author over the interpreter, part of a hierarchical structure of the universe, society, and human minds, dominates the approach of a religious reader to canonical texts. Assuming such a superior wisdom means also that it is hard to believe that an inferior reader, or even a community of readers, will ever be able to exhaust the multiple intentions implied in the canonical texts. Thus, it is not only the awareness of the riches of language, of its fluidity and ambiguities, that serves as the ground for ongoing interpretive projects, but also an assumption of the existence and activities of higher, even infinite forms of intelligences or divine attributes that are logocentric entities. It is not in history, as Gadamer would claim, but in an atemporal supernal reservoir that a Kabbalistic interpreter believes he will found his interpretations. Thus, Kabbalists operated with a radical trust in the text, rather than a basic mistrust in its author as the generator of the text, which characterizes modern deconstructive approaches. The horizontal intratextuality and intertextuality characteristic of recent secular approaches have replaced the vertical interchange between the reader and the metaphysical subject of his belief in religious hermeneutics.

A modern reader reads largely in order to express himself; a religious reader is looking much more to be impressed. Secular reading is an analytical, disintegrative process; it subverts much more than it integrates. Its agon is provoked by the self-imposition of the historical relations as generative factors. The gist of religious reading, on the other hand, is synthetic. It reflects a higher order, which is to be absorbed, imitated, or at least venerated.

I would say that earlier Kabbalah preferred the assumption that an infinity of meanings is latent in the gestalt of the divinely authored text over the view, found in several Christian texts, that the process of interpretation alone is infinite. According to the latter, each and every exegete is able to contribute his view to the exegetical tradition, whereas the text per se is very rarely regarded as infinite in its significances. Yet despite the indifference and even hostility of Christian religion toward language,[105] this did not preclude the emergence of the idea of infinite accumulative interpretations.

Indeed, it would be much more representative to describe the conceptions of the Kabbalists regarding the relationship between the Torah and man as requiring that the Kabbalist be assimilated to the Torah rather than vice versa. It is man who must accommodate himself to the infinite Torah rather than Torah to man. In addition, I would distinguish between the Kabbalistic emphasis on infinity of meanings and a view recurring in many other mystical literatures dealing with ineffable experiences. Kabbalistic texts do not emphasize a negative theology and rarely speak about experiences that cannot be rendered in words. The concept of interpretations found on high and waiting, so to speak, for the corresponding souls to actualize them does not allow ineffability, at least insofar as this important form of religious activity is involved. In lieu of the scholarly assumption that Kabbalah starts with a realm of unarticulated and inarticulable meanings,[106] I would say that the belief in primordially articulated meanings is quite representative of rabbinic and Kabbalistic literatures. In fact, the affinity between the specific interpretation and the root of one's soul, both of which preexist on high, emerged concomitantly in Safedian Kabbalah and points to a greater importance of the individual in the theosophical Kabbalah, a move that received an even greater impetus in Polish Hasidism. Unlike the earlier vision of the root of the soul in an upper world of Neoplatonic origin, which was accepted in thirteenth-century Kabbalah and remained a rather general principle, in Safedian Kabbalah this principle has become a much more vibrant issue which, together with other principles such as the more elaborated and individualized conceptions of metempsychosis, contributed to a vision of a more structured primordial psyche.[107]

We may portray the evolution of medieval and modern Jewish mysticism in the context of the infinity of canonical texts. In the thirteenth century the Bible was thought to possess infinite meanings; in these sources the question of the special nature of Hebrew was often addressed, and a correlation existed between the specific modes of writing of the Torah and infinities of meanings. In the sixteenth century the Zohar, a composition written in the thirteenth century but canonized only much later, was conceived of as possessing infinite meanings. The explanation has nothing to do with the special status of Hebrew, as this language is not relevant in the above discussion, but is related to the quasi-astrological understanding of the divine configuration. In Hasidism both views were preserved, but the kind of canonization characteristic of this mystical movement differs from the earlier two stages, given the fact that it concerns an oral performance whose canonization is now instantaneous. In this phase of Jewish mysticism there is indeed no need of an elaborate canonization process; students would debate the meanings of the sermon just after it was delivered. Canonical status was achieved by some of the Hasidic writings, like R. Shne'or Zalman of Liady's Sefer ha-Tanya or R. Nahman of Braslav's Liqqutei Moharan. Since the sermons were originally delivered by the Hasidic masters in Yiddish, a language very different from biblical Hebrew and even more so from the Zoharic Aramaic, it is not the status of the language that bears on the radical canonization but rather the status of the speaker (an issue addressed in more detail in Appendix 5).

The existence of views regarding the infinity of the canonical texts in systems of thought that do not assume a special status for a sacred language, as in the case of a philosopher like R. Yehudah Romano[108] and in Christianity,[109] invites a much more sophisticated explanation than one finds in recent speculations, based as such views are solely in the belief in the sanctity of Hebrew.[110] In fact, the recent surge in emphasis on the infinity of meanings of a text in Derrida's deconstruction does not rely at all on a sacred vision of language or text. Therefore, the scholarly overemphasis on this theory in order to understand some aspects of Kabbalistic hermeneutics is reminiscent of the modern secular reduction of Jewish culture to a cult of Hebrew language as a formative factor, irrelevant to the cultural content expressed in that language. Most of the Kabbalists, however, were concerned much more with the nature of the canonical text than with the special nature of language, which emerged in a rather specific historical moment as part of a polemical approach. The four reasons offered above demonstrate that a variety of nonlinguistic speculation can inform views assuming infinities of meaning, which have relatively understandable signifieds in what the Kabbalist believed was a different dimension of reality.

I would say that as long as the competition with the concepts of the ideal Arabic and perfect Qur'an was pressing and significant, a few Jewish philosophers and more among the Kabbalists were interested in dealing with the perfect language, and this is the reason for the importance of the many discussions of Hebrew as a perfect language in the twelfth and thirteenth centuries. Another reason for the emphasis on the sanctity of Hebrew was part of a reaction to Maimonides' vision of Hebrew as a conventional language.[111] Yet once the "danger" of, or competition with, Islam became less obvious, metaphysical, cosmological, and psychological speculations came to be introduced into Kabbalistic discussions, which also conceive of infinity as stemming from nonscriptural sources. In fact, a change takes place between the thirteenth-century discussions of infinity, as based mainly on the argument of a perfect language and its organization in the canon, and the sixteenth-century discussions, which are much more oriented toward other forms of explanation anchored in domains of Kabbalistic speculation that were much more developed in that century, such as theosophy and psychology. If during the thirteenth century Kabbalah was just beginning to build its complex theosophy on the basis of earlier, simpler theologoumena and mythologoumena and, together with Ashkenazi Hasidism, emphasize linguistic speculation, the sixteenth-century Safedian Kabbalistic schools already articulated extraordinarily complex theologies and psychologies, which become, together with complex theurgies, the focus of such speculation. In Hasidism the center of gravity moved dramatically toward emotional experiences, which became the source for and mode of validation of new insights in the mystical meaning of the texts.

To summarize: all the important components of the interpretive triangle—text, author, and exegetical devices—underwent decisive transformation in Kabbalistic hermeneutics. Also, in many Kabbalistic writings the nature of the interpreter's task differs from what was expected in earlier exegetical enterprises. The theosophical Kabbalistic interpreter is interested in the subtleties of divine life. He decodes the Bible as a mystical biography concerned with the infradivine infinite processes and the religious regulations that influence the function of these processes, rather than as a humanly directed document. Or, as in the prophetic Kabbalah, he views the highest interpretation of the Torah as the actualization of its infinite mathematical potentialities as they may assist in the expansion of the interpreter's consciousness of, or in the influence exercised by, the Godhead.

Therefore, Torah is either pushed in the direction of revealed divinity and some-times even identified with it; or, attracted in the opposite direction, Torah be-comes an instrument by which the union of man's intellect with God is at-tained.[112] The status of the Torah as an independent entity—such as we find in the talmudic and midrashic literatures—standing between man and God though sep-arated from both, vanishes. Likewise, in most forms of Kabbalah man's separate identity or self is jeopardized. The divine source of his soul, according to the sefirotic Kabbalah, or of his intellect, according to the prophetic brand, endows the Kabbalist with strong spiritual affinities to the Godhead. These affinities authorize, as they facilitate, the emergence of pneumatic exegeses to be defined against talmudic-midrashic, philologically oriented hermeneutics. The text be-comes a pretext for innovating far-reaching ideas, which are projected onto the biblical verses. The exegetical methods whereby these innovations are injected into the text differ considerably from the talmudic-midrashic rules of interpre-tation. The various forms of combinations of letters and gematria are entirely indeterminate and superflexible interpretive techniques. Hence they are liable to produce radically heterogeneous results. The looseness of these hermeneutic methods is counterbalanced solely by doctrinal inhibitions. When these inhibi-tions disappeared or were replaced by others, as was the case with the emerging of writings by Christian Kabbalists, they used highly similar Kabbalistic hermeneu-tics and easily drew the conclusion that Kabbalah adumbrates Christian tenets.[113] Thus, an emphasis on the importance of exegetical techniques for the shaping of the resulting interpretation should be balanced by taking into consideration the theological stands that allow rather limited spaces for interpretation. The more flexible the exegetical methods are—and they are both numerous and complex— the greater is the role of the theological inhibition in orienting the interpretations so as not to irritate the audience.

The Kabbalistic perceptions of the Torah as an absolute book that is both identical with and descending from the divinity supplied a point of departure from which the pneumatic exegete is able to discover its infinite significance, as we shall see in Chapter 6. The Hebrew Bible is viewed in some Kabbalistic discus-sions as an *opera aperta* par excellence, wherein the divine character of man finds its perfect expression even as it discovers God's infinity reflected in the amor-phous text. To put it another way: the Torah is a divine masterpiece, while Kab-balistic exegesis, and Kabbalah in general, should be understood as an attempt at unfolding both Torah's infinite subtleties and (paradoxically, to some extent) the Kabbalist's inner qualities. It is noteworthy that only those Kabbalists who belong to what I call "innovative Kabbalah"—R. Abraham Abulafia, R. Moses de Leon, R. Joseph Gikatilla, and partially R. Bahya ben Asher—formulated in explicit terms the principles of Kabbalistic hermeneutics. Moreover, there is a latent contradiction between the notion of Kabbalah, when it is perceived as a corpus of very defined esoteric theurgical-theosophical lore, as in the case of the perception in Nahmanides' school, and the existence of an articulate body of hermeneutic rules that tacitly assumes that the details of the Kabbalistic lore are not in the possession of the Kabbalists, who are presumed to apply those exegetical rules in order to reconstruct the Kabbalistic system.[114]

In sum, the question of the infinity of interpretations in Jewish mysticism should not be understood as the result of the influence of one single factor, namely the belief in the sanctity of the Hebrew language. Rather, we should allow as great a variety of explanations as the pertinent sources may indicate. Polemical factors like the resistance of some Kabbalists to philosophical allegorical interpretations, which are by and large monosemic,[115] and the assumption of a resonance between the nature of the author and the text are as good an explanation as the unproved theory that the sanctity of language invites a polysemic hermeneutics. The monolithic historical explanations that dominated the academic history of Kabbalah and reify complex matters—such as regarding Sabbateanism as stemming from just one factor, Lurianism, or resort to unilinear types of history and phenomenologies through terms like "messianic idea" or an "idea of the golem," or reducing the explanation to one basic "solution"—are as simplistic in these cases as they are in the attempt to understand the variety of concepts of textual and paratextual infinities.[116]

VI. On Multiplicity of Meanings in Judaism and Ancient Christianity

I have assumed that the Kabbalistic concept of infinite interpretations that are found in the Bible is related to concepts of infinity that emerged in the theosophical and cosmological realms. In midrash, however, this concept is not found, and the most we can detect there is the contention of indeterminacy. By and large the Kabbalists preferred the view that an infinity of meanings is latent in the gestalt of the divine text over the somewhat similar view, found in several Christian texts, that the process of interpretation alone is infinite.[117] According to the latter, each and every exegete is able to contribute his view to the exegetical tradition, whereas the text per se is only rarely regarded as infinite in its significances. Indeed, it would be much more representative to describe the Kabbalistic conception of the relationship between Torah and man as requiring the Kabbalist to be assimilated to the actually infinite Torah rather than vice versa. One example of such a process has been adduced above from a Hasidic statement, which also reflects faithfully the stands of some Kabbalists.[118] From a more detached point of view, however, it is human inventiveness that determined the nature and content of the interpretations offered by Kabbalists, even when they would claim the opposite. As we shall see in Chapter 12, there were, nevertheless, important cases where man's nature and deeds dramatically affected the structure of the Torah, and this too-human text was more easily understood by the human interpreter, as it mirrors him.

I wonder whether the divergence between the assumption that the text is infinite and the position that the possible interpretations are infinite does not reveal a basically different attitude toward the nature of the divine text. Some of the Kabbalists and the Hasidic masters conceive of the text as much more "divine" than the sacred text appears to be regarded in Christian literature. Although there are some statements as to the infinity of the scriptures in Christian literature, they seem to be rare.[119] However, one of the most influential texts in Christian spirituality, Augustine's *Confessions*, includes a passage that is noteworthy both for its intrinsic importance and for a comparative remark: "For my part . . . if I were to write anything that was to become supremely authoritative, I would choose to write in such a way that my words would resound with whatever truth anyone could grasp in them, rather than to put down one true meaning so clearly as to exclude other meanings, which, if they were not false, would not offend me."[120]

This apotheosis of polysemy is not only a matter of the sacred scripture but also an ideal to which even a human author may strive. It is part of an effort to deny one single, exclusive deep meaning in a manner reminiscent of many of the Kabbalistic passages above. We have seen that the sixteenth-century Kabbalists and those who were influenced by them claimed that each Israelite received one interpretation at the revelation at Mount Sinai, and at the end of time all the revealed and possible interpretations would exhaust them, thus restricting the notion of infinity. It seems, as Martin Irvine had formulated it, that in ancient Christian concepts of the sacred scriptures "this Text can never signify its totality—the sum of its productivity of meaning—in one instantiated act of interpretation, but continuously promises and postpones this totality through dissemination in a limitless chain of interpretations in supplementary texts. This model of textuality implies that a variorum commentary on the Scriptures compiled at the end of the world would still be incomplete, even though the claim of interpretations would be temporally closed, superseded by a signless, transcendental grammar."[121] According to this interpretation, the text is indeed semantically limitless, but also unattainable because of its postponing its semantic fulfillment, and thus it seems that it is the ancient Christian hermeneutics that comes closer to modern deconstruction than the Kabbalistic views on the topic. If Irvine is right, the ancient Christian vision of the scriptures' textuality is devoid of a transcendental meaning, while Kabbalistic and Hasidic masters would be more oriented toward a plenitude to be located in a past revelation. So, for example, R. Ze'ev Wolf of Zhitomir, a late-eighteenth-century follower of R. Dov Baer of Mezeritch, known as the Great Maggid, wrote as follows: "Our holy Torah comprises in itself much, since the promulgation by Moses and the generations after him until the advent of our Messiah, all the interpretations inherent in the [technique of] pardes[122] that are revealed and added by the sages of the time, it all comprises in itself from the voice of the shofar which has been heard at the Sinaitic revelation, as it is written,[123] 'and the voice of the Shofar sounded louder and louder,' and the reason for 'becoming louder' is that it comprises in itself so much."[124] However, according to some discussions earlier in Irvine's excellent work, Origen held that "the transcendental signified remained beyond the reach of all temporal sign relations yet is immanently manifest in all of them."[125] On the other hand, the Hasidic passage does not deal with a future development of interpretations that is endless, but an actualization of the contents already implicit within the divine voice heard by the Israelites. Thus, it is not a metaphysical or transcendental entity that is posited as the immediate source of meaning here below, but the divine voice that had already descended in the world and is continuously unfolding through human interpretative activity.[126] This pulsating voice, like the ever-emerging interpretations, does not require the hypothesis of a transcendental Torah which cannot be reached. Fugitive as are the spiritual truths achieved by listening to the voice or to the interpretation that emerges from the encounter of one's psyche's with the holy books, nothing is supposed to remain "beyond the reach."[127]

At least according to an interesting formulation of R. Pinhas of Koretz, when God revealed the Torah, the world became full of it, and thus there is nothing in the world that is not permeated by Torah.[128] It is in this context, however, that the Hasidic master claims that the Torah and God are one.[129] Kabbalists and Hasidic authors did not indulge in negative theologies, which left the core of the meaning as completely transcendent to human experience; in fact, the experience of the "ancients" may be understood as stronger than that of the "moderns," to judge by the leading assumptions that informed that experience: the text mediates the divine presence in the world and the possibility of a direct encounter with the mystic rather than deferring such an experience.

4

THE BOOK THAT CONTAINS
AND MAINTAINS ALL

The Torah is the perfection of all.
—*ZOHAR*, I, FOL. 234B

I. HISTORICAL AND ONTOLOGICAL IMAGINARY OF THE BOOK

Books are not simply literary objects to be arranged carefully on library shelves; neither are they simple mediators of ideas between minds or media for, to resort to Ricoeur's felicitous term, "proposed worlds."[1] They are also nebulas created by rumors, religious belief, wise advertisement, or, in more modern times, the consumption of a variety of critiques. They are units that constitute intellectual fashions, which in turn create predispositions toward the reception and digestion of their own and other books' content. Books, especially famous books, possess auras that may enwrap them long before most of their readers open them. The social imagination of certain elites prepares the ground for the acceptance, dissemination, and depth of influence of a book even before it has been conceived by its author. Even more so in the case of books dealing with religious topics that already permeate the faith of many individuals and the praxis of groups and movements. These books, which are founding documents of a religion, ideology, or intellectual movement—that is to say, canonic—are rarely consumed as pure literature and only seldom are able to evince their "proposed worlds" without the mediation of the imaginary that surrounds them and has been accumulated over the centuries and has conferred on them their particular status. In other words, books may be influential not only because of their distinct message but also because of the myths that accompany them.

The imaginary of the book may take two major forms: historical and ontological. The former is best represented by actual forgeries of books, what is often called pseudepigraphy and I would call "actual" pseudepigraphy, or by the invention of titles of books allegedly written in the past that in fact were never written, a phenomenon I shall call "hollow" pseudepigraphy. The historical forger assumes, or would like his reader to assume, that sometime in the past a more original, insightful, powerful, and authoritative mind was active, or he exploits a cultural image of it that is present in the society he is addressing, and as such its book should inspire a new perception of tradition, knowledge, magic or religion, or power. Hollow pseudepigraphy circles around mythical figures whose importance is advanced by enhancing its image by attributing some literary output to its cultural image. Both forms of pseudepigraphy have something to do with a feeling of a spiritual renascence, which is sometimes in search of validation. If there were nothing new to be offered in the present, no one would care to invoke the ghosts of ancestors. In some instances, however, the imaginary books are projected into the future, as is the case with the concept of Torah of the Messiah in rabbinic literature,[2] or with the concept of Torah de-'Atzilut in some forms of Kabbalah,[3] or the Testament of the Holy Spirit according to Joachim of Fiore.[4] Here the ideal writing is conceived of as completing the actual canonical book or books by means of the assumption of a final revelation. This projection, hardly a pseudepigraphical phenomenon, even less a forgery, is nevertheless part of what I call the historical imaginary of the book, for it is supposed to mark some turn in history.

Both the past-oriented and future-oriented imageries validate something in the present, but the strategy is connected to the belief in better times, either past or future, whose special knowledge passed to the present writer or the alleged, hollow pseudepigraph. The ontological imaginary of the book, at least in the way I suggest using the term, assumes that an actual or imaginary book already in existence is much more than a literary composition, profound and powerful as it may be, but is an extended metaphor for the structure and dynamics of reality or even of God. This form of book imaginary is much less concerned with validating a tradition, be it old or invented, or subverting one than it is with offering a new worldview. This mode of imaginary is much more current in literature, as in the works of Tommaso Campanella, Stéphane Mallarmé, Velimir Khlebnikov, Jorge Luís Borges, or Edmond Jabes.

In our generation the text (a reverberation of what I shall attempt to show, a very specific concept of the book) has been conceived of as embracing everything, as we learn from the famous pronouncement of Jacques Derrida, "Il n'y a pas rien dehors de texte." The text becomes a leading metaphor. In religions with a strong element of literary canonicity, however, the book may be regarded not only as a source of revelation and inspiration for human behavior but sometimes also as a comprehensive, all-embracing ontological entity, in some cases even the sustaining power of reality. Thus, while existent books are concerned less with ontology than with historical claims (such as validations of genealogies of knowledge) the building or aggrandizing of some historical figures in the past (such as Jesus Christ in Christianity) or in the future (such as the Messiah according to Jewish tradition and the Mahdi in Muslim tradition), the ontological approach deals mainly with an ever-present book. Distinct as they are, the two approaches nevertheless often overlap. A new religious insight, though attempting to anchor itself in hoary antiquity, may nonetheless attempt to advance some forms of insight in the nature of reality, and not only of history, just as the ontological imaginary may insist on a certain historical appearance of the ontological book in mythical time.

On the other hand, a historical imaginary may in time turn into an ontological one, and we shall be dealing with such examples below, in the case either of the Torah or of the Zohar as understood by mystics. Jewish mystical literature is replete with pseudepigraphical books attributed to men, angels, and God, most of them actual treatises, a few pertaining to the imaginary of some Kabbalists or to the category of the hollow imaginary. Among the pseudepigraphical writings we may mention Sefer Yetzirah, attributed to none other than Abraham or, according to another tradition, to a founding father of rabbinic thought, R. 'Aqivah; then, parts of the Heikhalot literature attributed to another leading figure of rabbinic literature, R. Ishmael, or even to one of the patriarchs, Enoch. Early in the Middle Ages one of the first Kabbalistic books was attributed to another important early rabbinic figure, R. Nehunya ben ha-Qanah. It is the famous Sefer ha-Bahir (Book of the Bahir) that shaped some of the developments of the nascent Kabbalah. Pseudepigraphical mystical literature was also known in late-twelfth- and early-thirteenth-century Germany, where the Hasidei Ashkenaz had access to material that is no longer extant. In the second half of the thirteenth century, pseudepigraphical literature flowered among the Kabbalists, a process that culminated in the composition of the most important book of Kabbalah, the Zohar.

The *Zohar* is a large-scale body of literature attributed, like many of the earlier forgeries, to a second-century rabbinic figure, R. Shim'on bar Yohay. Despite some doubts that arose when the first short treatises started to appear in public, the *Zohar* was accepted as authentic and managed to become a revered part of Jewish literature. It is a historical imaginary book, as its composition is projected back into late antiquity, into another place, second-century Galilee; part of this projection is to be understood as an attempt to confer an aura of antiquity to Kabbalistic ideas and thus to Kabbalah as a whole. Though claiming the authority of a revered figure, an authority derived either from his actions while living or from post-mortem revelations, the book does not claim the status of an ontological imaginary; that is, it does not pretend to be the container of the universe or the power that sustains it. These claims were, as we have glimpsed above and as shall see more immediately below, already known in the context of the Torah and sometimes affected also the view that the authors of the *Zohar* had seen the Torah. Thus, though a strongly historical pseudepigraphy, the *Zohar* was not eager to request the status of the cosmic book. I shall come back to this book in the latter part of my exposition, when its status will be treated as a cosmic entity.

Now let me introduce some earlier instances of ontological interpretations of the book of the Torah, which contributed to the emergence of the ontological imaginary of the book in Kabbalah. In these passages the Torah, which stands for the text par excellence, serves as a means not only for the transmission of religious messages but also, and perhaps in some cases quite prominently, for an extended metaphor for an ideal paradigm that informed the creation of the world at the beginning of time and sometimes also continues to inform—literally to give form, to existence.

II. THE DIVINE STRUCTURE AND THE BOOK

In the history of Jewish mysticism there may be discerned a gradual process of convergence of the divine being and the canonical book,[5] or, if one prefers a more literary nomenclature, a gradual convergence of the divine author and his book. In Chapter 2 we saw examples from late midrashic and Kabbalistic sources that evince partial identities between the two, but this was primarily related to the graphic isomorphism of the book and the author, as both were conceived mainly in anthropomorphic terms. Let me first attempt to explicate the problems and their solutions as envisioned by the Jewish mystics, in order to learn about an exotic vision that is not regularly confronted by modern literary criticism or by contemporary philosophies of texts, although the latter are nevertheless dependent on the former.

One of the hermeneutical problems that faced some of the Jewish mystics was the daunting quandary created by a double heritage: the biblical one, concerned with the display of the will of God as operating and visible on the scene of history and in the details of the revealed way of life, the commandments; and the growing importance of the fixed form of sacred history and ritual in a book that became canonical. Or, to formulate the issue differently: the Jewish mystics had to determine what is more important, the author's free will or the author's book. In modern, most conspicuously in postmodern, literary criticism, the author has gradually been marginalized, not to say killed, in order to safeguard the integrality and integrity of the book, and sometimes also the importance of the reader. It was a relatively simple enterprise, as most of the authors did not outlive their books.

In religious systems, however, it is easier to kill the book, important as it may be, than its divine author. Easier, but not easy, if the book becomes the founding text of the religious tradition. This is the case in rabbinic Judaism, where the canonical text was established as the most important source of authority, the paramount subject of study, and the main object of interpretation. In fact, the emergence of rabbinic Judaism can be described as connected to a renomadization that is reminiscent of an earlier type of worship centered on a portable sacred object, formerly the tabernacle, now a book. So, in such a tradition it is incumbent on author and book to coexist, and a modus vivendi should be ensured in order not to trivialize the book by relegating it to the status of one of the many possible literary products of the eternal author; but at the same time it is essential not to minimize the importance of the author, which ensures the importance of the book. This quandary becomes more acute in a minority culture, as the Jewish one was for most of its history, where other books, such as the New Testament and Qur'an, competed for the status of the final revelation. Thus, the battle over the book is much more central for a culture that gravitates around books, one that attempts to validate its canonical books but has to allow a significant role for the author.

One of the regular solutions for the tension between the two values is to subordinate one factor to the other, thus establishing a hierarchy between the two or, to resort to a phrase coined by a scholar of Islamic mysticism, "une distinction hierarchisée." Such a view sees the book as dependent on the author but somewhat reduces the dominant role of an author who is omnipresent.[6] This is the classical rabbinic stand which contends that the Torah is not found in heaven but is in the full possession of and is the legitimate responsibility of the rabbinic masters,[7] who apparently were more content to deal with the divine will as embodied in the specific literary expression they possessed without allowing further interference by the author. The rabbinic masters, and even less their mystical descendants, would not subscribe to Paul Ricoeur's theory about the eclipse of the author,[8] but rather assume an ongoing process of reading and elaboration on the book in the presence of the living author, yet without subscribing to his free will. What may be the precise difference between an eclipse of the author in Ricoeur and the presence of a living author in the consciousness of the religious reader—a living author who is not allowed to intervene in the act of reading, though he may be the ultimate goal of this act of reading—is an issue that I cannot dwell on here. Indeed, the phenomenology of reading is dictated less by modern assumptions about the actual death of the author than by the awareness and imagination of the reader, who may imagine the author as alive and attempt to enter into intellectual or spiritual dialogue him, even over centuries. This is especially so when the reader believes that the author is eternal and omniscient.

Although for a rabbinic master the "world of the text" and a certain distanciation between the author and the text, to use Ricoeur's terms, are plausible concepts, for the Jewish mystics the situation becomes much more complex. The mystics were part of a religion and culture which, at least in its elite forms, inherited a fascination with the book, but at the same time they were also pursuing the search for more direct contact with God, either as an author or as an entity before the very writing of the book, and these two forms of spiritual concern were a primary purpose of their mystical life.[9] Apparently they pursued a more vibrant relation with the supreme author, a direct contact with him, but could not, or perhaps refused to, circumvent the book as the canonical expression of the divine will, as the center of their culture, and as a divine entity that might mediate between them and the divine. However, a full-fledged mediation, by assuming a hypostatic status of the book, is only one of the solutions they accepted. The other was to conflate the book and the author, and this process of conflation is going to preoccupy us here.[10] In any case, the emergence of the main form of Kabbalah, the theosophical-theurgical one, dealing as it does with the details of theogenesis, namely the emanation system of the ten sefirot conceived of as divine powers and the processes that take place between them, can be described as a great concern with the authorial persona, as opposed to the rabbinic fascination with the book rather than its author.

III. THE BOOK AS AN INNER DIVINE ATTRIBUTE IN EARLY KABBALAH

1. *Sefer ha-Bahir*

The speculative corpora that emerged after the first millennium C.E. represent a return to the written Torah, the canonical Bible, in comparison to the rabbinic literature, both those works that preceded that period and those which followed it. Jewish philosophers and the great majority of Kabbalists invested most of their energy in presenting their worldviews as included in the Bible, much more so than in the rabbinic literature. Those corpora can be described as "protestant" to a certain limited extent, in comparison to the more "catholic" rabbinic literature, which put a great emphasis on the traditional lore and institutions. One of the changes that accompanied this protestant turn is, however, remote from the Protestant Christian emphasis on *sensus literalis*. In fact, philosophers' and Kabbalists' focusing of attention on the Bible was connected to a metaphorical impulse, alien (as pointed out by Susan Handelman) to rabbinic metonymic discourse. This change is already conspicuous in the earliest Kabbalistic literature.

Since the first documents of the theosophical-theurgical Kabbalah, the book of the Torah was conceived to be a main symbol in the various Kabbalistic symbolic codes. Already evident in *Sefer ha-Bahir*, one of the earliest Kabbalistic documents, the written Torah is the symbol for the sixth sefirah, Tiferet, while the oral Torah symbolizes the last sefirah, Malkhut. The union between the two, described as the result of the theurgical operation of the Kabbalist, was conceived of in sexual terms. Yet the precise status of the sefirot (a very rare term in this book) does not allow a simple identification of the Torah with the divine essence. If the sefirot are understood to be divine instruments, then the two books should be conceived of as preexistent to the creation of this world, though not automatically identical with the divine essence, and at the same time capable of being theurgically influenced by religious activities here below.[11] Elsewhere in the same book we find a pivotal passage dealing with Torah as a cosmic book:

> The attribute which is named Israel contains the Torah of Truth.[12] And what is this Torah of Truth? Something which indicates the true nature of the worlds and whose action takes place through the *mahashavah*, and it bestows existence upon the ten logoi, through which the world exists, and it is itself one of them. And He created in man [organs] that correspond to these ten, ten fingers. And when Moses lifted his hands and directed a little bit his intention to that attribute named Israel, in which there is the Torah of Truth, and hinted at it by the ten fingers of his hands that it maintains the ten [divine attributes], and if He[13] will not help Israel, the ten logoi will not be sanctified each and every day. This is why it is written, "and Israel prevailed."[14]

The cosmic dimension of the book of the Torah is conspicuous: it reflects the "true nature of the worlds." The precise nature of those worlds, however, is far from clear. Indeed, this is a difficult passage because it is based on a symbolic code whose details are not transparent. Is the "Torah of Truth" contained within the sixth attribute, Tiferet, which is almost invariably identified by Kabbalists as

Israel? Or, as Gershom Scholem has suggested, is it to be identified with the third sefirah?[15] What is the meaning of the Torah that operates through *mahashavah*, thought, an attribute connected in this treatise to a higher level within the sefirotic world?[16] Is there a primordial Torah in *Sefer ha-Bahir*, as Scholem claims,[17] which informs the lower Torah of Truth? How is this Torah one of the ten creative logoi and the origin of them at the same time? These and many other quandaries related to the content of this passage do not, however, attenuate the explicit statement dealing with both its reflecting the nature of the worlds and its bestowing their existence. We may portray the Torah of Truth as the starting point of the ten logoi, which in turn are the origin of the universe. This pyramidal structure with the Torah on top, which deserves more detailed discussion than can be provided here, underlies the paramount importance of a book for the constituency of the universe.

Let me address now the contention that the Torah is contained within a sefirah that has been designated here explicitly as Israel. Who precisely is the entity called by that name? And what is the possible relationship between it and the functions of the Torah it contains, as regards the cosmic nature of that Torah? Does Israel also contain the ten creative logoi? A pertinent object for comparison seems to be the following passage from 'Avot de-Rabbi Nathan: "He who saves one person [one life] is worthy to be regarded as if he had saved the entire world, which was created by ten logoi . . . And he who causes one person to perish is to be regarded as if he had caused the destruction of the entire world, which was created by ten logoi."[18] Moreover, in a passage very similar to the one from 'Avot, preserved in Hebrew by a medieval Ismaili author, it is said that "by means of ten ma'amarot the world was created, and by the Decalogue it stands."[19] This quotation is paralleled in a Jewish writing influenced by the Isma'iylia, which presumably reflects an older Jewish view, and by two short statements in *Midrash Tadsche'*, a later midrash that evidently includes earlier material as well, as some scholars have already recognized. According to one statement, "The world is maintained by the merit of those who study [the Torah] and perform the Decalogue; and the world was created by ten logoi, and its sefirot are [also] ten," and in the same context we learn also that "the world is maintained by the ten sefirot of Belimah."[20]

The strong affinity between the supernal attribute Israel, apparently corresponding to what the classical structure of ten sefirot designated as the sefirah Tiferet, and the Torah of Truth contributed, in my opinion, to the emergence of one of the most widespread views of the Torah in Kabbalah: the identification of God (represented by Tiferet), the Torah, and Israel. The origin and development of this triple identification, expressed by the Aramaic formula *qudsha' berikh hu', 'orayyita ve-yisra'el had hu'*, namely that God, the Torah, and Israel are one, have been studied in modern scholarship, but it seems that the possible relevance of the passage from *Sefer ha-Bahir* has escaped scholars.[21] Therefore, we may conclude that from the very beginning of Kabbalah, ten divine speeches found in the first chapter of Genesis were conceived of as both creating the world and maintaining it. That the first Kabbalists inherited this view and elaborated it in various ways is corroborated by the passage from *Sefer ha-Bahir*.

2. Torah as a Divine Pattern of the World in Theosophical Kabbalah

Let me address separately the two views of the Torah, as involved in the creation of the world and as maintaining it, despite the fact that the creative role and the maintenance function are closely interconnected. This combination of two operations commonly related to concepts of divinity is emblematic of the conception of the Torah as a divine being and of its more explicit identification with God in later Kabbalistic texts.

An important step in the development of the propensity to identify God and the Torah is found in the writings of thirteenth-century philosophically oriented Kabbalists. In several texts from the very beginning of the history of Kabbalah the Torah is regarded as identical to the divine mind, or divine wisdom, and as such it serves as the paradigm for the intradivine and extradivine emanative processes. According to other views, closer to medieval philosophy, the Torah is tantamount to the realm of ideas, namely the book is conceived of as identical to the spiritual world as it was variously envisioned by medieval thinkers. In some cases the Torah may be identical to the realm of ideas regarded as extradeical entities.[22] Let me adduce a few examples, out of the many available, for the concept that God contemplates Torah as a symbol of an intradivine pattern or attribute that comprises the ideas. First, from R. Jacob ben Sheshet, a thirteenth-century Catalan Kabbalist:

God was contemplating the Torah[23] and he saw the essences[24] in Himself, since the essences were in wisdom[25] [and] discerned that they are prone to reveal themselves. I heard this version in the name of R. Isaac, son of R. Abraham, may his memory be blessed. And this was also the opinion of the rabbi,[26] the author of [*The Book of*] *Knowledge*, who said that He, knowing Himself, He knows all the existent [creatures].[27] Nevertheless, the rabbi was astonished, in part 2, chapter 6 of the *Guide*, at the dictum of our sages that God does not do anything before He contemplates His retinue,[28] and he quoted there the dictum of Plato that God, blessed be He, does contemplate the intellectual world and He emanates therefrom the emanation [which produces] reality.[29]

R. Isaac, son of R. Abraham, is none other than R. Isaac Sagi Nahor, one of the earliest Kabbalists, a Provençal master who came to Gerona to propagate his brand of Kabbalah; there he became the teacher of some of the local second-elite authors, learned persons who did not play a central role in communal life. Ben Sheshet conflates two different discussions of Maimonides: one in *Mishneh Torah*, where the author presents his view, which stems ultimately from Themistius, that God comprises the forms of all the existents and thus cognizes them by an act of self-intellection;[30] the other in the *Guide of the Perplexed*, where Maimonides sharply opposes the "simplistic" interpretation of the midrashic dictum that God created the world by contemplating the Torah as the blueprint for reality. According to this Kabbalist, the two views seem to be identical, and he is surprised by Maimonides' inconsistency in accepting the first formulation while rejecting the second. Since the stand of R. Isaac the Blind, adduced before Maimonides' views were introduced, must be regarded as the truth in the eyes of ben Sheshet, Maimonides' second view is implicitly rejected, whereas the dictum of Plato, quoted in the *Guide* in order to oppose it, is taken by the Kabbalist to be the correct one.

Again, in the context of the midrashic view that God had contemplated the Torah when He created the world, R. Azriel ben Menahem of Gerona, a contemporary and compatriot of ben Sheshet, explains, in a manner that recalls the above-mentioned view of ben Sheshet:

> "The thirty-two wondrous paths of Hokhmah are the ten sefirot of Belimah[31] and the twenty-two letters."[32] And each of them has a separate path per se, and their beginning is the will, which precedes everything, and nothing is outside it,[33] and it is the cause of the thought.[34] And the sefirot and the paths and everything which will be created in the future out of them, [indeed] everything, was hidden within the mahashavah, and it is revealed in its paths, in the paths of speech[35] and the paths of deed.[36] And "He contemplates the Torah" [means] He contemplated the mahashavah, [namely] the paths that are included in it, and He drew each and every path out of its beginning[37] . . . and in the forms[38] of that mahashavah, the speeches and the deeds were figured,[39] since the mahashavah is the root.[40]

The existence of the roots of speech and deed in divine thought is compared by R. Azriel with the existence of form and hyle in divine thought according to the Neoplatonic sources he quotes. However, whereas the philosophers deal with entities alone as comprised in divine thought, the Kabbalist is interested also in the speech and deeds, therefore in dynamic processes as comprehended in the mahashavah. The view of letters as ideas found within Hokhmah is congenial with the view, expressed several times in ben Sheshet's writings, that identifies the second sefirah with the Torah, the latter being considered as comprising all the sciences.[41] This comprehensiveness is shared by the two Geronese Kabbalists, who thus confer on the canonical book the role not only of the perfect repository of Jewish lore but also of the book that comprises all knowledge in general. Unlike the first two layers of Jewish literature which we examined previously, the midrashic literature and Sefer ha-Bahir, where the Torah was indeed identified somehow with the divinity but retained its status as the characteristic type of religious knowledge of the Jews, the Geronese Kabbalists, influenced by some forms of Greek philosophy, regarded the ideal Torah as more universalistic in scope. Indeed, for them the book of God and the book of nature are one. This is the reason why R. Azriel claimed that "the words of the wisdom of the Torah and the words of the masters of investigation[42] mentioned above are both identical,[43] their way is one, and there is no difference between them but the terms alone, since the investigators did not know to designate the proper name to each and every part."[44]

Both ben Sheshet and R. Azriel conceived of the Torah as representing that divine attribute corresponding to the divine mind, the locus of all ideas that are contemplated by God as part of the emanative process. This is, however, the contemplation of an attribute that is part of the divine realm, no longer the contemplation of the Torah as an external pattern, as is the case in midrash. The Torah has, so to speak, been absorbed and become part of the configuration of the divine attributes. This identity between the Torah and one of the divine attributes is a step toward identifying the author with his book, though such a complete identification is still ahead.

I would like nevertheless to emphasize that in the writings of both Catalan Kabbalists the divine attribute contemplated by God is not just one among many. It is an attribute that encompasses the lower ones, and to a certain extent the Torah comprises most of the sefirot by virtue of its being identical with the locus of all the other sefirot. In other words, the first Catalan Kabbalists, apparently following their Provençal predecessor, envisioned the Torah as identical to the divine mind, and as such its content, the "world of the text" or noema[45]—is perfectly identical to the authorial intention, the noesis. No process of distanciation is possible, and the maximum that Kabbalists like these two authors could imagine is less than an absolutely faithful reproduction of the divine noesis in a mundane book; their assumption from the very beginning would be, however, that the objectification involves more material entities than those taking the emergence of the book to be identical to the divine mind. The received Torah is therefore not a reproduction of a more sublime form of book but an entity conceived of in terms of a book. Although in some cases Kabbalists would include the stage of a verbal discourse as preceding the constitution of the book—in fact the scroll—of the Torah, Kabbalists like Nahmanides speak of Moses as a copyist working from a supernal book.[46] By identifying the primordial Torah with the second sefirah, one that encompasses all the other lower sefirot and consequently the entire world, this Torah becomes a world-absorbing text.

IV. GOD AS TORAH OR TORAH AS GOD

In the writings of two Kabbalists who flourished at the end of the thirteenth and the beginning of the fourteenth century, we find a formula that conveys a total identification of the Torah, in many cases the Pentateuch, with God. The first text is a late-thirteenth-century Castilian treatise named *Sefer ha-Yihud*, which influenced the early-fourteenth-century Italian Kabbalist R. Menahem Recanati.[47] In his introduction to the *Commentary on the Rationales of the Commandments*, Recanati wrote: "All the sciences altogether are hinted at in the Torah,[48] because there is nothing that is outside of Her[49] . . . Therefore the Holy One, blessed be He, is nothing that is outside the Torah, and the Torah is nothing that is outside Him, and this is the reason why the sages of the Kabbalah said that the Holy One, blessed be He, is the Torah."[50] The identification of the author and the book reinforces the two values but also changes them. The book becomes tantamount to the divine, while the divine is now conceived of as the Torah. It seems to me that this is quite a logical development in a religion based on a book, but it leads to some forms of extreme mysticism. *Sefer ha-Yihud* is a work that, though extant in many manuscripts, did not attract the due attention of scholars. I would dare to say that this treatise is one of the most important Kabbalistic writings of the thirteenth century, one that had a special impact on all R. Menahem Recanati's writings. Recanati's book that includes the passage on the Torah as God is indeed extant in many manuscripts and was among the first Kabbalistic writings to be printed. Yet unlike other writings of this Kabbalist, which were translated into Latin and had a great influence on Pico della Mirandola's Christian Kabbalah, it was not translated into any European languages, and its striking identification of author and book apparently did not leave any mark on the development of modern hermeneutics. There is, however, one exception, and it is a major one.

Recanati's passage discussed above has been mentioned in a major study by Gershom Scholem dealing with the concept of the Torah in Kabbalah, originally delivered in German as a lecture at the Eranos Conference at Ascona in 1954. It was printed concomitantly in English and French translations in the UNESCO journal for the humanities, *Diogenes (Diogène)*. For our purposes the French translation (1955–1956), made by a very distinguished scholar of Judaica in Paris, Professor Georges Vajda, is the salient one.[51] in Vajda's translation the passage reads:

"Car la Torah n'est pas en dehors de Lui, pas plus qu'il n'est Lui-même en dehors de la Torah."[52] This is a faithful translation without being particularly literal. Nonetheless, the Hebrew original has nothing like "il n'est Lui-même en dehors de la Torah" because the term *Torah* in this phrase is an explication of a demonstrative Hebrew pronoun, *mimmenah*. In order to better understand the text, the demonstrative pronoun has been fleshed out and translated as if the Hebrew were "hutz me-ha-Torah." The difference is a matter of style, not content, but it nevertheless may show how the French phrase emerged. The fact that this statement about the identity between the Torah and God was available in French in 1957 may account for the emergence of one of the most postmodern statements in literary criticism: "There is nothing outside the text." Derrida could have had easy access to the French translation and could have absorbed it for his purposes, as he did in the context of another important statement by another Kabbalist.[53] In lieu of Recanati's "there is nothing outside her," namely outside the Torah, Derrida pronounced that "there is nothing outside the text," "il n'y a rien hors de texte" or, according to another version, "il n'y a pas de hors-texte."[54] Thus, he substituted the term and concept of Torah with that of text. Derrida's *De grammatologie* was first printed in 1967, ten years after the publication of the French translation of Scholem's article. The source of Recanati's phrase "there is nothing outside" used in a theosophical sense, namely that there is nothing outside God, is found already in the thought of R. Azriel of Gerona, who deeply influenced Recanati's theosophy.[55] However, while the Catalan Kabbalist was mainly concerned with a view of the divine will, the Italian one, though influenced by Castilian Kabbalah, expanded the pantheistic view to God Himself. In Recanati's writings, unlike those of R. Azriel, the concept of the divine will does not play an important role.

Interestingly enough, a contemporary of Recanati, the Provençal philosopher R. Levi ben Gershom, known as Ralbag or Gersonides, advanced a similar perception of the Torah: "Behold, the book that God wrote is the existence in its entirety, that is caused from Him . . . Existence is compared to a book because just as a book points to the ideality from which it was, in the same manner the sensible world points to the law of the intelligible universe, which is [the ideality of] God, from which the sensible world is."[56] Indeed, the philosopher refers to the all-comprehensive book as a parable for the divine creation; it seems quite plausible that it is not the dense textuality of the book which matters, but the fact that the divine ideal concept was materialized in creation, just as happens in the case of the author of a book. Unlike Recanati and his Kabbalistic sources, which refer explicitly to the identity between God and the Torah, here it is the created reality that is the divine book. Here the book is a simile for the whole reality, but it does not "absorb" God, as I attempted to show in other cases of Recanati's thought analyzed in Chapter 2. In other words, Gersonides' passage, which is reminiscent of ben Sheshet's ideas discussed above, is essentially logocentric. The text stands for a metaphysical or theosophical structure, defined by reverberations of the Platonic and Neoplatonic realm of ideas as understood in medieval Neoaristotelianism, and the qualities of text qua text, its special texture (as discussed in Chapters 2 and 3) are conspicuously absent.

V. SOME REFLECTIONS ON DECONSTRUCTION

Let me indulge for a moment in a comparison of Recanati's view with that of Derrida. For the Kabbalist, the book becomes more and more important, to the point where, in Recanati's most extreme formulation, it is conceived of as comprising God in itself. The book is conferred an extreme meaning, the all-comprehensive infinity of the divine nature, and it becomes the locus of all the sciences. I hope I do not exaggerate by assuming that despite the negation implied in the phrase "there is nothing," a quite positive meaning is ensured by the presence of the divine. For Derrida, however, God and all forms of metaphysical presence have been obliterated. His negative formulation, "il n'y a rien," seems to be a silent critique of the Kabbalistic insertion of God or metaphysics within the realm of the text. Yet despite the attempt to distance himself from the Kabbalistic formula and its metaphysical implications, and to allow the text a free and independent role void of any metaphysical presence, Derrida did not totally emancipate himself from the implications of the medieval source he adopted and adapted. After all, the fact is that the book remained the main metaphor for reality, and it survived even Derrida's attempt to get rid of God. I used the word *attempt* because my modest reading of Derrida has taught me that he conceives of the text as so pregnant with infinite meanings that his system is, after all, another reading, slightly secularized, of the formula of the Kabbalist: the canonical text is God— not a transcendental entity emanating meaning into a lower text, but an immanent divinity that ensures the infinity of meanings within the human text. The conservative medieval Kabbalist R. Menahem Recanati and the postmodern deconstructionist Jacques Derrida agree on one major point: the absolute centrality of the book. For the former, the book of the Torah is the transparent prism in which the infinite God is seen; for the latter, the text is the prism within which it is possible to discover an infinity of meanings. From Recanati to Derrida the nature of the infinity changed, but not the absolute statement regarding the all-inclusiveness of the text.

As to the relationship between author and book, in Derrida's formula the author has lost the battle with the book; he has been completely excluded. Or, to formulate it differently, the Kabbalistic fusion of the author with his book prepared the ground for the dissipation of the author within his text in the next stage, in Derrida's deconstruction, although the dissipating author is bringing within the text his most important attribute: infinity. The dissolution of the author within the text opened more room for the reader and his activity in shaping the content of the text he reads. The less distinct the persona of the author is, the more diffuse the meaning of the book will be. In addition, with the identification of text and author, the infinity acquired by the text left plenty of room for an attitude that I have proposed to call "innovative Kabbalah,"[57] which assumes that provided the presence of the infinite author in the text, it is possible to extract from it an infinity of meanings, an assumption that creates a strong reader. The assumption of an infinite God reduces the distinct characteristics of His persona as well as the distinctness of His messages, leaving the reader with the task of redefining, time and again, the content of the book as he reads it. It is not the eclipse of the author that opened the door for a creative hermeneutics in Kabbalah but, on the contrary, the assumption of his indelible omnipresence within the text that creates a process of omnisemiosis. While modern hermeneutics, especially French, takes as a defining characteristic of textuality the silence of the author after the completion of his work and regards it as decisive for the act of interpretation, some Kabbalists would opt for the possibility of a richness of interpretation as the effect of a pressing, though diffuse, presence.

To formulate this hermeneutical observation in terms closer to a sociology of knowledge, the absence of the authoritative author was necessary for a secular theory of reading in order to confer on the book the possibility of omnisemiosis. The less authoritative the author is, the greater the authority of the reader or the listener will be. In other words, the secular stand moved from an aristocratic and hierarchical attitude found in the religious views described above toward a more democratic one. By showing the development that preceded, and in my opinion also inspired, Derrida's postmodern vision of the centrality of the text and the reader at the expense of the author, I have attempted to insert it within a larger scheme of theories of text found in European culture and thus to attenuate its novelty. Indeed, if the above remarks have been persuasive, the Kabbalistic theories about the text should be given a certain place in the emergence of Derrida's view of the text, alongside those of Freud and Heidegger. This claim may be construed in Derridean terms as part of a larger project to allow a greater role to forms of knowledge that, though formulated and transmitted in Europe during the Middle Ages and the Renaissance, have been neglected or repressed by the historiography of European culture. Is it reasonable to ignore precisely those forms of speculation about the text that were more consonant with the postmodern form? Is the linguistic turn in postmodern thought to be understood solely in terms immanent to the Enlightenment, to Christian visions of the text, or to modern secular developments? Is the postmodern speculation under scrutiny here solely the culmination of processes that immediately preceded it, or may we assume that a more "chaotic" history, what I propose to call a panoramic approach to European culture,[58] should take into serious consideration ideas expressed by minorities like the Kabbalists, whose theories, repressed by modernism, found their way to the forefront when the more rationalistic mold of this thought began to crumble? If this more comprehensive approach is adopted by a modern historiography, the need to resort to historical appropriations of Kabbalah, or at least to phenomenological comparisons, will become more conspicuous. Postmodernism is not only a culmination of processes that immediately preceded it and are discernible in modern times, but also the move to the center of some much older forms of intellectual concerns characteristic of other periods in European history.

To put it in other terms, my reading of the history of the perception of the text as culminating in Derrida's deconstruction makes the Derridian contribution part of an ongoing and thus still-incomplete process of secularization, one that did not attain its most extreme object, as it still believes not only in meaning but in a multiplicity, if not an infinity, of meanings. Postmodern views attribute the source, however, not to a strong monolithic author who possesses an infinite mind but to the infinity of readers as a corporate community of individuals that succeed one another. The infinity of meanings of a text now unfolds in history, as Gadamer put it explicitly and as Derrida would agree in principle.

Modern deconstruction has turned its attention to the nature of the text as disassociated from its author but strongly dependent on the reader. Following the cultural crises in the elites involved in the Nietzschean and Freudian revolutions, the instability of meaning has become a crucial issue that betrays not only the fluid semantics of the interpreted texts and the eclipse of the author but also the flexible attitudes of the readers. A destabilization of classical philology's certainty of the possibility to ascertain the authorial intention or the idealism of meaning facilitated the emergence of more subtle, intricate, sometimes even oversophisticated discourses on the possibilities implied in the earlier discourses. This postmodern move toward the disclosure of the discrepancy between the poverty of the author and the richness of language is quintessential for and inherent in the secularization of the attitude toward literature that constitutes the reading in the nonpresence of the author. The unstructured elements of language, which are enchained by creative literary processes, never submit to the author but transcend his intentions by displaying a much greater spectrum of meanings than presumably he intended. It is a weak mind, genial though it may be, that attempts to enslave the variety of possibilities inherent in language as constituted by a long series of semantic shifts. This view of the secular text assumes a crisis in the former focus on the author and proposes a much greater interest in the contribution of the reader or, even more, the sophisticated interpreter. The interpreter completes the meaning by bringing his own riches to the interpreted text.

The secular attitude toward texts is a fundamentally democratic discourse. Sacred texts almost always imply strong authors. The concept of God or His prophets, or at least the authority of the ancient sages, supplies an authorship that provides much firmer bases for the belief that the canonical texts themselves represent higher forms of intelligence, if not absolute wisdom. It is this faith in the distinct superiority of the author, or even in that of ancient authors, over the modern reader (a reverberation of a medieval hierarchical structure of the universe, society, and intellects) that dominates the approach of a religious reader to canonical texts. Assuming such a superior wisdom means also that it is hard to believe that an inferior reader, or even a large community of readers, will ever be able to exhaust all the intentions implied in the "divine" texts. Thus, it is not only the awareness of the riches of language, of its fluidity and ambiguities, as Derrida assumes, that serves as the ground for ongoing cognitive and interpretive projects, but an assumption of the existence and pertinence of supernal, even infinite forms of intelligence that are in their original very close to Greek and medieval systems; they are quintessential logocentric entities but were interpreted by ecstatic Kabbalah linguistically as being sources of revelations that take linguistic forms. It is not in history or society but in the atemporal upper reservoirs of knowledge that a religious reader will found "his" innovative interpretations of a sacred text. Thus, it is a radical trust in the text, or more precisely in the plenitude or even semantic abundance of its linguistic components, rather than a basic mistrust in its author as the generator of the text, that characterizes many Kabbalistic views. This belief in the existence, omnipresence, and availability of the transcendent reservoirs of meaning, the supernal agent intellect which pulsates intellectual contents into the world that may be captured by well-prepared human intellects, that creates a logocentric way of thinking. Thus, the ecstatic Kabbalah can be defined as a vertical striving toward intellectual and mystical experiences interconnected with forms of eccentric exegesis.

The horizontal intertextuality characteristic of recent secular approaches has replaced the vertical interchange between reader and the subject of his belief or the reservoir of interpretations on high. A modern reader, too, sometimes reads in order to express himself. A religious one, by contrast, is more likely to read in order to be impressed. The former reading is analytical, disintegrative; it subverts much more than integrates. It allows readers to partake of the creative process during the reading process, and the different receptions atomize the world of the text by the intrusion of the multiple worlds of the readers. Its agon is provoked by the self-imposition of historical relations as generative factors. The gist of most cases of religious reading, on the other hand, is more synthetic. It reflects the search for a higher order, what Derrida would call a presence, to be internalized, imitated, or at least venerated. The reading process and synchronized rituals unify the individuals because of their common belief in an authoritative author, whose noesis is a message to be internalized. The very fact that in a religious society so many readers were perusing the very same book also contributed to the unifying nature of religious reading.

Let me point out, at the end of this short comparison between medievals and postmoderns, the more optimistic mode that transpires from the Kabbalistic attitudes toward the text. By assuming that the Torah comprises everything, the sacred text fulfilled the role of allowing religious readers, when they were so inclined, to adapt themselves to new intellectual developments and encounters. For them the text was not a prison that confines the reader, as Derrida would put it, but an opportunity for discovering more and more layers of divinity and, sometimes, reality. Indeed, as we shall see, according to the Jewish mystics it could even be a means of maintaining both God and reality.

VI. THE WORLD- AND GOD-MAINTAINING BOOK

One of the most important differences between the postmodern view of the text as a crucial metaphor and the Kabbalists' concept is the assumption that the canonical text not only constitutes reality but also maintains it. This type of text not only is a static paradigm, in the Platonic sense of an immutable supreme model, but continues to inform and sustain the entities created according to the inner structure of the Torah. More than the cosmogonic aspect of the text, the Kabbalists were concerned with the implications of such a stand as dealing with the post-creational process. In other words, the Kabbalists and the postmodern linguistic turn to some extent share the view that language, and the metaphor of the book, may account for the structure of reality. (The Kabbalists, however, unlike the postmoderns, claim that language not only noetically constitutes the world but also created it. This minimal agreement disappears where the more operational aspect of the book, namely its maintaining quality, is concerned.) Both use metaphor to explain a certain approach to reality, but they depart drastically when the possibility of affecting reality is addressed. I shall examine some instances where the book is conceived of as sustaining the world, in a non-Kabbalistic early-thirteenth-century text, in the Kabbalah of the renowned early-eighteenth-century author R. Moses Hayyim Luzzatto, and in some views found in early modern

Hasidism. Common to all these texts, and to many others that I cannot address here, is the pursuit of a validation of the book, of its study, and of the performance of the precepts taught in it. An exhaustive analysis of these vast and variegated materials is beyond the scope of this chapter, but several passages are adduced here to demonstrate that these texts regard the canonical book not only as a particularistic revelation but also as one having cosmic and ontological dimensions.

1. An Anonymous Ashkenazi Commentary on Haftarah

An anonymous and neglected commentary on the divine chariot, described in the first chapter of Ezekiel, is extant in two manuscripts.[59] It runs as follows:

> The pillar that sustains the world is called Tzaddiq,[60] and He sustains it by His right hand, as it is written, "The Righteous is the foundation of the world."[61] Ve-'ay'al in gematria is ha-gadol, because He is the great God. Shemo in gematria is va-sefer, "and the book," because by virtue of the book which is on high the world stands, and it is written, "He carves[62] his firmament[63] on water,"[64] ha-meqareh in gematria [amounts to] sefer gavoah [supernal book].[65]

This rather hermetic text requires some explanation. The Righteous mentioned here is none other than God, who is described as supporting the universe with his right hand. The right arm of God is mentioned explicitly in the phrase that immediately precedes this passage. The rest of the commentary relies on gematria, the assignment of numerical values to Hebrew letters, to establish affinities between significant words. One of God's cognomens, ve-'ay'al, whose origin is obscure, is thereby understood as tantamount to the Hebrew term for "the great," ha-gadol. Similarly shemo, literally "His name," is found to be tantamount to va-sefer, "and the book," as both phrases have the value 346. The affinity between the book and the divine name may point to a more precise relation between the Torah and the divine name, known from two texts written by Geronese Kabbalists, contemporaries of the anonymous author.[66] The world therefore "stands," or according to another plausible translation "exists,"[67] because of the book or the divine name. The author adduces as a proof text a verse from Psalm 104, which is interpreted as pointing to the book, a concept totally absent in the biblical verse. It is nevertheless projected there by a numerical calculation, which substitutes for the ha-meqareh, God as "the carver" of the firmament, the numerically equivalent phrase sefer gavoah, "supernal book," as both expressions amount to 350.

Thus, a supernal book identical to or at least closely related to the divine name is found on high, apparently as part of the divine creational process—Psalm 104 is a paramount creational text—but it also sustains the world. It should be mentioned that the verse from the psalm probably served as the trigger for the addition of the image of the book as the opening of a firmament, as a scroll is referred to in the Bible[68] and as is mentioned explicitly by this author at the very beginning of his own book.[69]

In fact, we should read the two parts of the quote—the first representing God as the Righteous who sustains the world and the second as the name and the book—as sustaining the universe in parallel. They not only follow each other but convey the same general idea. If this conjecture is correct, then the book is more closely related to God than to His name. God, His name, and the book all sustain the world. Indeed, the anonymous commentator was inclined to transform, by means of gematria, a variety of terms that prima facie have nothing to do with God into divine names.[70] The term "supernal book" thus becomes just one of many instances exemplifying the propensity to assign to God nouns that in the more common discourse are not related to Him.

2. Theosophical-Theurgical Kabbalah

In *Theses on Feuerbach* Marx and Engels described the difference between their approach and that of the philosophers as follows: "Up until now philosophers have only interpreted the world. The point now is to change it." This difference is parallel to that between the interpretations offered by medieval Jewish philosophers and some Kabbalistic schools, which can be described as theosophical-theurgical. The former were interested in understanding the structure of the universe as a religious duty, resorting also to the canonical texts as a source of inspiration. Many Kabbalists, however, had different agendas, which can be described as ergetic. One of the most ergetic explanations offered by Kabbalists for the study of the Torah is that Torah study has an influence on the divine realm, especially the relations between the divine attributes. This is already the case in *Sefer ha-Bahir*, where the two lower sefirot, Tiferet and Malkhut, which respectively represent the written and oral Torah, are described as united by the human act of study, and the number of examples to this effect is huge.[71]

Another important effect of the study of the Torah is the ascending human power emerging from the act of study, which affects the supernal potencies, as we learn in numerous Kabbalistic sources. Let me adduce one passage from Cordovero exemplifying the theurgical effect: "When [people of] Israel study the Torah here below they[72] come together in order to cleave to the secret of the innovated spirituality of the Torah[73] that ascends from the vapor of the mouth of man to the supernal worlds in order to link and unite them . . . like the joy of the bride and bridegroom who are united because of the secrets of the Torah, and they enjoy the supernal union . . . and this is certainly the account of Merkavah, that the [sefirot] of Tiferet and Malkhut are united together."[74] As in several other cases in theosophical-theurgical Kabbalah, the account of Merkavah is understood in terms of the union between the two lower sefirot. This union is achieved by the ascent of a spiritual force, created by the act of intense study, which changes the relationship between the divine powers. This view constitutes a version of the more widespread concept of the ascent of prayer on high and its impact there, and sometimes it takes the form of an inverse chain of being.[75] The theurgical aspect of the Torah and Torah study became one of the leitmotifs of Kabbalah, but there is no way to exhaust such a huge topic. The few examples adduced above should be supplemented by numerous other Kabbalistic discussions, medieval and modern, culminating in R. Hayyim of Volozhin's *Nefesh ha-Hayyim*, which was discussed in detail by Charles Mopsik in his *Les grands textes*.

3. Hasidism

Eighteenth-century Hasidic literature was full of linguistic speculation. Especially conspicuous is a concept that I have proposed to call "linguistic immanence," which portrays the divine presence in the world not only in terms of ontological emanation but also as the immanence of the divine language within all creatures, an immanence that ensures their persistence. Already the Besht, founder of what will become a movement, is quoted to this effect. A student of one of his main disciples, R. Shne'or Zalman of Liady, himself founder of an important Hasidic school, wrote in his *Sha'ar ha-Yihud ve-ha-'Emunah* in the name of the Besht[76] that letters and words that were creative of a certain entity (there the firmament)

> "stand upright forever within the firmament of the heaven"[77] and are clothed within all the firmaments forever, in order to enliven them . . . because should the letters disappear for a second, God forfend, and return to their source, [then] all the heavens would become nought and nil indeed, and become as if they had never existed at all . . . And this is also [the case for] all the creatures that are in all the worlds, higher and lower, even this corporeal earth, and even the aspect of mineral, would the letters of the ten logoi[78] disappear from it [the earth] for a second, God forfend, by means of which the earth was created . . . and the combination of letters that form the name *'even* [stone] is the vitality of the stone, and this is the case of all the creatures in the world, their names in the Holy language are the letters of the speech that are emanated from one gradation, which corresponds to stages of emanations, to another, from the ten logoi in the Torah, by their substitutions and permutations of letters according to the 231 gates,[79] until they arrive and are clothed within that creature.[80]

Significant parts of the passage already occur, anonymously, in a collection of doctrines of R. Shne'or Zalman's master, R. Dov Baer of Mezeritch, known as the Great Maggid,[81] although other parts are quite reminiscent of a passage quoted in a book by a younger contemporary of R. Shne'or Zalman, R. Hayyim Tirer of Chernovitz. Since the two masters were contemporaries and the latter does not mention the former, I assume that they drew from a common source that mentioned the name of the Besht. R. Shne'or Zalman's widely read text is important because it shows once again, and in a version somewhat different from that preserved by R. Hayyim Tirer, that the immanentist linguistics was attributed to the very founder of Hasidism. The Besht's view assumes that everything created by the ten creative logoi is maintained by the letters of the words that were pronounced in illud tempus and preserved in the first chapter of Genesis. However, all the other creatures, whose names were not mentioned there, like the stone, can subsist only by different derivations from the letters that constitute the ten logoi. Indeed, in the middle of the above passage, in a phrase we skipped earlier, we read:

> The earth was created during the six days of creation, it may return to absolute nothingness and nil, like before the six days of creation, and this is what the Ari [Isaac Luria], blessed be his memory, has said, that even in the mineral, like the stone and dust and water, there is an aspect of soul and spiritual vitality, namely an aspect of the clothing of the letters of the speech of the ten logoi, which are vitalizing and generate the mineral, such as it may exist, out of the nothingness and the nil of the preheptameronic situation, even if the name "stone" was not mentioned during the six days of creation, nevertheless vitality is drawn to the stone by the combinations of letters and the change of their order.[82]

What seems to me of special importance for the history of Hasidism is the paramount emphasis on a linguistic framework for the cosmology, not only as contributing to theological speculation but also as informing the mystical and magical acts of the founder of this movement and his most influential followers. More than any previous Jewish mystics, they seem to have construed a metaphysics of language, more precisely of the ten creative logoi, which enabled them to act and explain their actions as a skillful activation of language. Also interesting for the phenomenology of Hasidic mysticism is the interpretation of the vitalist stand of Luria, who assumes, following some earlier trends in Kabbalah,[83] the existence of soul and vitality even within the minerals, in terms of linguistic immanence. The transition from Luria's view to the Hasidic master's is indicated by the word de-hayyinu, translated above as "namely." What is important to note is the attempt to derive the existence of entities not even mentioned in the creation story by assuming that their name emerges from one of the divine logoi by means of transforming the order of the letters. This transformative process is one of the main practices in Hasidism, and I shall elaborate on it in Chapter 12.

Let me introduce now a quote from R. Hayyim Tirer of Chernovitz, one of the most learned among the third generation of Hasidic authors:

On each and every letter of our holy Torah thousands and thousands, in fact infinite worlds depend,[84] and their existence, vitality, and maintenance depend on the existence of the people of Israel, who sustain this [particular] letter in the Torah, this being the reason for [its] existence. And it is known what the Besht, his merits should safeguard us, said about the verse[85] "His Word stands upright forever within the firmament of the heaven" . . . and the Torah letters by means of which He has created His world . . . by these very letters the firmament has been generated, and until now these letters are the vitality and existence of the heavens and of the heavens of heavens . . . And if someone were to imagine the absence of the influx of the vitality of the letters for one moment, all the firmament would return to nothingness and nil.[86]

The letters that compose the creational discourse are, therefore, not only mediators of primordial events, components of myths describing the divine as an actor in the cosmological drama. The words that are included in Genesis are the eidos of the creatures, their essence and a form of divine presence. The created cosmos is dependent on the language as inscribed in the canonical book, which now not only is the blueprint of creation but also continues to be part of the continuous subsistence of the individual creatures. This is not, however, a static presence but one that depends on the worship of the people of Israel, who indeed are presented here as the people of the book—not a book that is imposed on them and venerated in servitude but one whose components are sustained by their acts. No doubt this is a fine example of the more particularistic vision of the Torah, which is described at the same time as a cosmic book; but now this book is coauthored by a particular nation, which saw itself as responsible for the religious and cosmic qualities inherent in the book.

What I find especially fascinating in this passage is the "absorptive" description of the individual letters of the Torah: on each of them infinite worlds depend. Thus, following earlier Hasidic views, R. Hayyim Tirer emphasizes the comprehensiveness of the linguistic units as organized in the canon over the cosmic reality. Long after the emergence of the concept of the infinities of worlds in the Renaissance, each fragment of the canonical text was conceived of as superior to the cosmic realms. For the time being, the last quote represents the apotheosis of the Torah from the point of view of the absorption of the cosmos within the all-encompassing text.

The above discussions were formulated superbly by Edmond Jabes, who wrote that "if God is, it is because He is in the book. If the sages, the saints . . . man and insects exist, it is because their names are found in the book. The world exists because the book exists, because existence is growing with its name."[87] It would be hard to find a more adequate expression of the world- and God-absorbing understanding of the book.

VII. Concluding Remarks

The propensity for identifying the book with the author, as described above in so many cases, should also be addressed from a more general point of view concerned more with the history of religion than with hermeneutics. There appear to be three stages in the development of the relation between author and book: in the biblical period, the divine author is mainly a speaker, and his being and activity transcend the importance of the message. In the rabbinic period, the canonical book reached a status that may transcend even the authority of the supreme author, though in some circles (those of the Heikhalot) the two factors are imagined not only as intertwined but also as overlapping. In the third phase, the mystical one, the two factors are even more closely linked, the mystic having not only identified them but presumably also experienced them as being together, as part of the process of study and ritualistic reading of the Torah. To a certain extent, the author now becomes more important than his book, despite the fact that the two are often deeply interconnected.

I have formulated the development of the relation between author and text in terms reminiscent of Gershom Scholem's famous proposal to distinguish three phases in the development of religion: the animistic phase, where there was no clear distinction between the divine and nature, and the divine could be experienced directly; the institutional phase, constituted by an abyss created between man and God and filled by an institutionalized structure, and the mystical phase, in which the mystic bridges the gap by his search for a more direct contact with the divine.[88] According to such a view, any religion that grows enough will eventually pass through the first two phases and reach the final, mystical phase. Nevertheless, Scholem did not offer even one concrete example that would explain in detail the nature of the premystical phases in Judaism. From perusing his treatment, one cannot be sure what historical period in Judaism, or what type of literature, is covered by the animistic or the institutional phase. Nevertheless, it seems obvious that the mystical element, occurring after the opening of the gap between God and man, is late. It attempts to overcome the institutionalized apparatus that appeared in the vacuum created by the withdrawal or "departure" of God. In the threefold scheme I have presented in this chapter, the book may play the role that the institution played in Scholem's scheme; the canonical book also mediates, and in the mystical phase is absorbed within, the divine. So far the two threefold schemes coincide. But unlike Scholem's scheme, which does not address the historical question as to precisely how and under what circumstances the second phase emerges from the first, nor how the third "emancipates" itself from the second, the above suggestion proposes to see the emergence of the second phase not as a "natural" development but as much more connected to a historical accident. If the Israelite temple was conceived of as ensuring the divine presence here below, its destruction was understood as a painful rupture between the mundane and the divine plane or a departure of the divine from the lower world. The book itself was, however, only rarely taken to be a final substitution for a destroyed temple and its sacrificial role[89] but rather was viewed as a much more democratic form of ritual different from the more restricted one, the sacrifices in the Temple. The centrality of the book in rabbinism and other forms of Judaism is, in my opinion, not merely an antidote or a substitute for the Temple, an escapist enterprise undertaken by an elite that has lost its ritualistic center or the geographical terrain, a manner of alleviating a trauma, but a novel religious strategy promoted by another type of elite, one compounded of rabbis and scribes, different from the priestly one, which was connected to the Temple. This is not simply an immanent evolution but a dramatic change that was facilitated, though not created, by a decisive blow to the topocentric religion inflicted from outside, the supremacy of one party, the Pharisees, over the more priestly elite.

Furthermore, the emergence of many of the medieval formulations concerning the nature of the book should not be understood simply as a result of a natural development; rather, they are due to the influence of Greek thought, especially Neoplatonism, as we have seen. Again, this is not necessarily the result solely of a systemic development within a certain religion. According to Isaac Baer and Harold Bloom, the move from the Bible to the rabbinic emphasis on the importance of learning is related to Platonic influence.[90]

Indeed, it will suffice to see the relatively more marginal role of the book in early Christianity, in the generations contemporary to the early rabbinic masters, in order to understand that biblical Judaism could evolve in more than one direction, the centrality of the book being more a conscious choice than anything like a natural development. The identification of the word with flesh and the placing at the heart of religion the vicissitudes of the fate of a semidivine figure, conceived of as the savior, is an adequate comparison for the possibilities open in Jewish circles around the time of the destruction of the Second Temple. Indeed, as scholars have already duly emphasized, in the Greek Bible the Christ has been identified with the nomos,[91] and thus the literal aspects of the book have been dramatically reduced in favor of an interpretation focusing on the details of the Christ's *via passionis*. It is less a matter of carefully reading the original Hebrew text and commenting on its details that entertained early Christian thinkers than one of building an elaborate theology around the life and nature of the Savior, to which the spiritual life of the Christian mystics has been devoted. The emphasis on faith and heresy, more than study of canonical texts and ritual deeds, constitutes the paramount redemptive acts. The more general idea of Torah as pointing to instruction[92] took the form of a scroll or book that exhausts the divine will according to rabbinic Judaism, or the form of a *nomos empsychos*, found already in Philo and apparently reverberating in early Christianity.[93] Views attributing an anthropomorphic structure to the Torah may, however, be found in ancient Judaism, and they become much more evident in theosophical-theurgical Kabbalah.[94] Yet the elements emphasized by the mystical understanding of the Torah were either its perfection and the identification with its perfect nature or the need to perfect it by human activity. To a great extent Jewish mysticism was much more fascinated by *via perfectionis* than it was by *via passionis*.[95]

5

MAGICAL AND
MAGICAL-MYSTICAL ARCANIZATIONS
OF CANONICAL BOOKS

In the previous chapters I analyzed views of the Jewish canonical texts that I describe as "absorbing." I use this term in order to convey the expanding comprehensiveness of the concept of the text which, moving to the center of the Jewish society, also integrated attributes reminiscent of wider entities like the world or God. This expansion facilitated the attribution of more dynamic qualities to the text conceived of as capable of allowing various types of influences on processes taking place in the world, in God, and in the human psyche. I would now like to examine some views found in Jewish magical and Kabbalistic literatures that demonstrate the existence of a more dynamic attitude toward the canonical texts. Let me start here with some aspects that may be called magical and then, in the next chapter, turn to the mystical aspects related to the study of the biblical text.

Jewish magic is a wide religious domain that had many autochthonous productions and adopted from outside further magical techniques and concepts. This is not the place to offer a comprehensive description of this vast field, and as our discussions will deal with one limited topic, the Bible and magic in the context of hermeneutics, they will perforce be rather preliminary and tentative. Given the importance of the Bible in different strata of Judaism, its sacredness attracted many magical interpretations of the role it might play. The best known is bibliomancy, which is based on the assumption that parts of the book may conspire to offer an answer to all sorts of questions, including practical ones.[1] In the present framework, however, I shall focus my remarks on matters that have some relevance to this topic, as part of a more comprehensive effort to integrate magic into the study of Jewish mysticism much more fully than has been done in the dominant lines of research.[2] Let me address, therefore, some examples of a descending type of magic, one concerned with bringing down spiritual entities from above in connection with the study of the Torah. Other forms of magic, related to the powers acquired through Torah study or the apotropaic function of studying the Torah, will not be treated in this context.

I. ANGELS OF THE TORAH: SOME MEDIEVAL REPERCUSSIONS

The assumption that there is an angel assigned to the Torah, and that Torah study is somehow related to the possibility of gaining access to such an angel, as formulated in the Heikhalot literature, is part of a gradual process of constellation that attributed to mundane entities, including canonical materials, a dependence on a higher governing power. This view was also alive between the time of composition of the Heikhalot literature and that of the late medieval and early modern texts, a period that will be the focus of the following discussions. As shown throughout the present book, secrecy is connected mainly with an orientation toward a spiritual verticality, and in this case we have a fine example wherein the knowledge of the angelic power assigned to the Torah, found in the supernal world, is a secret.

As we have seen, the reception of the Torah by Moses in heaven was described in several rabbinic and Jewish magical sources as preceded by a contest between him and the angels.[3] According to several early medieval Jewish sources, after Moses' "triumph" he was given, by the very angels that had opposed God's intention to reveal the Torah to him, some divine names. This linkage of reception of the Torah and disclosure of divine names is found explicitly in a passage from the magical book entitled *Shimmushei Torah*. I must stress, however, that the extreme difficulty in dating the composition of this treatise complicates any attempt to offer a more precise historical picture of the process of magical arcanization of the Torah. Nevertheless, my working hypothesis, based on analyses presented later in this section, is that this narrative structure is reflected already in the Talmud and thus suggests a tentative pedigree starting sometime in the third century C.E. That said, let us now turn to the most important discussion of this issue, found in the preface to *Sefer Shimmushei Torah*:

> The Holy One, blessed be He, has immediately called Yefeifiah, the Prince of the Torah, and he [Yefeifiah] gave to him [Moses] the Torah, "arranged in its proper order in every detail and kept [intact],"[4] and all the servant angels became his lovers and each and every one of them gave him a remedy and the secret of the names, which emerge from each and every pericope, and all their [magical] uses . . . and this is the [magical] use given to him by the angels, by means of Yefeifiah, the Prince of the Torah, and by Metatron, the Prince of the [Divine] Face. And Moses transmitted it to Eleazar, and Eleazar to his son, Pinheas, who is [identical to] Elijah,[5] the high and respectable priest.[6]

Several topics in this text are relevant for the concept of the Bible as possessing a magical and esoteric layer. The first is that there is an obvious relationship between an angel, Yefeifiah, and the Torah as a whole,[7] and between angels, pericopes of the Pentateuch, and their magical uses; whether such a nexus was elaborated in ancient Jewish texts in order to offer a comprehensive scheme for the whole biblical text, or whether there ever was a complete list of fifty-three names of angels corresponding to the pericopes, we do not know. It is evident, however, that *Sefer Shimmushei Torah*, which means "magical uses of the Torah," consists in a description of the "remedies," namely the medical and other uses of oftentimes incomprehensible names derived from various verses found in each of the pericopes of the Torah.

In this passage Moses is said to have transmitted the magical and linguistic secrets he received to his followers, in a manner reminiscent of the way the *Pirqei 'Avot*, an early rabbinic source, described the transmission of oral lore. This obvious attempt to provide a pedigree for magical-biblical knowledge also recalls the genealogies found in other books of magic dating from late antiquity.[8] In any case, the last part of the quote makes it clear that Moses' magical lore, consisting in the "secret of the names," has not been lost but is still available in the book dealing with this topic. This claim is not new, for it too appears in late-antiquity magical texts.[9] In *Sefer Shimmushei Torah* there is no explicit or even implicit thesis that the entire text of the Torah could or should be transformed into a series of divine names; only a few selected verses from each biblical pericope are treated as sources of magical names and portents of special power.

This is also the case in another book, the widely printed *Sefer Shimmushei Tehilim*, which deals with the magical uses of the Psalms and in structure closely resembles *Shimmushei Torah*. In both books the regular order of the letters of certain verses has been juggled to generate a magical name that has extraordinary powers. That is to say, rearranging the letters in some of the biblical verses reveals another manner of relating to the linguistic material, not as organs of transmission of knowledge or lore, but as a powerful magical force. By shifting from the usual run of nouns and verbs to the order of angelic and divine names, the biblical verses traveled dramatically, from a regular semantic organization of language to magical, in most cases meaningless but allegedly powerful names.

The relation between these two manifestations of the same linguistic material is not clarified in the extant magical sources. Was the magical order of letters conceived of as more important because it was more powerful? What are we to make of the conjunction of facts that the so-called Prince of the Torah (*Sar ha-Torah*) revealed the order of the Torah while the other, apparently lower angels delivered the magical and presumably secret aspects of the Torah? What is the relation between the plain order and the magical order of the text? Does the angelic hierarchy, which would subordinate the secret and magical to the plain sense and order, indeed reflect such a hierarchical relation between these two senses? Does such a hierarchy reflect a social situation or a specific social imaginary of the magical authors who produced the magical book, in comparison to the rabbinic "authorities"?

Several talmudic discussions seem to be pertinent for understanding the above passage and answering the questions just formulated. The implicit assumption in the Babylonian Talmud (BT), *Sabbath*, is that the gifts given by the angels are magical names, a view that does not correspond exactly to the assumption in *Shimmushei Torah* of a correlation between them and portions of the Torah.[10] Moreover, one may claim that while gifts, *mattanot*, are mentioned in another context in BT, *Sanhedrin*, fol. 91a, where Abraham is said to have given to the sons of his concubines the name of impurity, which is a lower mode of activity, the rabbis' understanding of the divine names in the talmudic passage in *Tractate Sabbath* does not elevate them to the status of a secret knowledge superior to that acquired by students of the Torah through the ordinary sequence of letters. If this is the case, we may ask whether the *Sabbath* passage does not include a polemic against views like those found in the *Shimmushei Torah* passage. Or, sociologically speaking, it is quite possible that the anonymous author of *Shimmushei Torah* belongs, like the authors of the Heikhalot literature, to a secondary elite.

On the other hand, the author of the *Sabbath* passage might have belonged to the primary elite, who were interested in emphasizing the superiority of the Torah in its ordinary order of letters against the claims of magicians, who attempted to offer another, more powerful and apparently superior secret reading of the Torah, in comparison to the regular rabbinic one. Thus, for example, in the early medieval midrash *Deuteronomy Rabba'*, Moses boasts, "I prevailed over the supernal pamalya and revealed their secrets [razeihem] to men and received the Torah from the right hand of the Holy One, blessed be He, and taught it to Israel."[11] The exoteric propensity of the rabbinic author is quite evident. There are no more secrets unknown to any humans; the Torah was revealed directly by God, not by an angel, high as it may be. Indeed, the distinction between the two readings suggested in *Shimmushei Torah* may best be understood against the background of double revelations, as found in sectarian claims advanced in such works as the *Book of Jubilees* and the Qumranic literature.[12] Especially interesting is the similarity between the contention found in *Jubilee* that an angel revealed the secret understanding of the Torah and the later rabbinic and magical theories discussed above.[13]

In the late twelfth century the relation between Moses, Torah, angels, and names was already known in Europe. So, for example, we learn from the anonymous Ashkenazi treatise on seventy divine names entitled *Sefer ha-Hesheq* that "pure and sacred names . . . were taught by angels to Moses our master when he ascended to heaven and received the Torah."[14] According to the opening sentence of another version of this book, "Whoever knows the seventy names of Metatron will be able to operate whatever he will desire . . . and he [Metatron] will reveal to you all the secrets of the Torah, and you will be capable of bringing a *maggid* according to your will."[15] The very expression *Sar ha-Torah* is explicitly mentioned elsewhere in the same book.[16] Assi Farber-Ginat has drawn attention to the nexus between the *Sar ha-Torah* practice and the Ashkenazi text, as well as the possible impact on the later concept of maggid.[17] Indeed, this term appears already in the most famous of the Ashkenazi speculative texts, *Sefer Hasidim*.[18]

However, the description of angels as princes of the Torah did not remain the patrimony of the rather marginal book *Shimmushei Torah* or of the various not-so-influential versions of *Sefer ha-Hesheq*. The first book, devoted to issues related to oneiric technique, was composed at the end of the first third of the thirteenth century in central France by a halakhic author, R. Jacob of Marveges, and was entitled *Questions and Responsa from Heaven*.[19] This book is quite unique in the vast rabbinic legalistic literature, for it aims at finalizing difficult halakhic issues by resorting to the assistance of revelations coming from angels speaking to the author in a dream. So, for example, one reads in this book a question closer than any other to mystical topics:

About the Holy Name of forty-two letters, whether it is permitted to make a magical use of it and invoke angels which are assigned to the Torah in order to understand whatever he studies and not forget what he learns,[20] and also for the purpose of invoking the angels assigned to richness and victory over enemies and over favorable treatment by high officers, or whether it is forbidden to use it[21] for any of these [purposes]? And they have answered: "Holy, Holy, Holy, is the Lord of Hosts,"[22] He alone will take care of your needs.[23]

The meaning of the answer is quite clear: the angels should not be addressed despite the fact that they are conceived of as assigned to the Torah; the ultimate source remains God alone. Interestingly, the manner in which the answer was formulated is also a biblical verse, as in many cases in this book, which should be decoded in order to understand the answer. In our case the tripling of the epithet "holy" points to the triple separation or distinctness of God: He alone is the source for the knowledge of the Torah, He will endow richness, and He will ensure victory. This is an oneiric interpretation of the Bible, a technique that was also accepted beyond R. Jacob of Marveges's book.

Apparently from this book, though perhaps also from some other parallel sources, the *Zohar* accepted the view that each and every pericope of the Torah has an angel that is assigned to it and that will protest before God if the reader of the pericope cuts its reading in an inappropriate manner.[24]

R. Abraham Abulafia, the ecstatic Kabbalist contemporary to the Kabbalists who wrote the *Zohar*, also mentions the *Sar ha-Torah*. In an untitled book which I contend should be attributed to him, it is said that "the secret of Metatron, whose name is Na'ar, is 'the angel of the Torah,' as is known from the secret of the calculation 999, the numerical value of *Metatron Sar ha-Panim*."[25] There can be no doubt that Abulafia did not subscribe to the mythic understanding that an angel waits to be conjured in order to reveal the secrets of the Torah. For him, as he mentioned elsewhere in the same book, the secret of the tenth angel is the secret of the Torah.[26] Metatron is not only the tenth angel but also the Torah, as we shall see in Chapter 11. In other words, Abulafia adopted the mythic imagery of the Prince of the Torah in order to propose a synthesis between philosophical and linguistic conceptualizations of an intellectual-linguistic entity.[27] Moreover, I assume that this "angel" is not only an ontological construct but also an entity believed to reveal itself to Abulafia, as we learn from another quote from the same book, where the angel says to him:

"I am the angel of the Lord of hosts, so and so, and it is the secret of the Garden of Eden [*Gan 'Eden*] that amounts to three names, YHWH *'adonai* 'elohim, whose vowels are the Prince of the Garden of Eden"[28] . . . and he will tell him: "I am the tree of life, the Garden in Eden from the east." And he will understand that God has sent to him His angel in order to help him by instruction, and to accustom him to the strong love of the Creator, by announcing to him the truth of the essence of the tree of life that is within the garden, and he is the "Prince of the Garden of Eden."[29]

Elsewhere in the same text Abulafia contends that from the "tree of life Torah," prophecy and commandments emerge.[30] On the ground of Abulafia's Kabbalistic system it is obvious that the divine names are not simply secrets to be mentally known but linguistic units that should be recited in order to change the consciousness of the performer. Here the ergetic aspect is conspicuous, for the Torah is understood as an influx whose reception is conditioned by the resort to mystical technique.

Perhaps the most detailed and comprehensive reverberation of the magic related to the angel of the Torah is found late in the Middle Ages in *Sefer ha-Meshiv*, a book that will concern us more in the next chapter.[31] God is reported to have instructed the anonymous Kabbalistic magician to resort to an ergetic device that will ensure the descent of the text that is not only a sacred revelation but also an interpretation of the Bible:

You should know that the secret causing the descent of the supernal book is the secret of the descent of the supernal chariot, and when you pronounce the secret of the Great Name, immediately the force of the "garment" will descend downwards, which is the secret of Elijah, who is mentioned in the works of the sages. And by this [secret] R. Shim'on bar Yohay[32] and Yonathan ben 'Uzziel learned their wisdom, and they were deserving of the secret of the "garment," to be dressed in it. And R. Haninah and R. Nehunya ben ha-Qanah and R. 'Aqivah and R. Ishmael ben 'Elisha' and our holy rabbi and Rashi and many others [learned] likewise.[33] And the secret of the "garment" is the vision of the "garment," which the angel of God is dressed in, with a corporeal eye, and it is he who is speaking to you . . . And the secret of the "garment" was given to those who fear God and meditate upon His name; they have seen it, those men who are the men of God were worthy of this state. And they were fasting for forty days continuously,[34] and during their fast they pronounced the Tetragrammaton forty-five times,[35] and on the fortieth day [the "garment"] descended to him and showed him whatever he wished [to know], and it stayed with him until the completion of the [study of the] subject he wanted [to know]; and they [Elijah and the "garment"][36] were staying with him day and night. Thus was it done in the days of Rashi to his master, and the latter taught him [Rashi] this secret [of the "garment"], and by means of it [the secret] he [Rashi] composed whatever he composed, by the means of his mentor and instructor. Do not believe that he [Rashi] wrote this down from his own mind,[37] for he did it by the secret of the "garment" of the angel and the secret of mnemotechnics, to explain the questions one is asking or to compose a book one wishes to compose, and [thus] were all the sciences copied, one by one . . . And this happened in the days of the Talmud and in the days of Rashi's master and in the days of Rashi too, since his master began this [usage], and Rashi ended it, and in their times this science[38] was transmitted by word of mouth, one man to another, and this is the reason all the sages of Israel relied upon Rashi, as at that time they knew the secret. Therefore, do not ever believe that he [Rashi] composed his commentary on the Talmud and on the plain meaning of the Bible out of his reason, but by means of this force of the secret of the "garment," and that [force] which dressed it, which is an angel, since by means of it he could know and compose whatever he wished . . . And those who were able to see it were like prophets, and in the time of the Talmud many used it.[39]

A more detailed treatment of the central issue of the garment must wait until Chapter 6. For the moment it is sufficient to point out that in the above passage the garment is presented as both an oracular technique, instrumental in answering questions, and a compository technique to which the rabbinic masters of late antiquity resorted in order to compose the Talmud and to which early medieval masters like Rashi turned in order to comment on both the Pentateuch and the Talmud. It goes without saying that these books, among the most exoteric in themselves, were believed by some circles in medieval Judaism to possess central secret layers. What seems of particular interest from our point of view, however, is the arcanization of the modes of their composition, not only of their content. In lieu of the exoteric view dominant in rabbinic literature concerning the unaided student, who is also the composer of midrashic texts, here the possession of a secret, reminiscent of the secret of the Torah in Heikhalot literature, is the precondition for composition. The mode of composition of the writings, which amount to a significant segment of Jewish classical literatures, by causing an angel, Elijah, to descend and reveal—in fact, to bring down—the composition, demonstrates that late in the Middle Ages theories about angels assigned to the most important intellectual activity in Judaism, compounding classical books and commentaries, were well alive and perhaps also put into practice by some Kabbalists. It is not entirely clear whether the theory of *Sefer ha-Meshiv* stems directly from a reading of and elaboration on the *Sar ha-Torah* composition, which stems from the Heikhalot literature, but the similarity in resorting to angels to produce more and more religious literature reflects the important role of magic in conceptualizing and validating religious activities. The anonymous Kabbalist whose views we discussed above was not a lonely voice in his generation; a contemporary, R. Isaac Mar Hayyim, described the emergence of the book of the *Zohar* as the result of revelations stemming from the angelic figure of Elijah.[40]

In this context we may offer perhaps another angle for understanding an important spiritual phenomenon in the sixteenth century: the emergence of the theories about the Maggid, an angelic mentor generated by the involvement in the study of some texts, especially the Mishnah.[41] This seems to be the inverse of the *Sar ha-Torah* practices: they do not preexist the text, and thus are not assigned to it, but are understood as emerging from the accumulated human energy involved in the process of study.

Mention of a Prince of the Torah can be detected as late as the beginning of the nineteenth century. In a hagiographic composition dealing with the deeds of the founder of Hasidism, an opponent of Hasidism, R. Abraham 'Abba', father of the famous R. Pinhas of Koretz (himself an important Hasidic author), told his son that he dreamed he had ascended to the paradise and then "the Prince of the Torah entered and repeated a Torah said by the Besht. When I awoke from my sleep I remembered it very well and I came here for that reason. And what I had already heard I heard again from his holy mouth."[42] The train of thought is tautological: the Prince of the Torah is preaching the Besht's Torah, in his name, before it had been pronounced here below. Presumably, the description of the Besht as being silent following his ritual immersion in preparation for the Sabbath, as we learn earlier in this story, is reminiscent of rites of purifications found in the Heikhalot literature. In any case, the Besht is described in the same book as performing the rites of bringing down the Prince of the Torah on Sabbath eve.[43] Thus, we may assume that the Besht was conceived of as expounding his teaching in the celestial academy before he did so here below. Its acceptance on high was therefore the supreme validation of the status of the Besht in the eyes of an opponent. In fact, a detail in the story, when the Besht scolded the opponent and ordered that the Torah scroll he was holding be taken away,[44] is illuminating from the point of view of the legend: on low the opponents—later to become the mitnaggedim—had the Torah taken away because they did not know how to hold it, and instead the nascent Beshtian lore is accepted on high. Moreover, I propose to see the confrontation between the two sides as involving two elites: the itinerant elite, represented by the Besht and described as keeping the Sabbath in a faraway community, and R. Abraham 'Abba', anachronistically described as an aggressive Lithuanian. Thus, the Prince of the Torah is deemed as involved in tipping the balance between the two elites in favor of the secondary one, or the secondary intelligentsia, as Jacob Katz called it.

Moreover, in the same collection of legends the Besht is described as having been asked by his companion to bring down the Prince of the Torah, an endeavor that he believes to be dangerous.[45] Given that the Besht's involvement with the Heikhalot literature is mentioned elsewhere in the same collection, as we shall see below,[46] we may conclude that many of the main forms of Jewish mysticism resorted to practices or concepts understood to enable intellectual gains from an angel named the Prince of the Torah. In fact, according to the same collection of legends, on the day of his death the Besht revealed to his son a secret name, which when invoked will bring the father down to study with his son.[47] This fragmentary survey of recurrences of the concept of *Sar ha-Torah* in some of the main schools of Jewish mysticism demonstrates that ancient techniques never died out; they changed forms, sometimes were forgotten and then revived, but hardly fell in complete desuetude.

It is worth noting that an ancient Jewish tradition dealing with the revelatory role of the angels in the transmission of issues regarding the Bible might have had an influence on the Muslim description of the angel Gabriel's revelation of the Qur'an to Muhammad over many years. Like the grand angel that played a central role in the ancient Jewish group deemed to be heretical, the Magharia sect,[48] which includes the revelation of the Torah, Gabriel is portrayed as the main intercessor between God and the recipient of the revelation, and has been identified in Muslim philosophical and mystical sources with various revelatory entities like the Holy Spirit and the Agent Intellect.[49]

II. R. YOHANAN ALEMANNO'S MAGIC OF THE TORAH

In addition to the angelic magic related to the Bible (apparently from Jewish sources), which assumes the performance of ritual for attaining secrets, books, and commentaries descending from the higher world, there are many more examples of turning to the Bible to obtain powers from above. Most of them resort to a type of magic that I propose to call *talismanic*, whose history in Judaism has been traced in the recent years.[50] Let me summarize the historical trajectory of talismanic magic insofar as Jewish mysticism is concerned:

First, talismanic magic was present in some writings of ecstatic Kabbalah, the astrologically influenced Kabbalah, and even the theosophical Kabbalah of the fifteenth-century Castilian Kabbalist R. Shem Tov ben Shem Tov. This initial stage of talismanic interpretation of language did not, however, affect the mainstream of Kabbalistic writings—the theosophical Kabbalah as represented in the Catalan

Kabbalah—either as formulated by the students of R. Isaac the Blind or as taught by Nahmanides and his Kabbalistic school, in the book of the *Zohar*, in many of the writings of R. Joseph Gikatilla,[51] or in the school of R. Joseph Ashkenazi and R. David ben Yehudah he-Hasid.

Second, beginning from the end of the fifteenth century talismanics were more substantially integrated in Kabbalistic literature, as we learn from the writings of R. Yohanan Alemanno and R. Moses Cordovero. The many followers of the latter Kabbalist disseminated this vision of language in numerous writings.[52]

Third, starting from the middle of the eighteenth century this view was adopted by many Hasidic masters from a variety of Kabbalistic sources, mostly Cordoverian. They elaborated on linguistic talismanics much more than the Kabbalists have done previously.[53]

In other words, as the evolving mystical literature of the Jews grew progressively more panoramic, the talismanic model became part and parcel of important segments of the Kabbalistic and, later, the voluminous Hasidic literature. In many, though not all, of the earlier forms of medieval Jewish mysticism the role of magic was attenuated,[54] whereas during the development of the different versions of Kabbalah the role of the talismanic theory of magic became more conspicuous and influential. The significant impact of this model of understanding the powerful text, which had important implications for the understanding of Jewish ritual in general, calls for a substantial reorientation in modern scholarship's understanding of how Jewish mysticism and the phenomenology of Kabbalah developed, as well as a shift in the methodology of future research. A greater effort should be invested by scholars of Jewish mysticism in studying ancient and medieval magic and astrology, in order to transcend theologically biased analyses of the Kabbalistic writings. Just as symbolic language is seen as a dominant feature of Jewish mysticism, talismanic language should be given a prominent place. Words of power were much more powerful in the general economy of Kabbalistic literature than modern scholars' mentalistic understanding of this lore has assumed. Let me first adduce a particularly interesting text, which reflects a strong magical understanding of the Torah. Its author is R. Yohanan Alemanno, a late-fifteenth- and early-sixteenth-century Kabbalist active for many years in Florence:

> After the external cleansing of the body and an inner change and spiritual purification from all taint, one becomes as clear and pure as the heavens. Once one has divested oneself of all material thoughts, let him read only the Torah and the divine names written therein. There shall be revealed awesome secrets and such divine visions as may be emanated upon pure clear souls who are prepared to receive them, as the verse said:[55] "Make ready for

three days and wash your clothing." For there are three preparations: of the exterior [the body], of the interior, and of the imagination.[56]

By reading the Torah and especially the divine names, the practicant perceives an initial infusion of power. This reading is preceded by a series of "preparations" reminiscent of the purifications performed by the Jews before they were given the Torah. The second stage of the process is described in the continuation of the above quotation. The Torah scroll itself becomes imbued with the spiritual force. At that moment "the writing of God, the spirit of the living God, shall descend upon the written scroll." By "the writing of God" Alemanno is referring directly to the revelation of the Torah at Mount Sinai as described in Exodus. A personal experience of the revelation of the law is a conventional thought in Kabbalah. What is new and striking in the process described by Alemanno is the similarity of the ceremony to the ritual of dedication found in many books of magic:

> When a man devotes a great amount of time, the intermittent becomes habitual. When he immerses himself in these things, then such a great efflux will come to him that he will be able to cause the spirit of God to descend upon him and hover above him and flutter about him all the day. Not only that, but "the writing of God, the spirit of the living God" will descend upon the scroll to such a degree that the scroll will give him power to work signs and wonders in the world. And such are the books called *segretti* [secret words], and all the incantations are the secret words that come from evil spirits. Therefore the Torah forbade these practices. The Torah of Moses, however, is entirely sealed and closed by the name of the Holy One, blessed be He. Therefore its powers are numerous and such is the book of Psalms. This is a great secret, hidden from the eye of the blind and the cunning.[57]

Alemanno thus resorts to a principle formulated by the early Kabbalists, especially R. Azriel, that the Torah is sealed in the divine name. This condition makes the whole difference between the licit magical use of the scroll of the Torah and the illicit resort to books of secrets, obviously books of magic stemming from demons. The similarity that Alemanno recognizes between the licit and illicit books, however, evinces the strong magical aspect of the way Torah can be used. Its recitation, when performed after purification, has two distinct results: the first can be described as mystical, as it is related to the purified soul and consists in revelations of secrets and divine visions. The second may be described as magical, as it is related to the descent of a divine spirit on the scroll that confers on the practicant powers to perform miracles. This capacity apparently involves the body as a main factor.

How does this magic, according to Alemanno, operate? The Kabbalist practicing the "licit" recitation is enacting the purification rituals in a regular manner until he causes the more habitual presence of the divine to descend on both man and the scroll. The accumulation of power in the scroll is fraught, however, with the potentiality of transmitting to man extraordinary powers. Thus, the scroll and especially the divine names become objects on which power is collected after it had been caused to descend by means of rites performed by the Kabbalist. In other words, the Torah becomes a talisman on which the supernal powers are captured. If we compare the passage from Alemanno to that from *Sefer ha-Meshiv* adduced earlier, we see two common denominators: the magician causes the descent of a supernal power, and this supernal power is related to the scriptures. Yet it is only in Alemanno that the scroll of the Torah serves as a talisman.

What is also crucial in Alemanno's text is the emphasis on the divine names, the less semantic aspects of the Bible. This understanding is corroborated by a comparison of the Torah to the book of Psalms, presumably because on these two parts of the Hebrew Bible alone a magical arcanization was available. Thus we may assume that the magical propensities inherent in the scriptures when fraught with power have to do with their having been understood as a continuum of divine names.

In another fascinating passage, found in an untitled treatise by Alemanno, the astromagical conceptualization of the Torah is even more evident. When elaborating on the third sefirah, Binah, which is assigned to the third celestial sphere dominated by Saturn, Alemanno describes that planet as

> supreme and noble, higher than all the other planets, which is the reason that the ancient sages said about it that it generated all the other planets . . . And they say that Saturn is the true judge and the planet of Moses, peace be with him.[58] The angel of Saturn is Michael,[59] the great minister, so called because of his great power in divine matters, and he is the ministering angel of Israel. And the astrologers who described Saturn say that it endows man with profound thought, law, and the spiritual sciences, prophecy, sorcery,[60] and prognostication and the sabbaticals and jubilees. The Jewish people and the Hebrew language and the Temple are under its jurisdiction. Saturn's major conjunction with Jupiter in the dominion of Pisces occurred to assist the nation and the Torah and its prophets. This planet endows the people with perfection in sciences and divine matters such as Torah and its commandments, out of its sublimity, because it is spiritual . . . It is concerned only with thought, understanding, and design, esoteric knowledge and divine worship and His Torah, and the Sabbath day is in its sway . . . and if

they will keep its spiritual rules and laws, it will impart a spiritual influx abundantly. But if they will not keep the way of God, it will spit out every-thing which is bad: prophecy will occur to the fools and babies in an insufficient manner, and to women and melancholics and those possessed by an evil spirit, and maleficent demons that obliterate the limbs and bad counsels and sorceries[61] and anxieties and erroneous beliefs.[62]

The Torah is therefore the ideal form of behavior which ensures the attraction of the spiritual forces onto the lower world. Although in the last occurrence of the term *sorcery* it has a conspicuously negative connotation, in its first occurrence the context seems to point in a more positive direction. In any case, the Torah, which points to a certain *regimen vitae*, is placed in the same category as astromagic, which is hinted at by the spiritual sciences, *hokhemot ruhaniyyot*.[63]

III. DRAWING DOWN HOLINESS

I would like to draw attention to an example of the transformation of a theme, found in Lurianic Kabbalah, from the theosophical-theurgical to the talismanic mode. It is the idea of the oral, linguistic efficacy of performing the biblical text as it has been accepted. Some Lurianic sources describe the holiness of the holidays as created by the reading of the liturgical parts. These Kabbalists hold that the reading induces the unification of the divine attributes and the descent of the divine power from the higher to the lower divine manifestations. However, ac-cording to R. Tzevi Hirsch Kaidanover, an influential early-eighteenth-century Polish rabbi later active in Frankfurt, the calling down by reading canonical texts takes place not within the divine realm but in the mundane realm, where the congregation, like vessels, is prepared to receive the supernal holiness. This move from theurgical toward magical activity assumes that a certain type of recitation brings down influxes, holiness, and light within or onto those who are prepared to receive them. The implications of this transformation are far-reaching for the understanding of some topics related to the Torah in Hasidism.

In R. Hayyim Vital's book *Peri 'Etz Hayyim* it is said that there is a difference between the holiness of Sabbath and that of the other Jewish holidays. Whereas holiness is inherent in the special time of Sabbath, so that the contribution of the Kabbalist's theurgical activity is negligible, for the other holidays it is prayer that causes the descent of divine energy within the divine realm. In other words, the holidays are to an extent created by the ritual of reading the liturgical texts related to those holidays, what is called in the classical sources *miqra'ei qodesh*. This phrase has two meanings in Hebrew: the first one, closer to the plain sense of the words, is "holy recitations." The second, offered by Vital, assumes that *miqra'* can mean "calling," a possible semantic interpretation of the verb qore'. Thus, when reciting the liturgical texts, the Kabbalist is also inducing a certain type of relationship between the configuration symbolized by the terms 'abba' and qodesh, namely the configuration that corresponds to the sefirah of Hokhmah and the configuration of Binah. The calling is the creation of this relation, which apparently has sexual connotations. Thus, certain intradivine processes were caused by the theurgical act of reciting a text, which contributes to the emergence of the ambiance that creates the holiday.[64] Vital's lengthy discussion focuses on the creation of the circuit of divine energy and illumination preeminently in the divine world, and the exposition involves very complex details as to the inducing of the relation between the divine attributes 'abba' and 'imma' and the influx that subsequently descends within the lower divine powers. This discussion is included in an elaboration related to Purim, a fact that seems related to the more historical aspect of that festival, which is not mentioned in the Pentateuch. Kaidanover devotes to the same distinction between the induced holiness of the festivals and the inherent holiness of the Shabbat a rather lengthy discussion. He also exploits the two meanings of the root qore', but his discussion is nevertheless unconcerned with the theosophical and theurgical aspects of the calling of the holiness by means of reading, though his focus is quite anthropocentric. I have no doubt that he did not invent the quasi-etymology mentioned above in the Lurianic source, and this is why I assume that Kaidanover (or his sources) has shifted from the theocentric interpretation expounded by Luria and followed by some other Kabbalists to a more this-worldly understanding of this distinction. According to Qav ha-Yashar there is a special world on high, which will be revealed only in the moment when the scroll of Esther is read (miqra' ha-megillah) and the blessing on the reading of the scroll is made.[65] This wondrous world, from which the soul of Mordechai comes, can be called to reveal itself, and an influx and illumination will then descend upon the head of the congregation that reads the megillah.[66] Each individual among the people of Israel should consider himself a well-prepared vessel (keli mukhan) upon which the divine spark and light will then descend.[67] Kaidanover uses the verb kavven to describe the self-awareness of the Jews that they are vessels for the descending divine power. This verb, which in Kabbalah stands for the directing of one's thoughts toward the divine, is used here to describe the status of man toward the divine.[68] In another context Kaidanover writes that when one recites the words of the Shema' (the public avowal of God's singularity and dominion) with intention, be-khavvanah, he ensures the descent of holiness on each and every limb.[69] Again, with respect to a liturgical text, the intention and the descent of holiness are described as part of one process. This special understanding of kavvanah should be compared to the uneasiness toward the praxis of the Lurianic understanding of the term.[70]

As Kaidanover admits immediately following the above discussion,[71] he found his views in the writings of R. Hayyim Vital. Yet because he does not cite his source explicitly, I am not quite sure whether it is also possible to find in Vital an anthropocentric understanding of the Lurianic discussions. In any case, the inclusion of such an understanding in a popular book, as Kaidanover's was, may be taken as a sign that it had become much more prevalent. This anthropocentric shift can be discerned in a series of Hasidic treatments of the double meaning of the term miqra'. I suggest that this shift has something to do with the impact of R. Moses Cordovero.[72]

IV. THE COMPLETION OF THE ZOHAR

As we have seen, for a later Kabbalist the book par excellence was not only the Bible but also the classic of Kabbalah, the Zohar. Composed at the end of the thirteenth and the beginning of the fourteenth century, the huge Zoharic corpus at the same time became a canonical and sacred book.[73] The special status of a book that is both a commentary on the Bible and a canonical and (according to some traditions) revealed text invited more magical approaches to the book. Here I would like to point out the existence of two ways in which this book is conceived to be a conduit of secrets from above, either by bringing those secrets down in terms reminiscent of magic activities or by drawing down parts of this book.

R. Moses Cordovero, a Kabbalist who prepared the longest extant commentary on the Zohar, wrote that

> because this compilation is composed from the attribute of Moses our rabbi, peace be unto him, that is [the sefirah] of Tiferet, in the secret of Da'at, and all its secrets flow from it, and it is called by its name, the Zohar . . . and because the book is related to his attribute, he must help with all his might to draw down the secrets, and he has the ability to be impregnated in R. Shim'on and make the secrets of the Torah flow in him . . . and this is the reason it is called the Book of Splendor, as its light is in the secret of Da'at, the degree of Moses our rabbi, peace be unto him, to him the springs of wisdom are open, and he draws them and transmits them from the [divine] pipes through the soul of Rashby, peace be unto him.[74]

Cordovero capitalizes on a concept explicated in much greater detail and in a systematic manner in his Pardes Rimmonim, which attributes, in good Neoplatonic terms, to each soul an organic connection between man's lower soul and his supernal one. This connection is designated as a channel.[75] R. Shim'on's soul was connected to the source of the Torah, Moses' attribute, the sefirah of Tiferet, and this is why he became instrumental in the drawing down of the secrets of the

Torah in his book, the *Zohar*. Cordovero also emphasizes R. Shim'on's corporeal preparations, which ensured his role as an appropriate transmitter.[76] The resort to the term *tzinor*, "pipe," the mention of drawing down, *li-sh'ov*,[77] and the term *hakhanah* "preparation," point to the impact of the talismanic magic I have described. Being connected to the supernal springs of wisdom and possessing a soul almost identical to that of Moses, the alleged author of the *Zohar* could bring down the secrets. This extraordinary understanding is not merely speculative, as one might conclude from the resort to the concept of Da'at, but a more ontic sucking from a supernal source by the mediation of the spiritual pipes. This process is understood, to be sure, in terms of both knowing secrets and illumination, but the result is much more concrete: a canonical book has been compounded. Given the more concrete aspects of the description of Rashby's body and mouth, I am inclined to accentuate the magical aspect of the descent of the *Zohar*, in addition to the spiritual aspects.

Despite a huge commentary on much of the Pentateuch and other parts of the Hebrew Bible, the *Zohar* forgoes comment on some important biblical books, including the books of the prophets and Psalms. Though no one felt that the *Zohar* is an incomplete writing, some traditions claimed that originally it was a much more extensive book.[78] Nevertheless, during the first centuries after the emergence of the *Zohar* there were no attempts to supply the missing parts, although attempts to imitate its style were not totally absent. Then at the beginning of the eighteenth century a young Kabbalist, R. Moses Hayyim Luzzatto, better known by the acronym Ramhal, started to compile Aramaic treatises that not only imitate the style of the *Zohar* but in some cases also claimed to supply commentary on those parts of the Bible that remained unaddressed by the *Zohar*.[79] It is not my purpose here to enter the complex issue of these writings but to bring the raison d'être of their composition, as indicated by their very author:

> When the *Zohar* is revealed, and when the treatises are accomplished, in an appropriate manner, the people of Israel will be redeemed completely. But the *Zohar* will never cease, because each and every day it will be increased and enhanced, and from it all the people of Israel will draw their maintenance, even all the supernal angels will be maintained, higher and lower. And when the wisdom [of Kabbalah] increases in the world, "because the world will be replete with knowledge"[80] each of Israel will taste its own taste from it, each according to his capacity.[81,82]

Let me start with the basic observation, well documented in Zvia Rubin's study of Luzzatto, that a messianic enterprise is involved in the completion of the *Zohar*. In later parts of the original, or what Luzzatto calls the "first *Zohar*," the idea that the *Zohar* will be revealed at the end of time is indeed found,[83] but there the assumption is that the revelation of the *Zohar*, already written but unknown even to Kabbalists, is a symptom of the advent of the Messiah. For Luzzatto, however, revelation means completion. The revelation of the mystical book is no mere symptom of the messianic advent but its *sine qua non* condition. By writing the missing parts, one brings about redemption itself. I shall return to the mechanism of writing and redemption later on. For now, let me address the issue of the role of the book in the messianic era. Luzzatto asserts that the people of Israel will, like the angels, draw their maintenance from the completed book. This is not a totally new development, since the "first *Zohar*" had already been described by Luzzatto in similar terms as supplying the maintenance of the world in the premessianic era: "The first *Zohar* is the *Zohar* that has not been completed, but there emerged whatever part emerged, and the world was illuminated by it until now, which is [the time] that the *Zohar* has finished its completion."[84]

The illumination of the world by a book is hardly a surprising concept in the context of the book of the *Zohar*. The term *zohar* means "radiance" or "splendor," and Luzzatto offers an interesting midrash on the term: it is not only the illumination of the few Kabbalists, a noetic function that informs the very few, but a cosmic purpose, the illumination of the world, which I take it to be very close to maintaining the world. Thus, it is completion of both the noetic function and the maintaining one that is invoked by Luzzatto in the context of his literary activity. But how is such a purpose fulfilled by writing the missing parts of the book? The Kabbalist offers an explanation: "By the completion this *Zohar* has become the second one, because by its means the communion of it to Israel was completed, and since the first *Zohar* has been completed, the Shekhinah has ascended and become united with her husband."[85]

The *Zohar*, an entity conceived of as descending from above, has reached the final status of being united to Israel here below apparently by its complete descent, while on high the union of the last divine configuration, the Shekhinah, with her male counterpart will be achieved. It seems that a certain form of reparation of a break between two entities is performed by the composition of the new parts of the *Zohar*. Its incompleteness is the symptom of other deficiencies on both the mundane and the supernal planes. The nontextual forms of incompletion, namely the historical, national, and theosophical, are therefore dependent on the textual incompletion. In one of his other Kabbalistic books Luzzatto writes that "power has been given to man so that he will be able to draw the power of the Shekhinah and her light downward, by means of his soul; and He gave all the things of this world to his use, because by this [use] they also are repaired and the power of holiness drawn by him is spreading also over them."[86]

Let me emphasize the plausibility of the affinity between the Shekhinah and her light, as drawn down by man, and the very concept of the Zohar as splendor or radiance. This idea is reminiscent of the passage where the illumination of the world by the Zohar was mentioned as descending from the firmament; indeed, in that context the Kabbalist is told by the prophet Elijah, "Rashby has opened the gates in the period when they were closed, and behold how the wisdom [of Kabbalah] was concealed from the world, but for one or two [persons], in a hidden manner. And Rashby opened the gates. What is the meaning of the gates? Obviously the gates of the firmament. From there your[87] Zohar emerges, the one called the 'Zohar of the Firmament,'[88] and there the supernal arcana are comprised within a supernal light, [and] by its means he made his Zohar, [which is] the first Zohar."[89] Given that the act of drawing down is conceived of as a human strategy used for achieving the completion of the Zohar, it should reasonably be understood in terms of enhancing the descent of light on low. This is no more than an elaboration of the biblical verse that served as a proof text: the attainment of the plenitude of knowledge on earth as part of the messianic scenario.[90]

V. CALLING GOD IN HASIDISM

Only in Hasidism has the potential relationship between reading and calling, with respect to the canonic text, been exploited more explicitly than it is in the Zohar. In order to better understand the somewhat later Hasidic discussions, let me start with a short survey of topics related to the practice of reading the Torah in early Hasidism. The founder of Hasidism, the Besht, was reported by his grandson, R. Moses Hayyim Ephrayyim of Sudylkov, to have taught the following:

> How is it possible to take[91] the Holy One, blessed be He, as if He will dwell upon man? It is by means of the Torah, which is indeed the names of God,[92] since He and His name are one unity,[93] and when one studies the Torah for the sake of God and in order to keep His commandments, and abstains from that which is prohibited, and pronounces the letters of the Torah, which are the names of God,[94] by these [activities] he takes God indeed, and it is as if the divine presence dwells upon him, as it is written:[95] "in all places where I pronounce the name of God," which is the holy Torah, which is in its entirety His names, then[96] "I will come unto thee and I will bless thee."[97]

By studying the Torah for the sake of the "name" or "names," the mystico-magical scholar is viewed as if "he thereby takes the name, and he draws onto himself the dwelling of the divine holy presence."[98]

R. Dov Baer, known as the Great Maggid of Mezeritch, one of the most important followers of the Besht, apparently continued and elaborated his master's assessment: "He [God] contracted Himself within the letters of the Torah,[99] by means of which he created the world . . . and the tzaddiq, who studies the Torah for its own sake, in [a state of] holiness, draws downwards the Creator, blessed be He, within the letters of the Torah,[100] just as in the moment of the creation . . . and by the pure utterances related to the study of the Torah he draws down God within the letters."[101] The divine transcendence, implied in the concept of infinity characteristic of the state of the deity before the moment of creation, is attenuated by an act of contraction, the self-limitation of the divinity within the particular letters of the Torah, which serves as the paradigm for the subsequent creation of the world. As a cosmogonic paradigm, those letters are also a reification of the divine in His contracted aspect. In fact, some Kabbalistic views and many Hasidic ones represent interesting cases of what I propose to call *linguistic immanence.*[102] The Torah as revealed to man, when studied by the perfecti, serves as the tool for the re-creation of the cosmogonic acts; study evokes and reproduces the first constitutive moments of the world by invoking the divinity into the letters. However, as the above text explicitly indicates, it is not the hieroglyphic, written aspect of the letters but their utterance, namely the individual performance of each of the letters by the righteous, that is involved in the process.

This invocation of the divinity by a phonic talismanics should not automatically be distinguished from a strong mystical purpose: the cleaving to the immanent God.[103] The Great Maggid expressed this view in various ways, and only a very few of them will be discussed here. In a collection of his teachings entitled 'Or ha-'Emmet we find what seems to me to be one of the most magical of the Hasidic formulations of manipulating God by means of the sacred text, again in the context of the divine contraction: "It is as if God has contracted Himself into the Torah. When one calls a man by his name, he puts all his affairs aside and answers to the person who called him, because he is compelled by his name.[104] Likewise God has as if contracted himself into the Torah, and the Torah is his name,[105] and when someone reads[106] the Torah they draw God, blessed be He, downwards toward us, because He and His name are one total unity with us."[107] The hidden affinity between God, His Name, and the Torah is a fundamental assumption that informed many of the Hasidic views of talismanic magic. Though close affinities, and sometimes even explicit identities, between these three topics appear in many Kabbalistic texts since the thirteenth century, only in Hasidic literature were the talismanic implications of such a view explicated in a rather extreme manner. Yet extreme as this magical assumption is, namely that God can be compelled by His name to descend, the mystical implication is also evident: the "callers" will cling to the descending deity and thereby attain a mystical union.

Similar views can be found in writings of one of the Great Maggid's most important students. R. Shne'or Zalman of Liady, the founder of the Habad or Lubavitch school, one of the most intellectualistic trends in Hasidism. R. Shne'or Zalman claims that the Bible is called miqra'

> because one calls [or reads] and [subsequently] draws down the revelation of the light of the Infinite, by means of letters, even if he does not comprehend anything at all . . . and the drawing down is by means of the letters precisely, and this is the reason that despite the fact that he does not understand the meaning[108] he is able to draw, whereas in the case of the oral Torah, clothed as it is within [the sefirah of] Hokhmah, he cannot draw down except on condition that he understands. In the case of the written Torah, however, he draws [down] even if he does not understand, as it [the drawing] does not depend upon understanding to such an extent [as the Oral Torah does], because the source of the drawing down[109] is higher than [the sefirah of] Hokhmah etc., it means that it [the drawing] is [done] by means of the letters, and this is why the written Torah is called miqra', because we call and [then] draw [down] by means of the letters.[110]

As mentioned above, the Hebrew verb qore', translated here as "call," can also mean "read." Here the reading of the Torah is understood more as a recitation, an actual calling to God, an invocation that is very powerful because it is accomplished by means of letters, whose origin is higher than the realm of Hokhmah, the second sefirah. Moreover, according to another passage, this drawing down is possible by virtue of a special feature of the biblical text: its constitution by a continuum of divine names.[111] A most interesting parallel to our passage is found elsewhere in the same treatise: "The whole Torah is [consists] in the names of God, blessed be He, which are the aspects of the letters of the Torah, and this is the reason that it is called miqra', which is derived from the term qeria'h [understood as "calling"], because he calls him by His names, and because of this He makes Himself available [poneh 'atzmo]."[112] In this context the hamshakhah, the act of drawing down, is also mentioned, defining the whole Torah as capable of drawing down from the sefirah of Hokhmah. Elsewhere in the same book the calling and the drawing down are again mentioned together.[113]

To remain in the same Hasidic school, in a collection of Hasidic traditions R. Hayyim Liebersohn quotes R. Shne'or Zalman's grandson, the mid-nineteenth-century master R. Menahem Mendel of Lubavitch, as declaring that "the study [of the Torah] and the [recitation of the] prayer, despite the fact that they [the students] do not intend the meaning of the words, because the letters are from the Torah, they [the words] are vessels for the dwelling of God."[114] This hyposemantic approach is reminiscent of the views of the Safedian Kabbalist R. Moses

Cordovero, who also emphasized the importance of performance while marginalizing the role of understanding. What seems more evident, however, in the Hasidic sources is the nexus between the act of recitation and the descent of the divine power into the continuum of the divine names. In more theological parlance, the proclamation of the divine by the ritualistic recitation of the Torah as divine names brings about the manifestation of the divine within this ritualistic performance. In the above quotes these two aspects are not distinct theological approaches but phases of a single, more complex process. Let me adduce now a quote from one of the most widespread books in Hasidism, studied in some circles up to the present day, Tanya' by the same R. Shne'or Zalman of Liady:

> To understand how the reader of the stories of deeds [that are found] in the Torah[115] is connected to the Life of the World,[116] according to what is written in [the book of] Kavvanot, fol. 16b, [you should know that] just as man is preoccupied here below [with the Torah], so is the configuration of the supernal man on high,[117] etc., and so it is insofar as the rumination[118] about the written letters [is concerned]. However, regarding the utterance, it should be said that it cuts a way through and ascends to the [world of] emanation itself, or to the [world of] creation by means of intellectual awe and love, or to the [world of] formation, by means of natural awe and love, and by means of the miqra' it ascends from this world to the ten sefirot of making, because it cuts off the airs etc. This is [however] not the case insofar as the rumination is concerned, which [affects] but the [supernal] configuration, which is the root of his soul etc. And what is written in the Zohar, III, fol. 105,[119] that the rumination does not affect anything . . . the thought remains there and adds there a great light, by the addition and the multiplication of the light within the [world of] emanation by means of miqra' and the practical commandments in the [world of] Making. The quintessence of the unification is on high, but its fruits [alone] refract on the lower world, by means of drawing a little bit of light from the small [configuration][120] downward, by means of the utterance and of the deeds, this not being the case for the rumination, which does not draw down anything.[121]

In this passage the medieval axiology, which conceives of thought as higher than both deeds and speech, is accepted by R. Zalman Shne'or of Liady. Thought, mahashavah, alone is able to reach the highest world of emanation and to have an impact on the augmentation of the light within this realm. Thus theurgy, namely the operation concerning the influence on divine realms, is a matter of activation of thought, which is conceived of as operating on high. Yet the magical act of drawing down a small part of the light is possible only by means of religious speech and deeds. Theurgy, expounded here in rather mentalistic terms, unlike in the same author's *Liqqutei Torah*, is understood as a precondition of magic, which may or may not follow the enhancing of the light within the divine realm. These two effects on extrahuman worlds depend on different acts performed by man.

The double occurrence of the term *miqra'* is important for understanding the whole passage. It is the performance of the *miqra'* that is the instrument of the ascent to the first and lowest of the four worlds characteristic of the later Kabbalah. From this point of view, it is certainly not the most sublime of the religious acts, yet it alone ensures the effective connection between human needs and the supernal energy that is prone to facilitate their accomplishment. According to this passage, the essence of the religious attainment is not magical but theurgical, the former being but a derivative benefit. The more abstract study of the Torah reaches the stage of the highest world, but the more mundane needs are attained by means of more material acts. It seems that the synthesis between the magical and the mystical moments, which was more organic in the writings of R. Shne'or Zalman's predecessors, is less visible in his own thought. This author, the initiator of the most intellectualistic trend in Hasidism, remains faithful to the medieval axiology recurrent in the writings of many philosophers as to the superiority of thought over deeds. Because of the inconsistency between the emphasis on the superiority of thought, which alone affects the highest realm within the divine according to the passage from the *Tanya'*, and the view expressed in *Liqqutei Torah*, which assumes that speech and letters stem from the highest sefirah, I propose to see in the latter a position much closer to the views expressed in R. Shne'or Zalman's entourage, while the former expresses more his own independent approach, which is inclined toward mentalism. The more magical approach, expressed in *Liqqutei Torah*, surmises not only a nexus between language and the highest sefirah but also one between language and the drawing down. Although the founder of Habad does not emphasize the thaumaturgical aspect of language, such a view may be adduced from a book by one of his younger contemporaries in Poland, who writes that "the genuine Tzaddiq performs miracles and wonders in the world because the supernal light is emanated onto his heart and the influxes go by his mediation, by the way of the five places of his mouth, because the mouth is the end of the head."[122]

While being a human channel for the transmission of the divine energy to this world, the tzaddiq is—according to some Kabbalistic texts but more eminently in Hasidism—also the activator and distributor of this energy. The divine dwells within the human personality, and sometimes in Hasidic literature it even takes possession of him. Thus the Hasidic theory of magic is based on the assumption of the possibility of a fusion between the divine descending power or the power found within the Hebrew letters, as performed orally during prayer or study of the Torah, and the magician. For our purposes, it is worthwhile to pay special attention to the emphasis on the role of the mouth: here the heart is the organ that collects the divine presence, while the mouth is the orifice whence the divine power goes out in order to perform miracles. Pronunciation is, according to this passage, the manner not of collecting but of distributing the supernal light. This apotheosis of the role of the mouth is typical of an orally oriented culture par excellence, as Hasidism is. This turn toward the oral aspects of the Bible and liturgy, evident already at the end of the fifteenth century in R. Yohanan Alemanno's thought, became more pronounced in the sixteenth century and culminated in Hasidism. Interestingly, it is since the beginning of the sixteenth century that the various Protestant Christian reformers and groups have emphasized the importance of reading the Bible aloud.[123]

The dwelling of the divine on human utterances is a mystical version of the talismanic view. According to the Hasidic view, however, the divine presence means much more than a talismanic attraction of the higher by the lower. The act of dwelling on man, more precisely on his mouth, is accompanied by a strong mystical experience: an anesthetic state, which includes both self-oblivion and union with God in an atemporal experience. The human body becomes the house of God, as God dwells on the words of the Torah and of prayer.

VI. CONCLUDING REMARKS

The direct experience of the divine presence, so crucial for this theory of magical text and language, is related to an attenuation of their importance as conduits of meaning. As we have seen in various Hasidic texts and their Kabbalistic sources, the centrality of meaning transcends both the plain sense and the esoteric sense[124] in favor of oral performances, implying the restitution of the primacy of the spoken language. La langage parlé, which amounts to a magical incantation of the divine emanation, is reminiscent of the move away from meaning in some developments in modern literary language, when the emergence of a langage poétique, in lieu of the langage classique, to use the terminology of Roland Barthes,[125] was described as accompanied by a monadization of language that opens it to the supernatural world: "Le simple recours à une parole discontinue ouvre la voie de toutes les Surnatures,"[126] Barthes writes. "Le geste oral vise ici à modifier la Nature, il est une demiurgie; il n'est pas une attitude de conscience mais une acte de coercition."[127] As in some forms of modern poetry, or in what Barthes has called langage poétique, so in the theory of language of some Jewish mystics who attributed to language a great importance, language has been monadized. Indeed, the Hasidic emphasis on a talismanic linguistic approach to the Bible or the liturgy was coupled by an atomization of language. The fascination with the magical power of language exercised such pressure on it that language disintegrated into its components.

This more activistic or ergetic approach to Hasidism differs from the more quietistic understanding of this lore. Hasidic mysticism has been envisioned by Rivka Schatz-Uffenheimer as including moments of suppression of linguistic performance in favor of a purely spiritual worship.[128] By doing so, she took the part of the philosopher in the above-mentioned dispute between him and the theurgist beginning in late antiquity. The Hasidic masters, however, ignorant as they were of modern predilections, took, in my opinion, the part of the theurgists. My position should be understood as differing substantially from the claims of Schatz-Uffenheimer, insofar as she deals, rather emphatically, with what she believes was a suppression of speech in some cases of mystical prayer; there can be no doubt that moments of sublime contact with the divine realm, which may also imply silence, are to be found in Hasidic literature, but the question is whether ritualistic prayer at its peak has been understood by Hasidic masters as culminating in a process that is solely mental, as Schatz-Uffenheimer argues. The dominant mode of thinking and acting, as expressed in the Hasidic texts, prefers, in my opinion, a strong and positive role for language in this kind of mysticism. This strong language is able, according to many Hasidic masters, to induce the dwelling of the divine presence in a manner that seems to be more direct than the claim of symbolistic Kabbalists. Indeed, the above analyses of talismanic canonic texts as one of the major models in Kabbalah should be understood as part of a much greater complexity, which includes both talismanics and theurgy. The Bible was not the only entity interpreted in such a way by the Kabbalists; the biblical commandments, the Temple, and the land of Israel, as well as other topics, have been reinterpreted in the same vein.[129]

Does the feeling that God is drawn into the human realm and experienced there, within the confines of the mundane world, detract from the more "classical" notion of mysticism? The answer depends on what definition of mysticism, and of the Godhead, we adopt. If the deity is regarded as a totally spiritual and unchangeable power that cannot be activated and influenced by human ritual, the talismanic interpretation of religion may be regarded as a self-styled form of magic, which lacks the "true" mystical trait of disinterested contact between two spiritual entities. This view, acceptable as it may be for some forms of spirituality and widespread though it is in studies on mysticism, should not be regarded as exclusive, just as the symbolic interpretations so recurrent in Kabbalah should not be accorded a higher axiological status than that of the talismanic or theurgical views of language.[130] Indeed, I am inclined to accept the self-consciousness of the medieval and modern authors as an important, though not unique, criterion for understanding their experience. For those talismanicians, the act of *devequt*, the experience of a mystical communion, or sometimes union, with the divine realm, has not been precluded by their emphases on talismanic perception of the Bible. And from my point of view as a scholar, I do not see an actual difference between the claim of a Western mystic that God is present within, or reached by human spirit, and the argument of a Kabbalist or a Hasidic master that God can rather be attained within or by the activation of human language.[131]

Indeed, given that the talisman as described above is constituted by the sounds uttered by the Hasidic master, and that God's emanation is brought down onto it, the categories of mysticism and magic often converge. The induction of the divine within the human body can be seen as both mystical and magical. These two categories, which may sometimes reflect distinct forms of religious attitudes, should not be too simply and drastically distinguished from one another. At least insofar as Jewish texts are concerned, magical elements present in many of the mystical writings do not by themselves attenuate their mystical characteristics. This seems to be the case already in the Heikhalot literature in early Kabbalah and, as we have seen, in later developments of Kabbalah and Hasidism.

It seems that the talismanic view of language combines within it traits of what the French thinker Jacques Maritain has called the magical sign and the sacramental one. Maritain views the magical sign as having as its end "the exercise of power over nature or over powers on which nature is dependent."[132] On the other hand, the sacramental sign "has as its end the interior sanctity to be produced in the soul."[133] In the account of the Hasidic view of text and its performance as discussed above, as well as of many of its Kabbalistic sources, Maritain's sacramental moment, which is comparable to what I have described here as mystical, precedes the magical moment. Indeed, to dwell once again on the interesting distinctions proposed by this French thinker, the magical moment of talismanic linguistics is more socially oriented, namely it is part of the influence that the Hasidic righteous claims he can impart on his followers, while Maritain characterizes the magical sign as "the nocturnal kingdom of the mind."[134] In my opinion, Thomas Merton's formulation of the effect of a mystical experience is more congenial to the way I have portrayed the relation between mysticism and magic. Merton claims that "contemplation, at its highest intensity, becomes a reservoir of spiritual vitality that pours itself out in the most telling social action."[135]

From this vantage point, the mystical moments that precede the magical acts, as well as the mystical overtones of talismanic linguistics recurrent in Hasidic literature, invalidate Martin Buber's unilateral "spiritual" interpretation of Hasidism as a distinctly nonmagical form of mysticism. The "rarified" and most "sublime" version of Hasidism in his otherwise very sensitive writings has overlooked the important role played by Kabbalistic theories of magic for the spiritual physiognomy of the different types of Hasidism.[136] Buber's own emphasis on the dialogical principle in Hasidism, as part of his broader philosophical project, has led to an underestimation of the technical role played by voice and recitation of the text in Hasidic mysticism.

6

TORAH STUDY AND MYSTICAL
EXPERIENCES IN JEWISH MYSTICISM

One who desires the Torah imagines he possesses all the beautiful things of
the world.
—R. ELIJAH HA-KOHEN 'ITHAMARI OF SMYRNA, *MIDRASH HA-'ITHAMARI*

I. THE MYSTIC AS ACTIVE READER

The biblical attitude toward the recipients of the divine message surmised rather
obedient personalities, envisioned as consumers of the revelation who yielded to
the divine will and fulfilled the religious imperatives, which were considered
semantically transparent. Living in what was believed to be a pressing presence of
the divine in daily life, a life punctuated by miracles, there was no significant role
for the religious creativity of the believer. With the emergence of the canonical text
as intermediary between the Author and the religious consumer, the situation
changed. According to rabbinic stands, the divine text not only mediates between
the two but also separates them. In fact, there was a dramatic shift between the
paramount role of the Author in the Bible and His modest place in the hermeneu-

tic process in rabbinic literature. In the latter, the most significant role moved to the interpreter, who was not only expected to study the divine revelation but, to use a famous phrase, to enhance the Torah and aggrandize it.

One of the modern contributions to hermeneutics argues that there are no texts but only readers. In a more moderate form, thinkers like Mikhail Bakhtin would say that beyond exploring the author's intention, there is an additional dimension related to the text: the creative comprehension that enriches humanity.[1] This may constitute a reaction to the type of assumptions characteristic of Hans-Georg Gadamer's and Paul Ricoeur's theories, which celebrate the view of a "matter of the text" or a "world of the text" as if it were a world apart, one that imparts the many modes of reading to readers. There are, however, different sorts of texts and different attitudes of readers toward these texts. Just as beauty is in the eyes of the lover, so the significance of a text is to a great extent in the mind of the reader. Both the reader and the lover react to a certain external reality, which is envisioned in accordance with the nature of their feelings.

In the case of canonical writings, however, the situation is much more complex. The religious text is conceived of not only as the writing of a certain divine author but also as the representative of a higher being in the mundane world. It is read not only to receive a message, be it ethical, ritualistic, or cosmogonical, but sometimes also to enjoy a feeling of closeness with the author, who is thought to be eternal. Thus, the religious reader brings along a vision of the author, sometimes shaped by earlier perusals of the same document, in order to read the document from this perspective. This is a rather tautological way of thinking, but it is nevertheless the clue for understanding the hermeneutical circle in many mystical encounters with sacred texts.

However, the image of the divine author changes with time, and a belated reader will encounter difficulties in matching his present image to a much earlier text, which demonstrates a rather different theology. These discrepancies have provoked tensions and subsequent attempts to mediate between the ancient and the modern. Later theologies have often been projected on earlier texts by resorting to the two-level meaning of the text, one of which is the arcane, imagined also to be hidden and more sublime. From such a perspective, reading a sacred text may be envisioned as entering into a new spiritual realm, an entrance that consists in the discovery of supreme knowledge or in the encounter with the divinity.

In some intellectual circles of medieval Judaism, the scriptures underwent a process of arcanization. However, the belief in or attribution of a secret dimension to the canonical texts, and its subsequent discovery by complex exegetical methods, is only rarely a purely intellectual exercise. The very belief in the existence of a secret layer or layers of a text that may be discovered and disclosed to others assumes the possibility of contacts with dimensions of reality that are only rarely the common experience of a religious person. I would say that the expansion of the significance of the text to such sublime realms sublime as that of divinity itself, of which we have seen abundant examples in Chapter 3, invites forms of experience that differ from the decoding of the plain sense of a text that deals basically with human affairs and from its conveying to others. Indeed, this more experiential reading of sacred text should be compared with the more general emphasis in modern literary criticism on the importance of experience in the process of reading, as formulated by Wolfgang Iser, who contends that "meaning is no longer an object to be defined, but is an effect to be experienced."[2] Even more so when the studied text is conceived of as divine or at least as stemming from the divine, as we had seen in Chapters 2 and 3. In the following, however, we shall be dealing with an event more complex than reading: interpretation, which involves, in the cases of Jewish mystics, not only an experiential moment but also an ergetic act, namely an act that allows understanding by the process of doing, which imprints the interpreted text with valences of their own. Let me inspect the experiential implications of the arcanization of the Bible and its decoding.

II. ON SECRETS AND MYSTERIES

Secrets are an integral part of life and as such are a part of many religious systems. Self-reflection will easily show that intimate experiences that remain in the realm of the inner life, and are hardly shared with others, do nevertheless contribute to one's idiosyncratic personality. Secrets are part of the self-definition of a religion, just as shadowy personal secrets contribute to an individual's self-perception. Again, just as in life, secrets in some religions grow with time and thus become much more numerous and even more formative. Later forms of some religions are also more inclined to include secret dimensions, a circumstance that should be taken into consideration when attempting to describe these religions. Processes that occurred in rabbinic Judaism represent an interesting example of the gradual and comprehensive process of arcanization of its contents.

It is the nature of these secrets, much more than their number, that is a constitutive factor of certain religions. Secrets of nature ostensibly differ from secrets of history, political secrets differ from theosophical ones, and secrets of sacred scripture differ from oral secret traditions. A typology of secrecy, the understanding of the cumulative importance of the various secrets, and of their changes and continuities, is therefore a precondition of a more sensitive description of the spiritual physiognomy of certain religions. With time religions evolve, and some of these changes may be discerned in the number and nature of the secrets that survive, are adopted from outside, or become influential. Though no accurate description can be generated by overemphasizing the importance of the domains of secrecy, ignorance or even only neglect of this area will produce a simplistic, sometimes monochromatic picture of certain religiosities. Though many scholars of religion, among them also students of Judaism, may attempt to avoid engagement with this realm of shadows, this seems to be more the effect of an Enlightenment preconception than a dictate of reason. Today we, who are a bit freer from those shadows generated by the century of lights than our predecessors were, may better encourage the exposition of the history and phenomenology of secrecy without too many apologetic and polemical concerns. I shall divide the more concentrated analyses of secrets in ancient Judaism, a topic that is indispensable for the later developments of medieval secrecy, into two parts: the first will deal with the more experiential dimension of believing in and finding a secret layer within the scriptures; the second, in the next chapter, will offer some historical observations related to the emergence of secrecy.

In a famous passage on the nature of the mystery experience, Aristotle distinguished between mystery and philosophy by describing those who had undergone the mystery rite as having been affected and suffering rather than as learning.[3] This experiential aspect of being initiated into mysteries is quintessential for these religions, even if one may argue that learning quite often involves some forms of experience. Thus, though I would refrain from overemphasizing radical differences between extensive corpora, I would claim that in ancient Jewish esotericism—with the notable exception of the Therapaeuts, Philo of Alexandria, and related Alexandrian Jewish phenomena where the importance of contemplation is more evident[4]—the experiential element was combined much more with the idea of learning than it was in the Greek mystery religion ambiance. Because of the loaded meaning of the term "mystery," as referring mainly to an experiential event and less, if at all, to learning, I have decided not to use this term in the following discussions and to prefer such terms as "secret" and "arcanization." The latter term can be understood as referring to both conscious and unconscious efforts to introduce secrets into the canonical texts, as the result of either a systemic development or a crisical situation.[5]

The systematic use of the term "secret" in the following discussions contends that the topics it covers are issues that can be understood in themselves and used in a technical way in order to reach certain magical and mystical effects; unlike the inexhaustible significance inherent in a mystery, there is an exhaustible feature in the concept of secret, either by understanding it or by using it. A secret therefore is something to be kept away from someone, though it be fathomable in itself.[6]

On the other hand, the term "mystery" stands, as I understood it, for a topic, a state of things or a deep personal experience whose ultimate meaning does not invite, or even totally escapes, a discursive explanation. This seems to be the way the term is used in ancient Greek and Hellenistic mystery religions and sometimes in Christianity.[7] So, for example, we learn from Tertullian's description of the Christian mystery that "in the old revelation this mystery of the Cross had to be cloaked in images. For had it been divulged naked and without images, the outrage would have been even greater. And the more grandiose this mystery of the Cross was to become, the more it had to remain in the shadow of images, in order that the difficulty of the understanding should forever impel men to seek the grace of God."[8]

It is a decoding of the earlier in accordance with the later, the fathoming of the shadows that will reveal their esoteric meaning only by another event, divine grace, as a condition of understanding, the need to transcend the visible—the image of the Cross, for example—in order to reach what is called its mystery, which means a move from the simple to the complex. Or, as Hugo Rahner put it, "the mystery of the Cross is God's great wisdom, discernible in the foolish little symbol."[9] A tension between the simple sense of the entity to become a symbol and the divine is operative in this type of symbolism that creates mystery.[10] In pagan mystery religion and, *mutatis mutandis*, in Christianity this experiencing of the mystery brings salvation and even instant transformation, as we shall see below. In this text I would like to point out the occurrence of the term "grace" as the purpose of the spiritual path. Thus, the religious discipline depends ultimately on the divine response, which cannot be fathomed. It seems to me that the concepts of mystery and grace are complementary, because no exhaustive understanding of the mystery is possible or even attainable by means of the human independent ratio. The emphasis on belief and faith in the unique nature of the *fatum* of the redeemer creates another attitude toward the core of a religion, which differs from the emphasis on the importance of the study of a book and the performance of its commandments—as understood by a particular elite—as in the case of rabbinic Judaism. The latter form or religion is more connected to a category that I have proposed to designate as *via perfectionis*, in comparison to the gist of Christianity, which I have proposed to call *via passionis*.[11] Needless to say, the terminology for pointing to those two different religious modalities does not imply any value judgment.

In my opinion, the concept of mystery, so important in both Christianity and mystery cults, does not play an important role in ancient Jewish texts, including the mystical ones, composed in Hebrew. Interestingly, the occurrence of the term *mystorin* in rabbinic texts—a conspicuous loan from the Hellenistic surround— often stands for a type of lore that can be explained and argued, such as the

Mishnah.[12] In other cases, when it stands for the divine name, the circumstance that its precise nature is not known to one is paramount, rather than the fact of its essential ineffability. In these cases the secretive, not the mysterious, character of the sacred name is referred to by *mystorin*.[13] Indeed, in one instance *mystorin* occurs in a passage paralleling a talmudic discussion where the term "[divine] name" is found. In a relatively ancient midrash it is written that "the serving angels had seen that the Holy One, blessed be He, gave the Torah to Moses, [and] they too gave him *mystorin*."[14] Elsewhere it stands for the sign, or perhaps process or ritual, of circumcision.[15] In all those cases it expresses the esoteric rather than the ineffable quality. Interestingly, this loan, which recurs several times in rabbinic texts, is never found in the texts that constitute the bulk of the Heikhalot literature, despite their frequent resort to secretive terminology. In other words, while the concept of arcanization as used in this book implies moments of secrecy or esotericism, the category of mysteriousness, absent from the Hebrew texts alluded to above, stands for the essentially unexplainable, and therefore the aspect of esotericism would be much less important, though it is not totally absent.

In line with this observation, I am inclined in most cases to prefer to translate the terms *raz*, *sod*, and *seter* as "secret" rather than "mystery."[16] This tendency is, however, applicable in the context of ancient Jewish mystical and nonmystical texts alone. In the medieval literature these terms reflect a much more complex situation where the sense of the mysterious is most often appropriate. I shall have more to say about the concepts of secret and arcanization in the next chapter. Let us focus in this chapter not so much on the content of the secrets as on the way they can be reached and expounded.

Though the form of some of the secrets in Heikhalot texts is quite unintelligible, as they consist in series of *nomina barbara*, they were used, according to some texts, as technical means to achieve intelligible goals: they magically facilitated the understanding of the plain sense and the increasing of the Torah, which may mean either expanding it or fathoming its content more deeply. It is a nonmysterious, in fact ordinary goal that is sought by the Heikhalot mystic by means of the secret. The power inherent in a restricted type of knowledge and practice assists the enhancement of the mental capacities so that the mystic can operate much more efficiently. The move is thus from the more complex, unfathomable *nomina barbara* to the simple. According to other texts (to be discussed below), a vision of God is reached by means of study, but also in these cases the mysterious element is absent. On the one hand, the mystery goal involves not only a transformation of the initiate but a radical change: a deep alienation from one's prior personality. So, for example, we learn from a statement by a participant in an Eleusian mystery rite:

"I came out of the mystery hall feeling like a stranger to myself."[17] On the other hand, in the Heikhalot literature the transformation would be more of one's way of perceiving the world: the intensification of one's spiritual faculties or a vision of the world as if new.[18] Again, while the mysteries invite various types of allegorization, mystical or more philosophical, because of their more amorphous content,[19] such a move is not part of the early Jewish esoteric literature or its understanding of the secrets.[20] Moreover, whereas in the mysteries the initiates undergo a drama, in which the already initiated also participate, as the central part of the rite, in the Heikhalot literature the initiation may start with a much more modest event and then move toward an internal shift within the mystic. These differences notwithstanding, it should be emphasized that both the mystery religions, Christianity and the Heikhalot literature, are Erlösungsreligionen, since by means of both mysteries and secrets a salvific state is achieved. They share a great emphasis on the immediacy either of the spiritual transformation or of the knowledge that the initiates are saved. These are instant or easy religiosities,[21] because both the mystery and the secret serve as a short circuit. The common use of strong techniques by mystery religions and by the Heikhalot mystics or the emphasis on faith in Christianity is indicative of their instant nature. Again, in both the mystery religions and the Heikhalot literature, magic is part of the ritual.[22]

III. ON EXPERIENTIAL STUDY OF TEXTS IN ANCIENT JUDAISM

Though dealing with secrets that can be exhausted and also transmitted I assume that their discovery in the canonical text and their disclosure of secrets to others involve an experiential dimension of fathoming the text. This guess is based on the existence of at least three texts found in the rabbinic and Heikhalot literatures which point out the possibility of a paranormal experience as the result of intensive study of the Torah. One is the famous dictum in Pereq Qinyan, the last chapter of the tractate 'Avot, where it is said, in the name of the second-century Tanna' R. Meir:

> Whoever busies himself in Torah for its own sake merits many things: and not only so, but he is worthy of the whole world, he is called friend, beloved; loves God, loves mankind. And he is clothed with meekness and fear, and he is fitting of becoming righteous, pious, upright, and faithful; it removes him from sin and brings him toward the side of merit. And they enjoy from him counsel and sound wisdom, understanding and strength, for it is said: "Counsel is mine, and sound wisdom; I have understanding; I have strength."[23] And it gives him dominion and the faculty of judgment. And they reveal to him the secrets of the Torah. And he is made, as it were, a

spring that ceases not, and a river that flows on, increasingly. And he becomes modest and long-suffering and forgiving of insult. And it magnifies him and exalts him over all things.[24]

The devoted student of the Torah is described here from several points of view with respect to his achievements: (i) his study contributes to an appreciation by external factors, as he becomes a friend and a beloved; (ii) the Torah adorns him with special gifts; (iii) secrets of the Torah are revealed to him by unspecified agents; and (iv) the student undergoes a transformation as the culmination of the prior gifts. The question may be raised as to whether these four achievements occur one after the other or in some way depend on each other—that is, whether understanding and strength not only precede the revelation of the secrets but also prepare the student for their reception. If this hierarchical arrangement of the achievements obtains, then we have a relatively early text testifying to the nexus between the possession of understanding and the reception of the secrets of the Torah, a theme that will be dealt with in the next chapter. The special intellectual faculty sometimes designated Binah has often been related to a very early concept found in another text of the tractate 'Avot to the effect that intellectual maturity is reached at the age of forty.[25] The higher intellectual faculty, designated by the verb BYN, is apparently a precondition of the reception of someone's else expositions of esoteric topics.[26]

According to another text, again found in a midrash, whose precise date is disputed by scholars, "if someone has read the Torah, the prophets, and the hagiographia, and studied the Mishnah, the midrash of halakhot and 'aggadot, and studied the Gemara', and studied [talmudistic] casuistry, for their own sake, [then] immediately the Holy Spirit dwells on him."[27] A close parallel to this passage is found in yet another midrash, apparently a fragment that according to some scholars belongs to the Heikhalot literature. In Midrash Mishlei it is said that God examines the scholars as to what they studied during their lifetime; after the whole range of biblical and rabbinic studies have been mentioned, a student who studied Talmud and still remembers it (mi she-be-yado talmud),[28] comes into the presence of God, who says:

Since you have studied Talmud, did you gaze[29] at the chariot, did you gaze at [my] greatness?[30] Since there is no delight in my world but in that hour when the scholars sit and study the Torah, and peer and look at and see, and ponder this immense Talmud, how my seat of glory is standing . . . the Hashmal[31] how does it stand . . . and more important than all the other [issues] is how I stand, from my toenail to the top of my head, what is the size of the palm of my hand, and what is the size of the fingers of my feet . . .

this is my greatness, this is the splendor of my beauty, that my sons acknowledge my glory, by this manifestation [middah].[32]

What is crucial from our point of view is the fact that the study of the greatness of God is not a special form of literature that culminates the rabbinic curriculum but rather a special mode of study of the whole range of classical texts. Much as in the midrashic sources, where study for the sake of study opens the student to a paranormal experience, so here the result of the special form of study opens the contemplative or even ecstatic vision of the gigantic size of the supernal world, including the gigantic divinity. Here peculiar topics of Shi'ur Qomah were seen to be achieved not by a resort to the special hymns and mystical techniques of the Heikhalot literature but by an immersion in the study of classical texts. This combination of textual studies with paranormal experiences, characteristic of the Heikhalot literature, is reminiscent of the 'Avot passage. I see no way to understand these passages, as well as others not adduced here, as pointing to a kind of spirituality that cultivates the study of texts as an aim in itself, or as absorbing some forms of information alone, while the mystical experience should be thought of as standing apart from the textual study. On the basis of this reading of a theory of mystical study, sometimes referred to as torah li-shemah, I prefer to see the use of the verb li-derosh in the mishnaic texts as pointing to an intensive approach to these three esoteric topics, and plausibly also to the texts related to these topics, which may culminate with an ascent on high.[33]

According to the Heikhalot fragment preserved in Midrash Mishlei, the mystic is able to see the divine glory during his study of the text. This is, however, not the only nexus between the two topics. In some midrashic texts, and in an important piyyut (song of praise) written apparently in the sixth century, two additional affinities between these topics surface. According to the midrashic sources, the Torah has been written on the divine arm or the divine forehead.[34] According to the piyyut, the Torah is of enormous size, just as that of the divine stature in Shi'ur Qomah.[35] Thus, the transformation of the classical texts into a certain type of transparent structure, by means of which it is possible to peer at the divine body, is not just an idiosyncratic view presented in a marginal fragment but is corroborated by additional and independent material. In other words, the mystical experience has been conceived, in some small circles at least, neither as separated from or alien to the rabbinic studies nor as an alternative to them. Thus, at least in the cases I have dealt with here, the texts have created a bridge between spiritual phenomena that modern scholarship considers to be well distinguished from each other. In my opinion, what is important in this bridge, or in the alternative to the complete separation, is the fact that literature and experience not only may coexist but also may constitute a certain continuum. It starts with the exoteric and communal but culminates in the esoteric and individual. It commences with the regular legalistic study but strives to transcend the plain sense by attaining the hidden structure of the supernal world as a reflection of the structure of the Torah. It conveys the idea that secrets, far from being alien to the letters of the canonical texts, are actually experienced by means of an immersion in the study of the content reflected by those letters. By this emphasis on literacy, the mystic achieves an aural or visual experience (or both) that infuses him with the secret depths of the written text. This stand should be compared to the view of the Prince or Angel of the Torah (Sar ha-Torah), an angelic entity that can be enticed by incantations to descend and to disclose the secrets of the Torah to the mystic.[36] Unlike the texts mentioned above, where study of the canonical literature is undertaken with intensity or devotion, in the Sar ha-Torah texts it is by means of a magical and thus hyposemantic approach to language and texts that the hypersemantic information is attained. So, for example, in one of the versions of Sar ha-Torah[37] it is written: "Get up and be seated before My throne, the way you sit in the academy. Take the crown, accept the seal, and learn the secret of the Torah: how you shall perform it, how you shall inquire into it,[38] how you shall use it. Raise the paths of your heart; let your heart gaze[39] into the Torah."[40]

I assume that the crown, keter, and the seal, hotam,[41] reflect the magically oriented approach to the Torah; they are also referred to in the verb phrases "perform it" (ta'asuhu) and "use it" (teshammeshu bo). On the other hand, the phrase "learn the secret of the Torah" (lamdu seder sod ha-Torah) seems to be paralleled by "inquire into it" (tidreshuhu). If this conjecture is correct, then the verb DRSh in this text, as well as another from the same treatise, has a distinct mystical value of discovering or expounding, perhaps in public, the esoteric meaning of the text. This enterprise is embedded, however, in a sequence of actions that includes magical ones. Not the semantic fathoming of the text, but rather some magical names and seals will accompany the mystical inquiry into the text. As the end of the above quote indicates, the study of and inquiry into the Torah culminate in a contemplation of the text, whose significance will concern us later on.

Let us turn now to another important instance where seal and crown are used in the context of Torah study. According to another Heikhalot text, God says that "this secret, that is one of the secrets that I have taken out of the house of my treasures, [and because of it] the voice[42] of your yeshivot[43] will be like calves of the stall,[44] without toil and labor, but [solely] by means of the name of this seal and the recitation of the crown."[45] Earlier in the same text it is said that by means of the seal and crown no 'am ha-'aretz—literally "people of the earth," here meaning the ignorant—will be found among those who use these means.[46] These texts have been mentioned in modern scholarship in order to characterize the nature of the Heikhalot literature. David Halperin has proposed to see this resort to magic as an indication of the lower status of the unknown authors.[47] Schaefer, on the other hand, surmises that the emphasis on magic detracts from the mystical, or more precisely the ecstatic, nature of the alleged experience that may underlie the Heikhalot literature.[48] Both scholars mention the easy magical way that circumvents the ordinary intense and laborious rabbinic study of the Torah.

Indeed, there can be no doubt that a simplification of Torah study is involved in the Heikhalot texts. Yet this simplification is introduced together with a goal other than purely legalistic discourse. This issue will be addressed below; suffice it to say here that it indicates that in the last text the magical technique does not replace study in the yeshivah but only facilitates it. The comparison of students using the seals and crowns to calves of the stall means, in my opinion, that study no longer involves great effort but is a rather easy way to attain the understanding and contemplation of the Torah within the framework of the yeshivah. In other words, magic does not totally subvert Torah study in all the Sar ha-Torah texts; in some cases it was conceived of as facilitating study, but without any increase in labor.

The verb tzofin, "gaze into," used in one of the above texts to convey the culmination of the study of the Torah, is reminiscent of the verb that occurs in many Heikhalot texts in the context of the contemplation of the Merkavah (the chariot in Ezekiel's vision), but more precisely recalls the passage from Midrash Mishlei mentioned above, where it is found again in the context of the study of certain canonical texts. The mystical nature of this last phase of the path can be extrapolated from a significant parallel found elsewhere in a text pertaining to the Heikhalot literature of Sar ha-Torah, where it is said that God, compelled by the protagonists of the Heikhalot literature, "has revealed to them the secret[49] of the Torah, how they will perform it, how they will expound[50] it, how they will make use of it. Immediately, the divine spirit appeared."[51]

The verbs in this passage parallel precisely those in the above-quoted passage from the same treatise. However, in lieu of gazing into the Torah, the appearance of the divine spirit is mentioned. This appearance is caused by magic but in itself seems to be a rather mystical experience, a circumstance that helps us better understand the mystical meaning of gazing in the other text. This is, in my opinion, not a mere reading but a rather experiential one fraught with revelatory potential. Again, in yet another passage belonging to Sar ha-Torah, if the merits of one's forefathers allow, "he may make use of the majesty of the crown and of this seal; and they are obliged to him, and he is exalted by the majesty[52] of the Torah."[53] The occurrence of the crown and the seal is reminiscent of the earlier text; and, as in that passage of Sar ha-Torah, so here a certain achievement, the glorification of the contemplator, is attained, apparently by absorbing the glory of the Torah. We may guess the nature of this gazing from a parallel text from the Heikhalot literature, where we learn that when R. Nehunya ben ha-Qanah, one of the main protagonists of the Heikhalot literature, "revealed the secret of the Torah; immediately my heart was illuminated like the gates of the Orient,[54] and the orbs of my eyes[55] gazed into the depths and the paths of the Torah, and nothing has been forgotten."[56]

The attainment of the secret of the Torah produces a special approach to the Torah, which involves both mystical contemplation, the gazing into the inner structure of the Torah, and magical attainment, the extraordinary memory.[57] The transformation of the inherent power of the eyes to contemplate the "depths and paths" of the Torah[58] into an actual act of contemplation implies a dramatic corporeal change reminiscent of the deep change involved in Enoch's transfiguration into an angel, which includes a drastic change in the orbs of the eyes.[59] The transformation of the eye when gazing into the Torah can be understood as the result of the disclosure of the greatness of God, His form or beauty (which is reminiscent of the vision of the Merkavah), found within the contemplated text. Indeed, the Torah is mentioned in many cases in a rather special manner that recalls the Merkavah: It has "chambers," hadrei torah, just as the Merkavah possesses hadrei merkavah. Thus we learn in this literature about the possibility of "the gazing into the chambers of the Torah."[60] Moreover, in the treatise Ma'aseh Merkavah, which belongs to this literature, it is written, in a rather awkward formulation, that "when Rabbi Nehunya ben ha-Qanah told me the secret of the chambers of the palace of the Merkavah, and the Torah as well, I shall not forget one of their chambers, and I saw the King of the world, sitting on the high and sublime seat."[61]

One possible reading of this rather obscure passage is that together with the secret of the chambers of the Merkavah, R. Ishmael, the recipient of this secret, was told something about the chambers of the Torah. This initiation had a double effect: he never forgot these secrets, and he saw God sitting on the seat. The fact that the two topics are discussed together suggests a certain affinity was existing between them. The mystical experience of seeing God is found here together with a more magical one, the extraordinary memory. These two issues do not appear, in this text, to be exclusive. It should be mentioned that the view that the Torah possesses chambers seems to be rather ancient; Origen indicates that he heard from a Jewish scholar a simile comparing the Torah to a house of many chambers.[62] Moreover, it seems that in Origen the very term "chambers" may, as Raphael Loewe has put it, stand for "a deep sense of intimacy."[63]

At this stage of our discussion, let us return to the magic of seal and crown.

There can be no doubt that both terms refer to magical names. Can we, however, propose a more precise explanation for the use of these two terms when dealing with the penetration into the recesses of the Torah? In my opinion, the transformative language that occurs when dealing with the experiential study of the Torah may corroborate the view that the seal and crown designate special forms of magical names that are used by the mystic as part of a journey, whether understood as metaphorical or not, according to the self-perception of the mystic. Like those who ascended to the Merkavah and attempted to defend themselves from the pernicious angels, so too those who invoked the Prince of the Torah had to protect themselves, by means of seals and crowns.[64] Likewise, it is possible to conceive the use of the crown and seal, in the context of the seat of glory, as a form of enthronement, a phenomenon apparently paralleled by the ascent of the mystic in other parts of the Heikhalot literature.[65] The seal, the seat, and the crown mentioned in the Sar ha-Torah texts conspire to allow one to attain both a mystical experience and magical powers. Their reception by the mystagogue shows that in this type of text, as in the ascent texts, the mystic has undergone a certain transformation, an apotheosis that will bring him closer to God, not only spatially but also essentially. In the Heikhalot literature God too is described as possessing a crown, a seal, and a seat.[66] There is a possible correspondence between the seal and crown on the one hand, and the phylacteries of the hand and head on the other.[67] If this was the intention of the texts, we may assume that, as in rabbinic passages where God is described as donning phylacteries, we may speak about a magical understanding of the ritual which is also fraught with more experiential overtones.

The Heikhalot literature was written in the Near East sometime in the middle of the first millennium C.E. It was transmitted to European Jewry, and the most important Jewish community was the small sect of Hasidei Ashkenaz active from the end of the twelfth century to the middle of the thirteenth century. The mystical aspects of the study of the Torah were also adopted and elaborated by those medieval masters. In the same vein as the above passages, we learn from Sefer ha-Hokhmah, an important thirteenth-century treatise on exegetical methods written by R. Eleazar of Worms, that the Torah enlightens its devoted students, and that "whoever darkens himself, day and night, in the light of the Torah,[68] [He] will enlighten his face, and he will have a splendor and ornament of the glory, 'the crown of the beloved'[69] . . . as it is said,[70] 'The wisdom of man will enlighten his face.' "[71]

The Torah is expressly viewed by R. Eleazar as tantamount to the face of the Shekhinah.[72] Therefore, the study of the Torah—and of the Talmud, according to a view to be adduced below—enables the student to become more similar to the supernal, luminous face of the divine presence and glory. An important text from the same book takes us a step forward toward a better understanding of the affinity between the human and the divine face. Just as Moses, when receiving the Torah, met God, whose face is conceived of as luminous, so too the medieval student of the Torah may be conceived of as meeting the light of the face of glory or of God. Later, in his *Commentary on the Torah*, R. Eleazar writes: "The [study of] the Talmud causes an ornament to man, and the 'countenance of his face' [qelaster panav] is bright like the splendor of the radiance of the great light, as it is said by the sages, 'Whoever studies the Torah, a thread of mercy is drawn onto him.'"[73]

Let me return to an important aspect of the phenomenology of the religious outlook of the Heikhalot literature. The mixture of mysticism and magic at the final moment of the path as proposed in those texts is crucial for the more balanced understanding of the religious goals of many of the Heikhalot texts. Gershom Scholem has emphasized the mystical goal of the ascent on high as quintessential for this type of mysticism, and Peter Schaefer, on the other hand, has emphasized the magical goal, at the same time drastically marginalizing the role of the mystical goals in the general economy of this literature.[74] Although some scholars have argued against such a drastic reduction in the importance of the mystical elements, some explicitly taking issue with Schaefer's views, the alternative that has been offered is a return to Scholem's stand as criticized by Schaefer, namely that the ascent to heaven is still paramount. I am aware of only one attempt to more carefully examine another possible way of understanding *Sar ha-Torah* as combining magic and mysticism.[75] In fact, one of the main proof texts for Schaefer's claim as to the magical nature of this literature has been his solely magical interpretation of *Sar ha-Torah*. I have opted, instead, for a mixture between the two goals.[76] Only when allowing a more balanced interplay and interface between the two ideals, the mystical and the magical, will the nature of the guiding goals of the Heikhalot literature be better approximated. Let me adduce one more example, regarding the mystical goal of the more magical of the texts in the Heikhalot literature. In the composition *Sar ha-Torah* we read:

> At the end of the twelve days, he may proceed to any aspect of Torah he requested: whether scriptures or Mishnah or Talmud,[77] or even gazing at the Merkavah. For he goes forth in a pure state, and from great abstinence and affliction. For we have in hand a teaching, a decree of the forebears and a tradition from the ancients, who wrote it down and left it for the genera-tions, so that the humble ones[78] could make use of it.[79] Whoever is worthy is answered by them.[80]

In lieu of using the "secret of the Torah," an ascetic path is introduced in this passage in order to open the way for an extraordinarily efficient, actually magical, study of the various canonical texts, which culminates in gazing at the Merkavah. I am inclined to understand the gazing at the divine chariot as the highest possible religious achievement, the peak of the studies that transcend the classical ones and attain the vision of God. Here the Merkavah stands, apparently, at the end of a spiritual path, such that the exposition of this subject is the most restricted one in the Mishnah and Talmud. At least insofar as the talmudic interpretation of the Mishnah on Hagigah is concerned, 'Elisha' ben Abuyah has contemplated the Merkavah, and this is offered as an interpretation of the term *sitrei torah*. Indeed, there are elements of magic and ascetics involved as crucial components of the path, a fact that does not, however, attenuate the contemplative goal of gazing at the divine chariot; as can be easily seen, this last text constitutes a partial parallel to the passage from *Midrash Mishlei* adduced above. I would like to ponder the relation between the study and the gazing; a possible reading would be that the verb *tzofin* means an activity that is restricted to the study of the text related to the Merkavah. Thus, a continuum between the study of the nonmystical texts and the reading of the texts dealing with the Merkavah would be ensured. Yet this possible reading is rather problematic for a variety of reasons. Let me start with a philological one: in the *Sar ha-Torah* text, the term used is *tzefiyyat ha-merkavah*. Only if we read this phrase as elliptical, namely as meaning the reading of the texts on the Merkavah which is designated as the gazing at the Merkavah, is such a proposal plausible. We would best be cautious with such elliptical readings, however, and resort to them only when necessary. Even if we allow it, for the sake of discussion, another stumbling block must be overcome. From the philological point of view, the verb TzPhH would have to be interpreted rather metaphorically in order to add to its basic meanings—look, wait, aspire—the meaning of reading or looking at a certain text. In theory such a significance is possible, but it has yet to be substantiated from the philological point of view, as well as by explaining why in this context such a reading would be more plausible. For the time being, until a different interpretation is fostered in a philological manner—and I am ignorant of such a possibility—I would advocate a more mystical interpretation of the *Sar ha-Torah* text, one that is consonant with numerous other instances in Heikhalot literature, where gazing at the Merkavah has scarcely anything to do with an act of reading.

Let me turn to one of the terms used in the Heikhalot literature, which appears in the quote above: *ha-tzenu'im*, the humble or, according to another possible translation, discreet ones. This term recurs in many sources in the context of mystical traditions, both ancient and medieval.[81] What is important for our discussion, however, is that this term occurs in a relevant context in the Talmud, Qiddushin, fol. 71a, where the transmission of the name of forty-two letters is allowed only to one who has special qualities, among them being that he is a humble person, tzanu'a, or, according to another statement found in the same passage, only to the humble ones among the priests, ha-tzenu'im she-ba-kehunah. This talmudic passage does not contain, in its form in the printed versions of the Talmud, any paramount magical element. In the Middle Ages, however, there existed a different version of this passage, as quoted by Maimonides in the Guide of the Perplexed, 1:62, and R. Todros ben Joseph ha-Levi Abulafia's 'Otzar ha-Kavod:[82]

> The name having forty-two letters is holy and sanctified and is only trans-
> mitted to one who is discreet,[83] has reached the middle of his life, is not
> prone to anger or to drunkenness, does not arouse criticism by his ways of
> life, and speaks agreeably with people. And he who knows it is heedful
> thereof and observes it in purity, is beloved on high and popular below. He
> is feared by the people, his learning is preserved by him, and he inherits the
> two worlds, this world and the next.[84]

The phrase translated by Shlomo Pines as "his learning is preserved by him" does not appear in the printed Talmud. The Hebrew is talmudo mitqayyiem be-yado,[85] which means that he does not forget what he learned. This seems to be a magical attainment, related to the extraordinary quality of the divine name, quite similar to the Heikhalot claims. At least from this important point of view, the similarity between talmudic and Heikhalot texts is paramount, an issue that should be remembered when comparing the attitude toward magic in the two cor-pora. Moreover, the tzenu'im mentioned in the Talmud are ostensibly part of the elite. One may argue, as David Halperin probably would do, that the Heikhalot literature adoption of the same term, in a similar context, is part of the appro-priation of the rabbinic elite's stands. Indeed, this is a possible explanation, but it may be no less plausible to assume that in the Heikhalot text, too, there is an effort to speak about an elite. In any case, this talmudic passage is just one of the many cases that erase sharp distinctions between the rabbinic and the Heikhalot attitudes to magic. Indeed, a valid comparison between the two types of literature should concentrate on their respective views of the same concepts and not resort to comprehensive statements about the nature of the two distinct sorts of literature.

In the Heikhalot texts there is a discontinuity between the nature of the tech-nique and the results. Magic, consisting in resorting to seals and crowns, and the knowledge of the secret of the Torah provoke the revelation of the inner structure of the Torah, but it bears emphasizing that the study of that structure is not mentioned. Not always in the Heikhalot texts are magical techniques a surrogate for conventional Torah study. It seems that the vision of the inner structure of the Torah, which implies a complex architectonics of chambers, paths, and depths, should also be viewed as a goal of the secret of the Torah.[86] If we combine this vision of the architectonics with the resort to the crown and seal, the rite that assumes the use of the secret or Prince of the Torah is even more reminiscent of the ascent on high, the enthronement and vision of the Merkavah. In any case, expressions that parallel those of the architectonics of the Torah are also known insofar as the Merkavah is concerned: the chambers of the Merkavah[87] and the depths of Merkavah.[88] Although I have not found the phrase *netivot ha-merkavah*, at least the expression *netivot 'arvot ha-raqia'* occurs.[89]

In the treatises belonging to the more restricted rabbinic orbit, however, the understanding of the secrets found in a certain text is attained by immersion in study of the same text. The rabbinic esoteric move is closer to what I have termed systemic arcanization, namely it may emerge from an intense preoccupation with text as a precondition of the attainment of its recondite layer. In other words, there is a move from the semantic toward the hypersemantic. The Heikhalot type of arcanization, however, is much closer to the crisical arcanization: it is imposed by an entity that is external to the recipient of the revelation and does not involve the prior profound absorption of the content of the text. Moreover, the few hermeneutical devices used to connect the theological stands to the sources, a rare situation in general, are part of what can be said to represent radical hermeneutics, like gematria.[90] Whereas in the rabbinic passages the studied text becomes transparent, a vehicle enabling the student to reach zones of knowledge and experience only after he has become familiar with the text, in the Heikhalot literature, which is less interested in interpretation of the canonical texts, there is a jump beyond the plain sense of the text to its secrets. The nature of the text, in this type of approach, remains semantically opaque, although its formal structure, referred to by the paths and the depths, is mystically attainable. It would be pertinent to compare these two attitudes toward the text to the Christian understanding of the Pharisean attitude. Unlike the Paulinian vision of the antagonism between letter and spirit, the rabbinic approach proposes a synthesis of the two. The mystical attitude, on the other hand, as represented in the Heikhalot literature, assumes a certain distance between the text and its secrets. In any case, the Paulinian view of the sacred text in ancient Judaism does not fit any of the main early postbiblical corpora: neither Philo nor the early rabbinic literature nor the Heikhalot treatises produced limited or comprehensive arcanizations. It would be better to assume that Paul was aware of at least some of the forms of early Jewish arcanization but attempted to solve the tension between his arcane reading of the Hebrew Bible as christological and other forms by proclaiming that actually there were no arcane readings at all.

Why such an arcanization, which operates by the transformation of the studied texts—according to the rabbinic sources—into mystical names has been ignored by modern scholarship is an issue whose detailed analysis transcends the present discussion. Such an analysis might, however, point to the acceptance of the classical Christian view of rabbinism as purely legalistic even by Jewish scholars,[91] to a vision of mysticism that disregards the possible mystical value of linguocentric spirituality,[92] and to the adoption of simplistic methodologies that encourage too stark a distinction between different types of literature that are contemporaneous, even in cases where I doubt they are helpful.[93]

IV. FROM SECRECY TO EXPERIENCE

If, according to some masters, understanding of a canonical text amounts to receiving secrets, these receptions were nevertheless preceded by a revelation, namely a certain form of mystical experience. Thus, ancient and some medieval approaches to the sacred text assume the ascent of the mystic, followed by the reception of the secrets, which sometimes consist in the magical names concealed within the biblical text. But whereas the ancient ascending experiences were related to different forms of body-shape experience, in the medieval Kabbalah the ascending entities were related to ontic extensions of human activities, like the voice, or in other cases *kavvanah*, the spiritual intention that accompanies ritualistic activities. Let me adduce an example that combines the two, from the mid-sixteenth-century Safedian Kabbalist R. Moses Cordovero:

> There is no doubt that the letters that compose each and every pericope of the pericopes of the Torah, and every gemara' and chapter[94] someone is studying which concern a certain mitzvah, have a spiritual reality that ascends and clings to the branches of this sefirah, namely that [peculiar] sefirah that hints at that mitzvah, and when the person studies the [corresponding] mitzvah or the chapter or the pericope or the verse, those letters will move and stir on high, on this reality [*metzi'ut*], by means of a "voice" and a "speech," which are Tiferet and Malkhut and Mahashavah and Re'uta' de-Libba'[95] . . . since Mahashavah and Re'uta' de-Libba' are as a soul to the "speech" and to the "voice," which are the [lower] soul [*nefesh*] and the spirit [*ruah*]. And behold, the voices and the realities of the letters [produced by] the twist of the lips bestow on them a certain act and movement [like that] of a body. And the reality of the letters ascends, and it is found everywhere on the way of their ascent from one aspect[96] to another, following the way of the [descending] emanation from one stage to another.[97]

This Kabbalistic master presents a comprehensive theory that involves the letters and voices together with their sources in the lower domain of the sefirotic realm, Tiferet and Malkhut, and their supernal sources, two higher sefirot, Maha-shavah and Re'uta' de-Libba'. On the psychological level they correspond to the two lower spiritual functions. This concatenation of the sefirotic, psychological, and linguistic conceptions explains, according to Cordovero, the possibility that the ascending letters might affect the higher sefirot. This dynamism of the letters, consisting in their capacity to ascend and their potential impact on the various sefirot, stems from the impetus conferred by human thought and will, which correspond to the divine thought and will. Intentional speech is an ascending human creation complementing the descending divine speech.

Another passage that embodies the relation between secrecy and experience is found in R. Hayyim Vital's influential book on the attainment of prophecy: "All the prophets followed him [i.e., Moses] by directing the people and by illuminating their eyes regarding the wisdom of the Torah and its secrets, by means of the divine spirit that enwrapped him. [Therefore] we conclude that prophecy and divine spirit must be in existence in the world, and this is an easy thing, provided that worthy men live."[98] It seems that the spiritual teachers who followed Moses were inspired and illuminated masters who taught the Jews the secrets of the Torah, which plausibly stand for the technique to attain prophecy, namely a mysti-cal experience. On this issue Vital appears to have been influenced by the pro-phetic Kabbalah of Abraham Abulafia.[99]

In an early modern form of Jewish mysticism, however, the study of the canoni-cal text itself has been conceived of as an avenue to a mystical experience. In one of the versions of the meeting between the Besht, the founder of eighteenth-century Polish Hasidism, and his most important disciple, the Great Maggid of Mezeritch, we read:

> He[100] asked me whether I had studied Kabbalah. I answered that I did. A book was lying in front of him on the table and he instructed me to read aloud from the book. The book was written in short paragraphs, each of which began: "Rabbi Ishmael said: 'Metatron, the Prince of Presence, told me.' "[101] I recited a page or half a page to him. The Besht said to me: "It is not correct. I will read it to you." He began and read, and while he read he trembled. He rose and said: "We are dealing with ma'aseh merkavah and I am sitting down." He stood up and continued to read. As he was talking he lay me down in the shape of a circle on the bed.[102] I was not able to see him anymore. I only heard voices and saw frightening flashes and torches.[103]

The passage is based on a certain ambiguity: the Besht asked his future disciple whether he studied Kabbalah, a question that may be understood as referring to the absorption of some topics related to the specific Kabbalistic lore. Thus, a fair understanding of the question and the answer is the acquaintance with some form of knowledge, which presupposes mental activity. Immediately afterward, however, the passage shifts its focus to the ability to recite a certain text, believed to be Kabbalistic, in a proper manner. Thus, an appropriate recitation of the mystical text is presented as its study. This shift is of paramount importance for understanding the new attitude toward the text: it is not so much the source of secrets as a tool for attaining an experience. Indeed, there is an affinity between the content of the text and the experience: the ancient text mentioned in the quote indeed deals with a revelation allegedly received by an ancient figure, R. Ishmael. This revelation was regarded, however, as much more articulated than what we learn from the Hasidic story. If the arcana were the purpose of the Heikhalot literature and the experience was instrumental, in the Hasidic text the arcana disappeared and the experience remained the main purpose of study.[104] This is but one major example of the process of dearcanization that is characteristic of the latest phase of Jewish mysticism.

Let me compare this conclusion, based on a rather legendary tradition, to a quote adduced in the name of the Besht by one of his contemporaries:

> Whoever prepares himself for study [of the Torah] for its own sake,[105] without any alien intention, as I was warned by my great teachers in matters of Torah and Hasidism, including [among them] my friend, the Hasid and Rabbi, who is the paragon of the generation, our teachers and Rabbi Israel the Besht, blessed be his memory, let his desirable intention concerning study for its own sake be to cleave himself in holiness and purity to the letters, in *potentia* and in *actu*, in speech and in thought, [so that he will] link part of [his] [lower] soul, spirit, [higher] soul, Hayah and Yehidah to the holiness of the candle of the commandment and Torah, [to] the enlightening letters, which cause the emanation of the influx of lights and vitality, which are true and eternal.[106]

Obtaining lights and vitality is the great achievement of the appropriate study of the Torah. Semantically they are rather inarticulate entities, important as they may be for the Hasidic mystic. The letters of the Torah are conceived of, as we have seen,[107] as conductors of divine power, and this power is one of the paramount ideals in Hasidism. Although the claim to adherence concerns quite distinct entities, the achievements are not described as discrete. No revelation is mentioned, no secrets disclosed.

Let me attempt to support this observation by pointing to a quote from the son of one of the earliest followers of the Besht, R. Mordekhai of Chernobyl. Having described the letters as containers of the divine light, he contends that they are "palaces for the revelation of the light of 'Ein Ṣof, blessed be He and blessed His name, that is clothed within them. When one studies the Torah and prays, then they[!] take them out of the secret places and their light is revealed here below. . . . By the cleaving of man to the letters of the Torah and of the prayer, he draws down onto himself the revelation of the light of 'Ein Ṣof."[108] The light of the infinite is again an energetic entity that can be caused to descend and have a positive impact on the mystic, but hardly ever in Hasidic literature would this term stand for a discrete mental topic. Penetrating to the core of the letters by the act of cleaving amounts to leaving behind the mental cargo of the word to which that letter belongs and achieving an encounter with the immanent divine force. The mentioning together of prayer and Torah study as conducive to the same result is quite emblematic. This means that what is crucial is not so much the semantic content of the texts to which one is adhering but unknown ciphers that organize those texts, whose efficacy is a matter of belief. The immersion of the student or the person who prays in the text as compounded of discreet letters enables a form of approach that is less dependent on the original content of the canonical texts and more guided by the spiritual propensities of the mystic.

The emphasis on the experiential dimension of the study of sacred texts is not restricted to the study of the Bible. A contemporary of R. Mordekhai of Chernobyl, R. Menahem Mendel of Premiszlany, contends that Kabbalistic literature is not a matter of esotericism but of ineffability stemming from its experiential basis. Explaining why the Kabbalistic lore has been described as hidden, he argues as follows:

Nistar is the name given to a matter that one cannot transmit to another person; just as the taste of [a particular] food cannot be described to a person who has never tasted this taste, so it is impossible to explain in words how it is and what it is; such a thing is called *seter*. Thus is the love and fear of God, blessed be He—it is impossible to explain to another person the love [of God] in one's heart; [therefore] it is called *nistar*. But the attribution of the term *nistar* to the lore of Kabbalah is bizarre, because for one who wishes to study [Kabbalah] the book is available to him, and if he does not understand he is an ignoramus, as [indeed] for such a person the Gemara' and Tosafot are also *nistar*. But the concealed matters in the *Zohar* and the writings of R. Isaac Luria are those based on the cleaving to God, for those who are worthy of cleaving and of seeing the supernal Merkavah,[109] like Isaac Luria, to whom the paths of the firmaments were obvious, and he walked on them [seeing his way] with his mental eyes, like the four sages who entered Pardes.[110]

Such an approach to esotericism is highly emblematic for Hasidism and important for the point I would like to reinforce: the process of arcanization, so characteristic of many types of Kabbalah, came to an end in Hasidism and to a great extent in Kabbalah in general, and the esoteric vision of Kabbalah is explicitly derided by this Hasidic master. The problems of communication created by the experiential basis of Kabbalah prevent any serious attempt to speak about this lore as esoteric. In the second half of the eighteenth century, when so many Kabbalistic books had been printed (and reprinted) and made almost as available as any other type of Jewish literature, the esoteric aura of Kabbalah faded, and with it the importance of secrecy.

Another type of Hasidic dearcanization is found at the beginning of the nineteenth century in a very influential writing. R. Qalonimus Qalman Epstein of Cracow distinguishes between the secrets of the Torah and the secret of God, mentioned in Psalms 25:14:

> It is necessary to understand the meaning of the secrets of the Torah. All Jews use this term, but what does it mean? It cannot refer to the science of Kabbalah and the writings of the Ari [Isaac Luria] of blessed memory and the holy Zohar, for a "secret" is that which cannot be communicated to others, whereas the Kabbalah, the writings of the Ari, and the Zohar can be imparted to others and explained very thoroughly to them. Consequently, these, having been revealed, are no longer secrets. What, then, is the secret that is impossible to impart? It is the "secret of the Lord," that is to say the essence of divinity that He was, is, and will be and that He is the ground and root of all the worlds. This cannot be imparted to another, but each man has his own degree of comprehension of the divine in proportion to his degree of understanding and the manner in which it is assessed in his heart.[111]

In lieu of the objective and communicable secrets of Kabbalah, the more vague and emotional experiences related to the apprehension and experience of God come to the fore in Hasidism. Its masters were not, however, content with offering their mysticism as a better version of Kabbalah but proposed another reading of Kabbalah consonant with the main propensities of Hasidic mysticism. This experiential rereading of the major books of Kabbalah, as advanced by R. Menahem Mendel of Premiszlany, is not entirely new or incorrect but addresses this lore as essentially nonesoteric. The last two quotes, whose main thrust is corroborated by many Hasidic statements, bear witness to a process of dearcanization that reached its climax in denying the secret dimension of the most important Kabbalistic corpora.

V. Bringing Down Interpretations

One of the most remarkable features of rabbinic exegesis was the exclusion of the divine from the process of interpretation. Allowing human interpretive activity its autonomy created the avalanche of exegetical literature contained in the Talmud and Midrash. This tide has been reversed, however, in many of the Jewish speculative corpora of the Middle Ages, as part of introducing more and more secrets as explanatory schemes.

The process of arcanization is connected, in some cases, with the resort to access to higher entities, which reveals the secret of the Torah. Rabbinic sources attempted to operate within the framework of the human, offering a double horizontal approach to the Bible, allowing the autonomous human intellect the capacity to penetrate the intricacies of the canonical text and discovering in that text matters concerning the social life. The process of arcanization, in contrast, created a twofold verticality related to the supernal nature of the source that reveals secrets and sometimes also to the projection of the secrets onto the supernal worlds. To a certain extent, the supernal entities reveal to the mystic secrets about themselves, the Torah being a mirror that reflects those revelations.

Let me start with a passage from an anonymous fifteenth-century Kabbalistic book compiled in Castile:

> One cannot comprehend the majority of the subjects of the Torah and its secrets, and the secrets of the commandments cannot be comprehended, except by means of the prophetic holy intellect, which was emanated from God onto the prophets . . . Therefore, it is impossible to comprehend any subject among the secrets of the Torah and the secrets of performing the commandments by means of intellect or wisdom or by *intellectus acquisitus* except by means of the prophetic intellect . . . by the divine intellect given to the prophets, which is tantamount to the secret of knowledge of the great [divine] name.[112]

There is an interesting irony in this passage. The introduction of the importance of the intellect, so characteristic of medieval Jewish philosophy, could have resulted in a strengthening of the autonomy of human speculative activity even beyond the rabbinic claim. This is not, however, the case in some forms of philosophical speculation that assumed there is an emanated or prophetic intellect, or holy intellect, higher than the one acquired by studies and speculations. This emanated intellect is just another term for the intention of imposing revelation as a superior form of spiritual activity to independent intellection. Thus, while the human intellect in *actu* is capable of understanding natural things, in matters of religion it is the emanated intellect that is indispensable.[113] Hence knowledge of the inner aspects of the Torah is conditioned on the attainment of the highest intellectual faculty, the prophetic intellect, which is seen as tantamount to a prophetic experience. Understanding the secrets is a function of blurring the gap between God as intellect and the human intellect; the latter acquires a divine, holy intellect, which is the sine qua non for fathoming the secrets of the Torah. The Pentateuch, a text thought to have been written under divine inspiration, can only be properly understood by re-creating an appropriate state of consciousness.

Of a totally different nature is the assumption that the Torah is studied in the celestial academy and that it is possible to obtain access to the results of these studies, which also contain secrets. To a certain extent this view is similar to that in the ancient apocalyptic literature and the Heikhalot, as we saw in Chapter 5. This approach sometimes assumes a pneumatic exegete, and the most interesting example with which I am acquainted is the vast corpus of Kabbalistic literature—in its extant form basically a commentary on the Pentateuch, composed in Castile around 1470—known as *Sefer ha-Meshiv:*

> You should know that the secret causing the descent of the supernal book is the secret of the descent of the supernal chariot, and when you pronounce the secret of the great name, immediately the force of the garment will descend downwards, which is the secret of Elijah, who is mentioned in the works of the sages . . . And the secret of the garment is the vision of the garment, in which the angel of God is dressed, with a corporeal eye, and it is he who is speaking to you . . . And the secret of the garment was given to those who fear God and meditate upon His name; they have seen it, those men who are the men of God were worthy of this state . . . and on the fortieth day,[114] [the garment] descended to him and showed him whatever he wished [to know], and it stayed with him until the completion of the [study of the] subject he wanted [to know]; and they[115] stayed with him day and night. Thus was it done in the days of Rashi to his master, and the latter taught him [i.e., Rashi] this secret [of the garment], and by means of it [the secret] he [Rashi] composed whatever he composed, by the means of his mentor and instructor. Do not believe that he [Rashi] wrote this down from his own mind,[116] for he did it by the secret of the garment of the angel and the secret of mnemotechnics, to explain the questions one is asking or to compose a book one wishes to compose, and [thus] were all the sciences copied, one by one . . . And this happened in the days of the Talmud and in the days of Rashi's master and in the days of Rashi too, since his master

began this [usage], and Rashi ended it, and in their times this science[117] was transmitted by word of mouth, one man to another, and this is the reason all the sages of Israel relied upon Rashi, as at that time they knew the secret. Therefore, do not ever believe that he [Rashi] composed his commentary on the Talmud and on the plain meaning of the Bible out of his reason, but by means of this force of the secret of the garment, and that [force] which dressed it, which is an angel, since by means of it he could know and compose whatever he wished . . . And those who were able to see it were like prophets, and in the time of the Talmud many used it.[118]

The garment, in Hebrew malbush, designates the transformation that every spiritual entity has to undergo when it descends to the nether worlds in order to reveal itself to men. This is also the case with the angels, like Elijah, who, according to the doctrine of Sefer ha-Meshiv, must use a garment when he descends into our world. However, if the revelation of Elijah was a commonplace in Jewish literature, sometimes even in relation to the revelations of doctrinal issues, as we learn from traditions related to the early Kabbalists, the doctrine of the garment is more specifically Kabbalistic and has a long history before Sefer ha-Meshiv, occurring, as in Neoplatonic sources, in contexts dealing with the descent of spiritual entities and their appearances to mortals, and perhaps also in formulations that are reminiscent of the Muslim view of tanzil.[119]

The precise mechanism of composition is described as copying, and the Hebrew verb stem used for it is 'TQ, which points to transmission of the sciences from their celestial source to our world by means of copying supernal books.[120] Indeed, this seems to be one of the techniques that the anonymous author of Sefer ha-Meshiv used to compose his own Kabbalistic commentary on the Pentateuch. Let me give an example of the magical nature of this copying of the books. In a magical recipe found in some manuscripts and belonging to these circles, three angels are mentioned by God as assigned to writing:

They are angels and servants from the order of the Tarshishim, and they consume fire and they will cause the descent of my force and strength. It is incumbent that they will be three: one in order to copy,[121] [and] he exists[122] in your imaginary faculty in order to copy from the book so that you should not become tired, and it is Hofni'el, the great prince, whose force is great in Torah, in order to copy. And this is the meaning of Hofni, it fills the hand of God.[123] He brings every hour [or time] you incantate to the book[!]. And Yikatvi'el, in order to write, and it is His servant and he will write everything that Yikatvi'el will inscribe. And it [the name] includes two yods, the supernal and the lower, which are inscribed, and it is the [divine] name, and it will write by the strength of God. And the secret of the third is Yihatmi'el, is sealing the twenty-two yods.[124]

To be sure, as this recipe claims, the technique of copying should be used in purity and for the sake of copying sacred books, *sifrei qedushah*, basically the books of the Hebrew Bible. The existence of such a technique demonstrates, however, that in other cases, too, the assumption was that a divine power is made to descend in order to help the copyist to reproduce the text of the sacred book. Moreover, some decades later another anonymous Kabbalist belonging to the same circle composed a series of concise commentaries on other parts of the Bible, especially a lengthy commentary on Psalms known as *Sefer Kaf ha-Qetoret*, on some scrolls, like the Song of Songs and Proverbs, on talmudic legends, and on liturgical pieces, and he likewise claims that those commentaries were descended from above.[125] The relationship between copying and causing the descent of a certain book is not clear to me. In any case, this propensity for causing the descent of supernal entities, including books and angels, culminates in claims that even the divinity may be drawn down by a certain magical technique.[126]

These passages and discussions should also be viewed from the more general standpoint of the history of the concepts of individual authorship.[127] If the commentary is an already existing composition, the commentator is not the original author but a tool or a channel for the apparition of a writing in the mundane world. No wonder the names of the author of *Sefer ha-Meshiv* and other members of this circle, whose Kabbalistic books are extant, remain unknown: they saw their activity as instrumental in transmission but did not consider themselves innovators. The only counterexample is the notorious R. Joseph della Reina, a Kabbalist known for his magical Kabbalistic activities, but not as a commentator.

Under the plausible influence of this type of magical Kabbalah, R. Shlomo Molkho, a fascinating visionary who flourished briefly at the end of the first third of the sixth century, confessed:

Sometimes in these days I see the celestial academy[128] of sages, and the books are open before them and they study the Torah and they discuss [issues concerning Torah], and they comment upon verses and statements of our sages, blessed be their memory.[129] And from their discussions I hear and learn something. And since I did not [previously] learn [Hebrew], nor was accustomed to the Holy language, I did not comprehend all their discussions. But from what I was taught there in that Holy Academy, I answer people who ask for interpretations of verses and statements,[130] which are seen as difficult to understand to the sages of [our] generation. And whoever wishes may ask me whatever he wants, to comment on recondite verses and statements, [for] with the help of God, I am confident that I may answer everyone who asks me in a satisfactory manner, sublime things which are sufficient for any intelligent person, which are not [written] in books [but] which I was instructed from heaven.[131] But I had never learned science from the mouth of a mortal master or colleague. And whatever anyone will ask me, I am allowed to answer, regarding the twenty four [i.e., books of the Jewish biblical canon], except the Book of Daniel.[132]

As in the quote from *Sefer ha-Meshiv*, here the oracular and the compository activities are mentioned together. Indeed, according to a statement adduced by a disciple of Molkho's in his name, "whoever studies the Torah for its own sake has the power to foretell the future."[133] The fact that Molkho was asked to respond to questions related to both the biblical verses and rabbinic statements should be highlighted, because it may betray an oracular attitude toward the rabbinic sources. The interpretations of this material would also, therefore, depend not only on the decisions of the rabbis below, but on a celestial academy whose discussions are caused to descend.

Molkho's view is coincident with that of his Christian contemporary Martin Luther, who contends that the understanding of scripture depends on the Holy Spirit and cannot be known before the revelation of that spirit.[134] Molkho explicitly acknowledges that his interpretations are not the result of previous studies, as he confesses his prior ignorance of Hebrew and apparently also of any substantial Jewish matters.[135] Additional instances of bringing down secrets related to the Torah and parts of the Zohar in the sixteenth and eighteenth centuries have been addressed above, and I would like not to repeat them here.[136] Let me turn, then, to some approaches that appear after the end of the eighteenth century.

In the previous section I discussed some Hasidic passages where the reward for the study of the Torah was not a mental revelation but a descent of power or light on the mystic. Representative as those passages are for the vast Hasidic literature, they do not claim that interpretations should and could be offered by Hasidic masters and communicated to their followers. As we have seen, this was a desideratum, although at least one Hasidic master contended that the Torah of the righteous should be interpreted in various manners by his followers.[137] But even when the question of offering an interpretation was addressed in Hasidic sources, it was much less a matter of mentalistic activities than of a mystical elevation to the source of all interpretations that generated the "new" interpretation. So, for example, we read in the influential book of R. Elimelekh of Lyzhansk that "when a tzaddiq wishes to comment upon a certain concept or biblical verse, before he begins to speak he shakes his [supernal] root, and the interpretation comes down to him from his root."[138] Building on Cordoverian and Lurianic psychological and theosophical views that were in turn influenced by Neoplatonism, R. Elimelekh assumes that interpretation is found already on high and is available by activating one's own spiritual source. This activation is possible because of the ontological continuum between the particular soul in the mundane world and its source within the divine one; a rope connects the two, either in order to stir the root or in order to serve as a channel for transmitting the interpretation.[139]

Indeed, the feeling of the Hasidic masters that they are offering interpretations already in existence beforehand, and that they attain these interpretations by a mystical discipline, is conspicuous in a relatively early testimony. Shlomo Maimon, a contemporary of the Great Maggid, describes the early Hasidic self-perception as follows:

Their sermons and moral teachings were not, as these things commonly are, thought over and arranged in an orderly manner beforehand. This method is proper only to the man who regards himself as a being existing and working for himself apart from God. But the superiors of this sect hold that their teachings are divine and therefore infallible, only when they are the result of self-annihilation before God, that is, when they are suggested to them ex tempore, by the exigence of circumstances, without their contributing anything themselves.[140]

These earlier passages point to concepts that were elaborated later by R. Nahman of Braslav, who expressed them in one of the most fascinating passages dealing with pneumatic exegesis:

Know that there is a soul in the world through which all the interpretations and the commentaries of the Torah are revealed . . . All the commentators of Torah receive [their words] from this soul. And the words of this soul are as hot as the burning coals, for it is impossible to draw forth words of the Torah except from one whose words are like the burning coals: as Scripture says, "Are not my words like fire?"[141] And when this soul falls from its rung, and its words become cold, it dies. When it dies, the interpretations that had come through it also disappear. Then all the interpreters are unable to find any meaning in the Torah. . . . He who wants to interpret the Torah has to begin by drawing unto himself words as hot as burning coals. Speech comes out of the upper heart . . . The interpreter [first] has to pour out his words to God in prayer, seeking to arouse His mercies, so that the heart will open. Speech then flows from the heart, and interpretation of the Torah flows from that speech . . . On this heart are inscribed all the interpretations of the Torah.[142]

I suggest understanding the phrase *yesh neshamah ba-ʿolam*, "there is a soul in the world," as a pun on the expression *nishmat ha-ʿolam*, the Neoplatonic view of the soul of the world, which is the origin of all the particular souls that descended in the mundane world. The attachment of the particular souls to the universal one is regarded in Neoplatonism—and this view reverberated in Hasidism[143]—as a mystical achievement, just as in R. Nahman's passage "all the interpreters" depend on the soul of the great interpreter, who is none other than the tzaddiq of the whole generation, namely R. Nahman himself.[144] The supernal heart, upon which all the interpretations are inscribed, is reminiscent of the universal soul but also of the Qurʾanic concept of a heavenly "guarded table," *al-lawh al-mahfuz* (see Qurʾan 85:22), upon which a more comprehensive Qurʾan was primordially inscribed, which ibn ʿArabi has compared to a heart.[145] The theme of fire is common to the Hasidic master and to the passage from R. Moses Hayyim Luzzatto analyzed in Chapter 3, and it may well be that they draw on a common earlier source, although a more emotional, in many cases an enthusiastic, turn is evident in the latter form of mysticism.

VI. STUDY OF THE TORAH AS RETURNING TO THE ORIGIN

The resort to the concept of the cosmic soul in order to explain the generation of the interpretations is part of a broader adoption of Neoplatonic cosmology and its mystical implication. Here we are concerned not with the various ramifications of the introduction of Neoplatonism for the transformations of the rabbinic ideals of perfection, but solely with the hermeneutical aspects of Kabbalah and Hasidism. So, for example, we learn from the medieval interpretations of a verse from Psalms regarding the perfect Torah, *torat ha-Shem temimah, meshivat nafesh*,[146] that the Torah is not only complete or integral but also causes the return of the soul, implicitly to its supernal source.[147] Whereas the biblical verse intends to point out that the Torah gladdens the soul of a man, or of man in general, and hence is a this-worldly experience, some of the medieval interpretations influenced by Neoplatonism introduced an other-worldly orientation, transforming study into an escapist enterprise. Thus, Torah study becomes to a certain extent a technique for personal redemption rather than a mental activity that strives toward an accumulation of knowledge. This is part of the vertical shift to which I have previously referred.

Let us inspect such an example, from the writings of a late-thirteenth-century

Castilian Kabbalist: "[King] David said that the Torah of God is perfect, etc.,[148] because just as God, blessed be He, returns[149] the soul to the body, so the Torah is emanated from Him and causes man to gain the life of the world to come, and this is *meshivat nafesh* . . . because the Torah is united with God, blessed be He."[150] The Torah is conceived of as offering an antidote to God's having caused the immersion of the soul within the body. Whereas God initiated the descent of the soul, the Torah causes its return to a place close to God: the next world. Neoplatonic themes are evident: the Torah is emanated and, I surmise, may function as a cosmic soul.

Let me turn to three sixteenth-century examples. R. Shlomo Alqabetz, an important Safedian figure, asserts that the Torah "brings us to a state of *devequt* with Him, may He be exalted, because when we cleave to her [the Torah], we also cleave to our Creator, since He and His wisdom are one."[151] Even more influential was the description of Torah study found in an important Lurianic book: "Concerning the study of Torah . . . all his intention must be to link his soul and bind her to her supernal source by means of the Torah. And his intention must be to achieve thereby the restoration of the supernal anthropos, which is the ultimate intention of the creation of man and the goal of the commandment to study Torah . . . As when studying Torah man must intend to link his soul and to unite her and make her cleave to her source above . . . and he must intend thereby to perfect the supernal tree [of sefirot] and the holy anthropos."[152]

Although explicitly antagonistic to philosophical thought, this Lurianic Kabbalist adopted a classical philosophical topos and envisions it as one of the peaks of the religious activity. Indeed, cleaving of the soul to its source is not the ultimate goal, as the return to the primordial source is portrayed as contributing to the reconstruction of the structure of the 'Adam Qadmon, namely a theurgical operation that strives for a more comprehensive perfection than the personal one. The supernal anthropos plays, at least in part, the role of the cosmic soul to which the individual returns.

This mystical interpretation of the study of the Torah becomes part of the Christian Kabbalah, as we learn from an influential book written in the middle of the sixteenth century by Sixtus of Siena. Sixtus defines Kabbalah as "a more secret exposition of the divine law, received by Moses from the mouth of God, and from the mouth of Moses by the fathers in continuous succession, received not in written form but orally. This [Kabbalah] returns us from the earthly to the heavenly."[153]

Let me now call attention to a few examples from Hasidic sources where the return of the student to the source by Torah study become a topos. R. Mordekhai of Chernobyl, a late-eighteenth-century Hasidic master active in Ukraine, asserts:

"If a man sanctifies each of his members and cleaves to the Torah, a cleaving of spirit to spirit, and he himself becomes a complete Torah, [then] 'this is the Torah of Man,'[154] because the man himself becomes Torah, and 'the Torah of God[155] is perfect,' [because] it has no imperfection, and it causes the return of the human soul to her source, and her source is restored in the supernal place."[156] The perfect man not only becomes a perfect Torah, but this perfect Torah is viewed as the divine Torah, clearing the way for the return of the human soul to her source within the divine realm. Here the Torah is deemed to achieve what the Neoplatonic philosophers strove for: the reversion of the particular soul to the source.

R. Moses Hayyim Ephrayyim of Sudylkov, a contemporary of R. Mordekhai of Chernobyl and the grandson of the Besht, wrote that "by study and involvement with the Torah for its own sake [or name], he can vivify his soul and amend his 248 limbs and 365 sinews, [and] cleave them to their root, and to the root of their root, which are the Torah and the Tetragrammaton, blessed be He, . . . all of this is [achieved] by the study of Torah for its own sake [or name] and for the sake of asking from the letters themselves, and I heard the interpretation of the Besht . . . from 'the secret of God' which is in them, which will help them [the students of Torah] to utter the letters with a firm utterance[157] 'for its own sake.' "[158] In this instance, unlike the earlier ones adduced from the Hasidic literature, the term "secret" does appear. However, it should be understood not in a mentalistic manner but as the presence of the divine energy within each and every letter, in the way that has been discussed already in Chapter 2. This energy will strengthen the student of the Torah, but nothing related to his becoming an expert transpires from this passage. Searching for an experience that is not intellectual in essence, the Hasidic masters strove to accentuate the sonorous aspect of the study in lieu of its visual one.

Let me turn now to some examples of the ascent of the products of the study of the Torah, or of the voiced Torah, which were deemed able to reach and cleave to the supernal realms. The founder of Hasidism, the Besht, was reported to have recommended that "during your prayer and your study [of the Torah] you shall comprehend and unify each and every speech and utterance of your lips, since in each and every [pronounced] letter there are worlds and souls and divinity, and they ascend and combine and unify with each other and with the Godhead, and afterwards they [the sounds] combine and unify in a perfect union with the Godhead, and the soul [i.e., your soul] will be integrated[159] with them."[160]

R. Shne'or Zalman of Liady, the influential Hasidic master active at the end of the eighteenth century, emphasized the importance of the vocal performance of Torah study as part of an experiential approach to the biblical text. In a passage already adduced and analyzed above,[161] this author presents a threefold hierarchy of human acts, which emphasizes the importance of the performative over the mental preoccupation with the miqra', the read Bible. Reading is, according to this text, bringing down divine powers within this world.

Another case of experiential study involves an explicit instance of union with the cosmic soul. In *Toledot 'Aharon* R. Aharon of Zhitomir, an early-nineteenth-century Hasidic author, when expounding the topic of the white letters,[162] describes the righteous as follows: "When someone recites[163] the speeches of the Torah and of the prayer out of love and fear, then they fly above and those letters cleave to the letters of the soul of the world, which are the light of the Infinite, blessed be He . . . and he[164] unites his speeches to the letters of the soul of the worlds, and he is united to the light of the Infinite, blessed be He, and there the letters are white, and there is no combination there, and this is the reason why the Torah is written black fire on white fire."[165] Again the study of the Torah is explicated in terms of recitation, in a manner reminiscent of the Besht's views. The pronounced words, however, are described as ascending on high and joining the supernal white letters, which are described explicitly as the letters of the soul of all the worlds. Thus, the letters vocalized by the student of the Torah may be conceived of as representing the human soul, which ascends and is united to the cosmic soul by means of Torah study. This study should be performed with emotion and dedication, in a manner reminiscent of the views discussed in Chapter 2 related to the view of R. Aharon's master in the context of the achievement of the messianic experience of reading the white letters.

R. Aharon of Zhitomir was a precise contemporary of R. Nahman of Braslav; in fact, R. Levi Isaac of Berditchev, R. Aharon's spiritual master, was a close friend of the young R. Nahman. R. Aharon's vision is that letters are the soul of everything[166] and so perforce the soul of the world. A proper study of the Torah is therefore an encounter with a spiritual power that permeates the text. When the student approaches the text after restraining his instincts, the letters of the Torah become prominent and are recombined,[167] and the student is thought of as "doing and building the letters of the Torah, and he merits hearing the voice of the Torah from above."[168] In fact, the genuine study of the Torah is intended to transform the student into a channel by which the supernal voice of the Torah is made available to others. However, this transformation of the student also involves a transformation of the order of the letters of the Torah. This is an interesting example of the strong reader becoming an author.[169]

An even more unitive experience related to the study of the Torah, reflecting the highly original nature of R. Nahman's mystical thought, is described as follows: "When one finally is integrated in 'Ein Sof, his Torah is the Torah of God Himself, and his prayer is the prayer of God Himself . . . there exists a Torah of God and a prayer of God. When a person merits being integrated in 'Ein Sof, his Torah and prayer are those of God Himself."[170] Mystical union, the integration of one's soul within the infinite, will change the status of the human verbal activities so that they become divine activities. This view is in line with the assumption concerning the experience of the Shekhinah speaking from the mouth of the mystic.[171] Mystical experiences are therefore one of the reasons for the claim of the divine status of Hasidic creativity. Torah here means the interpretations offered by a Hasidic master on religious topics, a terminology that will be dealt with below.[172]

This authority is described above as stemming from the contact with the divine, which implies a return to the primordial source. Another version of this theory concerning the Torah as return occurs elsewhere in R. Nahman's teachings, when he asserts:

> The quintessence of return depends upon the Torah. Behold, everything sacred comprises three things: impregnation, sucking, [and] mohin. As long as the thing is in potentia it is called impregnation, birth, and sucking. And when it is actualized in order to perform the necessary act it is called mohin. And when one studies the Torah the three things are also necessary. When one studies and concentrates his thought and heart on the Torah this is called impregnation, because he hides himself in it, just like an embryo in the entrails of his mother. And when he studies the Torah and understands it, this is called birth and sucking . . . And when he understands one thing from another, and he wants to innovate concerning it, this is called mohin . . . Thus, the understanding of one thing from another is called mohin, namely Hokhmah, and when he studies in such a manner, this is called return. And he returns the letters and the combinations which are his from all the worlds to their [proper] source and place, and he becomes a new creature.[173]

R. Nahman resorts to the term teshuvah, which can mean both return and repentance. In the above context, return is the intended meaning. How does this return take place? First, someone starts to study the text without really understanding it. This act is tantamount to immersion within the text, like an embryo. Indubitably, this stage is related to the theory of anamnesis, of Platonic origin, which entered Jewish sources in late antiquity. In its Jewish version, the embryo studies the Torah and forgets it at birth.[174] According to this passage, the Torah plays the role of the mother, within whose entrails the embryo begins his life. To describe the immersion, the Hasidic author resorts to the verb hit'allem, which I have translated as "hides himself." I assume that this occultation has a double meaning: it points to the fact that the embryo is not visible from outside and thereby alludes to the disappearance of the meaning of the text under study.

The emergence of the infant is a metaphor for the study of the text that involves understanding. By this point the infant is sucking from the Torah. The third mode of relation to the text is regarded not only as more advanced but also as more intriguing. Although the general terms of discussion involve the study of the Torah, now it is a second-order learning that is intended, one that is more self-sufficient, as it is grounded in the results of the second stage. The student is assumed to draw conclusions from the results of his prior understanding of the Torah.[175] I assume that this sort of study is related to esoteric understanding of the Torah. In any case, the study process is described as a spiritual renewal, for the student becomes a new creature.

Let me compare this passage to Paul Ricoeur's description of the relation between the reader and the text.[176] According to the French philosopher, loosing oneself is part of the capacity to enrich one's own self in front of a text, which impregnates the reader, thus enlarging his self. This seems to be the case where the occultation is concerned in the first stage. A return to an inchoate state is the reason for the possibility of rebirth, which is envisaged as causing the return of the self to the source. This self is enlarged by a certain manipulation of the text, which allows the emergence of letters and combinations, which he is required to return to the divine root.

The entire enterprise of the student, namely the different stages, starting with impregnation and culminating in mohin, represents an anthropocentric interpretation of the processes taking place, according to Lurianic Kabbalah, within the divine realm of partzufim, or configurations.[177] This means that the growth taking place cyclically within the theosophical realm is replicated by human rebirth taking place during the process of study, and the Torah is thus conceived of as nourishing the student's spiritual development.

VII. SEXUAL AND EROTIC UNDERSTANDINGS OF TORAH STUDY IN HASIDISM

In one of the most fascinating instances of personalizing the Torah in Midrash, the Torah is described as the daughter of the king, enclosed in a palace; whoever wants to approach the king is asked first to approach the daughter.[178] It is followed by another of the most famous passages in Kabbalistic literature, the parable of the beautiful maiden in the Zohar, which treats the study of the Torah in terms of erotic and sexual rapprochements between the student and the Torah, which is personified as a maiden living in a palace.[179] This experiential approach remained rather constant in a variety of later Kabbalistic, Sabbatean, and Hasidic texts, and it is naturally related to the feminine perceptions of the Torah.[180]

I would like to adduce two examples of this understanding of the eroticism of the approach to the Torah. The first is given in the name of the founder of Hasidism, the Besht, whose faithful student R. Jacob Joseph of Polonnoye wrote as follows:

> There is an aspect of blessing and curse not from the side of revenge because he had rebelled against the king but solely from the aspect of his not being in union with[181] the inner aspect of the Torah and the command-ments but by the intermediary of the adorned woman with the pertinent issues, for each and every one of Israel according to his aspect and desire, as it is written in the name of my teacher [the Besht] in the pericope Re'eh, see there, and it seems that it concerns another issue, as it is written in R[eshit] H[okhmah], the gate of love, chapter 4, in the account of *de-min 'Acco*,[182] that out of the desire of the lust of women[183] he was separated from the cor-poreality and turned to unite with the intelligibilia because of that separa-tion, so that he united himself to Him, blessed be He. See there and she is she. Because of it, it will be understood that the arrival of the blessing and the curse to you, namely the blessing being the lust of this world, He will give him from the aspect of the above-mentioned adorned woman, because his soul did not yet desire the intelligibilia. And then comes the curse.[184]

The founder of Hasidism interprets an earlier Kabbalistic story concerning the possibility of achieving direct contact with God by the elevation of an ignoramus's thought from lust for the body of a princess to cleaving to the intelligibilia and finally to the divine, in a manner reminiscent of the Platonic *elevatio mentis*.[185] The Platonic source of this story notwithstanding, it has been related, by the Safedian Kabbalist who preserved R. Isaac of Acre's story, to the study of the Torah by means of an a fortiori argument—if an ignoramus is able to cleave to God, so much more may someone who studies the Torah[186]—but he combines the two members of the argument in a rather complex manner. I assume that there are two main possibilities in the passage: one may cleave to the inner aspect of the Torah, a term that occurs frequently in Kabbalah and recurs in R. Jacob Joseph of Polon-noye's book as the study of the elite,[187] and thereby transcend the influence of curse or blessing. However, for those who study the external aspect of the Torah, the possibility of being under the aegis of blessing or curse remains. This less mystical manner of Torah study is conceived of as related to an affinity to the world or the corporeal—in contradistinction to the intelligibilia—and it is alle-gorized as a woman, resorting to the starting point of the story of R. Isaac of Acre.

Here the assumption is that the initial type of Torah study starts with the more mundane, concrete impulse, namely an adorned woman, but unlike the famous parable in the *Zohar*, where the study of the spiritual aspects of the Torah is still related to the princess, the founder of Hasidism is much more Platonically oriented, assuming that the erotic aspect of the study represents a lower type of relationship. In general, this discussion is reminiscent of the more widespread view in Hasidism, which contends that contemplation of the external aspect of a beautiful woman is conducive to contemplation of God.[188]

Let me compare this analysis of the Besht's view to a passage from one of the early Hasidic masters, R. Meshullam Phoebus Heller of Zbaraz, who distinguishes between two forms of love: the love of a man for a woman and the love of brother and sister. The former is described as transient, the latter as constant. It is possible, he asserts,

> to love the Torah because of the pleasure enjoyed by the student of wisdom who is accustomed to it always and has delight in its beauty, and this is similar to the pleasure a man has from a beautiful woman, and it is dependent upon a transient matter. However, the true love of wisdom is to be connected to the fact that the Torah is the vapor [stemming] from the mouth of God, blessed be He and His name, and it is a bone out of His bones[189] . . . and we are His sons, emanated from His will, blessed be He, and this means that we are brothers to His will and wisdom, and it is impossible to separate ourselves from it, and for this love study is necessary . . . We should return and cleave to God, blessed be He, by the brotherhood between us and wisdom, and by its means we shall come to our father in heaven.[190]

As in the earlier text attributed to the Besht, the love of the Torah may contain the pleasure that is reminiscent of sexual intercourse, though it may elevate to a more spiritual love, the brotherhood that unifies the entities that stem from the same root. In fact, I would suggest seeing in this passage another formulation of the identity between God, Torah, and Israel so recurrent in Hasidism.[191] Here, however, we find a formulation whose theological presuppositions are quite interesting. God is portrayed as possessing two different attributes: Hokhmah, wisdom, embodied in and by the Torah,[192] and will, which extends to human souls, understood as being emanated from the divinity. The idea is that like understands like, by virtue of their primordial organic unity. Understanding is therefore based on attraction, similar to Plato's view of the erotic attraction between the two parts of one body, a view that also reverberated in Hasidic mysticism.[193]

It seems that according to these two examples, which far from exhaust the variety of Hasidic approaches to the topic,[194] sexual impulses were regarded as involved in the initial stages of the study of the Torah, but a more advanced attainment was considered to be closer to Platonic eroticism. A starker differentiation between the initial and ultimate stages of study is involved in these two passages. The initial stages, related apparently to the more external aspects, should be transcended by cleaving to the divine as found within the Torah. Does such an approach assume the need of transcending textuality by seeking a trans-textual entity to which to cleave? Is Torah just an instrument for reaching higher forms of nontextual experience? Or is the innermost aspect of the materiality of the text tantamount to the divine, to which the Hasidic masters recommended cleaving? Those questions may be answered in more than one way, and the importance of one answer or another may have deeper repercussions for a follower of Jacques Derrida, who rejects the importance of "presence" within the text. In this context what seems most important is that a plenitude of experience was thought to be achievable by means of the different forms of study of the canonical texts.[195] Unlike Martin Buber's claims as to the importance of concreteness in Hasidism, the above examples point to an attempt to attain an experience that is much more reminiscent of the Platonic and Plotinian disentanglement from corporeality. Indeed, in one of the most fascinating treatments of the study of the Torah, an ecstatic death is envisioned as the apex of the experience of study. R. Yehudah Leib of Yanov, an early-nineteenth-century Hasidic master, testifies that "the fire of desire to cleave to His Torah is burning in him so strongly that [only] death will separate, as we heard and our fathers told us about some righteous, that when they comprehended the grandeur of the splendor of the Torah and the sweetness of its right hand, their soul cleaved to it and their [higher] soul departed, and they died. Happy is he who merits it."[196]

Indeed, I wonder if the much earlier formulation of Ramhal, who wrote that the "entire delight of the soul is nothing but the comprehension of the Torah,"[197] does not summarize both the more erotic ethos of mystical study and the experience of plenitude attained by this kind of study of the Torah.

VIII. CONCLUDING REMARKS

The above examples and discussions suffice, in my opinion, to make the claim that in many circles of Jewish mystics, from late antiquity to modern times, the study of the Torah was regarded as having strong experiential aspects. Those treatments, however, were much more prescriptive than descriptive, and one may argue that they constitute efforts to construct a certain attitude toward a most important form of religious activity, the study of the Torah. These claims cannot, therefore, automatically be viewed as pointing to what indeed happened in reality.

No doubt such caution is in order, and the two modes of discourse should not be confused. A question that seems to support the need for this distinction is why descriptive passages are not widespread. The answer can be put as follows: An important factor that created a reticence to plunge into autobiographical confessions has something to do with the basic style characteristics of the main stratum of Jewish literature, namely the propensity for an objectivistic discourse. As Erich Auerbach has pointed out, the Bible is much less concerned with depicting the interior landscape than it is with describing the external deeds. This proclivity for the external does not necessarily mean a depreciation of the internal states of mind or intimate feelings, but rather points to a cultural decision that the community is to be shaped by common denominators that are synchronized religious performances. This attitude remained crucial for the two main modes adopted by rabbinic literature: the midrashic-interpretive and the halakhic-legalistic. Both layers expanded on topics crucial for the Bible, and neither of them indulged in creating a more emotionally inclined literary genre. So, for example, the Halakhic discussions and prescriptions are concerned with the minutiae of the ritual, without elaborating on feelings that should accompany it or problems of intentionality. Again, I do not assume that there were no mystical experiences involved in some aspects of the religious life—prayer and the Torah study, to name two major examples—but those elements do not come to the fore. The technical aspects of the rabbinic approach were intended not to suppress the inner life but to liberate it from prescriptions involving deliberations on matters of faith and emotions. Although the creation of a solid common denominator by the Halakhic literature was crucial for the Jewish projects concerned with strengthening the notion of a corporate personality, the theological convictions and the feelings of the individuals remained their patrimony. The mystical literature analyzed above follows the same path: to instruct and prescribe, rather than confess or betray someone's inner life. Just as one cannot deduce from the prescriptive Halakhic literature whether one ever performed a commandment—though it seems that it is hard to deny such performance as a historical fact—so too I would not doubt the possibility that prescriptions to enjoy the study of the Torah inculcated expectations that were sometimes realized. Concerned as I am with the importance of the religious imaginaire as formative for the spiritual life, the documentation of the existence of such an imaginaire constitutes a major step in establishing the centrality of the Torah and its study for the mystical experiences of some Jewish elites.

7

SECRECY, BINAH, AND DERISHAH

I. SECRETS OF THE TORAH

In its biblical forms, Judaism is a rather exoteric and democratic type of religiosity. The emphasis on making the teaching of the revealed instructions open to all classes of Israelites and the paramount importance of making religious actions open, in most cases, to all members of the nation, marginalize during the biblical phase of Judaism the surfacing and privileging of mysteries and secrets. Some of the subsequent phases of Judaism can, however, be described as part of an ongoing process of arcanization, to use a term I adopt from Jan Assmann,[1] which means that the common texts and actions become fraught with "deeper" and, later on, multiple esoteric meanings. Secrets, in matters of religion as well as in other domains, reflect an important evaluation of a certain topic. If this assumption is correct, rabbinic Judaism would look for secrets more in texts than in other realms of reality. Articulated in a period when political power was part of the past, rabbinic esotericism is a matter of decoding the secret found in limited aspects of the text par excellence: the Torah. Unlike Platonic esoteric thinking, which embraces a form of secrecy that is much more political and is articulated in an environment that did not cultivate a canonic text, i.e., the Greek polis, rabbinic religiosity gravitated around a bibliocentric mentality. As such, the religious esotericism in rabbinic texts, and in those formulated in its immediate vicinity or within some of its circles, like the Heikhalot literature, rotates around the transmission of secrets believed to be within some few and limited texts, the way they are extracted from those texts, and how they are to be expounded to a few others.

This does not mean, at least in my opinion, that Jewish esotericism emerged solely from exercising forms of exegetical activity. I assume that in some cases "secrets" had penetrated Jewish circles from outside and were subsequently connected to the biblical texts by some sort of exegesis. According to recent studies, it seems that parts of Jewish esotericism, emerging in later periods, had significant affinities to much earlier esoteric traditions, especially of Assyrian and Babylonian extraction.[2] Yet some explicit beginnings of Jewish esotericism are to be found in a later—perhaps the latest—biblical book, the book of Daniel, as well as in the apocryphal literature of the Second Temple[3] and in the Qumran literature.[4]

The vast majority of the literary corpora extant in Hebrew are not esoteric, in the sense of the existence of a comprehensive arcanization of the biblical texts. This is conspicuous in the talmudic and midrashic literatures, which are palpably exoteric corpora; the Heikhalot literature, on the other hand, where esoteric elements are to be found in many cases, is not an interpretive literature that would expand on the idea of a comprehensive and pervasive secret sense of the entire biblical text. The several references to secrets in the apocryphal literature have to do either with secrets of nature[5] or with historical, namely eschatological, topics, as is obvious in the Qumran literature[6] and in the ancient apocalypses.[7]

On the other hand, many of Philo of Alexandria's biblical interpretations can be described as mystical, as some scholars have already pointed out.[8] Moreover, almost all the rabbinic discussions mentioning secrets, and some of the Heikhalot references to secrets, involve secrets that are at least formally related to some limited parts of the Bible.[9] The expression *sitrei torah*—the most widespread phrase describing Jewish esoterica—or the less well known *razei torah* and *sod ha-torah* point to a restriction of the greater variety of secrets in Jewish nonrabbinic literatures to topics included in the Bible alone. In other words, the secrets believed to be inherent in the Bible constitute the bulk of the secrets recognized as such by the rabbis or other Jewish elites.[10] This strategy allowed the absorption of several types of secrets one would like to adopt, with the condition of being able to offer, ingenuously, links between them and biblical verses. This development raises the importance of hermeneutics, the disclosure of secrets in the canonic texts as well as devices that facilitate their exposition.

I would like to emphasize the possible impact of this simple statement about the existence of a rather wide consensus over the existence of secrets in the Torah in late antiquity and early Middle Ages among Jewish elites. These elites waged intellectual and religious battle over the nature of these secrets and resorted to a huge and diversified array of exegetical methods; but the very invention of secrecy is not their achievement, as it is part of the processes I have described as arcanization. Neither Maimonides nor his Kabbalistic contemporaries nor the Hasidei Ashkenaz invented the concept of secrecy as inherent in the canonical texts of Judaism. Thus, the very concept of secrecy does not emerge as the result of a specific crisis, given the preexistence of the concept of secrecy to the different religious backgrounds of those thinkers. If there were crises that invited some forms of arcanization and the introduction of exegetical methods in order to extract these secrets from the canonic texts, this is a matter of a certain interpretation of the commonly accepted theory of secrecy.

Indeed, the preoccupation with exegetical devices is manifest in medieval Jewish mystical corpora created in different places and times, as the vast literatures of Hasidei Ashkenaz and ecstatic Kabbalah demonstrate.[11] The precise sources of some of the complex exegetical devices still await detailed analysis, which may well show their ancient extraction, even when the historical links have been uncharted for centuries.[12] In this framework I would like to deal with some expressions that betray these exegetical concerns in the context of studying secrets related to the Torah, or to show how the biblical text has been gradually enveloped by secrets. The nature of these secrets can be approximated by attempting to analyze the context in which they occur, followed by an academic discussion of the nature or the different opinions on the meaning of the Creation (ma'aseh bereshit) or the Chariot (ma'aseh merkavah). Here, however, I would like to adopt a different strategy and investigate two of the verbs that recur in the context of secrets, verbs that describe how one may decode these secrets or expound them. By adopting such a strategy, I will advance a claim about the nature of these secrets: they represent contents that are deeply connected to texts of the Bible but constitute a hidden understanding of some parts of this canon. This understanding could be fathomed and consequently is different from mysteries, which, even when presented as part of a ritual, can hardly be understood and primarily have a great emotional effect. Let me survey the use of two verbs occurring in biblical literature and their subsequent careers in the domain of Jewish esoterica.

II. Binah, or Understanding the Bible

The term *binah*, meaning understanding or discernment, and its derivatives occur many times in the Bible and postbiblical literature. They possess a variety of nuances, each developing successively. Here I should like to focus on one particular usage of the derivative verb, which signifies a deeper understanding that penetrates the superficial knowledge of a given topic. This fathoming of the meaning of a text, of a tradition, of a vision or revelation, sometimes involves the disclosure of the (often allegedly) implied secrets. Let me adduce the descriptions of this term in several scholarly studies and then add some texts concerning the extraction or reception of secrets in a context where Binah is mentioned. In the first chapter of Deuteronomy Moses tells the people of Israel, "Take wise men, of understanding, who are known among the tribes,"[13] in order to help him guide the people. Later in the same chapter, however, Moses indicates that he took "wise and known men,"[14] while *nevonim*, the understanding ones, are not mentioned at all. In some rabbinic discussions of the discrepancy between the verses, the claim is made that understanding men were not found in Moses' generation, an argument that implies that understanding is a very high spiritual attainment.[15] Against this view of understanding as higher than wisdom, represented by the Babylonian attitude,[16] the apparently Palestinian view was that wisdom is superior to understanding.[17] In another biblical discussion, a rather hypostatic view of Binah is found, which parallels that of Hokhmah, Wisdom. In Proverbs 8:14 Wisdom declares, "Counsel is mine, and sound wisdom, I am understanding, I have strength." This identity between the hypostatic Wisdom and Understanding is also found at the beginning of the same chapter: "Does not Wisdom call? And Understanding put forth her voice?"[18]

This sequence to the features of Wisdom is reminiscent of Isaiah 11:2, where the messianic figure is described in the following words: "And the spirit of the Lord shall rest upon him, the spirit of Wisdom and Understanding, the spirit of Counsel and Strength, the spirit of Knowledge and of Fear of the Lord."[19] It is quite plausible that, as in the phrase "spirit of the Lord," which implies a descent of the divine on the chosen man, so too the expression "spirit of Wisdom and Understanding" reflects a hypostatic status of those two concepts. An alternative reading may assume that the spirit of the Lord is a collective description of the six characteristics later enumerated; such a reading again implies a hypostatic status of Binah.

In the book of Daniel, however, the hypostatic stand seems to be absent, and the occurrence of the term *binah* has more to do with an epistemic claim; the meaning of *binah* in this book has been described by Gerald H. Wilson: "Bina in

Daniel therefore, unlike the wisdom literature, is not the end product of careful observation of experience through the analytic processes of the human mind. It is instead the knowledge which is beyond the ability of even the great hakam Daniel to understand and which must be interpreted by divine revelation . . . This increased emphasis in ch. 8–12 on instruction in esoteric knowledge sets Daniel's usage of these terms apart from that of biblical wisdom."[20] Indeed, the use of *binah* and *haven* in those chapters is very conspicuous, involving both the deeper understanding of the content of a vision[21] and of a book,[22] in both cases the eschatological secrets being evident. Moreover, the terminology of secrecy is found in Daniel 2:22, where 'amiqata', the profound secrets,[23] and mesatrata', the hidden things, have had a great influence on the subsequent Jewish esoteric nomenclature.[24] The two tendencies found in the biblical literature, seeing in the terms derived from BYN either the hermeneutical activity of understanding a text or a hypostasis on the high, have become the blueprints of the later Jewish esotericism. *Binah* as a noun represents the hypostatic approach, while the verbal forms, which may likewise imply the gift of understanding given by a higher entity, reflect the hermeneutical approach.

It seems that in this sense the verb occurs several times in the Qumran literature. In the *Manual of Discipline*, for example, it is said that at the end of time God "will cause the upright to understand the knowledge of the Most High, and teach the wisdom of the sons of heaven to the perfect way."[25] I take the understanding of the knowledge of God as higher than the knowledge of the wisdom of angels, referred to here as the sons of heaven. The strong hif'il verb form is understood here as the act of God, who causes the upright to understand, and not simply as an act of independent understanding of man.[26] The verb is used in this sense in a Qumran psalm, where it is demanded of God to grant understanding of the Torah, *havineni YHWH be-toratekhah*.[27] In another pertinent passage, found in the so-called *Apocalypse of Levi* as preserved by the Qumran community, we learn that the sage Hakim "understands the depths and speaking the enigmas." The first part of this quote translates the phrase *mitbonen be-'amiq[i]n*,[28] which has been translated into French as *comprendre les profondeurs*.[29] Elsewhere this treatise speaks of the "revelation of the profound secrets, which were not understood."[30] Several times in the *Scroll of the Thanksgivings* the sectarian confesses that he knows by means of the *binah* of God,[31] in the context of revelation of the wondrous secrets.[32]

Aside from this direct illumination of God, in the Qumran literature there is yet another relevant meaning of the verb, as Steven Fraade has noted: "In the Dead Sea Scrolls the verb *hevin* is commonly used to denote the prophetic enlightenment of the community by its priestly leaders and by God."[33] The same tendency to discern in the verb BYN a special form of understanding is found in David

Daube's analysis of rabbinic texts; following W. Bacher,[34] Daube assumes that BYN is "employed by the Rabbis preferably where the deeper meaning in question is of a secret, dangerous character."[35] He mentions several sources, including chapters 9 and 12 of the book of Daniel, and understands the instance of this verb in Daniel 9:2 as denoting "to get at the bottom of allusions made in the sacred books."[36] It seems that *binah* is a superrational faculty that is the organ of perception of the alleged inner or even esoteric meanings of a text. This also seems to be the term's meaning in a famous mishnaic passage dealing with the spiritual qualities of those to whom someone is allowed to expound the accounts of Creation and the Chariot; the recipient scholar is supposed to be "wise, and he understood by his own intellect," *hakham vehevin mi-da'ato*.[37] I assume that understanding, being a requirement for the reception of the most esoteric kind of knowledge in Judaism, somehow transcends the kind of elementary comprehension that comes from having an ordinary intelligence (*da'ato*). In a talmudic discussion (BT, *Shabbat*, fol. 31a) the understanding of one thing from another is described as proceeding from a preoccupation with wisdom. The talmudic list of qualities required in order to receive the secret topics also includes the phrase *navon lahash*,[38] which means "'one who understands [things] transmitted in a whisper,' namely one who is able to receive esoteric matters, which are transmitted orally, in a whisper."[39]

On the same page in the Talmud we learn that a young boy, Tinoq, "was reading the book of Ezekiel in the house of his master, and he was understanding[40] [the nature of] the Hashmal, and then a fire went out of the Hashmal and consumed him."[41] This text assumes that the book of Ezekiel, found in the house of a master, is an esoteric work and that its reading implies an esoteric activity.[42] Understanding therefore stands for a more advanced form of activity, and it alone seems to entail lethal danger. Thus I assume that it is an understanding not merely of the prophetic text but of the nature of an esoteric issue, the Hashmal[43] (apparently a kind of amber emanating light around the divine throne), which was interpreted as some sort of angelic powers in the Talmud.[44] Understanding is more than simply decoding the meaning of the mysterious Hashmal; it involves bringing someone into a direct relation to the entity represented by words in the text, and thus it creates a dangerous situation. I assume that such a reading also means fathoming the secret knowledge allegedly coded within the biblical text. This view regarding the story of the boy is corroborated by another story, also found in the Hagigah version, where the discussion of topics related to the Chariot induces the presence of the Shekhinah and produces some fiery phenomena fraught with danger.[45] R. Eleazar ben 'Arakh's exposition is lauded by his teacher, R. Yohanan ben Zakkai, in a rather interesting manner: he blesses the patriarch Abraham for his descendant's achievement, because the latter is able to "understand, and inquire and expound."[46] It seems, therefore, that according to those sources, the mere discussion of secrets pertaining to the higher world is instrumental in the emergence of extraordinary phenomena, which may endanger someone who is not prepared to encounter them.[47] An interesting statement, found in what is called the Hebrew Book of Enoch, claims that the book's protagonist is granted "all the secrets of the Torah, all the secrets of binah and all the depths[48] of the secret of Torah."[49]

It should be emphasized that in rabbinic texts, unlike Daniel, no divine revelation, in the strict sense of this term, is connected to binah, but rather permission for the transmission of an already existing, though apparently initially revealed, type of knowledge. In one of the Heikhalot texts the mystic is told that he "should understand what is in his heart, and be silent,[50] in order to merit the [vision of] the beauty of the Merkavah."[51]

The inner understanding, together with other acts, is therefore a prerequisite for mystical experience. In our case the mystical vision of the Merkavah, formulated in a manner reminiscent of the vision of God's beauty,[52] is preceded by the understanding of what is in one's heart. This expression is very similar to other expressions that also occur before an act related to the Merkavah. So, for example, in the Gemara it is said that "many have expected to expound the Merkavah, though they never saw it."[53] In the context of the discussion about a blind man's officiating in the ritual for the congregation, this sentence means that because of his blindness he could not view the Chariot and thus should not attempt to expound this topic to others. R. Yehudah's answer is that the vision of the Merkavah is not an ocular activity or achievement but depends on the understanding of the heart, 'ovanta' de-libba'.[54] At least in the view of R. Yehudah, the understanding of the Merkavah in the heart does allow even a blind person to expound related topics to others. What is the meaning of 'ovanta' in this context? In my opinion, the view of R. Yehudah is an alternative to the ocular vision, and though speaking about understanding, he actually refers to an inner vision. Thus, the above text from the Heikhalot literature, which is related to the Merkavah, opens the way to another, more external or, in the last case, public understanding concerning this issue, which we shall return to later on.

It is the understanding of the paramount importance of binah as pointing to instruction in esoteric knowledge, as included in the book of Daniel, which reverberates in a relatively late midrash 'Otiyyot de-Rabbi 'Aqivah, which preserved views and material from the Heikhalot literature: "You should know that binah is exalted in the eyes of God, even more than the Torah is, so that even if one reads the Torah, the Prophets, and the Hagiography, and studies Mishnah, Midrash Halakhah and

'Aggadah, Traditions and Tossafot, Moshelot and Ma'amadot, and all the orders of the Midrash, and has no *binah*, his Torah is as worth nothing, as it is written,[55] 'The *binah* of His wise men shall be hid.' "[56] I assume that it is not only intellectual capability—a very high one indeed, as it is considered to be higher than the Torah—that defines *binah* but also a peculiar power that penetrates complex issues. In my view, this passage does not afford a totally independent status to *binah*, but this capacity is exercised while studying the various parts of the Jewish canon.

A similar stand seems to be reflected in a well-known talmudic passage that elucidates R. Abbahu's quotation of the verse "The words of the Lord are pure words, silver refined in a furnace upon the ground, purified seven times,"[57] as follows: "Fifty gates of understanding were created in the world, and all were given to Moses save one, as it says:[58] 'Yet thou hast made him little[59] lower than a God.' "[60] The forty-nine gates seem to be related to a cosmological principle, which initially was not linked to the interpretation of the Bible. This seems obvious from the fact that the gates are depicted as created in the world. On the other hand, the reference to the verse concerning the sevenfold refinement can be understood, as some interpreters have already done, as meaning seven times seven.[61] Because this refinement is ostensibly related to the scriptures, a nexus has been created, by dint of this juxtaposition, between the gates, which apparently are a cosmological principle revealed to Moses, and the seven-times-seven ways to understand the scriptures.[62] Although no secret way of understanding is explicit here, the fact that only Moses was graced with such a gift shows that this is indeed a superior type of knowledge.

At the end of this short survey of the occurrence of the term *binah* in connection with secrets and secrecy, it would be in order to draw attention to two texts that assume a metaphysical existence of *binah*, in a way reminiscent of the biblical hypostatic views mentioned above. One is the famous talmudic passage dealing with the creation of the world by means of ten things, one of them being *tevunah*, a synonym of *binah*.[63] This is one of the sources of the Kabbalistic hypostatic notion of Binah as a sefirotic attribute of God. In the second passage, from *Sefer ha-Razim*, a third-century magical text,[64] the sun is invoked by the names of "the angels that cause men of knowledge to understand[65] and to discern[66] lore and obscure [things]."[67] Again the angels are portrayed as instructing men to understand secret lore.

III. BINAH: MEDIEVAL REVERBERATIONS

The use of the verb *haven* to point out a special, oftentimes more profound understanding of a text, occurs thousands of times in the Middle Ages, both in philosophical and in Kabbalistic literatures. Phrases like *ha-mevin yavin* and *ha-maskkil yavin* are commonplaces for an independent understanding of a topic conceived to be difficult, and their recurrence is so ubiquitous that it needs no detailed demonstration. Here, however, I would like to address but a few of the many instances of the special meaning of *binah*.

Let me turn first to a short text found in a manuscript whose precise background is unclear: "The perfect hasid, who has no evil thought, [namely] R. 'Aqivah was described as being worthy of [magically] using the glory of heaven,[68] and he was given Binah and he knew how to expound."[69,70] Here, as in the Mishnah of Hagigah, the presence of *binah* is a precondition for expounding esoteric issues. However, whereas in the Hagigah passage the recipient of understanding receives the exposition from another sage, here the understanding is a precondition for his own capacity to expound. This hierarchical distinction between *binah* and *derishah*,[71] both related to the transmission or exposition of religious secrets, also involves a magical moment: the power to use the divine glory, a quality attributed to R. 'Aqivah in BT, *Hagigah*, fol. 15b.[72] In this text both the faculty of *binah* and the activity of expounding are attributed to R. 'Aqivah, a figure whose name plays an important role in the Heikhalot literature as a mystic and in the midrashic literature as someone who expounded the scriptures in a rather peculiar way.[73] Indeed, this last quote is consonant with the one we saw earlier from 'Otiyyot de-Rabbi 'Aqivah.

This type of relationship between understanding and mystical experience is paralleled by a statement of R. Hai Gaon, an eleventh-century Jewish religious master, in a passage that deals with the Hagigah esoteric topics: "The whispers he is whispered,[74] and the general [principles][75] are delivered to him, and he understands them,[76] and from heaven he is shown[77] in the [most] hidden [part] of his heart."[78,79] Understanding is explicitly connected here to secrets shown from above. It should be emphasized that understanding is the human faculty that enables the mystic to comprehend the revealed principles, which facilitates the understanding of secrets. We can easily see here the two trends related to this verb—that of Daniel, emphasizing the need for revelation from above, and that of the superior understanding that enables the independent understanding of secrets. Here understanding concerns inductive knowledge; the principles are understood in their more detailed forms, and these forms, or contents, prepare the mystic for an understanding that precedes the vision of the beauty of the Merkavah. A contemporary of R. Hai Gaon uses the phrase *mevinei sodim*, namely those who understand the secrets.[80]

In a prayer pronounced before the ritual reading of the Torah on the New Year (Rosh ha-Shana) God is asked to grant "intelligence and understanding, in order to comprehend and understand the depths of its[81] secrets."[82] Again this verb occurs in a context ostensibly devoted to secrets, in a passage attributed to an eleventh-century rabbi,[83] R. Isaac ha-Levi, one of the Rashi's teachers, who describes the concern of the Ashkenazi Jews with the ritual poems thus: "They fathom[84] [in order] to understand[85] the commandment of the secret of our Lord, in the Torah, which has a pedigree and a [reliable] tradition [*qabbalah*] from a rabbi."[86] The occurrence of the verb *maʿamiqim*, "fathom," before the verb "to understand" seems to qualify the special understanding related to the "commandment of the secret of God," a rather obscure phrase. What is especially pertinent to our discussion is the fact that the secret not only is related to God but also is found in the Torah, according to the reliable tradition. Thus, the secret related to God can be extracted from the Bible by fathoming its meaning.

This also seems to be the meaning of *binah* in another passage, written by the poet R. Benjamin ben Shmuel, who lived in Lombardy in the early eleventh century. In one of his poems he put in the mouth of God the following verse, as a response to the Torah: "How shall I give your secret[87] to the immortals?[88] Is not the majority of your *binah*,[89] the matter of those [consisting of] flesh and blood, who decode them?"[90] I assume that the secret of the Torah is parallel to the majority of the *binah*, which is deciphered by mortals. If this juxtaposition is correct, then the *binah* of the Torah means in this case the secret of the Torah, which is to be penetrated by man.[91] In another poem this poet makes an explicit connection between the forty-nine gates and the tablets of the Torah, thereby establishing a rather hermeneutical role for the gates.[92]

The possible links between *binah* and secrets of the Torah served as the background for the emergence of a very complex treatment of the talmudic phrase "fifty gates of *binah*." This seems to be the case in another eleventh-century text, R. Moses ha-Darshan's *Bereshit Rabbati*, where eight thousand gates of understanding were mentioned as having been given to Moses and as corresponding to the books of the prophets, while five thousand gates of wisdom correspond to the five books of the Pentateuch.[93] Around 1217 R. Eleazar of Worms composed a lengthy treatise named *Sefer ha-Hokhmah*, on seventy-three exegetical methods of interpreting the Bible, designated as "gates of *hokhmah*." These gates are explicitly related to the Torah, on the one hand, and to fifty (sometimes forty-nine) gates of understanding, on the other. The meaning of these links is by no means clear, as various scholarly attempts to explain them show.[94] I am not sure that the *Bereshit Rabbati* view should not be addressed in this context. However, it seems that an interesting proposal in an article by Ivan Marcus may be relevant to our discussion.[95] Marcus surmises that the seventy-three methods of *hokhmah*[96] are intended as ways to reach the secret meanings of the Torah, meanings that are identical with the gates of *binah*.[97] Or, to formulate this affinity differently: it is by means of the gates of hokhmah, conceived of as technical devices, that the secret contents, the gates of binah, are allegedly extracted from the text. This resort to extrinsic methods to fathom the intrinsic secrets assumes that binah, or more precisely its gates, stands for the secrets of the text, in a manner reminiscent of some of the eleventh-century texts quoted above. Indeed, as a passage from Sefer Hasidim, a book composed in the milieu of R. Eleazar, indicates, the fifty gates of understanding are the goodness of God, which are hints and secrets placed in the Torah. They were dispersed there in order "to increase the reward of those who fear Him properly. They have to look for them, as it is written:[98] 'If you seek her[99] as silver, and search for her as for hidden treasures, then you will understand the fear of the Lord and find the knowledge of God.' "[100]

The verb in Proverbs deals with the search for binah, but in Sefer Hasidism this quest is undertaken within the text of the Torah. Once again, binah stands for the esoteric aspect of the Torah. Understanding is thus not a general quality, a general way of discerning, but the hidden aspects of the Torah. I would say that the cosmological background of a hypothetically earlier attribution of the comprehensive knowledge of Adam as possessing those gates was absorbed within a hermeneutics whose center is a text and the identity of whose protagonist was changed from Adam to Moses.[101]

The importance of understanding is quite obvious in Kabbalistic literature. This is a recurrent theme that cannot be dealt with in the present framework, given the hypostatic role attributed to the nouns binah and tevunah and the many functions that the sefirah to which they refer may serve. I would like to emphasize, however, the special importance of understanding at the beginning of Kabbalah, in the writings of R. Jacob ben Sheshet and Nahmanides. The Geronese Kabbalist R. Jacob ben Sheshet indicates that he received a tradition to the effect that the fifty gates consist of five sets of ten gates, each set explicating one of the five parts of the Pentateuch. Thus, we have strong evidence that from the very beginning of the Spanish Kabbalah, "gate" means a way of understanding the Torah.[102] Elsewhere, ben Sheshet mentions the gates in a context that is conspicuously related to the Torah. He identifies forty-nine gates with the written Torah, on the basis of the nexus with the talmudic discussion of the forty-nine ways of interpreting the Torah, and views the remaining gate as identical to the oral Torah. The two Torahs represent, respectively, the male and female aspects of the divinity, which should, according to the text, be unified.[103]

Nahmanides, as we have seen, juxtaposed the fifty gates of understanding with the forty-nine ways of expounding the Torah.[104] The relevance of this nexus becomes more obvious when he asserts that whatever was said to Moses in the framework of those gates has been written in the Torah, either explicitly or esoterically.[105] In general, however, Nahmanides should be seen as emphasizing the ontological view of the gates as related to various realms of reality.[106] Indeed, he repeatedly points out the need of understanding for the reception of the esoteric tradition, Kabbalah. So, for example, he mentions that his own words regarding Kabbalah "would not be comprehended by [way of] intellect and understanding, but from the mouth of a wise Kabbalist to the ear of an understanding receiver."[107] Elsewhere he insists that secret topics will not be understood[108] but by means of oral transmission.[109] In this vein, he asserts that "the secret of the account of Creation is profound, that cannot be understood from the pertinent verses but should be received orally . . . neither understood in a complete manner from the verses."[110] In those instances Nahmanides betrays an attitude to *binah* that is rather complex: understanding is needed in order to receive the secrets by way of oral transmission, but it is not a reliable organ for extracting secrets from the biblical sources. In one case, he uses the verb "understand" in the context of secrets, but at the same time he mentions that one must be meritorious in order to receive the secret.[111] This cosmological vision of the gates, which dramatically attenuates their exegetical role, seems to be fundamentally different from that received by ben Sheshet. In any case, it seems that Nahmanides was faithful to the mishnaic vision concerning understanding as the organ for receiving secrets, but not as an exegetical tool for extracting them from a text.[112]

In *Sefer ha-Yihud*, an anonymous thirteenth-century text, we read:

And the knowledge of the Creator, may His name be blessed and exalted, consists of eight sets of alphabets such as[113] va-yisa' va-yavo' va-yet which contain twenty-six letters. And before the Torah proper was given at Sinai, Moses was in Egypt. And it is accepted that Levi possessed a book of Kabbalah and he studied from it, as did those who preceded him . . . Moses studied the Kabbalah in its most complete form, with a pure spirit and a new heart, more so than any other man, and he attained certain knowledge of the Creator. Regarding him it is written,[114] "And there has not since then arisen a prophet in Israel like Moses whom the Lord knew face to face, not before or after." And so too we find in *Sefer ha-Mafteah* that before Moses returned to Egypt, the Holy One, blessed and exalted be His name, chose him from among the tribe of Levi so that he may serve Him. And Moses learned the entire Kabbalah from the alphabets, and his study of wisdom and knowledge and understanding refers to the letters and their vowels. And anyone who will understand and know and understand [sic] the power of the letters and vowels and their [visual] forms and the effects of their forms will understand and have knowledge of the blessed Creator.[115]

The emphasis on the linguistic elements points to the technical aspect of the Kabbalah, for according to this text the Kabbalist is able, by means of the secrets of letters, to reach an understanding of the divine on his own. In fact, the basic structure of this passage assumes that a secret knowledge that predated the revelation of the Torah includes wisdom. Moses prepared himself by study of the intellectual tools, which allows the understanding of the revelation to emerge only later. To a certain extent, acquaintance with the elements of the language and their secret meaning will open the way for understanding the revealed text. According to the anonymous passage Kabbalah, understood in a manner close to the elements of the ecstatic Kabbalah, preceded not only the Torah (in the case of the hero of that revelation) but also Jews in Egypt and, I assume, Jews in general, as it may point to an Adamic secret tradition that prepared the revelation of the exoteric canonic text.

The view that at the age of forty one achieves *binah*, together with the various formulations that connected the term *binah* with deeper understanding, including an understanding of the secrets in the biblical text, contributed to the emergence of the idea that secrets can be transmitted to one who has reached forty years of age or, alternatively, that this age is appropriate for studying secret topics.[116] So, for example, the age of forty has been connected by a thirteenth-century philosopher active in Spain, R. Shem Tov Falaquera, to the study of Maimonides' *Guide of the Perplexed*, which should be approached only at forty because of the vanishing of the fervor of youth at that age.[117] Moreover, Falaquera says, the topics dealt with by Maimonides are called *binah*. I am inclined to assume that the issues referred to by the vague term 'inyanim stand for the secret aspects of the *Guide of the Perplexed*.[118]

Abraham Abulafia, around 1280, defined the *mevin* as higher than the *hakham*, who is described as a student of books: "If he obtains it [knowledge] by [way of] the Kabbalah, that is to say as a tradition from one who has himself obtained it from the contemplation of the divine names or from another Kabbalist, then he is called *mevin*."[119] Higher than the *mevin* is the *da'atan*, who receives the content of his knowledge of reality from his own heart. Thus Abulafia interprets the mishnaic statement about *hakham, mevin mi-da'ato*, as pointing to three different stages in the intellective process, understanding being the second. Elsewhere in the same context Abulafia speaks about "the *binah* that is received from the mouth of the true Kabbalists,"[120] thus creating a clear identification between the concept of a received, apparently secret tradition and *binah*. According to this vision of Kabbalah, this means of acquiring lore is a rather mediocre approach which should, ideally, be transcended by independent speculations and revelations.[121]

In the 1280s R. Todros ben Joseph ha-Levi Abulafia, a central figure in Castilian Jewry and an important Kabbalist, emphasized the fundamental role of the knowledge of the esoteric tradition dealing with the structure of the Tetragrammaton in order to understand the mysteries of the Torah:

> Know that by the knowledge of the innermost [part] of the structure of its letters, all the secrets of the Torah and the prophets[122] will be explained and revealed to whoever will know it, each in accordance with what he will be announced from heaven to understand, one thing from another, and to return the thing to its [proper] essence. Happy is he who will be able to understand even one of the thousands upon thousands of mysteries and allusions that are inscribed in the innerness of the letters of the [divine] name for [the sake of] those who know. Oh we who see and do not understand what do we see![123] All the ancient and later masters of Kabbalah have sworn not to hint at issues [of Kabbalah], but they hint at their modest[124] disciples the notes of the chapters.[125]

From the perspective of the types of Kabbalah represented in their books, R. Todros Abulafia's thought has nothing to do with Abraham Abulafia's ecstatic Kabbalah. Despite the coincidence of their names, the two masters were not from the same family, nor did they share a common Kabbalistic worldview. Nevertheless, the quoted passage, dealing with the secrets of the structure of the Tetragrammaton as a compendium of the entire text of the Bible and thus its understanding as a sine qua non, is reminiscent of the ecstatic Kabbalist's emphasis on the importance of the Tetragrammaton and the centrality of revelation from above. Even more fascinating are the affinities between this passage and that of a student of Abraham Abulafia's, R. Joseph Gikatilla, who also assumed that the entire Torah is contained within the Tetragrammaton. (We shall explore this topic in Chapters 10 and 12.) Therefore, seeing the letters of the Tetragrammaton should be complemented by a more profound knowledge, the understanding, which is also related to the concept of revelation from above.

Within this limited framework it is impossible to treat all the avatars of *binah* and of the processes related to the understanding of secrets. They remained part and parcel of Jewish mysticism,[126] and a much more detailed survey is still a desideratum.

IV. DERISHAH: FROM ORACLE TO INTERPRETATION

Let me investigate a development that points to the peculiar nature of the rabbinic and Heikhalot methods of expounding Torah secret. Instead of the direct approach to the divine found in the prophetic literature, the mediation of the text and its study or the decoding the significance of a revelation is necessary in order to reach a realm of experience beyond the ordinary types of cognition. The first step of this development has been ably described by Michael Fishbane:

> Whereas the verb DRSh refers to oracular inquiry in Exod. 18:15, it is used as a term of rational legal investigation in Deut. 13:15, 17:4,9, and 19:18 . . . For whereas the expression "to inquire (lidrosh) of the Torah of YHWH" occurs in a mantic context of prophetic inquiry in 1 Kgs. 22:8, for example, and the expression "to inquire of 'Elohim" occurs in a mantic context of legal inquiry in Exod. 18:15 of "the Torah of YHWH." Here the text of the divine words serves, as it were, as an oraculum for the rational-exegetical inquiry.[127]

The shift from the oracular use of the root DRSh[128] in relation to God to the inquiry into the text in an exegetical manner is a development that assumes that the text substituted divine direct revelation. I would like to propose that these two forms of mantic understanding of the verb DRSh remained interconnected in some later Jewish texts, where the inquiry into the secret meaning of the Torah was instrumental in experientially discovering the divine within the text.[129] The canonic text functions, in many important instances in Jewish mysticism, as a means of recovering the divine by various forms of intense reading and studying the details of the revealed book. In my opinion, the overlapping of exegetical or hermeneutical experience, on the one hand, and mystical experience, on the other, is an alternative way of separating literature from experience or of making a sharp distinction between interpretation and ecstasy.[130]

So, for example, a possible nexus between the verb DRSh and secrets is represented by a reconstructed verse of Ben Sira: "He will inquire into the hidden aspects of the parable, and he will itratash[131] the enigma of the mashal."[132] It is not certain that the biblical texts are implied here at all, though at the beginning the torat 'elyon and the nevu'ot are mentioned (verses 1–2), while in verse 3 the sihat 'anshei shem and 'imqei melitzot, namely the depths of the metaphors,[133] are mentioned. The basic assumption here is that a parable has a cryptic meaning that should be disclosed by the sage. In any case, even if we assume that these verses deal with some biblical passages, there is no doubt that only a few instances in the Bible may be included in this category.

To demonstrate that esotericism has not been envisioned as an important preoccupation, it is sufficient to quote two well-known verses from Ben Sira III: "21: Things hidden from you [pela'ot] do not inquire into [al tidrosh], and things covered to you do not seek. 22: What you have been permitted to deal with do contemplate, but have nothing to do with things hidden [nistarot]."[134] This text is to be understood in the context of verse 18: "The graces of God are numerous, and to the humble[135] will He disclose His secret[s]."[136] This means that the verb lidrosh implies a deliberate but forbidden initiative to understand hidden things, which can nevertheless be disclosed by God. As Segal has proposed,[137] the term *pela'ot* may stand for the wonders of the Creation, as the parallel in *Ben Sira* XLIII:29 may indicate. Thus, the knowledge of secrets is a matter not of successful inquiry but of a revelation promised to those who are humble.[138] This warning has been repeated in many instances in rabbinic literature, which adopted this reticence to plunge into esoterica as a basic position.[139] Given the fact that a literary continuity between Ben Sira's view of esotericism and the rabbinic one is conspicuous, for the passage from this book is widely quoted in rabbinic sources, we may assume that the significance of the verb *lidrosh* is shared by some texts written in the middle of the second century B.C.E. and some written around 200 C.E. Indeed, the continuity related to the verbs that recur in the context of discovering and some-times exposing secrets shows that at least some consistency in terminology, and to a partial degree insofar as concepts are concerned, can be established.

In the Qumran literature we again find a use of this verb in the context of exposing an esoteric layer of the Torah. In fact, the institution of *doresh torah*, the interpreter of the Law, seems to be related, as S. Fraade has indicated, to an esoteric teaching characteristic of the Dead Sea sect.[140] This verb also plays an important role in the passages discussing the exposition of secrets in the mish-naic and talmudic material. In one of the passages, three topics were considered eminently esoteric: the *'arayyiot* (or, according to some versions, *sitrei 'arayyiot*), the secrets of incestuous relations; the account of the Creation (Bereshit); and the account of the Chariot (Merkavah).[141] An Aramaic version of the boy's story re-garding the Hashmal, mentioned above, indicates that the boy was expounding the matter of the Hashmal rather than understanding it.[142] Provided that under-standing precedes expounding, a condition found in this context, we may assume that two different forms of dealing with the Hashmal are involved: one, repre-sented by the Hebrew version, involves understanding, which means the boy's mental involvement with the topic and which may have an experiential aspect (hence the danger), and at the same time a transgression of the esoteric restriction on studying some texts, as we shall see below. The Aramaic version, however, insists on the disclosure of secrets rather than their understanding. It is the later stage of dealing with the Hashmal secret, the turn to the audience, the revelation of a secret, that incited the reaction of the Hashmal. Indeed, R. Shlomo Yitzhaqi, better known as Rashi, the famous eleventh-century interpreter of the Talmud, connected the two stages of the boy's activity, saying that *hayah mevin* refers to an activity that leads to an exposition of the Hashmal.[143] According to such an inter-pretation, the intention of the fathoming of this topic was its subsequent exposi-tion, apparently under the impact of the story on R. Eleazar ben 'Arakh, mentioned above. It seems quite plausible that the three esoteric topics point to particular well-defined parts of the Bible: as Origen pointed out, the first chapter of Genesis and the first chapter of Ezekiel. According to Origen, the third forbidden part of the Bible was the Song of Songs, which in my opinion is somehow related to incest.[144]

The possible implication of the mentioning of these texts is, however, far from encouraging for a theory of a comprehensive arcanization of the Bible. On the contrary, it displays a restrictive arcanization: it assumes that only these texts, out of the huge biblical corpus, should not be interpreted, and again the verb lidrosh is used to point out issues not to be dealt with in public. This restriction means that the Bible as a whole is not an esoteric text. Origen's formulation of his statement, namely that the rabbis had limited the study of the last three texts, which were not taught to the younger ones, ad ultimum reservari, assumes that the texts themselves, not only their secret interpretations, have been reserved for a later period of study. I propose to call this phenomenon unisemic arcanization. We may assume that it is something in the plain sense of those texts, as perceived by some rabbis contemporary with Origen, that was thought to be problematic, not its alleged esoteric level. It may well be that some more widespread topics in the ambiance of the Tannaites were considered to be harmful, and the very reading of the book of Ezekiel could serve as a trigger of interest in these issues.

However, the mishnaic text, which uses the term lidrosh in the sense of expounding secret topics, assumes that the secrets can be extracted from the texts or elaborated when received from someone else. These texts are therefore understood at least as bisemic. Interpretation is instrumental in the extraction of secret meaning from the text, or at least in its exposition. Yet both Origen and the Mishnah indicate the special status of many of the same texts. We may assume that their slight divergence nevertheless reflects a bifurcation of an early esoteric position on the special status of these texts.

While Origen speaks of age as a criterion for dealing with these texts,[145] the mishnaic passage regards the size of the restricted group as quintessential. Thus, we have two different criteria,[146] which may reflect the existence of different nuances—and perhaps more than mere nuances—in ancient Jewish understandings of the unique nature of some parts of the Bible. It follows that the act of expounding secrets requires not so much a special initiation but rather a higher type of intelligence, which will facilitate the understanding of the details of the elaborations on the secrets. Mental maturity in general is mentioned elsewhere in the context of revealing the secrets of the Torah in a text that apparently constitutes a possible parallel to Origen's claim. E. E. Urbach, in his study of the relation between Origen's interpretations of the Song of Songs and the rabbinic homilies,[147] mentions (in another context other than Origen's tradition) the view in the Palestinian Talmud that while students are young they should be taught *divrei torah*, apparently only the plain sense of the Torah. When they become more mature, however, the secrets of the Torah should be revealed to them.[148] No specific age has been mentioned, as in the case of Origen, nor does this text indicate the necessity of special intellectual preparation, as the Mishnah on *hagigah* implies. In any case, these discussions, both those preserved in the rabbinic texts and those found in Origen (but not those of the Heikhalot literature) appear to involve no special rite of disclosing secrets, no ascetic path, no total transformation of the personality by the disclosure of the secrets of the Torah or of the world. As we have seen in the discussion of 'Avot, the transformation of the student's capacities precedes the reception of the secrets of the Torah, although their reception contributes to further transformations.

The talmudic interpretation of the mishnaic term *lidrosh* assumes an ascent of the protagonists to the Pardes.[149] In my opinion, which I will elaborate elsewhere in much more detail,[150] the three topics in the Mishnah correspond to the three first Tannaitic figures—Ben Azzai on incest, Ben Zoma on the account of Creation, and Aher on the account of the Chariot—while R. 'Aqivah is related to the correct knowledge of the concept of *shi'ur qomah*. In other words, the esoteric topics of the mishnaic period have been interpreted by means of legendary material dealing with the ascent on high. Although the rabbinic masters who edited the Talmud did not disclose the details of the three topics, it is obvious that they had in mind experiential moments related to the inquiry into these issues. At least in the Jewish Babylonian sources, discussions on esoteric issues were understood as leading to paranormal experiences.

I do not know, and therefore I cannot claim, that the discussions of the three topics also involved an in-depth study of the biblical texts mentioned by Origen. This is an open question, but a positive answer seems to be more plausible than a negative one.

An important text that reveals the use of the verb DRSh in a rather magical context, is found in the Heikhalot literature: "[God] has revealed to them the secret[151] of the Torah, how they will perform it, how they will expound[152] it, how they will make use of it. Immediately, the Divine Spirit appeared."[153] The verbs in this passage precisely parallel those in the previously quoted passage from *Sar ha-Torah*. In lieu of the gazing into the Torah, however, the appearance of the divine spirit is mentioned. This appearance is caused by magical means but in itself seems to be a rather mystical experience, which helps us better understand the mystical meaning of the gazing in the other text. This is, in my opinion, not a mere mentalistic reading but an experiential one fraught with revelatory potential.

Unlike the important career of the verb BYN in Jewish mysticism, DRSh became part of the more general homiletic kind of interpretation, and during the Middle Ages it did not generally become associated with expositions of secret topics. An interesting instance of connecting secrets and expounding is found in a theosophical treatise by R. Moses ben Shem Tov de Leon, *Sefer Shoshan ʿEdut*, where it is mentioned that by means of some Kabbalistic secrets the Torah has been expounded.[154] The only instance I am acquainted with that regards the *derash* as an exegetical device concerned with mystical meaning is found in a mid-thirteenth-century treatise by R. Isaac ben Abraham ibn Latif, as proposed by S. O. Heller-Wilensky.[155]

V. Concluding Remarks

The two most important biblical books mentioned above in the context of Jewish esotericism are Daniel and Ezekiel, books composed in Babylonia. Significant esoteric topics are alluded to in Ezekiel, and the emphatic use of the verb BYN in reference to deeper understanding occurs in Daniel. Interestingly, complex exegetical devices corresponding, according to Stephen Lieberman, to those found in the Babylonian environment have been applied to the enigmatic verses of the book of Daniel.[156] These observations may contribute some modest insights toward locating some of the origins of Jewish esotericism in the ambiance of exile circles in Babylonia,[157] or circles influenced by them, an observation corroborated by rabbinic statements asserting that the "names of the angels" were brought from Babylonia.[158] One medieval tradition has it that a Babylonian figure, Abu Aharon ben Shmuel of Baghdad, allegedly brought some secrets to Europe.[159] On the other hand, Palestinian tradition's preference for *hokhmah* over *binah* was adopted by the Kabbalistic theosophical tradition, where the sefirah of Hokhmah always precedes that of Binah. In any case, it is also possible to see the third sefirah as an evolutionary stage, in comparison to higher sefirah of Hokhmah.

To speak in broader terms, the above survey, tentative and fragmentary as it is, may be important for sketching later developments in Jewish esotericism in general and of Jewish hermeneutics in particular, for two main reasons. A belief in an esoteric aspect or layer, or even a comprehensive esoteric meaning of Jewish canonical texts, is not new to the medieval thinkers. In believing in such a dimension, they did not innovate out of nothing but sometimes continued, at times guessed, and often invented or fabricated secrets because they already had sufficient grounds to believe that a secret dimension is predicated in reliable sources. When dealing with the different forms of arcanization—magical, philosophical, or symbolic—we should bear in mind that it is rarely a crisis that created the claim for a secret dimension, as is sometime argued,[160] but a much more complex situation that involved systemic, psychological, and sociocultural interactions.

8

SEMANTICS, CONSTELLATION, AND INTERPRETATION

I. Semantic and Parasemantic Approaches

In the present and following chapters I would like to address two different forms of Jewish exegesis, to be distinguished by whether they anchor themselves in the semantic or the parasemantic aspects of the interpreted text. The former is represented substantially by the midrashic writings, the halakhic treatises, most of the theosophical-theurgical Kabbalistic literature, and Jewish philosophical allegoresis. The parasemantic aspects of the interpreted texts, on the other hand, are put into relief by the Heikhalot literature, some late midrashim (like *Midrash Konen*), Hasidei Ashkenaz esoteric corpora, and some advanced stages of the exegetical enterprise of the ecstatic Kabbalah. Although both approaches strive to extract forms of meaning from the canonical texts, the difference between them is to be sought in the difference between the elements of the texts that are exploited more in the course of the interpretive moves. And though any attempt to distinguish too sharply between the two approaches, as if they occurred in totally distinct literary corpora, will inevitably become a futile exercise in abstract categorization, it is necessary to understand the different exegetical strategies that correspond to the different aspects of the interpreted material.

The biblical corpus, a literature that attracted the attention of persons concerned with ways of thinking, believing, or behaving much more than with questions of rhetoric, aesthetics, metaphysics, or history, was commonly approached as conveying major messages whose importance had to be anchored in as many parts of the canonical texts as possible. This attitude is associated with the creation of conceptual schemes that had to be imposed by means of various forms of ingenuous "translation" of an archaic language and worldview into new terms. Such an approach adopted basically semantic strategies for interpretation, to be defined as engaging the meaning of the separate linguistic unit, the word, or the sentence as the crucial object of interpretation. By doing so, one semantic entity is transposed onto another way of discourse that wishes to push forward a particular message.

By parasemantic hermeneutics I understand the interpreter's recourse to the assumption that even those elements of the text that are not commonly thought to convey a message in its original ancient context did so in a hidden manner. The size of letters, the graphics of the Torah scroll, the spaces between letters, are all interrogated in order to elicit even more recondite secrets.

The structured nature of the message to be conveyed via the biblical interpretation inherent in the semantic approach is public for at least two reasons. It may have some sources in speculative systems that are independent of the biblical text and so are available to an audience that does not depend on the interpreter who adopts it. A famous case is Maimonides' adoption of substantial Aristotelian concepts and some Neoplatonic views for his interpretation of the Bible. Again, to stay with this example, the interpreter may be concerned not only with the elucidation of an important ancient text but much more with shaping a certain religious worldview, and as such he turns consciously to the wider public. Strong semantic interpreters, namely those who adopt articulated conceptual frameworks, will only rarely insert in their writings discussions on parasemantic aspects of the text.

Parasemantic aspects seem to be much more idiosyncratic. They resort to textual elements which, though significant in the interpretive discourse, are not accepted as such by the ancient context and presumably by many of the interpreters' contemporaries. The semantic inchoateness of the interpreted material is therefore much greater. The choices made by the interpreter are fairly random and, more crucially, it is the syntactic structures of the text that vanish. In fact, in many cases even the structure of one word disintegrates because of the emphasis put on its separate components. As we saw in Chapter 2, even the white aspects of a text may become the starting point for speculation. Even more dramatically than in postmodern theories of hypertextuality, the order of the narrative has been severely attenuated in many Kabbalistic forms of interpretation, thereby allowing connections that are more nominal than syntactic. Emerging from a deep immersion in the biblical text, the numerous affinities established between different components of the Bible, conceived of as a hypertext, do not obliterate the ordinary sequence of letters, although the sequence is often ignored during the interpretive process. Neither did the widespread custom of creating literary collages by appropriating verses from different parts of the Bible (especially Psalms) for the daily Jewish liturgy involve any problematic attitude toward the biblical text.[1]

In this chapter I would like to deal with early examples of semantic interpretations that will later culminate in much stronger hermeneutical systems articulated in medieval Kabbalah. Parasemantic exegesis will be addressed much more extensively in the next chapter.

If postbiblical Jewish literature is a vast complex of different forms of commentary, the most influential mode of interpretation is referred to as midrashic. Like any generic term, it covers a vague category, a fact that does not free a survey of Jewish hermeneutics from having to confront the characteristics of this genre. Earnest and worthy attempts to do so are too numerous to list here, let alone to cover thoroughly,[2] but I would like to highlight some of the most salient features for the further development of hermeneutics in Jewish mystical literature. Let me start with the theological presuppositions of the genre.

Midrashic literature was informed by few theologoumena, which have never been presented fully explicated. Nevertheless, it can be generally envisioned as a literary corpus dominated by a personalistic view of God as deeply concerned with human affairs, a changing entity endowed with power and able to interfere in the course of history. Though similar to the major trends in biblical theology, the talmudic-midrashic one evolved under the hard circumstances of a people in exile, and the main theological trait not emphasized in the Bible is the identification of God with the vicissitudes of Jewish history. No longer is God a deity who rules history, as He does in the Bible, but rather one who willingly accepts the tragic fate of his elected people.

As distinct from the main line of the Heikhalot literature, and even more sharply from *Sefer Yetzirah*, *Shimmushei Torah*, and *Shimmushei Tehilim*, God in the rabbinic literature identifies Himself with the fate of Israel but separates himself from Israel's attempts to involve him in their efforts to examine the Torah.[3] The assumption (described in Chapter 4) that supernal powers will be involved in the process of learning and deciding the meaning of a religious text is quite alien to midrashic literature.

In the classical midrashim, the identification of the Torah with the divine is marginal; the major assumption is that after revelation the authoritative text is an independent entity, to be encountered as a sacred text, which can be interrogated in order to obtain answers to crucial religious questions. The separation between God and Torah notwithstanding, it seems that the nature of the rabbinic herme-neutical enterprise reflects the dynamic nature of God. In lieu of one frozen type of information that can be extracted from a biblical verse concerning, for example, the unchanging dimension of the divine body of Heikhalot theology,[4] in rabbinic literature the biblical text remains open to novel interpretations. This semantic openness can be explained in more than one way. From our vantage point it is the absence of an explicit and systematic theology that enabled a freer, hermeneutical attitude toward the text in the Talmud and Midrash.[5] I do not assume that these literary corpora are totally free of theological presuppositions; this would be too strong a claim. However, the absence of treatises dealing with theological matters in the strict sense is not an accident. I assume that the midrashists avoided such a theological move on purpose, for the strong theological bias of the Heikhalot literature and Sefer Yetzirah, which must have been known to at least some of the rabbinic masters, is evident. On the other hand, they avoided focusing on the parasemantic facets of the texts, such as gematria,[6] shapes of the letters, attribu-tions of huge dimensions to the biblical text, or identification of the Torah with supernal entities. It is the nonmetaphysical approach to the text that enabled the midrashists to maintain its relative openness, a move that is reminiscent of the more modern approaches. We may fairly apply Roland Barthes's description of the affinity between the langage classique and nature to the attitude of midrashic interpreters toward the Bible: "Que signifie en effet l'économie rationelle du langage classique sinon que la Nature est pleine, possédable, sans fuite et sans ombre, tout entière soumises aux rets de la parole?"[7] Midrashic language may well be viewed as a langage classique, whereas the Kabbalistic language accords in princi-ple with Barthes's description of langage poètique.

For a midrashic interpreter, the canonical text has to stand by itself; it has to open itself to the reader, who, on his part, is not supposed to be deeply indoctri-nated in any particular theology. The fateful correlation between a particular theol-ogy and predictable interpretations of specific texts was circumvented by the midrashists. They sacrificed, so to speak, the mysterious and magical attainment of their contemporaries in order to remain with the open text, which can be addressed to a larger community. By remaining faithful to the syntactic and semantic components of the text, the masters of the Midrash were able to communicate messages that could be adapted to the changing historical circumstances,[8] whereas the parasemantic elements generated meanings that remained beyond the scope of history and change. Whereas the Midrash is naturally related to the oral, fluid aspects of communication, the mystical and magical views of the Torah in the early Middle Ages were concerned much more with the unique, unchangeable messages to be extracted by means of eccentric hermeneutics precisely from the written form of the Torah.

To put it another way, infrastructural and hyperstructural readings of the text, found in the mystical-magical literatures, lose contact with the common people, with average consciousness and regular practice. The Torah as a huge hieroglyph can be contemplated as if through a telescope; the concern with the special significance of the separate letters can be compared to the reading of the Torah by means of a microscope. In both cases the specific texture of the text vanishes, especially its semantic parts. Dominated by their belief in the unique nature of the elements of language, the Jewish mystics could retreat into more formal, schematic, sometimes atomistic readings very different from midrashic semantics. The midrashists were reading the Torah with regular glasses, which may still distort the meaning of the text, but without exploding its inner syntax. Just as the regular fabric of life is disorganized by contemplative immersion and a too detailed penetration into the infrastructure of the regular objects, or by indulgence in cosmic speculation, so too is the case in the domain of the study of the texts. Special types of consciousness seem to be involved in mystical and magical interpretations of the Torah: transcendence of the mundane zone in the case of those who ascend to the Merkavah, or revelations stemming from the Prince of the Torah according to another text, or magical rites related to the use of the divine names extracted from the various biblical verses. These were not practices to be preached to the multitude, but attainments of the elite.[9]

Moreover, according to warnings found in rabbinic literature, the best known being the legend of the four sages who entered the Pardes, it is dangerous even for the elite to indulge in mystical and cosmogonic speculation. Midrash is a horizontal hermeneutics par excellence; hence the ethical focus of this literature. The basic situation of the Torah in this literature is that of a sacred scripture which stems from the supernal world but, according to the vast majority of texts, is descended and now found here below. When dealing with nature, Midrash envisions an encounter with it, not an explanation of its emergence from the higher world. However, the magical, the mystical, and the philosophical hermeneutics integrated substantial vertical elements. They bridged the gap between the supernal and the mundane either by creating an ontological nexus—emanation schemes, for example—or by elaborating on the theory of symbol as organically related to the supernal world, or by describing how to elevate the soul to its source, or by exploring the possibility of influencing the divine realm through magical or theurgical techniques. These are important and characteristic forms of Kabbalistic hermeneutics, as we have already seen in previous chapters.

II. On Two Divine Middot: From Midrash to Kabbalah

One of the best-known theologoumena in midrashic literature assumes the existence of two measures, *middot*, understood in many texts as two divine attributes, mercy and justice (or judgment). Though historically predating the earliest midrashic compositions, as we learn from Philo's recurrent resort to two divine attributes, and from other ancient material insightfully analyzed by Shlomo Naeh,[10] it may be that already the biblical material represents some distinction between the divine names as pointing to different theological approaches, as has been suggested by Israel Knohl.[11]

The midrashic interest in the various meanings of the divine names constitutes the incipient stages, already evident in Philo's many discussions on the topic, in a direction that will be fully exploited by the vast majority of Kabbalists. So, for example, we read in an influential midrashic text, *Pesiqta' de-Rabbi Kahana'*, about a passage from R. Meir, an important tannaitic author:[12] " 'The Tetragrammaton comes out of its place.'[13] It comes out from one attribute to another attribute, from the attribute of judgment to the attribute of mercy over Israel."[14] The gist of the passage is that despite the correspondence between the Tetragrammaton and the attribute of judgment, which is indeed a very rare identification, the Tetragrammaton is changing its regular activity and acts as an attribute of mercy. Thus, a distinction between the different passages in the Bible where the divine names occur is established; different divine powers are conceived of as operating in different passages that are related to divine actions. Though the "attributal" reading in the midrash does not bring together several biblical passages in order to define the Tetragrammaton as an attribute of mercy, this theologoumenon is accepted as a given fact and is put into relief without providing a more dense reading of the pertinent passages. Thus, it is an implicit constellation that works in the rabbinic perception of the meaning of the divine names.

Another formulation of the same dynamics appears in several midrashic sources as an interpretation of Ecclesiastes 8:1: "Who is like the wise man? and who knows the interpretation of a thing? a man's wisdom makes his face to shine, and the boldness of his face is changed." In *Leviticus Rabba'* this verse is interpreted as pointing to God, who is described as wise and as revealing the Torah to Moses. As to the last part of the verse, it is said in the same vein that it is a description of

God: "He is changing from the attribute of judgment to the attribute of mercy over Israel."[15] Apparently the shining face is the attribute of mercy, while the boldness of face stands for that of judgment.

These midrashic traditions constitute, in my opinion, attempts to translate the changes in divine will in terms that are more understandable. By resorting to the theology of divine attributes, a more "stable" system had been created, a system described at least once as somehow independent of God's will.[16] It should be mentioned that the rabbinic sources, like Philo in passages to be addressed below, assigned the role of governing to the divine attributes because by means of those attributes the world had been created. Some forms of ontological relations between the imagined attributes and the manner in which reality has been constituted and is ruled prepared the more detailed and consistent theosophical hermeneutics to be analyzed in Chapter 10.

These midrashic views are very modest indications of a process of gradual and more complex constellation of the biblical discourse, which will become paramount for the hermeneutical approach of theosophical Kabbalah. The "constellated" hermeneutics of some Jewish medieval literatures differs from the "disastered" approach of the Midrash and modern Jewish thinkers like Benjamin, Levinas, and Derrida, and comes closer to the concept of "systematics," to resort to Barthes's term.[17] According to a late midrash, Midrash Tadsche', which was committed to writing sometime in the eleventh century, "the two cherubim on the ark of testimony correspond to the two holy names: the Tetragrammaton and 'Elohim."[18]

One of the earliest Kabbalistic documents, a passage attributed (correctly, in my opinion) to R. Abraham ben David of Posquieres, combined the dichotomy of the two attributes with a more complicated theosophical scheme. At the end of an interesting passage dealing with the operations related to two attributes, he writes:

Since they were created du-partzufin, their actions are performed in cooperation and equality and in a total union,[19] without any separation. Furthermore, unless they would be created du-partzufin, no union would emerge from them and the attribute of judgment would not converge with [that of] mercy, nor would the attribute of mercy converge with [that of] judgment. But now, since they were created du-partzufin, each of them may approach his partner and unite with him, and his desire is to willingly unite with his partner, so "that the Tabernacle may be one."[20] A proof of this [view] is found in the [divine] names, which refer to each other, since Yod He[21] refers to the attribute of judgment and 'Elohim to the attribute of mercy, as in "Then the Tetragrammaton rained upon Sodom and upon Gomorrah."[22]

"The Tetragrammaton rained" [means] "He passed from one attribute to another attribute."[23]

This early Kabbalist resorts to the midrashic view of this specific type of relationship between the two attributes as a proof text for his view (analyzed elsewhere in some detail) concerning the emergence of the two distinct divine attributes from an androgynous unit and their possibility of cooperating because of it.[24] Presumably, the emanation of the sefirot Hesed and Gevurah from Binah—which is presumed to be the two-faced divine power, the du-partzufin—is the theosophical process that is described in ben David's text. As we shall see, a very similar stand is found in Philo of Alexandria. But unlike the Philonic view, which speaks solely of cooperation between the attributes, the midrashic proof text speaks of the possibility of transformations of one attribute into another, this being the illustration of the ideal of cooperation. In fact, the two processes, though similar, do not coincide.

R. Abraham ben David's grandson, R. Asher ben David, elaborates in his *Commentary of Thirteen Attributes* on the view of R. Abraham, though he takes the position one step further: provided that every sefirah somehow includes the other sefirot, the Tetragrammaton may refer to all the sefirot, as each divine power can be transformed into another. This is the case even where two diametrically opposed sefirot are concerned, since they too are united to each other.[25] Although the differentiation between the attributes was part of an attempt to account for the different types of divine activity, the exegetical difficulties and the dynamic vision of God conspired to attenuate the differences between them. By addressing the two Kabbalists' discussions, I have intended to point out both the continuity and the difference between the midrashic and the Kabbalistic understanding of the two attributes. Needless to say, discussions of the change from one attribute to another are quite widespread in Kabbalah, and I have not attempted to exhaust its later developments.[26]

The interest in the dynamic vision of the two divine attributes as changing into each other is found also in *Sefer ha-Hokhmah* of R. Eleazar of Worms, an Ashkenazi master who was, roughly speaking, a contemporary of R. Asher ben David.[27] In another writing he contends that "the Tetragrammaton is inscribed on the Seat of Judgment, and likewise on the Seat of Mercy and on the foreheads of the Cherubim, as it is written:[28] 'whose name is called by the name of the Lord of hosts who dwells upon the Cherubim,' and corresponding to it are the two [divine] names."[29] The fact that the Tetragrammaton is conceived of as inscribed on the two seats, presumably representing the two attributes, may be related to the transition from one attribute to another.

Let me attempt to describe the affinities between the vague prerabbinic and rabbinic theologoumena related to the divine attributes and the Kabbalistic and Ashkenazi passages adduced above. One way to address the quandary of the relationship between them is to claim arguments of continuity or discontinuity or, in more academic nomenclature, of coincidence of meanings philologically demonstrated or the resort of the Kabbalists to midrashic texts as mere proof texts. The other way would be to look to the affinities in terms of continuing an earlier vector, which assumes both exposure to the earlier text as religiously meaningful and at the same time relating the exegete's spiritual universe to components of the interpreted proof text. Thus we may assume that "mere" proof text may be sometimes better understood as a springboard.

Especially important for the later developments of the hermeneutics of the theosophical-theurgical Kabbalah is the dynamization of other aspects in the rabbinic understanding of the Bible. A fine example of what I would describe as a dynamic perception of a biblical event appears in *Mekhilta' de-Rabbi Ishma°el*, where Exodus 12:51, "Even that selfsame day it came to pass that all the hosts of the Lord went out from the Land of Egypt," is discussed as follows: "Whenever Israel is enslaved, the Shekhinah, as it were, is enslaved with them, as it is said, 'And they saw the God of Israel, and under His feet there was,' etc. But after they were redeemed, what does it say? 'And the likeness of the very heaven for clearness.' "[30]

The full biblical verse from Exodus 24:10 goes as follows: "(a) And they saw the God of Israel (b) and under His feet there was a kind of paved work of sapphire stone (c) and it was as the likeness of the very heaven for clearness." Part (c) expands and explains the content of (b), the subject of both phrases being the same, "a kind of paved work"; (c) merely complements the description of the "work" as "sapphire stone" by adding the attribute of clearness. The Midrash, however, perceives parts (b) and (c) as relating to two opposite situations: (b) is conceived of as describing the vision of Moses and the elders of Israel while still enslaved, a reading seemingly substantiated by an intertextual understanding of *livnat ha-sappir*, "paved work of sapphire," which the ancient exegete regarded as an allusion to *levenim*, "bricks,"[31] seen as a symbol of Jewish slavery in Egypt.[32] This pun allows one to attribute the state of slavery to God Himself: He, like the children of Israel, had bricks beneath His feet.[33] Especially pertinent is the tradition adduced in the name of *Midrash 'Avkir* by the thirteenth-century Ashkenazi master R. Eleazar ha-Darshan: "a kind of paved work of sapphire stone: it reflects the status of Israel, when they were treading the mortar with their feet; as though one could conceive it was above: In all their affliction He was afflicted."[34]

Once they had been redeemed, however, the vision changed: part (c) of the verse describes the new state of God when His feet were apparently "clear." The link between the two motifs is assured by the recurrence of the noun ʿetzem both in connection with the exodus from Egypt and in the context of the vision of God as clear.[35] An entire myth of the passage of Israel from slavery to freedom is here attributed analogically to God Himself, described in highly anthropomorphic terms. We witness an explicit case of participation mystique of the divine in the human experience of slavery and liberation; in the words of the sequence in the Mekhilta', "in all their afflictions He was afflicted."[36]

However, this changing perception of history and of the divine attributes can be more adequately qualified. In the same midrash we learn that God revealed Himself under two main attributes: mercy and judgment.[37] When the midrash wishes to exemplify the appearance of the attribute of mercy, it quotes part (c) of our verse. On the basis of this view, I would conjecture that the attribute of judgment is thought to be hinted at by the name ʾElohei Yisrael, the name ʾElohim usually being the common term for this attribute. Thus, our verse was regarded as pointing to a double revelation: of judgment and of mercy.[38] Moreover, even if this assumption proves to be incorrect, we still encounter a "dynamization" of the biblical verse: according to the Mekhilta', it refers to an entire process that occurs simultaneously on the historical and the divine planes. This intimate affinity between the two spheres of existence and their dynamics is forced on the verse, using current devices of midrashic hermeneutics. What distinguishes this particular interpretation from the more common midrashic ones is the correlation achieved between two processes—not states—which, while ontologically remote, are part of a higher dynamic structure. Here we are at the edge of myth, but a very specific type of myth. As R. ʿAqivah went on to say there, "Were it not expressly written in scripture, one could not say it. Israel said to God: 'Thou hast redeemed Thyself'—as though one could conceive of such a thing." The redemption of the Shekhinah depends, therefore, on the prior salvation of Israel.

III. Between Midrashic and Medieval Speculative Hermeneutics

Roughly speaking, medieval hermeneutics as represented by the most important practices adopted by philosophical, Kabbalistic, and Ashkenazi Hasidic literatures drastically deviated from midrashic, semantically oriented hermeneutics. The reason for such a bold departure seems to be related to the installment of strong theologies, which were not characteristic of midrashic literature and thought. All the above-mentioned types of thought were profoundly influenced by relatively elaborate theologies, which impinged on their peculiar manner of interpreting canonical texts. The midrashic approach is deeply exegetical, as it struggled with the semantic aspects of the text, only rarely allowing the impact of rigid extra-textual systems of thought. Although there cannot be any doubt that Midrash departs from some of the biblical ways of thought, it still remained immersed in the same domain of problems that preoccupied biblical thinking: the myth of exile and redemption, the myth of election, the deep concern with ritual and ethics. This is not so much the case in the medieval literatures mentioned above. More theologically inclined than hermeneutical, they incessantly struggled with the problem of how to import their respective metaphysical systems into the older texts, much more than attempting to embark on a sustained effort to interrogate these texts in order to discover solutions for their theological quandaries. This approach will be discussed in the next chapter under the name of intercorporality.

If the midrashic discourse is a large-scale enterprise in exhausting the possible implications of the "dark," namely ambiguous, parts of the canon, the super-imposition of elaborate theologies—Aristotelian, Neoplatonic, or theosophic—is characteristic of most medieval hermeneutics. By so doing, the speculative inter-preters of the Middle Ages infused their theologies in the midrashic interpretation of the Bible as well. To a great extent, the speculative interpretations were con-cerned with a comprehensive approach to Jewish religion as much as with a verse-centered approach. In their search for and emphasis on the hidden meaning of the various religious texts, some medieval writers helped to establish the idea of the plain sense of the scriptures, the peshat, a notion marginal to midrashic and talmudic thought. Midrash, on the other side, is not only a verse-centered ex-egesis but also an interversal hermeneutics,[39] which explores the significance of an obscure, controversial text with the help of another obscure, though perhaps less obscure, text. Interesting literary achievements of the midrashic discourse emerge peculiarly from the interval created by ambiguities inherent in some as-pects of various biblical verses.

In the greater intellectual systems of the Middle Ages the major effort is inter-cultural. Aristotle, Plato, the Muslim kalam, and some other forms of systematic thought were employed by Jewish thinkers in order to illuminate the obscurities of the Jewish tradition, biblical and talmudic-midrashic. It seems that only in a few cases in medieval Jewish literature can we detect a relatively faithful approach to midrashic interpretation, namely in some forms of Kabbalah. The more arrest-ing achievements of midrashic interpretation stem from the unexpected results produced through purely linguistic interpretive techniques; on the other hand, the speculative interpretations were based on the introduction of novel types of interpretation, allegorical or symbolic, or of older Jewish techniques that were marginal in the midrashic literature, in order to achieve expected results. The speculative approach was intended to clarify, as much as possible, the religious mechanism that governs not only perfect human behavior but also divine be-havior, by penetrating into the secrets of the higher worlds; in fact, both Kabbalah and Jewish medieval philosophy constitute different forms of demystification of the divine realm by comprehensive explanations.

Midrashic interpretation is interested in keeping the higher world a mystery of the divine will. Ironically, it is the midrashic approach that prevents any metaphysical discussion of the problem of *unde malum*, the origin of evil, in answer to the question of what the reason is for the terrible death of a righteous person like R. 'Aqivah: "Be silent, this what ascended into the [divine] thought."[40] The inventiveness of the midrashist is deeply rooted in his ability to manipulate the text as a literary work rather than a theological artifact, whereas the speculative attitudes envisioned their canon essentially as a fountainhead of theological truth and only secondarily as a literary creation. Freer from systematic theological constraints than the medieval Jewish thinkers were, the midrashists were able to respond to the same verse in different ways. A theology inclined to emphasize the divine will, namely an ever-changing power that cannot easily be formulated in itself but can only be glimpsed through its manifestation in a written document, informed a much more open attitude toward the text, one Handelman described as more metonymic. While a similar attitude may be found in some Kabbalistic schools, others, like their philosophical contemporaries, were concerned with exposing the one precise esoteric meaning of the canonical texts. This openness of Midrash to different though quite loose theological stands allowed a more creative hermeneutics. This is why modern research was able to propose relatively comprehensive descriptions of the theologies of the medieval speculative Jewish literatures, while the study of midrashic thought still awaits reconstructions of the different trends of thought in the midrashic and talmudic texts.

In the following I shall try to substantiate my skeptical attitude toward the view that Kabbalistic hermeneutics in general is more faithful than other medieval literatures to the midrashic approach. There is no doubt that several Kabbalistic schools are as distant from the midrashic approach as the medieval philosophers were. Among examples are the Provençal Kabbalah and its Geronese repercussions; it would be very difficult to find midrashic approaches in the writings of R. Isaac Sagi-Nahor, one of the paragons of early Kabbalah. The dry, monosemic, theosophical symbols and discussions may perhaps reflect earlier esoteric traditions, extracted by R. Isaac's predecessors from traditional texts that preceded him by decades, but his own hermeneutical approach is very technical. He relates the various elements of the canonical text, the words of the daily liturgy or the sentences of *Sefer Yetzirah*, to the theosophical *termini technici* without any substantial effort to explain the semantic relationship between them. A bit more hermeneutical is the approach of his student, R. Ezra of Gerona, but his follower, R. Azriel of Gerona, seems to return partially to the way of R. Isaac the Blind, even intensifying the technical use of philosophical terminology. The ʿIyyun literature, whose affinities to R. Azriel of Gerona were already acknowledged by scholars, rarely bothers with interpreting substantial parts of the canonical texts. Somewhat similar to them are the writings of the ha-Kohen brothers, two important Kabbalists flourishing in the mid-thirteenth century. They commented on a series of topics, such as the letters of the alphabet and the biblical cantillation sign but, with one exception, not on the canonical texts. Abraham Abulafia's writings are deeply concerned with the mystical and philosophical issues, but his interest in the midrashic approach is rather scanty.[41]

What remained of the major Kabbalistic schools of the thirteenth century are the book of *Bahir*, the Kabbalistic school of Nahmanides, and the book of the *Zohar*. Though in radically different ways, it seems that only in these three cases is there a strong awareness of Midrash as a powerful source of creativity. The *Bahir*, sometimes referred to as the *Midrash of R. Nehunya ben ha-Qanah*, indeed uses some midrashic strategies.[42] This awareness is evident in R. Yehudah ben Yaqar's *Commentary of the Prayer* and, to a lesser extent, in Nahmanides' writings.[43] It gradually disappeared in the writings of the followers of Nahmanides, in the late thirteenth and early fourteenth centuries. In later Kabbalah, as represented by the Lurianic literature, the midrashic approach is even smaller, as the use of the *termini technici* prevail in an unprecedented manner. The more the symbolic approach was attenuated by its absorption into a comprehensive and detailed myth, the less can we expect a resort to a midrashic attitude toward the interpreted texts.[44] It seems, therefore, that only the *Zohar* has consciously intended to accept the literary genre of Midrash, as even some of his titles demonstrate: *Midrash ha-Neʿelam*, *Midrasho shel Rashbi*, *Midrash Va-Yehi ʾOr*. Much more significant, however, is the actual structure of the Zoharic discourse, which reflects a deep affinity with rhetorical strategies of Midrash.[45] The absence of technical terms, the presence of rhetorical locutions, and the implicit theology that emerges out of the interrelated biblical verses pervade important segments of the *Zohar*, transforming them into part of a medieval Midrash. What seems to be characteristic of the Zoharic theology, and to a certain extent some important segments of other theosophical-theurgical kinds of Kabbalah, is the fusion between the static and the anthropomorphic theology typical of the Heikhalot literature, on the one hand, and the more dynamic, powerful, and personalistic attitude of midrashic-talmudic thought, on the other. The static shape of the divine *shiʿur qomah* was "activated," at least on some levels, by the biblical and midrashic views of God as will and power that can augment or diminish.[46]

The reintroduction into Jewish theology, toward the end of the twelfth century, of the dynamism found in mystical literature had a deep impact on Kabbalistic hermeneutics. The ongoing processes taking place between the various divine attributes, which are more than the metamorphoses of the divine limbs, allowed a much more creative and dynamic reading of the Bible as reflecting the supernal processes into the decoded polysemic texts.[47] To the extent that the formal elements remained important in Kabbalistic theosophy, they can also be detected in the peculiar emphasis on the shapes of the Hebrew letters, which became a real fascination of the theosophical Kabbalists.[48] This correlation is obvious in *Sefer ha-Temunah*, which surmises that the alphabet is the real countenance of the divine configuration, referred to as shi'ur qomah.[49]

The strong presence of more articulated theologies among the Jews is therefore the major factor in preventing the development of midrashic discourse in the Middle Ages. When the focus of the literary discourse is divided between the inner tensions of the semantics of the text and the strong intellectual superstructure that in most cases emerged outside the tradition that produced the text, the midrashic approach is radically weakened. Some Kabbalistic writings, particularly the Zohar, remained close to the midrashic discourse only when they were able to disguise the existence of an elaborate theosophy, which was commonly expressed by other Kabbalistic writings in complex, novel nomenclature. Whether the diametrically opposite Kabbalistic and philosophical approaches to the canonical texts are the result of a deep spiritual crisis,[50] or more variegated explanations for the emergence of the new modes of interpreting the texts are more pertinent, it is obvious that the medieval thinkers distanced themselves from the nonconstellated thought of Talmud and Midrash.

The attenuation of the role of Kabbalistic theosophical terminology, sometimes by its psychological interpretation, enabled Polish Hasidism to regain some of the charm of the midrashic discourse. Yet even in the cases of those Hasidic masters who did not use Kabbalistic terminology, it is rather difficult to find a classical midrashic treatment of the texts. The reappearance of orality in the Hasidic groups, in the form of sermons delivered by Hasidic leaders, was a watershed, which contributed to a certain transcending of the medieval ideological superstructures in favor of simpler and more fluid theologies informing a simpler and more flexible hermeneutics. It seems that simpler theologies invite a simpler hermeneutical and exegetical approach, whereas the more comprehensive and systematic theologies support more complex and eccentric exegesis and hermeneutics. (This issue is addressed in some detail in Appendix 3.) Indubitably, Martin Buber was right when he considered Hasidism an attempt to deschematize the mystery, namely religion, which became more schematic and mechanical in Lurianic Kabbalah.[51]

IV. PHILO OF ALEXANDRIA AND SYMBOLIC EXEGESIS

I would like now to offer an explanation of the emergence of those types of symbolism characteristic of theosophical-theurgical Kabbalah. My main claim is that the ascent of new theologies that strive to validate themselves attracted material from the sacred scriptures in order to use them as proof texts and thus retrojected themselves into the earlier sacrosanct texts. This move is even more conspicuous when it takes place within a polemic ambiance. Here I shall deal only with a few examples, which seem to me to be the earliest late-antiquity appearances; the later and more widespread resort to symbolism in medieval Kabbalah will be dealt with in a separate chapter. I would like to emphasize that I make no claim to have found a beginning or the precise historical origins of a certain type of symbolism. Rather, I am concerned with the types of cultural and religious situations that invite a different form of metaphorical expression.

A survey of the developments related to Jewish mystical exegesis cannot overlook the fundamental fact that the first extensive commentaries on many parts of the Bible were produced by Philo of Alexandria before the articulation of rabbinic literature in written form. Written in Greek in a center of Hellenistic culture, Philo's commentaries were destined to have a lasting impact on the emerging Christianity, which was responsible for the preservation of his manuscripts. Though transferred to Caesarea, a center of patristic and rabbinic scholarship on the shores of the Mediterranean Sea, those manuscripts did not attract the attention of Jewish masters, and the name of Philo and his commentaries was destined to disappear from the horizons of Jewish thought and exegesis for a millennium and a half. If he had any influence on medieval Jews, a supposition which in my opinion remains to be proved, it is a matter of mediated transmission, perhaps by Christian thought, rather than of direct acquaintance with his writings in the original or in translation. This rejection of the Alexandrian exegete by all the rabbis is part of a cultural decision, which preferred other forms of thought and writing.[52] For our purposes, however, the emergence of articulated allegorical and symbolic approaches to the Bible in antiquity should be seriously taken in consideration from both the phenomenological and historical points of view—even more so when the exegete is seen by many leading scholars to be a mystic.[53]

Phenomenologically speaking, the emergence of commentaries that are concerned with extracting from the sacred scriptures a set of ideas that were influenced by various Greek philosophies in their terminology and concepts was described as a radical move. Philo is indubitably such an interpreter and has been described by Gerald Bruns as a radical interpreter.[54] Philo's oeuvre represents a dramatic development whose specific characteristics shaped the form of Western religious thought for many generations. His thought has been seen by Erwin Goodenough as part of a more widespread phenomenon, a Jewish mystical stream that was antirabbinic in nature and resorted to symbols. Were Goodenough's theory accepted, it could provide material for a strong and influential form of ancient Judaism that would constitute a parallel to medieval Kabbalistic symbology and invite historical reflections about possible affinities between ancient and medieval Jewish forms of symbolically inclined mysticism. However, the material Goodenough presented in his numerous volumes on Jewish symbols, as well as in his *By Light, Light*, did not support his claim of a widespread and uniform mystical trend in Judaism.[55] Yet this critique does not invalidate Philo's mystical inclinations or his resort to symbolism in his vast oeuvre. His mystical leanings and exegetical stands, unlike Goodenough's argument for an ancient stream of mystical Judaism developing alongside Philo, are not a scholarly reconstruction.

Historically speaking, the hermeneutical phenomena embodied in Philo's books might have remained isolated events with no repercussions in Judaism. The claim of the impact of Philo's exegesis on a layer of Zoharic literature was advanced by Samuel Belkin but rejected firmly by Scholem's school.[56] This rejection of a specific claim does not, however, negate the possibility that phenomenological affinities should be pointed out, and this indeed is what Scholem did on a number of occasions, when he called attention to fascinating resemblances between the Alexandrian exegete and Kabbalistic hermeneutics.[57] Moreover, the historical nexus between Philo and medieval Jewish mysticism should not be totally rejected. I would suggest keeping an open mind to various possibilities that would explain parallels or even influences. As I have attempted to show elsewhere, there is at least one striking instance when the similarity between a passage from R. Abraham ben David, one of the first Kabbalists, and a view expressed in Philo.[58] Furthermore, an interesting parallel can be drawn between a passage from Rabad's son, R. Isaac the Blind, dealing with eschatology, and a passage from Philo.[59] Here, however, it is not the possibility of historical linkages that concerns me but the phenomenon represented by Philo's symbolic exegesis. Needless to say, the following observations do not attempt to offer an overall survey of Philo's exegesis,[60] nor even a comprehensive analysis of his resort to the term *symbol*. The goal of the present discussion is to put into relief the existence of a special type of symbolism that relates biblical material to divine powers and events, in a manner reminiscent of the later theosophical-theurgical Kabbalah. Let me start with Philo's discussion of the biblical cherubim as symbols of the two divine attributes. The three texts adduced below have often been quoted together, though I could not find any sustained discussion that addressed their hermeneutic implications and their relevance for later Kabbalistic symbolism.

In *De Cherubim* we read:

> With the one God who truly Is are two all-high and primary powers, Goodness and Sovereignty. Through his Goodness he engendered all that is, through his Sovereignty he rules what he has engendered, but a third uniting both is intermediating Logos, for it is through Logos that God is both ruler and good. Of these two powers, Sovereignty and Goodness, the cherubim are symbols, but of Logos, the flaming sword is the symbol.[61]

Elsewhere, again when discussing the nature of the cherubim, he claims:

> For it is necessary that the Powers, the Creative and Royal, should look toward each other in contemplation of each other's beauty, and at the same time in conspiracy for the benefit of things that have come into existence. In the second place, since God, who is One, is both the Creator and King, naturally the Powers, though divided, are again united. For it was advantageous that they be divided in order that the one might function as creator, the other as ruler. For the functions differ. And the Powers were brought together in another way by the eternal juxtaposition of the names[62] in order that the Creative Power might share in the Royal and the Royal in the Creative. Both incline toward the Mercy Seat. For if God had not been merciful to the things which now exist, nothing would have been created through the Creative Power nor be given legal regimentation by the Royal Power.[63]

For the history of the emergence of the symbolic mode of interpretation in theosophical-theurgical Kabbalah, it is important to point out the organization of two crucial issues in the biblical text according to the ontology that informs Philo's thought based on the activity of two divine attributes: the Creative and the Royal. These attributes are symbolized by the two cherubim and the two divine names.[64] More consequential from our point of view, however, is the relationship between the two cherubim: they are not conceived of as statically pointing to the two divine powers but rather embody in their status a principle that informs their emergence: just as their substance is identical to that of the seat of mercy—according to the biblical description—and inclines toward it, so too the attributes emerged from the divine substance and cooperate with each other. Thus, both the structure and the processes related to the divine powers are thought to be inherent in the structure and position of the cherubim. The two divine attributes and their manner of activity inform many of Philo's discussions. Of special importance for understanding the nexus between exegesis and mysticism is Philo's confession regarding the topic of cherubim. He indicates that "it [the interpretation] comes from a voice in my own soul, which oftentimes is god-possessed and divines where it does not know. This thought I will record in words if I can. The voice told me that while God is indeed one, His highest and chiefest powers are two, even goodness and sovereignty . . . For this is a divine mystery and its lesson is for the initiated who are worthy to receive the holiest secret."[65] The mysterious interpretation of the cherubim therefore resorts to symbolism that is nourished by an inner voice or a divine revelation, which creates the nexus between the theological scheme and its biblical counterpart.

Let me compare Philo's symbolism and allegory with the main stream of Jewish medieval allegoresis. The latter is concerned more with psychological, political, and natural (physical and metaphysical) topics than it is with relations and processes taking place in the divine realm. Inspired by a negative theology adopted by Maimonides, Jewish allegorists were not particularly concerned with transforming the linguistic units of the biblical text to signs dealing with the divine realm. Philo, however, was much more open to envisioning the sacred scriptures as conductive to a positive knowledge of the divine realm.[66]

Yet although these are examples of symbolic interpretations that elevate some of the biblical accounts to the status of narratives that reflect events on high, related to the divine realm, Philo did not resort to symbolic interpretations of this kind very often. More commonly he regarded the biblical words as pointing symbolically to inner processes, an exegetical matter close to medieval psychological allegoresis.[67] Nevertheless, Philo testifies that a more comprehensive symbolic approach is to be found among some persons he knew: "I heard . . . from inspired men who take most of the contents of the Law to be visible symbols of things invisible, expressing the inexpressible."[68] It is quite interesting that already Philo presents the nexus between inspiration and symbolic interpretation. Apparently, the secret or symbolic cargos of the sacred scriptures are not discovered by an analytical approach to the text but depend on a divine revelation. According to another text, Philo seems to have had access to much more symbolically inclined trends of biblical exegesis: "There are some who, taking the laws in their literal sense as symbols of intelligible realities, are overprecise in their investigation of the symbol, while frivolously neglecting the letter."[69] Therefore, we may distinguish between Philo's own symbolic interpretations, which are apparently more limited and moderate insofar as the biblical text is conceived of as pointing to the divine realm, and a more comprehensive arcanization that took the form of symbolic decoding of substantial parts of the biblical text, a trend toward which Philo adopted a reserved attitude.

For the history of the emergence of the symbols that point to divine attributes and events, it is important to mention the symbolic exegesis of Valentinus, who explained the Greek Bible as a symbol for a celestial history for which Jesus' life is a lower replica.[70] This form of exemplarism was also adopted by Origen.[71]

V. Monoimos the Arab: A Forgotten So-Called Gnostic

Let me turn to another early form of symbolism, one that is more static than the standard Kabbalist symbolisms. In a presumably late-first-century Gnostic text by Monoimos the Arab, as quoted by Hippolytus of Rome, we read about an anthropomorphic entity that is both a monad and a decad, a tittle of the letter iota:

> The monad, [that is] the one tittle, is therefore, he says, also a decad. For by the actual power of this one tittle are produced duad, and triad, and tetrad, and pentad, and hexad, and heptad, and duad, and ennead, up to ten. For these numbers, he says, are capable of many divisions, and they reside in that simple and uncompounded single tittle of the iota. And this is what has been declared:[72] "It pleased [God] that all fullness should dwell in the son of man bodily."[73]

What interests me in this passage are the strongly speculative aspects of the tittle of the iota, which is described by referring to mathematical assumptions, characteristic of the short passages that survived in Monoimos' name. The monad generates all the numbers, which are all comprised in it, and the theological aspect, the identification of the monad/decad with the Christ. There is nothing symbolic involved in this passage, hence it does not organize any literary discourse in terms of an entity found on another level; the verse from the Greek Bible refers to an entity that is also referred in Monoimos' text. In another passage, however, the type of discourse changes dramatically. The tittle of the iota attracts plenty of literary description:

> That one indivisible tittle is . . . one tittle of the iota,[74] with many faces,[75] and innumerable eyes,[76] and countless names, and this [tittle] . . . an image of that perfect invisible man . . . constitutes a perfect son of a perfect man. When, therefore, he [Monoimos] says, Moses mentions that the rod was changeably brandished for the [introduction of the] plagues throughout Egypt—now the plagues, he says, are allegorically expressed symbols of creation—he did not [as a symbol] for more plagues than ten shape the rod. Now, this [rod] constitutes one tittle of the iota, and is [both] twofold [and] various. This succession of ten plagues is, he says, the mundane creation . . . With that one tittle, the law constitutes the series of ten commandments,

which expresses allegorically the divine mysteries of [those] precepts. For, he says, all knowledge of the universe is contained in what relates to the succession of the ten plagues and the series of ten commandments.[77]

Let me start with the simple observation that the organizing entity is a linguistic sign: the tittle of a small letter. Its tenfold nature—I assume because iota/yod is the tenth letter in the Greek and Hebrew alphabets—allows such a resort to it as a suitable symbol. Thus, both tenfold and anthropomorphic, it brings together other types of decads: the ten plagues, the ten commandments, and perhaps some version of ten creative speeches, reminiscent of the divine logoi, ma'amarot, in rabbinic literature. However, organizing the various decads may be a simple creation of affinities based on a formal criterion that operates on a strictly horizontal level, bringing together material found in the text, and may be strictly mundane, as they point to events taking place here below. Yet this is evidently not the case in this passage, for there is a conspicuously and decisively vertical dimension to the decads mentioned in the Bible: the reference to a metaphysical decad, the anthropomorphic "son of man," who is likewise intimated by the tittle of an iota. In my opinion, the emergence of these affinities is facilitated by the ascent of the centrality of metaphysical thinking over textual thinking and the power of the ontic structures to organize textual ones. In short, the above text represents an impulse that is crucial, though not exclusive, in Philo, in Gnosticism, and in some ancient Christian theologies, to validate ontic schemes by attracting earlier texts into a web of relationship that would present the schemes as central. Since ontic schemes and hermeneutical grids were new, the discrepancy between the new organizing schemes and the "attracted" material was a matter of necessity, and it created ambiguities that contributed to the mysteriousness of the supernal structures and invited a more symbolic approach to the scriptures. Or, to capitalize on Bruns's suggestion that in Christianity the Old Testament has become a secret book pointing to events related only in the New Testament, with the Christ as performing a midrashic exegesis by reading himself in the Hebrew Bible as the secret of the Bible,[78] we may say that a similar logic occurs in Judaism insofar as other theological innovations seeking to be anchored in scripture are concerned. More dramatically, we can see in the last two major chapters in the history of Jewish mysticism the attraction of biblical material to the hermeneutical grid constituted by the new ideals. In Sabbateanism the canonical writings become a vast domain for discovering references to Sabbatai Tzevi, just as in Hasidism the nature and role of the tzaddiq permeate the interpretive projects of this literature.

Before addressing the issue of symbolism in the last passage, let me turn to an additional text. When describing a certain epoch, a representative Gnostic text contends that "the eon of the truth, being a unity and multiplicity, is honored with little and great names according to the power of each to grasp it—by way of analogy, like a spring which is what it is yet flows into rivers and lakes and canals and branches, or like a root which extends into trees with branches and fruit, or like a human body which is partitioned in an indivisible way into members of members, primary members and secondary [ones], great [and] small."[79] As in the case of Monoimos, unity and multiplicity coexist in the same entity, which is again described, perhaps this time metaphorically, as a human organism. More interesting, however, and quite representative of the Gnostic discourse, is the emphasis on the many names by which the same entity is designated, as the tittle of iota is described as possessing innumerable names. Those names do not have to be biblical, but in Monoimos' texts it is biblical material that is attracted by the supernal entity as part of an effort to aggrandize the status of the described entity. Or, to put it sharply: Philo as well as Christian and Gnostic texts emerging in religious polemical contexts, either in relation to Judaism or among themselves, strove to reorganize the Hebrew Bible, and sometimes also the Greek one, around hypostases, whose existence and status in a particular spiritual environment could be demonstrated by resort to the scriptures.

Let me adduce another Gnostic example: "God, the ruler of the eons, and the powers,[80] separated us wrathfully. Then we became two eons, and the glory in our hearts deserted us, me and your mother, Eve."[81] The emergence of the hypostases of Adam and Eve is quite important in itself. But I am interested here more in the new, apparently Platonic, reading of the first chapter of the Bible. The biblical God, described in benevolent terms when separating woman from man, becomes here, like Zeus in Plato's Symposium, a wrathful ruler. This is the well-known Gnostic inverse reading of the Bible. The Hebrew Bible is converted, or inverted, to tell a story that is fundamentally taking place elsewhere, on another plane. The surge of hypostatic thinking may well be part of an ancient Jewish trend that nourished some parts of the Christian and Gnostic hypostatic discourses. So, for example, there is the assumption of the pair of entities existing before the Creation in Pseudo-Philo, Liber Antiquitatum Biblicarum 60:2, which is considered to be a syzygy of powers which, historically speaking, preceded and probably influenced their Gnostic counterparts.[82] Also, the numerous early Jewish speculations about the Hokhmah contributed to Gnostic and some later Jewish conceptualizations of hypostatic discourses.[83] Moreover, the history of major theological terms in rabbinic literature like Shekhinah and knesset yisra'el, not to speak of the divine attributes and the Torah, point in this direction.

The passages adduced from Monoimos include expressions of mysteriousness and symbolism which seem to me to be significant for a history of the much later

Kabbalistic symbolism. First and foremost, a nexus has been made between the ten commandments and the plagues, which are textual topics informing ritual and sacred history with cosmic powers, namely creative actions, and a complex supracosmic power, the son of man. The biblical material is described as symbolic and allegorical, although the content of these symbols and allegories is not specified. One may imagine that a more specific correlation between the various decads might have been established by Monoimos but accidentally not quoted by Hippolytus, or that Monoimos never offered a greater correspondence, yet neither of these contentions can be corroborated from the extant material.

An aspect that attracted our attention earlier appears here in an interesting version: the cosmic, comprehensive, and absorbing understandings of the biblical text. According to Monoimos, the ten commandments contain all the knowledge of the universe. Moreover, they reflect the decad within the son of man, who in turn reflects the higher entity that is the supreme divinity. A certain hierarchy seems inherent in Monoimos' passages: the highest level, the perfect man, apparently a term for God; then the son of God, who comprises in himself both the monadic and the decadic natures. I assume that the ontic move from the father to the son of man means the transition from a noncreative monad to a creative one, as the son is also the decad. The decad within the son constitutes the mysteries reflected in the Decalogue and, by parallel, in the ten plagues, which in turn reflect the process and the knowledge related to creation. All these decads are reflected also by two symbols: the tittle of the iota and Moses' rod. We may assume that both the other parts of the Bible (aside from the Decalogue)[84] and the universe represent the greater plurality which is thought to emanate from the decad, in a manner reminiscent of the rabbinic view of the ten creative ma'amarot. If this analysis is pertinent, we may advance one more suggestion for understanding Monoimos: the son of man reflects the father but also comprises the lower decads, and the ten commandments and ten plagues reflect the higher decad of the son but also comprise, respectively, the entire law and the multiplicity of created beings. Indeed, the comprising of the multiplicity within the decad is expressly pointed out in the discussion of the monad as generating the ten figures. Such a reading assumes an implicit theory of emanation, reminiscent of the later Neoplatonic emanative theory, but this issue cannot be dealt with here.[85] Thus, there emerges a theory of participation, which would attribute to the lower aspects of the hierarchy a certain sharing of essence with the higher one. This hypothesis would assume that the literary decads, those represented by the biblical discussions dealing with the plagues, namely the rod and the creative logoi, share something in common with the son of man, in addition to their numerical identity.

Thus, by knowing or reflecting on mundane entities like the graphical forms of the tittle of an iota and the rod, and by understanding their connection to the biblical decadic accounts, one is able to ascend to the higher decad, that found in the son of man. Let me point out that, according to what I conceive to be a plausible interpretation of tittles of letters in a rabbinic text, they point to divine secrets, as the tittle does in Monoimos.[86]

The sources of those hypostases, decadic or not, that are related to the biblical text are a matter of speculation. Perhaps the hypostases reflect some form of spiritual experience.[87] Yet even if this is the case, our main concern here is not to explain the emergence of hypostatic thought but to point to the importance of the semiotic process of "attraction" or translation of the biblical material to these hypostases because of a belief in the correspondence between them, which will culminate in a symbolic thinking.

Let us adduce one more ancient text, a passage written by Justin the Martyr:

I shall give you another testimony, my friends . . . from the scriptures, that God begat before all creatures a beginning, [who was] a certain rational power [proceeding] from Himself, who is called by the Holy Spirit, now the Glory of the Lord, now the Son, again Wisdom, again Angel, then God, and then Lord and Logos; and on another occasion He calls Himself Captain, when he appeared in human form to Joshua, son of Nun. For He can be called by all those names, since He ministers to the Father's will, and since he was begotten of the Father by an act of will; just as we see happening among ourselves; for when we give out some word, we beget the word; yet not by abscission, so as to lessen the word [which remains] in us, when we give it out; just as we see also happening in the case of a fire, which is not lessened when it has kindled [another] but remains the same; and that which has been kindled by it likewise appears to exist by itself, not diminishing that from which it was kindled.[88]

This passage should be seen in the context of the sort of Christology that was expounded in several parts of Justin's Dialogue,[89] where the assumption is that Jesus Christ issued from the Father in a manner that does not create a division between the two entities.[90] Here the details of theological discussions are less important, and we shall concentrate on the semiotic aspects of the passage: the divine that has been emanated from the Father is described by resorting to many names stemming from the various biblical passages. One entity, at least superficially different from God, is understood to be the reference of various parts of the Bible that resort to various names.

VI. Rabbinic, Kabbalistic, and Hasidic Decadologies

The schematic correspondences based on decads in the quasi-Gnostic passages adduced above are reminiscent of statements found in rabbinic literature in general, although I am especially interested in parallelisms between ten ma'amarot and the Decalogue.[91] In a late midrashic text, Midrash Tadsche', it is asserted that "when the Holy One, blessed be He, spoke and delivered the ten commandments, He started with the first letter of the alphabet in order to talk with them, as it is said, 'anokhiy. The first letter of the commandment[92] is aleph and the last is yod. From one He started until ten, the entire numeration, so that they shall know that the Holy One, blessed be He, fills the entire world, and He is the first and the last."[93] The anonymous Jewish author of the late midrash is mentioning the mathematical speculation of the first and the last figure, one and ten, in order to describe the divine presence is the world, in a manner which seems quite reminiscent of the passage above where Monoimos resorted to quoting from the Epistle to the Corinthians. Later in this midrash the correspondences between the plagues and the commandments are explicitly expounded: "The world is maintained by the merit of those who study [the Torah] and perform the Decalogue; and the world was created by ten logoi [ma'amarot], and its sefirot are [also] ten . . . The world is maintained by the ten sefirot of Belimah."[94]

What is interesting for a history of hypostatic thinking in Judaism is the convergence of rabbinic ideals, like the study of the Torah and the performance of the commandments, with hypostatic entities: ten sefirot and ten ma'amarot. I assume that at least the sefirot are to be seen as ontological entities, which correspond to the metaphysical structure of the son of God, conceived of in Monoimos' passage as comprising a decad. Here too it would be difficult to find a precise correspondence between the specific contents of the three decads. If we compare the perceptions of the decads in the quasi-Gnostic text and those in Midrash Tadsche', two of the major differences, from the point of view of our discussion, are the absence of the mysteries and the strong accent put on performance and its impact on the external world: the maintenance of the world. If the Gnostic-Christian text of Monoimos attempts to move the son of God to the center and his decadic nature expresses perfection as well as correspondences to authoritative verses, in the rabbinic ambiance the centrality is given to offering a cosmic stand for the religious performance. The performative aspect of the ritual and its relation to hypostases on high, as found in Midrash Tadsche' and its parallels, invite the assumption that a more dynamic approach to the meaning of correlations between the lower entities (the horizontal material in biblical texts) and the higher entities is already adumbrated in the late midrashic material, though it may reflect much earlier developments. As we know, the late midrashic treatises sometimes reflect much older material from the ancient pseudepigraphic literature, rather than the earlier and more classical midrashim.[95] Indeed, it seems that in eleventh-century material preserved in the circle of R. Shlomo Yitzhaqi (Rashi) it was claimed that the correspondence between the ten creative logoi and the ten ordeals of Abraham explains why the world is maintained. There is no doubt a very interesting pun: to withstand a certain ordeal is expressed by the root 'MD, which is precisely the root that is used to point to the act of maintaining the world.[96]

Let me address now a later view that expresses the concept that the entire Torah is contained within the ten commandments, as are all the creatures. In the Zohar we read:

> R. Eleazar taught that in these ten words all the commandments of the Torah were inscribed,[97] all the decrees and punishments, all laws concerning purity and impurity, all the branches and roots, all the trees and plants, heaven and earth, seas and abysses. Behold, the Torah is the name of the Holy One, blessed be He, and just as the name of the Holy One, blessed be He, is inscribed in the Decalogue, so too the Torah is inscribed in the Decalogue, and these ten words are the name of the Holy One, blessed be He, and the Torah in its entirety is one name, the Holy Name of the Holy One, blessed be He, indeed.[98]

Let me start with the difficulty in finding a precise translation for the term 'amarin, which has been translated above as "words." It stands for the ten words of the Decalogue, according to the passage that precedes this one. Yet 'amarin also has a cosmic overtone, just like the term ma'amarot, because creatures are mentioned together with the Torah. The question is, How may we understand the details of the text? Does it speak about a series of identifications, which equate the divine name, the Decalogue qua ma'amarot, the Torah and all the creatures, or may we suggest a more hierarchical reading? I would favor the latter option and suggest that we may distinguish between God, represented in the text as "the Holy One, blessed be He," His name, then the Decalogue qua ma'amarot, and then the Torah and the creatures. The Torah is identified with three different entities in this hierarchy: the name, the Decalogue, and the laws. If the suggested pyramidal hierarchy indeed represents the stand of the Zoharic text, we have an interesting parallel to Monoimos' views. If so, the divine name plays a role similar to that of Jesus in Monoimos. In any case, it is obvious that the ten 'amarin organize both the Torah and creation according to ten categories. Moreover, if we assume that the ten 'amarin stand for the ten sefirot, a view that is found in many medieval Kabbalistic sources,[99] and that the latter constitute an anthropomorphic structure, then the similarity to Monoimos' view is even greater.

Indeed, a similar explication of the unfolding of plurality from unity, reminiscent of Neoplatonic theories of emanation,[100] is found in quite Neoplatonic language in an important nineteenth-century Hasidic master, R. Yehudah Arieh Leib of Gur:

> First there was only the Decalogue and afterwards when they[101] descended from their rank the entire Torah was added to them and then they descended even more . . . and the oral Torah has been promulgated . . . as it is written in Sefer ha-Yashar by R. Tam[102] and according to the cleaving to the Creator, blessed be He, plurality is diminished and they come to the unity . . . and this is also the case of the Torah whose basis is the twenty-two letters, and in a particular manner the four letters of the name of God, blessed be He, who is the principle of everything. However, the plurality stems from the various combinations of letters. But when someone merits he comes close to the unity.[103]

The mystical approach to God coming near to him parallels the reduction of the plurality of the canonical texts. Thus the reduction of the texts implies the attainment of the highest textual configuration: the Tetragrammaton. Ontology and textology, according to the Hasidic master, reflect each other. This approach exemplifies the exploitation of the theological and textual hierarchies in order to illustrate mystical attainments. Plurality on the ontic level is conceived of as paralleled by the literal complication of some letters that are described as combined. The combinations of letters do not serve, in this and many other Hasidic texts, as techniques to reach the divine, as is the case in Abraham Abulafia's system, but they reflect the descent of unity in plurality and thus the distancing from the divine. Indeed, ecstatic Kabbalah was less concerned with portraying the different parts of the biblical texts as allegories of different ontic levels. It is obvious, however, that the transition from the combinations of letters in general to the combinations of the letters of the divine name in particular was viewed as an advance in the techniques at the disposition of the Kabbalists.[104] In other Hasidic texts, combinations of letters were regarded in a much more magical manner, as acts by means of which the perfecti are able to create worlds.[105]

From the point of view of the emergence of Kabbalistic theosophical symbolism, structured as it is around the ten sefirot, the possible (though, in my opinion, not plausible) contributions of Gnostic speculations, the statements in

Sefer Yetzirah, and the rabbinic materials represent only rudimentary elements that informed a dramatic development that marks the difference between the pre-Kabbalistic and the Kabbalistic material. The components of the decads that where related to biblical material were distinguished from each other by both names and properties, which are able to attract specific aspects of the biblical lexicography to a certain supernal power. Only the systematic differentiation between the ten powers, which allowed some forms of dynamics and the impression of the literary material with the valences found in the supernal system, created the specificity of the main trend in Kabbalistic theosophical symbolism.

VII. Ancient Traditions on Constellation and Divine Names

The question should be asked as to whether the variety of decads found in Jewish pre-Kabbalistic material did not include one dealing with the ten divine names. Such a view would narrow the gap between the simpler constellations of the midrashic authors, based on two divine names, and the much more complex one found in Kabbalistic literature. In a passage preserved by Origen, whose importance for understanding this aspect of Jewish tradition is paramount, it is said that "the names Sabaoth and Adonai, and all the other names that have been handed down by the Hebrews with great reverence, are not concerned with ordinary created things, but with a certain mysterious divine science[106] that is related to the creator of the universe."[107]

Two important details for better understanding the history of Jewish magic and mysticism are found in this passage: that divine names not only are powerful, which is the gist of the whole passage, but also are part of a divine, secret science concerning God. Speaking in the plural, this leaves us with the impression that if Origen's testimony is correct, it was a matter not only of magic but also of a much more elaborate form of mysterious lore that we are told was found among the Jews. Just before the passage quoted above, Origen mentions that the above tradition "is a consistent system, which has principles known to very few." The detailed nature of this system, unfortunately, is not indicated by Origen. However, as John Dillon has proposed, there may be an affinity between the two Hebrew names in Origen's book and the occurrence of precisely these names in some Gnostic texts, where they point to hypostatic potencies.[108] Especially important in this context is the occurrence of these two divine names, which point to but a sample of a more complex secret doctrine, in *On the Origin of the World* as part of a group of seven androgynous beings. As I have attempted to show elsewhere, in this Gnostic source there is a passage, immediately before this discussion, which testifies to the impact of Jewish mythical traditions paralleled later in Kabbalistic writings.[109] It should be emphasized that Origen's testimony concerning these two divine names is at least partially corroborated by earlier traditions related to Moses and extant in the magical papyri.[110] However, I assume that Origen hints at much more than we already know from Philonic and midrashic sources. He claims that the numerous divine names constitute a part, or perhaps even the whole, of a secret lore dealing with the nature of the creator. It seems that the assumption, for the time being hypothetical, that different divine names reflect different divine attributes or aspects is not too far fetched.

This preoccupation with the various divine names as part of a secret tradition concerning the nature of the divine realm is strikingly reminiscent of some forms of Kabbalah, more precisely that of R. Joseph Gikatilla's Sha'arei 'Orah. More salient for our discussion, however, is the very mentioning of a tradition that has been "handed down with great reverence." This phrase plausibly points to a ritualistic transmission, which included some details in addition to the very pronunciation of the divine names. Reverence seems to be especially important in this context. It should be mentioned that the passage from Origen does not deal with the Tetragrammaton or with the name of forty-two letters, but with two other names, a fact that shows that the talmudic discussion in Qiddushin, dealing with the transmission of divine names, tells us but part of the story regarding the secret transmission of divine names.[111] If the midrashic pattern that dominates some of the discussions of the divine names as reflecting divine attributes had been expanded to additional divine names in ancient secret doctrines, such a hypothetical development could have prepared the floruit of a much more complex theosophy related to the divine names. Such a hierarchic vision of the biblical material as composed of more secret, powerful, and sacred material that is related to divine attributes, and the other part of the Bible which is apparently less concerned with theology, does not recur in rabbinic thought, which emphasized the unhierarchical structure of the canonical texts, but flourished in circles that prevailed in nascent Kabbalah.[112] I surmise that the gradual emergence of a code constituted by ten divine names could be related to a standardization of the lists of divine names found in the opening sentences of Sefer Yetzirah,[113] or in lists of divine names that should not be erased,[114] and contributed to the establishment of a decadic code that culminated in the different schemes of ten sefirot as themselves divine or as divine instruments.[115] In any case, such a decadic structure of ten sefirot was already active in organizing the exegesis of the Song of Songs, as we learn from an important introductory passage by R. Ezra of Gerona. This early Kabbalist contends that he received traditions that connect some key words of the Song of Songs as if pointing to sefirot.[116]

Finally, other decads emerged that strengthened the importance of decads of divine names. For example, the existence of lists of ten vowels, which were conceived of as fitting the special target of resorting to the Tetragrammaton, or ten different colors, to be used as part of a process of visualizing the letters of the ten Tetragrammata, emerged in a theosophical system that regarded the ten sefirot as too sublime to be used as a hermeneutical code.[117]

9

RADICAL FORMS
OF JEWISH HERMENEUTICS

I. ON INTRA- AND INTERCORPORALITY

The eleventh through thirteenth centuries produced the most important exegetical literature of the Middle Ages and made a substantial contribution to the canonical writings in this genre. Rashi and his French followers, Abraham ibn Ezra, Nahmanides, and the Zohar represent the best of the medieval commentaries that not only became classics but also illustrate different intellectual attitudes toward the Bible and epitomize the main forms of Jewish spirituality of the period. Rashi was the master of the plain sense; the renowned philosopher and astronomer Abraham ibn Ezra opened vistas for understanding the Bible in terms of new forms of knowledge previously marginal in Judaism; Nahmanides and the Zohar contributed mystical and mythical understandings of the biblical canon.

These influential commentaries have attracted the attention of numerous scholars, and many fine studies of their exegetical approaches are available.[1]

In this chapter, however, I shall be dealing with other forms of exegesis that also generated commentaries on the Torah, although they remained on the margin of Jewish culture, as the recent first printing of some of them indicates.[2] In these commentaries, produced by authors belonging to Hasidei Ashkenaz and by the founder of ecstatic Kabbalah, Abraham Abulafia, there are substantial elements of what may be called radical hermeneutics, a phrase I adopt from the title of an excellent book on modern deconstruction.[3] By radical I mean two different things. One is an aggressive attitude toward the interpreted text that dissolves its common literal structure, and sometimes the common structure of a particular language, a strategy I shall call deconstructive radicalism, which affects the "expression-plane."[4] The other meaning is the introduction of conceptual elements that are alien to the semantic fields of the interpreted text, an attitude that may be termed semantic radicalism, which in Kabbalistic texts is either allegorical or symbolic. This radical attitude brings together terms and concepts stemming from two or more different forms of thought as expressed in different literary corpora, an approach that will be called intercorporal hermeneutics. The term intercorporal points to the relationship that is established by means of hermeneutical devices between two intellectually different corpora stemming from different cultures and often written in different languages. Intercorporality involves a complex intellectual life that consists in a recognition of the reliability and authority of two different traditions. The process of translating one term into the intellectual framework of another system is not merely participation in "an event of tradition," as Gadamer would put it, but creation of a third tradition, which to an extent unifies the corpora involved in the intercorporal hermeneutics. The expectation that both the biblical text and the Greek philosophical traditions will accord meant, for medieval as well as some Renaissance thinkers, that a third form of thought, close to the concept of prisca theologia, informs the esoteric meaning of the Bible and Greek philosophical thinking. It is the interplay of two or more heritages that was at work in some of the major medieval exegetical enterprises that concerned us in previous chapters and will continue to hold our attention. In other words, expectations of the existence of levels of Jewish traditions, which are conceived of as esoteric and much richer from the point of view of the realms they cover, informed the interpretive moves of many of the hermeneutes under scrutiny here. More unified forms of knowledge, reminiscent of Gadamer's "fore-conception of completeness" or more specifically what has been called a "Jewish-Greek" approach, is conspicuous in the medieval philosophy of the Jews but also reverberates in various forms and doses in some of the Kabbalistic exegetical enterprises. It is a new form of organization of knowledge that is introduced by the intercorporal attitude, which unifies at the same time as it reduces the various intellectual traditions used in medieval exegetical interactions. Rather than regarding interpretation as the retrieval of ancient, original knowledge that guides the present, interpretation may be well seen as constructing a sense of broader relevance incorporating strata of human knowledge that corroborate and mutually enrich each other.

I would like to distinguish my understanding of intercorporality from the widespread concept of intertextuality. The latter points to what I have proposed to describe as intracorporal relations. In the forms of intertextuality expounded by Julia Kristeva and in Harold Bloom's agonistic theory, a prior relation between the writer and the text that the writer absorbs, destroys, or displaces is presupposed. However, the intercorporal relation, despite the rhetoric of the interpreters who resorted to it, can be designated a false or imaginary intertextuality. By false I mean the assumption that many Jewish commentators in the Middle Ages made that all the sciences are found in the text of various details of the Torah and that it is possible to derive them from the "adequate" exploration of the structure of the sacred scriptures. His assumption as such is a false one, though his thought and writing themselves may well be defined as intertextual. Thus, paramount intertextual writings, which I describe as intercorporal, may be based on assumptions describing false or imaginary intertextualities.

Unlike the intracorporal readings, which may elucidate one term by means of another found in the corpus or at least in the same culture (within a different corpus sharing similar conceptual presuppositions), the intercorporal reading changes, or at least significantly enriches, the conceptual cargo of one of the terms in contact with each other. While the intercorporal interpretation is a strong semantic deconstruction of the initial meaning of the text, the intracorporal one implies a weaker deconstruction of the initial meaning, despite the hypertextual approach. The latter may consist in a strong deconstruction of the linguistic fabric of the text, although semantically the deconstructive process is often less aggressive. In the discussions below I shall consider the Hebrew Bible as one literary corpus, a position that is simplistic given the document theory, which distinguishes between different layers in this collection of texts. If this approach is adopted, the intertextual interpretations found even in the Hebrew Bible may sometime consist in intercorporal exegesis. However, from the point of view of later traditional interpreters, both Jewish and Christian, the Hebrew Bible is a single, rather homogeneous body of writings, and intertextual interpretations are intracorporal.

Although the Hebrew Bible and the rabbinic literature are, from many points of view, different literary corpora, from the intellectual point of view they overlap on many basic issues, and the many intersections among them will therefore be treated not as intercorporal but, to a great extent, as intracorporal. On the other hand, the Christian interpretation of the Hebrew Bible can be described either as intracorporal, if one accepts the Christian view that the Hebrew Bible prefigures events in the Greek Bible, or as intercorporal, if one does not accept this view, and the two texts are conceived of as representing different religious outlooks.

Let me return to the two types of radicalism mentioned above. They cannot be dealt with in detail here, and I shall be focusing my analysis more on the first type. (More on this issue may be found below, in Chapter 11.) However, before addressing deconstructive radicalism, let me offer a short survey of the framework of my discussion. Beyond the specific contributions in content, which are decisive for the whole subsequent history of Jewish hermeneutics, the medieval period contributed unprecedented forms of awareness concerning three components of the hermeneutical process: the nature of the text, the nature of the hermeneute, and the nature of the methods. Only the last topic is represented in earlier rabbinic sources in the form of extended discussions, even treatises, dealing with thirteen or thirty-two measures or methods of interpretation.[5] Interestingly, the thirteen measures of exegesis have become part of the ordinary Jewish liturgy and are recited in the morning prayer. The medieval systematic reflections on these issues are part of large-scale reformulations of Judaism after the encounter with Islamic and (to a lesser degree) Christian theologies. Moving from a much more "organic" form of creativity, from a less polemical and more text-centered religiosity as found in the rabbinic literature represented by the Talmud and Midrash, the medieval forms of Judaism express an acute awareness of the challenges other cultures and religions increasingly presented. One of the principal answers to these challenges is the process of arcanization.

Arcanization took place in one of the major religions, which was mostly exoteric in its initial phases, namely biblical and early rabbinic Judaism. During its long peregrinations, however, Judaism assumed some of the most complex esoteric expressions known in any religion. Yet the hermeneutical aspects of this pivotal process have remained on the fringe of modern Jewish scholarship. The process of arcanization adopted more than one form, and its vigor and extent seem not to be paralleled by developments in Christianity and Islam. The former, shrouded in mystery, was reluctant to adopt significant forms of esotericism; the latter, less concerned with mystery, was also less interested in religious secrets. This pendulum swing from exotericism to esotericism in Judaism is a remarkable development that found expression in some major forms of Jewish literature which, though sometimes related or reacting to each other, constitute divergent forms of thought. Those major corpora are Jewish philosophy, represented by two main twelfth-century authors, R. Abraham ibn Ezra and Maimonides, and the huge interpretive literature devoted to their writings; Hasidei Ashkenaz, the Jewish masters active in the Rhineland at the end of the twelfth and beginning of the thirteenth centuries; and Kabbalistic literature, in its various schools and versions. In different forms these three modes of esotericism remained influential until the middle of the seventeenth century, when other currents, which may be described as dearcanizing moves (whose origins are earlier), started to neutralize the effect of some of the strongest arcanizing propensities. In the eighteenth and nineteenth centuries the main innovative forms of Jewish literature, like Polish Hasidism or the Lithuanian Musar literature, were basically indifferent toward the contents of the earlier processes of arcanization. They moved toward an emphasis on inner spiritual development rather then preoccupations with theosophical entities and processes.

II. MEDIEVAL HERMENEUTICAL CORPORA

The processes of arcanization contributed to new conceptualizations of the canonical texts, exposed in lengthy and authoritative commentaries that embodied the details of the esoteric interpretations. Significantly, the emergence of this interpretive literature was paralleled by the simultaneous emergence of systematic treatments of hermeneutics, including new forms of interpretation. This is the case in Abraham ibn Ezra's introduction to his commentary on the Pentateuch,[6] the important Hasidei Ashkenaz commentator R. Eleazar of Worms's *Sefer ha-Hokhmah*,[7] the Kabbalistic fourfold method of interpretation known by the acrostic *pardes*,[8] and R. Abraham Abulafia's explications of his sevenfold method of interpretation.[9] The processes of arcanization triggered the emergence not only of the first systematic treatments of modes of interpretation (my focus here) but also of articulated views of the nature of the text and its interpreter. Systematic hermeneutics was articulated as part of a greater process of arcanization of the canonical texts. The new forms of interpretive literature attempted to justify their extraction of the secrets from the plainly exoteric text and to explicate the relationship between the new forms of interpretations and the earlier, more traditional ones. These claims may be thought of as double justifications: one, of the exegetical method and its integration into the culture of the community; the other, of its results within the larger life of the religious community of the hermeneutes, which share the same canonical texts and forms of religious life. Traditional communities encouraged, or at least selected, the more integrative approaches, which do not attempt to discredit or minimize the already existing exegetical approaches but rather strive to capitalize on their achievement and enrich the religious patrimony of that community. Although there sometimes are tensions between the traditional and eccentric exegetical modalities, by and large the more integrative approaches become the more influential ones.

Relating new speculative contents to ancient texts is a complex issue, and the modes of adaptation vary from one corpus to another. We may assume a certain affinity between the type of topics propelled within the text and the methods of these associations. We may generally distinguish between three main forms of extracting or finding secrets within the canonical texts: the numerical, the symbolic, and the allegorical. While the later two methods represent forms of thought most characteristic of Jewish literature in the Middle Ages, the first is well represented in much earlier Jewish sources. Before offering some historical reflections on the numerical devices, let me touch on nonnumerical ones. Both symbols and allegories adopted semantic strategies when approaching the interpreted text. The meaning, or plot, of the commented verse is conceived of as hinting at an additional plot involving layers of existence and experience that are believed to be of a higher religious order than the narrative told on the plain level of the text. One word on the plain level is understood as a code for a concept found on the symbolic or allegorical level, and thus one narrative is exchanged for another narrative. To a certain extent this exegetical development takes extratextual information as the clue to fathoming the hidden and sublime meanings of the canonical text. Thus, one semantic unit, usually a word, is deemed by the interpreter to point to a concept, often stemming from other cultural or intellectual layers than the interpreted text. We may describe this interpretation as intercorporal, which means that bodies of literature are understood to correspond to each other. Unlike intertextual interpretations, which presuppose the impact of one text on another while both texts stem from the same intellectual or literary tradition—one poem influences another, one narrative has an impact on another—the intercorporal interpretation consists in the imposition of the axiology of one corpus on another, which constitutes semantic radicalism.

Numerical interpretation, however, is much more intratextual. It assumes hidden numerical correspondences between linguistic elements found within the same text. In other words, the text is believed to elucidate itself, and the role of the interpreter is to discover these hidden numerical affinities. Although the discovery of such affinities may be conducive to new narratives, this is rarely the case. Unlike the narrative approaches, which infuse new meanings into older texts, frequently the numerical approaches were adduced in order to reinforce the uniqueness of a sacred text. This is the case in the conservative tone of Hasidei Ashkenaz hermeneutics, which found numerical relations between different words in the Bible or between words and pericopes in the Bible and those in the liturgy. By the very disclosure of the structural and formal correspondence, the divine wisdom is revealed and the belief in its perfection strengthened. In the following sections of this chapter, I will propose short surveys of how these radical techniques were in fact used in some of the commentaries on the Pentateuch, as part of the emphasis on an interpreter-oriented ergetic hermeneutics that I believe is characteristic of some Jewish mystical schools. The point I aim to make is that the existence of a multiplicity of radical methods allowed the interpreter a gamut of alternatives from which to choose.

III. GEMATRIA

The best known of the radical hermeneutical devices in Jewish mysticism is gematria. Recently it has been the subject of several articles,[10] the last two emphasizing the relevance of this device for mystical experience. Therefore, I shall concentrate here on points that still require clarification, relating to gematria and hermeneutics.[11]

In the texts with which I am acquainted, the Jewish exegetes calculated the numerical value of words, not in order to indulge in Pythagorean speculation as to the special cosmological valence of the number, but for two main reasons. First, they wished to compare (more rarely, to contrast) one word or phrase with another. The numerical calculation leads to a semantic speculation created by producing an encounter between different words or phrases that possess the same numerical value. The chemistry between the different words is believed to be anchored into a primordial affinity that may be demonstrated by pointing out the numerical identity, but the semantic encounter nevertheless emerges from the semantic values of the words, not from their numerical valence. Second, by transforming words into numbers they hoped to extract some sort of theological information. The most famous instance of such a use of gematria in ancient Jewish mysticism is the precise measurement of the divine body, deduced by calculating the numerical valence of a biblical phrase describing God.[12] By and large, this method is conservative, for it attempts to make an extra sense of the biblical material that coexists with the plain sense of the verse. This is not the place, however, for a detailed analysis of the different uses of gematria in Jewish mysticism, so I shall restrict my remarks mainly to two corpora: Hasidei Ashkenaz literature[13] and the ecstatic Kabbalah, two forms of thought that attributed a decisive role to gematria. In his "gate of gematrias" R. Eleazar of Worms, an early-thirteenth-century Ashkenazi mystic, describes this interpretive technique as follows: "Gai in Greek means number, and matria—wisdom. Another interpretation: Gai means valley, matria means mountains, namely if you throw the mountain into the valley, it will be equal. So also you should do to the Torah, and you should find out what the sages said, in the Midrash or in the Talmud, by way of gematria, or by way of allegory[14] . . . But you should not resort too much to gematria—because even the clowns do so—lest people deride you."[15,16] In spite of his own warning, R. Eleazar of Worms offers several examples of possible uses of this method: "'Elohim is equivalent to *zeh dayyan;*[17] *ve-'eloheikha* in gematria [is tantamount to] *be-din.* Another thing: *'elohim* in gematria [is tantamount to] *ha-kisse',*[18] and this is the reason why the sages said that this name stands for the 'attribute of judgment.' "[19]

The divine name is related to two main concepts: judgment and the throne. Both are part of the patrimony of traditions received by R. Eleazar, and whether he invented the particular gematria or inherited them, we still witness an intra-corporal strategy that creates numerical relations between elements that coexist in the same conceptual system. The introduction of the concept of the chair or throne is an elaboration on the view (found *inter alia* in the Babylonian Talmud, *Pesahim,* fol. 54a) that the divine throne preexisted the creation of the world. Thus, a mythic vision of the creation of the throne, and its importance to the extent that it is designated by one of the divine names, is emphasized by resorting to gematria. Someone may claim that a semantic radicalism may be discerned in the nexus between a created entity (the throne) and a divine name. Although both indeed preexisted creation, the special nexus of their juxtaposition in this account may significantly shift the meaning of one of the two words. In principle such semantic radical hermeneutics may be possible, but I doubt this is the case in this instance, because a semidivine, feminine status of the throne is already found in the Heikhalot literature.[20]

What seems to be more radical, however, is the change of the grammatical status of *'elohim* from subject to object—no longer the creator, as is the case in the Bible, but the creature. This approach, which may be linguistically radical, is conceptually conservative, for no new concept is introduced by means of the gematria. All the terms linked by the device of gematria were already part of a certain way of thinking. Yet this does not mean that gematria cannot generate new ideas by putting together two elements that were previously unrelated. The numerical method is instrumental in creating unexpected encounters for readers who are less cognizant of the different layers of Jewish tradition. The identification of the attribute of judgment with the divine throne is a plausible example of such an innovation, as I am unaware of the juxtaposition created by two already existing equations: *'elohim = kisse'* and *'elohim = middat ha-din,* which produced the identification of *middat ha-din* with *kisse'.*[21] Creativity may therefore be somehow prompted by means of gematria, although it alone rarely creates radical interpretations.

The most important example of this conservative approach toward numerical calculation in Kabbalah is found in Nahmanides' sermon *Torat ha-Shem Temimah*:

> Let no one deride me[22] because I rely on the calculation of the value of the letters called gematria, and think that it is a vain matter, because someone might change the allusion in verses into a pernicious matter by means of gematria. The truth is that no one is permitted to deal with numerology [in order to] deduce from [numbers] something that occurred to his mind.[23] But in the hands of our masters [there was a tradition] that [some] gematrias were transmitted to Moses at Sinai, and they are a reminder and a sign to the subjects transmitted orally together with the remnant of the oral Torah; some of those[24] deal with the subjects of *haggadot*, others with issues of *'issur ve-heter*.[25]

The intracorporal nature of the material involved in the numeric affinity, according to Nahmanides' view, is obvious: it is the oral Torah that comprises the topics related by numerical calculations, which function as mnemonic techniques. This attitude warrants the conservative nature of these calculations. What is conspicuous here is the apprehension attending innovations that may invade the Jewish discourse by allowing free resort to numerical calculations. In fact the gematrias themselves are part of a tradition, and Nahmanides plausibly insists that new ones should not be invented. We may describe Nahmanides' approach as expressing an implicit concern with losing control over the halakhic processes, which are determined by nonnumerical rules, despite the fact that gematria was included in the classical list of rabbinic hermeneutics. Out of concern with preserving a religious status quo, which emphasizes the paramount importance of the ritual, the numerical technique is invoked only in order to conserve the achievements of earlier generations.

However, in Kabbalistic numerical hermeneutics, as represented in the writings of Abraham Abulafia, numerical methods are much more radical. Abulafia uses exegetical devices to deconstruct the text before reconstructing it, only then infusing it with new meanings, in a manner reminiscent of what we have proposed to call the intercorporal approach. Therefore, numerical approaches may be either conservative or radical.

As I have mentioned, the general trend of symbolic and allegorical approaches is conservative insofar as the structure of the text is concerned but radical because of the intercorporal tendencies. The numerical approaches of Hasidei Ashkenaz are radical from the standpoint of addressing elements in the interpreted text as disassociated from their immediate context by obliterating the canonical order for the sake of an intertextual interpretation. Intracorporal interpretations can extract the same term or different terms from their context in order to relate them according to a common formal feature, such as gematria. The fabric of the text is sometimes obliterated. In ecstatic Kabbalah, however, we find the radicalism of the intratextual approach as well as that of the intercorporal.

As I am concerned here only with numerical hermeneutics, let me illustrate the above statements by some examples. In one of his commentaries on Maimonides' Guide of the Perplexed, Abulafia addresses the concept of gematria in some detail:

> The gematrias comprise issues related to measures[26] and the geometrical forms[27] and the numbers. But there are persons who claim that the number[28] is not comprised [in this category]. But I know that the term *gematria* stems indubitably from Greek, because they call the earth *yay*[29] and call the measure *metron*, and therefore its meaning is "the measure of the earth" and the name of the number is likewise so. And also in our language *middah* means measuring,[30] and measuring is the number. But the number is found also in thought, and this is the reason why it is called calculation[31] and measuring is predicated on something which has a size in reality which is greater[32] either by its length or its breadth or its height. And the line [and] the point and the letter tell us the secrets of all the names, which represent reality.[33] And we know that just as reality easily shows the philosophers the essences of things, all the letters too represent to us[34] the essence of things in an even easier manner. This is why we have [esoteric] traditions which represent more easily the attributes of God, blessed be He, and His governance and providence, and His influx, and the existence of His actions, and what he [the Kabbalist] hears from it is something that the philosophers cannot attain even after a long toil, and after lengthy times and many studies, because about holy names you will hear [here].[35]

Abulafia's book is a linguistically oriented commentary on the most logocentric book written in Judaism up to that time, the Guide of the Perplexed. Thus, it is a conscious enterprise to submit Maimonides' intellectualistic classic to forms of interpretation that stem from the earlier Jewish exegetical arsenal of what could be called eccentric hermeneutics, which Maimonides himself would have rejected.[36] For Abulafia gematria, but not the combinations of letters, is fundamentally related to the understanding of reality. This does not mean that Abulafia did not consider this method exegetical. As we shall see, he expressly did consider it so from the very beginning of his literary activity. He discusses philosophy as revealing the essence of reality and sees Kabbalah as able to obtain the same information more easily, and to enjoy additional forms of gnosis unavailable to the philosophers. At least in the first case, the difference between philosophy and

Kabbalah is only a matter of measure, not category. Gematria for Abulafia, like geometry for the Greeks, involves an understanding of reality, namely a nontextual hermeneutics, applied to the book of nature. For the Greeks, however, the main avenue is a matter of measuring nature by means of lines and points; for Kabbalah, however, it is the letters and the names that allow easier access to the same subject: the essences of reality. At least from this point of view ecstatic Kabbalah differs from the attitude of the theosophical-theurgical Kabbalists, who were looking symbolically at reality through the prism of the Torah as an absorbing universe, as we shall see in the next chapter.

Yet whereas Greek philosophers measured external reality and systemized their findings accordingly, Kabbalah obtains information from a text, from letters and names, as interpreted by means of gematria. From this standpoint the Greek approach is basically logocentric, for it assumes that language not only represents reality feebly but that it does not provide the best way to achieve understanding. Hence the information harbored by sacred texts is, for the Kabbalist, superior to natural science. Abulafia and many other Kabbalists would say that although there is nature outside the text, nature is best found within the text alone. To what extent there is an identity between essences in reality and the Hebrew letters, or to what extent letters are the most important channel for arriving at the transcendental essences, is less evident. This is a complex issue, and I do not believe that a simple answer does justice to the intricate discussions of Abulafia's numerous texts. If the former answer emerges as predominant, the logocentric view will somehow be attenuated while the second possibility will enforce logocentric interpretation of ecstatic Kabbalah.

The divine attributes, the middot, and the knowledge of the essences found in reality are related to each other, as both are obtained by means of the linguistic rather than the geometric technique. Thus, for Abulafia geometry illustrates the Greek naturalistic attitude toward reality while gematria is presented as the Jewish attitude that prefers the book of God to the book of nature. How gematria both serves as an exegetical technique and facilitates understanding of divinity and existence we may learn from Abulafia's very first book: "Divine names[37] change the nature,[38] [as they] are the throne,[39] and this is the secret of [the verse][40] 'the finger of God,'[41] namely the finger changes nature[42] by virtue of the mentioned 'Elohim, which is the attribute of judgment."[43,44]

In order to better understand Abulafia's exegetical move, let me adduce the interpreted verse: "This is the finger of God: and Pharaoh's heart was hardened." The Egyptian magicians explain the intervention in nature represented by the plagues as the work of the divine finger. The semantic field of the verse has to do with miraculous changes in the course of events for the purpose of bringing about a historical event: the deliverance of the people of Israel. In fact, neither the concept of nature nor a term that might convey it was available in biblical Hebrew. Abulafia introduced the term *teva'*, a medieval neologism denoting nature, which in the definite form *ha-teva'* is numerically equivalent to the divine name *'elohim*. The biblical verse deals, therefore, with the intervention of the finger of God in nature. Prima facie we witness here an intercorporal interpretation, which links a certain intervention to the mode of thought that deals with a regular path of events (nature), and the breaking of that path; therefore the rapprochement between the biblical and Greek corpora is achieved by means of gematria. We witness not only a radical semantic form of hermeneutics but also a deconstructive radicalism, which affects the grammatical structure of the text, for the following reason. The Hebrew phrase *'etzba' 'elohim* is a construct form, and *'elohim* is part of the phrase "finger of God." But by adducing the gematria of *'elohim* as nature, the biblical phrase is disassembled so that the finger is understood to intervene within the *'elohim*, which is tantamount to nature. Thus it is not simply a matter of exchanging one word for another, *'elohim* for *teva'*, but an extraordinary move that construes a whole drama between the two nouns, which originally are part of one expression. In other words, it is a syntactic aggression that divides two parts of one grammatical construct in order to introduce a term that represents a concept alien to the original corpus. What seems most important in our case, however, is not so clear from the careful formulation of the quoted passage: nature is identical with the divine attribute of judgment, and it appears, on the basis of many other passages, that no change can be assumed to take place, because nature is conceived to be unchangeable.[45]

In another discussion the same author indicates that "The name *'elohim* comprises [several meanings]: it is an appellative for the totality of the natural forces; it is part of the names of the first cause, and it refers also to an attribute of Him, by which He, glory to Him, is separated from other entities."[46] The verb translated as "comprises" is *kolel*, which, like the appellative, *kinnuy*, is numerically equivalent to *'elohim*, each having the value 86. If *'elohim* points to natural forces, then the intervention was neither extraordinary nor miraculous but natural. Therefore the introduction of the term *teva'* constitutes both a violation of Hebrew syntax, a move I propose to describe as deconstructive radicalism, and semantic radicalism, because the meaning of *teva'* dramatically altered the message of the verse. In fact, someone may even argue that the volitional theology of the Bible has been replaced by a more naturalistic understanding of reality.

To put it differently: the canonical text is understood as dealing not only with a particular instance in history when God intervened and changed the regular course of events by a miracle. In fact, the sacred scriptures are understood as pointing to a new form of discourse, one that deals with the question of nature, its stability, and the relations between the natural order and divine attributes. Again the emphasis is not on the numerical structure, because the number 86 is not attributed to any specific quality per se, as representing a certain cosmological feature. What is more important is the relationship that is established between a divine name and a term dealing with Neoaristotelian physics. This move, which is represented by many other examples in Abulafia's writings and those of his followers, takes the use of gematria a long way from its cautious application in Nahmanides. In lieu of establishing affinities between intracorporal elements and thus strengthening a closed system, as is the case in Hasidei Ashkenaz and Nahmanides, Abulafia uses this device so as to put the closed system in relation with other corpora, in a manner reminiscent of the allegorical strategy adopted by Maimonides and his followers. However, while the latter were more conservative from the linguistic point of view, because they did not attribute an important noetic role to language, the ecstatic Kabbalist introduced a mysticism of language that allows more precise affinities between alien concepts and traditional terminology. Moreover, among the most outstanding characteristics of Abraham Abulafia's writings is the relatively large-scale resort to gematrias that involve a variety of alien words, mainly Greek but also Latin, Basque, Turkish, and Arabic.[47] The more universalistic approach that is conveyed by this practice is in stark contrast to Nahmanides' approach.

According to a statement in the introduction to Abulafia's *Commentary on the Pentateuch*, which deals with a biblical story "they [the words of a verse] are taken within the philosophical approach, [they] become related to each other in a general manner, and not in all particulars. Whereas according to the methods of Kabbalah, not [even] one letter is left unused [by the commentator]."[48] The hyperliteral approach that takes into consideration each and every letter of the interpreted text is basically different from the allegorical method of interpretation, which is more concerned with the general narrative than with the details of the interpreted text. While the conceptual additions to the contents of Jewish thought made by the ecstatic Kabbalist by means of gematria stem largely from Greek thought, the technique derives from Hasidei Ashkenaz, as well as some Greek and ultimately Babylonian sources.

IV. Numeric Exegesis: A Fragmentary Prehistory

I have explained the medieval systematization of the exegetical methods as emerging together with esoteric literatures—philosophical ones related to Hasidei Ashkenaz or Kabbalistic ones. Is there any significant affinity between elaborate arcanization and systematic hermeneutics? The praxis evident in these literatures demonstrates that this seems to be the case. But if so, we should speak about a double process of arcanization: that of the content of the scriptures, which originally was exoteric, and that of the exegetical methods, because these were conceived of as part of the esoteric literature, although earlier they were part of the rabbinic, exoteric literature. Such an arcanization of the exegetical devices is possible, though not necessary. Let me deal a bit more with the esoteric nature of the exegetical methods and the possible solutions for their emergence in the Middle Ages.

Some form of exegetical thought may be discerned earlier in R. Yehudah he-Hasid's *Commentary on the Pentateuch*, where the term *sod* is used in order to point to esoteric interpretations.[49] In his writings, however, no systematic treatment can be detected. According to his disciples, R. Eleazar of Worms, the author of the first extant treatise on Ashkenazi hermeneutics, *Sefer ha-Hokhmah*, also called the book *Secret of Secrets*, and it consists in seventy-three methods of interpreting the Bible, which he enumerates, explains, and exemplifies copiously.[50] He points out explicitly that these techniques, which involve a variety of numerical methods, were part of an esoteric tradition he inherited from his master, R. Yehudah he-Hasid. He claims that the "fifty gates of understanding"—a classical rabbinic phrase[51] which in my opinion sometimes points in R. Eleazar's writings to non-rabbinic issues[52]—represent the realm of secret, *sod*, which is decoded from the biblical text by means of the seventy-three gates of wisdom.[53] The fifty gates of understanding represent the conceptual arcanization. The seventy-three gates, however, are also seen as part of the esoteric tradition.[54] Thus, the exegetical methods elicit not only secrets from a text but also secret topics in themselves. If, historically speaking, R. Eleazar is right and indeed he has been initiated into a series of exegetical norms by his master, as he explicitly claims, his exposition of these norms is a matter not of arcanizing exoteric norms but simply of revealing and to an extent exotericizing them after they had been handed down as part of an esoteric tradition. Again, if this claim is true, a substantial body of exegetical techniques has been transmitted as if it were esoteric topics. Among these techniques, the numerical ones, including gematria, played a very important role.

A similar situation may be discerned in Abraham Abulafia's description of the advanced stages of his sevenfold hermeneutic system. When describing his three last forms of interpretation, he sees them as the secret ones, and all three involve deconstructive radicalism[55] as they dissolve the commented text into its basic elements in order to build up new words, which are conceived of as "the meaning" of the interpreted text. These interpretive techniques, which include gematria as part of the sixth technique,[56] are described as "the hidden path of the Kabbalah."[57] Therefore, the claim of two of those Jewish mystics who committed to writing the deconstructive radical methods, which include gematria, was that they inherited an esoteric tradition. Yet on the basis of the resort to gematria in rabbinic sources, and its inclusion in rabbinic exegetical methods,[58] this claim of esotericism is a difficult one to maintain. Indeed, as R. Eleazar mentioned in one of the passages quoted above, even the clowns would use gematria. If these masters did not receive such a technique as esoteric, their claim would be superfluous, given that the method itself was already well established and therefore not in need of authoritative sources.

What, then, is the weight of such a claim for esotericism? Any possible answer depends on the earlier existence of traditions that would describe the technique of gematria as esoteric. Only if the existence of such a claim—or, even better, claims—could be demonstrated might the claims of the medieval masters carry some historical weight. But such a claim cannot be found in the rabbinic sources. Nevertheless, it was part of the very ancient Mesopotamian lore. As Stephen Lieberman has shown, some of the interpretive techniques that are very similar to the rabbinic, exoteric ones, including the techniques that correspond to gematria, were part of the esoteric lore in Mesopotamia.[59] Lieberman compared the Mesopotamian material to the Jewish material that is closest in time, namely the rabbinic sources. He demonstrated in a virtuoso manner the similarities between some ancient techniques and rabbinic ones, but did not address the question of the discrepancy between ancient esoteric techniques in Mesopotamia and the quite exoteric rabbinic material that was informed by them. (This does not, of course, invalidate his conclusions.)

May we portray a historical development that started with the esoteric Mesopotamian technique, then made an exoteric move in the rabbinic texts, and then underwent arcanization in Hasidei Ashkenaz? Such a development is certainly possible, although it is far from plausible. One of the main reasons for my reticence to embrace this scenario is R. Eleazar's claim that he indeed inherited the interpretive techniques as an esoteric tradition. Thus, although the gap in time between the ancient non-Jewish techniques and the medieval Jewish ones is much greater than in the case of the rabbinic sources, there still are two reasons to make the historical claim of an affinity between the two claims plausible. One, the common esoteric nature, has already been mentioned. The second reason is much more complicated.

Lieberman has described some intricate interpretive techniques used in Mesopotamia, but nothing so complex is known in the rabbinic sources. Although he was aware of more complex "Kabbalistic" forms of numerical interpretation[60]—in fact, those of Hasidei Ashkenaz—he did not follow up on the possibility that the more complex systems, though historically later, are nevertheless closer to the

Mesopotamian material he adduced. One might suppose that similarities between corpora written in such different geographical areas, composed in different languages, and belonging to different literary corpora should not be compared, and they even constitute less plausible candidates for an attempt to establish a historical nexus between them. This is indeed a cautious approach, and the problems created by neglecting it may be quite serious. But there is no reason not to suggest possibilities that cannot, for the time being, be proven by means of standard approaches.[61]

One last interesting observation: according to a recent proposal, the Aramaic form *gematrin*, found long before the twelfth century, is related to the Greek *grammateia*, which denotes "a scribal means of writing secretly."[62]

V. *TEMURAH* AND *TZERUFEI 'OTIYYOT*

Let me describe briefly other exegetical techniques[63] that are part of what I propose to call deconstructive radicalism: changing the order of the letters of a certain word or words in order to create a combination that is supposed to clarify or reveal the meaning of the original. The numerical calculation does change either the letters of a given word or even their order but enriches the word's semantic cargo by confronting it with another, or other, numerically equivalent word or words. Just as in the case of allegorical and symbolic interpretations, the stability of the interpreted text is preserved, but the more comprehensive discourse is fragmented by a strong extraction of a word and the infusion of an additional meaning on the basis of nonsemantic reasons. Thus, the hermeneutical norm of gematria stands somewhere between semantic and deconstructive radicalism, for it overemphasizes the basic linguistic components at the expense of the more comprehensive linguistic units, namely words or sentences.

Other forms of exegesis are even more radical, however. The most interesting of them, and of a paramount importance for some techniques found in Jewish mysticism, is the combination of letters.[64] First, as we saw in Chapter 1, it was more a cosmogonic technique already central for *Sefer Yetzirah* but also known in talmudic texts and influential on subsequent developments in Jewish mysticism and magic until late Hasidism, as we shall discover in Chapter 12. R. Abraham Abulafia contends in his first book, written in Spain in 1273, that

> under this category[65] there are gematrias and calculations,[66] etc., . . . and
> *temurah*, that is, the exchange of one letter for another, and its substitution,
> and its replacement for another, like the letters 'a[leph], h[et], h[e], 'a[yin], and
> the similar letters, all have substitutes. And this is a glorious lore,[67] to be
> done everywhere in an appropriate manner, without adding or diminishing;

and the combinations of letters is the permutation of one letter to another, without substituting them at all, like 'adam, 'amad, dama', da'am, mada'. And this is also a very glorious lore, and by means of these things the secrets of the Torah will be revealed, but not in any other ways.[68]

The Kabbalists use either of two devices. One involves manipulating the letters of a single word, changing their order or exchanging one letter for another, techniques described under the umbrella term temurah. The other, more complex technique is combination of letters, tzerufei 'otiyyot, by which a variety of letters, either those of the Hebrew alphabet in general or those belonging to different words, undergo change.[69] The method of gematria is explicitly described as different from combination of letters, although both are techniques for discovering the secrets of the Torah. To put it in a more radical way, an ecstatic Kabbalist may or should apply to the same word a variety of modes of radical hermeneutics, which in principle are, according to Abulafia, infinite in number.[70] Indeed, Abulafia regards the principle of combination of letters as the essence of language itself, and therefore it is not only an exegetical norm but also the very structure of language. In several instances he adduces the gematria tzeruf 'otiyyot = shiv'yim leshonot, namely the phrase "combination of letters" is numerically tantamount to the phrase "seventy languages," a figure that points to the totality of languages.

We may assume that this passage, as well as many other texts of Abulafia's, had an impact on the introduction to an early-sixteenth-century treatise on ecstatic Kabbalah composed by R. Yehudah Albotini in Jerusalem, in which we read:

the paths of combinations of letters and their permutations . . . which is a glorious lore,[71] from which the secrets of the Torah will be revealed; and the different types of gematrias . . . to know the supreme and wondrous name, and they are also like a ladder to ascend to the degree that is the most sublime of all the degrees, to bring and to cause the descent of the influx from God, blessed be He, which cause that man will attain the divine spirit, and to the degree of prophecy, by means of the paths of hitbodedut[72] and asceticism.[73]

The phrase "glorious lore" is absolutely identical to that occurring in the passage from Abulafia. In both cases knowledge of the secrets of the Torah is mentioned in the context of gematria and combination of letters. I am inclined to see in Abulafia's book the source of the later treatise. Yet despite this similarity the sixteenth-century Kabbalist adds to Abulafia's claim the explicit view, which may be inferred from Abulafia but apparently was never expressed by him, that gematria may cause the descent of the divine influx and perhaps a mystical experience. Such a claim recurs in several contexts in ecstatic Kabbalah and talismanic discussions as an attribute of the process of combination of letters,[74] but it seems that Albotini is the first who explicitly combines this issue with the resort to gematria and to mystical experience.[75] In both cases the interpreted word supplies only the prime matter for the creative game of the Kabbalists, who permuted letters in a variety of ways. Indeed, in defining Kabbalah Abulafia wrote : "The true Kabbalah which is in our hands is [claims] that whoever is not cognizant of the combination of letters[76] and is not very experienced and has examined them[77] and also in the calculation of the letters[78] and their separation [from one word][79] and their conjugation,[80] and their reversal[81] and permutation,[82] and their exchange,[83] as it is written in *Sefer Yetzirah*[84] according to our path, he does not know God [*hashem*, or the Name]. Therefore, it is impossible to comprehend reality but by means of the names."[85]

The exegetical techniques are therefore not only a matter of interpretive norms but also paths for attaining knowledge of God in general—in Abulafia's writings, I would say, an experimental knowledge of God. However, in addition to the religious valence of hermeneutic radicalism, knowledge of God, and even the achievement of mystical experiences, Abulafia introduced a more scientific achievement: comprehension of reality. Yet although in the last quote the two topics are mentioned together, in other instances these two achievements do not coexist so easily. So, for example, in one of his later works, after enumerating the books that constitute Aristotle's *Organon*, Abulafia claims that he studied them in depth; but then he mentions the existence of a superior wisdom, "the path of the knowledge of the permutation of letters, which is more excellent than that [of Aristotle], its essence having been explained in the commentaries on *Sefer Yetzirah*." The Kabbalistic way, which is tantamount to Abulafia's own ecstatic Kabbalah, is regarded as superior to Aristotelian logic, as the former is the science of the "inner [and] superior logic" while the latter is an "external and lower aspect" in comparison to Kabbalistic logic.[86] Several times in his writings Abulafia described the sixth and seventh ways of interpreting the Torah by means of various eccentric techniques, some of them ergetic.[87] And though not in a systematic exegetical treatment, all these techniques were put in practice by a variety of Kabbalists.

Let me adduce one more example of the belief that combination of letters is an exegetical technique for understanding the arcana in the Torah—in addition to the Torah's mystical function—from a book by a student of Abulafia. In *Gate of Vowels* R. Joseph Gikatilla wrote: "The entire Torah is woven [*ne'ereget*] from letters, as if you will say that the word *bereshit* emerged when someone mixed these six letters with each other, by the mixture of these letters and the understanding of the depth[88] of their permutation[89] and their combination[90] the prophets and vision-aries penetrated the mysteries of the Torah."[91] The idea of the woven Torah also occurs elsewhere in Gikatilla's writings,[92] and in both cases the assumption is reminiscent of the various descriptions found in Plato's *Cratylus* (387e–388c, 425a, 431b) and *Sophist* (259e, 262c).[93] Yet if for Plato the texture created by weaving is a matter of combinations of words, for Gikatilla it is the letters that provide the threads of the linguistic fabric. In any case, both authors compare the texture to the creation of the world.[94]

Let me now adduce one of the most important formulations regarding the discovery of the secrets of the Torah by means of combination of letters, as explicated by one of the most influential Kabbalists, the Safedian rabbi Moses Cordovero. In his widespread *Pardes Rimmonim* Cordovero, allowing a wide range of hypertextual readings of the Bible, contends that

> the knowledge of the secrets of our Torah is by means of the *tzerufim* and *gematria'ot* and *temurot* and *rashei teivot* and *sofei teivot* and *tokhei teivot* and *rashei pesuqim* and *sofei pesuqim* and *dillug 'otiyyot* and *tzeruf 'otiyyot*. And those matters are sublime and hidden and their secret is sublime [sic] and we have no power to comprehend them because of their outmost concealment be-cause they [the secrets] are shifting in accordance with these paths to the infinite, in a limitless manner.[95]

This passage represents a moment of canonization of the ancient exegetical practices by a famous theosophical Kabbalist, who absorbed significant aspects of the ecstatic Kabbalah in his influential compendium. Despite the fact that in this passage, and in its context, Cordovero argues that those techniques are almost unknown and will be revealed in the eschaton, he describes them in some detail immediately afterward. There is no plausible reason to doubt the impact of ec-static Kabbalah on this passage from Cordovero, and my assumption, to be elabo-rated in Chapter 12, is that the Safedian Kabbalist adopted exegetical techniques and concepts of the Torah stemming from Abraham Abulafia and his followers.

However, what is important for some of the contentions about to be presented in the next chapter is that Kabbalists were rarely concerned with ineffability or ontological transcendence, while expressions of noetic insufficiency related to the understanding of the divine realm are rather poor. In the last quote there is a clear example of noetic insufficiency, yet it is concerned not with the divine structures or powers but with secrets of the Torah and techniques of its interpretation. In fact, there is nothing reminiscent of the *theologia negativa*, but because of the assumption that there is a huge number of mathematically oriented exegetical methods, the secrets shift frequently and the human mind is unable to follow them. It is essential to pay attention to Cordovero's remark that the secrets shift with the methods of interpretation. This is a recognition that the secrets depend on methods which in themselves can be understood and controlled. Although such an approach does not involve acknowledging that secrets are projected, the affinity Cordovero established between methods and secrets constitutes a step in the direction of the strong reader or interpreter.

VI. BETWEEN ASHKENAZI AND ECSTATIC-KABBALISTIC HERMENEUTICS

Though technically identical, the Ashkenazi use of deconstructive radicalism is different from that of the ecstatic forms of deconstruction and their reverberations. We have seen the difference between the intracorporal and intercorporal approaches. Here I would like to suggest another major difference between the two main medieval hermeneutical treatments. The seventy-three techniques enumerated by R. Eleazar of Worms are conceived of as equally important or esoteric. We may describe R. Eleazar's list as horizontal, for it does not attempt to offer a hierarchical distinction between the numerous methods of interpretation.

R. Abraham Abulafia, on the other hand, offered a very careful structure of seven modes of exegesis, arranged in what I propose to call a vertical hierarchical structure. The first three stages, or lower level, is the plain sense, the fourth the allegorical one, and the last three Kabbalistic. The verticality of the exegetical norms on the list is strengthened by its social implications, because the lower stages are explicitly intended for the vulgus (the common people), the fourth for the philosophers, and the last three to the few elite. Ontologically speaking, the different social groups were considered to be interested in the more material, philosophical, and spiritual topics, which stand also for the ladder of beings which brings men to God. Moreover, the higher the exegetical method on the exegetical ladder, the greater the ergetical character of the technique.

Let me adduce a clear example of the strong hierarchical propensity of Abulafia's hermeneutics:

> This knowledge should be taken by the righteous from the Torah according
> to its plain sense, in order to perfect his righteousness, but if he wants to
> become a pious man, he should approach it by means of the path of the
> philosophical-esoterical one. However, if he desires to prophesy, he must
> approach it according to the "path of the names," which is the esoteric path,
> received from the divine intellect[96] . . . If you want to be righteous alone, it
> suffices that you will follow the paths of the Torah, on the path of its plain
> form. If you wish to arrive at being pious alone, it suffices that you will know
> the secrets of the Torah in the manner of the men of inquiry, together with

your being righteous. However, if you want to be prophets, it will suffice to follow the path of the prophets, whose path was to combine the [letters of the] entire Torah and to approach it by the path of the holy names, from its beginning to the end, as it reached us in a true Kabbalah regarding it [the path] that "the entire Torah is [consists] of the names of the Holy One, blessed be He,"[97] together with being perfect in the first two paths.[98]

The affinity between the linguistic path of the names, which culminates in the practice of a discipline that involves at the lower stages both gematria and combination of letters, and prophecy is a central point in Abulafia's system, just as it surfaces in the passage from R. Joseph Gikatilla quoted above. How may such a view be integrated into the innovative exegetical system of ecstatic Kabbalah? In my opinion, the immersion in exercises involving linguistic techniques, the ergetic practices, was envisioned as capable of inducing an ecstatic state of consciousness when text and language took over the mystic's consciousness. Just as a modern deconstructive thinker would consider language as taking over the author and thus obliterating the importance of the authorial intent, so too some of the Jewish mystics claim that their interpretations are transmitted to them by higher entities with which they either communicate or identify. In the case of Abulafia, not only was the main technique that was believed to induce mystical experiences basically linguistic, but also the agent intellect was conceived to be primordial speech.

The intellectual hierarchy suggested in this passage from Abulafia therefore strengthens the hermeneutical one. The hierarchical structure emerges out of an attempt, found also in other forms of Kabbalah (especially in Castile), to integrate into one structure a variety of forms of literature, as we may learn from an analysis of the fourfold *pardes* interpretations.[99]

The Ashkenazi esoteric literature was less open to integrating significant bodies of alien material, what I call intercorporality, and the need to deal with problems of hierarchy was less evident. The Ashkenazi masters had to choose between equally important exegetical strategies, which were applied in most cases intratextually, while some of the Spanish Kabbalists had to establish the superiority of Kabbalah in an intellectual ambiance that was permeated by a variety of bodies of thought. Thus its hermeneutics is sometimes arranged hierarchically, exploiting and emphasizing the differences between the corpora and the need for different exegetical strategies pertinent to these corpora, and sometimes conceived of as horizontal and intercorporal, as striving to point out the alleged correspondences or, to use a Renaissance term, hidden concordances between historically and conceptually diverse corpora. It should be mentioned, however, that despite the sometimes quite artificial interpretations of the sacred scriptures by means of a variety of Greek philosophical systems, these semantically radical interpretations became an integral part of the conceptualization of Judaism; in other words, they were significantly incorporated. This dynamics of incorporation, which absorbs the concepts that were introduced by intercorporal hermeneutics, is one of the most interesting processes in the intellectual expansions of Jewish thought. That is to say, the profound absorption of the attainments of intercorporal exegesis created subsequent forms of new intracorporal interpretations.

The eccentric hermeneutical techniques described above mainly on the basis of the thirteenth-century corpora were accepted as part of Jewish and Christian Kabbalah. Some of Abulafia's foremost passages describing his views were incorporated in Sefer ha-Peliy'ah, a classic of Kabbalah written late in the fourteenth century in the Byzantine Empire.[100] This is evident from the important role the exegetical techniques play in the most influential exposition of Kabbalah, Johann Reuchlin's De Arte Cabalistica. Even more detailed is the treatment of thirty-two exegetical techniques used by Kabbalists offered by Nicolas le Fevre de la Boderie in a work attached to his brother Guy's translation of Francesco Giorgio Veneto's De Harmonia Mundi.[101] Written in French and printed in Paris in 1588, it made available to a wider audience an exhaustive description of numerous Kabbalistic exegetical techniques, some taken from Abulafia's writings. As we have seen, in their generation a distinguished Safedian Kabbalist, R. Moses Cordovero, incorporated many of the Ashkenazi and Abulafian eccentric techniques in his widely influential Pardes Rimmonim, thus offering a synthesis between the Spanish Kabbalah and the techniques that were much less in vogue in the Iberian peninsula. Whole gates of Cordovero's classic book are devoted to explanations of the meaning of individual letters and to the presentation of interpretive techniques which became the patrimony of much larger audiences once the book was printed in 1584.[102] Under his own direct influence, as well as that of his students and of Sefer ha-Peliy'ah, the eccentric techniques were adopted and used almost constantly in Polish Hasidism.[103] They even appeared in the writings of a close disciple of R. Elijah of Vilnius, R. Menahem Mendel of Shklow, who was acquainted with some of Abulafia's most important works, from which he quoted from time to time, and absorbed the ecstatic Kabbalists' hermeneutical approaches.[104]

IO

THE SYMBOLIC MODE IN THEOSOPHICAL-THEURGICAL KABBALAH

I. Introduction

The biblical and the rabbinic literatures are devoid of substantial symbolic propensities, if by symbolism we understand a way of reflecting the divine attributes or worlds by means of a sustained exegesis of the sacred scriptures. The emergence of forms of Kabbalah that display a vigorous symbolic mode of interpretation, and the composition of a book that is informed by a symbolic code and becomes canonical, are therefore sharp departures from the royal road of expression and interpretation dominant, previously, in those forms of religious literature.[1] Interestingly, even after the ascent of this figurative mode in some Kabbalistic writings, symbolic expressions or interpretations did not radiate beyond the Kabbalistic writings—to Halakhic treatises, for example—and even in thirteenth-century Ashkenazi Hasidism these Kabbalistic modes of expression were put on a pedestal as part of the process of dearcanization.[2]

As mentioned in Chapter 8, symbolic exegesis as practiced by medieval Kabbalists has many earlier parallels and perhaps even some ancient sources. The floruit of Kabbalistic symbolism, however, is to be located in Castile in the second half of the thirteenth century,[3] the very same period determined by Umberto Eco as the time when the more vague symbolic and allegorical modes collapsed, under the influence of Thomas Aquinas' restriction of allegorical interpretation to the understanding of scripture alone.[4] Is the synchronicity between the two semiotic developments, the scholastic restriction on the one hand and the Kabbalistic expansion of symbolism on the other, a matter of simple coincidence? Is the upsurge of symbolism in theosophical Kabbalah at the very time when it started to collapse in Christian theology as a comprehensive attitude to reality the result not only of two different processes but also totally independent events? In this chapter I shall attempt to answer this question by resorting to an explanation of the nature and emergence of the Kabbalistic symbols that differs from that of the dominant scholarship, an explanation that will take into consideration Eco's theory of symbolism as a textual code. Yet so that we may better understand the solution about to be offered, let me survey the scholarly view of the nature of the symbol in Kabbalah and the circumstances of its emergence.

II. MODERN THEORIES CONCERNING THE SYMBOLIC MODE IN KABBALAH

There can be no doubt that symbolism (and here I use the term in a very loose manner) plays a major role in Kabbalistic discourse. A variety of symbolic systems, which differ from each other both in details and in principle, are found in many of the Kabbalistic books. Recurrent as it may be, symbolism is not, however, ubiquitous in Kabbalistic literature. As I have already pointed out elsewhere, there are whole Kabbalistic corpora which are not symbolic, as for example the ecstatic Kabbalah of R. Abraham Abulafia and the linguistic Kabbalah of the early R. Joseph Gikatilla and R. Moses de Leon.[5] Nevertheless, the recurrence of symbols in some important Kabbalistic corpora, together with other factors, has convinced some scholars of Kabbalah to formulate what I would call a pansymbolic understanding of Kabbalah, namely an assumption, repeated piously by Scholemian scholars, that Kabbalah cannot be imagined without the symbolic perception of reality as a whole.

However, even the scholarly treatments of symbolism in those forms of Kabbalah that indeed express themselves symbolically have been very general and simplistic. Attempts to define Kabbalistic symbolism in toto without paying attention to historical developments within different schools of Kabbalah, without any effort to develop a systemic understanding of the various symbols within each of those schools, without a detailed history of even one Kabbalistic symbol, and without considering the many other possible approaches to such a vast literature as Kabbalah represents, means that a more sophisticated theory of Kabbalistic symbolism is still an important desideratum of the scholarly treatment of this mystical literature. Only recently has a more detailed study of one Kabbalist's view of symbol been undertaken, and an attempt to describe the symbolic semiosis of one word been made.[6]

We may distinguish between three main types of explanations for the emergence of Kabbalistic symbols in modern scholarship. One sees symbols as expressing the mystic's encounter with the divine; another centers on a discourse shaped as part of a reaction toward cultural-religious processes; and the third has to do with the encounter between Kabbalists and history.

1. Noetic Insufficiency

The more dominant definition of the Kabbalistic symbol in scholarly literature is related to what I shall call *noetic insufficiency*, namely the impossibility of the human mind, and perhaps of human experience in general, to encounter and express an entity understood as the ultimate. In this Neokantian approach the Kabbalistic symbol is, according to Isaiah Tishby, the "representative of an occult, or hidden, entity or process, that is neither revealed in itself at all nor can it be expressed in a direct manner."[7] The symbolized entity can neither be apprehended nor expressed in itself, but solely by means of the symbol.[8] Tishby is but echoing a view expressed by Scholem, who claimed, in one of his pertinent statements, that "the Kabbalists do not start from the idea of communicable meaning."[9] Indeed, this overemphasis on the radical transcendence of the referent to which the symbols point is one of the leading principles that informed the pansymbolic school that Scholem established.

Insofar as scholarship on Kabbalah is concerned, this definition is formulated in a way that insinuates that the modern scholars who proposed this formulation accept the Kabbalistic axiology, that they assume the existence of a hidden entity that reveals itself or is intuited by means of symbols. I would stress, however, that the Kabbalists themselves were far from been so reflective in their description of what may be termed the symbolic mode. In fact, the above definitions are sometimes imposed by scholars on the Kabbalists, as if reflecting their experiences of the ineffable.

Another view of the Kabbalistic symbol that will concern us here was also expressed by Scholem, explicitly in the context of an experience but implicitly with respect to the nature of the language of the mystics:

What exactly is this "secret" or "hidden" dimension of language, about whose existence all mystics for all time feel unanimous agreement, from India and the mystics of Islam, right up to the Kabbalists and Jacob Boehme? The answer is, with virtually no trace of hesitation, the following: it is the symbolic nature of language which defines this dimension. The linguistic theories of mystics frequently diverge when it comes to determining this symbolic nature. But all mystics in quest of the secret of language come to share a common basis, namely the fact that language is used to communicate something which goes way beyond the sphere which allows for expression and formation: the fact also that a certain inexpressible something, which only manifests itself in symbols, resonated in every manner of expression.[10]

This beautiful passage has all the qualities of a grand statement, including that it is to a certain extent true.[11] There can be no doubt that the symbolic mode of expression is a recurrent phenomenon in mystical literature in general and also, in many cases, in some important forms of Kabbalah. Nevertheless, the passage contains what seems to me to be an overstatement, an overemphasis on the centrality of the symbolic mode, at least insofar as the Jewish mystical visions of language are concerned: it is a pansymbolic view of Jewish mysticism, which is hardly sustained even by the Kabbalistic texts alone. Indeed, Scholem's formulation takes into account only one aspect of the symbol, the referential, as part of an experience that the mystic attempts to communicate. He speaks expressly about the mystical experience as generating symbols.[12]

However, it seems that a different aspect of Kabbalistic symbols, the performative one, has been neglected by modern scholarship. Only recently has attention been paid to the active role of language beyond its being a transparent agent. So, for example, the magical theories of language, like the talismanic one,[13] would only rarely fit the emphasis on the symbolic (or referential) nature of language, inclined as these magical theories are toward the performative aspects.[14] For some Kabbalists, words are not only the extensions of the divine attributes into the lower worlds, hints at the unknown that reach the human soul remote as it is from the divine, initiations into divine mysteries. Although these descriptions of the role of language may be appropriate for some forms of Kabbalah, in many cases they do not fit the total variety of views of language in this lore.

While the referential approaches can in some cases define the initial phase of the theosophical-theurgical path, they cannot exhaust a fundamental aspect of some Kabbalistic theories of language: their performative, or manipulative, or effective understandings. Only after a Kabbalist, especially a theosophical-theurgical one, has understood the symbolic cargo of a particular word may he be attracted, or invited, to apply this mystical insight to the performance of the ritual, not only as reflecting higher truths but also as part of an endeavor to affect supernatural realms. If there is an organic link between the symbols and their source, as is the case in some of the Kabbalistic views of symbols, this link works not only downward but also in the upward: the symbol as the divine presence within the lower world is not only the feeble reflection of the supernal into the mundane but also the beginning of an ontological chain that facilitates the transmission of the human influence on high. It is an energetic entity, functioning as a speech act no less than a communicative unit. In fact, the coexistence of these two aspects, the symbolic and the performative, is to be accepted as a crucial feature of some major forms of theosophical Kabbalah.[15] As I shall suggest below, the sequence of understanding the symbolic valence, as a precondition for resorting to the performative aspect of language, represents the sequence in the Kabbalistic literature from its beginning; I assume, however, that the theurgical-performative acts predated the emergence of the symbolic vision of the Bible and the commandments.

2. Symbols and Crises

Scholars have proposed an alternative to this vision of experience as the source of symbols: the assumption that symbolization is motivated by the feeling of a crisis in the canonical text, in sacred language, or in tradition generally. Symbolization is therefore described as the way some Kabbalists attempted to safeguard the values they believed in, when those values were deemed, according to scholars, to be endangered by religious insufficiency. These scholars asserted that some aspects of Judaism were "dubious" in the eyes of the early Kabbalists.[16] Symbolization was conceived of as adding a spiritual aura to the texts and was understood as highly important for saving them from the alleged crisis.[17] Moreover, by offering the "symbolic-mystical" interpretation of Judaism, the Kabbalists were deemed to be able to recover from this alleged crisis or "depression," to escape the dominion of Satan and open the path to a luminous way of life.[18] It seems very plausible that the attribution of such a dark starting point for Kabbalistic creativity is the combined result of the importance given to Gnosticism in Scholem's studies, on the one hand,[19] and to the impact of the Shoah on modern Jewish scholars, on the other.[20]

Fascinating though this theory may be, as applied to the specific historical circumstances of the late twelfth and thirteenth centuries, when the symbolic mode began to crystallize, and to the specific geographical area that hosted them, I find it hardly plausible. Its appearance is representative of a modern development of the conception of Jewish history as haunted by crises and presided over by a demonic power, as formulated by Scholem, but it is less in accord with the understanding of hermeneutics in the Middle Ages.

3. Historical Symbols

Let me address now the claim that another crisis, this time more historical than cultural, has been instrumental in the symbolic interpretation of Judaism. According to Scholem, the historical experiences of the Jewish people during the exile were crystallized into powerful mystical symbols which, having been disseminated later to the larger masses, were able to affect the course of Jewish history. In formulating the first part of his claim, Scholem called attention to "symbols of a very special kind, in which the spiritual experience of the mystics was almost inextricably intertwined with the historical experience of the Jewish people. It is this interweaving of two realms, which in most other religious mysticisms have remained separate, that gave Kabbalah its specific imprint."[21]

Here we have an interesting attempt to propose a correlation between the Kabbalistic symbol and the cumulative historical experiences of the people of Israel, which informed the mystic who produced, in his experience and its expression, a fusion between the personal and the collective experience. This is the reason for the mysterious affinity between the Kabbalistic symbol and Jewish national history. Moreover, Scholem explains the correlation between the two realms rather lucidly when he asserts that "the more sordid and cruel the fragment of historical reality allowed to the Jew amid the storms of exile, the deeper and more precise the symbolic hope which burst through it and transfigured it."[22]

Consequently, a deep continuity between the historical experience of the Jews and Kabbalistic symbolism, or at least a part of it, is assumed to be crucial for understanding this branch of Jewish mysticism. The tears of a lachrymose history crystallized into Kabbalistic symbols, which served as mirrors within which Jewish history receives its meaning. The mystic's consciousness becomes a mysterious alembic for this alchemical transformation and also the agent that transmits, symbolically, the meaning of history for his generation.

But insofar as the Kabbalah of the sixteenth century is concerned—the most powerful arsenal of historical symbols, according to Scholem—no new symbols that can be called historical are mentioned. In fact, I believe that some historical events may perhaps have deepened the significance of some preexisting symbols, but it seems to me very implausible to assume, on the basis of these statements, that historical experiences have also created new symbols. Their origins therefore remain obscure, to be traced in the preceding phases of Jewish mysticism, which predate the expulsion of the Jews from Spain. This seems to be the case with the concepts of *tzimtzum* and the breaking of the vessels.[23] It is important, however, to dwell on the phenomenology of Scholem's description of the fusion of horizons which allegedly takes place in the case of the mystic's production of Kabbalistic symbols. In his view, the symbols that lay at the heart of Kabbalistic myth are those of exile and redemption, "which assumed such vast dimensions with the Kabbalists and accounts for their prolonged historical influence."[24]

I would like to address the possible manner of the transformation of traditional concepts like exile and redemption into Kabbalistic symbols. In Scholem's explanation, two crucial elements conspire in the formation of the symbol: one, the historical experience of the nation (or a significant portion of it), probably condensed into a concept like exile and redemption, to take Scholem's examples; the other, the inner experience of the mystic, who combines and recirculates these concepts in the form of symbols that express simultaneously the experience of the nation and the individual. The assumption would be that the traditional concepts, which encapsulate the historical experience, were experienced by the mystic without any formative conceptual mediation, thereby allowing a direct suffusion of the collective experience with that of the individual. Yet this seems to allow for a direct, unmediated relationship between the mystic, in our case the Kabbalists, and those concepts epitomized by certain words. It is possible to argue that in most cases a Jewish mystic will experience not a concept or word open to accept a new meaning in accordance with his own peculiar experience, but a concept or word already loaded with Kabbalistic significance in the Kabbalistic texts in existence before a certain Kabbalist became immersed in such symbols as productive of experiences. It is Kabbalistic theosophy that impinged directly on the concepts used by the Kabbalists qua mystics and not, as far as I can tell, an epitome of historical experiences. If we push the formative role of historical experience as the basis of (at least some) Kabbalistic symbols, then we must allow the impact of history on Kabbalah from its very inception, when the first Kabbalistic symbols emerged, an argument that does not fit Scholem's assumption as to the indifference to history in the early Kabbalah.

However, as Hans Jonas has pointed out, the doctrinal framework is to be surmised as an important contributor to mystical experiences, in the case of ancient mystical systems and experiences. I assume that this is also the case insofar as some other medieval bodies of mystical literature are concerned.[25]

On the other hand, I would not separate so sharply the genesis and significance of the Kabbalistic symbols from that which we may encounter in other forms of mysticism. Scholem assumed that such "historical" symbolism, allegedly characteristic of Jewish mysticism, would seem "strange to students of Christian mysticism, since it does not fit into the categories of 'mysticism' with which they are familiar."[26] Yet if we are correct as to the importance of preexisting theological and philosophical concepts for the formation of Kabbalistic symbolism,[27] there is no categorical difference between the manners in which Jewish and other mystical symbolisms have emerged. In all these cases it would be reasonable to inspect the respective theologies and related types of literature in order to uncover the literary sources of the mystics. Jewish theology was concerned with the problem of the history of the Jewish nation since the Bible, just as Christian theology was concerned with the story of Christ since the New Testament; the two respective types of mysticism have integrated within their symbolism theological concepts that may or may not be related to a "real" historical event or events. In lieu of two constitutive components of the emerging Kabbalistic symbols, as proposed by Scholem, I would therefore allow three: the traditional concept, for example *galut*, understood as a national event or situation; the Kabbalistic-symbolical significance of that concept, in this case the exile of the divine, in many cases the Shekhinah as the prototype or reflection of the national exile; and finally the mystical experience of the Kabbalists, a feeling or state of personal alienation, an inner *galut*. This last element is an event which, important as it may be, is nevertheless imponderable in connection with the formative moment of the symbol, and as such it is difficult to speculate on its relative importance.

Another issue related to the phenomenological aspect of the Kabbalistic symbols is the decisive role of the complex of "exile-redemption" symbolism in the general economy of Kabbalistic symbolism. Scholem himself apparently implies that this peculiar type of symbolism is relevant for a later stage of Kabbalistic thought; moreover, even in the case of Lurianic Kabbalah, the question of whether the exile-redemption problematic is really the heart of the system can be debated. A highly complex literature, Lurianic Kabbalah can be read in different ways while allowing emphases on various key concepts, the exile-redemption polarity being only one of them.

One last point: Scholem and his followers view Kabbalistic symbols as forms to understand reality as a whole. This is a sweeping view, which is best represented in Tishby's claim, which he made without adducing any corroborating evidence, that "the Kabbalistic symbols are not only means for understanding reality, or ways of expression, but the entire reality is conceived of as a texture of symbols for divinity, and the vision of the existents without understanding the significance that is hidden within them, is a flawed vision."[28] Such a view presupposes a homogeneous universe that is symbolized in toto; it ignores the importance of hierarchical thinking in the Middle Ages and in human imagination in general. It should be stated categorically that, relevant as the scholarly discussions of symbolism may be for understanding the phenomenological core of some important trends in Kabbalah, their overemphasis oftentimes obliterates the uniqueness and value of some other, nonsymbolic Kabbalistic trends.

The common denominator of the different explanations for the emergence of Kabbalistic symbols is the assumption that the Kabbalists were expressing forms of deficiency and attempts to overcome them by resorting to another approach, the symbolic one. The Kabbalists were haunted by their own inability to express themselves, or by the radical and more general impossibility of expressing the divine fullness, or by their awareness of an imminent or immanent crisis in their tradition, or by the expression of a specific historical crisis, the expulsion of the Jews from Spain and Portugal at the end of the sixteenth century. In the following, I shall offer an explanation that assumes that Kabbalists, in their attachment to the religious texts and ritual praxis, attempted to find instances of experience of plenitude; sometimes this plenitude was understood in terms of symbolic interpretations of the basic religious elements, by resorting to their preliminary acquaintance with the structure of the divine realm. This plenitude is connected with the conviction, which initiated numerous exegetical enterprises of projecting or "discovering" within the most common Jewish texts, that there is a wealth of symbolic and other meanings and powers in the traditional texts, and that the Kabbalist is able to uncover it.

III. KABBALISTIC SYMBOLISM AS AN EXEGETICAL CODE

My basic proposal for understanding both the emergence and the ongoing relevance of the symbolic mode in Kabbalah has to do with a more systemic development that explains the relations between modes of thinking about divinity, on the one hand, and modes of understanding canonical texts and acting religiously, on the other. The first mode, the hermeneutical one, offers insights into the esoteric meaning of the Jewish canonical texts; the other, the theosophical-theurgical— mode, offers rationales for ritualistic Jewish activity. I propose to pay attention to the emergence of the hermeneutical role of the Kabbalistic symbol or, to use Eco's category, the view of the symbols as part of a code that attempted to counteract another hermeneutical code. In describing the confrontation between the allegorical code, espoused by Jewish philosophers, and the symbolic code, embraced by theosophical Kabbalists, I assume that the latter responded to the former. Thus, I see both as part of a more comprehensive process, the arcanization of the canonical texts, which also involves other forms of hermeneutics contemporary to the two mentioned above, like the more mathematically oriented hermeneutics of Hasidei Ashkenaz.[29]

At the beginning of the thirteenth century Maimonides, the most important Jewish philosopher in the Middle Ages, offered the first large-scale effort to introduce an allegorical understanding of most important aspects of Jewish ca-nonical writings and rituals.[30] Insofar as the hermeneutical aspect of his project is involved, the Hebrew Bible was understood in such a way that the anthropomor-phic and anthropopathic expressions recurrent in the Bible become allegories for states of being and forms of cognitions that will obliterate the "improper" under-standings of the canonical scriptures. This was indeed a far-reaching enterprise given the predominantly nonfigurative nature of most Jewish discourses as occur-ring in both the Bible and rabbinic literature. Moreover, the monosemic under-standing of such diverse Jewish sources as the different parts of the Bible and some late-antiquity and early-medieval Jewish sources that constitute the rabbinic literature consists in a leveling of different meanings and nuances, restricted now by the medieval master to point to one allegorical significance. The reductive nature of philosophical allegory, which allowed the interpreter to discover a firm and well-defined significance of the text when interpreted on the allegorical level, is already obvious in Maimonides, two generations before the floruit of Aquinas.

Composed in order to guide the perplexed Jewish intellectuals, Maimonides' masterpiece, Guide of the Perplexed, imposed itself as one of the most influential writings in Judaism, although its main attainment is the introduction of Greek modes of thought (under the influence of Arabic philosophy) into Jewish thought. Especially conspicuous is the impact of Greek views in the domains of physics, metaphysics, and psychology. In a long series of discussions, especially in the first part of the Guide, Maimonides created a rather comprehensive "deciphering" of "problematic" terms and imposed an allegorical mode that remained influential for many centuries. What is quintessential for Maimonides' allegorical mode is the belief that it is possible to find out the one "correct" allegorical meaning, a presupposition anchored in Aristotelian noetics.[31] If one is capable of fathoming the ultimate meaning of the Bible, there is nothing more that remains to be known. This is a monosemic code, which uses a form of ratio facilis inspired by the elaborate Aristotelian writings extant and available to the medieval master. The biblical terms were considered to point to equivalents that were already well defined and articulated in lengthy discussions by the Greek and Arabic thinkers, an attitude that I have termed intercorporal.

This determined allegorical code, which covered a variety of domains—metaphysics, physics, and psychology—inspired many Jewish intellectuals in the Orient and Europe, although other Jewish authors vehemently protested against Maimonides' views, including the introduction of allegorical interpretations. Controversies exploded in various parts of the Jewish world, some of them con-stituting the most ferocious polemics of the Jewish Middle Ages. Some of Mai-monides' opponents attempted, as part of a more comprehensive kulturkampf, to eradicate the allegorical mode altogether by launching direct attacks against the *Guide of the Perplexed*. Other critiques were less direct and were addressed to Maimonides' followers, who were described as weakening the role of ritualistic language because of the mentalistic attitude to prayer.[32]

It is within this tense spiritual ambiance that more comprehensive Kabbalistic systems of symbolism emerged. Their greater vagueness is the result of a more flexible attitude toward the exegesis of the texts—a stand anchored in midrashic hermeneutics—and of its establishing a nexus between a theology that was much more nebulous and dynamic than the Aristotelian one exposed by Maimonides. Though in part a reaction to Maimonides' and his followers' hermeneutics, the Kabbalistic view of the symbol is not a complete innovation but much more systematic elaborations on succinct, fragmentary, and obscure mythologoumena found in Jewish writings and traditions that preceded the emergence of Kabbalah.[33] In other words, the symbolic hermeneutics of the Kabbalists is best understood as an attempt to counteract the allegorical monosemic code, historically of an alien source and viewed as such by traditionalists, which was conceived of as subverting the plain sense of the sacred texts. This seems to be the situation already at the beginning of Kabbalah, and it continued to be a spur in some of its later developments.[34]

The crystallization of the symbolic mode in Kabbalah is, if this explanation is adequate, part of a comprehensive conflict between Aristotelian noetics, which had been applied to the sacred scriptures, and a growing theosophical system stemming from earlier Jewish sources and Neoplatonic ontology, which invited a different noetics, more Neoplatonic in its propensity, and a more nebulous and polysemic approach to the canonical texts. Indeed, the most important Kabbalistic corpus resorting to symbols, the *Zohar*, composed at the end of the thirteenth and the early fourteenth centuries, has been described by scholars as a reaction to Maimonides.[35] This general observation is pertinent insofar as symbolic exegesis is involved. In order to better understand the scriptural nature of the symbolic code, let me make some remarks about their nature, with reference to Eco's semiotics.

In many forms of Kabbalah the symbol may be defined as a word that stands for an absent thing, and in some cases even for an entity no longer in existence in this world. Let me emphasize the absence as crucial in a symbolic system that is exegetical, which, unlike the symbols as understood in a variety of negative theologies, is concerned more with the hidden though existent divine entities. The scholarly views of symbol in Kabbalah, as surveyed above, assume that the symbols reflect the hidden divine realities, which otherwise are unknown. The present theory assumes the opposite: the theosophical system was known to many of the Kabbalists, and they used the sefirotic and sometimes angelic and demonic structures to make sense of the quandaries of the canonical texts. Thus, the linguistic unit should be understood as a combination of ratio difficilis and ratio facilis. As ratio facilis, a Kabbalistic symbol points to what the Kabbalist believed to be an ontological entity, a divine attribute whose nature was defined when it was introduced in Kabbalah. The fragmentary, dynamic, and obscure nature of the theosophical system, however, invited a more complex situation: the transformation of a biblical word into a symbol for a sefirah means not only infusing a figurative meaning into that word but also transferring meaning from the word to the imaginary entity on high. Thus we are closer to the concept of ratio difficilis—even more so if the scholarly assumption is that the sefirotic realm is re-created and modified each time someone enriches it by the semiotic process connected to it. In other words, the more the theosophical system is articulated and the more the interpretation of the biblical linguistic material becomes automatic, the more we face a ratio facilis, which brings the Kabbalistic symbols closer to philosophical allegory. Historically speaking, Kabbalistic symbolism moves from a semiotic phenomenon closer to ratio difficilis to one more typical of ratio facilis.[36] Indeed, if this suggestion is corroborated by further research, the widespread opposition between symbol and allegory, which permeates the scholarly treatments of figurative language in Kabbalah, should be transcended by an assumption that the two forms of ratio describe fluctuations within Kabbalistic semiotics, which better describe what happened in the field. Indeed, if earlier Kabbalah is closer to the ratio difficilis, we may speak, using an expression coined by Martin Buber to describe Kabbalah in toto, about a schematization of the mystery in later Kabbalah, when the semiosis of ratio facilis is much more evident.

The Kabbalistic resort to a ratio difficilis at the beginning of Kabbalah is the result of the absence of a crystallized Kabbalistic theosophy and the effort to maintain as strong a role as possible for the plain sense of the Hebrew original of the Bible. Allegorical exegesis was adopted by thinkers whose propensity was for a conventional theory of language. The ratio difficilis confers on language a greater importance, and in the case of many of the Kabbalists who emphasized the vision of Hebrew as a natural or divine language, a symbolic approach was more evident. Language was not a means to convey a message, which is found too in other forms of literature, like medieval philosophy, but also part of the message itself, in a manner reminiscent of Roman Jakobson's view. This is conspicuously the case for R. Joseph Gikatilla, who emphasized the divine nature of Hebrew[37] yet also wrote an influential book on Kabbalistic symbolism.[38] This nexus between symbolic interpretation and the vision of language as nonconventional is part of a broader phenomenon in Jewish mysticism, that of relating the unlimited semiosis to the special nature of Hebrew, which we examined in Chapter 3.

So, any biblical figures—David or Abraham, for example, were understood as symbols of the various divine powers, known as sefirot. Thus, in order to move from the signifier to the signified, a Kabbalist had to rely either on a word, which points alone toward the higher entity it symbolizes, or on a concept that emerges from the various contexts of this word. In some cases the concrete entity no longer exists, and therefore its significative function as a representative here below of the supernal sefirah was conceived of as having been taken over by the word that pointed to it. The persona of David the king, for example, who was regarded as a representative of the last sefirah, the kingship, Malkhut,[39] is no more approachable as an entity here below. Thus, solely the word David is the possible conduit of the meaning which points to the last sefirah. Yet at least for most stages in the development of Kabbalah, the theosophical Kabbalist knew the significance of the last sefirah, and he determined according to this preexegetical knowledge the symbolic valence of the biblical word, whose real reference was no longer available. A whole literary universe, mostly biblical, compounded of dead persons, destroyed cities, shattered temples, defunct rituals, such as the crucial rites of sacrifices, a universe once thought to signify symbolically the supernal theosophical powers and processes, was now approachable only by means of linguistic designators whose valence was determined by the theosophical knowledge of the Kabbalist. Much more than revealing the nature of deity, the Kabbalistic symbols decoded what was conceived of as the symbolic meaning of the scriptures.

Let me analyze one important symbol in some detail: Jerusalem, which was considered in both biblical and rabbinic sources to be the unifying place between the mundane and the divine realms, an omphalic locus. However, for medieval Kabbalists, the vast majority of whom had never seen the city, the word Jerusalem was now the starting point for the transition to guessing the higher divine reality. Yet even in cases where the symbolizing reality still existed, but was distant and not approachable in the foreseeable future, the situation was not essentially different. Jerusalem, for example, was a city still functioning during most of the Middle Ages but practically unknown, at least in a direct manner, by those Spanish Kabbalists who also viewed it as a symbol. Thus, the various concepts of the city were in many cases the result of a construct on the basis of the biblical passages; only rarely did they rely on reports of pilgrims, and almost never, I would say, were they the result of a direct encounter with the geographical and historical reality of the city. As such, Jerusalem as a symbol functions on two levels: as a present, available literary symbol or as a *symbolum in verbis*, it works because of the special nature of the biblical text, which was understood by the Kabbalists as reflecting the divine sphere of existence; and on an ontological level, as a *symbolum in factis*, the temporally absent and geographically remote city represents a spiritual and thus cognitively remote divine power. These two symbolic channels were supposed to lead, independently of each other, to one and the same divine entity, in most cases the last sefirah, Malkhut.[40]

To understand how two such different entities—a name (a linguistic unit) and a city designated by that name—may help one to reach the invisible divine power, the Kabbalist would assume that there is a profound affinity between the name and the entity it designates, a phenomenon that can be described as a linguistic immanence.[41] That is to say, the word *Jerusalem* is not merely a conventional name for the city; by the structure of the word, and in a variety of ways, it summarizes the very essence of the mundane city and at the same time points to its supernal, divine counterpart. The triad of a name, a geographical entity, and a superessential divine attribute that governs both the name and the geographical entity is therefore a rather common grouping that informs many symbolical processes in Kabbalah. However, given the fact that the starting point of the vast majority of Kabbalistic symbols is the biblical texts and their intricacies, whose counterparts in the historical or geographical realms were either no longer in existence or geographically very remote and beyond the scope of the more ordinary medieval Kabbalist living in Europe, Kabbalistic symbolism should be defined as predominantly inspired by authoritative texts and their religious values and as functioning by means of the linguistic units that constitute these texts. By and large, Kabbalistic symbolism has very little to do with attempts at symbolizing natural reality, as the scholarly pansymbolic school claims, but is fundamentally a code to interpret the canonical texts while ignoring forms of realia that are divorced from the contents of the sacred scriptures. Rhetoric about the absorbing nature of the Torah is certainly not absent in the theosophical Kabbalah, as we saw in Chapter 4, and it provides the nexus between claims of symbolizing everything via the absorbing characteristic of the Torah. Nevertheless, we should distinguish carefully between rhetorical claims and the general practice as carried out in voluminous treatises like the *Zohar*.

This preoccupation with the canonical writings is, in my opinion, the main reason for the recurrence of the symbol of Jerusalem in Kabbalah and the total absence of symbolic values for cities like Lunel, Posquieres, Narbonne (in southern France), Barcelona, Gerona, Burgos, Avilla, and Toledo, which hosted the first stages of the development of Provençal and Spanish Kabbalah. This is also true of the Italian and Ottoman cities that hosted the expelled Kabbalists. On the other hand, even nonbiblical cities like the remote town of Tiberias,[42] mentioned in rabbinic legends, have acquired symbolic meanings, but this is not the case for the immediate urban reality of the European or North African Kabbalists themselves. One final example may strengthen this observation. The most important center of late Kabbalah, Safed, which hosted an unprecedented pleiade of famous Kabbalists, only very rarely turned into a Kabbalistic symbol despite the vastness of the Kabbalistic literature composed in that city. In fact, I am acquainted only with one exception.[43] On the other hand Rome, a place where theosophical Kabbalists did not create especially important works but which was conceived of as the place of the demonic powers in Jewish apocalyptic literature before the emergence of Kabbalah, was seen symbolically as pointing to a demonic entity in the Kabbalistic literature.

In other words, symbolization was ostensibly part of a sustained exegetical and spiritual, rather than a historical or naturalistic, reorientation of Kabbalists. It was more an attempt to enrich the value cargo of the canonical texts than an attempt to find a meaning for the events that an individual Kabbalist living in the thirteenth or sixteenth century witnessed, by endowing the historical events with symbolic valences. Although such a spiritual reorientation was achieved obliquely by the enrichment of the canonical texts, it seems that this indirect strategy may account for the manner in which the spiritual life of Kabbalists was substantially affected by the symbolizing processes. Neither the calm times of the emergence of Kabbalah and its floruit in thirteenth-century Spain, on the one hand, nor the socially catastrophic and sometimes psychologically traumatic events of the expulsion from Spain, on the other, produced a direct form of spiritual reaction that might be translated into the emergence of new symbolics, which may argue for an impact of history on Kabbalistic symbolism. The concept of historical symbol, in the sense of a Kabbalistic symbol epitomizing the historical experience of the Jewish people, seems to me to be as significant as the nonbiblical "geographical" nonexistent symbolism.

The theosophical Kabbalists are to be understood as striving not for a comprehensive symbolism of natural or historical reality but for a comprehensive symbolization of their canonical writings and actions. Outside the canon there is no need for symbolic valences. Indeed, when dealing with the symbolism of evil, some Kabbalists were more creative, inventing demonic names that are hard to detect in the extant traditions. Yet even this modest inventiveness may well be part of our ignorance of the magical and demonic sources that may have inspired the Kabbalists.

Let me adduce a short passage and a succinct analysis to exemplify the imposition of the theosophical structure on the biblical material. In a *Commentary on Ten Sefirot*, apparently written in the fourteenth century, we may learn about the way Kabbalistic symbolism functioned: "Mount Zion is so called because the tenth [sefirah] is called the heavenly Jerusalem, which receives an emanation from *ha-tzaddiq yesod 'olam*,[44] which is called *tzion*. For just as in the earthly Jerusalem is Mount Zion, a tower defending the city, so too is in the heavenly Jerusalem the Mount Zion, its spouse, protecting it from the accusers, so that they will not enter it."[45]

That the ninth sefirah, Yesod, designated Tzion, points to the phallic element in the sefirotic realm is obvious, and this issue cannot be extracted either from the real geography of Mount Zion or from the biblical passages dealing with Jerusalem and Zion. It is part of the structure of many Kabbalistic theosophical constellations, which emphasizes the polarity between the male and female elements and between the holy and the demonic. Thus, the theosophical structure is imposed on the biblical phrases Mount Zion and Jerusalem, as symbolizing respectively the male and female powers. Moreover, the theosophical picture that construes the last sefirah as endangered by demonic powers striving to enter the divine realm is imposed on both biblical text and any geographical reality. Sexualization and demonization are among the theosophical ways of organizing the supernal constellation of divine powers, which are imposed on the biblical texts; polarity and collaboration are paradigmatic relations that characterize the sefirotic world, and these relations are imposed on the biblical texts. This move can be defined as a shift from the strong symbol, as described by Eco in the case of the Neoplatonic and Kabbalistic approach, to a much more allegorical approach.[46]

What are the implications of the previous observations for our understanding the general structure of Kabbalistic symbolism? First and foremost is its paramount linguistic character. Nature, present events, towns where Kabbalists lived, rivers they were seeing, or contemporary personalities are almost totally excluded from the realm of theosophical symbolism. From this point of view, Kabbalistic symbolism is quite different from that described by Mircea Eliade in his "Methodological Remarks," where he emphasized the nonlinguistic symbols as reflecting the nature of real religion. Symbolism in Kabbalah is by and large the result of a postreflective stage, because it combines a learned attitude, as represented by the immersion of the Kabbalists in the sacred scriptures, with their beliefs in a supernal structure of the divinity. There was much more direct contact with the literary material than with reality. So, for example, the most insignificant of the Edomite kings mentioned in the Bible becomes infinitely more important for a theosophical Kabbalist than the most potent of the Spanish kings.[47] The latter never became part of the Kabbalistic systems of symbols even as demonic powers. They were not given a share in "eternity" because their names are irrelevant, as no divine immanence is going to dwell in their letters; they can serve no mystical purpose, and even a modest demonic role was denied them. A mystical life concentrated on texts and language may be so strong as to be self-sufficient and in no need of external validation, basically independent of the need to structure the external reality by means of the types of order that inform their view of the canonical texts.

This overall vision of the nature of Kabbalistic symbolism runs against the modern scholarly understandings of this subject. It problematizes Scholem's recurrent emphasis on the relation of some of the Kabbalistic symbols to historical events, what he called "historical symbols"; it problematizes even more Tishby's extreme formulation as to the comprehensive cosmic nature of Kabbalistic symbolism. I doubt this comprehensiveness because even the symbolically oriented Kabbalists were able to express themselves in forms that are not symbolic. Some of the early Kabbalists were first elite scholars, very creative and serving as guidance to their communities. Since their creativity also encompasses nonsymbolic modes like halakhic writings which continue the traditional genres in a very intense manner, and given the absence of an awareness of a crisis either in their explicit writings or in our historical records, I prefer to envision those thinkers as far from being in a crisis or from reacting to a crisis or even from perceiving others as in such a crisis. I would expect the introduction of symbolic expressions precisely in their halakhic writings in order to strengthen their authority, yet that did not happen. Moreover, even if sometime in the future an initial crisis were detected insofar as thinkers in southern France and Spain are concerned, the question is, Why does symbolism, a mode of thinking not counted as a significant mode in the rabbinic forms of literature, become so deeply rooted in other geographical areas, like Italy for example, and in other periods of time? This fact demands a much more comprehensive explanation related to a constant that will unify the spiritual concerns of at least segments of the Jewish intelligentsia living in all the places and periods of times. Such an explanation involves an approach other than a historicist one, an approach that relates the emergence of a vital form of expression to a feeling of crisis and decline in very specific circumstances.

As I have suggested elsewhere, the emergence of more complex semantic and parasemantic discussions of the Hebrew language may have something to do with polemics and apologetics related to ideas expressed by Muslim theologians about the perfection of the Qur'an and the Arabic language.[48] Such a debate does not, however, mean that the Jewish thinkers were necessarily in a spiritual crisis. The question, then, is whether a crisis should not be discerned in the lives of those who formulated the crisical theories. So, for example, we read in Tishby's explanation of the role of the symbolistic mode:

> especially those of the last generation who were expelled from Paradise into
> the great desolation . . . are wandering on the paths of life, divided and

perplexed, without compass and without a way. The nice idyll of the vision-aries of the enlightenment dissipated like smoke, reality revealed itself in its demonic, threatening face. The eon of anxiety, which the Kabbalists and those like to them apprehended in their time and in other times, returned again, an eon of discomposure and breakdown of values. The crisis of values that takes place in the great world did not skip over the small Jewish world at all. We were standing, feeble and ill and without solid values. Our generation, as men and Jews, as individuals and as a community, is pushed toward the chasm, and before him there is a crossroad: to roll down to the slope of nihilism or to elevate by a spiritual elevation and discover the existing values, hidden within the external shattered reality. It is possible that a profound study of the wisdom of Kabbalah, and especially the mean-ing of the symbolistic approach to the values of Judaism, will be able to illumine our eyes and help us in the search for the exit from the great perplexity.[49]

I wonder whether the earlier Kabbalists experienced such shocking historical experiences as Tishby did, experiences reflected quite conspicuously in this pas-sage. Attempting to combat what he considers the "discomposure and break-down of values" in the world in general and the Jewish world in particular, Tishby sought to learn from the symbolic strategies of "wise" Kabbalists.

IV. THEOSOPHY, SYMBOLS, AND THEURGY

My working hypothesis has been that symbolism flourished after the acceptance of some rudimentary versions of theosophical systems that preceded the emer-gence of the historical Kabbalah. A skeletal view of the ten sefirot as pointing to divine powers is a much older concept, whose details were analyzed in Chapter 8, where likewise I discussed the nexus between theosophy and theurgy in ancient Jewish texts, a view recently corroborated by much more detailed analyses.[50] This sefirotic decadic system served as a metaphysical constellation for some small parts of Jewish tradition, and with time it constellated greater and greater seg-ments of Judaism, according to its theosophical Kabbalistic vision. Let me suggest this attraction of the theosophical and the theurgical in connection with an inter-pretive mode at the very beginning of theosophical-theurgical Kabbalah. In his *Commentary on the Song of Songs* R. Ezra asserts that "it is incumbent upon us to interpret, in accordance with our way, from what [divine] attribute each and every mitzvah is."[51] The interpretive mode is quite obvious: "in accordance with our way" means, in my opinion, the theosophical Kabbalah, whose hypostatic stric-ture offers the possibility of interpreting the commandments. While R. Ezra is ready to explicate the precise dependence of the commandments on the divine Chariot (the Merkavah), namely the sefirotic realm, in the school of his compatriot, Nahmanides, only the very general affinities between the commandments and the Merkavah are mentioned. Nahmanides himself prefers not to speculate about the mystical significance of this topic.

Happily, R. Shlomo ibn Adret, Nahmanides' most important disciple, has dedicated to this talmudic dictum an important discussion, in which he complains that the understanding of ma'aseh merkavah in the vein of Greek philosophy is dangerous, because it weakens the performance of the commandments. His assumption is that the deed is the starting point, and from it one should understand the intelligibilia hinted at within the deed: "and this is the issue of the Merkavah, since the matters alluded to by the commandments are ma'aseh merkavah. And Abbayei and Ravva have been preoccupied [solely] by the interpretation of the commandments . . . how precisely should they be performed . . . but not to explain and disclose the rationales hinted at within them . . . while R. Yohanan ben Zakkai has performed the commandments in fact, and he has concentrated his attention on contemplating their complexion."[52]

The ergetic dimension of the commandments is necessary in order to disclose the depth of their content: the Merkavah. The rationales cannot be apprehended except through the act of the commandment itself as the starting point. This is an explicit rejection of the intellectualistic approach, inspired by the Greek philosophy, which emphasized the abstract intent of the commandment rather than its performance. I assume that this was also the perception of at least one Kabbalist, an early fourteenth-century author, R. Meir ibn Avi Sahulah, who wrote in his Commentary on Sefer Yetzirah: "Despite the fact that our knowledge is limited and we cannot comprehend the issues according to their precise depth,[53] it is incumbent upon us to inquire into the issues in accordance with our comprehension, and to follow the way trodden by those called, in our generation and in those of the former generation, for two hundred years [by the name] Mequbbalim. And they call the wisdom of the ten sefirot and some few rationales of the commandments by the name Qabbalah."[54]

The main quandary in this passage is our limited understanding of the depth of the Torah or of the commandments. The solution suggested by this Kabbalist is a tradition he dated as older than the scholarly dating of the emergence of Kabbalah, one that related some of the commandments to the ten sefirot, a relation I refer to as consisting in a nexus between theosophy and theurgy.[55] Thus, a hypothetical affinity between some ritualistic aspects of Judaism and the ten divine powers predated the emergence of the symbolic systems as we now know them, which may be described as an expansion of the affinities between these powers and some commandments to a much broader range of biblical material, including much that has nothing to do with the commandments. In an ambiance where the philosophical-allegorical exegesis was applied extensively on the nonritualistic parts of the Bible, it is easy to understand this expansion insofar as the refraction of the theosophical topics in the Bible is concerned, just as the theurgical explanation was committed to writing in order to counteract Maimonides' historical and psychological explanations of the commandments.[56] It is reasonable to assume, on the basis of the reading of early Kabbalah, that the theurgical views, namely those correspondences between the deeds and the divine powers, were monosemic and only later, in the less theurgical visions, did symbolism become more polysemic.

The symbolic mode as described above emerged and remained vital as long as the theosophical way of reflecting about divinity was in vogue and was related to the performance of the commandments, conceived of as having an impact on the divine, an impact to be described in the following as theurgy. In my view, Kabbalistic symbolism is also a means of relating ways of thinking and experiencing the divine powers, conceived of as susceptible to human acts, whether mental, linguistic, or ritualistic. The emergence of this mode was a systemic process, by which I mean an inner development of a Kabbalistic system that expands on either the theosophical or the hermeneutical level, or insofar as the explanation of the commandments is concerned. Thus, a more complex theosophy invites a more detailed symbolism to account for the different aspects of the divine powers, and a more detailed explanation of the commandments invites more complex symbols for making sense of the variety of acts involved in the ritual. An expansion of symbolism is, in my opinion, part of the expansion of the theosophical and theurgical ways of thinking and experiencing. Such an account is less concerned with detecting historical and cultural crises or dealing with the ineffable than it is with attempting to correlate symbolism with other forms of discourse characteristic of the Kabbalistic corpora under scrutiny. Or, to put it in negative terms: those literary bodies of Kabbalah which are neither theosophical nor theurgical will be less interested in symbolism, if they are interested at all. In Chapter 8 I discussed the historical aspects of the emergence of symbols; now let me address some phenomenological aspects of Kabbalistic symbolism.

The methodological proposal that should guide an interpretation of the Jewish rites and symbols as understood by some Kabbalists should assume that they are functioning on more than one level:[57] on the one hand the operative, seen as devoid of the need for mystical intention, Kavvanah, which includes the corporeal components, the pronunciation of words, and making of gestures; and on the other the spiritual, which consisted in mental or spiritual operations known as mystical Kavvanah. To borrow Victor and Edith Turner's terminology for the nature of the symbol and ritual,[58] it would be plausible to approach the Kabbalistic material reflecting a manifest, operative level as the "sensory pole" of the rite, and the theosophical-symbolic level would be its "ideological pole." Likewise, we may assume the existence of the experiential moment, namely that spiritual event which may accompany the performance of the ritual but is at the same time not identical to the explanation or explanations offered for the ritual. It is the repercussion of the sensory pole onto the inner state of the Kabbalist, and it may be the most unstable and imponderable aspect of the Kabbalistic performance of the ritual. The two other aspects, the sensory and the Kavvanah, can be more easily transmitted, one being part of the halakhic regulations and the other being part of the concepts of Kabbalistic theosophy and theurgy. However, the impact of the performance, and perhaps also of the mystical intention accompanying the performance, on the inner life of the Kabbalist was, I assume, much more fluid and vague.

According to most of the theosophical-theurgical Kabbalists, the sensory facet of the rite, when performed by a righteous person though not necessarily a Kabbalist, is fraught with a spiritual aspect of its own, independent of the mystical intention of the operator. This attitude is consonant with the general positive attitude toward *peshat*, the plain sense of the scriptures, as it is expressed in the vast majority of theosophical-theurgical Kabbalistic writings. Yet a Kabbalist can add his particular symbolism and activate the rite in a theurgical direction without deflating the spiritual cargo of the sensory pole. It would be convenient to distinguish between the spiritual cargo, which the Kabbalist attributes to the very performance of the ritual, and the spiritual impact that this performance may have on the Kabbalist himself, as the two do not necessarily coincide. While the assumption that there are some automatic reverberations to the act of fulfilling the commandments will be related to an ideological assumption, the impact on the Kabbalists' psyche is relatively marginal for the Kabbalistic literature which, like the Halakhic one, was less inclined to expatiate about the feelings of the mystic. I shall address first the question of the sensory pole and then turn to the ideological one, leaving aside for the moment the psychological aspect, important though it may be for the mystical understanding of the ritual.

It is possible to approach the problem of the plain level of the rite with the aid of a modern theory of ritual and symbols. A modern anthropologist has stated her interest in "the kind of use to which people put their symbols in everyday life, as regulators or as channels of power. That is, we would attend to their ideas about ritual efficacy, and less to the structure of their theoretical orientations."[59]

An issue that should be treated separately, but is nevertheless related to the present study, is the question of symbolic efficacy, *efficacité symbolique* in the formulation of Claude Lévi-Strauss and Charles A. Bernard.[60] The major question therefore is: Was theosophical Kabbalah creating its myths and symbols out of a "theosophical contemplation of God's secret life considered as the central religious reality," as Scholem put it,[61] or is it possible to allow an important role also to the experiences of performing the ritual and of decoding canonical texts as a starting point for creating symbols and myths?[62] Is Kabbalistic symbolism solely a matter of expressing experiences or is it also, perhaps even more, a matter of impressing the canonical texts with new valences that emerged out of the application of a speculative constellation to a text, thus betraying, at least in many cases, a strong exegetical enterprise? If the answer to this question is yes and we assume that the expressive mode was dominant, we would expect, as Scholem and Tishby have indeed assessed, a much wider range of realms supplying material for symbolism, which consequently would draw from a great variety of sources, both religious and nonreligious. But if the "impressive" approach is adopted, the strong preponderance of the biblical and rabbinic sources is more easily understood. If this is the best answer—and it is my preference—the "codic" and semiotic nature of the symbolic enterprise becomes more evident. I would certainly not deny the possibility that mystical experiences are involved in the relation between the Kabbalists and the sefirotic realm, but I would say that those experiences were facilitated by the articulation of the supernal world in traditional terms without assuming that those experiences were automatically the source of the process of symbolization. Or, to put it differently: the mysticism of encounter with the symbolized realms may be screened by too great an emphasis on symbols, whereas the mysticism of the Bible is enhanced by the discovery of the symbolic discourse. The divinization of the Bible, in fact its identification with God in some Kabbalistic writings (as described in Chapter 2), is an integral part of the process of its symbolization, and it opened the door for an experiential hermeneutics.[63]

At least insofar as most of the theosophical Kabbalists are involved, once the sefirotic system was more crystallized, they applied its details to the canonical texts, whose exegetical problems they attempted to solve. In fact, a perusal of the dozens of commentaries on the ten sefirot will reveal that they consist in indexes intended to organize the main biblical terms in accordance with each of the ten divine attributes. This literary genre, which has been studied only from the bibliographical point of view, is a major source for the study of the history of Kabbalistic symbolism and its exegetical function. Therefore, from the very beginning of Kabbalah in the late twelfth century, the order of the divine attributes shaped the structure of the discourse, which consisted in collecting symbols under theosophical categories.[64]

V. CLOSED VERSUS UNLIMITED SEMIOSIS

Let me return to the initial question concerning the floruit of Kabbalistic hermeneutical symbolism in the period when it declined in Christianity as a comprehensive attitude toward reality. The question may be reformulated: Why was Maimonides' authority not able to impose itself in Judaism as strongly as Thomas
Aquinas' authority did in Christianity? After all, both masters attempted to reduce
more flexible forms of interpretations to stable allegorical, monosemic readings
of the Bible. Moreover, it is obvious that it was Maimonides' reading of some
portion of biblical terminology that shaped Aquinas'. Thus, at least one affinity
between the two different phenomena can be established. Aquinas continued
Maimonides—though certainly not Maimonides alone—on various topics,[65] presumably also in introducing a more rigid understanding of the Bible, while the
theosophical Kabbalists, aware as they were of Maimonides' interpretive technique, refused to do so and adopted a more polysemic and symbolic hermeneutics. Maimonides is therefore to be viewed as the common factor that inspired, at
least to a certain extent, two different hermeneutical processes: Aquinas' closure
of allegory so that it deals only with the biblical texts and the theosophical Kabbalists' openness toward symbolism.

Aquinas, a critic of some forms of Neoplatonism,[66] is the counterpart of the
contemporary theosophical Kabbalists, who were much more open to this form of
thought.[67] In Spain the locus for the upsurge of Kabbalistic symbolism, even the
most Maimonidean thinker, R. Shem Tov ibn Falaquera, the single commentator
on the *Guide* in thirteenth-century Spanish philosophy, was immersed in Neoplatonic thought, as his translations from *Fons Vitae* by Shlomo ibn Gabirol (Avi-
cebrol), his resort to Avicenna's writings, and his recurrent quotes from the
Plotinian so-called *Theology of Aristotle* amply demonstrate. Thus, the Neoplatonic
propensity of the theosophical Kabbalists facilitated a more symbolic and more
flexible hermeneutical approach.[68]

This is even more so in the case of a follower of Maimonides, the most ardent
disciple of the great eagle among the thirteenth-century Kabbalists, R. Abraham
Abulafia. He wrote in his last book, *Sefer 'Imrei Shefer*, in the context of a critique of
theosophical Kabbalists, that they "claim they received from the prophets and the
sages that there are ten sefirot and by their means He created the entire world.
And they[69] designated each and every sefirah by names, some of them being
homonyms,[70] others proper names. And when we asked them [to explain them],
those who know them were unable to say what these sefirot are, and to what [kind
of] entity these names refer . . . and their names[71] are well known from their
books, but they are very perplexed[72] concerning them."[73]

Perplexity is the main spiritual phenomenon Maimonides wanted to combat in his *Guide of the Perplexed*, which meant for him a corporeal misunderstanding of the biblical descriptions of God. Abulafia conceived of his Kabbalah not only as higher than Maimonides' philosophical achievement,[74] which solved only some of the theological problems, but also as better than the theosophical Kabbalists' attempt to relate biblical terms to the divine powers. He points out the vagueness of those Kabbalists' conception of the divine attributes. He was interested in the divine name, or names, much more as means to a technique of attaining an experiential encounter with God than as a philosophical conceptualization that resorts to negative and positive attributes. I would say that for Abulafia, the theosophical Kabbalists resort to symbols as pointing to a theory of positive attributes—a position that may endanger monotheistic theology[75]—because of its creating theological quandaries, whereas his own Kabbalah strove to transcend the knowledge of the positive attributes by a direct encounter with the divine. While the theosophical Kabbalists believed in the value of the symbolic under-standing of the biblical text as pointing to God and so as validating their attach-ment to the classical texts, Abulafia's Kabbalah regards this positive attitude as endangering what he viewed as the ongoing enterprise of transcending structured language, the ordinary, structured psychological states, in order to attain an ec-static experience. If for the theosophical Kabbalists symbols reveal, for Abulafia they confuse, because they screen the divine by imposing the inertia of ordinary linguistic units, which is the necessary substratum of symbolism. Abulafia's de-constructive attitude is the very inverse of the attempts of theosophical Kabbalists to cultivate the discovery of a symbolic meaning for solid linguistic units. There-fore, Abulafia, although a disciple of Maimonides, was at the same time one of the most extreme exponents of an orientation that does not prefer a monosemic approach to the Bible but, even more than the unlimited semiosis of the symbolic Kabbalah, systematically attempted to transcend any fixed meanings.[76] Thus, al-though deriding Kabbalistic symbolism, Abulafia did not embrace Maimonides' monosemic allegoresis.

In the above passage Abulafia mentions the Kabbalists' claims that they had inherited a theosophical tradition, stemming from ancient times, dealing with the structure of the divine world. At that time the theosophical Kabbalists assigned names—that is, symbols—to these divine powers. If my interpretation of Abulafia is correct, then we have contemporary evidence for the way Kabbalistic symbols emerged: they fleshed out linguistically the details of the theosophical tradition dealing with the ten sefirot. Moreover, according to another passage from this Kabbalist, found in the context of the above text,[77] the theosophical Kabbalists were initially persons interested in rabbinic topics who were not satisfied with rabbinic studies and started studying philosophy (in that context Abulafia mentions Maimonides), and when disappointed with philosophy, they became Kabbalists. Thus, at least implicitly, Abulafia claims that Kabbalists were not only acquainted with Maimonides' work but also unsatisfied with it. This is not a mere typological abstract discussion. We have additional material, of a much more biographical nature, which corroborates this claim.[78]

In contemporary Christianity, Aquinas' more monosemic approach may be seen as part of the strengthening of the much older synthesis between biblical Judaism and Greek views, which was in favor of theological and dogmatic stands; in Judaism, Maimonides' dogmatism, both theological and hermeneutical, was a newcomer which emerged under external influences after a long period of resistance from Jewish authors to adopting Greek thought. Provided the nondogmatic nature of rabbinic Judaism and the lack of one recognized central authority in matters of religious thought, the imposition of Maimonides' hermeneutics encountered resistance and spurred attempts to offer alternatives much more consonant with an open hermeneutics that is less systematic.[79] It is in the second half of the thirteenth century that concepts of infinities of the Bible started their more sustained career in Kabbalah.[80] Maimonides' introduction of Aristotelian noetics, and thus of monosemic allegoresis, was welcomed by Aquinas but combated by all the contemporary theosophical Kabbalists. Their various reactions to the challenge posed by Maimonides are a plausible explanation of the synchronicity of the different forms of treatments of symbolism in the two religions.

The reasons for the emergence of what I propose to call the innovative Kabbalah are too complex and diverse to examine thoroughly here.[81] It will suffice to say that the unprecedented resort to symbolism in the Zohar did not create an ongoing effort by Kabbalists to innovate but receded rather soon with the book's canonization at the beginning of the fourteenth century.[82] In lieu of the dynamic symbolism characteristic of this book,[83] a more scholastic attitude toward the huge Zoharic literary corpus emerged.[84] With the establishment of the most comprehensive symbolic code, quandaries related to the understanding of the Bible were dealt with by inspecting the Zohar, which became the subject of an increasing number of commentaries. In other words, Kabbalistic symbolism started with some monosemic symbolic approaches, moved toward a much more polysemic approach in the second half of the thirteenth century, and returned to much more monosemic forms of symbolism with the canonization of the Zohar.

VI. ON THE EMERGENCE OF MEDIEVAL KABBALISTIC SYMBOLISM

Kabbalistic symbols are rarely significant as separated signifiers. A corollary of the emphasis on the exegetical nature of the symbols is the fact that they strive to elucidate not separate words but sentences or even longer forms of discourse. Ideally, a Kabbalistic symbol does not stand alone. It is part of two different axes, one vertical one, the other horizontal. Along the vertical axis I describe the Kabbalistic perception that the symbol represents something found originally on another level. This seems to be a basic feature of theosophical-theurgical Kabbalah. The symbol is also, however, part of a literary plot, in fact a double one: at its sensory facet it points to things embedded within the classical material that is decoded by the different components of the theosophical system; on its ideological pole it refers to the processes and myths taking place in the divine or sometimes the demonic world. Kabbalistic symbolism emerged as part of the expression of the emerging theosophies in traditional nomenclatures, but without a better articulation of the supernal and demonic structures it would be difficult to speak of stable symbolic systems.

How did this development take place? Or, to put the question differently: Can we assume a priority of the emergence of theosophical structures over the resort to a symbolic approach to be characteristic of some Kabbalistic schools? In my opinion, the answer is yes, although the extant material often portrays an overlapping of a theosophical stand and symbolic forms of expressions. I wonder whether the most important documents capable of depicting the evolution that culminated in the emergence of Kabbalistic symbolism are available, either because of the importance of the oral aspects of this evolution or because of some of its esoteric aspects. As we have seen, Abraham Abulafia already adumbrated the thesis that symbolism emerged from attempts to explain the earlier, more conceptual theosophical structures. I have no idea how he reached such a conclusion, but it deserves a close examination on the basis of an analysis of earlier traditions.[85] Indeed, there is some ground for supposing that a decadic theology was found early in circles closed to Judaism, and that anthropomorphic structure attracted a few topics in the Bible as related to it. On a larger scale, this type of semiotic process took place from the beginning of Kabbalah, with the ascent of a dynamic decad as the center of the theosophy of some Jewish circles. The very history of the decadic theosophy in Judaism is complex, and I assume that it did not start with the first documents identified by scholars with the nascent Kabbalah.[86] Yet what seems to me to be crucial for understanding the history of Kabbalistic symbolism is to be aware of the importance of one of the main contributions of Kabbalah to the literary genres in Judaism: the plethora of commentaries on the ten sefirot. There are almost 150 extant commentaries that organize the different biblical words according to the ten sefirot.[87] They thereby contributed, more than any other literary genre in Kabbalah, to the emergence, dissemination, and study of symbolism and to the interpretation of the classical texts from a symbolic perspective.

What process is reflected in the ascent of this new literary genre? In my opinion, it has to do with the ascent of the decadic theosophy related to the ten sefirot but devoid of authoritative support of the classical texts, with the exception of *Sefer Yetzirah*, where the concept of ten sefirot initially emerged. An early-fourteenth-century Kabbalist described the emergence of Kabbalah as consisting in a theory of ten sefirot and rationales for some of the commandments. This may indicate not two different and unrelated topics but a relationship between two crucial realms of religious thought and activity. This is an interesting hypothesis for the emergence of the theosophical-theurgical Kabbalah. This initial and limited affinity expanded, however, into a more general one, which includes not only a few ritualistic aspects of the Bible but increasingly broader parts of the canonical text. In other words, the biblical text gradually became constellated by a certain understanding of a theory that stems from *Sefer Yetzirah* in a mode of interpretation that characterizes most of the exegesis of the theosophical-theurgical Kabbalah, just as the combinatory theory of this book will dominate most of the exegesis of the ecstatic Kabbalah.[88] This development is quite remarkable from the phenomenological point of view: a text that is basically indifferent to biblical and rabbinic thought provided the conceptualization that, in a certain understanding, will become the center of the exegesis of the most important Jewish documents in Kabbalah.

Let me address now an example from a late-thirteenth-century text by R. Joseph of Hamadan which testifies to the process of expansion of a presumable earlier Kabbalistic theory, as argued by R. Meir ibn Avi Sahulah. In *Commentary on the Rationales for the Commandment* R. Joseph wrote:

> Happy is he, and blessed his lot, who knows how to direct a limb which corresponds to a limb, and a form which corresponds to a form in the holy and pure chain, blessed be His name. Since the Torah is His form, blessed be He, we were ordered to study the Torah, in order to know that archetype of the supernal form, as some Kabbalists have said: "Cursed be he who does hold up all the words of this Torah"—to the congregation . . . so that they will see the image of the supernal form, moreover, the person who studies the Torah, that he sees the supernal secrets and he sees the glory of God, literally.[89]

The identification of God with the sefirot, on the one hand, and with the Torah, on the other, created the climate necessary for the attraction of biblical material to the different terms that denote the theosophical divinity. Terms like "archetype of the supernal form," "holy and pure chain," or "glory," which all point to the system of ten sefirot,[90] represent the divine structure that is imprinted on the

Torah, and in virtue of this identity the Kabbalist is asked to identify words with ontic structures. The theory of correspondence is a stronger way of speaking about representation, since the word not only signifies or symbolizes a divine power by its semantic valence but also points to it by its graphic structure. Moreover, as I understand R. Joseph's text, the structure is not only symbolized but also impacted by the "corresponding" human limb, a concept that adds the theurgical aspect to the symbolic-theosophic nexus.

Let me now turn to another example of the strong nexus between theosophy, symbolic exegesis, and theurgy related to a biblical text. In a manuscript treatise by R. Joseph Gikatilla entitled *The Secret of the Cherubim*, belonging to the later phase of this Kabbalist's thought, we read:

[1] The secret of unity is not found until the tenth sefirah of Malkhut, and from Malkhut downward there is the secret of separation. And this is the secret of the "river that goes out of Eden to water the Garden, and from there it separates and becomes four heads."[91] And from Eden to the Garden there is the secret of unity, and everything is done by the river that waters the garden-beds of the Garden from the emanation from Eden.

[2] Happy is he who knows to unify the branches of the Garden to the river, and the river to Eden, then everything becomes a true and perfect union because of him, and behold, he is repairing all the pipes and draws the supernal waters throughout the pipes to all the garden-beds, and waters the mountains . . . and about this man it is said, "and the righteous is the foundation of the world"[92] . . . and by him the sefirot were unified and the supernal waters were drawn and running through the pipes of the [divine] will through the channels, and water all the garden-beds of the Garden, and all the worlds were blessed by him . . .

[3] And because "Abraham was keeping the guard of God" and drew the blessings through the pipes and the channels from Eden, which is the [sefirah of] Keter, until the Garden, which is Malkhut, then all the worlds were nourished by all the blessings in the world . . .

[4] When a righteous one who knows how to unify the true unity is found in the world, and he unifies the branches with the root and waters the garden-beds of the Garden, by[93] him all the worlds are blessed and nourished . . . And all this is connected to the man who knows the secret of Malkhut until Keter, and all that is lower than Malkhut receives blessing and influx and maintenance, each and every one according to its species and its way. And this is the secret of [the verse] "Or let him take hold of My strength, that he may make peace with Me."[94,95]

An analysis of the structure of discourse may be relevant for our thesis. Gikatilla starts with the theosophical definition: what is conceived of as the world of unity, namely the world that consists of the ten sefirot and is identical to the divine realm. Then he describes the nonsefirotic world, the world of separation, and introduces the Genesis verse that reflects these two worlds. In order to imprint the theosophical code within the biblical text, some semiotic moves are introduced. A construct phrase, *Gan ʿEden*, Garden of Eden, has been understood as symbolizing the two extremities of the world of unity, and thus the entire sefirotic realm is symbolized by the Garden and Eden. In other words, *Gan ʿEden* is the symbol of the divine pleroma. We may refer to as a systemic symbol, because it represents not one single sefirah or process but the entire complex of the divine realm. From this point of view *Gan ʿEden* is similar to the symbol of the menorah, the supernal man, or the tree of sefirot. Those symbols comprehend a more "anatomic" structure, and also a "physiological" one, or one pointing to the shape of the structure, the theosophical element, and to its mode of acting, more related to the impact of theurgy.

In addition to representing the sefirotic system, however, the biblical description of the separation of the river into four branches is understood as symbolizing the world of separation, which is located beneath the divine world. The water is related to the concept of emanation, which abounds and descends beneath the pleroma into the world of multiplicity.

The succinct theosophic-symbolic description in the first paragraph opens the discussion of the theurgical discussion in the second. Man is ordered to unify the divine world that is separated by Adam's sin. As a consequence of the reparation, the unity in the supernal system will ensure the descent of the influx onto the world of multiplicity. This is the gist of the third paragraph, where Abraham is described as the paragon of the theurgical activity. The fourth paragraph generalizes by commanding everyone to become righteous and unify the divine world in order to supply the lower worlds with an abounding influx. The righteous is conceived as the connoisseur who knows the secret of Paradise, its pipes and channels, and also knows how to unify all its components. By ensuring unity, he creates the sine qua non condition for the circulation of energy within the divine system, and from there onto the lower worlds. The repair of the divine pleroma is the quintessence of the religious obligation of the righteous, who is described both as the foundation of the world and as someone who strengthens the divine system. As the above passage indicates implicitly, by resorting to the terms "righteous" and "guard" (and more explicitly elsewhere in the same treatise), the regulation of the circuit within the intradivine and extradivine realms depends on the performance of the commandments. They are the main modi operandi of the theurgical Kabbalist.

Thus, we have a semiotic movement from the symbolic-theosophical interpretation of the verse to a theurgical understanding of the implication of the
theosophical interpretation, as exemplified by Abraham, and finally a more general demand that everyone act according to the paradigm established by introducing the supernal system within the biblical text. A symbolic interpretation may
therefore invite thought, as Paul Ricoeur suggested, but the Kabbalists, as exemplified by Gikatilla's and R. Joseph of Hamadan's resort to the phrase "happy is
he who knows," were concerned more with the performative than the cognitive
implication of theosophical symbolism. Thus, the major move in the emergence
of Kabbalistic symbolism can be portrayed not as allowing some Kabbalists access to an otherwise inaccessible sublime realm by means of reading the Bible,
but as "making sense" of the Bible by a code that was gradually articulated and
became elaborated by the interaction with the interpreted material. The formative
role of experiences is never mentioned in any of the dozens of extant commentaries on the ten sefirot I have carefully perused.

This process of attraction of biblical material by each of the ten sefirot should,
however, be seen in a rather dialectical manner. I assume that the decadic theosophy in its nascent phases was defined quite poorly from the theological point of
view. Presumably, some of the characteristics of each of these divine manifestations were shaped in the process of attracting biblical and other classic material
into the symbolic semiotic process. The more a certain divine power attracted
material that became symbolic, the richer and better defined theologically it became. This dialectic process notwithstanding, I assume that the relative importance of a particular sefirah from the point of view of its systemic location—higher
or lower within the hierarchical scheme, or more or less influential on this world—
shaped the number and nature of the material that was attracted, thus allowing
an important role to the theological scheme. So, for example, the last sefirah,
Malkhut, conceived of as closer to and ruling over this world and at the same time
as feminine, attracted concepts related to kingship, like Diadem ('Atarah) and
Queen (Matronit), both feminine nouns, but also male terms like David and Solomon, to adduce but two outstanding examples. The structure of the code had an
impact on the semiotic process by imposing valences important within the framework of the code on the interpreted material, even when the context would resist it
from some points of view. On the other hand, I assume that an attracted symbol
like 'Atarah affected the function of the divine attribute it symbolized, which was
described as ascending from the lowest point to the highest one, following some
descriptions of 'Atarah in earlier Jewish traditions.[96] Or, in a more general manner, the establishment of strong affinities between the sefirotic schemes and the
biblical material, both dealing with history and, even more decisively, with the

divine imperatives, introduced more dynamic valences into the theosophical skeleton that initially attracted the classical Jewish material.

VII. SEFIROT, SYMBOLISM, AND EXPERIENCE

As I have pointed out, I prefer the priority of the theosophical development to the experiential one as an explanation for the emergence of Kabbalistic symbolism. This preference is corroborated by a survey of the overwhelming majority of the commentaries on the ten sefirot. With the exception of two of them, both composed by R. Joseph Gikatilla, all 150 commentaries are arranged in descending order, which means that the first sefirah to be discussed is the highest, Keter, and the last is the lowest, Malkhut. These lists of symbols parallel the theogonic process or emanation, so that the most primordial manifestation is treated first and the latest is treated at the end.

The exceptional nature of Gikatilla's approach in his books *Sha'arei Tzedeq* and *Sha'arei 'Orah*—the latter being the most influential commentary on the ten sefirot—was not explained by the Kabbalist, and a better understanding of his work invites, therefore, an explanation. To guess the significance of Gikatilla's adoption of the ascent strategy, it would be advisable to refer to a short commentary that was not mentioned in the extant discussions on the ten sefirot, a passage from an epistle written by R. Abraham Abulafia a few years before the composition of *Sha'arei 'Orah*. Several times Abulafia, formerly Gikatilla's teacher, expounded his views on the ten sefirot, which differ substantially from those of his predecessors and contemporaries among the Kabbalists but nevertheless follow the descending pattern.[97] At least once, however, he adopted the ascending pattern, in a discussion that may help us answer the significance of this pattern:

Man can cleave to each and every sefirah by the essence of the influx expanding from its emanation on his sefirot,[98] which are his attributes[99] . . . And it is necessary to mentally concentrate[100] [in order to attain] an apprehension, until the expert Kabbalist attains from them an influx of which he is aware.[101] This is so, given the fact that the written letters are like bodies, and the pronounced letters are spiritual [by nature] and the mental [letters] are intellectual and the emanated [letters] are divine . . . and out of [his] concentration[102]—to prepare the power of the bride to receive the influx from the power of the bridegroom, the divine [letters] will move the intellectual ones and—because of the sustained concentration and its greatness and power, and the great desire [of the Kabbalist] and his forcible longing and his mighty infatuation to attain the *devequt* and the Kiss[103]—the power of the bride,[104] and her name and her essence, will be positively known and preserved for eternity, since they were found righteous, and the separated [entities] were united[105] and the united ones were separated[106] and the reality is transformed,[107] and as a consequence, every branch will return to its root and will be united with it and all spiritual [entity] [will return] to its essence and will be linked to it, "and the Tabernacle will become one,"[108] "and the Tetragrammaton[109] will be the king of the entire world, and on that day the Tetragrammaton will be one and His name one,"[110] and if he will do so to the order of the sefirot and the structure of twenty-two letters, "and join them one to the other to make one stick, and they shall become one in thy hand."[111,112]

The fascination with the ideal of *devequt*—the cleaving to the divine or to the Agent Intellect—rather than the emanative scheme, dictates the order of the discussion. The "ascent" of the mystic to the higher realm invites the survey of the divine powers in ascending order. In other words, whereas for the theosophical Kabbalists the emanative process was one of their main concerns, for the ecstatic Kabbalist the return of the mystic to the source of his soul is the main focus of his mystical preoccupations. Indeed, the ecstatic Kabbalist openly indicates that the mystic, the "recipient of the names of the sefirot, should make an effort to receive the divine influx from them themselves,[113] in accordance with his attributes. And he should cleave to each and every sefirah separately, and he should integrate his cleaving with all the sefirot together, and will not separate the branches."[114]

Let me clarify that for Abulafia, at least in some cases, the names of the sefirot are related to the divine names, which serve as part of his mystical techniques for reaching experiences of ecstasy,[115] rather then the knowledge of the divine powers or an attempt to influence them as in the theosophical-theurgical Kabbalah. Although the ecstatic proclivities of his former master never became the focus of his Kabbalah, Gikatilla was nevertheless interested in both prophetic phenomena[116] and the mysticism of the divine names. So, for example, in *Gate of the Vowels* he wrote that "the letters of the Tetragrammaton, blessed be He, are all of them intellectual, not sensuous letters, and they point to an existent and lasting issue, and to every entity in the world, and this is the secret meaning of [the verse] 'and thou that did cleave to the Lord your God are alive every one of you this day,'[117] namely that those who cleave to the letters of the Tetragrammaton are existing and lasting forever."[118] Here the cleaving to the divine name is conceived of as a mystical ideal, as in Abulafia's Kabbalah. Therefore, I assume that Gikatilla, despite the deep transformation in his Kabbalah, retained the importance of the mystical path as related to an ascending description of the ten sefirot. Like Abulafia, Gikatilla here emphasizes the important role of the divine names. Although adopting the literary genre that was cultivated by the theosophical Kabbalists, Gikatilla nevertheless somehow remained faithful to an approach that can be found in ecstatic Kabbalah.

Abulafia's adoption of the ten sefirot as an ascending chain does not imply a reference to them by means of symbols. He is not interested, as we have seen, in symbolism as practiced by the theosophical Kabbalists. Rather, symbols serve as an expansion within the world of man, who is able to capture the divine influxes on his own body or spirit. This example demonstrates that the sefirot can serve the mystical path, including the unitive experience, without resorting to symbols at all. Man's constitution is the main channel for connection with the sefirot and the hidden meanings of the Hebrew words.

In Gikatilla's book, however, the situation is much more complex. Although the capturing of the divine on the human body is still evident, the core of his book is definitively symbolic, assuming not only a knowledge or experience mediated by symbols but also the possibility of cleaving to the divine powers.[119] An alternative channel to the divine remained open even in one of the most theosophical and symbolical treatises in the entire Kabbalistic literature. Therefore, there is no reason to allow to the symbolic system the role of the single path open for the Kabbalist to establish contact with the inner life of the divine realm.

VIII. THE HIDDEN LAYER OF TORAH AS A MAIDEN

The most famous of the Zoharic discussions of the nature of the biblical text, as well as of its modes of interpretation, in a fascinating parable in which the Torah, on its esoteric level, is symbolized by a young maiden and the accomplished Kabbalist is envisioned as her lover.[120] The different rapprochements between the two are indicative of the four ways of interpretation, which culminate in the symbolic-theosophical mode, which is paralleled in the parable by the marriage of the two. The erotic union between the lover and the beloved does not invalidate the earlier forms of communication between them, and the Zohar emphatically indicates that the plain sense is not abolished by the arrival to the esoteric one. The involvement of the mystic with the text is to be understood, on the basis of the parable, as a very experiential reading, a penetration of the body of the text, which has obvious sexual connotations. It is quite emblematic that the Zohar, unlike other Kabbalistic literature before it, and unlike its contemporaries, uses the view of a female human body in order to make its point. This reading has implications related to the nature of the interpreter as the strong reader in comparison to the weaker text. According to the parable, the Kabbalist is the master of the palace and the husband of the Torah. It should be stressed that although the geometrical metaphors are characteristic of R. Abraham Abulafia and the younger R. Joseph

Gikatilla,[121] and the resort to the male body recalls the later Gikatilla, the Zohar creates a view of the beloved that is reminiscent of medieval courtly love.[122]

An interesting reverberation of the maiden parable is found in a vision of the eighteenth-century mystic Emmanuel Swedenborg:

> There appeared to me a beautiful girl with a fair countenance, advancing quickly towards the right, upwards and hurrying a little. She was in the first bloom of youth—not a child nor a young woman. She was dressed attractively in a black shining dress. So she hastened cheerfully from light to light. I was told that the interior things of the Word are such when they first ascend. The black dress stood for the Word in the letter. Afterwards, a young girl flew towards the right cheek, but this was only seen by the interior sight. I was told that those are the things of the internal sense that do not come into the comprehension.[123]

The girl when veiled is compared to the literary level of the Torah; in both cases, the initiative is taken by the girl, who approaches the man. It is perhaps significant that the second girl's dress is not mentioned; she may correspond to the woman who discloses her secrets in the Zoharic parable. I would therefore suggest that Swedenborg has adapted Kabbalistic material in his visions. Significantly, the most striking difference between Swedenborg's version and that of the Zohar is that while for the Christian mystic the gist of the parable is to understand as related to Holy Scripture, for the Kabbalist its focus is on experiencing this meaning and thereby becoming the "husband" of the Torah.

This integrative, or inclusive, approach of the authors of the Zohar notwithstanding,[124] in the later layer of the Zoharic literature, the so-called Sefer Ra'ya' Meheimna' or Book of the Faithful Shepherd, there are important examples which posit Kabbalah at the top of the Jewish curriculum in a way that is ostensibly disjunctive. So, for example, when dealing with the four types of interpretation, the anonymous Kabbalist assumes that the only correct understanding of the Torah is the Kabbalistic one, while other forms of interpretation are not only inferior but sometimes even deleterious.[125] It is in this context that an explicit relationship between the four methods of interpretation and the story of the four sages that entered the pardes is established, to the effect that only one of the sages, R. 'Aqivah, has a correct approach to the Bible, namely a Kabbalistic one.[126]

IX. MASSIVE REMYTHOLOGIZATION OF THE BIBLICAL TEXT IN THE ZOHAR

The biblical literature constitutes a fabric of complex crosscurrents, which consist in efforts to demythologize earlier traditions and to propose another myth, that of the divine will. The demythologization of some earlier elements, however, was never complete; even where attempts were made to obliterate the mythical contents of some traditions, vestiges of the mythical imagery are still evident. Those vestiges served as starting points for the mythopoeic imagination of the *Zohar*, which created, and sometimes even re-created, myths out of the biblical verses and truncated phrases. I shall discuss one passage of the *Zohar*, part of *Midrash ha-Ne'elam*, which exemplifies this trend in Zoharic use of the Bible:

When a man departs[127] the angels cause the soul to ascend to the distance of three hundred years, as it is said in our sages,[128] "from the earth to the firmament there are five hundred years," and they cause the soul to ascend to the highest heaven and they say: if the soul has [done] a virtuous deed she will ascend. But before she ascends, they set her in a place where there are thirty-two thousands of thousands of paths, some of them straight, others awkward, and all of them are called "traps of Death" and "ways of Sheol." And on each and every path there is a consuming fire, and they say to each other: "If you should see any soul entering any of those ways, tell me." And there is another way, and over this way a power [is in charge], which is similar to a dog, and when the soul enters any of those paths the Dog sees it and immediately barks, and when the noxious [powers] and the pernicious angels [mal'akhei habbalah] hear its voice they know that there is a soul [arriving there] and they immediately arrive and seize the soul, and they sling her, as it is written,[129] "and the souls of thine enemies shall He sling out, as out of the hollow of a sling," until they throw her to Gehenna. And David, king of Israel, blessed be his memory, implored the Holy One, blessed be He, that He should rescue him from the Dog, as it is said:[130] "Deliver my life from the sword; my only one from the Dog." Is it possible that David, king of Israel, would be afraid of a dog? But of that power [was he afraid] which is called Dog. And they said that the souls of [the children of] Israel do not enter that place and these paths, and this Dog does not damage them, as it is said:[131] "But against any of the children of Israel not a dog whet his tongue."[132]

The special understanding of the Dog, mentioned in two biblical verses quoted in the text, shows how the Zoharic imagination worked. On the one side, David, the quintessential hero of the Bible and the author of the Book of Psalms, is afraid, according to a verse from Psalm, of the Dog. This fear is interpreted as pointing to the extraordinary nature of the Dog: it is not an ordinary animal, which would not impress the heroic king, but a personification of an evil power. Thus, a dramatic encounter between the soul of David and the mythical Dog is created. This encounter, in which the soul is at risk, takes place in the underworld or perhaps in a kind of purgatory. If thus understood, however, the Dog of the *Zohar* is reminiscent of Cerberus, the dog that in Greek mythology is the guardian of Hades. Thus, the *Zohar* imports a Greek mythologoumenon in order to better understand a verse of the Bible, yet in doing so it not only clarifies a verse but creates a new myth. How is the image of the Zoharic Hades, or Jewish Gehenna, produced? Again, by means of biblical verses and expressions. So, for example, the phrases "ways of Sheol" (Proverbs 14:12) and "traps of Death" (Psalms 18:6) are personified in a way that creates a new myth. These, together with the verse from Samuel, produce a concatenation that creates a web of dramatic events related to the odyssey of the soul in the underworld. Whereas in their biblical sources they have a half-metaphorical and sometimes even half-mythical status, here they become proper names for pernicious powers that populate a labyrinthine underworld. To a certain extent, the Zoharic reading of these mythical prebiblical vestiges reinvests them with mythical values.

Let me draw attention to an important semiotic phenomenon that structures this Zoharic text, a phenomenon I call hypertextuality. Immersion in the Jewish scriptures, in some cases knowledge of them by heart, was part of what was called study, *limmud torah*. This close acquaintance made it possible to retrieve material dealing with a given topic or even a given word and to create a discourse that is not intertextual but hypertextual. In our case it is the resort to the word "dog" (*kelev*) in different biblical contexts and the importing of the mythological Cerberus that produced the fabric of the passage. In other words, interpretation was part of the potential hypertextuality, which was facilitated by intense study.

X. SEXUAL POLARIZATION AS A ZOHARIC EXEGETICAL DEVICE

One of the most outstanding characteristics of Zoharic exegesis of the Bible is the exploitation of biblical stylistic parallelism between different parts of a verse in order to introduce a polar reading, in many cases involving the polarity between male and female. This approach is related to the comprehensive arcanization of the biblical text, as it implies that the acceptance of a mere repetition of synonymous terms would diminish the semantic charge of the text. By reading a dual vision into the parallels in the verse, which are synonyms in the biblical style, the *Zohar* creates a drama that often implies a sexual or erotic mythical event occurring in the sefirotic realm. However, central as this exegetical device is for Zoharic hermeneutics, it is not new with the *Zohar*; it is already present in several instances in early-thirteenth-century theosophical Kabbalah, such as R. Ezra of Gerona's *Commentary on the Song of Songs*. The new development is to be highlighted against the basic tendency that is evident in the generations of commentators that preceded the emergence of Spanish Kabbalistic exegesis. So, for example, Rashi's famous commentary on the Song of Songs interprets some of the organic descriptions of the lover as referring to parts of the Torah or components of the Temple. Against this traditionalistic propensity, the more erotic hermeneutics represents not only a return to an impulse found in some early forms of Jewish religion but also the spiritualization of Judaism via the process of symbolization.

I would now like, however, to show how the *Zohar* exploits the embryonic possibilities created much earlier by *Targum 'Onqelos*, one of the Aramaic translations of the Bible:

> "Great is the Lord and highly to be praised, in the city of our God, in the mountain of his holiness."[133] When is the Lord called "great"? When *knesset yisra'el* [the congregation of Israel] is to be found with Him, as it is written, "In the city of our God is He great." "In the city of our God" means "with the city of our God" . . . and we learn that a king without a queen is not a [real] king, and is neither great nor praised. Thus, so long as the male is without a female, all his excellency is removed from him and he is not in the category of Adam, and moreover he is not worthy of being blessed . . . "Beautiful for situation, the joy of the whole earth: Mount Zion, the side of the North, the city of the great King." "Beautiful for situation, the joy of the whole earth" stands for the excellency of their [sexual] intercourse. "Beautiful for situation" [stands] for the Holy One, blessed be He, who is the Righteous, [who is] "the joy of the whole earth" and then it is the delight of All, and *knesset yisra'el* is blessed.[134]

Let me start with the Zoharic interpretation of the terms describing the city of Jerusalem. *Yefeh nof*, a beautiful view, is understood as a symbol for divinity, more precisely the ninth sefirah, Yesod, which is the male divine power par excellence, identified with the *membrum virile*. This limb, which is to be used only in holiness—an imperative recurring frequently in the *Zohar*—is representative in the Zoharic symbolism of the quality of righteousness, both the divine (the ninth sefirah), and the human. This sexual reading is fostered by the occurrence in the same verse of the term *masos*, translated here as joy and delight, which occurs in several other Jewish texts in the context of the desire of the bridegroom for the bride.

Indeed, the erotic connotation implied in the reading of *yefeh nof* as a bridegroom is not completely new with the *Zohar*: it is inspired by the Aramaic version of this verse: "Beautiful, like a bridegroom who is the delight of the inhabitants of the whole earth." The biblical *masos* has been translated into Aramaic as *hedwatah*, which is followed by the term *kol*, a fact that inspired the emergence of the Zoharic phrase *hedwetah de-kullah*. I suspect that the term "earth," *ha-'aretz*, was understood by the author of the *Zohar* as a symbol for Malkhut, which is synonymous with *knesset yisra'el*, all of them serving as symbols for the feminine divine manifestation.

Let us turn now to the Zoharic interpretation of another biblical verse in the above passage, which also adopts a sexual polarity. This time the pattern of interpretation, similar to many other passages in Kabbalah, involves differentiating between the meaning of two divine names: the Tetragrammaton, signifying the Lord and standing for the sefirah of Tiferet, the male divine attribute, and 'Elohenu, referring to Malkhut or the female attribute. As we saw in the previous chapter, this differentiation is not new but reflects much earlier exegetical processes. The novelty here, and the focus of the exegetical effort, is rather on the word "great," which articulates the relationship between these attributes. Greatness is not conceived of as an inherent quality of the male but is acquired through his relation to the female; only by the act of intercourse is the quality reflected in the words "great" and "praised" made applicable to the male, whereby a male becomes a "man." The sexualization of the relationship between the divine attributes is a well-known Kabbalistic exegetical device, which presupposes a special concern with a duality within the divine world, to be discovered even in those places in the Bible where synonyms were misinterpreted as pointing to different entities.[135]

Beyond the investment of divine names with sexual qualities, common in theosophical Kabbalah, the above passage from the *Zohar* adds something more specific: it deals with the way that the greatness and excellency of the male is attained, in both the human and the divine realms. The gist of this exegetical endeavor is the appearance of a quality through the establishment of a certain relationship. The ultimate message of the *Zohar* is not, however, the mere understanding of the condition for perfection; while its symbolism may indeed invite acts of contemplation, awareness of certain theosophical and anthropological ideas does not change man. In order to attain both his own perfection and that of Divinity, a Kabbalist must act appropriately, otherwise the very purpose of the exegetical process is not fulfilled. The experiential aspect of apprehending the Zoharic exegesis is therefore only the first step toward the ultimate goal inherent in the approach of the author; understanding is, for the Kabbalist, an inescapable invitation to act, otherwise the male would not reach the status of man, nor would he be able to perform the theurgical activity intended to influence the supernal syzygies.

This definition of man is adduced in a very peculiar context: how to understand the occurrence of the term *'adam* ("man") in the verse "If any man of you bring an offering to the Lord."[136] Symbolism is therefore, at least in the Zoharic exegesis, to be viewed as part of an effort to deepen the significance of the biblical text and at the same time the understanding of human ritualistic activity, regarded as theurgical and thus oriented toward having an impact on the higher world. Symbolization is therefore much more than the disclosure of a static meaning implemented in certain words, a disclosure of the rigid designator, to use Saul Kripke's term, for a divine power.

We may therefore distinguish three distinct steps constituting the inner structure of the text: (1) "gnostic" perfection, which stands for the understanding of the theosophical and theurgical significance of the verse; (2) an operative achievement, namely the acquisition of the status of man, which involves an ongoing way of life together with his wife, just as two sefirot are to be brought together by the Kabbalistic way of life; and (3) the induction of divine harmony by the Kabbalist, as a perfect man, through the performance of the commandments. As in the parable of the palace of the maiden, according to the Zohar even the fathoming of the depths of the biblical text has an experiential aspect; the second step, that of becoming a complete man, is to be seen not as the attainment of a static perfection but as a dynamics to be cultivated in relation to the wife.

To return to the aforecited passage on Jerusalem: the plain sense of the second verse is apparently obvious—that the Lord is great and, as a separate assertion, that His mountain is located in His holy city. The former is a theological assessment, unconditional and absolute; the latter indicates that the sacred mountain is located geographically in the sacred city. The relationship between God's greatness and the sacredness of the mountain is not even alluded to; these two theological statements can easily be understood separately, and so I assume that there is no intention of describing any peculiar dynamics between God and His city. Even though the biblical conception of the holy city as the city of God is quite explicit, no changing pattern of relationship is implied by this assertion: it is chosen forever. The pattern of relationship is a vertical one: divine holiness, stemming from the supernal world, is imposed on a material entity, which is thereby metamorphosed into a sacred center. The Zohar radically changes this pattern: the vertical relationship is transposed on the divine plan, where it can now be viewed as the horizontal relationship of two sexually differentiated entities, both of which are divine attributes. In order to determine the relationship between the two parts of the verse, the Hebrew prefix be-, "in," is interpreted as meaning "with"; the dynamics that emerges from the sexualization and interrelation of the two divine names found in the biblical verse creates the specific quality of Kabbalistic exegesis, in comparison with other types of Jewish exegesis. Theosophical Kabbalah alone could put into relief divine attributes, whose affinity with one another gradually turns into myth—sometimes only semi-myth, at other times full-fledged myth. The transformation of the vertical relationship into an intradivine polarity does not, however, obliterate the previous vertical understanding of the relation of God to the city.

As we have already seen, the corporeal reality was not ignored by the Zoharic Kabbalist but was interpreted so that it would not detract from its substantiality. Unlike other symbolic modes, the specific symbolic mode as cultivated in the bulk of the Zohar does not supersede the material reality or the interpreted text; it only adds a new layer of significance. The real city is holy because it represents a higher entity of female nature, in the lower world. This is a "horizontal descending symbolism,"[137] which on the level of corporeal reality turns into a vertical symbolism, as a Kabbalist would put it; or, as a modern reader would formulate it, the vertical relationship of God and His city is transformed into an ascending symbolism on the horizontal divine level without attenuating its primary significance.

With the development of Kabbalistic hermeneutics, however, there are a few cases where the interpreted material, rabbinic or of alien extraction, is assumed to be incomprehensible or unimportant on the plain sense and the symbolic interpretation alone is thought to offer a certain meaning.[138]

XI. ON THE VICISSITUDES OF KABBALISTIC SYMBOLISM

The preeminent role of symbolism in the Zoharic literature and in Gikatilla's later theosophical writings ensured the reverberation of this form of exegesis in numerous other Kabbalistic books that belong to the theosophical-theurgical school of Kabbalah. This floruit of symbolism is evident in the generation following the composition of the two Kabbalistic corpora, in what can be described as "mosaic" exegetical writings that capitalized on the developments in the preceding generation. This new wave includes R. Isaac of Acre, R. Joseph of Hamadan, R. Joseph Angelet, R. Menahem Recanati, R. David ben Yehudah he-Hasid,[139] and the anonymous Kabbalist who composed the later part of the Zoharic literature: the author of Sefer Tiqqunei Zohar and Ra'ya' Meheimna'. Some of these Kabbalists were aware of the coexistence of different symbolic systems in their mainly eclectic writings. Yet in their drive to develop more complex theosophies, they were sometime capable of accommodating the diverging symbols by applying them to different layers in the divine worlds.

The outburst of symbolic thought in the Zoharic literature and among contemporary Kabbalists left a decisive impression on the subsequent history of Kabbalah. Shortly after its appearance, various attempts were made to decode the precise symbolic meaning of Zoharic discussions, and a large literature arose containing translations, commentaries, and dictionaries of Zoharic terminology and symbolism. The canonization of the Zohar generated this body of writings, which enriched Kabbalistic literature and enhanced the understanding of the

Zohar but only marginally contributed to the further development of symbolic thought in Kabbalah. Few Kabbalists imitated the Zoharic symbolic language, and even fewer added anything new to the symbolic structure of Kabbalah. The Zohar thus became a canonical monument, to be explained rather than continued. "Innovative Kabbalah," as reflected in the Zohar, had a splendid but brief life; the conservative factors in Kabbalah, which were now focused on the doctrine of the Zohar, began the process of systematizing its fragmentary, ambiguous, and at times contradictory thought.

A major example of this trend appears in the literary activity of R. David ben Yehudah he-Hasid. By the end of the thirteenth century he had undertaken a Hebrew translation of parts of the Zohar, in which the rendered text was commented upon by means of the addition of letters above the words which alluded to the sefirot. The greater part of this supercommentary reflects Zoharic symbolism, but sometimes a non-Zoharic symbolic usage was superimposed on the text. Moreover, many words that were not intended to function as symbols were interpreted as such,[140] a technique that turned the Zoharic text into a baroque agglomeration of symbols wherein the peculiar dynamics of the Zoharic composition is lost. Paraphrasing Emile Mâle,[141] we may say that true symbolism holds too large a place in the Zoharic text for it to be necessary to seek it where it does not exist. This relatively indiscriminate, mechanical superimposition of symbols clearly indicates that the Zohar had become a canonical work whose words must be symbolized, just like the words of the Bible. The spirit of Zoharic symbolic creation, rather than symbolic interpretation, was lost.

R. David was not only the first translator of the Zohar but also its first, or at least one of its earliest, commentators. In his commentary on 'Iddra' Rabba', entitled Sefer ha-Gevul, he attempted an extremely complex exegesis of this treatise, illustrated by endless circles and figures that obfuscate rather than illuminate the significance of the text. The works of R. David, together with those of R. Joseph ben Shalom Ashkenazi, hence opened the way for a comprehensive symbolization of each and every issue, thereby serving as an intricate and complicated intermediary between the subtle symbolism of the Zohar and the baroque symbolism of Lurianic Kabbalah. R. Moses Cordovero and R. Isaac Luria, the two great exegetes of the Zoharic literature active in sixteenth-century Safed, succeeded in combining these sometimes disparate symbols and mythologoumena into more comprehensive and coherent conceptual systems, whose influence on later Jewish theosophy was tremendous. Cordovero was concerned to offer a survey of the different forms of thought found in the vast Kabbalistic literature before answering the quandaries in a sometimes innovative manner. He often quotes, analyzes the different stands, and looks for solutions that will be decided in favor of one position or

another or offer a new idea. Luria, on the other hand, was much more interested in offering a long and detailed scheme that covers all of existence, from
the 'Ein Sof to the vision of the end of history. In Luria's system, symbols become
enchained in a huge theosophical myth, so that they less and less serve exegetical
aims.

Jewish symbolism, however, only secondarily benefited from these developments. Symbols rarely maintain their freshness, ambiguity, and allusiveness when
they become integrated into a more elaborate and detailed theological structure,
which can be called overtheosophication. The greater the area that Kabbalistic
theosophy conquered for itself, the less vital space remained for symbolic élan.
No wonder that Lurianic Kabbalah, the most complicated Jewish theosophy, produced only marginal discussions on symbolism and practically no significant
commentaries on the ten sefirot. The scholastic structure of Safedian Kabbalah
had a pernicious effect on the evolution of symbolism. The floruit of Kabbalistic symbolism may be located, therefore, between two stages in the history of
theosophical-theurgical Kabbalah at its very beginnings in the thirteenth century
and its sixteenth-century maturation. The age of Kabbalah's youth, so to speak,
was a brief period of flowering, whose vigor and enthusiasm faded[142] as the more
articulated, sophisticated, "mature," and conservative theosophies became ever
more prominent.

For the more theologically oriented generations of Kabbalists before the Zohar,
the Kabbalistic tradition was the bearer, to borrow from E. T. A. Hoffmann, of
"the mysterious language of a distant spiritual kingdom, whose marvelous ac-
cents resound within us and awaken a higher intensive life."[143] In the Zoharic
literature, however, it is obvious that some Kabbalists learned the motifs of this
mysterious melody and were capable of composing novel variations while at the
same time creating new ones. This new work is the Zohar, which constitutes both
the first major outpouring and the climax of Kabbalistic symbolic creation.[144]
Only later do we find some interesting usages of symbolism in such literary
creations as the Aramaic poems composed by Luria and recited during the three
meals of the Sabbath.[145] Another outstanding symbolic literary creation is R.
Nahman of Braslav's collection of stories, whose subtle and allusive symbolism
contributes substantially to their mysterious and allusive atmosphere.[146]

II

ALLEGORIES, DIVINE NAMES, AND EXPERIENCES IN ECSTATIC KABBALAH

I. Interpretive Allegory in Jewish Literature

As we have just seen, some modern scholars assumed the ubiquity of the symbolic mode of expression in Kabbalah as a whole, even portraying it as completely different from allegorical types of expression, which they regarded as representative of Jewish philosophical literature. Indeed, interpretive allegory, or allegorization, is one of the outstanding spiritual imports into the exegetical arsenal of Jewish hermeneutics. Despite Philo of Alexandria's great contributions to the emergence and development of allegorical exegesis in early Christianity and, to a lesser extent, to allegory in Western medieval exegesis, his exegetical approach to the Bible was completely rejected in the rabbinic forms of exegesis as represented by the classical midrashim and in talmudic treatises. It was a millennium after

Philo's death before the next significant instance of interpretive allegory in Judaism was discernible, but then it was mediated by the renascence of Greek philosophies in the Arabic Middle Ages, and did not represent a direct and substantial influence of Philonic exegesis. This means that the medieval philosophers faced a situation similar to Philo's: they had access to some forms of Greek corpora—now in Arabic translations—and they appropriated them in order to ascribe a philosophical allegorical meaning to the sacred scriptures. Thus, medieval Jewish philosophy may be described as basically a Jewish-Greek amalgam, which had an impact on some aspects of Kabbalistic exegesis and metaphysics.

With the emergence in the mid-eleventh century of formative influences of Neoplatonic philosophy in Shlomo ibn Gabirol, known in the scholastic literature as Avicebron, we find explicit vestiges of such allegorical interpretations, which apparently were much more numerous than the scant extant material testifies. Although only few examples of an allegorical approach to the Bible have survived from his writings, and the precise extent of his allegorical exegesis is unclear, there can be no doubt that the new rapprochement between Greek thought and the sacred scriptures took a form that is quite reminiscent, though probably independent, of the earlier ancient encounter as represented by Philo's allegoresis. However, even in ibn Gabirol's allegorical interpretations, which were quoted in an influential work, R. Abraham ibn Ezra's *Commentary on Torah*, the impact was marginal.

It is only with the wholesale absorption of Aristotelian terminology at the end of the twelfth century and its exposition in what became the classic of Jewish philosophy, Maimonides' *Guide of the Perplexed*, that allegorization, or the allegorical mode of interpretation, became part of a more accepted approach to the Jewish canonic writings.[1] To be sure, the Aristotelian allegories, even when espoused by an accomplished and authoritative Jewish master like Maimonides, did not pass without strong resistance and sometimes sharp polemics from some Jewish elites. An intercorporal exegesis, as I defined this approach in Chapter 9, invited the dominant role for terms and concepts previously unknown in classical Jewish texts and conceptually different from the worldview of rabbinic thinkers. Indeed, fiery debates, which continued for centuries, accompanied the penetration of Aristotelian-oriented exegesis, and such a critical attitude toward it may still be discerned late in the eighteenth century among the opponents of Hasidism. In between, however, a series of appropriations of allegorical interpretations can be found not only among the followers of Maimonides, such as the various authors from the ibn Tibbon family, but also in other circles, including some of the more conservative ones, in the camp of Kabbalists.

The main example is Abraham Abulafia's allegorical exegesis. He was not, however, an exceptional voice in this camp: some of the treatments of R. Azriel of Gerona, many of R. Isaac ibn Latif's biblical interpretations, some of the early writings of R. Moshe de Leon and Joseph Gikatilla, the last three of them Abulafia's contemporaries, display strong affinities to Maimonidean allegorizations of the biblical texts. This is also true of one of the most influential Kabbalistic commentators, R. Bahya ben Asher, and of the *Commentary on the Talmudic 'Aggadot* by ben Asher's master, R. Shlomo ibn Adret (known by the acronym Rashba). The extent of the influence of allegorical exegesis in Kabbalah still awaits close inspection. Such an examination should be quite fascinating, as it will have to take into consideration the manner in which this exegetical device has been integrated within the more complex hermeneutical system of the Kabbalists. While in general the medieval philosophers had to work with a twofold method of exegesis based on the plain sense and the allegorical sense, the latter conceived of as esoteric, for many Kabbalists the philosophical allegory was already a cultural and spiritual fact, and they had to integrate it within much more complex systems that included additional exegetical dimensions.[2]

As a rule, Kabbalistic exegesis is much more complex than the regular philosophical exegesis. Whereas the latter was almost exclusively indifferent or even critical toward the Kabbalistic methods, the former was often quite inclusive, as we shall see in the next chapter. This inclusive propensity is more evident when we compare it to the much more exclusivistic attitude of rabbinic authors since the Middle Ages, who would reject both the allegorical and the symbolic-Kabbalistic types of exegesis. What was the reason for the indifference and even rejection or sharp criticism of allegory by some Jewish thinkers (including Kabbalists), on the one hand, and its later integration, on the other? Any monolithic answer would be a simplification if not a blatant distortion. In dealing with a millennium and a half of Jewish exegesis, it would be dangerous to reduce the reticence of hundreds of writers to one major motive. Nevertheless, as concerns allegory, one such observation presents itself: if the etymology of allegory suggests the telling of two stories through one medium, with respect to rabbanism allegory would mean the creation of a universe of discourse that parallels and so competes with the sacred scriptures. The plain sense would have to compete with the other narrative, whose conceptual dimensions stem from a universe of discourse imported from outside, emphasizing the importance of the abstract, cerebral, natural, or orderly in lieu of the much more concrete, imaginative, irregular, and voluntaristic approach found in the biblical texts. As I shall attempt to show, even the types of esotericism informing the two modes of writing were different: they were much more linguocentric in the case of Judaism, where the secrets are often related to texts (*sitrei* torah), whereas in the Greek form of Platonic esotericism, which was the most influential form in the West, the secrets were much more political than scriptural.

Generations of encounters between Jewish thinkers and alien forms of discourse, whose eidetic structures were different from the biblical and midrashic ones, convinced many Jewish thinkers that one truth is, or at least should be, shared by what has been conceived by them as the various authoritative corpora.[3] Interpretive allegory was conceived of as the main means of illuminating this allegedly shared conceptual universe, and there is no doubt that this form of allegory, as cultivated in the Jewish philosophical literature, was an important agent for introducing into Judaism a more universalist type of discourse. I use the term *universalist* because the Greek manner of reasoning was accepted by a much greater intellectual audience as the higher view of discourse, as the pagan, Muslim, and Christian writings show. The *allos*, or "other," has been Judaized, just as Jewish elements have been allegorized. Any fundamental spiritual enterprise has its price, however; it enriches but also excites fears and implies dangers. There is much of reductionism in universalism, as the latter is but an expression of a majority or more powerful culture. Allegory can be seen as a powerful agent of acculturation, but just as often it is an agent of cultural assimilation. The particularistic trends, so conspicuous in Jewish literature, have been instrumental in this rejection of the allegorical forms of discourse.

Let me formulate those cultural and religious fears in the Jewish camp in more hermeneutical terms. Interpretive allegories emerged in the Hellenistic period when attempts were made to interpret the Homeric literature in terms of speculative systems that had little in common with the mythology described by Greek poets. The emergence of the allos within Greek society—the independent, individualistic, even elitist thinkers who sometimes confronted the common religious beliefs, sometimes simply followed another form of intellectual logic based on what was called nature—invited moments of reconciliation between the public domains of agreed-upon myths and the elitist attainments. The more linguistic realms of the mythos, with greater national or local specificities expressed in not only the written but also the oral repetitive culture, encountered spiritual systems, namely systems created and sustained by the logos, the mental or cerebral forms of activity. The allegory was indeed the claim that the accepted myths of the Greek societies are but other formulations of the philosophical truths elaborated by the elite. Although this is an "elevation" of the mythos to the degree where it becomes a trader of an inherent logos, allegory is a violent invasion of one form of discourse into another, namely the imposition of the logocentric onto the linguocentric. The inner problematics, tensions, discrepancies, and idiosyncrasies naturally found in the revered texts, traditions, beliefs, or imaginations have been not only enriched by allegorical interpretations but also, at the same time, "solved," which in fact means simplified. The linguistic incoherence of the imaginative has been trapped in much more logocentric webs of philosophical coherences. It seems that the official representatives of Greek myths and archaic religions, if there were such authoritative exponents in the early Hellenistic period, were weak or indifferent enough not to protest against the elevation of their mythology to the rank of a hidden philosophy of nature, or perhaps were satisfied by such a development.

The move of the sacred book to the center of Jewish religion during the period of the Second Temple brought to the forefront a new class of intellectuals, the *soferim*, who—together with the later Pharisees, who generated the rabbinic elite— were bibliocentric and to a certain degree linguocentric elites.[4] Their intellectual project was much more inclined toward public disclosure than toward discovery. The book under their scrutiny was written in a language partaken of by people, whereas the Hellenistic philosophers employed much more a silent language of nature or a complex philosophical text studied by the very few elite. The project of the rabbinic elites was to transform the Bible into a shared, founding, formative, or inspiring source that would amplify the richness of the divine text either by expanding on its (allegedly implicit) meanings through various forms of commentary or by consciously preserving different and sometimes diverging and conflicting interpretations as equally relevant and worthy of study. It is random expansion rather than deliberate simplification, pluralism rather than coherence, that marked the main effort of the rabbis in the exegesis found in the midrashic and talmudic literatures. It should be stressed that this was a very qualified and restricted expansion, a calculated and controlled pluralism, but nevertheless the main effort was toward collective interpretations that amplified the mythical elements in the Bible rather than reducing them so as to imply the existence of a coherent speculative system.

One of the elements that seem to be crucial for the floruit of the multiplicity of interpretations was to leave outside the discussions the more general ontic, metaphysical, psychological, and naturalistic presuppositions that presumably nourished the rabbis' interpretive discourses, and to present the results as if they emanated directly from the written source or oral traditions. Rabbinic Judaism did not develop, apparently as a result of a deliberate choice of literary genres, any elaborate theologies, philosophies, astronomies, physics, magic, alchemies, or psychologies. This does not mean that rabbis were not aware of alien forms of thought or that they did not share some of them; they may even have been inspired by them when operating within the linguistic exegetical realm.[5] But the religious importance of the allos was explicitly denied or derided or, in other cases, silently integrated, so that its independent status was regarded as irrelevant for the exegetical project. The absence of significant philosophical and astronomical terminologies in the talmudic-midrashic literature is one of the outstanding pieces of evidence for the marginalization of the structures of thought that were potentially competing with the rabbinic literature.

The case is quite different, however, when considering the vast speculative projects of Philo or the more modest ones of ibn Gabirol, Maimonides, or Leone Ebreo, who in their deep differences (apparently not incidental) from the rabbinic form of discourse were phenomena of the Diaspora, both in the adoption of speculative systems and in the choice of the language in which to compose their allegorical writings. Here I would like to examine one case of the integration of allegoresis within the hermeneutics of a specific Kabbalistic school, the ecstatic one, and point out the problematics created by attempts to offer a synthesis of an allegorical and a Kabbalistic approach. The main topic in this instance consists in linguistic units, the divine names, of utmost importance, or at least of formal status, in Jewish literature. Being ways to designate the deity, the linguistic units that are considered to be divine names represent the more sensitive part of the sacred language, as is evident from the many interdictions related to their performance, in both written and oral forms, in the regulations found in the rabbinic literature. My intention is to examine a few Kabbalistic approaches to the status of the divine names as representing either the most important points of resistance of the scriptural in the face of the allegorical or their allegorization by Kabbalists.

II. DIVINE NAMES IN JEWISH MYSTICISM

Discussions about various divine names permeate most of the literature of Jewish mysticism. The immense literary corpus, and even the considerable bibliography, have yet to be organized in a manner that would facilitate a comprehensive typology of the use of the divine names. Insofar as the mystical literature since the Middle Ages is concerned, I would suggest a fivefold distinction between the different ways Jewish mystics used the divine names:[6]

(1) The divine names were taken to be important components of techniques to achieve mystical experiences, as is the case in late-twelfth- and early-thirteenth-century Hasidei Ashkenaz, Abraham Abulafia's ecstatic Kabbalah and its various repercussions, until Polish Hasidism.[7]

(2) The divine names were taken to be an indispensable part of theurgical operations, especially those performed during prayer. By theurgical I mean recourse to techniques, most of them nomian, in order to have an

impact on the relations between the divine powers, the sefirot. This view is found from the very beginning of Kabbalah and has reverberated in a long series of discussions.[8]

(3) Jewish magic in general, and Kabbalistic magic in particular, have resorted to the divine names as powerful and paramount linguistic units. Incantations, amulets, and talismans are often replete with words that are taken to be divine names, even when they are much closer to *nomina barbara*.[9]

(4) The divine names were understood as pointing to the structure of the universe, as a type of scientific formula.[10]

(5) The resort to the concept of divine names is evident in a great variety of hermeneutical approaches from the ancient Heikhalot literature up to eighteenth-century Polish Hasidism. The biblical text has been understood as consisting of a texture different from that engaged in the traditional reading of the canonic text.[11] An understanding of the new structure of the biblical text as consisting of divine names was thought to reveal an esoteric layer of the scriptures, which retrieves the various paranormal powers inherent in it: the technical-mystical, the theurgical-symbolical, and the magical.

The first four categories of understanding and using the divine names reflect, in my opinion, a deeper differentiation in the spiritual concerns of Kabbalists and Hasidic masters. I have proposed in the introduction to distinguish between three models corresponding to the first three categories: the ecstatic, the theosophical-theurgical, and the magical, respectively. I hope to elaborate on the relevance of this theory of models for understanding the ecstatic Kabbalists' attitude toward divine names. In the limited framework of this chapter, however, I would like to concentrate on some aspects of the history of the later hermeneutical attitude toward the biblical text as possessing this particular quality, that is, of consisting of a series of divine names. The explication of the hermeneutical principles that were inspired by this view may help us understand some important issues related to the development of Kabbalah as a much more diversified mode of thinking. An additional reason for focusing on this aspect is that this approach has been understood in modern scholarship as quintessentially reflecting the entire Kabbalistic attitude toward language.

III. EMERGENCE

The assumption that powerful names emerge from the verses of the Torah is expressed in *Ma'ayan ha-Hokhmah* by the verb *yotze'im*, which literally means "go out." This means, in the above context, that a certain linguistic exegetical technique is able to extract from a regular verse something that is found in it. A similar view appears in a passage of *Midrash Konen*, where God is described as opening the Torah and taking out three names from it.[12] The opening of the Torah and the taking out of names seem to reflect a certain understanding of the emergence of the names from the text, which is now envisioned as a box where the names are deposited and kept secret. This implies another type of imaginary, as opposed to that of *Ma'ayan ha-Hokhmah*, where the secrets, though also closely related to the text of the Torah, are disclosed by an external agent which teaches Moses where in the Bible to find the verse that generates the name pertinent for curing some malady or remedying a certain problem. In *Midrash Konen*, however, the Torah is conceived of as preexisting creation and as the source of the creative processes, by means of three divine names found in it. Let me call this approach *intratextual*, meaning that the additional layer of understanding some parts of the Torah is generated not by the introduction of an elaborate nomenclature whose conceptualization is extraneous to the interpreted text—an approach I shall call *extratextual*—but by a rearrangement of the linguistic units that constitute the interpreted text. The above cases are instances where the process of arcanization does not involve importing concepts that are linguistically extraneous to the text, as the allegorical and the symbolic forms of interpretation do, but entails rearranging the linguistic units that constitute the canonical text.

IV. NAHMANIDES' TWO READINGS OF THE TORAH

Already among the Jewish Rhenish pietistic masters, the so-called Hasidei Ashkenaz, there was a tradition and practice related to the belief that the Torah is a continuum of divine names.[13] In some instances such a view underlies the concepts of certain halakhic texts.[14] In Nahmanides' hands there were two different traditions regarding the Torah and the divine names included therein: one stemming from *Sefer Shimmushei Torah*, the other circulating already at the beginning of the thirteenth century in some circles of Jewish writers in Europe but still not attested in a book that would carefully explicate its significance. According to one of Nahmanides' expressions of the two traditions:

> The entire Torah is replete with the names of the Holy One, blessed be He, and in each and every pericope there is the name by which a certain thing has been formed or made or sustained by it. And in this domain there is a book called *Shimmushei Torah*, and it explicates in connection with the pericopes their [magical] use and the name that emerges from it and how it emerges and how to use it [the pericope]. But[15] there is a [secret] tradition

to the effect that the names written in that book are much more numerous than those [explicitly] written in it, because the Torah, from *bereshit* to *le-ʿeinei kol yisraʾel*, is entirely names, for example, *berosh yitbaraʾ ʾelohim*, and others similar to it . . . and from it Moses, our master, blessed be his memory, knew whatever a creature can know and understand.[16]

Nahmanides was therefore aware of the existence of two somewhat different traditions: one, still extant in *Sefer Shimmushei Torah*, which presents a limited number of magical names, and another, claiming the existence in ancient times of reading of the entire text of the Pentateuch, from the first to the last words, as a series of divine names. While the former tradition is concerned more with angelic names, the tradition mentioned in the context of the continuum was dealing, according to Nahmanides, with divine names, but not angelic ones. It should be emphasized that Nahmanides does not oppose or criticize the magical aspects of the Torah, but he believes that they indeed were known by Moses and, according to the continuation of this passage, were known and practiced by the "pious men of [former] generations."[17]

The passage that most influenced numerous Kabbalists in their concept of the Torah as a continuum of divine names is found in Nahmanides' introduction to his *Commentary on the Pentateuch*, where he uses some formulations identical to those found in his above-quoted sermon but adds some crucial comments. So, for example, after adducing the dictum that the Torah is a continuum of divine names as a "[secret] tradition of truth," he writes that "it was possible to read it [the Torah] according to the path of the [divine] names, and it was possible to be read, according to our reading, as concerning the Torah and the commandment, and it has been given according to Moses according to the path of the division [of the text] of the reading of the commandment, and it has been transmitted to him orally according to its reading as [divine] names."[18] By recourse to the term "reading," *qeriʾah*, but not to "going out," as in his sermon, Nahmanides comes a little bit closer to an exegetical approach, although in his case, too, it is not the human effort to understand the text that conveys its ultimate meaning but a revelation that has been imparted to Moses. The two readings are therefore strongly distinguished by Nahmanides: one deals with the regular Masoretic division of the text and consequently reflects the understanding of the Torah as dealing with the commandments; the other, transmitted orally, deals with the divine names. In the case of the former, Nahmanides uses the form "our reading," therefore implying the common rabbinic approach to biblical texts. Although the oral tradition has been given to Moses, it has apparently been lost since that time and is no longer available, at least not in its entirety. This last conclusion refers to the more comprehensive vision of the entire Torah as a continuum of divine names. Thus, an oral tradition, which is at the same time described as a true one, concerning the manner of transforming the entire text into divine names has been hinted at, but the sole concrete example given for such a reading has been restricted to three verses in Exodus, taken from much earlier Jewish texts.[19]

The source that passed the oral tradition on the divine names to Moses is quite unclear: Nahmanides uses a passive verb form, which obfuscates the nature of the transmitter: Moses was given, nimsar, but the giver is not identified. By a comparison to *Sefer Shimmushei Torah*, where the multiplicity of angelic names is attributed to a revelation from an angel, I would not be surprised if additional sources corroborated such an interpretation. The alternative, that God himself revealed both the Torah and the divine names, is certainly still possible but is not warranted by an explicit text. This reluctance to speak about a secret tradition is crucial in this master's overall conception of Kabbalah: any Kabbalistic traditions already revealed may in principle be lost but not invented. The more playful interpretive approach to the canonical texts, found in many instances in the rabbinic tradition, is marginalized by one of the most important representatives of the rabbinic culture in the Middle Ages. So, for example, we learn in the sermon quoted in an earlier chapter that the resort to gematria is to be very limited.[20]

Although the loss of a tradition is not invoked in this passage, the attempt to restrict the free inventiveness of mathematical interpretations is obvious. What seems to me interesting in the case of Nahmanides' approach is to point out the very existence, in hoary antiquity, of a tradition related to divine names, but not to claim that it is extant. Therefore, even if Nahmanides himself explicitly calls this tradition qabbalah shel 'emmet, a "Kabbalah of truth," nevertheless this is not the mystical tradition he himself inherited and transmitted, which is presumably much more focused on the theurgical and theosophical aspects of the Bible. Despite the essential difference between the path of names and the path of commandments, as they have been explicated by Nahmanides they have something very substantial in common: both emerge out of the same conglomerate of letters which, having been written primordially as a sequence of discrete letters, could be divided in more than one manner. The criterion for this division could not be another text that preceded the Bible but must be a matter of a revelation. The revelation is intended to instruct the legislator in the secrets of the two readings, which are constituted by the very act of division. In my opinion, an intratextual approach underlies the two readings, since no extratextual conceptual parallel is invoked as involved in the different divisions of the sequence of letters.

To approach the common denominator of these readings from a more modern literary point of view, we may see the sequence of Torah letters as a structure that interacts with the reader: a rabbinically oriented mind will see in the sequence the source of the ritualistic understanding of the Bible, while someone who possesses a secret tradition will see in the very same letters a series of divine names.[21] Moreover, in Nahmanides' mind the double reading of the Bible—for its plain, exoteric sense and its esoteric, "names"-level sense—does not include an implicit depreciation of the former by an elevation of the latter. In my opinion, the main content of the Bible was regarded as the revelation of the commandments, as we may learn from Nahmanides' designation of Moses as the "prophet of the commandments."[22] Unlike the interpretive allegory of the medieval Jewish philosophers, whose writings were often haunted by the danger of secretly preferring the intellectual, esoteric content over the more historical and ritualistic content, Nahmanides was less bothered by this possible implication of his proposal.

V. INTERPRETIVE ALLEGORY: BETWEEN THE PATH OF COMMANDMENTS AND THE PATH OF NAMES IN ECSTATIC KABBALAH

Nahmanides records the existence of a sublime but now only partially available tradition in which the Torah as divine names is considered the exclusive patrimony of Moses and, because it is not extant but very fragmentary, is regarded as irrelevant to a postbiblical interpretive project. In Nahmanides' vision of Kabbalah, there is no place for reconstruction of a lost tradition, as this would automatically involve a process of reasoning that he had explicitly banished from understanding Kabbalah. We may assume, on the basis of Nahmanides' introduction to his *Commentary on the Pentateuch*, that the sublime Kabbalah that conceived of the biblical text as a continuum of divine names was lost forever. However, this somewhat antiquarian and conservative approach was appropriated in a much more creative manner by another school of Kabbalah, the ecstatic one, in the decades immediately following the death of the Geronese Kabbalist. In the writings of Abraham Abulafia and some of his followers, the passage from Nahmanides' introduction about the divine names is quoted several times, always in positive terms but without implying that the details of this tradition are no longer available. This absence is not incidental: it reflects the feeling among the ecstatic Kabbalists that Nahmanides, whose writings they explicitly cite as their source, has offered them an approach to the Torah that is very relevant, indeed the core of their Kabbalah, which is often called the "path of [divine] names." The divine name consisting of forty-two letters was thought by Abulafia to be derived from the first forty-two letters of Genesis, which starts with the letter *bet* and ends with the letter *mem*, *mem-bet* being the name of forty-two letters.[23] This "fact" is described by Abulafia as part of the view that "the entire Torah is [consists] of divine names of the Holy One, blessed be He, and this is an intelligible proof for a Kabbalist."[24]

Although Abulafia does not explicitly maintain that he applies Nahmanides' principle, his formulation is identical to that of the Geronese Kabbalist. Yet unlike the example offered by Nahmanides, who does not claim that his description of the division of words in the first verse is any more than a guess at the original reading according to the "path of names," in the case of Abulafia the name of forty-two has been conceived of in some already-existing magical and mystical texts as a divine name. What was regarded as lost (whether in whole or in part) by Nahmanides was retrieved by Abulafia. Nahmanides himself was wary of allegorical interpretations.[25] Although he was acquainted with Maimonides' naturalistic exegesis, the thrust of his approach was quite different. Nahmanides was not a radical interpreter, because he neutralized the possibility of reading the Torah as a continuum of divine names in the present and rejected philosophical allegories. Abulafia, on the other hand, was a radical interpreter for two reasons: he envisioned both possibilities as accessible, and he brought together Maimonidean and Nahmanidean theories, namely the allegorical path and the path of the names. It is quite evident, however, that while these two masters were among the pool of sources that influenced Abulafia's Kabbalah, Abulafia was acquainted with additional elements similar to Maimonides' allegory and Nahmanides' path of names but independent of these two thinkers. He knew, on the one hand, R. Abraham ibn Ezra's *Commentary on the Pentateuch*, which contains allegories, and medieval Neoaristotelianism in its Arabic, Jewish, and perhaps also Christian variations, and on the other hand was familiar with *Sefer Shimmushei Torah* and the Hasidei Ashkenaz views, where divine names play an important role in thought and praxis.[26] Nevertheless, from the specific formulations used by the ecstatic Kabbalist, it is obvious that he regarded Maimonides and Nahmanides as the cornerstones of his approach to the secrets of the Torah.[27]

Let me briefly discuss another text of Abulafia's, already adduced in Chapter 9,[28] where these two approaches were conjugated to create a particular type of hierarchy. I take the reading of the Torah in this passage on its plain sense as standing for Nahmanides' "path of commandments," which fits the rank of the tzaddiq. The last path, defined in terms copied from Nahmanides, is the highest one, and although Nahmanides restricted it to Moses, for Abulafia it is a matter not only of all the prophets in the past but also of those persons who strive to become prophets in the present by resorting to combinations of letters and divine names. The introduction of the theme of combining letters within the Nahmanidean view seems to be new with Abulafia, and it had some interesting reverberations in subsequent Kabbalistic and Hasidic theories, which will be discussed in some detail in the next chapter.

The second path, however—the esoteric path, which follows the philosophical path—is absent in Nahmanides but very close to the manner in which Maimonides was understood in the Middle Ages: an esoteric philosopher. What is important in the very last sentence is the cumulative and the integrative nature of the prophetic path: in order to become a prophet, one must be a righteous and pious man who combines ritual and mental accomplishment—namely a philosopher. Philosophical understanding of the Torah, an approach that resorts to allegory, is not a stage to be transcended by the aspirant to prophecy but an approach to be maintained even when traveling the path of the prophets. As indicated in this quote, philosophical understanding of the Torah is a process that culminates in perfect knowledge. It represents the moment of the purified understanding of God à la Maimonides, which is a condition for uniting with Him or receiving a message from Him. The regular religious performance of the righteous, the mystical moments of prophecy (namely ecstasy), and the contemplative ideal, which involves the allegorical understanding of the Bible, were all given a secure place in his system. The insertion of the interpretive allegory between Nahmanides' path of commandments and the path of names is far from being a mechanical attainment: as we shall see shortly, the allegorical approach did not always remain a separate technique but was sometimes combined with the path of names. What seems more important, however, is that it radiated on Abulafia's perception of Nahmanides' paths. So, for example, Abulafia's attitude toward the meaning of the commandments is significantly different from that of the Geronese master and much closer to a Maimonidean intellectualistic understanding of the role of Jewish ritual. No less interesting, though, is the fact that philosophical esotericism has also affected the other form of Jewish esotericism: the linguistic one.

VI. Interpretive Allegory and the Path of Names

For both Abulafia and his student R. Nathan ben Sa'adyah, who composed Sha'arei Tzedeq, allegorical understanding of the Torah precedes the prophetic reading and is necessary for its attainment. How, then, did the ecstatic Kabbalist understand the relationship between the two as exegetical techniques? According to a statement in Abulafia that deals with a biblical story discussed earlier in his text, the allegorical approach is more general, whereas the Kabbalistic approach takes into consideration each and every letter of the interpreted text.[29]

The move from allegorical to Kabbalistic techniques of interpretations involves, according to the Kabbalist, a gain from the point of view of textual understanding. Allegory, or the metaphorical approach, because it deals with broad concepts, means understanding the relationship between the various elements in a biblical pericope in a general manner, which would presuppose that some elements of the text remain beyond the scope of the exegetical allegorical approach. Only Kabbalistic exegesis, according to Abulafia, can exhaust the plenitude of the text without skipping any of its components and thus in principle take fully into account the textual idiosyncrasies. Abulafia expresses this idea in the strongest terms: "Not one letter is left without being used" during the exegetical enterprise.

Let me explore in more detail the implications of that statement. A hyperliteralistic[30] approach seems to inspire Kabbalistic exegesis à la Abulafia, who does not regard the letters or names as an authoritative source for religious behavior, as Nahmanides' path of commandments is, nor as a magical source, as may have been Nahmanides' understanding of the path of names, but as a source of experience. The minute examination of the text, its dissection into its constitutive letters and subsequently their rearrangement into new formulas, displays an extreme devotion to the text at the same time as it opens the door to exegetical freedom. The constraint of taking all the consonants into consideration may, unlike the looser allegorical approach, produce paralyzing moments; indeed, as understood in ecstatic Kabbalah, all the letters of the interpreted text should be involved, but the exegete enjoys a great freedom to manipulate the text, so that it is quite possible to find more than one way of construing a Kabbalistic interpretation. In a passage particularly relevant to this question, Abulafia writes:

> This issue has been said in two pericopes, which have been comprised together according to the plain sense and commented upon according to the [way of] wisdom [namely philosophy], with few additions of Kabbalistic words; it is necessary indeed to return to this in order to demonstrate all these issues also according to the [path of] names. However, should we approach this path, according to what we have received from it, [as dealing with] the forms of the names and the [letter] combinations and gematria and notariqon, and those like them from the paths of Kabbalah, we would not be able to write all these issues that we have received by this Kabbalistic path related to the knowledge of the names, even if all the heavens would be parchments, and all the seas ink, and all the reeds pens, and all the beams— fingers, and every moment of our days as long as the years of Methuselah. A fortiori there are [Kabbalistic] paths that we have not received and we do not know anything about.[31]

This Rabelaisian passage expresses the nature of Kabbalah according to this Kabbalist. It consists in innumerable techniques of interpretation, each providing a comprehensive and detailed interpretation of the text; this is the reason why even in a Kabbalistic commentary on the Torah the Kabbalistic exegete is able to offer but a few of the infinite Kabbalistic interpretations.[32] The concept of Kabbalah as found in the school dealing with the divine names is therefore not that of a forgotten or fragmentary lore, a closed corpus, but an open field that actually expands in accordance with any additional effort by a Kabbalist to understand the details of a text. The common denominator of all the Kabbalistic exegetical techniques mentioned in this passage is that they are intratextual: they exploit the literal resources of the text without importing conceptualizations that would create a certain concatenation of the different words of the text, as allegorical exegesis does. Eccentric and radical as these forms of exegesis may be, they nevertheless rely exclusively on the alleged potential inherent in the linguistic fabric of the text. Although the contents found in the allegorical approach can be exhausted, the Kabbalistic contents are conceived of as inexhaustible. From this point of view Abulafia, as a Kabbalist, is closer to the midrashic approach, not only because he echoes, in an exaggerated manner, the statements found in rabbinic sources, but also because of the emphasis on intratextuality. Unlike midrashic intertextuality, which is much closer to the modern deconstructionist stand, the intratextual approach is not particularly sensible to the morphemic aspects of the text. Whereas the midrashic, allegorical, Kabbalistic-symbolic, and deconstructionist approaches resort to a certain form of textual narrative because in general they preserve the grammatical functions of the words involved in the biblical narrative, in the intratextual approach this is far from obvious. The reliance on the smaller linguistic units, the phonemes, is more apparent in the intratextual approach, which, detached from external conceptualization, texts, or plots, reconstructs the deconstructed text from the constitutive phonemes. This is quite an innovative reconstruction, which is able to take into account all the original letters, or their substitutes, and weave them into the fabric of the new text.

In discussing the three angels who revealed themselves to Abraham, Abulafia mentions that their acts are conspicuous in the scriptures and that the issue of prophecy has been already clarified in Maimonides' *Guide of the Perplexed* "and other books of wisdom [namely philosophy] in a manner sufficient for those who wish to know them, if they will peruse them carefully. And the men of speculation [namely the philosophers] would apply the names of the forefathers[33] to the human intellect, and the rest of the names would refer to the powers beneath it, some closer to it and some farther away. They would refer everywhere to the Tetragrammaton and other divine names as designations of the agent intellect."[34] The allegoristic interpreters would therefore interpret the proper names, those of the forefathers and those of God, as pointing to various forms of intellect, the human and the separate one. In other words, this extratextual interpretation is quite reductive, transforming the particulars into a general terminology. From this point of view the allegorist may not be able to give an account of why the intellect or God is designated by one biblical term or another. Being part of a universalistic approach—after all, the intellects, human and cosmic, are transliteral and transnational entities—they transcend the peculiar designations found in the scriptural texts. In fact, an even better understanding of the dramas connected with these intellects can be found in the Averroistic treatises on the intellect, which served as sources of inspiration for some of Abulafia's own psychological allegories. The biblical text is understood as drawing its allegorical sense not only from another series of texts, the philosophical ones, but also from texts originally written in another language, often stemming from another culture and oriented toward a much more unified and simplistic axiology. What seems, however, to be even more striking in the allegorical approach is the absence of God: His names were allegorized as standing for the Agent Intellect, and the whole spiritual enterprise took the form of an intraintellectual affair involving the relations between the human and separate intellects.

It should be mentioned that in some cases it is quite difficult to distinguish between the human and separate intellects, and sometimes even between them and God, provided that the realm of the spiritual is continuous. This view, adopted by Abulafia in some discussions, offers a restricted domain of intellectual events as recurring in a variety of biblical stories. It is this extreme psychologization that is "remedied" by the overemphasis on divine names found in the path of names. Although the allegorist speaks of very important and positive psychological events, he nevertheless deals with a lower God, a fact that is transcended by the imposition of the Kabbalistic discourse. In other words, the ecstatic Kabbalah's adoption of interpretive allegory presents itself not as an alternative to the negative approach of the Jewish allegorists but as a higher form of interpretation that forcefully reintroduces the divine into the spiritual enterprise Abulafia calls prophecy.

In the same context Abulafia offers an example of allegorical interpretation that corroborates his argument:

> The men of speculation have determined that the name Lot is an allegory for the material intellect and that his two daughters and wife refer to the material realm. And we are instructed that the angels are the advisers of the intellect. They are the straight paths that advise the intellect to be saved from the evil ones, which refer to the limbs [of the body], whose end is to be consumed in sulphur and heavenly fire—this is the full extent of the parable.

This is in accord with what they say, that the Torah would not have deemed it important to relate such a matter, even in the event that it actually did occur, for what is the point of such a story for the man of speculation?[35]

The gist of the allegorical approach is to construe a parable, which represents naturalistic events, in order to save the significance of the biblical story. By resorting to an axiology based on the psychomachia, the allegorist exegete is able to save the embarrassing canonic text from the semimythological story and confer on it an aura of philosophical content. Allegory saves the text from its meaning by assuming that another meaning should be imposed which stems from a type of nomenclature alien to the original text. This extratextuality, unlike midrashic intertextuality, finds the solution to the canonical text by exchanging the archaic or antiquated meaning for another meaning, which often violates the original one. The uneasiness with the plain sense is expressed rather convincingly by Abulafia's typology of the attitude toward language among philosophers: "It is conceivable in only one of three ways: either it is construed on its plain sense, or it may be a parable, or it occurred to Abraham in a dream in the manner of prophecy."[36]

The alternatives opened by the philosophical approach are different, but the conclusion is the same: either the plain sense is preserved, but then the philosopher has nothing to learn from such an obsolete story; or it did not happen in the historical sense, and the canonic text is to be explored for deeper meanings. This is done either by interpreting the text allegorically, in the manner we have just seen, by transforming it into a veiled philosophical discourse that should be decoded, or by relegating the story to the realm of prophecy or prophetic dreams. In any case the Bible on its plain sense is philosophically insignificant.

Let me elaborate more on the last possibility, again by adducing a passage from Abulafia: "And if it is a prophetic dream, or a prophecy itself, it is worthy of being written in order to instruct the prophets in the methods of prophecy, and what may be derived from them regarding Divine conduct, and in any case the prophet will be able to see in it parables and enigmas."[37] Thus, the last approach, paralleling the path of the names, may provide an insight into how to reach a prophetic experience or how to know God. Indeed, Abulafia indicates in the same context that "the explanation of the Kabbalist is that they are all names and therefore worthy of being recorded."[38] He is not worried by the obsolete meaning, nor does he solve the problem by renewing the meaning by substitution. The text is elevated to the highest status, of becoming a continuum of divine names. The ecstatic Kabbalist makes quite different claims from those of the allegorist. Abulafia's approach deals with the last three of seven paths, and all three may be described as an intratextual or intercorporal approach. According to Abulafia, "every Kabbalist will invoke the name in all places [in the Bible where it occurs] as instructed by means of any of the divine attributes, because this is true and right, and this is the reason why it is necessary to inquire into names and to know, each and every one of them, to which attribute it points, because the attributes change in accordance with each and every issue. And it is known that God does not at all possess attributes that will change from one to another, but the attributes change in accordance with the nature of the creatures that are [necessarily] emanated from them."[39]

While the allegoresis of the philosophical interpreter will reduce the plethora of divine names or proper names to describe one entity, the intellect, in its various states, the ecstatic Kabbalist claims that different names correspond to the variety of creatures here below that emanated from God. On high there are no attributes that change, a critical hint at the exegetical practices of some forms of theosophical Kabbalah, but the different manners of action are projected on the divine realm from the differences in the nature of the creatures. From this vantage point the variety of names is not a case of redundancy; they should not be reduced to the status of synonyms but respected in their singularity, in order to discover a higher complexity on high. In any case, what is crucial in this last quote is the express need to respect the textual multiplicity of names, much more than the allegorist was capable of doing. It is the concern with the particulars that inspires, at least in principle, the ethos of the path of names. The absoluteness of the details of the text, much more than of its meaning, inspires the linguocentric Kabbalistic approach, which is to be contrasted even with Kabbalistic exegesis focused on symbolic interpretations of the morphemes. This concern with intratextuality differs, therefore, not only from allegoristic extratextuality but also from the midrashic and, very often, Kabbalistic symbolistic penchants for intertextuality.

Let me compare this approach to allegoresis as a kind of exegesis pointing to a general truth beyond the details of the text to the way the Christian spiritual commentaries on the scriptures were understood in the Middle Ages. According to Beryl Smalley, the spiritual attitude toward the Bible produced "many commentaries containing little exegesis," because the truth was conceived of as an infinite space to which the spiritual man is able to look through the physical surface of the text.[40] This is also true insofar as allegorical medieval interpretations are concerned; those interpreters knew the truth in advance, before the details of the text had been interpreted, a phenomenon I have called semantic radicalism. Yet whereas the Christian spiritualists knew the "truth" to be attained by their exegesis from their theological doctrine, the Jewish allegorists were inspired by the various trends of Greek thought as mediated and transformed by Arabic philosophy. Sometimes Kabbalists would say that the resort to flexible exegesis, like the combinations of letters, should be balanced by checking the results against the views of the "Torah," namely the Jewish religious accepted wisdom. New and oftentimes flexible exegetical methods invite validating structures to prevent the emergence of overly idiosyncratic results.

VII. AN ALLEGORIZATION OF NAHMANIDES' STAND

Whereas Abulafia was inclined to restrict the allegorical approach to a relative lower role in the general picture of his hermeneutical system, as the fifth of seven modes of interpretation, one of his disciples went a further step in allowing allegorical exegesis a somewhat greater role. Toward the end of the thirteenth century R. Nathan ben Sa'adyah, a Kabbalist belonging to the ecstatic school of Kabbalah who composed the book *Sha'arei Tzedeq*, wrote:

Anyone who believes in the creation of the world, if he believes that languages are conventional [then] he must also believe that they [the linguistic conventions] are of two types: the first is divine, i.e. an agreement between God and Adam, and the second is natural, i.e. based on agreement between Adam, Eve, and their children. The second is derived from the first, and the first was known only to Adam and was not passed on to any of his offspring except for Seth, whom he bore in his image and likeness. And so, the [esoteric] tradition [*ha-Qabbalah*] reached Noah. And the confusion of the tongues during the generation of the dispersion [at the tower of Babel] happened only to the second type of language, i.e. to the natural language. So eventually the tradition reached 'Eber and, later on, Abraham the Hebrew. Thus we find regarding *Sefer Yetzirah*, whose authorship is attributed to Abraham, that the Almighty revealed Himself to him.[41] And from Abraham the tradition was passed on to Isaac and then to Jacob and to his sons [the tribal ancestors]. And our forefathers were in Egypt, but the Kabbalah was in the possession of the elders of the nation, and the thing remained with them until the birth of Moses, who was at home in the house of the king, and he learned many sorts of alien lore [namely philosophical and scientific lore], and despite this fact, because of his predisposition to receive, his mind did not rest before his father, Amram, had given to him the tradition that was with them from the forefathers, blessed be their memory. And what happened is that he went out in the field and secluded himself in the desert, the "Lord of All revealed to him" in the bush and informed him and taught him and related to him the most wondrous things which remained with him until the [revelatory] event at Sinai, when He introduced him to the inmost secrets of the science of the letters . . . until he became acquainted with the essence of these letters, revealed to us from his cognition, and the essence of their distant [supernal] roots, and Moses, blessed be his memory, had arranged the Torah as a continuum of letters, which is [corresponds to] the path of [divine] names, which reflects the structure of the supernal letters; and [then] he divided it [the text of the Torah] in accordance with the reading of the commandments, which reflects the essence of the arranged lower entities.[42]

Let me start with the obvious: the Kabbalist, explicitly quoting the aforementioned passage from Nahmanides' introduction to *Commentary of the Pentateuch*, also distinguishes between two readings of the Torah, according to the path of names and the path of the commandments. Unlike Nahmanides, however, he offers an ontological distinction between the two forms of reading: the path of names reflects a metaphysical-divine realm, whereas the path of the commandments refers to a physical or human-oriented one. This understanding of the two paths is partially corroborated by a passage from one of Abulafia's own writings, where he distinguishes between what I assume is the states of the divine names that are "not combined"; that is, the order of the letters remained in its pure form and deals with things that do not perish, belonging to the account of the Chariot, a strong parallel to the "structure of the supernal letters" in the passage from *Shaʿarei Tzedeq*. On the other hand, the "combined" names, the forms of the names that do not preserve the original sequence of the letters in the divine names, stand in that passage from Abulafia for the account of Creation, which consists in transient entities, corresponding in the passage from *Shaʿarei Tzedeq* to the lower things.[43] Nahmanides' path of commandments is understood in Maimonidean terms as pointing to the world of generation and corruption, whereas the path of names stands for the account of the Chariot, namely for some form of Aristotelian metaphysics. According to another passage from the anonymous Kabbalist, the supernal letters correspond or are related to the world of names, whose existence is obscured in the thought of those who behave in accordance with the philosophical lore, which is equated with the attribute of judgment and with nature, while the messianic time will reinstate the reign of the world of names, understood as standing for the attribute of mercy.[44]

R. Nathan, like Abulafia yet somehow different from him, sometimes uses philosophy and Kabbalah against themselves, sometimes conjugating them with each other, creating a more comprehensive scheme. Nahmanides' distinction between the two paths may indeed have something to do with the distinction between the account of the Chariot and the account of Creation, as some later Kabbalists would hint at.[45] I wonder, though, whether Nahmanides' own understanding of the two accounts has anything to do with their Maimonidean interpretation, which looms under the hints of the passage from Sha'arei Tzedeq. I have opted for a theosophical interpretation of Nahmanides' two paths by alluding to a symbolic reading of the two accounts as pointing to the sefirot Hokhmah and Binah,[46] while the ecstatic Kabbalist has separated them in accordance with Maimonides' distinction between metaphysics and physics. In other words, the ecstatic Kabbalist has allegorized Nahmanides' discussion by imposing a distinction, found in Greek philosophy, between the world of eternal entities and that of generation and corruption on Nahmanides' view: the commandments have become allegories of issues found in this lower world, while the names were conceived of as allegories for the transcendental world. However, by such a dramatic shift the path of names or, according to another passage, the world of names is no longer conceived of as a lost tradition but is connected to an ever-existing and never-changing reality, which is indeed obscured nowadays but will be recaptured in the messianic time, when the prophecy will return.[47]

Someone may assume that on this point the differences between Nahmanides' implicitly lost tradition and the ecstatic Kabbalist's utopian knowledge are not so great, as both posit an absence in the present. Such a reading, however, is questionable; R. Nathan ben Sa'adyah, like Abulafia before him, has obfuscated Nahmanides' ambiguity concerning the question of the availability of the divine-names tradition and opted for the possibility of possessing it already in the post-Mosaic era—not only in the messianic time but in the lifetime of this Kabbalist himself. In other words, though offering somewhat different interpretations of Nahmanides' "sublime" tradition, the two ecstatic Kabbalists believe that they still possess what Nahmanides contends was lost long ago, in hoary antiquity.

The specific point of view of this project, pertinent to the hermeneutical move just analyzed, is the shift from a nonallegorical passage, which may have some symbolic value, namely that of Nahmanides, to an allegorical understanding that introduces clear philosophical concepts conceived to explicate the meaning of their Kabbalistic tradition. But the most conspicuous move of this Kabbalist, in comparison to Nahmanides and even to Abulafia, is the description of the history of Kabbalah. For Nahmanides, the path of names is a revelation given to Moses and presumably since then entirely forgotten. In the above passage, however, the Kabbalah is said to have already been disclosed to Adam and transmitted thereafter until the time of Moses. Thus, it is not a purely Mosaic or Sinaitic lore but an Adamic revelation, which already presupposes, despite its esotericism, a more universalist status.

What fosters this universalism of Kabbalah, however, is the picture of Moses as someone immersed in the study of many sorts of alien lore well before he was initiated in the Kabbalistic secrets. This remark is quite unusual in the Kabbalistic literature and should be understood on more than one plane: historically speaking, Moses is described, at least initially, as the product of Egyptian culture, a fact that could be ignored or marginalized by a Kabbalist but instead is remarked upon. Next, the assumption that Moses' study of alien lores—in the Jewish Middle Ages a derogatory term for philosophy—did not preclude him from receiving Kabbalah means that for the Kabbalists there is no unbridgeable gap between the two forms of thought. Indeed, as we learn from the succinct autobiography of this Kabbalist, he himself has studied and immersed himself in philosophy before becoming a Kabbalist, and I see the above description of Moses as an *apologia pro vita sua*. This was by no means an exception in the group of secondary intellectuals who played a major role in the emergence of the creative Kabbalah, as we shall see. Moreover, given that Moses is the model for the accomplished mystic and his life is understood as paradigmatic for mystics, we may infer that for this Kabbalist the study of philosophy before the study of Kabbalah is not a historical accident, either in the case of Moses or in R. Nathan's own case. Rather, this order of study can be understood as an ideal curriculum. Consequently, just as in the case of the passage from Abulafia's *Mafteah ha-Hokhmot*, so in *Sha'arei Tzedeq* philosophy and allegorical understanding of the Torah are not incidents in the cultural history of Judaism but a necessary and positive step toward the attainment of prophecy.

VIII. ALLEGORICAL COMPOSITIONS AND DIVINE NAMES

Another important use of philosophical allegory is the allegorical composition. Unlike the few instances discussed above (and many others found in Jewish philosophy and some Kabbalistic books), where the interpreted texts were not composed by authors who envisioned their writings as fraught with allegorical meanings, and where the interpretive allegory is in fact an interpolated allegorization, few Jewish treatises are written as allegories from the very beginning.

In the same years that the *Zohar* was composed in Spain as a symbolic text, R. Abraham Abulafia produced in Italy and Sicily a series of "prophetic writings," in which his revelations were committed to paper and interpreted allegorically. In my opinion, the subsequent philosophical interpretations, which are more allegorical, are only rarely a matter of later and insignificant addition to a text that initially had another literary and conceptual structure; rather, these interpretations represent an explication of conceptual elements already coded within the text. Unfortunately, the nature of the extant material and its neglect by modern scholarship means that a more detailed analysis of the literary and hermeneutical aspects of Abulafia's activity on this point remains a desideratum. This lamentable situation is exacerbated by the fact that most of the so-called prophetic books have disappeared and only their commentaries, made by Abulafia himself, are available; meanwhile, the single original prophetic text extant, a poetically oriented treatise named *Sefer ha-'Ot*, is not accompanied by a commentary. Nevertheless, it is still possible to investigate the allegorical composition and the author's interpretation, because sometimes the commentaries quote sentences from the original prophecies before offering the interpretation. Let me analyze one such instance, found in a book relating a revelation that occurred in Rome in 1280:

And the meaning of his saying "Rise and lift up the head of my anointed one" refers to the life of the souls. "And on the New Year," "and in the Temple"—this is the power of the souls. And he says: "Anoint him as a king"—anoint him as a king with the power of all the names. "For I have anointed him as a king over Israel"—over the communities of Israel, that is the commandments. And his saying "and his name I have called Shadday, like My name," [means] whose secret is Shadday like My name, and understand all the intention. Likewise his saying "He is I and I am He," and it cannot be revealed more explicitly than this. But the secret of the "corporeal name" is the "messiah of God." Also "Moses will rejoice," which he has made known to us, and which is the five urges, and I called the corporeal name as well . . . now Razi'el started to contemplate the essence of the messiah and he found it and recognized it and its power, and designated it David son of David, whose secret is Yimelokh . . . the heart of the prophet.[48]

The revelation is cast in rather traditional terms: "anointed one," "New Year," "Temple," "king," Moses, David ben David. They are interpreted, however, in rather spiritual terms: "life of the souls," "power of the souls," "the names." The allegorical approach is quite obvious in the phrase dealing with Razi'el's (Abraham Abulafia's) contemplation of the "essence of the messiah," namely the spiritual change that causes the union between man and God, and the transposition of the divine name to the human being, which is expressed in "designated it David son of David." It is Abulafia's choice to select David ben David as the personification of the powers of the soul and of the kingship, meaning spiritual growth and experience of the divine. Another clear hint at the conscious construction of a text that should nevertheless be interpreted esoterically is found in connection with the phrase "Shadday like My name," presumably an innovation of Abulafia's, followed by the warning "and understand all the intention." The allegorical mode is found not so much in the interpretive aspect, though it is also there, but much more in the construction of a narrative concerning the inauguration of the king in the Temple, at the New Year, as pointing to nontemporal and nonspacial events. What is important in this quote is the introduction of the names within the framework of the allegorical decoding. The divine names, when transferred from God to man, designate, not allegorically but quite directly, the union between the human and the divine.

In some instances it is possible to see in the transference of names a sign of a deep transformation. This is already the case in ancient Jewish mysticism, where the paragon of the Jewish mystics, Enoch, became an angelic being named Metatron and in addition received seventy divine names. Whereas the ancient texts refer to a corporeal translation on high, an extension of the body, which in my opinion is part of an attempt to restore the lost stature of Adam, in ecstatic Kabbalah the transformation takes place mainly on the spiritual level, as in the above passage. It is not a classical installation of a king, or of the king-messiah, that is dealt with here but the spiritualization of man, who will master his body and inclinations and become his own savior. Ancient mythology of the king-messiah, whose corporeal status was changed by his installation by means of coronation and anointment, implying a deification of the king in flesh and blood, was interpreted as pointing to the spiritual change in the consciousness of the mystic, who is able to become deified in spirit.

In the above passage Abulafia offers an allegorical reading of the ancient ritual by describing the ancient installation ritual in his own words, which were selected so as to imply, by their very precise structure, their allegorical meaning. So, for example, the four strings of numerically identical terms presuppose that words included in the corporeal description of the king-messiah are equivalent to their allegorical explications. Let me start with the main string: *rosh meshihi* (head of my anointed one) = *hayyei ha-nefashot* (life of the souls) = *u-ve-rosh ha-shanah* (and on the New Year) = *u-ve-veit ha-miqdash* (and in the Temple) = *koah ha-nefashot* (power of the souls) = *timshehehu ke-melekh* (anoint him as a king) = *mi-koah kol ha-shemot* (from the power of all the names) = 869. The corporeal aspects, the head of the messiah, the time and the place, are translated into spiritual terms related to the soul, on the one hand, and the divine names, on the other. (This latter nexus will recur in another passage of Abulafia, as we shall soon see.) However, the precise numerical equivalence of so many elements in a rather short text demonstrates quite convincingly that the narrative dealing with the corporeal aspects was carefully designed to include the allegorical interpretation as an organic translation of the meaning of the ancient mythological installation of the king. In other words, the prophetic tracts have a twofold structure: they consist in a short, rather apocalyptic and "primitive" narrative that corresponds, on another level, to the spiritual development of the soul; and the allegorical reading of them is compulsory, given the numerical identity of the various parts of the passage.

This twofold strategy of composition seems to be unique to Abulafia's way of writing, and it stresses the intratextual feature of his approach. Unlike regular philosophical allegory, which is dependent on external terminology from Arabic and Maimonidean sources, in Abulafia the implication is that only within language is it possible to find the solution of the meaning, because one concept is connected to another not only by the narrative syntax but also by the numerical value that sends the reader to the corresponding term in the allegorical interpretation. According to such a composition, allegory is a much less conventional but quite integral type of relationship that is built into the structure of the text.

Let me, for the time being, move on to the second string: yisra'el = qehillot [congregations] = ha-mitzvot [commandments] = 541. The numerical value 541 is a very common gematria in Abulafia's writings, whose key is found not in this string but in numerous other passages in Abulafia's writings, including an important discussion in the context of the above-quoted passage from Sefer ha-'Edut.[49] The missing clue is the concept of Agent Intellect (or Active Intellect), the last of the ten intellects, which informs all cognitive processes in this world. Its meaning is influenced by Neoaristotelian interpretations (disseminated in Greek, Arabic, and Jewish philosophies) of Aristotle's rather ambiguous nous poetikos, which has usually been rendered in Hebrew as sekhel ha-po'el, a phrase whose gematria is 541. According to some passages, Yisra'el (Israel) represents not only a particular nation on the mundane plane but also a spiritual essence identical to the Agent Intellect, which is regarded as the sum of all the forms found here below, a concept also referred to by the term qehillot. Thus, we may again interpret this string as dealing ostensibly with corporeal aspects but hinting at spiritual ones. However, just as the theme of the names has been introduced in the first string, I assume (again with support from many other passages) that Yisra'el also stands for another concept, yesh ra'al, a reinterpretation of the consonants YSR'L to which Abulafia and some other Kabbalists in his entourage often resort. Yesh means simply "there is," and the gematria of the remaining word, ra'al, is 231. This figure represents all possible combinations of two letters of the Hebrew alphabet, as described in some versions of Sefer Yetzirah, the source for many of the combinatory techniques that were to develop in Judaism. This combinatory technique not only was of mathematical import but was also pregnant with mystical and magical valences, for by combining and reciting the 231 combinations, one is able to create a golem or to reach a prophetic experience. Thus, in addition to the allegorical implications of the name Yisra'el, as standing for a metaphysical entity whose conceptualization stems from Greek ontology as understood by Arab and Jewish thinkers, it is quite plausible that the prophetic dimension of Kabbalah is also implied here. Indeed, this assertion is crucial for understanding the whole passage. The anointment of the head of the messiah, discussed in the first part of the quote, implies a descent of the oil as part of the unction, a process that is paralleled by the descent of the ideas, or forms, from the Agent Intellect onto the mind of the prophet.

Moreover, in an important passage in another prophetic writing of Abulafia's, the Agent Intellect, the human intellect, and the persona of the historical messiah were all described as messiah. While the historical person parallels the path of the righteous and the human intellect the path of the philosophers, the Agent Intellect may stand, as it often does in Maimonides and Abulafia, for the source of prophecy and hence may imply the path of prophecy. Thus, the intellectual development of the intellect—or the souls—in our passage is understood in soteriological terms, implying a messianic experience attained, according to Abulafia, by means of the combination of letters and recitation of divine names.

This nexus between the body of the messiah, his intellect, and the source of intellection is paralleled by the third string of gematrias in the passage under scrutiny here: *ha-shem ha-gashmi* (the corporeal name) = *mashiah ha-shem* (the anointed of the name) = *yismah mosheh* (Moshe will rejoice) = *hamishah yetzarim* (five urges) = 703. The first three phrases all contain the consonants *h*, *sh*, and *m*, either in *ha-shem* (God, "the Name") or in *mosheh* (Moshe). The meaning of this occurrence is quite explicit in a passage from Abulafia's *Sefer ha-'Edut*: "Moshe knew God [*ha-shem*] by means of the name [*ha-shem*], and God [*ha-shem*] also knew Moshe by means of the name [*ha-shem*]."[50]

In other words, by means of the recitation of the divine name Moses knew God and God knew Moses, or, in the terms of the passage under discussion, by means of the name Moses became the anointed of God. The phrase *ha-shem ha-gashmi* stands for the name of Moses and the names of the forefathers that have become, by means of a complex linguistic transformation, divine names.[51] On this point, however, we must pay attention to the gist of the passage: though speaking of Moses and his transformation into the messiah, his cleaving to God, Abulafia also mentions the forefathers' names, and by doing so he includes the name of Abraham. If we recall an earlier quotation from a prophetic book addressed to Abraham, which is hinted at in this passage by the angelico-theophoric name Razi'el—both names amount in gematria to 248—there can be no doubt that the messiah hinted at here is none other than Abraham Abulafia, who claimed to be a messiah. This is also implied in the fourth string: *david ben david*[52] = *yimlokh*[53] = *lev ha-navi'* (heart of the prophet) = 100 means that the entity named David son of David will reign. A few lines earlier in this book, however, God mentioned the anointment of Abulafia as a king. Abulafia sees himself as David son of David. I assume that the second David is none other than the Agent Intellect, and the phrase "David the son of David" stands for the union between the human and the separate intellects.

This reading may be corroborated by a third expression in the above passage, ve-'anokhi hu' (I and He), which amounts to 99, a figure that for the Kabbalists is practically identical to 100. Thus, the whole discourse is not merely an allegorical composition showing how one may become a messiah by reciting divine names. It should be understood also as telling, on a more esoteric level, not only the atemporal truth about the spiritual path, understood in soteriological terms, but also the very temporal truth—and perhaps an issue as important for Abulafia as the atemporal one—namely, that Abulafia himself is a messiah and a prophet. Allegory here is not only a compositional technique, an interpretive device, but also, and more eminently, an esoteric means to point to one's own extraordinary mystical attainment and redemptive role in history. The mystical attainment is clearly alluded to by the phrase dictated to Abulafia by God, "He is I and I am He," which should be understood as pointing to a mystical union between the human and the divine.[54]

Allegory may, therefore, play a more general role in telling the story of all the souls striving for the spiritual redemption and extreme mystical attainments, as indeed it does in many of Abulafia's writings. In some of his discussions, however, it stands for his own soul in a more esoteric way. Spiritual allegory, which is the expression that seems to me more appropriate for both decoding the biblical text and composing one's own narrative, may designate a special application of allegorical techniques for self-expression rather than for a more general exegesis and literary composition dealing with atemporal truths. What is important in this instance of spiritual allegory, however, is that the mystical path and the mystical attainment were not expressed solely by intellectualistic terminology drawn from the medieval philosophical patrimony, but also by resorting to linguistic devices and to personal and divine names that are intertwined with more classical forms of allegory.

IX. INTERPRETATION AND MYSTICAL EXPERIENCE IN ECSTATIC KABBALAH

The import of a plethora of new terms in order to convey the intellectualistic and experiential understandings of the Bible is part of what I described above as the intercorporal enterprise.[55] The massive resort to it was one of the reasons for the tensions created by the emergence of extensive writings, including Jewish philosophical exegesis, and it became more prominent during the debates related to the second Maimonidean controversy. Although Maimonides' disciples claimed a faithful approach to the Jewish heritage, their opponents described their exegetical enterprise as heretical.[56] To what extent the allegorists were sincere in offering their intercorporal interpretations, or to what extent allegorical interpretation was regarded as alien to the Kabbalists, is a very complex issue that transcends our concern here. There can be no doubt, provided the inclusive approach of many Kabbalists, that theosophical Kabbalists like R. Bahya ben Asher, his master the Rashba', and sporadically other Kabbalists as well, adopted this exegetical path.[57] This is even more the case, as we have seen in this chapter, for the ecstatic Kabbalists.

I would like to address now the question of the perception an ecstatic Kabbalist could have while offering interpretations of the Bible. As we have seen, Abulafia resorted to the verb hadesh, which can be translated as "innovate" or "create," to point out the inventive aspect of exegesis.[58] Two additional discussions may illuminate the perception of the interpretive moment. The first stems from Abulafia's Sefer Gan Na'ul:

> It is incumbent to revolve the entire Torah, which is [consists] in the names of the Holy One, blessed be He, and it is incumbent to innovate new wonders on each and every letter and on each and every word, from time to time. And it is incumbent to inquire into one word and connect it to another, and then leave the second and look for a third to connect it with it [the first], and then another, sometimes at their middle, sometimes at their beginning, sometimes at their end, sometimes by their numbers and sometimes by their permutations, until he will exit from all his initial thoughts and will innovate other, better than them, always one after another. And despite the fact that he does this while the holy name is sealed within his blood, he will not feel until it will move from its place and the blood will not run from his face by the attribute of judgment together with that of joy, he did not achieve anything from the prophetic comprehension. But it is known that when the Name, whose secret is in blood and ink,[59] began to move within him, and he will feel it, as one who knows the place of a stone which is within him, he will then know that the knowledge of the Name acted in him, and it began to cause him to pass from potentiality to actuality, and since then he will be judged by all the attributes.[60] And he should stand forcefully in the war with them, because they are the emissaries of the supernal, testing and examining his power . . . and he should always implore the Supreme Name to save him from the examination of the attributes, so that he will be considered innocent in the supernal court.[61]

An interesting chain of interpretive methods is expounded here. First and foremost is the claim that each and every letter should be the subject of an effort of interpretation. This atomizing exegesis does allow, according to some statements by Abulafia, the contention that each separate letter is a world in itself.[62] This method does not, however, involve the most cherished of Abulafia's exegetical techniques: the combination of letters of the canonical text. When presenting this technique he offers a more complex, detailed, and experiential account. First the contemplative exegete moves from one word to another as they appear in the biblical text; then he associates the beginnings of each of these words to one another, or their middles or their ends. This second device is itself an exegetical technique, found earlier in Ashkenazi Hasidism but put in practice by Abulafia under the name *seter*—which means "secret"—whose consonants stand for the three major constituents of the exegetical method: the end (*sof*), the middle (*tokh*), and the beginning (*rosh*).[63] It should be mentioned that Abulafia not only proposed it as an exegetical model to be applied to the Bible but also used it to compose a short esoteric text that may be understood only when resorting to this type of exegesis.[64] Moreover, these three elements play a role in Abulafia's mystical technique.[65] This and other exegetical practices are intended to remove old thoughts and invite new ones, a process that is the reason why he resorts to the term "innovation."

The physiological aspects of the process described above are less transparent. Abulafia's language is not very clear, and in the following I offer what seems to me to be a plausible understanding of the text. Abulafia assumes the existence of two stages: during the first one the divine name is sealed in the blood, but he does not feel it, and the blood does not run from his face. I assume that during this stage the practicant is still aware of himself, the divine power or name not having taken possession of him. This stage is described as preprophetical. As only the blood is mentioned, I assume that this stage is connected with the plene spelling of the Tetragrammaton.[66] On the other hand, during the second stage the practicant is aware that the divine name is activating or moving him, but this time both blood and ink are mentioned, a fact that for Abulafia means the activation of both the imaginary faculty (the blood) and the intellectual one, which is referred to explicitly and connected to the ink.[67] Indeed, the advanced stage conducive to a mystical experience is described elsewhere by the ecstatic Kabbalist as follows:

The hairs of your head will begin to stand up and to storm. And your blood—which is the life blood which is in your heart, of which it is said,[68] "for the blood is the soul," and of which it is likewise said,[69] "for the blood shall atone for the soul"—will begin to move out because of the living combination which speaks, and all your body will begin to tremble, and your limbs will begin to shake, and you will fear a tremendous fear, and the fear of God shall cover you . . . And the body will tremble, like the rider who races the horse, who is glad and joyful, while the horse trembles beneath him.[70]

This physiological process is explained in more spiritual terms immediately beforehand: "And his intellect is greater than his imagination, and it rides upon it like one who rides upon a horse and drives it by hitting it with [a whip] to run before it as it wills, and his whip is in his hand to make it [the imagination] stand where his intellect wills."[71] I assume that these two stages described in *Sefer Gan Na'ul* are reflected, using more specific terminology in the above-mentioned *Sha'arei Tzedeq*, where the terms *rashut 'enoshit* and *rashut 'elohit*, respectively, point to the human power or authority and the divine one.[72]

How are these events related to interpretation? Obviously, there is a move from the canonical sequence of letters in the Bible to one that is conceived of as a continuum of the divine names. This move may point to the first stage, where the name is sealed in the blood. The second stage assumes a prophetic experience during which the mystic encounters different powers, described as divine attributes, and has to withstand these encounters. This is what the text says explicitly. However, on the basis of many discussions in Abulafia's writings my assumption is that these powers are intensifications of the human faculties, like imagination and intellect, regarded as separate entities in Neoaristotelian psychology. Withstanding such an experience is tantamount to an examination or ordeal. These processes of examination are reminiscent of the biblical ordeals of Abraham and the prophets. Indeed, in one of his prophetic books a supernal power is reported to have told Abulafia, "You have been victorious in my war, and you have changed the blood of my forehead, and its nature and color, and you have stood up to all the tests of my thoughts. Ink you have raised, and upon ink you shall be aggrandized; the letter you have sanctified, and by means of the letter and wonder you shall be sanctified."[73]

Thus, the changing of the blood into ink is the basic metaphor for the intellect's overcoming the imaginative power. Whatever the precise affinities between the transformation of the ordinary order of the text into divine names, and the physiological and spiritual transformations undergone by the exegete, it is obvious that a radical transformative exegesis induces strong transformative experiences. By structuring the biblical text into divine names, the mystic is inviting God into his blood, is activated by the divine presence, receives prophetic inspiration, and is ultimately united with the divine.

How is this prophetic inspiration achieved through the exegetical process? Let us have a look in another book of Abulafia's:

After you find the appropriate preparation for the soul, which is knowledge of the method of comprehension of the contemplation of the letters, and the one who apprehends it will contemplate them as though they speak with him, as a man speaks with his fellow, and as though they are themselves a man who had the power of speech, who brings words out of his mind, and that man knows seventy tongues, and knows a certain specific intention in every letter and every word, and the one who hears it apprehends it in order to understand what he says, and the one hearing recognizes that he does not understand, except for one language or two or three or slightly more, but he [that one] understands that the one speaking does not speak to him in vain, except after he knows all the languages; then every single word within him is understood according to many interpretations.[74]

The dialogical aspects of Abulafia's mystical experiences have been analyzed elsewhere, and I would prefer not to dwell on them here. My main concern is status of the letters as revealing. This experience is achieved after some preparations, as is indicated at the beginning of the passage, and I consider them to be pertinent for the concept of interpretation as understood by Abulafia. Of special interest is that the letters of the Bible do not address the recipient of the revelation solely in Hebrew, but their message should be decoded in all the possible languages.

Let me now turn to a third example of the nexus between exegesis and mystical experience. One of the most widespread treatises of ecstatic Kabbalah, the anonymous *Sefer ha-Tzeruf*, which is extant in many manuscripts in two Hebrew versions and in a Latin translation by Flavius Mithridates, includes a comparison between man, described as microcosmos, and the Torah:

Likewise in the Torah and its letters there are intelligences and intelligibles,[75] active and recipients of power, like the intellect that moves the sphere [or circle], which is the [hylic] matter that receives the power or the intellect that moves it, and actualizes it to the form, which is *in actu* that creates its meaning.[76] So also are the plain senses of the Torah and the form of the letters like the matter, and by the motion of the intellect the secrets planted within them are created out of them.[77] This is the reason why the sage allegorized them,[78] telling interpretations and allegorical things.[79] And the purpose of the general principle of all of them is that from the attainment of the wisdom you should understand that [you] are the supernal chariot for the Purpose of Purposes, blessed be He and His name. And the plain senses are like the matter of the sphere, and the form and the mover are the intellect and the intelligible found within it. And the motion within the mover is the intellect. Behold, this is the secret of the doer, of the matter, of the form, and of the purpose. The intellect is the doer, the matter is the form of the letters and the plain senses of the words. And the form is the intelligible understood or cognized from them. And the purpose is the Purpose of the Purposes, blessed be He and blessed be His name. And behold that the sphere corresponds to the heart, and it is the words, and it is the intermediary, and it is the praise allotted to it, not as a necessary thing but as a possible one. And by this several secrets will be clarified, elucidated, accumulated, if you are an illuminated one.[80]

What is the underlying vision here? I assume that the Aristotelian vision, in its medieval Averroistic version, inspired the entire passage: the matter, namely the letters of a word, includes within it all the possibilities, which are actualized by the human intellect, which manipulates the letters so that meanings, the intelligibles, emerge. This explanation is paralleled on the cosmic level by the extraction of forms from the matter by the motion of the sphere, according to medieval Neo-aristotelian theory. The forms emerging from this motion correspond to the meaning, or the allegorical interpretations, extracted from the words or letters. So far we have accounted for three of the four causes that Aristotle surmised are to be found in any action: doer, matter, and intelligible form. The last and most important one is the purpose, which in this case is God, described explicitly as the Purpose of Purposes. How is this purpose described within the interpretive enterprise? As the anonymous Kabbalist put it expressly, the ultimate purpose of all the interpretations is to guide someone to become the chariot of God, to become close to Him, which means, in my opinion, to attain an experience of adherence to God. By doing so, the mystic reaches the experience attained by the forefathers, who were described in a famous midrashic dictum as the chariot of God.[81] In fact, the mystical experience is also understood by Abulafia as similar to the Mosaic and prophetic one, which were the source of the canonical texts. So, for example, he wrote in an untitled treatise:

> It is already known that from the tree of life prophecy, Torah, and commandments come. Because from where should these three come if not from the [place] of the secrets of the sacred letters, and who will receive them if not the tongue found between the two hands? Behold, I had already announced to you the wonders when disclosing the secret of the three worlds, the supernal, the median [the celestial world], and the mundane . . . and the tongue between hands [it is said][82] "All the time will your clothes be white

and oil on your head should not lack." Man asks himself, What is the oil on my head? and he himself answers saying, On my head there is the Torah, the median [ha-ʾemtzaʿyit].[83,84]

Thus, all the interpretations should be understood as leading to the same main principle: the attainment of a mystical experience. Such an experiential understanding of the Chariot, the Merkavah, is found in later Kabbalah and in Polish Hasidism.[85] However, unlike Abulafia's more instrumental approach to the role of the Torah as conducive to an experience that strives to cleave to a totally spiritual or intellectual entity, Hasidic texts analyzed at the end of Chapter 6 invite a less instrumental function.

X. TWO LEVELS OF THE TORAH

Let me attempt to explicate the way in which Abulafia would understand the relations between the two levels of the Torah: the plain sense, represented in some important cases as the Torah of blood, or imaginative-exoteric sense (see Appendix 2), and the intellectual sense, the Torah of ink, or intellectual-esoteric sense. In some passages in Sitrei Torah Abulafia contends that it is impossible to invalidate either of the two senses:

> Today there are five thousand and forty years since the time that the world was both created and eternal. And if it is created alone it is not important to speak about, because everything that teaches at the beginning of thought that the plain sense of the Torah is true without having a parabolic meaning, we shall believe it immediately without any doubt, as it is, and it is sufficient. And if it is eternal from one point of view, and eternal from another point of view, there is no need to speak about it, because the aspect of the creation suffices in order to innovate the plain sense of our Torah. And if it will teach the aspect of eternity according to the esoteric sense we shall lose nothing, namely the secrets of the Torah. Because the whole intention is to prove the truth according to comprehension and to remove the absurd thought from the hearts. Because if the world is eternal and we believe in creation it would be a lie, and so too if it is created and we believe that it is eternal. But since we believe in the development[86] of the creation, as it had been testified to by the true Torah . . . we should not worry about determining which of the two ways is the true one.[87]

Thus, Abulafia believes that a synthetic approach is better than any of the two more puristic alternatives. In fact, he hints at the fullness involved in the complexity of the assumption that the world is both eternal and created. This is the attitude of the prophets and the prophetic Kabbalists, and it is the reason for the superiority of this form of understanding. Again, in another quote, he indicates:

> According to its essence the Torah comprises two sorts of reality, and both are good. They are the plain and esoteric senses, both being true; and this should be understood from the existence of the body together [with the soul][88] which are together, one is created and one is eternal, this is the exoteric and that is the esoteric, as if this is the parable and that is the signified, but both are together. And this wondrous hint should be sufficient for you.[89]

Earlier in the same book he writes:

> The plain sense of the Torah is a definitive truth, and its secrets are an ultimate truth, and both together are one in their essence. You should understand and contemplate this secret and its words one by one. You should know the source of the thing, [and] by which concept it should be conceptualized according to the human intellect, and what is worthy to be believed in accordance with the influx stemming from the divine intellect, related to the three issues I have hinted at: the innovation of the world and its eternity, the parable of the new and primordial Torah, and the plain sense of the Torah and its esoteric sense.[90]

We see that Abulafia, the spiritualist who attempted to build a mystical system that teaches ways to transcend normal consciousness takes pain to assert that the plain sense is also good and necessary, though certainly not as important as the esoteric one. This line of argumentation is also found in the writings of one of Abulafia's anonymous followers, the Kabbalist who composed *Sefer ha-Tzeruf*, which has been mentioned above.[91]

Before turning to some more general observations, I would like to point out the affinity between Abulafia's spiritualistic hermeneutics and that found in a series of Jewish commentaries written in Arabic starting in the beginning of the thirteenth century in Egypt and then later in the Middle East by descendants of Maimonides and others. Under the strong impact of Sufi hermeneutics and mystical techniques, the Jewish authors, most eminently R. Abraham Maimuni, offered spiritual allegories that resemble some of Abulafia's interpretations.[92] The extent of the impact of those developments on Kabbalah is still a matter of dispute. Although I consider it to be evident in the case of ecstatic Kabbalah as it has been formulated since the end of the thirteenth century, in the generation of Abulafia's students outside Spain it is hard to substantiate the influences on the earlier phase of Kabbalah in general. Such a possibility should not, however, be neglected.[93]

XI. TORAH AS AGENT INTELLECT

One of the major developments that nourished Jewish mysticism was the growing interest in late antiquity and in medieval literature of the role played by themes related to Enoch, a marginal figure in the Bible. Enochic themes become more and more important, especially when Jewish mystics were looking for a model for human transformation during a mystical experience, following the dictum "Enoch is Metatron."[94] The metamorphoses of Enoch into the angel Metatron and the different functions attributed to that angel in Kabbalistic literature has already attracted the attention of scholars, and much more should be done in this field.[95] R. Abraham Abulafia is indubitably one of the Kabbalists fascinated by the angel Metatron. He took upon himself the mystical name Razi'el, related to Metatron, which in gematria is the numerical equivalent of his given name, Abraham,[96] but also speculated about the various identifications of Metatron with the supernal Torah as the cosmic Agent Intellect.[97] Some of Abulafia's Metatronic discussions have antecedents in early mystical literature, although he consistently interpreted the mythological figures of Metatron allegorically, as pointing to intellectual matters.[98] Such a tradition has to do with the identification of Metatron with the scroll of the Torah, adduced by R. Abraham ibn Ezra in the name of unknown persons: "There are those who say that the angel is the Torah scroll, for the verse states, 'My name is within him.'"[99,100] Although ibn Ezra himself rejected this view, and I am unable to corroborate this tradition. Nevertheless, it is obvious that through ibn Ezra's commentary this tradition remained part of the Jewish tradition. Abulafia's writings contain various formulations dealing with the identity between an intellectualistic concept of Torah and the Agent Intellect. I have brought up elsewhere numerous discussions of this issue from Abulafia's writings and his immediate sources, and I would like to add here one more passage, found in an untitled manuscript. When interpreting the verse u-vaharta ba-hayyim[101] Abulafia asserts that "there is a great secret pointing to that upon which the life of people depend, whose secret is the tenth angel, and it is the secret of the Torah because the [word] 'And thou should choose [u-vaharta]' amounts to ha-torah. And ba-hayyim is a secret, and is the knowledge of the Tetragrammaton, Yod He' Vav He'. Behold, the secret of the Torah is life which depends always upon the Torah."[102]

There can be no doubt that the tenth angel stands for the tenth cosmic intellect, which is identical to Metatron. Real life is to be understood in the context of Abulafia's writings as the life of the human intellect, which depends upon the Agent Intellect, namely the supernal Torah. This spiritual dependence of the human upon a supernal angel is reminiscent of Muslim spirituality, which resorts to an angelology, especially as expounded in ibn 'Arabi.[103] However, immersed as

Abulafia was in numerical exegesis, he founded his passage on the identity between "life," namely the sublime attainment of the intellect, and the union with
the divine name, as be-hayyim and the numerical value of the consonants of the
Tetragrammaton plus their plene spelling amount to the same sum, 70 or 71.

Let us move now to another formulation, which deserves a more detailed
analysis. In one of his commentaries on the *Guide of the Perplexed* Abulafia wrote:

> The soul is a portion of the divinity, and within her there are 231 gates [*yesh
> ra'al*], and it is called "the congregation of Israel" that collects and gathers
> into herself the entire community under her power of intellect, which is
> called the "supernal congregation of Israel," the mother of providence,
> being the cause of providence, the intermediary[104] between us and God.
> This is the Torah, the result of the effluence of the twenty-two letters.[105]

I chose this passage in order to show how one short discussion is able to
encode a variety of conceptual corpora. Let me start by remarking that this is a
rather uncharacteristic passage: Abulafia was concerned with the intellect, not
with the soul, and the divinity of the soul is quite weird in an Aristotelian or
Maimonidean system, which Abulafia shared to a very great extent. I assume that
here, as in some other cases, there is a vestige of an earlier tradition that was not
sufficiently adapted to Abulafia's way of thought. In any case, the soul is conceived
to be a portion of divinity in a way reminiscent of Neoplatonism and theosophical
Kabbalah. This divine soul harbors the 231 gates that point to the primordial
Torah (as we shall see in much more detail in the next chapter), and Abulafia
mentions Torah explicitly at the end of the passage. Moreover, we may assume
that either Abulafia or his source did not intend human souls in general but the
souls of the people of Israel, for two reasons: the phrase *knesset yisra'el* occurs twice
in the passage, and the Hebrew consonants that R'L, which denote the 231 gates,
are part of the word *yisra'el*, as Abulafia and the young Gikatilla repeat so many
times in their writings. It is quite reasonable to assume that the two terms *knesset
yisra'el* stand for the human intellect and the supernal one, which is identical with
the Agent Intellect and the human intellect.[106] The feminine terminology used by
Abulafia to designate the Agent Intellect is also strange in his mystical axiology,
where the source of knowledge is regarded metaphorically as masculine. Perhaps
the resort to such a reference has to do with an earlier Kabbalistic source, which
stems from another way of thinking. This quote may be understood as pointing to
a triunity of God, soul of Israel, and Torah, in the vein of the famous but much
later formula *qudesha' berikh hu', 'Orayta' vi-yisra'el had hu'*, which has been mentioned several times in earlier discussions.[107]

Abulafia's Kabbalistic system, as represented in the two passages, brings together five different forms of speculation derived from diverging corpora: the anomian theory of linguistic combinatory, stemming from *Sefer Yetzirah* and represented here by the 231 gates and the twenty-two letters, and the resort by Hasidei Ashkenaz to combinations of letters and gematria; the nomian concept of the Torah; the Heikhalot concern with Metatron; and the philosophical interest in the Agent Intellect and the rabbinic term *knesset yisra'el*. However, the conceptual layers that determined the meaning of the complex of ideas emerging from the last passage—and many others in Abulafia's writings—are two: that of *Sefer Yetzirah* and its followers and medieval Neoaristotelianism, which means two types of anomian thinking. I would say that while the philosophical corpus expands and changes the conceptual cargo of the three other layers, *Sefer Yetzirah* and mathematical methods provided the exegetical means that brought these diverging layers together. Or, to return to one of the recurrent claims of the present work: the broader the expansion of the conceptual cargo of a certain corpus or corpora, the more eccentric the exegetical methods that have to be put to work.

XII. ALLEGORY AND SYMBOLS

In ecstatic Kabbalah, following Neoaristotelian medieval literature, allegory was conceived therefore not as an alien form of discourse but, on the contrary, as an important method for interpreting Torah, for reinterpreting some forms of Jewish postbiblical esoteric tradition, and even for composing Kabbalistic writings. From this point of view there is no radical difference between Maimonides' allegorization of ancient Jewish esotericism and the ecstatic Kabbalist's allegorization of Jewish canonical writings. In any case, after Maimonides' powerful introduction of allegoresis in Jewish medieval exegesis it became difficult for many Jewish intellectuals, for good or for bad, to neglect it, and as soon as this approach was accepted, it moved into many realms of exegesis of the sacred scriptures.

The allegorical impulse expanded and entered more and more domains of Kabbalah as this form of mystical literature developed. This is not the place to elaborate on the strengthening of some allegorical impulses in some forms of early-seventeenth-century Kabbalistic interpretations of Lurianic Kabbalah, which escalated the role of allegoresis just a generation after the acceleration of the resort to the variegated mythical aspects of Kabbalah in the thought of the famous Safedian master.[108] Thus, although we may refer to a preponderance of symbolism in some important forms of Kabbalah, the theosophical-theurgical ones, and of allegory in a few others which, though less central, were still influential types of Kabbalah, no definitive attribution of this form of exegesis solely to Jewish philosophers, on the one hand, and its absence or rejection in Kabbalistic literature as a whole, on the other, is historically or phenomenologically accurate. Instead of attempting to distinguish sharply between Kabbalah, as a generic term, and philosophy—again a rather reified description insofar as so many of the Jewish medieval sources are concerned—or between allegory and symbolic forms of discourse, I propose to strike a different balance that will conceive the vast domain of Kabbalistic literature, as is the case with Jewish philosophy, as much richer, much more open and variegated, and much more capable of absorbing different forms of exegesis.[109] Such a variegated picture of the phenomenology of Kabbalah will facilitate a better answer to the emergence of spiritualistic allegoresis in eighteenth-century Hasidism. Far from a neutralization of elements in Lurianic Kabbalah done by Hasidic masters as an answer to the crisis created by Sabbateanism, some elements in Hasidic exegesis are similar to and perhaps also influenced by ecstatic Kabbalah.[110]

12

TZERUFEI ʾOTIYYOT
Mutability and Accommodation
of the Torah in Jewish Mysticism

I. Four Modes of Torah Mutability in Kabbalah

The absorbing quality of the Torah, a trait related to many of the issues we have addressed so far in this book, assumes that the nontextual reality either is a small part of the broader textual reality or is sustained by it. This nontextual reality was conceived of as consonant with the textual one and as reflecting changes taking place within it. The leading assumption has been, nevertheless, that the textuality of existence is informed by the temporal and hierarchical priority of the concept of the Torah, whose structure and content reality is believed to imitate. In one way or another creatures were regarded as being accommodated to the structure of the primordial Torah, not vice versa. This type of relationship was inspired by a rather static vision of the Torah. The eternity and immutability of the Torah was considered to be one of the principles of Judaism, especially since its formulation in the sixth and seventh tenets of Maimonides' Thirteen Principles of Faith. One of the main elements of this principle is the concept, established long before Maimonides, of inviolability, which means that no single letter should be added to or subtracted from the sacred scriptures.[1] Kabbalists and Hasidic thinkers also adopted this view, as a plethora of examples corroborate. So, for instance, we learn from an interesting formulation of R. Moses Hayyim Ephrayyim of Sudylkov that "the Torah is eternal, and it is found in every man and in every time."[2]

This traditional and highly influential view notwithstanding, various Kabbalistic schools envisioned different sorts of textual alterations and mutations that the Torah has undergone or will undergo in the future. In rabbinic thought it is possible to discover some forms of mutability that did not move to the center of medieval speculations. So, for example, there is an assumption that the very characters in which the Bible is written, the so-called old Hebrew alphabet, were changed in the time of Ezra the scribe into the Assyrian alphabet. Moreover, the sins of Israel, as distinguished sharply from Adam's sin, were believed to have affected the structure of the Torah. The nature of the alterations that will be addressed below, however, reflects much of the deep structure of the system within which they were formulated. The very possibility of substantial changes in crucial aspects of reality should be admitted in order to allow changes in the Torah. I would say that in more static speculative systems like Maimonides' thought, which assumes a perfect deity who does not change, it is hard to allow meaningful changes in the structure of the Torah.

The various expressions of Torah mutability in Jewish mysticism fall into four main categories: the astrological, the eschatological, the Neoplatonic, and the combinatory. In the scholarly discussions of topics related to the mutability of the Torah, those views have been described without a clear distinction between the different models,[3] and I believe that the entire issue deserves a much more thorough discussion. I shall devote most of the discussions below to the last of the four categories. First, however, let me succinctly introduce the other three and offer some examples that will help to highlight the divergences between them.

The most famous type of Torah mutability has been addressed several times in modern scholarship and is related to certain forms of the theory of *shemittot* (sabbatical years) and *yovelim* (jubilee years), namely cosmic cycles of seven thousand and forty-nine thousand years, respectively. I shall designate this attitude as astrological, because the structure of this Kabbalistic thought is deeply indebted to astrological concepts of order. According to some statements of Kabbalists as early as the end of the thirteenth century, but more conspicuously in the fourteenth and fifteenth centuries, each shemittah is presided over by a sefirah of the seven lower sefirot; the nature of the creation and the processes that take place during this period are affected by the special qualities of that sefirah. This stand implies the specific nature of the Torah, whose decrees change in accordance with the corresponding sefirah. In those cases in Kabbalistic literature, especially the mid-fourteenth-century Byzantine *Sefer ha-Temunah*, where the governing sefirah is Gevurah, the attribute of stern judgment, the laws of the Torah are considered to be very harsh. The assumption is that in the future eon the text of the Torah will change and adopt more lenient laws.[4] According to this particular version of the cosmic cycles, the present sefirah is the worst, as are, therefore, the laws of the Torah. The antinomian leanings of this book were duly detected by Gershom Scholem, and they are the result of the impact of astrological views, quite widespread in the Middle Ages, that envisioned changes in religion as due to astrological changes taking place cyclically in the celestial world. The changing of the structure of the Torah relevant during a certain eon reflects, therefore, a supernal shift that does not constitute a progressive development but varies with the specific natures of the various sefirot.

What seems to me to be characteristic of this model is that, eschatological as this view is, the envisioned change does not consist in revelation of the secrets of the Torah but in the successive emergence of other texts, which have their own secrets. Moreover, the basic eschatological stand of this model can be described as *macrochronic*, as it deals with cosmic units of time, beyond the scope of individuals and even nations.[5] Radical as this theory may appear, it influenced a series of influential Kabbalists, like the anonymous author of *Sefer ha-Peliy'ah* and R. David ibn Avi Zimra, whose *Magen David* is permeated by discussions on the mutability of the Torah.

The second category of Torah mutability may be roughly described as eschatological: changes occurring at the end of time will require the revelation of a new Torah, which differs from the old one and is thought to be much more sublime. Here, the change takes place within history, unrelated to cosmic upheavals, or in what I propose to call *mesochronos*.[6] This view is preceded by a famous division of mesochronos into three equal periods, each consisting of two millennia: one of chaos, the other of Torah, and the third of Messiah, a view found in both Jewish[7] and Christian sources.[8]

This view reverberated in the theosophical Kabbalah, especially in the Zoharic one, where there are two different theories. The first occurs in the main body of the Zoharic literature, particularly in those forms that belong to the 'Iddra', the most secret of the Zoharic treatises. It deals with the aspect of the Torah that is "the soul of souls," Torah of the Ancient of Days, *torah de-ʿattiq yomin*, or the Torah of the Occult Primordial Entity, and stands for the Kabbalistic layers of the Torah or for the Torah of the World to Come; or, according to other texts, ʾorayyta' *de-ʿatiqqaʾ setimaʿ*, a utopian vision of the Torah that consists in secrets that will be revealed in the messianic eon.[9] The second type of eschatological mutability is epitomized by the terms *torah de-beriyʾah* and *torah de-ʾatzilut*, which stand, respectively, for the present Torah, which is the law obeyed by persons described as slaves or servants, and the ideal one, which is pertinent only to the Kabbalistic elite. As they occur for the first time in the later layer of the Zoharic literature, their importance may be related to the acute messianic impulse characteristic of this Zoharic layer.[10]

Let me adduce one passage dealing with the Torah of Creation, which is important for some of the subsequent discussions. The anonymous author asserts that this kind of Torah "is the garment of the Shekhinah. And if man were not created, the Shekhinah would remain without covering, like the poor. Consequently, whoever sins strips, as it were, the Shekhinah of her garments. And this is man's punishment. And whoever fulfills the commandments of the Torah clothes, as it were, the Shekhinah in her garments."[11] The Torah of Creation, as explicated in this passage, constitutes a need of the Shekhinah, but it could appear only when man was created. This form of law constitutes the interaction between the divine need and human religious obligations. This is not a divine text but an accommodation to the needs of man and the Shekhinah. What seems me important to point out, however, is that this is not an accommodation to the sinful nature of man, and from this perspective the attitude toward this lower form of Torah is quite positive. Yet according to other discussions in this layer of the Zoharic literature, the Torah of Creation represents an adaptation of the exalted Torah of Emanation and is much more accommodated to human beings' sinful nature,[12] although the precise process of adaptation is not clear. This view was later developed in R. Moses Cordovero's Kabbalah, as we shall see. It should be mentioned that these two kinds of Torah had a long and influential career in Kabbalistic literature, especially in the Sabbatean one, and the main phases of their development have already been treated by many scholars.[13]

In this context it should be mentioned that the concept of the Torah of the Messiah, which was regarded as immanently subversive and radical, does not always involve a dramatic change but may serve as a conservative idea. This is the case in the manner in which R. Jacob Emden described one of the functions of the Messiah: "He should illumine the world during the exile by his Torah, so that the world will not perish."[14]

The third category, the Neoplatonic one, assumes that the revelation of the Torah is a matter of the descent of a spiritual entity into this corporeal world, a descent that is a materialization and clothing of the inner soul into a body and a garment. Unlike the midrashic view that the Torah is now found solely in the mundane world, some Kabbalistic sources, beginning with the *Book of Bahir*, refer to a supernal Torah, which is identified with a variety of divine attributes and as such coexists with the Torah as revealed here below.[15] The revelation of the inner meaning of the Torah consists, therefore, in the retrieval of the spiritual core by removing the coarse, embodied aspects of the Torah. Either in the present, for the few mystics, or in the eschatological future, for the entire nation of Israel, this removal is considered to be possible and conducive to mystical experiences. I adopted the term *Neoplatonic* for this category because it is possible to discern the impact of Neoplatonic terminology in many of the Kabbalistic discussions, as the description of the descent of the Torah is imagined as part of the process of emanation, which is characterized precisely by the Neoplatonic process of descent and materialization, the *processio*, versus the ascent and spiritualization, or *reversio*.[16] So, for example, we learn from an anonymous Kabbalistic text, apparently composed at the end of the thirteenth century or early in the fourteenth century in Castile, dealing with the "Secret of the Tablets of Law," that "things are emanated; when they are on high, in the spiritual world, they are spiritual and subtle; when they are in the world emanated from the supernal one, they are more shaped.[17] And when they are in the corporeal world, they are corporeal. So the Torah [too] is in all the worlds: when it is in the intermediary world it is more spiritual, and when it is in the separated world it is more spiritual, and so on until the [sefirah of] Hokhmah, which is the cause of the Torah."[18] The ontic descent of things, a version of *processio*, is complemented by the Torah that is described as ascending to its source in the second sefirah. This description assumes that while the emanational process created this world, it is by means of the Torah that it is possible to achieve the *reversio*.

It is interesting, though not surprising, that the view of Torah as an entity read or deciphered differently on the different levels of reality found its way into Christian thought. According to Emmanuel Swedenborg,

> The whole sacred scripture teaches that there is a God, because in its inmost content there is nothing but God, that is, the divine which proceeds from time; for it was dictated by God, and nothing can go forth from God, but what is Himself, and is divine. The sacred scripture is this in its inmost content. But in its derivatives, which proceed from the inmost content but are on a lower plane, the sacred scripture is accommodated to the perceptions of angels and men. In these also it is divine, but in another form, in which it is called the divine celestial, spiritual, and natural, which is the inmost and is clothed with such things as are accommodated to the percep-

tion of angels and men, shines forth like light through crystals, but with variety according to the state of mind which a man has acquired, either from God or from himself.[19]

It is not unlikely that the similarity between this Christian visionary's perception of the sacred scripture and the Kabbalistic one is the result of the influence of Jewish texts.[20] Those are but few examples, which can easily be multiplied, as to the theory that the Torah had to accommodate itself to the various ontic levels in order to be understood.[21]

The fourth model, the combinatory type of Torah mutability, contends that the pristine Torah was composed of exactly the same number of letters, arranged in the same sequence as they are in the common biblical text, but their combinations differ from that of the present one. The revealed Torah constitutes a different sequence of the same number of letters, one that reflects the nature and order of the present world, and the assumption is that in the future another order of letters will be achieved reflecting a new type of reality. Though similar to, and sometimes even almost identified with, the Neoplatonic theory of the descent of the Torah, the theory of letter combination as the main explanation for the appearance of the mundane Torah should be understood as basically a linguistic process. Throughout the preceding chapters ample space has been devoted to combination of letters as a method and concept widespread in Kabbalah and Hasidism. Both the technical aspects recurrent in ecstatic Kabbalah, which employed recitations of combinations of letters in order to attain mystical experiences, and the more creational and cosmological aspects prominent in Hasidism conspire to allow a unique role to this method in Jewish mystical thought, one that was not sufficiently acknowledged for the time being.[22]

Important as the differences between these models are, however, I would like to emphasize that many discussions in the Kabbalistic literature do not reflect adherence to clear-cut categories but combinations between two or more categories. More common is the conjoining of the Neoplatonic and combinatory models of mutability, and many examples will be adduced below. The first two models were combined more often in some Sabbatean circles.[23] The eschatological and the combinatory models of accommodation, too, were sometimes combined with each other.[24]

II. FROM THE SUPERNAL TO A MUNDANE TORAH

Kabbalists, however, were more flexible. Let me adduce an interesting passage written by R. Samuel de 'Uzeida, a mid-sixteenth-century Safedian author, where the Torah has not been revealed in its entirety:

The Holy One, blessed be He, did not deliver all the Torah in its entirety, because Moses was not prepared to receive it in its entirety, because it is written,[25] "Yet thou hast made him a little lower than ʾElohim," etc., and this is the reason why it is said that "Moses received," because [the disclosure] has been in accordance with the recipient in order to let us know that the revelation is according to the preparation and the receptacle that was there, and so it has been received . . . and it has been said that Moses received the Torah without *he*,[26] which would mean that he received the Torah in its entirety, but this was not the case . . . namely that what he received was the Torah but he received only a part of it, not its entirety.[27]

This passage is an excerpt from a widespread well-known text that has been widely studied for centuries. It is not exceptional but is corroborated by other parallels, including another famous commentary on the treatise ʾAvot, by R. Moses Alsheikh,[28] and the Hasidic interpretation of R. Isaac Aizik Yehudah Safrin of Komarno.[29] Those passages are but a few examples of the assumption of the existence of the Torah on a higher level, and its substance or content did not transpire in its entirety with the Sinaitic revelation. The basic assumption is that there is an ontological gap between God and His Torah, apparently because of their infinite or perfect nature on the one hand, and the human recipient, exalted as he may be, on the other hand. Complete transmission is impossible because of the limited nature of even perfecti like Moses.

Each of the two different Kabbalistic schools that traveled throughout the history of Kabbalistic literature, the theosophical-theurgical and the ecstatic, addressed one of the main quandaries related to the relationship between the primordial and the revealed Torah. The emergence of detailed theosophies, characteristic of the main strands of Kabbalah, created a certain tension between the evaluation of the mundane entities and their supernal, more spiritual archetypes. Though substantially influenced by Neoplatonism, the theosophical-theurgical Kabbalists were less inclined to a Platonic, paradigmatic, and static worldview but tended to emphasize the importance of human deeds performed here below for the processes taking place in the divine realm, not to speak of the reverence toward the book of the Torah, although it is conspicuously an artifact produced by human copyists. As seen in several cases above, and especially in Appendix 3 below, the supernal existence—in fact, preexistence—of the Torah has received substantial treatment in the Kabbalistic literature, and the underlying question as to whether the belief in the existence of a supernal, primordial, pure Torah detracts any authority from the lower Torah, which was revealed at a specific point in time and is embodied in the material world, remains to be addressed by scholars of religion.[30] I would formulate the emergence of an inner tension between a model of thought based on the assumption of a primordial Torah, related to its metaphysical status, and another based on the search for the religious plenitude as connected to the study and performance of imperatives related to the formulation of the Torah as it was revealed here below.[31] Kabbalists adopting the strategy of the theosophical-theurgical school were more inclined to describe the descent of the supernal Torah in terms of embodiment and darkening, or of the spiritual being materialized, in a manner that should be classified as Neoplatonic.

Another way of explaining the transition from one level of existence of the Torah to another was to hold that the letters of one Torah had been permuted into a new order, a technique commonly described as *tzerufei 'otiyyot*. This view is prevalent in ecstatic Kabbalah and, as we are about to see, had an impact on both Safedian Kabbalah and Hasidism. The theosophical-theurgical theme of the embodiment will be dealt with below only marginally, to the extent that it has been put together with the combinatory theories describing the descent of the Torah. I have described this technique, when used as part of the interpretive process, as deconstructive radicalism,[32] but with the descent of the Torah from one plane or another by permutation of its letters it can be called *creative radicalism*, because the pristine Torah is materialized as part of the creational process. In some cases the descent takes the form of the immersion of the linguistic elements in matter, a theory I refer to as *linguistic immanentism*.

I would now like to draw attention to a development that culminated in a mid-nineteenth-century version of the Hasidic cosmological vision of combinations of letters of the Torah, one that elaborates on early views attributed to the Besht, to R. Shne'or Zalman of Liady, to R. Levi Isaac of Berditchev, or to R. Hayyim Tirer of Chernovitz, already discussed above.[33] R. Israel Friedmann of Ryzhin was reported to have embraced a cosmological view that assumes that each of the worlds is informed by a unique combination of the six hundred thousand letters of the Torah, and a passage on this idea from his writings will serve as our main object of study in this chapter. In order to better evaluate his specific view, however, let us start with some earlier Kabbalistic and Hasidic discussions on the descent of the Torah by embodiment or by letter combinations which indubitably informed his thought. These discussions elaborate on some tendencies that had been emerging in Kabbalistic literature since the late thirteenth century but reached their apex in Cordovero's writings and those of his followers among the Kabbalists and the Hasidic authors.

Let me distinguish first between two major forms of combinatory accommodation. According to the triangular model, the core of the Torah is the divine name, and the Torah in its entirety is the explication of that name, which involves elaborate ramifications of its meaning. This model is closer to the Neoplatonic type of accommodation. The other model, represented by a double-line theory, assumes that there is no limited core of letters in the Torah but that exactly the same number of letters constitutes the two distinct "lines" of the Torah by allowing various divisions of letters in different words. According to this approach, the Torah in its original form is a continuum of divine words.

III. EXPLICATION, OR THE TRIANGULAR CONCEPT OF THE TORAH TEXT

In Gikatilla's *Sha'arei 'Orah* an important theory concerning the structure of the linguistic elements of the Torah contends that all ten divine names, which point to the ten sefirot, depend on the divine name, the Tetragrammaton. On each of these ten divine names depend numerous cognomens referring to angelic powers. Each cognomen organizes many other linguistic elements in the Bible, which refer to more mundane affairs.[34] This linguistic triangle, with the Tetragrammaton at the top and all the regular words at the bottom, assumes a certain transformation of the fewer and higher elements into lower ones, a process also described by the metaphor of the lower as the garment of the higher. In other words, the semantics of the different parts of the Torah is to be understood as informed by a strictly hierarchical structure, with one word pointing to God as comprising all the other words. The semantic order of the Torah therefore parallels the ontic structure of reality in its entirety. According to *Sha'arei 'Orah*, the Torah is a map of signs that represents the whole spectrum of being, but it does so by assuming a web of relations on the linguistic level that reflects the ontological.[35] Gikatilla does not, however, go into the details of the processes involved in transforming the higher linguistic elements into lower ones, or what he calls the weaving of the biblical text.[36] He offers no specific explanation as to the way in which the divine name is explicated by all the other words, nor how he imagined that it comprises all those words, although it is obvious that he refers to a combinatory technique.[37]

Gikatilla's basic assumption is that the texture of the Torah consists quintessentially in diverse ramifications of the letters of the Tetragrammaton; the Kabbalist who is able to understand how those ramifications emerged is able to envision the divinity of this sacred text and to cleave to God. The Kabbalistic reading of the text means the ability to use the sefirotic tree as a framework for the retrieval of the way in which the four letters of the divine name inform the ten divine names, and so on. According to Gikatilla's parable, the king, who stands for the Tetragrammaton, reveals himself to the people in war by donning a heavy garment, but gradually he removes his clothes when closer people are with him, and finally he reveals himself naked to his wife. It is possible to watch the innermost essence of the Torah, an experience that involves reducing the plurality of the diverse words of the Torah to the one original root. Here the linguistic journey from the ordinary words to the Tetragrammaton parallels the ontic *reversio* of the Neoplatonic thinkers. In late Gikatilla, the Neoplatonic model is associated with a combinatory model, though not one that deals with restructuring the division of the Torah letters in the way we shall see in the texts analyzed in the following paragraphs.

According to a passage from R. Moses Hayyim Luzzatto, the Torah consists in the text that emerges from the combinations of the letters of the divine name, the Tetragrammaton, which is the symbol of the sefirah of Tiferet, and each of the twenty-two letters of the Hebrew alphabet, which points to the sefirah of Malkhut. This view, apparently stemming from Abraham Abulafia via Cordovero's writings, addresses the explication of the divine name which becomes the Torah by resorting to the process of letter combination.[38] Indeed, according to another passage, the revelation of the Torah to each of the participants at Mount Sinai took different forms, or facets, which are no more than different "combinations of the secrets of the names."[39] This explanation is also applied to the emergence of the stories found in the Torah.[40] Interestingly, Ramhal adopts Abulafia's technique of combining letters to reach a mystical experience for quite a different purpose: to describe how the Torah emerged from within the divine realm. As we have already seen, this triangular perception of the Torah reverberated in Hasidic texts.[41]

IV. R. Abraham Abulafia and R. Nathan's *Sha'arei Tzedeq*

In addition to the triangular structure of the Torah as evolving from one simple linguistic unit into the full-fledged biblical text, there was another Kabbalistic tradition that conceived the relation between the primordial Torah and the revealed one as two textures constituted from the same number of letters and differing from each other by their various letter combinations. Already found in a premetaphysical manner in Nahmanides' position regarding the two paths of reading the Torah, as analyzed in Chapter 11, the theory I would like to survey here is adumbrated in various passages from Abraham Abulafia and in a passage from R. Nathan's *Sha'arei Tzedeq*. Let me first introduce, however, an important text known to the Ashkenazi Hasidim and to Abulafia. In a late midrash dealing with the creation of the golem, we find the first case of explicit juxtaposition of *Sefer Yetzirah* and its combinatory practice and the Torah:

> By *Sefer Yetzirah* God created His world . . . At the beginning, when He created the world alone, and the thought emerged to create the world, He was strengthening the foundations of the earth and it did not subsist until He created the Torah [and] *Sefer Yetzirah* and He gazed into it and understood its wisdom and He immediately created the world. His eyes were gazing at *Sefer*

Yetzirah and His hands were roaming[42] and building within the world . . . like a man who builds a building and has a book and contemplates it, so did the Holy One, blessed be He, when He created the world. And he finished it[43] and put it in the Torah . . . And when Abraham understood [*Sefer Yetzirah*] his wisdom was enhanced and he studied the entire Torah. So did the Holy One contemplate *Sefer Yetzirah* and create the world.[44]

This passage relates the anomian technique of *Sefer Yetzirah* to an understanding of the Torah and should be seen as one of the major sources for later developments in this direction. To a great extent, the quintessence of the hermeneutics of ecstatic Kabbalah can be seen as the reading of the Torah in a combinatory manner, part of which was inspired by *Sefer Yetzirah*. Abulafia recommends, "Read the entire Torah, both forwards and backwards, and spill the blood of the languages. Thus, the knowledge of the Name is above all wisdoms in quality and worth."[45] The phrase "forwards and backwards" points to the movement of a circle on which letters had been inscribed in order to allow their permutation, a view found already in *Sefer Yetzirah*. Thus, we have here a parallel passage to other discussions of Abulafia's dealing with the circle of the Torah, *galgal ha-torah*. About this syntagm we read:

The circle of the Torah, namely the permutation of the twenty-two letters, and their weight, and their metathesis, and their combination according to the two hundred and thirty-one gates . . . Behold the principle of the reality of up and down, of front and back,[46] from which emerge good and delight [on one side], evil and affliction [on the other], whatever you may choose by your permuting of the circle of the letters, and take. Because two pericopes there are in your hand, "life and death I set in front of you, and you should choose life."[47] And this is the secret of [the verse] "the tablets were written on both their sides,"[48] namely they are written front and back.[49]

It is easy to see how the concepts of *Sefer Yetzirah* concerning combination of letters were mingled with the concept of choice characteristic of the Torah. Here the Torah is less a matter of commandments or a nomian text and much more a technique of combination that raises the possibility of choosing between different types of messages. Elsewhere in the same book the more ecstatic nature of the exegetical technique is explicated: "I know that by necessity you should attain the knowledge of the Name and you will speak with the Agent Intellect and it will speak with you in accordance with your strength.[50] First you should operate when under [the impact of] this supernal and divine comprehension, you should begin to permute the Torah."[51,52]

It is extremely interesting that R. Nathan's *Sha'arei Tzedeq* makes an explicit nexus between the path of the names, which reflects the supernal letters and their metaphysical roots, and the path of the commandments, which reflects the structure of the lower entities. According to this view, the structure of the Torah as transmitted in the common form mirrors the mundane beings and processes, although its text constitutes a reorganization or recombination of the same letters that reflect a supernal order.

I take this distinction to corroborate an interpretation offered by Abulafia in juxtaposing the account of the Chariot, understood as the combination of the divine names, and the account of the Creation, which deals with words that represent transient beings: "You must know that on the one hand the Names, in their form of combination, are likened to the phenomena that subsist and pass away and on the other hand to those that endure. Indeed, those that endure are called the 'work of the Chariot' and the others are called the 'work of the Creation,' and the secret of this is 'ivrit."[53] The passage is based on the equivalence of the numerical values of the word 'ivrit, "Hebrew," and the phrase ma'aseh merkavah, "work of the Chariot," namely 682.[54] This implies that the phenomena that endure do so by means of the holy names, which exist only in the Hebrew language. This assumption transforms Hebrew into the intellectual language, since only that language has the ability to express the intellectual nature of unchanging existence. Hebrew is construed as the metaphysical language, and that is the reason God chose it.

According to a passage written in the circle from which R. Abraham Abulafia emerged, Moses was introduced to the secrets of the "science of the letters," which point to their supernal sources. This is a supreme form of Kabbalah, and R. Nathan contended that "Moses learned the entire Kabbalah from the alphabets, and his study of wisdom and knowledge and understanding refers to the letters and their vowels. And anyone who will understand and know the power of the letters and vowels and their [visual] forms and the effects of their forms will understand and have knowledge of the Blessed Creator."[55] Thus, it is the profound knowledge of language in its alphabetical order that constitutes a vision of Kabbalah at the beginning of the second half of the thirteenth century. I see no other way to understand this relation of the alphabets to the Torah than by assuming that the letters of those alphabets were combined into verses. To turn to a quote from *Sha'arei Tzedeq*, Moses then arranged the Torah as a continuum of letters that constitute divine names which reflect "the structure of supernal letters," and only at the end did Moses divide this continuum into another one, which is designated as the path of the commandments. We may distinguish between four parallel levels of existence connected to the Torah: (i) the supernal roots of letters, or the ontic level, which is close to God; (ii) the discrete letters on high, or the supernal letters; (iii) the Torah as a continuum of divine names; and (iv) the Torah as a textual structure dealing with commandments and sacred history. It is worth mentioning in this context that a contemporary of R. Nathan, and himself an ecstatic Kabbalist, R. Isaac of Acre, is the first to have expounded a fourfold theory of cosmogony, which parallels a fourfold exegesis.[56] The author of *Sha'arei Tzedeq*, less inclined to metaphysical discussions, did not elaborate on his structure of reality, but it is possible that the four states of the existence of letters point to a fourfold cosmogony. It is in the immediate context of the discussion of the path of commandments that we learn that this sequence of letters constitutes the back and the present structure of the Torah, while the path of the names is its front or face structure. The former is described as "very weak and found nowadays in our hands, and we need it and we revolve[57] and sometimes we receive [a revelation], sometimes not."[58] This theory is reminiscent of a passage of Abulafia's adduced earlier in this section.

Elsewhere in the same book we read:

> The entire world is governed in accordance with [the laws of] nature, which indicates the attribute of judgment. Thus, the world of Names is suspended and obscured, and its letters and combinations and its virtues are not understood by those who conduct themselves in accordance with the attribute of judgment . . . and this is the secret [meaning] of the cessation of prophecy in Israel; [for prophecy] inhibits the attribute of judgment. [And this continues] until the one whom God desires arrives, and his power will be great and will be increased by being given their power. And God will reveal His secrets to him . . . and the natural and philosophical wisdoms will be despised and hidden, for their supernal power will be abolished. And the wisdom of the letters and Names, which now are not understood, will be revealed.[59]

Kabbalah is thus described as an immersion in the structure of language, as it was before the emergence of the biblical canon. Departing from Nahmanides' stand and following Abulafia's view as expressed in his *Hayyei ha-'Olam ha-Ba'* and *Commentary on the Pentateuch*,[60] R. Nathan introduced the theory of combinations of letters within a more conservative position, as formulated in Nahmanides, which in fact preceded this Kabbalist, one that deals with another division of the same sequence of letters but not with the combinations of those letters in new structures, as the ecstatic Kabbalists thought.

In sum, the supernal letters, which apparently are understood to be discrete entities, are first combined so as to constitute divine names and only then divided into commandments, a process that should be understood as an accommodation of the Torah letters to mundane affairs. Let me emphasize the specificity of this sort of explanation of the emergence of the revealed Torah from the pristine Torah: in the two cases we may speak about two parallel lines that contain exactly the same number of letters, whose sequence is identical but the separation between units of letters that become words differs. If we take into consideration that in ancient times the scroll of the Torah was written with consecutive letters not separated into words—a fact that allows modern scholars of the Bible plenty of room for exegetical imagination—the later Torah, as it has come down to us, is based on a separation between the words.[61] Thus the ancient manner of writing the text created allowed numerous readings of the same sequence of letters. This transition has been projected onto the more primordial plane by many Kabbalists, as we shall see in more detail below.

Let me adduce now a version of this stand found in one of the most influential writings of Christian Kabbalah: Johann Reuchlin's *De Arte Cabalistica*. Although I am not sure that the following passage was influenced by Abulafia's writings, I see the Abulafia's way of thought as the closest parallel to Reuchlin's view. Concerning the mystical potency of the Torah, which is capable of elevating the human mind to the supernal world, Reuchlin wrote:

> At first—the Kabbalists assert—"God wrote his Law onto a fiery globe, applying dark fire to white fire." As Ramban Gerondi says, "it appears to us through Kabbalah that Scripture came into being in black fire on white fire." Hence in Deuteronomy 33: "From his right hand is a law of fire for them." The letters, so they say, were confused and jumbled up at that stage, although studious men could look at them and speculate with careful consideration until, under the influence of the Holy Spirit, they have no difficulty in picking and choosing letters from every place possible after thorough scrutiny, and then collecting and forming them into particular words, to show good for the virtuous and bad for the sinner. So Moses, under God's instruction, reduced all the letters to order for telling to the people. Everyone then knew what the laws were and could keep them, and the Law was divided up into books and put into the ark in the same form as Moses had received it from the Lord. Moses did not explain to the vulgar the art either of ordering and varying the order of the letters or of sweetly interpreting Sacred Scripture to elevate the mind, even though he had by then received that art from the Divine Majesty.[62]

According to Reuchlin, the order of the Torah letters was "*confusae ac inglomerate.*" I wonder if behind the Latin words one should perhaps discern a Hebrew source describing the situation of the primordial Torah letters as *tohu va-bohu* ("unformed and void," Genesis 1:2). Such a hypothetical source may allow us to draw a parallel between the material creation that started with the confused pre-existent matter arranged as part of the move from chaos to cosmos, on the one hand, and the arrangement of the disordered letters and the emergence of the Torah dealing with ways of religious behavior, on the other. I use the word "disorder" in a relative manner having nothing to do with the sequence of letters as found in the revealed Torah, regardless of whether those letters are divided into words. According to Reuchlin, Moses or the Kabbalist is not dividing the same sequence of letters into words different from the original, but the double-line stand implies that the same letters will occupy different places on the two lines, because the process of selecting letters occurs in different places in the text, a method that can be identified with combination of letters.[63] Here the creativity of the interpreter is much greater than it is in those texts adduced earlier from the ecstatic Kabbalists, although the exegetical technique is not essentially different. Reuchlin creates in this passage a certain tension, even an opposition, between the regular, rabbinic students of the Torah and the mystical reading that elevates the mind to the supernal world, in a manner reminiscent of ecstatic Kabbalah. Indeed, the very description of Kabbalah as the technique or rearranging the letters of the Torah, which Reuchlin advances immediately after the above passage, demonstrates his close affinity to Abraham Abulafia's thought.[64] Moreover, as in the ecstatic Kabbalistic school, the process of reading the Torah is informed by a mystical experience, the Holy Spirit guiding the exegete.[65] The Christian Kabbalist implies, however, that Moses' technique for composing the Torah is not a lost science but is the very essence of Kabbalah and may be used again to create new forms of ritual instruction. No doubt the fluidity of the primordial text is much greater in Reuchlin's passage than in any other of the texts I am acquainted with, including the later examples adduced below, and the role of the interpreter becomes much greater. Indeed, it is a strong ergetic drive, inspired by a superior power, that informs the restructuring reading of the Kabbalist.

Let me address the manner in which the superior line is conceived. The Torah letters, if indeed this concept is adequate for this passage at all, are circular, as the word "globe" shows. I am not sure that the original intention of the hypothetical Hebrew source was a globe or a sphere. I suppose that the original word was *galgal*, which may point to either circle or sphere and which Reuchlin translated, in fact mistranslated, as "globe." The resort to two colors, or two fires, in order to point to the substratum and the letters may have something to do with the manner in which R. Isaac of Acre envisioned the Torah (see Appendix 2, par. IV). If we assume that the lower line is composed from the scroll of the Torah, we may speak about a theory of two circular lines that parallel each other, although this parallelism does not consist in keeping the same sequences of letters.

V. R. JOSEPH BEN SHALOM ASHKENAZI

The double-line theory is reminiscent of a text written by an influential Kabbalist active at the end of the thirteenth century or the beginning of the fourteenth, R. Joseph ben Shalom Ashkenazi. In one of the most influential Kabbalistic treatises, a commentary on *Sefer Yetzirah*, R. Joseph writes that "the circles were void and the letters moved within the letters so that all the languages and speech were combined from them, as well as all the 613 commandments. And this is the Torah that preceded the world [Binah].[66] And it is the name of God, because there is no interruption or corporeal combination,[67] because all are sacred, and the Tetragrammaton is within it."[68] R. Joseph deals with the combinations of letters by means of twenty-two concentric circles within which Hebrew alphabets were inscribed;[69] their movement creates the combinations of letters, apparently called the corporeal combinations, which produce the ordinary sequence of letters constituting the mundane Torah, which differs from the supernal one, where the letters are found in a continuous manner, as we learn also elsewhere in the same treatise.[70] This compact existence of the Torah letters was regarded as forming the name of God. By resorting to this view of the Torah, R. Joseph ignores Nahmanides' tradition of the Torah as divine names—which, as we have seen, was interpreted by the ecstatic Kabbalists—and accepts instead a position found in the writings of his contemporaries, R. Ezra and Azriel of Gerona, and recurring in the *Zohar*.[71] I assume that the unit of one name has something to do with the mode of writing the letters of the alphabets without interruption. It should be mentioned that the concept of combination of letters as connected to the sefirah of Binah is found in a Kabbalistic Ashkenazi commentary on *Sefer ha-Yihud* written by an anonymous Kabbalist well acquainted with peculiar Kabbalistic views characteristic of R. Joseph ben Shalom Ashkenazi.[72]

According to a statement found in another of R. Joseph's writings, "the conjunction between the letters will change in accordance with the deed, thought, and speech of the children of Israel . . . because all the movement of man and his speech, deeds, and thought are written and done on the supernal letters."[73] This view is not necessarily related to the passage from his *Commentary on Sefer Yetzirah*, but if such a nexus can be established—and I see that as possible—then a view close to that described above in connection with *Sha'arei Tzedeq* can be plausibly reconstructed. On high are Torah letters, whose conjunction depends on human deeds. As such, the corporeal combination of letters reflects the nature of the realm that induced that combination. This syntagm is, in my opinion, of great importance for subsequent Kabbalistic and Hasidic theories of combination of Torah letters and recurs in R. Moses Cordovero's classic book *Pardes Rimmonim*.[74] It assumes a certain impact on a development taking place between letters found on a very high level, this development reflecting consequently the nature of the deeds of the human being. I would suggest calling this approach *theurgical linguistics*, to be compared to theurgical theosophy, which contends that human deeds can affect divine powers. This attitude had a huge impact on Hasidic thought and practice, and examples of the assumption that combinations of letters can affect the supernal realms abound in this literature.[75]

VI. SOME SIXTEENTH-CENTURY KABBALISTIC VIEWS

It seems, however, that the most interesting forms of dealing with the linguistic accommodation can be found in a variety of sixteenth-century Kabbalistic treatments. Let me start with a prolific Kabbalist active in Jerusalem and Syria in the middle of the century, R. Joseph ibn Tzayyah. In *Sefer Tzeror ha-Hayyim* he writes:

> The Torah, according to the secret of the twenty-two letters and its combinations [as] it has been combined according to the commandments, has been revealed in order to purify Israel by them . . . and in it the 231 gates were combined: the letter 'aleph with all the letters, and all the letters with it . . . because the entire Torah, and its combinations done in this manner, is an inner and spiritual matter just as it is in our hand today, without receiving any addition or subtraction, neither a change nor a permutation [is allowed], and it is eternal and stands forever, and within it the entire world is found; and it [the Torah] is subordinated to the ten commandments . . . and you should understand that all the matter of the combinations of the Torah and its stories and the order of the manner in which the commandments were promulgated, all are inner matters, which are interpreted in different forms and modes. This is why you should find that in it there was written, according to the secret of its combination, "if a man dies in a tent," [already] two thousand years before the creation of the world, when death had not been exacted upon the generations[76] . . . all its words are hidden.[77]

This is an interesting synthesis between the combinatory theory of *Sefer Yetzirah* and the sanctity of the order of letters concerning the commandments. A Kabbalist well acquainted with the views of ecstatic Kabbalah, ibn Tzayyah is quite reluctant to allow the possibility of combinatory changeability of the Torah. He insisted that the preexistence of the ordinary sequence of letters to the creation of the world invites the possibility that a view which would assume that cosmogonic and religious processes might have been able to affect the primordial sequence, inflicting a change that expresses a theory of accommodation, existed already before ibn Tzayyah and is reflected in the formulations of Cordovero and his school, as we shall see immediately below. In other words, I assume that a view close to Cordovero's had been in existence several decades earlier and is refuted by ibn Tzayyah.

One of the topoi dealing with the revelation of the Torah to Moses is the rabbinic legend, found in various sources, where the angels are described as opposing the revelation of the Torah to man. Moses is portrayed as telling the angels that the Torah is not pertinent to their status because it deals with human affairs. The angels, convinced by Moses' argument, not only allow the revelation of the Torah but, as we have seen, give Moses some gifts, which should be understood as a metaphor for holy names.[78] This legend was interpreted quite often in the Middle Ages, and the various interpretations deserve a detailed survey, which cannot be made here (although in the next section one specific interpretation salient to our discussion will be adduced). R. Joseph al-Ashqar, a Kabbalist active in Tlemcen, North Africa, in the 1520s and 1530s, argued that the angels possess a Torah different from the one to be revealed to Moses, and they mistakenly opposed the revelation of "their" Torah. In describing the difference between the two forms of Torah the Kabbalist wrote:

> The angels were reading the Torah according to the path of the combinations of holy names,[79] and they thought that the Torah would be revealed to Israel in this manner. And this was considered to be impossible, as how is it possible that six hundred thousand men, in addition to younger persons, would be able to comprehend all the combinations of letters? And since the Holy One, blessed be He, announced to Moses the manner in which he would receive the Torah, namely that the very Torah letters, from which the names of the *havvayyot*[80] have been combined, would be the letters of the [revealed] Torah, but He will not resort to the same combination, but He will clothe the letters differently, and He will combine the letters in another way, like the exodus from Egypt and similar issues . . . and the angels knew that the Torah would be clothed by matters of *peshat*, which is like a body, and the matters of the combinations of names would remain [the patrimony] of the few elite, which are similar to a soul hidden in a body.[81]

Two motifs are clearly related in this passage: the two forms of Torah differ because they consist in different combinations of letters and because the lower constitutes a clothed form of the higher. Again, as in some of the above passages, the divine names constitute the preexistent Torah, whereas the stories emerged out of the restructuring of the supernal order of Torah letters.

It is difficult to pinpoint the precise source that influenced al-Ashqar. Since there are no traces of ecstatic Kabbalah in his book, it is implausible that one of the sources quoted above from this school served as his starting point. Rather we may assume a source in Spain, which inspired both this Kabbalist and one of his contemporaries, R. David ibn Avi Zimra. A much younger contemporary of al-Ashqar, ibn Avi Zimra interpreted the same legend as the Kabbalist from Tlemcen did, as follows: "We have received an explanation of this quandary[82] that the entire Torah is [consists] of divine names . . . the Torah was written in the front of God according to the path of His names, blessed be He, without any division of words, without vowels or cantillation marks . . . And its reading was very spiritual, not corporeal."[83] According to this view, the angels agreed that the Torah would be revealed to human beings because they understood that only the corporeal aspect was to be transmitted, while the spiritual one, based on divine names, would not been disclosed. We may assume that the Torah was conceived of as existing on two different levels at the same time: on high, in the front of God, and on low, as revealed now. Such a view is similar to an argument that a late-fifteenth-century Jewish thinker, R. Isaac 'Arama, made in his influential sermon,[84] and that later appeared in R. Yoshi'ah Pinto's commentary on the talmudic 'aggadot entitled *Me'or 'Einayyim*.

VII. R. Moses Cordovero and His Impact

Some of the views we have surveyed influenced many Kabbalistic discussions, one of the most consequential being R. Moses Cordovero's elaborations on the topic of the Torah.[85] He explicitly resorts to the triangular view found in Gikatilla's *Sha'arei 'Orah*, and he was acquainted with Abulafia's *Hayyei ha-'Olam ha-Ba'* and with R. Nathan's *Sha'arei Tzedeq*, which he attributes to Abulafia.[86] No doubt he knew the eschatological model of the two layers of the *Zohar* and had access to R. Joseph Ashkenazi's commentary on *Sefer Yetzirah*. The Safedian Kabbalist resorts to a theme that is very characteristic of his thought in various writings, whereby he portrays the descent or the clothing of the Torah as its becoming more material; the higher level of the existence of the Torah as divine names is related to the concept of lights, while the lower is associated with that of darkness.[87] Several times Cordovero employs the verb TzRF, namely "to combine," in order to explain the transition from the higher linguistic elements to the lower ones. We may describe this process as an accommodation of a supernal and luminous pattern to the qualities of the different worlds while changing the structure of the letters as part of this metamorphosis.[88]

Using the metaphor of the various metals that are imprinted by a seal, *hotam*,[89] or paradigm, *temunah*, which stand for the Torah, Cordovero attempts to account for the corporeal stories and parables of the Torah. Two different elements are involved in his description of the transition from the higher world to the lower one: the model remains the same, but it takes a coarser form because of the nature of the lower world, or the metal, and adds another element. This seems to be inconsistent with the former element, namely that there is a change in the model itself, as letters changed places and even were replaced in the process of combination. This inconsistency notwithstanding, it is plausible that Cordovero believed that the coarse nature of the lower world triggers changes understood as combination of letters, which produces parabolic discourses.

Let me adduce a passage that exemplifies Cordovero's view on the accommodation of the Torah structure while descending to this world:

> The original combination of letters in the Torah before the fall did not include the interdiction of *sha'atnez tzemer u-fishtim* but the same consonants in another combination, namely *satan 'az metzar ve-tofsim*, a warning to Adam not to exchange his original garment of light for the garment of serpent's skin, namely the qelippot named *satan 'az*, "insolent Satan."[90] Further, the words embodied a warning to the effect that these powers would assuredly bring fear and affliction [*tzarah ve-tzuqah*] upon man and attempt to gain possession of him [*ve-tofsim*] and thereby bring him down to hell. But what brought about this change in the combination of letters, so that we now read *sha'atnez tzemer u-fishtim*? It came about because when Adam put on the skin of the serpent his nature became material, thus necessitating a Torah that gave material commandments. This called for a new reading of the letters to convey the meaning of a commandment. And so it is with all other commandments based on the corporeal and material nature of man.[91]

This passage, recorded in R. Abraham Azulai's *Hesed le-'Avraham*, presents a moderate form of accommodation: the Torah is understood to have had a sublime message intended for Adam before his fall but changed the message afterward. Thus, the Torah was conceived of as dealing with human matters, either in its pristine form, which corresponds to the spiritual and innocent Adam, or with the fallen man in its new combinations of letters. Cordovero exemplifies the pristine message as one that can be deduced by combinations of letters, but this recombination does not lead to a version of the Torah that consists in divine names. The specific type of combination exemplified by Cordovero involves restructuring the letters of some words by moving one of the letters from one word to the next one without changing the sequence of letters found in the Torah text. It is not a matter of adding letters to one word or subtracting them from another but of restructuring the order of the very same letters. Such a theory calls into question the importance of the symbolic mode based on the concept of rigid designation, since the main semantic anchoring is considered to be the ever-changing nature of the mundane world rather than the essence and structure of the divine one.

Unlike in this passage, which ascribes a distinct semantic valence to the primordial Torah, in other passages Cordovero offers a vision of this Torah, and of the future Torah, as unknown and unknowable in the present. Indeed, the human intellect is understood as unable to penetrate the sublime meaning of those forms of Torah.[92] Cordovero insists, however, that dramatic as the change in the understanding of the meaning of the Torah will be in the future, the nature of the commandments will not be affected at all.[93]

The most explicit combination of the Nahmanidean stand and the Abulafian one is found in *Ha-Shelah*, one of the most influential books dealing with Kabbalistic issues: "The secrets of the Torah and the combinations of its names[94] will be revealed in the future, because now the letters are arranged [according to the order of] the Torah that is in our hand. But in the future the Torah will be new, but not new really, God forfend, but only its letters will be combined so as to [point to] another matter, as it was on high before it was given, as it has been explained in Nahmanides' introduction to [his commentary on] the Pentateuch."[95,96] Especially interesting is the formulation offered by this same Kabbalist, who asserts that "just as man materialized himself, so too the Torah materialized itself," and then he continues to refer to a Cordoverian discussion.[97]

In the first quote R. Isaiah Horowitz offers a stand that indeed takes into consideration Cordovero's view but still relies on Nahmanides. Unlike the Safedian master, Nahmanides never spoke about a preexistent Torah that consists of separate letters, but he assumed the existence of two different forms of combinations of letters: the secret one and the revealed one, the latter dealing with the path of the commandments. Never, to my knowledge, did Nahmanides contend that there would be a return to the secret combinations of the Torah letters as divine names, a point that seems to be introduced into the view of the Catalan Kabbalist by the second quote.

In the late seventeenth century, in a short quotation from an anonymous source found by R. Elijah ha-Kohen 'Ithamari of Smyrna and preserved in his influential compendium *Midrash Talppiyyot*, we read: "The Torah was before the Holy One, blessed be He, in [the form of] letters, six hundred thousand letters which were not arranged in the form of words. And because Adam sinned He arranged the letters so as to point to matters that were caused by sin, like '[This is the Torah of] Man, when he dies in a tent'[98] . . . and many like these. However, had Adam not sinned those letters would have been arranged in other words. End of Quotation."[99]

According to this text, the assumption is that the discrete letters were arranged by God to represent the nature of the state of things in the eon before the sin. Thus, the nonconjugated letters were combined in a manner that reflects the situation created by the sin. It should be emphasized that according to this passage, the contention is that there was no order before sin, if by "order" we mean a sequence of letters in specific words. The single form of structure is constituted by the sequence of the same letters, each of them standing alone. On the other hand, there is no express claim in the passage that disorder related to the letters of the primordial Torah is implied according to this anonymous quote. R. Elijah added a remark at the end of the quote, again reflecting a Cordoverian concept:

> Behold, in the future when the sin of Adam will already be forgiven and things will return to their original state, the very Torah of our master Moses, blessed be his memory, with the number of its letters, without any subtraction or addition, arranged according to other words, as it was worthy to be arranged had Adam not sinned, and this is the new Torah that God preaches to the righteous, namely the very Torah of Moses, or it is possible that the arrangement of the words as they are arranged now, "Man, when he will die in the tent," . . . God preaches them by disclosing their intention despite the fact that then there will be no death, and He interprets it in another manner, and this is the new Torah indeed, a concealed and very profound thing which is an innovation for the listeners.[100]

It is obvious that R. Elijah makes an effort to clarify his attachment to the rabbinic vision of the perfection of the Torah, understood here as keeping intact the number of the Torah letters. The meaning of God's teaching another reading is found elsewhere in a passage by R. Elijah, in a quotation from a lost treatise of his, preserved in a book by HYDA'. The latter quotes first a passage from R. Bahya ben Asher on the nonvocalized scroll of the Torah,[101] and then writes:

> And the Rabbi, our master R. Elijah ha-Kohen, may his memory be blessed, the author of *Shevet Mussar*, and more [books], has written in a manuscript treatise [Quntres]: It should be assumed that this [nonvocalized] Torah, which was in front of the Holy One, blessed be He, before it was delivered to the mundane realm, its letters were in the [same] number in His front, but it was not formed into words as is the case today. And the reason for its arrangement [in words] is [to reflect] the way the world behaves. Because of Adam's sin, He arranged the letters in the front of Him, according to the words describing death and the levirate and other issues. Without sin there would have been no death, and He would not have arranged the letters into words telling another issue. This is the reason the scroll of the Torah

is neither vocalized nor divided into verses, nor does it have cantillation marks, thus hinting at the original state of the Torah, [consisting in] a heap of unarranged letters. And the purpose of His intention is that when the king messiah will come and death will be engulfed forever, there will be no room in the Torah for anything related to death, uncleanness, and the like, then the Holy One, blessed be He, will annul the words of the scroll of the Torah, and He will join a letter of one word to a letter of another word in order to create a word that will point to another matter. And this is [the meaning of] "A new Torah will proceed from Me."[102] Is not [however] the Torah eternal? [The answer is] the scroll of the Torah will be as it is now, but the Holy One, blessed be He, will teach its reading according to the arrangement of the measure of the letters that He will be joining to each other to form one word, and He will teach us the [new] division and the joining of the words. End of quote from above R. Elijah ha-Kohen, may the memory of the righteous be blessed; [quoted] in a shortened manner.[103]

Three different states of the Torah are mentioned here: (i) the original or pristine state, when the letters were discrete, no words having been formed at all, since there was no world, nor any processes to be reflected by conjoined structures of the Torah letters; from this point of view there is a parallel to the stand of *Sha'arei Tzedeq*;[104] (ii) the present Torah, which consists in words reflecting the actual human condition; and (iii) the future Torah, which will differ from the present one by consisting in new words and from the primordial Torah by the fact that the Torah letters are nevertheless destined to constitute words. None of the three versions of the Torah reflects another except by dint of possessing the same number of letters, which follow each other according to the same sequence. Nevertheless, the latter two forms of the Torah are much closer to each other, not only because words are involved in both but also because the scroll of the Torah will remain the same, but God will teach the manner of a different reading of the same scroll. On the grounds of the earlier quotes from R. Elijah, we may assume that the new Torah was in fact the option of the combination of letters that might have emerged had Adam not sinned.

Let me focus for a moment on the concept of the primordial Torah, which consists of exactly the same number of letters arranged in the same order as the other versions but existing separately. The word "heap," *tel*, which appears in this passage alone, constitutes the single significant addition to the series of discussions of our theme. Whatever the role of this term in the economy of the above passage may be, it should not be understood as essentially changing the significance of the passage. I would argue that the idiosyncratic phrase *tel shel 'otiyyot*—

or, in the passage to be adduced below, *tel 'otiyyot*—is reminiscent of the widespread interpretation of the word *talppiyyot* as *tel she-kol ha-piyyot ponim 'elav*,[105] the hill (namely the authority) to which all the mouths are turning. This suggestion has something to do with R. Elijah's compiling *Midrash Talppiyyot*, an encyclopedic treatise on Kabbalistic matters arranged according to the order of the letters of the Hebrew alphabet. It may be assumed that the primordial Torah is conceived of as semantically vacuous, because each of its letters stands alone, while the two latter forms of Torah point to either the human or the divine realm.

The quote from R. Elijah's manuscript treatise has been commented on by Scholem, who declared this text to be a "daring formulation," for reasons which he did not elaborate.[106] The perception of the passage as daring is complemented by his claim that HYDA', who quoted R. Elijah's passage, "protested in horror against so radical a thesis," all because of the former's piety.[107] Just as it is hard, in my opinion, to find a real break in R. Elijah's views with the already existing Kabbalistic theories, so it is difficult to find any horror in HYDA''s reaction. What he says immediately after the above passage is worth quoting: "But I, in my paucity, say that what he wrote, that the Torah was in front of God as a heap of letters [*tel 'otiyyot*], if it is not a saying of the rabbinic sages, [then] it is not accepted by my short knowledge. But the Torah in its entirety is [consists of] the names of the Holy one, blessed be He, and those letters were written as a combination of holy names. And the words of the sages are 'The Torah in its entirety is [consists] of names of the Holy One, blessed be He.' But the sin caused those letters to be written by those words."[108]

HYDA' correctly distinguishes between the view that the primordial Torah consisted in divine names and that of R. Elijah, who argues that it consisted in a heap of discrete letters. Emphasizing that he is not acquainted with a reliable source for the latter view, HYDA' indicates that he does not accept it. Given the very respectful attitude toward R. Elijah, as seen in the manner in which he has been cited, I fear that Scholem's portrayal of HYDA''s reaction as one of horror is quite exaggerated. As HYDA' himself indicated after the last quote, his views on the theme under scrutiny here were detailed elsewhere, in his commentary on the prophetic readings, the *haftarot*:

It is known that the Torah has clothed itself in these stories because of the sin of the calf, though this very Torah is [consists] in combinations of holy names[109] and supernal secrets which are not read like those words that had been divided in other words which are stories, but the letters that will come are profound, supernal secrets [found] on high and combinations of holy names. But in the future we shall be worthy of studying the Torah from the mouth of God . . . and the Torah will be [consist] in combinations of holy names and secrets of secrets and these letters will be the very same, but in lieu of stories there will be holy names and wondrous allusions. And this is the sign of what is written by our sages, that "This Torah will be a vanity in comparison to the Torah of the Messiah."[110] The meaning of this is that the sequence of these words is stories, and it is vanity in comparison to the Torah of the Messiah because the letters will then be read in accordance with combinations of holy names, because then we shall study the Torah as if from His mouth, not by the mediation of an intermediary[111] . . . but in the future the Torah will not have those stories, but these letters will constitute combinations of names and secrets of secrets.[112]

When the mediator is active in delivering the Torah, it consists in combinations of letters that reflect his nature. When God is revealing the Torah directly, however, He expresses in its structure His spiritual nature. HYDA' assumes that the primordial Torah will be similar to or identical with the one to be revealed in the eschatological future. Thus, the Torah in all its forms is conceived of as pointing to some form of structured reality. Therefore, I see no reason to portray this thinker as reacting in horror or indignation to R. Elijah's resort to the term "heap." Indeed, as Scholem himself admitted on the same page where he mentions horror, HYDA' himself expressed a view that is "scarcely less radical."[113]

VIII. R. MOSES HAYYIM LUZZATTO

One of the most original among the eighteenth-century Kabbalists, Ramhal of Padua, paid attention to the Nahmanidean formula in his writing, advancing an interesting interpretation of his own. According to his view, the Torah as a continuum of divine names points to that form of the Torah by means of which the world has been created. Moreover, this view on the series of divine names is related to the concept that by this Torah miracles have been performed by the righteous, including resurrection of the dead. This form of the Torah is described as *tzerufei ha-beriy'ah*, combinations of creation.

The path of the commandments, on the other hand, is conceived of as the combination of letters that is conducive to the worship of God, *tzerufei ha-'avodah*. Provided Ramhal's eschatological conviction, this path represents the last combination of letters, which will repair all the other previous forms of Torah, which are described as combinations of letters.[114] This point dealing with reparation, *tiqqun*, seems to be characteristic of his view. He claims that "because of the reparations, that man repairs the Torah by preoccupation with the combination of their worship, they will cause the extension of the Torah to them from the aspect of the influence and comprehension."[115] Thus the combination of letters which one performs means drawing down an aspect of the Torah from its root, a branch that constitutes one's own Torah.[116] From time to time Ramhal mentions the view that the Torah is compounded of 231 combinations.[117]

IX. SOME HASIDIC VIEWS

From the very beginning of Hasidism the Cordoverian theory of the Torah was absorbed and adapted. A more precise version of it than the one quoted above from *Hesed le-'Avraham* can be found, anonymously, in R. Gedalyah of Lunitz's *Teshu'ot Hen*.[118] None other than the Besht is reported, in this collection of traditions printed at the end of the eighteenth century, to have said:

> It is true that the holy Torah was originally created as a mixture of letters.[119] In other words, all the letters of the Torah, from the beginning of Genesis to the end of Deuteronomy, were not yet combined into combinations of words as we now read, such as the words "In the beginning God created" or "go from thy land," and so on. These words, on the contrary, were not yet present, for the events of creation that they record had not yet taken place. Thus all the letters of the Torah were indeed mixed in mixtures,[120] and only when a certain event occurred in the world did the letters become combined so as to form the words in which the event is related. When, for example, the creation of the world or the events in the life of Adam and Eve took place, the letters formed the words that relate these events. Or, when someone died, the combination "and so-and-so died" came into being. So it was with all other matters: as soon as something happened, the corresponding combinations of letters came into being. If another event had occurred [instead], other combinations would have arisen. For know that the holy Torah is God's wisdom, which is infinite.[121]

This Hasidic source seems to be much more concerned with an ethical issue than are most of the Kabbalistic texts adduced above, which have a more metaphysical orientation. The concern with free will may be understood as underlying some of these formulations, because a preexistent and paradigmatic Torah, which serves as the model for both the emanated and the created universes and also absorbs subsequent human history, creates a tension between the content of a text that emphasizes free will and its new ontological and overdetermining status. The attainment of the status of an ontic zone by the Torah fixed the structure of the world, and of the events taking place in the world, and clashed with the dynamic attitude of the biblical and rabbinic forms of Judaism.

Let me address the special terminology employed in the above passage. I have translated as "mixed in mixtures" a phrase including two words derived from the root 'RV. Scholem, in contrast, rendered it as "incoherent jumble of letters," so as to fit the manuscript text of R. Elijah of Smyrna dealing with the heap of letters. I see no special reason, however, to emphasize the incoherence, because the verb form *meʿuravin* should be understood as pointing to combinations of letters, without any negative implication. This is already the case in a passage from R. Joseph Gikatilla's *Shaʿar ha-Niqqud*, as printed in *'Arzei Levanon*, at folio 39b (quoted earlier)[122] and again at folio 37a. The Besht was influenced by this treatise with respect to one of the most important topics: the cleaving to letters.[123] This more neutral understanding of mixture is perfectly consonant with the way most of the Cordoverian sources were formulated and seems to me to be much more plausible, given that any sequence of discrete letters is neither coherent nor incoherent. Rather, I would suggest seeing the status of all the Torah letters as forming a single word, a theory reminiscent of R. Joseph ben Shalom Ashkenazi's view of the Torah as one name. Cordovero also mentioned the possibility of making combinations of letters of the entire Torah, although he attributed these infinite combinations to God—the new Torah—and not to the Messiah.[124]

I have not found clear expressions of accommodation theory in the second generation of Hasidic masters, although it seems that R. Jacob Joseph of Polonnoye was acquainted with it.[125] In any case, this author is reported by his disciple R. Gedalyah of Lunitz to have transmitted a tradition in the name of the Besht: "When the Messiah comes, let it be soon in our time, he will interpret [*yidrosh*] the entire Torah, from its beginning to the end, according to all the combinations [found] in each and every word. Afterwards, he will construe the Torah as one word and the combinations will amount to infinity, and he will interpret all these combinations."[126] This quote, which presents the Messiah's study of the Torah in quite an Abulafian manner,[127] is interpreted by R. Gedalyah within the context of the Cordoverian theory of Neoplatonic-combinatory accommodation, with which he was well acquainted, which also assumes that it is possible to reach the understanding of the Torah before Adam's sin.[128] Elsewhere in the same book this emphasis on the Neoplatonic-combinatory view is combined with the eschatological model relating to terms that reflect the concepts of *torah de-beriyʾah*, the revealed Torah that starts with the letter *bet*, and the future *torah de-ʾatzilut*, called the Torah of the 'Aleph because it will start with that letter, a theory he claimed to have seen in some unidentified books.[129]

The basic assumption of this quote deserves a more detailed discussion. I assume that the Messiah is understood to combine the letters of each word, and of the entire Torah as one single word, and to explain them not as part of a continuum or sentence but as constituting one semantic field. My understanding is that all the combinations of the letters of one word, when taken together, form a discourse that should be investigated in itself, rather than as part of a narrative. This is much more conspicuous where the Torah's becoming one long word is concerned, since in this case there is no way to assume the existence of a biblical narrative. This mode of interpretation is found in R. Abraham Abulafia, as I have attempted to show elsewhere,[130] and it was also adopted by the early Gikatilla.[131] In *Ha-Shelah* there is an example of permuting the letters of one word to build a narrative based on the different combinations of letters, and this passage was quoted in an early Hasidic treatise, R. Benjamin of Zalisch's *'Ahavat Dodim*.[132]

What may be the meaning of this theory of interpretation? Given that two basic elements count in this process, the fixed number of letters and the attempt to exhaust their combinations, I would explain the last passage as an instance of "operational validity."[133] If meaning is not a given message transmitted by means of a text but is created in pure textual contexts, for the Hasidic master, as for his Kabbalistic forerunners, the meanings that emerge out of a given set of letters are related to the ergetic mode of interpretation that exploits the semiotic potential of those letters, creating a discourse out of those combinations. In such a manner a maximum exploitation of the linguistic material available emerges from the above passage, one that intervenes in the given structure of the text in order to liberate the potential meaning enchained by the ordinary sequence of letters. This creative and liberating ethos is the main reason for the importance of the combinatory technique. Indeed, in a collection of R. Yehiel Mikhal of Zlotchov's teachings, the Besht is quoted in the following context:

> If he is strongly united to the holiness, he is able to elevate profane things to [the level of] holiness by means of the lore of combinations of letters which is known to the holy and divine Besht, blessed be his memory, and to his disciples, who possess the divine spirit . . . But the *tannaim* were in the possession of the divine spirit and they possessed this lore in a perfect manner, [namely] the combinations of the letters, and they spoke in accordance with the divine spirit, and they [the topics] are secrets of the Torah, and everything stems from their cleaving to the supernal holiness, because of their righteousness.[134]

Thus, it seems that the formulations of the three quotes in the name of the Besht, which deal with the combinatory interpretation of the Torah, come close to Abulafian views of combinations of letters as a way to interpret the Torah, which are associated in two cases with the more dominant theories stemming from Cordovero's school.

In the third generation of Hasidic authors, R. Levi Isaac of Berditchev, whose views on the Torah have already attracted our attention,[135] asked a pertinent question:

> Since the Torah preexisted the world, how is the verse "And Timna' was the concubine"[136] or all the other stories of deeds[137] before the creation of the world? It is certainly true that the Torah in its entirety is [consists of] the names of the Holy One, blessed be He, and there were within it combinations of letters, arcana and recondite secrets which were never seen by eyes but by means of its [descending] emanation[138] to this mundane world, when they were clothed in a thick garment, and so too the stories of the Torah. But he to whom God has given the gift of knowledge, of understanding, and of intelligence, and whose veil of blindness has been removed from his eyes, will see wondrous things in the Torah.[139]

In the circle of this master we find another, more explicit reverberation of the theory under scrutiny here. R. Aharon of Zhitomir wrote:

> The Torah is preexistent and before the creation of the world it was written in front of God as combinations of names and it was solely letters. It is only when the time came that the Torah should be clothed in deeds according to the time, and become combinations of letters according to the needs of the time. And the archangel takes the letters and combines them for himself as he wishes, namely "Every son should be cast into the River [Ha-YeLWD Ha-Ye'WoRaH]."[140] Before the creation of the world the combination of the letters was 'aVYR Yah wa-HMY [a reference to the supernal air]. Then the archangel came and combined [the letters as] Ha-Ye'WoRaH ["into the River"] you should throw, and he confuses the mind so that he will not elevate the letters to the primordial intellect.[141,142]

R. Aharon seems to be the first to exemplify the theory we have discussed above. Unlike Cordovero's text, where the pristine Torah is not described as dealing with divine names, the Hasidic master's example strives to substantiate precisely this point. He interpreted the biblical phrase dealing with a historical issue, *Ha-YeLWD Ha-Ye'WoRaH*, which means "the male born to the Nile," by resorting to combinations of letters and gematria, as pointing to "the air of Yah" namely the air of God[143] and of MY, the last two letter pointing, apparently, to the sefirah of Binah. According to another passage MY is indeed related to *mahashavah*, thought, to the primordial Torah, or to its secrets.[144] Perhaps, the name Yah stands for the sefirah of Hokhmah and thus the passage refers to the two sefirot related to the primordial Torah.[145] The noun *Ha-YeLWD* is equivalent in gematria to *MHY*, namely 55.[146]

What is quite novel in this passage, however, is the introduction of a median entity that performs the "descending" combinations; angels are conceived of as changing the order of the supernal letters, which form sequences of divine names, into phrases that point to historical events. In any case, also according to this master it is conspicuous that the nature of the lower world dictates the type of combinations the governing angel is operating. In fact, the author assumes the existence of many angels, which are appointed on the seventy nations and regulate the profane history, and I am inclined to see in his discussions a reverberation of the triangular structure of text and reality as proposed by R. Joseph Gikatilla. Those angels are conceived of as preventing the mystical student from returning to the initial combinations of letters by elevating the verses of the Torah to their primordial status as divine names. According to another passage from the same author, the elevation of the letters to the primordial intellect, *qidmat ha-sekhel*, is related to the white letters, which are not combined, an issue that has been discussed above in some detail.[147] In a way reminiscent of the texts discussed above about the *Sar ha-Torah*, the angel of the Torah, here too the angels are related to some parts of the Torah or even create them by combining letters. The pernicious role of the seventy angels in mediating the Torah is reminiscent of earlier views, which were not connected to the accommodation theory but regarded the negative aspects of the Torah with the angelic powers governed by Sammael.[148]

A contemporary of R. Levi Isaac and his disciple, R. Yehudah Leib of Yanov, also addressed the emergence of the revealed Torah following the combinatory model. He asserts that the meaning of the Torah, apparently the primordial one, cannot be exhausted, but "it has been revealed out of the great occultation[149] so that those letters of the holy names emerged and were combined, as it is written in books . . . Beforehand the letters were united and merged in a complete union, as it is written that 'Bezalel knew how to combine the letters by which heaven and earth were created'[150] . . . this is the revelation from the great darkness."[151,152]

It seems that this Hasidic master points to printed books, *sefarim*, where at least part of the passage is found. Unfortunately, I have been unable to uncover those books. The basic assumption is that the primordial Torah consisted in letters that were strongly connected to each other and were found in darkness and occultation. The nexus between the two terms is implied in this passage and is explicit in another passage, where they are identified with primordial thought[153] and *tohu va-bohu*.[154] Moreover, at this level the Torah of unity is described as consisting in divine names.[155] I wonder if the term *mahashavah qedumah* in this book does not parallel the term *qidmat ha-shekhel*, which occurs in many other Hasidic texts, both pointing to a certain form of unconsciousness, which produces the revealed

Torah, paralleling the conscious. According to this Hasidic master, the secrets of the Torah, which I take to be identical to the unconscious, can be perceived by the sense of sight, when a veil separating sight from the secret level will be removed, while the plain sense can be perceived by hearing.[156] It seems plausible that this removal is connected to the transition of the Torah, as found in darkness, to the revealed and luminous level.

A stand reminiscent of R. Yehudah Leib of Yanov's passage is found in the works of his contemporary, the Hasidic writer R. Isaac of Radvil, who claimed that the new Torah to be revealed consists in a content hidden within the existing Torah, which is the garment of the future one.[157] This new revelation means, according to R. Isaac, the recognition of the divine immanence everywhere in the world.[158] This immanence is attainable even now, by means of purification.[159] The printer's introduction, by the way, is replete with elements taken from the Cordoverian theory of the accommodation of the Torah to the human material condition.[160]

The most elaborate and complex treatment of the accommodation theory of Torah letters is reported in a Hasidic book first printed in 1880 and attributed to R. Israel Friedmann of Ryzhin. (It is difficult to confirm the correctness of this attribution; that in the following discussions I refer to R. Israel as the author should not be taken as a sign that I have been able to substantiate it.) I shall translate parts of his neglected discussion and point to its affinities to earlier treatments in both Kabbalah and Hasidic literature:

> The holy Torah precedes the creation of the world by two thousand years . . . the "two thousand years" emerge out of the sefirot of Hokhmah and Binah[161] . . . and its precedence points to the grandeur of its concealment and its [not being] comprehended by the thought of men, as the sefirot of Hokhmah and Binah belong to the three first sefirot . . . and the secret of the Torah emerges from the supernal Hokhmah[162] . . . And R. Shimeon bar Yohay said that by means of the Torah the Holy One, blessed be He, created the world, and this is according to the secret of the six hundred thousand letters. And for each and every world, the combination of the six hundred thousand letters, which stems from the combinations of the divine names, corresponds to the greatness and the strength of its luminosity[163] so that it[164] will illumine it[165] and cause the descent of the good and the great light so that it may behave according to light so as to maintain that world . . . The combinations of six hundred thousand letters are numberless, in accordance with the number of the worlds, which are numberless and limitless . . . By the [primordial] Torah the Holy One, blessed be He, created the

Torah, [and] the world is maintained by it. And then [there was] the descent [of the Torah] to this world, to the six hundred thousand souls, each of which has a letter in the Torah that draws the influx and the vitality and the illumination to the soul that is related to it in order to maintain it and vivify it according to the secret of the maintenance. This is why you should find that in the ten generations between Adam and Noah the corporeal and thick deeds are made explicit. This is so because they were close to the sin of Adam and the impurity of the serpent, there was not in them and in the light of their soul strength to receive the light of the Torah,[166] [concerning] the combinations of the words [related] to the deed[s] of the commandments, because of the materiality of their body and the deficiency[167] of the light of their soul because of the sin of Adam, so that the vessel should not be broken because of the abundance of the oil that causes the extinction of the candle. And it was necessary that the combinations of the letters be according to the combinations of the words of the deed[s] of corporeality so that they will have a possibility of receiving, and it sufficed to them in accordance with the deficiency of the light of their soul. So also concerning the ten generations between Noah and Abraham which distanced themselves a little bit from the sin of Adam; the light of their soul was enhanced, and they were purified from the materiality and the thickness of their body. Then the letters of the holy Torah were combined so as [to reflect] the stories of Torah that are more subtle in comparison to the prior ten generations from Adam to Noah, but then was added a little bit of the light of the Torah according to the addition of the good deeds of the commandments of the seven commandments of the sons of Noah, because the light of their soul was enhanced . . . and there was a possibility that they would receive the light of the Torah according to the combinations of a few of the commandments so that the vessel would not be broken, in a manner that was not so in the previous ten generations. Also in the generations of Abraham, Isaac, and Jacob, and the twelve tribes who distanced themselves even more from Adam's sin, and it has been cleaned up in [the case of] Abraham, and has been lustrated in [the case of] Isaac, and purified in [the case of] Jacob, and then the materiality of their body has been purified very much, especially when standing under Mount Sinai, when the impurity of the serpent has entirely stopped, and the light of their soul was enhanced so that they had the possibility of receiving the light of the Torah . . . of the positive and negative commandments, and it has been lustrated to them and combined in the form of the stories of the Torah, as the light of their soul has been enhanced. The conclusion [to be drawn] from this is that the six hundred thousand letters of the holy Torah are illumining in the supernal worlds in the combinations of the names of each and every world according to the grandeur of its luminosity. Each and every world according to a combination different from the other world according to the grandeur of its luminosity. And the entire Torah is illumining there without a garment, solely as combinations of the holy letters with subtle and luminous lights. Only the descent to this corporeal world necessitated its combinations according to corporeal deeds, and [included] positive and negative commandments . . . and our master Moses, blessed be his memory, because he purified his matter and his body completely . . . and he reached the rank and degree that is higher than that of the angels, the serafim, and the ofanim, so that the angels were jealous of him when he received the Torah.[168] And by his purification of his matter and body he knew the entire Torah according to the combinations of the names [found] in all the supernal worlds without any garment and cover whatsoever . . . and it is known that the Shekhinah was really speaking from the throat of Moses because he was the prepared vessel[169] for the very dwelling of the Holy One, blessed be He, in him by the complete purification of his body and his matter.[170]

This passage deals with several paths of progress that conspire in the complete revelation of God from the throat of Moses.[171] There is the gradual purification of the bodies, which starts with the lowest point, the sin of Adam, which inflicted the presence of the impurity of the serpent, and slowly reaches its apex when Moses becomes a pure vessel. R. Israel mentions the three decades of generations as significant temporal units for the rhythm of purification, with Moses as the culmination of the process of spiritualization. The purification of the body enables the reception of a more spiritual form of Torah: it is only in the second decade that the commandments of the sons of Noah become significant, and only in the third decade has the Torah been revealed. Thus, the structure of the Torah is consonant with the material preparation of the generations, because a spiritual manifestation of the Torah letters is likewise prone to destroy the unprepared body. This means that the structure of the Torah itself changes with time, and the modes of the combinations of letters accommodate to the state of the recipients. This is quite unlike the more widespread concept of accommodation, which assumes that divine teaching has been adapted to the level of understanding of a certain generation or age. In our case, however, the accommodation is that of the uninformed Torah letters, which are understood to adopt the properties of a particular period in human history.

This form of historical accommodation is to be understood as part of a more comprehensive attitude toward the concept of accommodation, which includes a more ontological approach that assumes that the specific combinations of the letters of the Torah reflect the status of each and every world. Thus, the original or primordial Torah letters illumine in the supernal world while they are not yet combined in words but are combined with lights.[172] However, the descent of the Torah in worlds lower than the world of 'Atzilut, which are nevertheless described as being supernal, involves a double process: one of combining letters with themselves and the other regarding the covering of the lights. Thus, whereas the creational process, or the ontological accommodation, starts with the spiritual and moves toward the more coarse or material, the historical accommodation moves in the opposite direction. Man is capable, as was the case in Moses, of transcending the human status and becoming the vessel of the direct divine presence. The cosmological descent of the spiritual letters and the materialization of the Torah do not create an unbridgeable abyss between the primordial Torah and human existence. It is as if the spiritualization of the human body undoes the descending creation by preparing the substratum for the dwelling of the divine presence.

Let me return to the role played by the process of "descending" or creative radical combinations. They are the clue to the different ways of accommodation of the pure Torah to the nature of each of the lower worlds, and of the ascending accommodation of the human to the divine. In both cases the same root is used: TzRF, which in its different inflections can stand for combination and for purification.[173] In his experience Moses combined the two forms of spirituality: he purified his body, which was prepared to encounter the pure divinity, and achieved the knowledge of the entire gamut of combinations of Torah letters, including its primordial status.

Let me draw attention to the special treatment R. Israel has given the concept of the primordial letters of the Torah. When dealing with some of his Kabbalistic and Hasidic sources, Gershom Scholem suggested the resemblance between those Jewish mystical views and Democritus' and Aristotle's presentation of the doctrine of the atomist about the stoicheia, which means both letters and elements.[174] Analysis of the treatments of letters in the two contexts, however, discloses many more differences than affinities. The most important is that the elements serve, according to the Greek thinkers, as formative components of the more complex entities, which cannot be regarded as emerging except as the result of the combination of preexistent elements. In the Jewish texts, however, the lower and complex entities and processes emerged first—Adam, serpent, sin, etc.—and then they induce the occurrence of the new combination of letters that reflects the essence of the newly created entity. This explanation of the relation-

ship between the material entities and lower events and the corresponding linguistic formulations within the Torah contradicts the much more widespread and
opposite assumption that the name of an entity represents its core or its form, as
has been discussed above.[175] This anti-Platonic move attributes to the human and
the mundane a pivotal role for the mode in which the Torah is formulated. Rather
than imposing or inspiring human behavior here below, the structured forms of
Torah are understood as reflecting it by the special types of combinations the
Torah letters acquired. Unlike the more common Kabbalistic theories that describe the Torah as the divine shadow[176] or divine impression, *roshem*,[177] some of
the texts above adopt a special form of accommodation.

Let me call attention to another attitude toward combinations of letters in
Hasidism. R. Ze'ev Wolf of Zhitomir's 'Or ha-Me'ir betrays a fascination with the
method of combination of Torah letters, which is unparalleled in Hasidism from
the point of view of the recurrence of this concept. According to one of the
numerous discussions regarding this method, the Hasidic author argues that by
contemplation of biblical verses new combinations of letters emerge, which reflect the religious status of the contemplator; if he is a perfect man the new
combinations will be holy, but if his deeds are wicked they will be ugly.[178] Again,
the Torah letters adopt a sequence that reflects a heterogeneous process: whereas
for the ecstatic Kabbalist, for Cordovero and his many followers, and for the
Hasidic masters the restructuring of the Torah letters into the Torah verses represents the nature of human deeds in the hoary past, R. Ze'ev Wolf claims that such a
restructuring is still taking place today. From this point of view he does not accept
the historiosophy expounded by R. Israel of Ryzhin, which attributed to definite
historical periods different types of letter combinations that are characteristic of
them. It is one's spiritual achievements, and not one's point in history, that
determines the combinations one will make.

In another passage the same Hasidic author describes a process that leads
from the stories of the Torah, portrayed as material combinations, to the cognomens and then to the divine names, a process that is understood as the ap-
okatastasis of the Torah to its primordial status in the luminosity.[179] Here the
Hasidic master resorts to Gikatilla's triangular structure of the Torah in order to
describe the technique for reaching the initial status of the Torah or to undo the
process of descending accommodation; material combinations are elevated to
spiritual combinations and finally to the sefirah of Hokhmah.[180]

The reflecting aspect of the Torah as combining preexistent letters in order to
relate some states or events should be dealt with in the context of the passages
addressed in Chapter 6 as to the description of Torah study as conducive to
experiences of plenitude, especially in some elite circles, mystical or philosophi-

cal. Experiences of plenitude should be understood as connected to deep convictions that the Torah, as it is transmitted to its students nowadays, reflects on its inner or esoteric level, a richness that can be fathomed, and its attainment allows a paranormal experience. However, if the Torah is understood to reflect, at least in some of its parts, the deeds, not to say the sins, of mankind, the question arises as to whether there may exist a deeper sense that allows experiences of plenitude. Indeed, someone may distinguish, following the passage attributed to R. Israel of Ryzhin, between the different parts of human history and the corresponding "depths" of the Torah, which are conceived of as increasing with time. Yet, even when such a "progressive" approach is adopted, it is hard to ignore the emphasis on the heterogeneity of the canonical text and the relativization of at least those "historical" aspects of the Bible. This passage rejects or at least marginalizes the well-known view, which had repercussions in Hasidism, that the forefathers performed the commandments of the Torah long before its revelation at Sinai.[181]

A perusal of Kabbalistic and Hasidic literatures may, however, allow an understanding that somehow attenuates this tension. The ancient myths concerning the lives of Adam and of the forefathers, although containing many details that seem to be meaningless if understood as reflecting solely the choice and the fate of a certain specific individual, assume a more sublime significance if they are imagined as paradigmatic for later historical developments or, to use a better known term, as typological. The biblical sacred history was understood as reflecting higher processes.[182]

Especially revealing for the understanding of the special status of the Torah in the above passages are the divergences between R. Israel's quote and the views addressed in Chapter 3, where the understanding of the infinite views of the Torah depends on the souls as shaped by the different worlds from which they emerge. If according to the theory of accommodation all the readers of the Torah are destined to understand it in a rather homogeneous manner, given the conception that it reflects one basic situation here below, according to the "absorbing" perspective each and every reader understands it differently.

The Hasidic concern with the revelation of the primordial Torah through the combination of letters has an interesting counterpart in a passage from R. Isaac Aizik Haver, an accomplished Kabbalist who compiled one of the most comprehensive compedia dealing with Kabbalistic views of the Torah. According to Haver, in its sources[183] the Torah is "limitless and without measure, but when it descends to this lower world it reveals itself according to the combinations of letters and words, just as the letters are written on the white parchment, while they are black."[184] Thus, the white component of the Torah is reminiscent of the source and the hidden, whereas the black letters and their combinations represent the revealed aspects. Here it is obvious that the infinite and spiritual Torah becomes more corporeal by its descent. It is hard to imagine a more concise combination of the Neoplatonic model of accommodation and a combinatory model.

X. RADICALNESS AND DISTRIBUTION

Let me return now to Scholem's different evaluation of the views of R. Elijah of Smyrna and HYDA', in which he regards Elijah's mentioning of the "heap" as a radical thesis. The fact that the later Kabbalist argues that he is not acquainted with such a view is a plausible demonstration that indeed this view is not found in extant Jewish sources. After looking for years for a parallel for such a stand I have found only one case that may be relevant for our discussion. It is a very special Kabbalistic treatise written and printed long before R. Elijah was born, namely Reuchlin's passage analyzed above.

Let me characterize these two sources. One is a Christian text that reflects, in my opinion, a now lost Jewish source apparently stemming from Abulafia's school. The second is a lost manuscript that survived only because of the unparalleled erudition and curiosity of HYDA'. Why did those two sources remain on the margin of the Kabbalistic discourse, with possibly a minor impact on the view of R. Yehudah Leib of Yanov? I assume that the reason for this marginalization of the nonsemantic view of the primordial Torah is an uneasiness with the attribution of a semantic vacuity to the Torah letters. Although the view of the Torah as divine names does not offer an ordinary type of meaning either, the assumption in this case is that some form of semantic relationship nevertheless exists, even if God alone is cognizant of this supreme significance. Thus, in the vast majority of the above texts the normal semantics of the revealed Torah is but the garment of an even higher semantics, and the marginalized traditions assume the augmentation of the semantic cargo when the Torah letters become the ordered Torah. In other words, the more linguistic speculations of *Sefer Yetzirah*, when combined with nomian trends of thought, had to adopt some forms of meaning beyond the cosmogonic role of the combined letters. The concept of the Torah in so many cases absorbed the anomian vision of *Sefer Yetzirah*. Thus the Torah was identified with the 231 gates and assumed the role of the permuted letters of *Sefer Yetzirah*.

This succinct history of the exegetical technique of combination of letters in the context of the accommodation and mutability of the Torah has its main stages, which may help us understand something about the history of Kabbalah and perhaps beyond. The centrality of this exegetical technique in Abraham Abulafia's ecstatic Kabbalah and the circle of Kabbalists from which he emerged is evident beyond the texts adduced in this chapter and the previous one. This is also the case in Christian Kabbalah and in R. Moses Cordovero's *Pardes Rimmonim* and the writings of his followers. The last major stage in this history is Hasidism, which continued the views expounded in the first two schools. Does this preponderance of the combinatory method tell a greater story? The answer is not simple, for we have examined but a small portion of the discussions about *tzerufei 'otiyyot*, those dealing with the different changes related to the emergence and new revelation of the Torah. An insufficient spectrum of topics connected to this topic has been inspected. Nevertheless, I believe that a tentative suggestion should be advanced, one that will have to be corroborated by additional analyses related to the topics of accommodation and mutability.

This concept is absent in the many Kabbalistic schools that did not cultivate the exegetical technique of *tzerufei 'otiyyot* and the related views of Torah accommodation as described in the combinatory model. They include the Provencal and Geronese Kabbalah, the Castilian Kabbalah related to the Zoharic literature, the Lurianic Kabbalah—with the exception of the Sarugian branch—and most of the nineteenth-century Mitnaggedim.[185] These more nomian forms of Jewish mysticism assume that the codified messages should be extracted from the canonical texts without altering their order in any substantial manner. Given that manipulations of Torah letters intending to create new words that would contribute to the discovery of new meanings was marginal in the nomian trends, the disclosure took the form of symbolic exegesis.

There are, nevertheless, three quite interesting cases in the nomian forms of Kabbalah which are pregnant with theosophical-theurgical thought: two classical Kabbalistic books, the early-fourteenth-century *Sefer Tiqqunei Zohar* and the late-fourteenth-century *Sefer ha-Peliy'ah*, and some of Ramhal's views. These three cases adopted combinations of letters as a significant method of exegesis and may be described as serving as sources for anomian or even antinomian attitudes. I see this affinity between a much freer attitude toward the order of letters in the Bible and antinomian overtones as significant for more profound structures. It should also be pointed out that the Kabbalistic schools that adopted the combinatory approach were more inclined to revelatory experiences, as is obvious from the very literary framework of the two above-mentioned books and from Ramhal's literary activity. This conceptual complex, emerging from the juxtaposition of flexible exegesis, of the changing text of the canonic, and of paranormal experiences, seems to inform more anomian forms of interpretations, which is not the case in other Kabbalistic schools.[186]

13

TRADITION, TRANSMISSION, AND TECHNIQUES

I. NAHMANIDES: FROM TRADITION TO TRANSMISSION

So far we have examined the different ways in which the worlds of the sacred texts were imagined by various Jewish mystical thinkers and how they interpreted those books. In the past few chapters the emphasis has been on explicating the exegetical techniques, which offered the strong exegetes the possibility of discovering, in fact rediscovering, religious worlds that had previously been adopted by the Kabbalists, or sometimes by their philosophical sources, from a variety of relatively late intellectual and literary corpora—mostly Greek thought as translated and adapted in Arabic and, less frequently, Latin. We should be aware, however, that only very rarely was the exegetical encounter one between a Jewish intellectual in the Middle Ages who possessed some exegetical skills—and was able to apply some exegetical techniques—and a book that he read for the first time late in his life. It is plausible to assume that in the Jewish mystical literature the act of interpretation is always a reencounter, or even a series of reencounters, with a literary world that had already been absorbed by the mystic but is now approached from dramatic new angles. It would be better, therefore, to speak about different transformations of religious elements already digested in a more superficial or naive manner early in one's life, rather than of an encounter between two different worlds. What intervened between the childhood studies of the Bible, practiced by all those who later became Jewish elites, and their more mature enterprises as biblical interpreters varies from one person to another. We may, simplistically, define those developments as a result of absorbing a great amount of rabbinic culture, which adds substantial elements to the biblical world, or nonbiblical corpora, which include magical, Kabbalistic, or philosophical conceptualizations. The interim worlds between the naive reading of the Bible in childhood and the more sophisticated approach to the same book in adulthood comprise both technical exegetical methods and intellectual worldviews. Those additional worlds were acquired either by study done in groups, or by the reception of some forms of tradition, or by independent study. This means, to follow the type of relations that in Chapter 9 I designated as intercorporal, that information significantly different from the interpreted text is imposed on the world of the text as part of the interpretive project. This reencounter is determined by elements that the interpreter may conceive of as part of the tradition within which the ancient text was deemed to have been embodied, and is understood by the mystic to be intracorporal, or what I suggested calling false intertextuality.

While from a genetic, historical point of view that an academician would accept, the process of interpretation is much more innovative than exegesis, for many Kabbalists—including the innovative Kabbalists—interpretation is much more a matter of disclosure. I would like to emphasize, however, that even in Kabbalistic circles dealing with the secrets of the Torah, the guiding approach was not always exegetical. In addition to the emphasis on the need to interpret in order to extract the hidden sense from the plain sense of the Torah, there was a Kabbalistic attitude which, though stressing the importance of the text of the sacred scriptures, nevertheless did not allow the resort to exegesis in order to extract the secrets of the Torah. Instead, a unique emphasis on the reliable transmission of secret concepts was cultivated.

Thus, we may distinguish between three main types of approach to the problem of the origin of *sitrei torah*. One is the midrashic, with its emphasis on the semantic attitude that culminated in the Kabbalistic literature in the *Zohar*. Another is the parasemantic, which emphasizes a variety of aspects of the text, as found in Hasidei Ashkenaz, Abraham Abulafia's numerology, and the individuals and schools influenced by them. In these, the midrashic approach is minimal. The third approach, to be compared below to the second one in order to highlight its phenomenological structure, assumes that secrets were communicated orally and illumine the plain sense without being extracted from it by the Kabbalists. This is also a nonmidrashic, and to a great extent nonexegetical, attitude, although it pretends to deal with secrets of a text. From the point of view of the further developments of Kabbalah, the more midrashic and combinatory techniques of Kabbalistic interpretation moved to the center, whereas the more esoteric predisposition in Nahmanides' circle, with its monosemic semiotics, remained less influential until the emergence of Lurianic Kabbalah.

In the following I will attempt to expose the differences between the conceptual transmission, which is concerned with Kabbalistic concepts to be passed along by the masters, and technical transmission, which deals less with content than with methods as the subject matter of the act of transmission. Unlike the purely informative and sometimes the operative implications of scientific information, religious secrets involve the perpetuation of a primordial revelation that often becomes concretized in a certain way of life, within which the secrets receive their full significance. Transmission, which may deal with information in its restricted sense, involves much more than acquisition of knowledge for a religious person. For such a person, direct contact with the informant apparently means receiving details of a modus vivendi that may be summarized—only partially, if at all—in distinct categorical concepts. The existence of the famous rabbinic concept and praxis of shimmush talmidei hakhamim, namely a life in the presence of the great sages, which means attending them and learning thereby how to behave as well as to have their personality impressed by that of the masters', is relevant for our discussion. Tradition, which includes transmission of more specific conceptual or exegetical-technical information, therefore mediates between the two major moments of relation to the Bible: the beginning of its study and the later moment of interpretation. These two points are, to be sure, part of a much more continuous experience of reading and reflecting on the Bible that spans over decades. We may describe this experience as life in front of an ever-changing perception of the sacred text, which includes moments of more dramatic developments that will culminate in a crystallized commentary. To resort to Gadamer's terminology, the text with whose horizon the Jewish mystic is fusing his own religious horizon is itself part of the horizon early in the life of the future mystic. In our case, the interpreted text and the tradition that informed interpretation are often inseparable.

Moreover, the informant who initiates someone into the Kabbalistic lore may provide, in addition to secret information, details concerning manners of behavior, which are also transmitted mimetically and sometimes represent a religious framework for the secrets. This is the reason why religious transmission would often put a greater emphasis on the authority of the informant, but also on the religious and psychological makeup of the receiver, on the very rite of transmission—in some cases an act of initiation—than the scientific transmission, which focuses only on the objective correctness of information.

Religious information is only rarely judged as merely correct in itself, as if following its inner logic; it is also supposed to be congruent with a more general religious outlook or worldview and praxis of the informant, and at the same time be significant for the recipient. On the other hand, the transmission of the peculiar form of the religious modus vivendi involves, at a very deep level, the remembering of the primordial revelations that reverberate in the way of life that serves as the background for the secrets. This primordiality, which is but one of the aspects of authority, seems to be quite irrelevant for the scientific manner of looking at reality. It is the novelty that seems to ensure a more correct picture of reality, rather than the antiquity of a certain piece of information. The authority of the religious informer is derived from the authority of his instituting founder. In the case of Kabbalah, there is more than one candidate for the role of founding figure of the macrochain: Adam, Abraham, and Moses. It is Moses who is portrayed as the prototype of the recipient and the transmitter of the secret lore, and in many cases the Kabbalah is depicted as stemming from the "mouth of Moses." In conceptual transmission, namely when the content of the esoteric tradition consists in some concepts conceived of as secrets, the assumption is that the primordial context—paradisiacal knowledge or Sinaitic revelation—which produced the canonic esoteric text, conceived to be secret on another level, should be perpetuated because of its intrinsic importance and relevance, while the religious achievement of the receiver is relatively marginal.[1] The receiver is to become part of the longer chain of tradition and, to a certain extent, be instrumental in the preservation of tradition as the central religious value. He is more a vessel than a creator of secrets. On the other hand, in those types of esotericism or mysticism which are more experiential in the sense that they consist in techniques of exegesis and of inducing mystical experiences that are viewed as ideal attainments, the importance of authority is indeed drastically diminished. It should be emphasized that these more experiential traditions assume that the ancient masters practiced both magical and mystical—designated above as prophetical—types of lore. Their unquestionable religious authority confers an aura of holiness on the Kabbalah as a sublime lore, and the Kabbalistic texts that promote this image of antiquity are less concerned with the actual praxis of the Kabbalist in the present, at least according to the way the Kabbalist presents himself explicitly in his writings.

Relying on the achievement of the ancients conceived of as mystics and magicians was quintessential in order to foster the status of nascent medieval Kabbalah. It is the search for authority, more than specific contents or anything else, that counts in some Kabbalistic contexts. Therefore, between the recipient of secrets and the interpreted text there was a process of mediation by tradition. Let me adduce an important text to this effect, from an introduction by one of the paragons of medieval Judaism, R. Moses ben Nahman, known as Nahmanides. He warns the reader of his *Commentary on the Pentateuch*: "I bring into a faithful covenant and give proper counsel to all who look into this book not to reason or entertain any thought concerning any of the mystic hints which I write regarding the hidden matters of the Torah, for I do hereby firmly make known to him that my words will not be comprehended nor known at all by any reasoning or contemplation, excepting from the mouth of a wise Kabbalist into the ear of an understanding recipient; reasoning about them is foolishness; any unrelated thought brings much damage and withholds the benefit."[2]

Nahmanides emphasizes the need to receive the meaning of the Kabbalistic hints alluded to in his commentary by oral transmission from an expert master,[3] otherwise any speculative reasoning as to their contents will be damaging. His argument is based on the duality of an affirmation of the antiquity, yet without providing the detailed praxis or concepts that were allegedly ancient. He does not mention ancient books in order to underline the antiquity of his stand, but describes Moses as the single available source for an authoritative oral esoteric lore. It should be stressed that although oral transmission is a prerequisite for understanding Kabbalah, according to this Kabbalist there must also have been other parameters connected to the Kabbalistic lore. It would be bizarre to assume that everything that is transmitted orally becomes, for Nahmanides, Kabbalah in the sense that it is an esoteric discipline.

At least one further dimension of the traded lore is implicit in the above quote: it has to be related to hints concerning topics of the Torah. In other words, the oral tradition has to address issues appearing in the canonic writings, as we learn from another passage from Nahmanides: "Indeed, this matter contains a great secret of the secrets of the Torah, which cannot be comprehended by the understanding of a thinker, but [only] by a man who gains them, learning [them] from the mouth of a teacher, going back to Moses our master, from the mouth of the Lord, blessed be He."[4] It should be stressed that here, unlike in the previous text, the emphasis is on the informant, while the qualities of the receiver are not mentioned at all. In yet another text, a sermon on Ecclesiastes, Nahmanides declares that "these issues[5] and others similar to them, their essence cannot be understood properly by his own reason[6] but by [means of] Kabbalah. This issue is explained in the Torah to whomever has heard the rationale of the commandment by Kabbalah, as it is proper, a receiver [meqabbel] from the mouth of [another] receiver,[7] until Moses our master, from the mouth of the Lord."[8]

We may infer that according to Nahmanides' rhetoric,[9] and in my opinion also according to his practice, esoteric issues understood as Kabbalah have to be transmitted orally.[10] This Kabbalist would sometimes, however, adduce a few theosophical topics, including explicit mention of the names of the sefirot, without leaving the impression that he reveals some esoteric knowledge. In general, I would propose that it would be better not to automatically identify any recourse to theosophical terminology with the esoteric Kabbalah Nahmanides claimed that he does not reveal. This is an issue worthy of detailed treatment, which cannot be undertaken here. In other words, it may well be that the theosophical content, which serves modern scholarship as the principal criterion for the definition of this kind of mystical lore, did not serve as the main organizing parameter in Nahmanides' vision of Kabbalah.

Nahmanides does not address the possibility of allowing the beginning of the tradition with any other figure except Moses. He alone is mentioned in the above quotes, and his role is also implied in another important discussion. When addressing the question of where the supernal palaces, the Heikhalot, or the account of the Chariot, mentioned in the text of the Torah, were, he asserts that despite his not knowing, he assumes that "there was an oral tradition" which reached to the time "when Ezekiel and Isaiah came and linked it" to the biblical verses.[11] This emphasis on the central role of orality for the transmission of Kabbalah seems to have occurred for two different reasons: one is an actual practice that I assume is reflected in the above quotes, namely the factual handing down of secrets related to the Torah in small groups in the circle of Nahmanides.[12] The other is the conscious attempt of the main halakhic Jewish elite in Catalonia, what I propose to call the primary elite in thirteenth-century Kabbalah, to keep to itself the secrets of the law. Nahmanides does not mention, in his many writings, an important Jewish esoteric term already found in the talmudic texts: rashei peraqim, the heads of the chapters, general hints or perhaps some principles concerning esoteric issues.[13] This implicit rejection, or at least dramatic marginalization, of such an important rabbinic term reflects his view that Kabbalistic lore should not be elaborated but rather transmitted or, more exactly, reproduced faithfully.

Nahmanides' warning, in my opinion in both theory and practice, is an extreme effort to intimidate the resort to exegetical techniques capable of extracting secrets from the sacred scriptures independently. According to Nahmanides, the gematrias are not an exegetical technique but a tradition stemming from Mount Sinai.[14] His views on the topic of Kabbalistic exegesis, and those of his school, open the question of the world of the text, as understood by Paul Ricoeur or Michael Riffaterre, as self-sufficient. Without the continuous influence of the secret tradition stemming from the author, the reader is regarded as unable to fathom the deepest layer of at least some of the parts of the text. If the sacred scripture is self-sufficient for the vulgus, this is not the case insofar as the elite is concerned. A profound understanding is conditioned by a form of authoritative human transmission that is independent of the canonical text. This need for an authoritative and uninterrupted contact with the intention of the author, mediated as it may be by a long series of accomplished masters, opens the question—which is even more pertinent for many coded texts—as prone to be included in the philosophy of textuality as formulated by Ricoeur. After all, if in the case of the Bible it was no more than an imposition of codes stemming from spiritual universes different from that of the Bible, in many cases authors compose books that are based on codes, and it may happen that this code is not transmitted within the book itself. The orality of the secret tradition in fact created a school, Nahmanides' school, or what Stanley Fish would call an interpretive community.[15]

Nahmanides' emphasis on the strict necessity of transmission of the secrets of the Torah from the first elite to the novices creates a strong authoritative role for the mediating master and is structurally reminiscent of the Catholic emphasis on the importance of institution and tradition.[16] It did not encourage the emergence of Kabbalistic commentaries on the Bible, despite the fact that Nachmanides himself wrote a commentary on the Pentateuch which is, statistically speaking, only peripherally Kabbalistic. The students of his immediate disciples produced commentaries—in fact, supercommentaries—on the Kabbalistic secrets of their master, but we may scarcely speak of independent Kabbalistic thinking in his school.[17] By perusing both Nahmanides' views as adduced above and the supercommentaries of the late-thirteenth- and early-fourteenth-century Kabbalists, I learned that the esoteric topics are to be described, as I translated the term above, as secrets, namely views that may be transmitted, and not mysteries, as Scholem implicitly assumes.[18]

Let us move to a much more "Protestant" approach, which allows the creative individual a greater role as standing before the biblical text when armed less with the arsenal of tradition and much more with a sense that he is asked to offer an interpretation resorting to exegetical techniques.

II. R. ABRAHAM ABULAFIA: TECHNIQUES AND EXEGESIS

The last third of the thirteenth century is the period of the emergence of the most elaborated hermeneutic systems of Kabbalah. Some fourfold exegetical systems, like those of R. Isaac ibn Latif, R. Joseph Gikatilla, R. Moses de Leon, the Zohar and Tiqqunei Zohar and that of R. Bahya ben Asher, on the one hand, and the sevenfold system of R. Abraham Abulafia, on the other, offer strong evidence of the deep interest in techniques of interpretation, hermeneutical devices, and comprehensive conception of the nature of the text and the interpreter, to an extent incomparable in discussions found in the earlier stages of Kabbalah. Writings of other Kabbalists, like R. Joseph of Hamadan in the late thirteenth century and R. Isaac ben Samuel of Acre at the beginning of the fourteenth century, though not always expressing an explicit and systematic hermeneutics, present a vital concern with different esoteric methods of understanding the sacred scriptures (see Appendixes 1 and 3).

These innovative Kabbalists can be described as belonging to the "secondary elite," namely educated individuals who were in continuous search of new types of thought and often uneasy with their intellectual starting points: the authoritative philosophical theology of Maimonides or, more rarely, even the views of another great authority, Nahmanides. All this stands in sharp contrast to the role played by their contemporaries, the "primary elite" and Kabbalists, too, who were leading figures in Catalonia and Castile. So, for example, Nahmanides in Gerona and R. Shlomo ben Abraham ibn Adret in Barcelona, and R. Moses ben Shimeon of Burgos and R. Todros ben Joseph ha-Levi Abulafia in Toledo, were accomplished Kabbalists, active either on the public plane as important legalistic figures or as social leaders of their communities; in none of these cases is there any evidence of interest from their side in systematic hermeneutics. None of them, however, even reproduced the systematic expositions formulated in their generation. I believe that this clear-cut distribution in distinct groups—on the one hand, the secondary elite interested, on the other the primary elite uninterested in presentations of systematic hermeneutics—is highly significant for a better understanding of the Kabbalistic conceptions of hermeneutics.

This prominent concern with hermeneutics is evident not only in practice but even in the manner in which Kabbalah is defined by the secondary-elite Kabbalists. Abraham Abulafia, for example, enumerates the three principles of Kabbalah as "letters, combinations [of letters], and vowels. Their acronym is 'ATzN, which can be permuted as Tzo'N . . . The combination turns the letters, and the vowels turn the combinations, and the spirit of man, given by God, turns the vowels until they cause the emergence and the illumination of the concept that is proper to any intelligent Kabbalist."[19]

According to other Kabbalists, who were part of the spiritual milieu of Abulafia, Kabbalah consists in linguistic methods like those of ginat—an acronym denoting gematria, notariqon, and temurot (permutations of letters), namely the "garden of the nut," a metaphor for mystical speculation.[20] Both Abulafia's emphasis on language and the various mechanical combinations of its elements and his acquaintances' emphasis on the more formal aspects of the manipulation of texts involve technical instructions concerning how to play with language and texts which are much easier for students to master than the esoteric concepts that constitute the inner religious core of the canonic writings. Indeed, emphatic as Abulafia, like other Kabbalists, is on the importance of secrets, he is also aware that, unlike others, he is much more inclined to reveal them rather than keep them. This is why he declares, in a rather rare example of conscious Kabbalistic exotericism, that "despite the fact that I know that there are many Kabbalists who are not perfect, thinking as they are that their perfection consists in not revealing a secret issue, I shall care neither about their thought nor about their blaming me because of the disclosure [of Kabbalah], since my view on this is very different from and even opposite theirs."[21]

Immediately afterward Abulafia "discloses" the view that ma'aseh merkavah, the account of the Chariot, which is one of the most important esoteric topics in Jewish mysticism, should be understood neither as a visionary experience, as in the first chapter of Ezekiel, nor as an allegory for metaphysics, as in Maimonides, but as a matter of combination of letters of the divine names, as technique of interpretation and perhaps also a mystical technique.[22] Elsewhere Abulafia describes the perfect student, who is entitled to receive the entire Kabbalistic lore: "Since this man does not need a master in order to hand down the Kabbalah and what he finds written in this book about it will suffice . . . and if he finds a master it is fine, and if not he should go over what is written in this book."[23] Abulafia was therefore eager to recognize that his book, the latest of his writings that are dated, can substitute for the tradition and the transmission. He did not, however, claim an absorbing status for his book, as he understood it as a conduit of techniques, not of concepts.

The various hermeneutic systems expounded by late-thirteenth-century Kabbalists were intertwined with novel approaches to canonical texts; by applying their exegetical methods, Kabbalists were deemed to be able to extract new Kabbalistic views or elaborate on already existing Kabbalistic theories. This innovative type of Kabbalah constitutes a considerable departure from the dominant perception of Kabbalah as an ancient and precious esoteric lore consisting of certain concepts or explanations of particular aspects of the canonical writings, to be transmitted and preserved without changes. In other words, the emergence of the fourfold exegetical method, as well as Abulafia's sevenfold exegetical system, at the end of the thirteenth century coincides with the nascent innovative Kabbalah. From the perspective of the history of Kabbalah, the understanding of the affinity between the pardes types of interpretation and the creativity that characterizes the contemporary Kabbalah is of paramount importance, as we shall see in Appendix 1. Transmission has now been reduced to disclosing different methods, exegetical or conducive to mystical experiences, much more than to instructing someone in specific secret contents. This is one of the reasons why Nahmanides' conceptual transmission has been able to constitute a distinct Kabbalistic school that orally perpetuated his content secrets for at least three generations after his death. Nothing similar is known in the various forms of innovative Kabbalah.

The traditional nature of transmitted material may be regarded, when speaking in abstract terms, as interfering with, if not in some cases obfuscating, personal experience. The acceptance and the veneration of the cherished concepts of the past could be understood as obliterating the immediate contact with what the mystic would conceive of as ultimate reality. Indeed, the question as to what extent mystical experiences are constructed by what is widely described as tradition or have some degree of independence from traditional material is part of an ongoing controversy in some academic circles.[24] I am not concerned with that issue here, because tradition, in the context of the controversy, is defined not as oral transmission but in much more general terms as language, concepts, religious literature, and ritual. Rather, I shall focus my brief discussion on the impact of the emphasis on experience on the status of transmission, according to the views of a few thirteenth-century Kabbalists.

According to a treatise by R. Nathan ben Sa'adyah, an author belonging to ecstatic Kabbalah, "The essence of this issue cannot be conceptualized *ex definitio*, nor discussed by mouth, even less in written form, and this is the reason it is called Kabbalah and heads of chapters,[25] namely the principles, as the meaning depends on the receiver to [understand it] in detail and divest [his soul from corporeality] and delight. The Kabbalah is not transmitted but [by way of] heads of chapters alone."[26] The importance of the conceptual content of Kabbalah is explicitly mitigated here: the impossibility of transmitting it is essential, and this is why the more general principles alone are provided by the informant master, while the details are shaped by each and every recipient. The experiential aspect is viewed here as quintessential. The issue of delight and sweetness comes up several times in this treatise, and the very assumption of the author is that Kabbalah has a strong experiential aspect, which should not be discussed argumentatively but approached as practical lore.

R. Nathan ben Sa'adyah confesses that after his rather modest studies of philosophy he encountered "a divine man, a Kabbalist, who taught me the path of Kabbalah by heads of chapters. And, notwithstanding the fact that because of the little I knew from the science of nature it[27] seemed to me to be impossible, my master said to me, 'My son, why do you negate an issue you did not experience? Indeed, it would be worthwhile to experience it.' "[28] This emphasis on the criterion of experiment and experience is not unique with this Kabbalist. Another one, R. Abraham Abulafia, who may be none other than the "divine man," mentions in one of his writings that the study of the most important treatises that informed his thought did not induce mystical experiences in him, but only when he decided to approach revered texts, like *Sefer Yetzirah* and Maimonides' *Guide of the Perplexed*, the two most important sources of Abulafia's Kabbalah, in a more experiential manner.[29] In a passage from *Sefer ha-Hesheq* Abulafia classifies the oral Kabbalistic traditions as the lowest form of Kabbalah:

> In order to understand my intention regarding [the meaning of] *qolot* [voices] I shall hand down to you the known *qabbalot*, some of them having been received from mouth to mouth from the sages of [our] generation, and others that I have received from the books named *sifrei qabbalah* composed by the ancient sages, the Kabbalists, blessed be their memory, concerning the wondrous topics;[30] and others [other traditions] bestowed on me by God, blessed be He, which came to me from ThY[31] in the form of the daughter of the voice,[32] these being the higher *qabbalot* ['elyonot].[33]

This is one of the few instances where Abulafia explicitly mentions his reception of oral traditions from some masters. Only in one other case, when speaking about the reception of esoteric traditions concerning the secrets of Maimonides' *Guide of the Perplexed*, does Abulafia again mention an oral tradition.[34] For an ecstatic Kabbalist, the orally received traditions are lower than those received from the "mouth of the Agent Intellect." Indeed, the very resort to the metaphor of a mouth for the relation of the human to the cosmic intellect is very significant, because it transposes the image of the transmission here below, or from the horizontal level to a vertical type of relationship, namely the intellectual connection of the mystic with the divine world.[35] Moreover, this metaphor may indicate that the Agent Intellect was conceived of as a master, or the master par excellence, as Hindu mystics understood the guru to be a cosmic power.[36]

This emphasis on the spiritual supernal source of Kabbalah according to the ecstatic Kabbalah, as opposed to a flesh-and-blood teacher in Nahmanides, is just one of the differences between the conservative Kabbalah of the Geronese master and the innovative one formulated by Abraham Abulafia: the revelation is the prerogative not only of the ancient masters, especially Moses, as Nahmanides and his school would contend, but also of the medieval mystics, whose recent revelations can be regarded as even higher than those of the old masters by their resort to techniques conceived of as Kabbalah.[37] Abulafia's aforecited passage is based on two different traditions: the ancient Jewish one found in the Talmud, which mentions the transmission of the esoteric lore to those who are wise (hakham) and understanding (mevin) by his own mind (mi-da'ato).[38] Abulafia has differentiated between these three terms, which should be understood in the talmudic context as a unified intellectual activity, as if they pointed to three different activities. These activities are connected to the well-known distinction between acts committed in writing, those committed orally, and those committed mentally, a division that is crucial for the mystical technique of this Kabbalist.[39] As in the above quote, so too the oral recitations of the divine names and the written permutations of letters are inferior to their inner pronunciations.[40] It should be added that Abulafia also mentions traditions he has received orally, "from the mouth of the sages of his generation."[41] Thus, although this form of acquiring Kabbalah plays a certain role in his system, Abulafia attributes to it only a limited and not very high role. I would say that the concept of revealing the conceptual secrets of the Torah, as in Nahmanides, is much less crucial for Abulafia's understanding of the oral teachings than is the teaching of the techniques for attaining mystical experiences. The master, who plays an important role in Abulafia's Kabbalah, is supposed to serve mainly as an external catalyst.[42] Elsewhere, Abulafia offers this description of Kabbalah: "The purpose which is intended by the ways of Kabbalah is the reception of the prophetic, divine, and intellectual influx from God, blessed be He, by means of the Agent Intellect, and the causing of the descent and the blessing by means of the [divine] name on the individual and on the community."[43]

Whereas the image Nahmanides wants to project is that of a reliable transmitter of esoteric traditions, Abulafia would be much more pleased to be viewed as the receiver of Kabbalistic traditions by means of divine revelations in the present. Nahmanides' perception of Kabbalah revolves around the founding experience of Moses in a glorious past, Kabbalah being conceived of as the extant reverberation of that constitutive experience; with Abulafia, however, this humanly transmitted lore is a lower form of knowledge that should be transcended by means of what he believes to be much higher forms of reception in a glorious present: those from the source of all knowledge, either the Agent Intellect or God. Abulafia would like to short-circuit the chain of human transmission by establishing direct contact with the spiritual source. He is much more concerned with the present and the imminent future, while the past is significant mainly insofar as it provides examples to imitate, techniques to shorten the way to the divine, rather than fixed concepts to be passively accepted and transmitted. In other words, the role of the human authoritative master, expert in some esoteric concepts, who was considered to be quintessential in the primary type of elite, becomes less important in the secondary elite, who is much more concerned with examination and the preparation of the recipient.

It is emblematic of this change of focus that we know very little about the masters of the secondary-elite Kabbalists, like Isaac ibn Latif, Joseph Gikatilla, Moses de Leon, Joseph of Hamadan, and Abraham Abulafia; in most instances even their names have escaped modern scholarship. In the case of the conceptual Kabbalah we can much more easily trace the identity of the masters: thus we may assume that R. Jacob ben Yaqar, Nahmanides, R. Shlomo ibn Adret, R. Shem Tov ibn Ga'on, R. Meir ibn Avi Sahulah, R. Yom Tov Ashvili, and R. Yehudah Campanton shared, mutatis mutandis, the more conservative form of Kabbalah, which was handed down from master to disciple for a century and a half.[44] Whereas the conceptual Kabbalah is concerned with tracing the vestiges of those primordial experiences by studying and preserving the remnants of the secret tradition transmitted to the exemplary figure (often Moses), the experiential Kabbalists would rather emphasize their personal mystical testimony or the avenues open to realize such an experience, namely the mystical techniques. To summarize: whereas Nahmanides' school mainly played the role of curator of an esoteric lore, Abraham Abulafia, like such other innovative Kabbalists as Gikatilla and de Leon, should be viewed much more as artists who transformed Kabbalah from a traditional lore into an art.

III. PARTICULAR VERSUS UNIVERSAL TRANSMISSION

The shift in the late thirteenth century from conceptual transmission to technical transmission, which is more experiential and exegetical, involves an additional and, in my opinion, essential change in the nature of Kabbalah. Conceptual transmission is very deeply related to the text, precisely to the Hebrew Bible and eminently to some of the idiosyncratic qualities of the Hebrew text, its eschatology and its ritualistic content. In short, it is a particularistic approach. The transition, however, from the interpreted text to the secret message included in it, at least as it was cultivated by Nahmanides, is not an interpretative or midrashic one but much more a matter of confidence in the authoritative human source. Nahmanides, one of the most important figures in medieval Jewish exegesis of both the written and the oral Torah on what he argued to be their plain sense, was reluctant to expand on the symbolic-theurgic traditions he claimed to have inherited.

On the other hand, technical transmission, being freer from the particularistic approach, assumes that a gifted receiver can manipulate the more general methods either for an exegetical project or for the sake of attaining a mystical experience. By distributing the general principles, either in an oral or in a written manner, and by not entering into details, the secondary-elite Kabbalists revolutionized the dominant and more conservative concept of Kabbalah. Their exotericism marked the start of a massive interpretive project. Let me adduce two more examples dealing with the importance of the "heads of chapters" from ecstatic Kabbalah. One of Abulafia's followers, the anonymous Kabbalist who composed *Sefer ha-Tzeruf*, wrote that "whatever is transmitted concerning this lore is heads of chapters, and this is why it needs the intellect, and it is called intellectual Kabbalah[45] because it is not like the other sciences, namely the propadaeutic ones, which are transmitted alone . . . But it is impossible to transmit this lore, known as Kabbalah, in toto in an oral manner, nor even in written form, even for thousands of years. And whatever efforts a Kabbalist makes in order to interpret, everything is [still] a hint and a head of chapters."[46] The emphasis on the necessity of human intellect in order to understand the Kabbalistic lore while criticizing philosophy as being too scholastic a science is a unique feature of this text. In a Platonic vein, Kabbalah is conceived of as an invitation more to decode, to elaborate, to expand, than to repeat faithfully. The resort to the concept of head of chapters, namely the principles that are by definition starting points rather than final statements, is quite representative of ecstatic Kabbalah. The recourse to philosophy, despite the fact that the anonymous author criticizes it, can be understood as the synthesis between the microchain of the linguistic Kabbalah, which apparently preceded ecstatic Kabbalah, and Neoaristotelian philosophy, especially as expounded by Maimonides, which is part of a macrochain, the thought of the Greek master transmitted by the Arab thinkers as accepted by a major Jewish philosopher in the Middle Ages. This is the main achievement of Abraham Abulafia, an ardent student, teacher, and commentator of the *Guide of the Perplexed* but also profoundly influenced by some Jewish traditions related to the linguistic techniques of *Sefer Yetzirah* and the Ashkenazi Hasidic masters.

But let us return to the "heads of chapters." Abraham Abulafia writes in one of his epistles that "despite the fact that Kabbalah is transmitted to every illuminatus in general, not every listener and receiver is able to actualize it, because what it is transmitted from it [the Kabbalah] are but heads of chapters, to whomever is wise, and understanding from his own knowledge."[47] Kabbalah becomes, in many circles, much more an open-ended theory, whose contents can vary, be enriched, and also often reflect the personality and concerns of the Kabbalists as much as the nature of the religious tradition within which it emerged. The appearance of the issue of actualization is crucial for understanding the whole relationship between Kabbalah and philosophy: Kabbalah should be understood as a type of information in *potentia* that is waiting to be actualized, a term stemming from Aristotelian epistemology. From the perspective of the medieval attitude toward things in *actu* and in *potentia*, there can be no doubt that the former is considered to be much higher than the latter. In other words, the general principles, the headings, serve as potential indicators, to be elaborated by the gifted Kabbalist according to his own aptitude. Unlike Nahmanides' approach to this esoteric lore, which in principle does not leave room for its conceptual expansion by the next Kabbalist, in ecstatic Kabbalah such an expansion is accepted as inevitable. The ecstatic Kabbalist would orally receive the methods for expansion, either of his consciousness as mystical techniques or of the various understandings of the Torah by means of exegetical techniques.

On this point let me adduce one more quote, which emphasizes the great importance placed on the preparation of the recipient: "The secrets of the Torah, and the secrets of reality and the foundations of the commandments, are not told except orally, from a perfect person to someone who is worthy of receiving the perfection, face to face, after the test and the trial, [regarding] the intention of the receiver, if he is meritorious and it is right to transmit [them] to him or not."[48] The fact is that many quotes from Abulafia's *Sefer Shomer Mitzvah* adduced here in the context of transmission are not a matter of accident or of my focusing on this forgotten treatise. In my opinion the problematic of transmission is central in this book, because the Kabbalist dedicated it to one of his students, R. Shlomo ben Moses ha-Kohen, who left Sicily, apparently in order to return to his native Galilee. This seems to be the reason for the recurrent emphasis that the major form of transmission is oral, while the written one is a lower form. Although Abulafia dedicated some of his other books to his students, they were written on the occasion of Abulafia's leaving his students, not vice versa.

IV. GRADUAL TRANSMISSION

Both the conceptual and the technical transmissions took into consideration the spiritual development of the receiver. Different as these two types of transmissions are, they nonetheless agree on the view that the esoteric traditions should be delivered only gradually. This is the case in the school of Nahmanides, where we learn that some secret topics are not to be revealed even to a Kabbalist before he reaches the age of forty, and then only in an oral manner.[49] Such an attitude seems to be not only reasonable in itself but also fostered by statements found in rabbinic tradition to the effect that some issues should be revealed only quite late in the program of studies.[50] This stand is made explicitly in Abulafia's *Sefer Shomer Mitzvah*:

The Kabbalist is not allowed to reveal [the secrets of Kabbalah] and explain them in his writing, but he should disclose one span and cover the other two. But when the prepared person worthy to reveal to him orally is available, he should first reveal two spans of the tradition and cover one. And if he [the receiver] will receive it and really desire to complete what he has begun, some topics should be revealed, in accordance with his capacity to receive them, and they should not be hidden from him, because they are by nature hidden and occult and covered by essence.[51]

Elsewhere in the same treatise we learn that

despite the fact that the wondrous secrets emerge out of their numbers, their secrets should not be taught except orally, and only after much labor concerning the essence of the paths of Kabbalah, so that the knowledge of truth should not occur to the receiver randomly. But it is necessary that at the beginning he should make great efforts to [follow] the ways of Kabbalah and their paths, which are the ways that open the gates of the heart, in order to understand the truths. It is necessary that whoever wants to come within the depths[52] of truth, according to the Kabbalah, should at the beginning lay the foundations for the wisdom and understanding within his heart.[53]

Abulafia conditions the disclosure of the most advanced hermeneutical method, the seventh one, on the prior oral reception of the knowledge of the names of forty-two and seventy-two letters and the transmission of "some traditions, even by heads of chapters."[54] Moreover, the importance of systematic studies, including oral instructions and apparently technical exercises, which are mentioned in some of Abulafia's writings and those of his followers, assumes that the more regular religious behavior is less pertinent as a way to reach the depth of Kabbalistic secrets. Likewise, the end of the quote from *Sefer Shomer Mitzvah* may imply the necessity of the study of philosophy as an important step toward understanding Kabbalah, because Abulafia believed that philosophy can help purify, as Maimonides' philosophy does, the central theological concepts, which were misunderstood by some readers of the Bible. His Kabbalah therefore deals more with a gradual intellectual and spiritual development, which culminates with a deeper penetration of the "secrets" of the Torah, rather than cultivating studies within a certain elitist group for a long period and assimilating his religious worldview to the group's secrets, to its ethos and way of behavior. In short, the technical transmission opens the door for a much more individualistic type of experience, as it delivers the clues for an independent mystical path. Like the great eagle,

Abulafia believed that it is possible to reach the secrets by activities independent of human aid.

V. ENCOUNTERING THE TEXT AND SELF-RECOGNITION

The issue of the similarity between man and the Torah has been addressed in the preceding pages and will be addressed also below in Appendix 2. Indeed, R. Hayyim Vital describes his master, R. Isaac Luria, as the "Torah scroll of the Ashkenazis."[55] In the theosophical-theurgical Kabbalah, it was the anthropomorphic structure of both God and Torah that served as a common denominator. In the ecstatic Kabbalah, however, what were regarded as the main constituents of man provided the basis for the affinities: the organic, material structure represented by blood, and the spiritual aspects, like imagination and intellect, represented by blood and ink. The conflict between these two aspects of human psyche, and their ongoing battle, the Aristotelian psychomachia, attracted Abraham Abulafia's attention, as it did that of some Sufi masters.[56] The study of the Torah creates a dialogical situation wherein a revelation of a human form allows a conversation that has revelatory implications.[57] Abulafia's paraphrase of the 'Avot dictum that we see from the Torah presupposes a visual though imaginary experience, starting with the study of the Torah à la Abulafia. The canonical text and its imaginary apparition therefore enhance the human experience. From this point of view, study of the text is a much easier technique for spiritual progression than study of nature by philosophers, as Abulafia is eager to point out.[58]

Let me compare this aspect of Abulafian hermeneutical thought to Paul Ricoeur's thesis as to the meaning of encountering a text. The French philosopher asserts:

> To interpret is to explicate the type of being-in-the world unfolded in front of the text . . . Ultimately, what I appropriated is a proposed world. The latter is not behind the text, as a hidden intention would be, but in front of it, as that which the work unfolds, discovers, reveals. Henceforth, to understand is to understand oneself in the front of the text. It is not a question of imposing upon the text our finite capacity of understanding, but of exposing ourselves to the text and receiving from it an enlarged self, which would be the proposed existence corresponding, in the most suitable way to the world proposed . . . As a reader, I find myself only by losing myself. Reading introduces me into the imaginative variations of the ego. The metamorphosis of the world in play is also the playful metamorphosis of the ego.[59]

Ricoeur proposes a moment of loss of self-control in order to be able to enhance one's self by exposing oneself to the text. Only this loss will enable a

fruitful encounter and shape the reader's ego by augmenting it. Ricoeur emphasizes this nonegoistic ability to read, stemming from the New Testament, elsewhere in his writings too, and it may help us understand his view to adduce one
more quote: "The reader does not submit the meaning of the text to his own finite
capacity of understanding, but . . . lets himself be exposed to the text, in order
to receive from it a Self. By Self I mean a non-egoistic, non-narcissistic mode
of subjectivity which responds and corresponds to the power of a work to display
a world."[60]

In the sense of standing in the front of the text, Ricoeur's theory is reminiscent
of Abulafia's. What seems to me even more striking, however, is that both the
medieval Kabbalist and the modern philosopher speak of a broader "world of the
text" that allows the enhancement of the ego. They both agree that the world of
the text is greater than the individual interpretations that are elicited by the reader-
text encounter. Interestingly, both speak about the confrontation with the text,
especially as we learned from a quote from *Sefer ha-Hesheq*.[61] Yet whereas Ricoeur's
proposal is to see the very existence of the discourse, especially the written text, as
decontextualizing itself from the author, the particular circumstances, and the
audience for whom the author intended his work, and as continuously recontex-
tualizing itself for various audiences, Abulafia, like many Kabbalists, would say
that the raison d'être of a religious text is to become a conduit for all the potential
readers, so that they can reach the author who looms behind the ordinary order of
the text as accepted in the community. Though many Kabbalists would accept the
concept of the continuous recontextualization of the Torah, especially as it is
conspicuous in the theory that all the sciences are contained within the Torah,[62]
and the two decontextualizations from particular circumstances and audiences,
they would think it deleterious to contemplate an author-oriented decontextual-
ization. More than the classical assumption that the text reflects the intention of
the author and interpretation strives to reach it through the message of the text,
the Kabbalists would say that it is the author himself, not only his intentions, that
should be reached through the strong reading of the text.

Let me attempt to extrapolate from the more extreme example of Abulafia's
thought to a better manner of approaching the relationship between the different
Jewish corpora mentioned above. I would construe the speculative and mystical
literatures of the Jewish Middle Ages as standing in front of the earlier, canonical
Jewish writings, being inspired by them but also dramatically attempting to project within them their systems of thought. Although such a double attitude may
appear to be a pure contradiction, the conscious and unconscious processes of
adoption and adaptation, to which exegesis contributed greatly, reduced stark
opposition to tensions, or to a double sense, which expresses one view as the

plain sense and another on the esoteric level. And though many of the medieval corpora continue spiritual vectors found in earlier sources, the filling of the vague mythologoumena and theologoumena was often done by resorting to more systematic themes found in the speculative systems residing in their intellectual and religious environment.

VI. PERFECTING THE TORAH

The task of the Kabbalistic interpreters is to be understood largely in terms of projecting new religious worlds within the canonical texts. Although these projections, conscious or unconscious, commonly took the form of commentary, one major example assumes that the oral Torah, understood as intellectual, clarifies the written one, conceived of as more hylic. The famous early-seventeenth-century rabbi Yehudah Loewe ben Bezalel of Prague, known as the Maharal, writes as follows:

> Everything created during the six days of creation needs amendment and action . . . The Torah has been given from God, blessed be He, by a prophet, but the rank of the intellect is higher than that of the prophet, as it has been said, "The wise man is higher than the prophet,"[63] and this is the reason he has said that the action of the intellect is higher than that of nature . . . because the action of the intellectual man is higher than nature, so the act of the intellect is higher than that of prophecy. This is why the sages are the amendment and the perfection for the Torah,[64] even if it was given by Moses on Mount Sinai . . . because everything needs an amendment by man, who is [an] intellectual [entity]. So it is that the intellectual Torah, which arrived to Moses by prophecy, did not arrive in such a clear manner and in a refined manner by words that are explicit, and because of the sages the Torah is the clarification and the refinement of prophecy.[65]

The intellect of the wise men is directed not just to explaining the content of the written Torah, nor is their activity one of purification alone. The sages are also completing or perfecting the Torah, in a manner reminiscent of Eco's open work.[66] Although this is an act of interpretation, the sages subsequent to Moses are adding to the canonical text. The Torah is thus a natural entity that invites the refinement of the ongoing tradition viewed in a rather intellectual manner. The Maharal resorts to the duality of intellect versus nature in order to create the hierarchy of the oral versus the written. This hierarchy assumes the ongoing completion of the latter by the former—an actualization, I would say, of potentialities inherent in the written text. The later interpreter therefore continues the initial revelation, perhaps even on a higher level, all this as part of a natural development also taking place in the case of other entities that need additional acts for their completion.

This appreciation of the sage is formally an interpretation of the talmudic dictum on the status of the sage in comparison to the prophet, but the gist of the Maharal's view is the attribution of so low a status to the written Torah as being in need of intellectual completion. In keeping with some of the earlier discussions, the approach to the interpreter of the written Torah becomes much more powerful, as he, not God, becomes the source of the perfection of the Torah. This author is not a Kabbalist, although he was acquainted with Kabbalistic views. Nevertheless, his view corroborates my contention that an interpreter could claim, even without being a Kabbalist but being a rather traditional and conservative thinker, the status of completing the Torah, a view that is in line with the theory of the strong reader.[67] The Maharal's passage demonstrates that more extreme formulations, like those found in Abraham Abulafia's writings and those influenced by him up to Hasidism, do not constitute a problem even in traditional circles of the Jewish first elite.

14

CONCLUDING REMARKS

The different forms of Kabbalah demonstrate the existence of significant instances of linguocentric forms of mysticism. They not only emphasize the holiness of Hebrew language, in a way that is reminiscent of two important forms of
Muslim and Hindu mysticism or of the importance of the text, as is the case in
many kinds of mysticism, but also assume that it is within language and through
the text—though not exclusively—that the mystical experience can be attained.
Many authors whose writings constitute the mystical literature of Western Christianity envisioned the human soul and the introvert path as the major locus of the
mystical experience and the technique of its attainment. Nature mysticism, re-

ligious or secular, prefers the extrovert path, as it sees the external world as the place of the mystical encounter. In many cases, God Himself is the space of His encountering man, and this type of mysticism can be viewed as theocentric. In the various forms of Kabbalah, there are numerous cases where performed language and texts are the main locus of the mystical encounter, in a manner reminiscent of Gadamer's assertion that belonging takes place in language.[1]

However, unlike all other forms of mysticism, where the locus of the experience existed long before the mystical experience, the linguocentric and bibliocentric forms of mysticism start, in some cases, with the creation of the locus by the mystic himself, as a sine qua non of his mystical experience. This propensity assumes an active approach, because without human initiative the locus of the experience cannot even be shaped. The speaking man, not God—as in more theocentric types of religiosities—is the main bridge-builder. Language can be envisioned as an expression of the soul, of the subjective, which nevertheless takes place in nature, namely in space, and is intended, according to some views, to attract God within it. Viewed thus, linguocentric and bibliocentric mysticism is a more comprehensive approach than the other kinds of mysticism mentioned above. Unlike soul, nature, or God, which can be experienced and were often presented as moments of solitary experience, language- and text-oriented experiences have a prominently connective social role, and the type of mysticism I have described above assumes that God may be encountered precisely by means of the most social of human tools. If the written text, which has been crucial for generations of Kabbalists, has been viewed as an iconic representation of the divine, for some other Kabbalists and for many of the Hasidic masters it is precisely the tool for overcoming the distance between themselves and God, for reducing the importance of textual semantics that has caused a certain alienation, or *verfremdung*, to use Ricoeur's term, by establishing the direct encounter by proclamation and manifestation. The move from a hypersemantic mysticism to a hyposemantic one, so clear in the transition from Kabbalah to Hasidism, is one of the reasons for the much greater diffusion of the latter than the former among the masses.

The arcanization of the canonical book in Judaism should be understood as a characteristic move within the broader framework of a linguocentric spirituality. This form of spirituality should be recognized as a category in itself, though similar to some forms of spirituality less known in the West.[2] Too often, in my opinion, the academic requirement of allowing each type of spirituality its own modus operandi and modus existendi has been ignored by scholars; the history of the assumption that the letter kills the spirit not only is part of ancient and medieval Christian attitudes toward Judaism but sometimes creeps into scholarly books as well. So, for example, we read about the recurrence of the term "Torah" in the Heikhalot literature, "Too often we hear of the 'book' in which all the mysteries are written and which one should learn and not forget."[3]

Indeed, the sacred book and its secrets often played a paramount role in Jewish spirituality, a role in some respects similar to that which the Christ and the mysteries of his via passionis played in Christianity and Christian mysticism. It seems that the biblical religion, with its emphasis on the exoteric, has produced at least three different religiosities that departed from this emphasis: the Christian one, revolving around mysteries; the Qumranic one, emphasizing eschatological secrets; and the rabbinic one, which includes an arcanization of the canonic texts. It seems that the Christian emphasis on mysteries and the Qumranic exegesis revolving around eschatological interpretations represent attempts to transcend the unconditional importance of the interpreted book by gravitating toward topics that are supposed to happen in the future, after the completion of biblical history. Mysteries, revealed in the life and death of the Christ as expressed in another canon, the New Testament on the one hand and eschatological sermons of the *doresh ha-torah* on the other, leave a more modest role to the variety of topics expressed by the text of the Hebrew Bible. The widespread refusal to indulge in detailed and public presentations of the secrets of the Torah in rabbinic circles encouraged each of the members of the elite to return to the canonical text in order to understand it with his own spiritual capacities and share his findings only with the few. Inspection of the medieval mystical literature of the Jews, which has strong esoteric proclivities, shows a shift in the meaning of the terms *sod*, *raz*, and *seter*, which received a much more mysterious significance in comparison to their ancient occurrences.[4]

The gist of many of the discussions above was that some medieval Jewish corpora, especially the mystical ones, were more prone to resist the impact of the logocentric Greek speculations by emphasizing the dense textuality of the sacred scriptures in their Hebrew original. I would prefer, therefore, not to insist on a simplistic synthetic nature of Kabbalistic literature but to suggest instead the creation of hierarchical organizations that allow the less logocentric elements a greater role than they have in philosophical corpora. Indeed, we may assume that biblical thought created more particularistic approaches, which inspired a predisposition not to adopt logocentric thought so easily, even in the Middle Ages. So, for example, we learn from the testimony of the late-twelfth-century bishop of Exeter, Bartholomew:

> The chief cause of disagreement between ourselves and the Jews seems to me to be this: they take all the Old Testament literally, where they can find a literal sense, unless it gives manifest witness to Christ. Then they repudi-

ate it, saying that it is not in the Hebrew Truth, that is in their books, or they refer it to some fable, as that they are still awaiting its fulfillment, or they escape by some other serpentine wile, when they feel themselves hard pressed. They will never accept allegory, except when they have no other way out. We interpret not only the words of Scriptures, but the things themselves, in a mystical sense, yet in such a way that the freedom of allegory may in no wise nullify, either history in the events, or proper understanding of the words, of Scriptures.[5]

The English bishop is correct insofar as the marginality of the allegorical mode in Jewish rabbinic literature is concerned. However, the resistance to allegory in Jewish writings started to diminish dramatically in exactly the period when the above passage was written. What seems fascinating about this quote is that it was composed at a watershed: the very beginning of the ascent of Jewish allegorical and mystical exegesis, and the beginning of the decline of Christian mystical exegesis, to judge from the history of Christian mysticism as surveyed in Bernard McGinn's three volumes. McGinn's approach, which put special emphasis on the hermeneutical aspects of Christian mysticism, can be read as follows: the first two tomes reflect the concerns of authors active from the beginning of Christianity to about 1200, who were mainly interested in exegesis, whereas the third, covering the period from 1200 to 1350, reflects a less sustained exegetical enterprise. In Christian mysticism, however, the move from the metaphorical understanding is not to a more literal one but to a more direct experience which owes less to the study of the minutiae of the sacred texts. I would say that starting from the ancient myth of the inspired nature of the translators of the Septuagint, which could allow the Greek text as important a role as the Hebrew original enjoyed in ancient times and continued to enjoy in medieval Jewish mysticism, the sanctity of the precise literary formulations continuously diminished. It survived only insofar as the Hebrew text is concerned, not because of the relatively late theory of Hebrew as a sacred language but because of the much earlier and stronger impact of the logocentric theories adopted by ancient and medieval Christian thinkers. It would be sufficient to compare Philo's version of the story of the miraculous translation of the Bible into Greek to the story of an early-sixteenth-century Christian printer who denied the possibility of translating the fullness of meaning, dependent as it is on each and every letter and word of the original Hebrew.[6]

On the Jewish side we find the inverse move. The ancient literatures that may be described as mystical, the Heikhalot literature, and *Sefer Yetzirah* are not exegetical corpora, and although the first was concerned with the Torah and its multiplication and secrets, no commentary on the Torah emerged from these circles. From the beginning of the thirteenth century many mystical commentaries emerge at the same time in the Near East, under the impact of Sufi mysticism, in the circle of Maimonides' descendants,[7] in the Rhineland circle of Hasidei Ashkenaz, and somewhat later in the century in the various schools of Kabbalah in Spain and Italy, and these new exegetical trends had a lasting impact on many of the subsequent commentaries on the Bible. Thus, at least as regards the development of Jewish medieval and later forms of Jewish mysticism, the Bible and its interpretations move to the center of the spiritual concerns, as the performed ritualistic language constitutes techniques to reach mystical experiences as well as their locus. Interestingly, the expansion of the Jewish symbolic exegesis took place in a period when Christian theologians restricted the allegorical interpretation, as we saw in Chapter 10.

This recentralization of the Bible in both the philosophical and Kabbalistic circles is part of the struggle over the "authentic" secrets of the Torah between the competing elites. However, the various forms of competition over the meaning of those secrets only highlight the centrality of the canonical book. This issue is crucial from another point of view as well. Kabbalists and Hasidic masters become recluses only rarely in the history of Jewish mysticism. Their impact has much to do with the fact that among their major concerns were the special interpretations they offered of the Bible and the commandments, thus sharing with their community a vital common denominator. In lieu of a much stronger emphasis on the nature of the inner experiences in other forms of mysticism, it seems that Kabbalists and Hasidic masters formulated their religious life and much of their manner of expression in terms provided by the Bible as a main semantic reservoir.

II. JEWISH, GREEK, AND JEWISH-GREEK

In modern scholarship there are voices that attribute to biblical and rabbinic attitudes toward text and textuality a unique status in comparison to the Greek attitudes. The most articulate expressions of this trend are found in books by Susan Handelman, Jose Faur, and Shira Wolosky.[8] The most extreme voices in the opposite direction are those of Isaac Baer and Harold Bloom, who speculated about the hypothetical centrality of Platonism for the emergence of the rabbinic attitude toward learning.[9] There can be no doubt that most of the rabbinic corpus, committed to writing in milieus replete with Hellenistic thought and literature, should not be completely separated from their immediate intellectual environment, and this point has been made in a large number of studies, especially those of Saul Lieberman. Without denying the obvious, however, I see no reason to subscribe to either of the two extreme alternatives. My contention has been that the Kabbalistic concepts of hermeneutics reflect both the earlier Jewish attitudes revolving around the text and the adoption of more logocentric attitudes, especially during the Middle Ages. Let me attempt to integrate some of the topics discussed above into a more comprehensive picture.

On the side of the separatists, let me adduce a passage by Hans Jonas, concerning the uniqueness that he attributes to biblical thought as compared to philosophy: "There was an anti-metaphysical agent in the very nature of the biblical position that led to the erosion of classical metaphysics, and changed the whole character of philosophy . . . The biblical doctrine pitted contingency against necessity, particularity against universality, will against intellect. It secured a place for the contingent within philosophy, against the latter's original bias."[10] Indeed, Jonas's formulation is reflected in the emphasis some Kabbalists had put on the concrete and particular aspects of the text, namely its parasemantic facets, as we had seen in ample examples above.[11] Those particularistic elements were mitigated, however, when they encountered Greek thought, in the specific forms it took in translations, commentaries, and syntheses produced in the Islamic and Christian worlds. Those approaches emphatically introduced more vertical and hierarchical schemes, which contributed to more instrumental approaches to the canonical texts. In some cases, like R. Abraham Abulafia's hermeneutical scheme, the allegorical exegesis was presented as lower than the more hyperliteralistic exegetical methods, and this may be also the case in the manner in which philosophically oriented interpretations were sublated by Kabbalistic methods, as we shall see below in the case of pardes, where the second method, remez, may stand for allegory.[12] Moreover, as Frank Talmage suggested, the term haggadah, which appears in a Zoharic discussion dealing with ways of interpretation and is lower than the Kabbalistic method, stands for a form of rationalistic interpretation.[13] How should we understand those syntheses?

Harry A. Wolfson suggested considering the history of European philosophy from late antiquity to Spinoza as a series of encounters between Greek philosophy and the sacred scriptures, starting with Philo and reverberating through the Middle Ages in different forms of syntheses.[14] Looking back to some of the discussions above, we may describe Jewish medieval thought from the perspective of different forms of confrontation between the two, mitigating the resort to the idea of synthesis and instead adopting, along the lines of Gadamer's and Derrida's thought, a greater awareness of the creative tension between the two. The great impact of the combinations of letters on Jewish mysticism, on the one hand, and on seminal figures in European thought like Ramon Llull,[15] Christian Kabbalists like Pico della Mirandola,[16] Giordano Bruno,[17] and their repercussions in Leibniz[18] and other European thinkers, on the other, deserve a separate study that will document in detail the accumulative impact of the infiltration of Kabbalistic material in the fabric of modern thought on language and text.

Our methodological assumption, which informed some of the passages above, is that significantly different corpora[19] interacted substantially in medieval and Renaissance Europe. On the one hand, the arrival of some forms of Greek philosophy beginning in the eleventh century to Europe via Syrian, Arabic, and then Hebrew translations created the speculative systems that attempted to integrate the varieties of Neoaristotelian and Neoplatonic, and some forms of Stoic and Pythagorean, speculation into theological systems that may be described as Jewish-Greek. From the second half of the fifteenth century, however, new corpora impinged on the medieval forms of speculation, owing mainly to the translations of Marsilio Ficino and a few others. Those corpora interacted with the older ones and were instrumental in the rather rapid dissolution of the medieval forms of thought.

The interactions between these corpora—religious, philosophical, mystical, and magical—involve hermeneutical moves that gradually transformed the intercorporal relations into intracorporal ones, thus creating a series of Jewish-Greek syntheses. I have attempted to point out the tensions between the logocentric and textocentric approaches in the high Middle Ages, which produced not only speculative writings but also systematic descriptions of hermeneutical rules. Later these corpora became influential in Renaissance culture and found their way into modern European culture through Renaissance influences and those of modern scholars of Kabbalah, like Adolph Frank in the nineteenth century, but more eminently through the writings of Martin Buber and Gershom Scholem.

III. SOME MODERN REVERBERATIONS

Let me turn again to modern implications of some of these discussions. The writings of Walter Benjamin, Maurice Blanchot, Harold Bloom, Jorge Luis Borges, Jacques Derrida, Umberto Eco, and George Steiner, who resorted sporadically, or even systematically, to hermeneutical concepts found in Kabbalah, point to the emergence of a new awareness that hermeneutical patterns of the Jewish late antiquity, especially Midrash, and Middle Ages, especially Kabbalah, may contain significant food for reflection on the extremities the interpretation of sacred texts may reach even in a religious society.

Modern radical hermeneutics, as exemplified in Derrida's deconstruction, should be seen as a phenomenon that both emerged as the result of modern trends in European philosophy and was inspired by models already in existence in antiquity, the Middle Ages, and the Renaissance. It is difficult to strike a proper balance between the two sources, and it is not my intention even to attempt to treat such a delicate subject here. It is necessary to point out that in Derrida's

Dissemination a sentence by R. Abraham Abulafia dealing with the combination of letters as the special form of logic has been quoted verbatim. It runs, in the English translation, as follows: "The Kabbalah is not only summoned up here under the rubric of arithmosophy or science of the literal permutations . . . The science of letter combinations is the science of superior interior logic . . . it also cooperates with an Orphic explanation of the earth."[20] As we saw in Chapter 9, Abulafia's statement about letter combinations is part of a confrontation between the Greek and Jewish forms of logic. Indeed, my analysis of Abulafia's thought somehow confirms Derrida's general assumption (based on Levinas's writings) as to the reticence toward metaphysics in some forms of Judaism.[21]

Like the ecstatic Kabbalists, who strove to explain reality and not only the sacred texts, Derrida views Kabbalah as "an Orphic explanation of the earth." Although this quote corroborates Abulafia's double vision of Kabbalah as a higher philosophy and a mystical discipline, it includes a phrase that cannot be deduced from Abulafia, "an Orphic explanation," which is related later in Derrida's discussion with another form of Kabbalah, the Lurianic. Thus, Derrida was aware of the Kabbalistic technique of combination of letters, although we should be aware that he was also influenced, at least in *Dissemination*, by Stéphane Mallarmé and his view of *Le Livre*.[22]

Let me reflect on the possible impact of these discussions on the modern form of deconstructive hermeneutics. In Derrida's description it is basically a semantic form, as he emphasizes the fluctuation of meaning of words in a given text rather than the instability of the text itself. To the best of my knowledge, the intertextual reading is a form of soft radicalism, as it put in relation texts that are much closer to each other than in intercorporal hermeneutics.[23] Being non-harmonistic, Derridian radicalism is, because of its "différancial" nature, soft in comparison to religious intercorporal hermeneutics, which believes that all the different corpora involved in the hermeneutical project share the same basic meaning, despite the apparent terminological discrepancies. This is the case in both Philonic and Maimonidean hermeneutics and in the Renaissance versions of the *prisca theologia*. Less concerned with the importance of a stable meaning—see Derrida's crucial denial of presence—semantic radicalism is attenuated by the fluctuation that may be discerned in the different meanings of a text. To clarify what I mean: the greater the conceptual differences between the corpora that are imposed on each other, the more radical the hermeneutical presuppositions involved in the exegetical process.

So, for example, the introduction of a totally different meaning for the word 'elohim (as "nature" by means of gematria)[24] far beyond the semantic flexibility that disestablishes a permanent meaning of a given text, à la Derrida. The combination of semantic radicalism with deconstructive grammatical and linguistic radicalism, as exemplified above by the literary corpora of Abulafia and his followers—and pertinent examples may easily be multiplied—produced forms of deconstruction that are reminiscent of what modern scholars would call radical hermeneutics. Those scholars, however, were less concerned with the instability of the text as such, although Mallarmé's Livre played an important role in some of Derrida's discussions. The ecstatic Kabbalist challenges equally the structure of the text and its traditional meanings. Yet while modern deconstruction attempted to get rid of the former Archimedean points of metaphysics, theology, and authorial intention as anchors of and sources for meaning, it sometimes remained confronted with a relatively stable text that is the anchor or springboard for the whole hermeneutical project.[25]

The mystical forms of radicalism, however, are more aggressive than the modern form in their approach to the text, precisely because they not only accepted a certain type of metaphysics and the existence of a God, for example, but also assumed the possibility of free access to Him. By resorting to mystical techniques nearly identical with the exegetical ones described above,[26] both R. Eleazar of Worms and R. Abraham Abulafia believed that they might enjoy, and indeed claimed to have enjoyed, mystical experiences, which presumably offered them the authority to "find out" the esoteric meanings of a text by resorting to the most eccentric of hermeneutical strategies imaginable. In fact, the actualization of the human spiritual potential that brings about the mystical experience is related to one's ability to actualize the plethora of meanings, mostly esoteric, conceived to be dormant within the interpreted text.

At least insofar as Abulafia is concerned, this actualization of the intellect, which is often described as a union with the divine, does not take the form of the return to the origin, the repetition of a blissful situation, the retrieval of lost meanings—all these in the Platonic vein—but much more the perfection of the activity of the human intellect. It is not a repetition, a return, a reconstruction, but a breaking through of the intellectual faculties from the material and imaginary ones, conceived of as obstructing perfect intellection or union with the absolute spiritual. Undoing the regular ties between the linguistic components of the interpreted text is paralleled on the psychological level by untying the knots that connect the soul to matter. It is a simultaneous liberation of the intellect from the bonds of the potential meanings of the sacred scriptures and from routine as embodied in the traditional understandings of religion. From this point of view, interpretation involves existential as well as textual hermeneutics.

Moreover, as in forms of modern deconstruction that attempt to exploit all the linguistic potential of the text, Kabbalists too, as we have seen, argued that they prefer a detailed literal analysis in order to do justice to the minutiae of the text, unlike the more general and logocentric attitude of the philosophers, who were in search of philosophical allegorical readings. Abulafia, in his fourth way of interpretation, would see allegory as a licit manner of understanding the Bible at a certain stage of one's spiritual development, and from this point of view he did not combat it. However, he definitively saw in the peculiar immersion in exercising linguistic exegetical techniques a higher spiritual achievement. From this perspective logocentrism was transcended by a linguocentric attitude, which nevertheless does not attempt, as in the case of other Kabbalists, to oppose this exegetical praxis categorically.

While traditional radicalism in Kabbalah was ready to deconstruct the text in order to find God by a more direct experience within the very performance of ritual language, modern deconstruction had first to kill God or transcendental meaning in order to divinize the text. Modern radicalism in the domain of metaphysics or theology—the Nietzschean statement of the death of God—introduced a pivotal new constant in culture: the text. Its infinite riches are actualized mainly by discovering the principle of the fluidity of meaning. Indeed, ecstatic Kabbalah seems to parallel forms of radicalism that distinguish modern deconstruction from other modern forms of hermeneutics. So, for example, both share the assumption of the fluidity of the text, as opposed to much more stable approaches to the text. There is a strong emphasis on the complete and intact text in some forms of modern hermeneutics; to paraphrase Paul Ricoeur, the status of the book is that of a screen between the author and the reader, while in the religious visions of the text the sacred book is the nexus between the Author and the mystical reader. Indeed, I assume that Ricoeur has expressed a quite modernistic understanding of textuality when he declared that "the book divides the act of writing and the act of reading into two sides, between which there is no communication."[27] Unlike Derrida and Ricoeur, however, the ecstatic Kabbalist regards the sacred book as one of the most important modes of union and communion with a transcendent divine.

The deconstructive hermeneute, on the other hand, becomes the prophet of a text that is now more and more accessible to the ordinary reader but whose contents are conceptualized by scholars as more and more opaque. He is now conceived of as mediating not between God and the religious group but between the text, whose meaning becomes more and more remote, and the reader. Indeed, I think that what happened in the Derridian conception of the text is the dissolution of a strong ontological vision of the text, as represented by Kabbalah, and its transformation into a philosophy of a total absence, as we shall see also more below.

Modern deconstruction has turned its attention to the nature of the text as disassociated from its author but as strongly dependent on the reader. Following the cultural crises in the elites involved in the Nietzschean and Freudian revolutions, the instability of meaning has increasingly become a crucial issue, which betrays not only the fluid semantics of the interpreted texts and the eclipse of the author but also the flexible attitudes of readers. A destabilization of classical philology's certainty in the possibility of ascertaining the authorial intention facilitated the emergence of more subtle, intricate, sometimes even oversophisticated discourses over the possibilities implied in the earlier discourses. This modern move toward the disclosure of the discrepancy between the poverty of the author and the discovery of the richness of language and text is quintessential for and inherent in the secularization of the attitude toward literature. The unstructured elements of language, which are enchained by creative literary processes, never subsume to the author but transcend his intentions by displaying a much greater spectrum of meanings than presumably he intended. It is a weak mind, genial as it may be, that attempts to enslave the variety of uncontrollable possibilities inherent in language as constituted by a long series of semantic shifts. This view of the secular text assumes a crisis in the former concept that focuses on the author, proposing instead a much greater interest in the contribution of the reader or, even more, the sophisticated interpreter. Readers and interpreters complete the meaning by bringing their own riches to the interpreted texts.

The secular attitude toward texts is a fundamentally democratic discourse. Sacred texts, however, almost always imply strong authors. Either the concept of God, or that of His prophets, or at least the authority of the ancient sages, supplies an authorship that provides a much firmer basis for the belief that the canonic texts in themselves represent higher forms of intelligence, if not absolute wisdom. It is this faith in the distinct superiority of the Author, or even in that of ancient authors over the modern reader (a reverberation of a medieval hierarchical structure of the universe, society, and intellects) that dominates the approach of a religious reader to his canonic texts. Assuming such a superior wisdom also means that it is hard to believe that an inferior reader, or even a large community of readers, will ever be able to exhaust all the intentions implied in the divine texts. Thus, it is not only the awareness of the riches of language, of its fluidity and ambiguities, that serves as the ground for ongoing interpretive projects, but also an assumption of the existence and pertinence of supernal, even infinite, forms of intelligence that in their original Greek and medieval systems are quintessential logocentric entities but were interpreted in ecstatic Kabbalah linguistically and as sources of linguistic revelations. It is not in history or society but in the atemporal superior reservoirs of knowledge that a religious reader will establish "his" innovative interpretations of a sacred text that stem from these reservoirs. Thus, it is a radical trust in the text, or more precisely in the plenitude, even semantic abundance, of its linguistic components, rather than a basic mistrust in its author as the generator of the text. This belief in the existence, omnipresence, and availability of the transcendent reservoir of meaning, the supernal Agent Intellect, which pulsates intellectual contents that may be captured by the well-prepared human intellects, is paramount for his system. Thus, the ecstatic Kabbalah is a vertical approach toward intellectual and mystical experiences and forms of exegesis, an issue that was discussed in some more detail in Chapter 11.

The horizontal intertextuality characteristic of recent secular approaches has replaced the vertical interchange between the reader and the subject of his belief. A modern reader reads, sometimes, in order to express himself. A religious reader is looking much more to be impressed. The former reading is analytical, disintegrative; it subverts rather than integrates. Its agon is provoked by the self-imposition of historical relations as generative factors. On the other hand, it seems that the gist of most of the religious reader-situation is synthetic. It reflects the search for a higher order, which is to be internalized, imitated, or at least venerated.

The deconstructive approach attempts to establish itself in a space between Greek logocentrism and Jewish ethical openness toward the other, as expounded by Emmanuel Levinas. Being a philosophy of hesitation that deliberately refuses to choose between the two, Derrida's deconstruction is critical toward aspects of both.[28] Concerned with establishing a unique space from which a critical stance could be elaborated, this is a speculative project intended to create a much freer reader and interpreter. In Abulafian hermeneutics, another system that stands between the Jewish and Greek conceptualizations, there is a definitive propensity for accepting both while being critical of some aspects of the two attitudes toward reality and understanding each in the light of the other. So, for example, the supernal intellects and their influx here below, crucial topics in Abulafia's worldview and mysticism, were understood in linguistic terms as speech or primordial speech, a very significant departure, though not a total divergence from Greek logocentrism.[29]

For the radical traditional hermeneute as exemplified by Abulafia's exegetical methods, modern deconstruction, as put in practice, would be quite a modest intellectual enterprise, because the main purpose of the hermeneute is not to decipher the divine secrets of the Torah but to bring about the identification of his intellect with the Author Himself. The ecstatic Kabbalist escapes subscribing to the logocentric attitude of the Arabic and Jewish philosophers who influenced him by moving his own logos to the center and attempting to become the source of the ever-changing esoteric meanings.[30]

To be sure, the above discussion is not a call for the traditional forms of radicalism, nor an attempt to support modern theories of deconstruction by claiming that they have a much earlier pedigree. All have, in my opinion, their extremes of strong and weak points. I have attempted to point out only the moderate nature of modern radical hermeneutics by introducing another corpus for comparison, mainly the ecstatic-Kabbalistic one. Less concerned as I am to point out the conceptual or historical filiation between the medieval and the modern views (although I believe that I have been able to demonstrate them), I am much more interested in contextualizing Derridian deconstruction within a European development. After all, in this book we have examined medieval texts composed in Germany, Spain, and Italy in the thirteenth century, and although they were composed in Hebrew, their main strategies transpired in several ways in Western languages, Latin and French, already in the sixteenth century. An approach that emphasized the pertinent contribution of texts that were in possible contact with the interpreted text, as deconstruction is, may be interested in investigating the possible importance of corpora that were somehow available to the formulator of deconstruction.

I do not claim that modern deconstruction is a continuation, extension, or distortion of more radical Kabbalistic forms of deconstruction, but that given some developments in the critique of meaning—from the Nietzschean and Freudian perspectives and of metaphysics and theology from a variety of angles (including Nietzsche and Levinas), some Kabbalistic views attracted the attention of Derrida—as was the case with Harold Bloom's literary theory—who basically should be situated within European philosophical-critical developments. Nevertheless, without attempting to transform ecstatic-Kabbalistic hermeneutics into a pioneer of modern deconstruction, I would assert that the fundamental situation of a confrontation between logocentric and textocentric modes of thinking is found already in the attempts of those Kabbalists who had to choose between the linguocentric mystical traditions[31] and the newly introduced Greek logocentric thought within the intellectual horizons of some elites in European Judaism. As Abulafia put it, there are two paths: "the path of the *Guide*; and [the other] according to my own path, that is the path of Kabbalah . . . the paths of Kabbalah which are the secrets of *Sefer Yetzirah*."[32,33] Despite the divergences between the two, Abulafia nevertheless attempted to interpret the former in the light of the latter.[34] This confrontation and its solution represent an important instance of the awareness of the divergences between the two and at the same time an attempt to overcome them. From the perspective of later developments in hermeneutics it is possible to describe some aspects of modern European thought as a contest between two modes of thought: one assuming the discovery of a truth that is independent of textuality, the other creating a dependence of various messages on a canonical text.

IV. NEGATIVITY OR PLENITUDE

The bibliocentric nature of medieval and later Jewish mysticism should be addressed in the context of the elites' vision of religion as conducive to experiences of plenitude. Moving the center of the exegetical and mystical experiences to mental and emotional processes related to an available and approachable book opens questions that had been answered in the earlier scholarship in a too definitive manner. My claim is that various forms of negativity nourish some of the modern approaches to the nature and function of the book in Jewish mysticism. Emblematic of the dominant attitude is a statement found in the last of Scholem's *Ten Non-Historical Theses*, where he defined Kafka's secular Kabbalah as reminiscent of "the strong glance of the canonical, the perfection that destroys."[35] I see in this, the very last sentence of his theses, the quintessence of a profound negativity, one that recognizes the perfection of the canonical as well as its destructiveness. I contend that perfection in the context of canonicity reflects the view of the Torah as perfect, as reflected in the verse from Psalms, whose mystical interpretations were discussed earlier in some detail.[36] I read the glance as related to Kafka's "Before the Law," where the glimpse of the Law is emanating. Canonical, luminous, perfect as the Torah was for the Kabbalists and many other Jewish masters, according to Scholem it was conceived of as hardly attainable, even destructive. This contradiction between the conservative aspects of Scholem's description of Kabbalah and its antinomian aspects has been duly pointed out by Harold Bloom, who even summarized one of Scholem's theses as follows: " 'God Himself is the Torah'; so also Torah cannot be known."[37] Indeed, the third thesis claims—as Scholem did in some other instances—that the written Torah cannot be approached, while the oral Torah, which is identified with tradition, is wrapped in darkness.[38] In both cases, forms of negativity are quite obvious. They have much to do with what Bloom calls Scholem's revisionist description of Kabbalah, which is strongly influenced by both Kafka's and the Sabbateans' sorts of negativity,[39] by his own search for catastrophes,[40] and by his Gnostic leanings.[41]

A perusal of the different types of Kabbalistic literature as I know them does not, however, corroborate Scholem's descriptions emphasizing the transgressive and negative aspects as either comprehensive or representative. I do not deny their existence, but assert it only in cases where I have specific and detailed reasons to do so, as I pointed out in Chapters 2 and 12, for example. Neither am I interested in negating their phenomenological specificity, and I quite understand the predilection and the attraction that scholars had and still have toward them.

Nevertheless, this academic proclivity for radical and anarchic elements does not mean that they are representative or that they are common in the general economy of Jewish mystical literature. I cannot engage here all the sources and problems involved in such a misreading of Kabbalah. Some of them have to do with the emphasis on the importance of negative theology adopted in academic descriptions of Kabbalah.[42] In this context it suffices to remark that the paramount role played by expressions that are understood as icons of negativity in modern scholarship of Kabbalah—radicalism, paradox, dialectics, antinomianism, anarchism—merits a separate study and may indeed be related to themes stemming from Hegelian and Marxist thought that entered the intellectual apparatus of Scholem and thus the basic language of modern Kabbalah scholarship.

I would like only to adduce a few examples that further demonstrate what we have already seen in many passages adduced and analyzed in this book: the positive, constructive role that the concepts and study of the Torah played in Kabbalah and Hasidism, which include an apotheosis of human activity. The strong interpretive techniques adopted by Kabbalists indicate an activist approach, which has nothing to do with a "danger zone" imagined by Scholem as characteristic of the Kabbalistic vision of the Torah. I would say that the stronger the belief in the perfection of the Bible, the more it activated stronger exegetes who elicited stronger interpretations, which were part of creating experiences of plenitude that sometimes are described as the few realizing in the present the beatitude preserved for the many in the eschatological future. The contemplation and learning of the Torah was one of the paths for attaining what the Jewish mystic imagined to be the maximum religious perfection, and for the elite it would be hard to find examples of what Scholem described as "life in deferment."[43] Were I to reformulate Scholem's thesis, I would opt for a vision of the "strong glance of canonical, a perfection that absorbs."

The innovative techniques adopted in Kabbalistic hermeneutics are part of a profound transformation characteristic of some forms of Judaism, culminating in what Jacques Riviere calls "a kind of assault on the absolute"[44] that changes the Jewish view of man as well as of language. Like many phenomena in modern literature, some forms of Kabbalah consist in an attempt to transmute reality through the power of words.[45] Both activities are part of "a vast incantation towards the miracle."[46] Some of the Kabbalistic techniques are, in my opinion, much closer to Dadaist and Surrealistic visions of creative activity than they are to Kafka's or Celan's ambiguity and negativity.[47] Kabbalists and the Hasidic masters did not wait in front of a sealed Law but initiated forms of religious activities thought capable of ensuring an experience of the divine. If Kafka chose a simpleton as the protagonist of his magisterial "Before the Law," there is no reason to identify the passivity of someone who is an ʿam ha-ʾaretz to the much more constructive approaches of the Jewish elites.[48] In other words, a vision of Kafka as representative of a secularized Kabbalah is based on a comparison of things that are incomparable.

If, however, we inspect the general thrust of the Kabbalistic attitude toward the Torah, we find a much more activist approach, which is incompatible with the passivity of Kafka's protagonist. So, for example, according to one of the most influential among the Kabbalists, R. Moses Cordovero, it is man alone, not even angels, who is "able to add enigmas to the Torah, or to reveal any secret of its secrets, but man alone, whose soul is seizing in [or by] the Torah and becomes as a bucket by his soul, to draw the secrets of the Torah from its source in the sefirot . . . and the quintessence of the understanding of the Torah is found in the people of Israel, who will cause its descent by their soul, spirit, and higher soul from its source and will draw it from the pit of the depths of the secrets of the Torah, and this is the reason why each of the six hundred thousand souls of the people of Israel had, each of them, an inheritance in the Torah."[49] Another activistic contention is found in the same context, where the same Kabbalist claims that "everything is delivered to the deed of man, and according to his talent he will draw within them[50] inestimable influx which cannot be described, all in accordance with the preponderance of the deed, because he acts in accordance with the Torah and the commandments, because of the seizure of the soul, spirit, higher soul of emanation, to Torah and commandment."[51]

Cordovero is quite a traditional Kabbalist, a synthetic and systematic mind who summarizes many of the earlier impulses found in Kabbalistic literature, and thus he had an impact on later developments, more preeminently Hasidism. He presents no paradoxical or negative understandings of the Torah, but a series of Kabbalistic models that allow a much more positive and activist attitude toward the Bible. In place of the rather illusive role of the negative aspects attributed to the Torah, the different models—theurgical, magical, and ecstatic—contrived to build different understandings of the Torah, of its study and its interpretations, which only marginally hosted negative appreciations of the Torah. A presentation of the strong interpreter is well deserved by the view of the Besht's grandson, R. Barukh of Medzibezh, who thus describes the study of the Torah:

> The principle is that everyone has first to hear in his heart . . . and afterwards to study what the heart is hearing . . . God said ʾanokhiy, and it is incumbent on man to hear in his heart and afterwards in the Torah . . . They[52] have seen

what has been heard, namely they have seen in the Torah what they heard in their heart . . . He brings a blessing within the Torah and illumines within it, and this is the meaning of the Torah that is studied for its sake, to illumine in the Torah what he has heard in his heart . . . and if he did so, then the Torah will illumine in his soul, and this is the meaning of [the dictum] "the Holy One, blessed be He, and the Torah and Israel are one."[53]

Over the centuries, some of the Jewish masters have heard much in their soul, apparently what they had first learned from books, and were able subsequently to illumine the Torah. Or, to resort to an expression by R. Ze'ev Wolf of Zhitomir, the righteous are "drawing down, generation after generation, allusions and speeches, according to the need, and innovate a new meaning."[54] Indeed, the Bible ceased to be an ancient and revered book, but was a live document, whose revelations are still continuing, as the same Hasidic master put it, following Ha-Shelah: "The reason for our blessing of the Torah by [the formula] 'He gives the Torah' is to show that the Holy One, blessed be He, is still revealing the Torah as He did then, in antiquity, at the holy assembly, at Mount Sinai."[55]

The feeling of the Hasidic master is that the revelation of the Torah was not only a historical event, the promulgation of a law, but a spiritual trigger that had continued to inform religious life ever since. This has been made clear by R. Yehudah Arieh Leib of Gur, who asserts that God "has given the Torah to the sons of Israel, and in addition to it He really implanted within us the power of the Torah, so that man will be able to innovate words of Torah and to combine the Torah letters."[56]

The Kabbalistic and Hasidic forms of plenitude do not suit the Kafkaesque negativity, and I assume that this is also the case with Derrida's emphasis on absence and indeterminate openness of the text, which are related to a limitless delay of the significant. If infinity is found in the fact of textuality, for Derrida it is mainly a matter of a fluidity that will never reach a stable meaning even for the one interpreter, so that we may assume a continuous process of relative frustration, in comparison with the renewed Kabbalistic readings, which assume an infinite number of stable meanings, each of them pertinent to one of the Israelites, as we saw in Chapter 3. For modern deconstruction, undecidability is the main form of encounter with the fluid text, and this undecidability creates a cumulative infinity. Skeptical as Derrida is that a finite object can incorporate infinity, he would resist the Kabbalistic claims of the positive infinite in the Torah in the way the Kabbalists understood it.

As Jonathan Smith has pointed out, the canon, one of the main concepts that have informed our discussions, should be understood against the background of two processes: closure, which defines the corpus that becomes canonical, and ingenuity, which is related to the exegesis that opens the closed text to new and particular situations.[57] The emergence of the state of closure demands, especially in the case of groups active in many different religious, intellectual, historical, and social circumstances, efforts at adjustment, and this is one of the reasons for the proliferation of radical hermeneutics, as represented by such a diversity of eccentric exegetical methods. Their application prevented what has been called the closural reading, allowing, to resort to Derrida's phrase, "an infinite and infinitely surprising reading."[58] But assuming, as some of the Kabbalists did, that they were infused by a primordial type of interpretation, they would not easily reject the closural reading as far as the individual is concerned, allowing to community a much more open type of reading. I would like, however, to compare modern deconstruction's emphasis on the possibility of an infinity of readings to the Kabbalistic emphasis: the latter emerges in many cases from the assumption that the readers are assuming that some of the main features of a text are not noted in the text itself—the vowel signs, for example. Even more so when the combination of letters is involved. When doing so, the reader is coming with a certain semantic cargo that elicits a particular manipulation of the linguistic material. The Kabbalist, like all readers of the Torah scroll, operates with an unfinished text—indeed, with less unfinished texts when other books written in Hebrew are concerned. Because of his contribution to the shaping of the text, the Kabbalist brings a certain fugitive truth, which nevertheless is neither an undecidable reading nor an approach to the text as indeterminate.

Not so the modern deconstructive reader: for him the text is a given, and his experience of reading consists in a discovery of gaps, absences, and tensions inherent in the text. Like the author himself, the modern interpreter is caught within the fluxing net of language and textuality. The predetermined texts, appearing as a given to the modern reader, create the feeling that he is a prisoner of a huge comprehensive textual system that is overwhelming on one side and fluid on the other. Despite the belief in the absoluteness of the canonical text, the traditional readers who have been described above felt the liberty to innovate by approaching the interpreted texts by means of rather aggressive exegetical techniques. It seems that belief in a supreme author does not have to inhibit a rich reading of the sacred text but may allow exegetical radical moves that would otherwise be much more difficult. This type of religious imaginaire was, in my opinion, crucial for shaping the possibility of the strong reader, one who is so absorbed in the interpretive project that he would efface himself. World-absorbing and divine-absorbing concepts of texts were conceived by thinkers and interpreters who were already absorbed by the study of those texts.

APPENDIX 1

PARDES: THE FOURFOLD
METHOD OF INTERPRETATION

I. THE EMERGENCE OF PARDES

Jewish mysticism, like other forms of religious mysticism, was in permanent search of objective validation. Personal experience and sometimes mystical intuition, important as they might be for the spiritual life of the individual, strove also to anchor themselves in the collective experience of the community, basically by resorting to a reinterpretation of the canonical writings.[1] Accordingly, the hermeneutic enterprise in Kabbalah is a main component of this mystical lore. Centered much more on the Bible than the Christian mystics were, and perhaps more even than the Sufis, the Kabbalists offered a plethora of mystical interpretations whose relationship to the already existing corpus of traditional nonmystical interpretations of the scriptures is complex and deserves further clarification. The major expression of this attempt to establish an explicit scheme that explicates the hierarchical relationship between the different types of Jewish exegesis is known as *pardes*, an acronym that designates a fourfold system of exegesis used mostly in Kabbalistic writings. *Pardes* stands for *peshat* or plain meaning, *remez* or hint, sometimes designating allegorical explanations, *derash* or homiletic exposition, and *sod* or secret (namely symbolic) interpretation. In the following I shall present some reflections about the background of the emergence of the fourfold hermeneutics as it was advocated by Kabbalists and the significance of its structure.

There are two main scholarly explanations for the emergence of pardes exegesis among the Kabbalists at the end of the thirteenth century. Wilhelm Bacher maintained that the Kabbalists adopted and adapted the Christian fourfold theory of interpretation,[2] whereas Peretz Sandler asserted that this exegetical system emerged as the result of an inner development starting with twelfth-century Jewish exegesis.[3] At first Gershom Scholem adopted Bacher's theory, but later he did not explicitly reject the view of Sandler.[4]

I, too, believe that Sandler did not make a very strong case. On the other hand, it is rather difficult to accept the Bacher-Scholem theory because of the simple fact, pointed out first by Sandler and more recently by Frank Talmage and A. van der Heide, that in crucial details the Kabbalistic fourfold method does not correspond to the Christian fourfold method.[5] Although it is always possible that one particular Kabbalist might accept an alien type of exegesis, Christian or Muslim,[6] it seems to me unconvincing to assume that several Kabbalists accepted, exactly at the same time and apparently independently, a very similar exegetical method. We must look for a common factor that will explain the concomitant resort of several Kabbalists to these exegetical methods. Can we accept as reasonable the explanation that independent Kabbalists would accept, in the same period, an alien type of exegesis, without having more substantial factors in common?

The obvious fact that those who exposed such a fourfold method of exegesis were Kabbalists is highly significant. However, in the last quarter of the thirteenth century, when this system emerged, it designated methods which were applied separately in various types of Jewish literature. The plain sense was the main subject of the rich exegetical literature produced by the school of exegetes in northern France in the eleventh and twelfth centuries. There was already a voluminous homiletic literature produced between the third century and the early Middle Ages. Jewish philosophers starting using allegorical interpretation in the eleventh century, and its floruit can be established in the thirteenth century. Finally, Kabbalistic—that is, symbolical-theosophical—interpretations of the Bible and other canonical Jewish writings were already known at the middle of the thirteenth century. Pardes incorporated a variety of types of Jewish literature that had already been in existence when this system was first articulated. The latest type of literature was Kabbalah, and it is no accident that the exponents of this mystical lore were those who first expounded the method of pardes.

We have, however, sufficient evidence to suggest that some of the Kabbalists who proposed pardes or other systematic exegetical methods underwent a certain spiritual development before they became Kabbalists. There can be no doubt, as pointed out by Isadore Twersky,[7] that Isaac ibn Latif, Moses de Leon, Joseph Gikatilla, and Abraham Abulafia were interested in Jewish philosophy before they became Kabbalists. They clearly were well acquainted with the Bible and its plain interpretations as well as with the midrashic literature. Thus the personal spiritual development of some of those Kabbalists who expounded pardes or similar systems is highly relevant for the acceptance of such peculiar methods, even if such acceptance resulted from having appropriated a foreign method. Because of the emergence of the additional, mystical type of Jewish literature in Spain, the peculiar biography or curriculum of some of the Kabbalists also included Kabbalah; the other three bodies of literature were considered to be a preparation for the study of the mystical lore. Consequently, in order to better understand the ascent of systematic hermeneutics in Spanish Kabbalah, it is not sufficient to notice the possible alien sources; it is equally important to inspect the cultural framework within which the new hermeneutics emerged as well as the spiritual biographies of those Kabbalists who articulated it.

Two related conclusions can be drawn from these observations. Kabbalists presented, as van der Heide has suggested, the fourfold method in a very specific manner in order to confer on their mystical lore the privileged status of an exalted type of knowledge.[8] By including the other three non-Kabbalistic types of interpretation in the fourfold system, the Kabbalists accomplished two different, though complementary, achievements: they safeguarded a place of honor for their peculiar lore, at the same time preserving the traditional modes of interpretation as necessary stages for the development of the ideal approach to the canonical texts. Jewish mysticism was not portrayed as an alternative to the already existing bodies of Jewish literature; it was conceived of as their culmination. This inclusive character of the Kabbalistic fourfold system of interpretation avoided the centrifugal tendencies characteristic of some non-Jewish types of mysticism.[9] This is also true in the case of Abraham Abulafia's sevenfold exegetical system. As we might imagine, it is his peculiar sort of Kabbalah, the ecstatic one, that is considered the source of the highest methods of interpretation. In the various expositions of his hermeneutics Abulafia does not discredit or oppose the symbolic types of Kabbalistic interpretation, but he posits his own mystical approaches to the text as superior.[10] Again we can see both the conservative and innovative character of the

Kabbalistic hermeneutic systems: they are always inclusive, allowing an important role for all the existing achievements of Jewish cultural creativity as preparatory approaches, while presenting the respective mode of interpretation that corresponds to the Kabbalistic system in whose framework it was articulated as the highest one. De facto, however, we may describe specifically Kabbalistic exegesis itself, according to the versions found in the different layers of the Zohar, as integrating elements from the other three sorts of exegesis, despite mutual tensions. I would like to emphasize that the Zohar does not resort systematically to the four exegetical methods as separate types of interpretation but uses various elements together as part of the Zoharic interpretation of the Bible.[11] No doubt the author or authors of the Zohar were aware of the contributions of the various layers of Jewish exegetical literature to the formation of the Zoharic text. The second conclusion, which derives from the first, is the relative conservative nature of even some of the innovative types of Kabbalah. Far from being ready to regard the previous stages of Jewish exegesis as obsolete or superfluous, the innovative Kabbalists strove to integrate them into more comprehensive exegetical systems, safeguarding their importance and survival[12] even when some of the Kabbalists, like Abraham Abulafia, would consider the "lower" types of exegesis as pertinent for the vulgus alone.[13] Kabbalists attempted to articulate their hermeneutics in concert rather than in conflict with traditional hermeneutics. This responsible attitude toward the spiritual heritage of Judaism ensured the special role of Kabbalah in those Jewish circles that were not identical with the Kabbalistic groups proper.

Nevertheless, there are examples of discussions that posit Kabbalah as indispensable for the proper interpretation of a text. A pun related to the word pardes will easily illustrate this. R. Hayyim Yoseph David Azulai, better known as HYDA', commented in his Midbbar Qedeimot: "Whoever believes only in the plain sense of the Bible, peshat, is indeed a fool, as a permutation of the consonants of peshat 'demonstrates': tipesh." Moreover, he continues, without the secret, namely the Kabbalistic interpretation, designated by the s in pardes, the three first consonants of this word would form the word pered, an ass.[14] Important as the first three methods may be for the accomplished Kabbalist, in themselves they do not suffice for the real understanding of the text. In fact, without the knowledge of Kabbalah the exegete is no more than an ass. Notwithstanding that the regular attitude toward the "lower" ways of exegesis was not negative, a perusal of the vast Kabbalistic interpretative literature conspicuously reveals that in general the Kabbalists were not inclined to propose plain, homiletic, or allegorical interpretations of their own. While acknowledging in principle the importance of the "lower" modes of interpretation, the Kabbalists did not see themselves as obliged religiously to provide the whole range of explanations suggested by the pardes system. Moreover, with the significant exception of R. Bahya ben Asher's *Commentary on the Pentateuch*, the Kabbalists contended themselves with providing Kabbalistic commentaries par excellence, not compilations of heterogeneous types of exegetical material.[15]

Let me address another facet of the pardes method. According to several discussions dating after the late thirteenth century the four methods correspond to the four tannaitic figures who entered the pardes, a spiritual adventure out of which only one person, R. 'Aqivah, returned safely.[16] According to the talmudic story and its parallel in the Heikhalot literature, three other figures, Ben Zoma, Ben Azzai, and 'Elisha' ben Abuyah, were damaged in varying degrees by a spiritual adventure whose peculiar nature is rather obscure.[17] For our purpose it is important to emphasize that R. 'Aqivah, who corresponds typologically to the Kabbalistic method of interpretation, is the only person who returned safely. Thus, at least implicitly, the Kabbalistic method of interpretation is regarded as the single safe type of exegesis, whereas the other three involve, again implicitly, different sorts of dangers. Nevertheless, the underlying purpose of this correlation is not to recommend that the masses use Kabbalistic exegesis but to emphasize the elitist nature of this type of spiritual preoccupation. R. 'Aqivah alone was able to emerge from the dangerous experience of pardes undamaged; the study of Kabbalah, albeit proposing a safe type of exegesis, also involves dangers that should not be overlooked. As such, mystical hermeneutics is to be restricted to the very few, an assumption characteristic of the whole history of Kabbalah.

Another interesting relationship was established between the four methods of exegesis and the four cosmic layers or worlds, designated in Kabbalah by the acronym 'BY': 'Atzilut, Beriy'ah, Yetzirah, 'Asiyah. (I will have more to say on this correspondence, in an earlier context, in Appendix 3.) Consequently, the *sod* corresponds to the world of 'Atzilut or Emanation, the *derash* to the world of Beriy'ah or Creation, the *remez* to the world of Yetzirah or Formation, and the *peshat* to the lowest world, that of 'Asiyah or Making. According to Lurianic texts, neglect of one of the senses of the Torah induces a certain damage in the corresponding cosmic level.[18] Thus, it becomes obvious that even the Kabbalist should not disregard the lower types of interpretations. Explicitly, the Kabbalistic onto-hermeneutics of the Torah leads the mystic to the divine world of emanation. The pardes system involves a certain version of *scala mentis ad Deum*; the Kabbalist, gradually immersing himself in the various aspects of the text, is at the same time fathoming the depths of reality; the Bible became a tool for metaphysical exploration. At the core of this text stands, according to many Kabbalists, the divinity or one of its manifestations, and the dynamism of the divine life can be extracted by the explication of the rich secret meanings of the infinite divine text. The hermeneutical enterprise of the Kabbalist brings him, according to this ontological concord, to an experience of the divine; in exploring the text, the Kabbalist enters the highest spiritual domain.[19] A Kabbalistic reading of the Torah apparently meant, at least for some Jewish mystics, more than a determination of a certain potential meaning of the text; by creating or extrapolating this significance, the Kabbalist also experienced it. In other words, some of the important stages of Jewish mysticism envisioned mystical exegesis not only as a manner of extracting novel significances from a text by propelling some theological or theosophical views into it, but also—and in some cases this was perhaps the main purpose of the enterprise—as a way of encountering deeper levels of reality.[20] The experiential aspects of Kabbalistic hermeneutics is a subject that has been dealt with above; some of its facets are reminiscent of the modern phenomenological type of reading, which emphasizes understanding as an experiential moment over the analytical "objective" approach.[21]

II. KABBALISTIC HERMENEUTICS AND ELITES

The last third of the thirteenth century is the period of the emergence of the most elaborated hermeneutical systems of Kabbalah. Some fourfold exegetical systems—those of Isaac ibn Latif, Joseph Gikatilla, Moses de Leon, the *Zohar* and *Tiqqunei Zohar*, and Bahya ben Asher, on one hand, and the sevenfold system of Abraham Abulafia on the other—bear clear witness to the deep interest in techniques of interpretation to an extent unseen in discussions found in the earlier stages of Kabbalah. Writings of other Kabbalists, like R. Joseph of Hamadan in the late thirteenth century and R. Isaac ben Samuel of Acre at the beginning of the fourteenth century, though not expressing an explicit and systematic hermeneutics, similarly present a vital concern with different esoteric methods of understanding the scriptures. The common denominator of the intellectual formation of most of the aforementioned authors is the fact that, despite their good formation as Kabbalists, none of them can be considered an important Halakhic figure, and it is far from clear whether their Halakhic formation included in-depth studies of the legalistic literature. Moreover, insofar as I am acquainted with the biographies of these authors, none of them played a leading or even a significant role in Jewish communal life. There is no evidence that any of these Kabbalists was involved in the internal affairs of his community. The innovative Kabbalists[22] can be described as belonging to the secondary elite, educated individuals who were continuously searching for new types of thought and were uneasy with the authoritative philosophical theology of Maimonides or the perception of Kabbalah by another great authority, Nahmanides.

All this stands in sharp contrast to the role played by their contemporaries, the "primary elite" and Kabbalists who were leading figures in Catalonia and Castile. So, for example, Nahmanides in Gerona and R. Shlomo ben Abraham ibn Adret in Barcelona,[23] and R. Moses ben Shimeon of Burgos and Todros ben Joseph ha-Levi Abulafia in Toledo, were accomplished Kabbalists, active in the public sphere as important legalistic figures or leaders of their communities; in none of these cases is there any evidence of interest from their side in systematic hermeneutics. I believe that this clear-cut distribution of distinct groups—the "secondary elite" interested or the "primary elite" uninterested in presentations of systematic hermeneutics—is highly significant for our understanding of the Kabbalistic conceptions of hermeneutics. The hermeneutical systems were closely related to novel approaches to the canonic texts; by applying the exegetical method, Kabbalists were able to extract new Kabbalistic views or elaborate on the preexisting Kabbalistic theories. This innovative type of Kabbalah constitutes a considerable departure from the dominant perception of Kabbalah as an ancient and precious esoteric lore, to be transmitted and preserved without changes. In other words, the emergence of the fourfold exegetical method, as well as Abulafia's sevenfold exegetical system, coincides with the nascent innovative Kabbalah. From the vantage point of the history of Kabbalah, understanding the affinity between the pardes types of interpretation and the creativity that characterizes the contemporary Kabbalah is of paramount importance.[24] It would be an exaggeration to assume that all the previously unknown themes appeared as the result of hermeneutic activity; I have no doubt that we must also attribute the plethora of unknown Kabbalistic views to the surfacing of ancient mythologoumena, for reasons that are not always clear. I assume, however, that we had better attribute to the hermeneutic processes substantial contributions to the much more variegated landscape that the late thirteenth-century Kabbalah presents to scholars.[25]

III. THE POLYMORPHISM OF THE SECRET SENSE

The level of sod, or secret interpretation, was not restricted by the innovative Kabbalists to a single type of exegesis. Although the prevalent sort of Kabbalistic exegesis was symbolic-narrative,[26] in Kabbalistic literature there are also several nonsymbolic approaches to the divine text understood as secret senses:

(1) The monadic understanding of the Hebrew language and implicitly the Bible. According to this view, which has ancient sources and by the intermediary of the Kabbalistic material became prevalent in Hasidism, each and every letter is a universe in itself. The atomization of the semantic units into letters thought to designate divine names, the entire system of sefirot and the whole alphabet, diminished the importance of

the specific sequence of the letters in the Bible, in favor of the immersion of the Kabbalists and, later on, the Hasidim in the inner world of the letters. It is as if the interpreter were contemplating the text through a microscope.[27]

(2) The hieroglyphic, iconic, or ideogrammatic understanding of the whole text as a picture of the supernal divine system. This view is closely related to the anthropomorphic view of God in Heikhalot literature and its metamorphoses in the Kabbalistic view of the ten sefirot as constituting an anthropomorphic structure. It is as if the exegete were using a telescope to see the whole text as one unit.[28]

(3) The Kabbalistic understanding of the white forms of the letters as pointing to a higher reality, in comparison to that symbolized by the black forms of the letter. This view, related somewhat to the hieroglyphic view, has been examined earlier, in Chapter 2.

(4) A variety of mathematical approaches to the text, which consist of methods like notariqon, gematria, temurah, and tzeruf 'otiyyot, as well as other variations of these exegetical techniques.[29]

The symbolical-narrative as well as the static symbolical and the nonsymbolical types of interpretations allowed the Kabbalist a relatively free choice in his hermeneutic project. The accumulation of the various exegetical techniques in the late-thirteenth-century Kabbalah was fateful for its development. One of the views characteristic of some of the Kabbalistic systems designated as innovative Kabbalah is the claim that the Torah, being a divine text, is infinite and thus it is possible to extract from it innumerable meanings. This view, whose roots can be detected at the middle of the thirteenth century, was not accepted by the conservative Kabbalists, namely those persons who did not adopt the method of pardes. Nevertheless, it is recurrent in the writings of the Kabbalistic innovative hermeneutes. Through the mediation of Christian Kabbalah this view could have an influence on modern theories of the open text. The central assumption of the Kabbalistic understanding of the divine text, namely that, like its author, it is infinite, could be supported better if it were possible to return to the text and reinterpret it mystically time and again.[30] Some of the innovative Kabbalists assumed that it is possible to apply more than one Kabbalistic type of interpretation at a time, and this implies that the text was understood to offer a whole range of mystical meanings all at once.[31]

In other words, mystical interpretation is not to be understood as explicating the infinite meanings of the texts solely as part of an evolving historical process that assumes the accommodation theory of revelation or related types of adaptationist theories. Although sometimes the Torah was indeed described by Kab-balists using theories of accommodation, as has recently been shown by S. D. Benin,[32] even the lower, mundane manifestation of the Torah was thought of as pregnant with an infinity of meanings. Regularly the assumption that the divine message has accommodated to the peculiar period of time or level of evolution points to the revelation of one hidden type of meaning implicitly excluding the concomitant existence of other similar types of meaning. In the case of the Kab-balistic theory, even when the theory of accommodation was in fact adopted for one reason or another, this did not vitally affect the coexistence of a plurality of symbolic or nonsymbolic messages in the same text for the same person. More-over, the general impression is that innovative Kabbalists, though sometimes using accommodationalist formulations, were not eager to acknowledge a lower-ing of the status of the Torah by attributing to it only one significance that alone will inform the religious life of a generation.

IV. HASIDISM

The last phase of Jewish mysticism, Hasidism, was less interested in the external shape of the text. Instead it emphasized the paramount importance of vocal realization; the real letter, and text, was the oral one, a dramatic change of em-phasis in comparison to many of the Kabbalistic discussions.[33] Nevertheless, as we have seen, the idea of the infinity of the significance of the Bible occurs several times in Hasidic texts; interestingly, Kabbalah was now seen as a very profound lore, which can scarcely be fathomed. To a certain extent, this mystical lore was put on a pedestal; one of the most arresting expressions of this attitude was that, according to R. Yehudah Leib ha-Kohen of Anipola, even the plain sense of Kab-balah is unknown because of the vicissitudes of the exile, a fortiori the *remez*, *derash*, and *sod* of pardes.[34] This formula was interpreted by this Hasidic master as an exclusive device. It now points not only to the levels of the biblical text but also to the depths of Kabbalah, especially the *Zohar*; Kabbalah, which meanwhile was sanctified as a revealed lore, should be explored by the same criteria as the Bible itself.[35] In Hasidism the plain sense of the Bible as exposed by Rashi is regarded as preeminently mystical;[36] the symbolical level of interpretation is no longer the forefront of exegesis, as it focuses its expositions on the effort to disseminate devotional and psychological interpretations of Judaism.[37] The neutralization of several important aspects of Kabbalistic theosophy rendered superfluous or mar-ginal the complex Kabbalistic hermeneutics expounded by the medieval innova-tive Kabbalists. In fact, in one of the discussions of pardes, the *peshat* was explic-itly connected to one of the most widespread mystical ideals of Hasidism, the *hitpashetut ha-gashmiyyut*, the divestment of materiality.[38]

APPENDIX 2

ABRAHAM ABULAFIA'S
TORAH OF BLOOD AND INK

I. INTERPRETING AN ANCIENT RABBINIC DICTUM

In the previous discussions I resorted several times to the various writings of R. Abraham Abulafia to describe his contributions to Kabbalistic hermeneutics. Nevertheless, those quotes do not represent the breadth and depth of his concepts. Some of that material has been treated separately elsewhere, especially in my monograph devoted to Abulafia's hermeneutics. Here I would like to present a translation of a fascinating passage dealing with the "absorbing" status of the Torah, found in one of Abulafia's commentaries on Maimonides' *Guide of the Perplexed*. It constitutes one of the thirty-six secrets that Abulafia claimed that Maimonides hid in his book and the ecstatic Kabbalist contended that he reveals. The title of the secret is *sippurei ha-torah*, "stories of the Torah." Maimonides himself had already criticized those who deride the stories of the Torah, but he did not offer any specific speculative theory as to how to counteract such derisions.[1] This phrase was often discussed in Abulafia's lifetime as part of the response of theosophical Kabbalists to real or imaginary derisions that philosophers hurled at the simple-minded contents of the biblical stories. This is the case in R. Moses de Leon's Kabbalistic responsa, some discussions of the Zohar, and perhaps also a passage from de Leon's *Sefer ha-Rimmon*.[2] Whereas the theosophical Kabbalists solved the quandary by resorting to symbolic decoding of the various biblical narratives, elevating the mundane stories to the status of an inner-divine drama (see Appendix 3), this avenue was not available to Abulafia, who followed, *mutatis mutandis*, Maimonides' Aristotelian theology. What did Abulafia offer, as a Kabbalist, to the Kabbalistic understanding of the biblical stories? Let us first translate the salient passage:

[1.] The twenty-two letters of the Torah are the sanctum sanctorum on which it has been written at the end of Tractate *'Avot* what our sages, blessed be their memory, said:[3] "The son of Ben Bag Bag said: Turn it and turn it because everything is in it and you are within it in its entirety, and you shall see in it and you shall not stray from it, because there is no better virtue[4] than it." And the son of He' He' said: "The retribution is in accordance to the sorrow." And see what the rabbi, blessed be his memory, commented in his commentary.[5]

[2.] But we had received and we indubitably know that the two double names which had been mentioned at the end of the above-mentioned spiritual treatise, which was composed according to the views of the great rabbis, the saints of the earth, blessed be their memory, are double in order to disclose wondrous secrets. And after they warned us concerning all the good virtues and every intellectual rank, they returned to clarify the purpose of the intention and hinted to us the secret of the combination of the twenty-two letters, and said that the entire world is within the Torah and we are all of us in the Torah and from within it we see and from it we do not stray, and there is no better virtue than this. And they called it "virtue" because it indeed points to all the other virtues, supernal and low, and according to its virtues everything behaves, and it is a virtue and a "measure against measure." And "if all the measures were annulled, the measure against the measure is not annulled"[6] and will never be annulled and the secret is "the attribute of judgment" and "the attribute of mercy," and this is why they finished their statement with [the phrase] "the retribution is in accordance with the sorrow." And they said that it is good [*tovah*] because its numerical value is twenty-two, and this is also the secret of Bag Bag and the secret of He' He' together amount to *tovah*.[7] And the secret of half of the measure against the measure is *GaB 'AH GaB 'AH* which [amounts to] *'AHWY* and the secret of Ben Ben is a witness, and everything is appropriate. But I am not allowed to disclose more than this but face to face and mouth to mouth. However, the sagacious Kabbalist will understand it from his own mind. Indeed, the secret of "measure against measure" is *ha-'anan* [the cloud], *ha-me'ayyen* [the one who speculates] and *ha-meniy'a* [the activator] and its secret is *'av gilgul*. And if I shall come to announce to you the secret you should understand it easily from the statement of God to Moses:[8] "Behold I come to you in a heavy cloud." And all the blood [*ha-dam*] is manifest [*galuy*] and on it has the book of the Torah been written, on the parchment [*ha-gevyil*] whose secret is *mid[d]ah* and its matter is *'ed dam 'ed dam*[9] and you should understand it in depth.

[3.] However, I am adding to what I said announcing to you that each and every letter found in the Torah, even when part of the story regarding whatever happened to whomever is mentioned in it, is an endless matter in regard to what can be understood concerning that letter and what is found in it. The mind of man will never exhaust the understanding of even the paths of a tittle of a yod, because there are heaps of heaps of halakhot,[10] even more so in [a matter that] is more important. And so did the rabbi mention in the chapter Heleq, and said there concerning what David said:[11] "Open my eyes and I shall look the wondrous of thy Torah" concerning the eighth tenet where it is said that in "each and every letter"[12] in the Torah there are great secrets and sciences for whomever God, blessed be he, caused to understand them. However, the ultimate wisdom[13] of the Torah cannot be comprehended as it is written,[14] "its measure[15] is longer than the earth, and broader than the sea," and so he said in relation to all the commandments. And it is similar, in my opinion, to what Nahmanides, blessed be his memory, said in his commentary on the Torah, and as I referred above, that the entire Torah is [constituted] by the names of the Holy One, blessed be He. Thus, what would be the need, after all this, to interpret to you the essence of the stories of the Torah, since it had been disclosed completely that even a matter of small significance is a divine name.[16]

This is a dense and, in part, coded text, whose precise content is not conspicuous from a superficial reading. As Abulafia indicates, there are issues that one should understand by himself since he cannot commit them to writing, because they necessitate an oral transmission. This is a rather exceptional case of esotericism uncharacteristic of Abulafia's more exoteric approach. What is this secret matter that he can expound orally but did not want to do in a written manner? It is not a matter that is difficult to understand, as he explicitly indicates, and thus is related neither to ineffability nor to a quality of mysteriousness.[17]

The understanding of the "secret" depends on decoding the various gematrias found in the passage and explaining their meaning. The most important is the gematria of the words that amount to twenty-two, the number of Hebrew letters. Thus, the word tovah, pointing to the high status of the turning over, namely of the combination of letters, amounts to twenty-two. This is also the case with the names of the two rabbinic authors quoted in the passage from 'Avot: Bag Bag He' He', which amounts to twenty-two. There should be no doubt: these calculations have nothing to do with the plain sense of the ancient text. The ecstatic Kabbalist has ostensibly introduced the concept of twenty-two letters and manipulated the ancient material in order to convey the fundamental status of the turning of the Torah as a combinatory technique. Moreover, in one of the hints in the above passage, he introduces what he conceived of as the hidden divine name 'AHWY—a combination of two other divine names[18]—which amounts, again, to twenty-two. Abulafia therefore described the preoccupation with the Torah as if it consists in a process of permutation of its letters, as the ultimate mystical ideal.

Another crucial gematria in the passage is forty-nine. It is the numerical value of the most recurrent word in the passage, middah, which has been translated above sometime as "virtue" and sometimes as "measure." Indeed, this is a very polyvalent word in Hebrew, and it is difficult to assess its precise meaning in all its occurrences above. In any case, Ben Bag Bag had described the study of the Torah as the ultimate virtue. Its numerical value is forty-nine, as is that of gevyil, "parchment," and galuy, "manifest." What is of much greater importance, however, is the apparently less significant gematria of ha-dam, "the blood," or 'ed dam, "vapor of blood," which amounts to forty-nine. An attempt to relate the significance of these words by gematria is crucial for our understanding of Abulafia's intention, and I shall make such an attempt now only in part. Basically, the significance of the numerical affinities is that the manifest aspect of the Torah, the parchment, is related to blood, and I shall elaborate on this issue below.

A third gematria that plays a certain role is that of seventy-two, the gematria of 'av and of gilgul—another word for combination of letters.[19] It is presented as part of the biblical verse portraying the apparition of God to Moses in a cloud. The biblical archaic imagery is interpreted by Abulafia as indicating esoterically the achievement of the revelation of God by means of permutations of letters, especially as seventy-two points to the important divine name of seventy-two units of three letters, which is a main component in Abulafia's mystical technique as presented in his books *Hayyei ha-ʿOlam ha-Baʾ* and *Sefer ha-Hesheq*.[20]

Abulafia resorts to an additional gematria that organizes some of the statements above: 175. This is the numerical value of the phrase *mid[d]ah ke-neged mid[d]ah*, measure against measure, and of each of the words *he-ʿanan, ha-meʿayyen,* and *ha-meniʿya*. The last two words point perhaps to the importance of the speculation, understood by Abulafia as activating, *ha-meniʿya*, the letters that are studied or interpreted. *He-ʿanan* is the construct part of the phrase in the verse which includes *ʿav*. The significance of these gematrias is rather positive. (The meaning of the recourse to the "measure against measure" will be elucidated below.)

Yet another string of numerical equivalences is constituted by the following Hebrew phrases: *tav dam = demut = nafshekha = kashfan = keshafim = shofekh dam*, each of which amounts to 450. All these words imply a rather negative valence.

II. The Code of an Ecstatic Kabbalist

What is the common denominator of many of the gematrias adduced above? They introduce another code while claiming that they decode the significance of the archaic request of immersion in the study of the Torah: the authentic study is not the repetitious perusal of the canonical text to discover all the meaningful messages there. The imperative *hafokh* should be understood in *ʾAvot* as turning everything up, like turning a stone over, to discover under it the relevant messages. In Abulafia, however, *hafokh* should be understood as an act intended to affect the disintegration of the studied matters. Indeed, in one of the passages analyzed above we encountered the word *hippukh* as a technical term for combination of letters.[21] It is the permutation of the letters of the Torah, which amounts to a deconstruction of the canonical sequel of letters and words, in order to achieve a mystical experience, which is related also to the speculative, namely philosophical, preoccupation.

What would be the relation Abulafia envisions between the plain study of the Torah, following the ordinary sequence of letters, and his own manner of study, in fact what he regarded as interpretation? This seems to me to be the basic question underlying the above passage. After all, it is only in the normal sequence of letters that stories are told in the Bible. By restructuring the order of letters, the stories disintegrate or disappear. Abulafia created a quandary between the canonical sequence of letters, which is fundamentally semantic as it is structured in words and sentences, and the discrete letters that interact between themselves. This approach introduces a moment of chaos, a dissolution of the ordinary sequence, at least before another sequence possessing some semantic valences is construed. To formulate the question differently: Is the maximum religious effect achieved when resorting to the words of the Torah, or is it attained when dealing with its separate letters? Or, from the point of view of authority: Is the received tradition of the sequence of the text also the supreme structure, or is the mystic able to put forward other types of linguistic order, provided he resorts to the same letters?

On one hand, the answer is simple: Abulafia himself, in paragraph 2, paraphrases the apotheotic description of the Torah in 'Avot, as quoted in paragraph 1, as an entity that encompasses everything. Thus, the answer would be that the canonical order understood as Torah is of paramount importance, and apparently no other indication is to be found in the above passage. On the other hand, this apotheosis of the regular status of the text would not invite expressions of such an unusual esotericism from a Kabbalist like Abulafia. I assume that the clue to the hidden message of the passage is found in the significance he attributes to the word "blood." After all, the meaning of writing the Torah on the blood is not clear, and this strange claim should be viewed as a clue to the proper understanding of the passage. I suggest understanding the blood as pointing to the plain, manifest sense of the Torah. The problem, however, is how this sense is understood in connection to blood. In order to fathom Abulafia's understanding of this word let me adduce some instances where he clarifies it. In his *Commentary on Sefer Yetzirah* he puts it blatantly: "And within the blood is Satan and within Satan is blood."[22] Elsewhere, in a passage from *Sitrei Torah*, Abulafia writes:

> Adam and Eve [amount] in gematria [to] "My father and my mother," and their secret is blood and ink.[23] The latter points to the name YHWH[24] and the former points to the combination of this name and it is recited Yod He' WaW He'. And know that the innocent has a sign inscribed on his forehead, and the guilty is inscribed on his forehead with a sign.[25] To one the sign of blood, to the other the sign of ink. And the secret of the sign of blood is being born,[26] and its matter of sign-blood and its secret is image,[27] which means that it preceded the existence of man, and from it your soul emerges, and all our sorcery will turn to the path of sorceries, and whoever does so spills blood. And the secret of the sign of ink is parturient.[28] Behold there is one form born and another form that gives birth . . . and the secret is that Adam and Eve are two but [also] are one, and the witness is "He created them male and female."[29]

The passive and active elements are described in pairs, which include, on one side, Adam, male, ink, parturient, innocent, and the Tetragrammaton and, on the other side, Eve, female, blood, soul, sorceries, image, being born, and the compounded letters of the Tetragrammaton. There can be no doubt as to the superiority of ink over blood. There can also be no doubt, however, that the two opposing elements complement and, to an even greater degree, unite with each other. Thus, the plain sense of the Torah, referred to by "blood," and the imaginary faculty referred to by *demut*, "image,"[30] allude to the common order of the letters of the Torah. This is the starting point, material and passive, or the substratum represented by the parchment. The dynamic aspect, however, is represented in the context of the text of the Torah by the ink. Therefore, the passive, which can be understood as Satanic—in the manner in which Maimonides envisioned Satan as imagination—or imaginative, is the lower plain sense, the manifest one, which should be transcended in order to reach the esoteric intellectual or spiritual meanings. I assume that the polarity between the two forms of existence is also implied in the phrase "measure against measure." Since one of the two measures relates explicitly to blood, it is possible that the opposite measure refers to the intellect. In such a manner we should understand the significance of the two attributes, mercy and judgment, as standing not for divine modes of acting in the world but for human actions.

III. CONTEMPLATING LETTERS AND NAMES

In Abulafia there is an inversion of the axiology we found in passages cited in Chapter 2 belonging to theosophical forms of Kabbalah where the white aspects, or the parchment as substratum, were conceived of as superior to the black aspects of the Torah scroll. There the primary, primordial, passive elements were given priority, while for Abulafia what the mystic creates by combining letters counts more. In order to make such a claim he had to allow the individual letters valences of their own. He could do so by resorting to several mystical and magical sources.[31]

He chose, however, to do so by resorting first to Maimonides' contention concerning the depth of the Torah, not to a Kabbalistic one. Indeed, paragraph 3 is, in part, the philosophical "justification" of the practice of letter manipulation. Whereas the second paragraph starts with "but," implying a possible tension between the manner in which Maimonides interpreted the relevant part of *'Avot* and the Kabbalistic tradition, the third paragraph greatly attenuates it. After all, in *Sitrei Torah* Abulafia strove to demonstrate that he reveals secrets of the great eagle, not theories found in mystico-magical books, which were understood by Abulafia to be different from Maimonides'. In his earliest commentary on the *Guide* he wrote explicitly that there are two paths, "the path of the *Guide* and [another one] according to my own path, that is the path of Kabbalah . . . the paths of Kabbalah which are the secrets of *Sefer Yetzirah*."[32]

There can be no doubt that Abulafia perceived the combinatory theories as belonging to *Sefer Yetzirah*. However, he compares Maimonides' view on the inexhaustibility of the Torah to Nahmanides' dictum about the Torah as a series of divine names, an issue already discussed above.[33]

Let me attempt to elucidate the difference between the Tetragrammaton and its being written in a plene manner. The simple form of spelling the Tetragrammaton corresponds to the ink, the plene or compounded one to the blood. Indeed, in one of the discussions on blood and ink Abulafia emphasizes that blood stands for death and mixture.[34] This distinction may point to the necessity to transform the biblical text by various devices, such as the gematria *ve-dyo* = 26 = YHWH, into expressions of the divine name.[35] This possibility is reminiscent of the more general principle found in the work of Abulafia's student, R. Joseph Gikatilla, that all the words of the Torah are ramifications of the Tetragrammaton.[36] It is quite plausible that Abulafia had access to an earlier tradition that also inspired Gikatilla. Such an assumption would involve the ongoing interpretive attempts to extract the divine names from all the biblical verses by all possible exegetical techniques. In any case, this might have been a mystical ideal that informed Abulafia's own literary activity. In one of his prophetic books, *Sefer ha-Haftarah*, God is reported to have revealed to Abulafia, "I innovate a new Torah within the holy nation, which is my people Israel. My honorable name is like a new Torah, and it has not been explicated to my people since the day I hid my face from them."[37] This is a quote from a book composed in the same period as *Sefer Sitrei Torah*. I assume that the name mentioned herein is the very same one mentioned in paragraph 2: 'AHWY.[38] Thus, God revealed to Abulafia another Torah, which is identical, as in some other earlier Kabbalistic sources, with the newly revealed name of God. Indeed, the assumption that one can receive a revelation that is similar to Moses' revelation was not exceptional in Abulafia's thought. He contended that his prophetic book should be read as part of the Sabbath ritual, after the reading of the Torah, as one of the prophetic books, and this is the reason he entitled it *Sefer ha-Haftarah*.

IV. TORAH AS AN ENCOMPASSING ENTITY

Let me now address the "absorbing" aspect of the Torah as expressed in *Sitrei Torah*. It is obvious that Abulafia offered a paraphrase to the formulations found in the *'Avot* treatise. It is also evident, however, that his formulation is much more comprehensive, because his vision is much more ontological and anthropological: the Torah contains all. What does such a far reaching theory mean in his thought? In order to answer this question, let me quote a parallel discussion, written nine years later, from Abulafia's commentary on the Torah:

The Torah shows to us today everything depicted[39] in front of us, supernal and lower things,[40] everything is known in accordance with it when you will be willing to follow it in accordance with the divine, prophetic intention, and fathom it in an appropriate manner, as it is said: "Turn it and turn it, because everything is in it, she is entirely within you, and you are entirely within it, and by it we see, and from it you should not stray." And insofar as our matter dealing with esoteric issues is concerned we should compare the Torah to the menorah and its lamps, because the lamps are the very Torah because it illumines every spirit from six extremities, and the four directions of the world, and it is the median[41] between all [things] in gematria[—]and according to the subject matter. Without Kabbalah, what are we, and what would our life be! This is why it is said: "Blessed be He who precedes the [creation of a] medicine to the malady."[42] . . . He left us a remnant related to the Torah and the language. This is the reason it is incumbent to inquire into the understanding of the Torah in a manner that man will know himself within it, like someone who contemplates a mirror in order to see his face and himself and the other within it, and from there he who looks into it will ascend to the contemplation of God, blessed be He, and referring to this speculative principle they said: "When you make the lamps ascend in front of the menorah, all the seven lamps will light up."[43]

The comparison of the Torah to a mirror is fascinating for several reasons. One is that it helps us understand the manner in which man is included in the Torah, according to the two main passages discussed here. It is a comprehensive entity that allows one to contemplate oneself and also others. How may such a statement be understood? As we have seen, the Torah incorporates both intellectual and imaginary aspects, which correspond to man's two most important spiritual faculties. It is by interpreting the Torah that these faculties may be actualized. So, for example, we read in Abulafia's *Gan Na'ul*: "When the name, whose secret is in blood and ink, began to move within him, and he will feel it, as one who knows the place of a stone which is within him, he will then know that the knowledge of the name acted in him, and it began to cause him to pass from potentiality to actuality."[44] Therefore, the discussions of blood and ink are not related to the divine name in an exegetical manner alone. For a Kabbalist whose main mystical practice is related to combining the letters of the divine name, using also the written medium, what seem to be scholastic numerical affinities may have, initially or post factum, an experiential dimension; in this regard we had the opportunity to discuss above the activation of the blood during the mystical experience.[45] In any case, the last quote is also helpful in elucidating the possible meaning of the word *ha-men'ya*, translated here as "the activator": it is the divine name, which is described in the last quote as *mitno'e'a*.

Abulafia's assumption that the Torah encompasses man means that the scriptures contained two levels, the imaginary and the intellectual. Such an understanding opens the possibility for these human faculties to be actualized by activating linguistic possibilities found in the text. This practice is, as Abulafia contended in the quote from *Sefer Mafteah ha-Sefirot*, conducive to self-knowledge, the tests and examinations mentioned in one of the passages dealt with above,[46] and then to the knowledge of God. From this point of view, the Torah is more comprehensive than man, as a mirror is, but this parable does not imply a visual contemplation of oneself within a text. A metaphorical concept of comprehensiveness is implied here. It seems, however, that the concept of the Torah as encompassing man, evident in Abulafia's recurrent use of the phrase "you are entirely in the Torah," also had more graphical expressions. R. Isaac of Acre, a Kabbalist whose contact with Abulafia's views was quite significant, describes Moses' vision of the Torah as follows:

I awoke from my sleep and suddenly I saw the secret of the saying of the rabbis concerning Moses, our teacher's writing of the Torah, that he saw it written against the air of the sky, in black fire upon white fire.[47] This is that, when a man ascends a very high mountain standing within a broad flat valley without any hills or mountains within it, but only a great plain, and he lifts up his eyes and they look about and he gazes at the firmament of the heavens close to the earth, around around, to the place of the sky close to the earth, as it appears to his eyes, this is half the circle, and is known in the language of the sages of zodiac signs as the circle of the horizon. This was seen by the soul and intellect of Moses our teacher, surrounding him from above as the entire Torah, from the letter *bet* of *bereshit*, which is the first letter, to the *lamed* of *yisra'el* written in one complete circle, each letter next to its neighbor, surrounded by parchment.[48] That is to say, it is as if there were a hair's breadth between one letter and the next, for all the air that is around the letters of the Torah is entirely within the circle, and between each letter and outside of the letters there was white fire dimming the circle of the sun, and the letters themselves were of black fire, a strong blackness, the very quintessence of blackness. She [Moses' soul] gazed at them here and there to find the head of the circle or its end or its middle, but did not find anything . . . For there is no known place by which to go into the Torah, for it is wholly perfect. And while he yet gazes at this circle, she combines on and on into strong combinations, not intelligible ones.[49]

The image of the Torah as a circle is not new with R. Isaac. To give a few examples: the early-twelfth-century R. Yehudah Barceloni implies it in his *Commentary on Sefer Yetzirah*,[50] and one of R. Isaac of Acre's contemporaries, R. Joseph Angelet, formulated it as follows: "The book of the Torah is required to be round,[51] for just as in a ball one cannot detect its beginning and its end, so in the Torah is its beginning fastened to its end."[52] Moreover, as we saw in Chapter 12, at the end of the fifteenth century Johann Reuchlin reported Nahmanides' words at the beginning of his *Commentary on the Torah*, concerning the writing of the Torah in black fire upon white fire, adding that the Kabbalists had a tradition that the Torah was written in a "sphere of fire," *globum igneum*.[53] I assume that the Christian Kabbalist had access to a certain understanding of Nahmanides' introduction to the *Commentary on the Pentateuch*, which was combined with a statement in Nahmanides' *Commentary on Sefer Yetzirah*, to the effect that the first and last letters of the Torah form one word, a view we examined earlier.[54]

None of these authors spoke about the sphere or circle of the Torah as a real, ocular vision. Such a cosmic simile for the Torah emphasizes, on one hand, its perfection and comprehensiveness, while on the other hand there is a feeling of impenetrability. It is not only the picture of the hermetic closure of the huge circle of letters so close to each other,[55] but also the last sentence dealing with the unintelligible combinations of letters. What concerns me most in this context, however, is the statement that Moses considered himself, in his spiritual senses, to be encompassed by the Torah, although later on in the same text the Kabbalist indicates there is no way to enter the Torah. The description of the mountain as standing at the center of the horizon assumes that Moses saw himself as being at the middle of the circular Torah. I assume that the circular Torah embodies, in R. Isaac's view, two hypostatic powers, the sefirot Hokhmah and Binah, as we shall see in Appendix 3, while the penetrable Torah, that which is studied here below, is the available book as extant in the reproductions of the copy first made by Moses.

The encompassing nature of the Torah in those two ecstatic Kabbalists should be compared to the somewhat later vision of R. Menahem Recanati concerning the all-encompassing nature of the Torah, which we discussed earlier.[56] Although they are, presumably, unrelated historically, they nevertheless point in a direction that late-thirteenth-century Kabbalah opened: to include everything that matters in their Kabbalistic system within the Torah.

APPENDIX 3
R. ISAAC OF ACRE'S
EXEGETICAL QUANDARY

In the following I would like to translate and analyze in some detail an interesting text by R. Isaac ben Shmuel of Acre, a Kabbalist of vast knowledge and substantial influence. I find the following passage relevant to several topics that we have addressed, especially the nature of Kabbalistic symbolism, the relationship between Kabbalistic symbolism and philosophy, and the nature of Kabbalistic hermeneutics. R. Isaac had an inquiring mind and was a prolific and itinerant Kabbalist, active in the late thirteenth and early fourteenth centuries, who moved from Acre in Galilee, where he made his first advanced studies, to some cities in Spain and then, presumably, to northern Africa. He was acquainted with a variety of Kabbalistic schools and wrote some books in which the various types of Kabbalah are combined in several ways. The following text is written largely in the vein of symbolic Kabbalah, mostly as it was practiced in the schools of Gerona and Barcelona in the mid-thirteenth century, though I suspect a secondary influence of Ashkenazi Hasidism or Abraham Abulafia's Kabbalah:

[1.] I, the young Isaac of Acre,[1] have been reading the portion of Genesis in the secrets of the Torah by our master Nahmanides, blessed be his memory. And while reading that the Torah preceded the creation of the world by two thousand years, and that a black fire was written on a white fire,[2] I understood the secret of this matter and I thirsted to placate the wrath of the difficult questions of the philosophers who said that the number of the days and years depend upon time, and time depends upon the motions of the sun and moon and stars, as it is said: "let them be for signs and for seasons, for days, and for years."[3] Because upon their motions and revolutions the measures of time depend, and how can we mention years before the existence of the sphere? Despite the fact that their argument is true, they did not merit to know the intention of our sages, blessed be their memory. You should know that just as heaven is higher than earth, double is the height of the intention of our sages in their sayings in comparison to the understanding of the philosophers.

[2.] Their intention is related to the secret of the ten sefirot of Belimah found in the [letter] 'aleph of 'ABYA'[4] in accordance with the path of the true truth[5] because from the secret of the intentions of the blessings that world hints at the [sefirah of] Tiferet, and the ten sefirot of Belimah are the foundation of all matters, and the essence of all numbers, and there is no end to the details of their number, because they are more numerous than the hair of the head and understand that the letters of "ten" ['eser] are the same as the letters of "hair" [se'ar] because they are more numerous than the hair of the head and you will find in them the secret of 18,000 worlds.[6]

[3.] And since you know that the [sefirah of] Tiferet is the world, you should understand the intention of the sages, blessed be their memory, when they claim that[7] one should always[8] enter the measure of two openings and then pray. But when one prays in a place where there are neither openings nor houses, what should he do? Therefore you should know that despite the fact that one should always cause the adherence of the thought of his intellect to the unique Lord, he has also to put before his eyes the attribute of T[iferet] all day and all night long . . . T[iferet] includes the six [sefirot], and since the thought of man is [fixed on] T[iferet] all day long, when the time of prayer arrives—and all men who are fearful of God are eliminating the matters of the world from their heart—because T[iferet] is the secret of the world, as it is written that his heart and the eyes of the thought of his intellect adhere to the place of the supernal simplicity[9] and the complete unity, he has to enter two openings in order to come to the house of the supernal YHWH which is the B[inah], the secret of the complete unity and the proper simplicity, because the simplicity of the three supernal [sefirot] in comparison to Ti[feret] and the six extremes is comparable to the simplicity of the soul in comparison to its palace,[10] and to the simplicity and sanctity of the seventh day in comparison to the six days of the week. And the two openings are the [sefirot of] G[edulah] and P[ahad], which are [situated] between B[inah] and T[iferet]. And provided that the essence of the intention of the sages, blessed be their memory, is not [concerning] the corporeal sensibles, which are the openings of the sensible houses, but are certainly the secret of the supernal emanation, the emanation of the divine secret, they did not say that it is incumbent to enter two openings but said the measure [of two openings], namely that he should enter into the thought of his mind the measure of these two openings.

[4.] I shall return now to my first place and say that each of the ten sefirot of Belimah comprises all the ten sefirot and thus they amount to a hundred. And each comprises a hundred and thus they are a thousand, and each of them comprises the whole thousand and thus they are ten thousand. And the secret of *shannah* [year] is sefirah and the essence of the place of the Torah is H[okhmah], which is the beginning of the emanation and the beginning of all the creatures, and this is why the Torah said,[11] "God created me at the beginning of his way," the beginning being Hokhmah,[12] we see that all their sayings are true to the intelligent believers who merited to understand my intention in a proper manner. And those two thousand years by which it had been mentioned that the Torah preceded the world hint at Hesed and at Binah, and this world is T[iferet], as it is said that immediately with the emanation of Hokhmah the Torah was emanated because H[okhmah] is the Torah, and the Torah is H[okhmah] and it was written by black fire on the white fire, not by a fire as it is believed by those of little faith who speak about the righteous in a boastful manner, thinking that all the sayings of the sages, blessed be their memory, all concern the sensible fire and concern the [two thousand] years that they are dependent upon the motions of the spheres of the firmament and of the planets. However, this is a fire that is not a fire, as it is said by the sages, blessed be their memory:[13] "When you arrive at the stones of pure marble do not say: Water, water, etc. Because there are neither stones of marble nor water." So too is the matter of this fire: the black fire hints at the attribute of judgment, which is B[inah], and the white fire hints at the attribute of mercy, which is H[okhmah]. Behold that our eyes see that within the secret of the supernal emanation, the Torah preceded by two thousand years, namely two 'alephim, two units . . . the divine thought, *shannah* is the secret of sefirah, whose secret is *mahashavah*,[14] because these two units are H[okhmah] and B[inah], before the world was created, before the emanation of T[iferet], and it has been inscribed on H[okhmah] which is the white fire, [and] the attribute of Mercy, which are blank and white like white paper, by black fire, on B[inah] which is the black fire, the grand attribute of judgment . . . similar to the black ink.

[5.] And when arose in the thought[15] that the unique Lord desired to create the [sefirah] of T[iferet] . . . He emanated the MShH—M[etatron] S[ar] H[a-Panim]—certainly the emanated MShH, the supernal Moshe, who copied the Torah from a primordial book, from the two primordial sefirot which preceded in the [realm of] emanation, and this is the written Torah, and this is the secret of the *waw*[16] which unites all the six extremities. And this is the reason the majority of the verses of the Torah of Moses start with *waw*, and concerning T[iferet] which is the secret of the written Torah our sages, blessed be their memory, said that "the simile of the supernal Hokhmah—which is [the sefirah of] H[okhmah]—is Torah,"[17] which is the T[iferet].[18]

Although R. Isaac describes his reading of Nahmanides' commentary on the Torah, it is obvious that therein he did not find sufficient answers to the quandaries posed by the philosophers. The rabbinic dictum describing the preexistence of the Torah involves the prior creation of the celestial bodies that determine time. While not accepting the centrality of philosophy, Nahmanides' commentary does not constitute a sustained attack on allegorical interpretations, nor a Kabbalistic disclosure of the symbolic-theurgical layer of the Bible which constitutes Nahmanides' Kabbalah. Thus, to follow the philosophers whose quandary is presented as containing some truth, he would admit that the rabbinic dictum is based on an inner contradiction. It is this contradiction that bothers the Kabbalist and urged him to make an effort to solve it. Let me start by explicating the emergence of the quandary. A rabbinic text attempting to exalt the Torah asserts its preexistence to the moment of creation. A precise span of time between the moment the Torah came into existence and the moment the world was created is mentioned, but such an issue did not bother rabbinic authors as they were not particularly concerned with ontological problems like the nature of time and the relation between time and creation. However, the emergence of Jewish philosophy, which introduced preoccupations with the nature of time and space, opened the question of measuring time, and in the vein of the Aristotelian definition of time as the measure of the movements of the spheres, the rabbinic dictum became immediately incoherent. It is this clash between the archaic religious vision and the philosophical causality that prompted R. Isaac to search for a solution. This is a conspicuously apologetic effort to make sense of the rabbinic dictum that inspired the exegetical exercise in paragraphs 2, 3, and 4.

The Kabbalist approaches the quandary by disentangling the nexus between world, namely material world, and time, namely two thousand years. If the term "world" in the rabbinic dictum does not denote the created world, and if time in years is not the measured time, then the causality of the philosophers is not relevant in this case and no contradiction can be discovered in the rabbinic statement. R. Isaac "achieves" this end by a process symbolic of these two elements to another realm, where the causality put forward by the philosophers does not hold more. R. Isaac interprets "world" and "two thousand years" as symbols for sefirotic powers. There the philosophical causality is substituted by an hypostatic hierarchy, which installs another type of process. How does this symbolic reading operate?

The term ha-ʿolam occurs in the first dictum, where it has been translated as "world." It also occurs, however, in the second rabbinic dictum, in paragraph 2, as part of an adverbial construct, le-ʿolam, translated as "always." This second dictum is interrogated by R. Isaac and brought to the point of absurdity: What is the meaning of the sages requiring someone always to enter the measure of two openings if there are cases where one prays in a desert, for example? "Always" means that there is no prayer exempt from this entrance. Yet since in rabbinic sources there is no exemption from prayer on architectonic grounds, it follows that "always" should be understood metaphorically. This means that the phrase le-ʿolam is to be interpreted in the rabbinic dictum, according to rabbinic logic, as a metaphor. This argument is necessary in order to put forward the metaphorical understanding of ʿolam in the first dictum. Thus, the philosophical critique of one rabbinic dictum compelled R. Isaac to claim that the plain-sense reading of the rabbis is also problematic in another case where the term occurs, and that in general the rabbis' dicta should be interpreted according to another interpretive code, the sefirotic one.

Before going into the details of this interpretation, it is important to point out that although reading a Kabbalistic book—R. Isaac expressly indicates that he read Nahmanides' Sitrei Torah[19]—the answer to the quandary was not found there; nor does he claim that he had ever received an oral tradition that could solve his quandary. In this passage, unlike many other passages in the same book, R. Isaac does not contend that he received a revelation that could help him solve the exegetical problem. In this case he describes himself as standing, as a Kabbalist, alone before the derision of the philosophers, armed not with a specific traditional deciphering of the dictum but with a symbolic code that he applied to the difficult text. I believe that this situation, *mutatis mutandis*, is characteristic of a good many instances that provoked symbolistic interpretations of the semantically or intellectually difficult parts of Jewish tradition. Here, unlike the other cases, we have a report of the starting point of the interpretation, not only its final results.

Interestingly, R. Isaac starts his interpretation not by resorting to Kabbalistic cosmogony or theogony, as the chart that will allow the symbolic elevation, but with a ritualistic statement by the rabbis which has been interpreted, plausibly before him, in a symbolic manner. The experience of the lived ritual apparently is more immediate for him than general speculations. The experience of having the divine name before his eyes all the time, namely the sixth sefirah, is conceived of as a common one. This sefirah is symbolized, however, as he reiterates time and again, by the term "world." In this case "world" stands for the mundane preoccupations that should be transcended by mental elevation in the moment of prayer. In other words, the sefirotic realm that is the object of mystical uninterrupted adherence during the time of human awareness, the sixth sefirah, is low in comparison to the sefirotic powers that are involved in the shorter but more intense experience of mystical prayer. Then the Kabbalist has to transcend the lower sefirot in order to reach the highest divine unity or simplicity. Although R. Isaac does not resort in this context to the term 'Ein Sof, the Infinite, there is no doubt, on the basis of many other discussions in his writings that a Kabbalist should fix his mystical intention on the Infinite and even cleave to it.[20] This move from the lower to the highest divine levels should, however, be understood according to the second rabbinic dictum as involving the Kabbalist's entrance through two openings. Here, too, the Kabbalist insists on the need to read the rabbis metaphorically: the rabbinic dictum does not indicate, as he stresses, the imperative to enter physically through two openings but the measure of two openings. In Hebrew "measure," *shi'ur*, is a term that was part of the famous expression *shi'ur qomah*, the measure of the [body] of God. R. Isaac himself dealt several times with this phrase, and I assume that for him the very occurrence of the term *shi'ur* invited an elevation of the significance of the phrase to the sefirotic realm.[21] Therefore, he claims, the rabbinic dictum is again to be read metaphorically. This is the case, according to R. Isaac, of another, more famous rabbinic passage, which deals with the mystical ascent to the supernal world: the passage, found in various versions, concerning the four sages who entered the pardes. In this case the rabbinic formulation includes a negation, "do not say," which the Kabbalist interprets as indicating a metaphorical reading of the terms "stones of marble" and "water." In other words, R. Isaac accepts, at least to a certain extent, the stand of the deriding philosophers, who claimed that the corporeal reading of the rabbinic sources renders these statements incoherent. Yet while the philosophers are described as persons of little faith, who see only the contradictions without making the effort to provide an alternative spiritual explanation that would solve the problem, the Kabbalah is conceived of as being able to supply such an answer, and R. Isaac attempts to do it.

What is the metaphorical reading of the two openings? They stand, according to the symbolic system that R. Isaac adopts in that passage, for the two sefirot, Gedullah and Pahad, that mediate between the sefirah of Tiferet, the world, and the higher sefirah of Binah, which belongs to the supernal triad of divine unity. The entrance is therefore not necessarily a corporeal move but is paramountly a mental tour of the divine architectonics that starts, during prayer, with the lower sefirot and ascends to the higher level.

The ascending hierarchy that informs the mental process related to the liturgical ritual—found in a Kabbalistic source quoted by R. Isaac in another book[22]— serves R. Isaac's purpose in describing the descending theogonic hierarchy, which will provide the solution for the initial quandary. The preexistence of the Torah to the world is interpreted by him as an ontic, not a temporal, priority. It is not time that plays the defining role in the relationship between the Torah and the world, but the emanative primordiality of the supreme hypostases related to the Torah in comparison to the hypostasis that symbolizes the world. The Torah is identical to the second sefirah, Hokhmah, although according to other statements this sefirah is to be conceived of as the white fire, or the substratum on which the black letters are written, letters that are identified with the third sefirah, Binah. Thus, the Torah as an entity identical with these two sefirot is found on a level higher than the world, the sefirah of Tiferet, and as such it precedes it ontologically, and perhaps even temporally, if time were allowed to play a significant role in the process of emanation.

Indeed, it seems that the issue of temporality bothered R. Isaac enough for him to attempt to do away with this aspect of the rabbinic dictum. He resorts to the gematria of the word for year, shannah, in order to identify it with sefirah and mahashavah, namely a hypostatic being. Also, the other word implying a measure of time, 'alppayyim, "two thousand," is decoded as pointing to two 'alephs standing for the two sefirot, Hokhmah and Binah. Again temporal quantity, two thousand years, is forced to refer to hypostatic entities.

So much for the hermeneutical details of the above passage. I am inclined, however, to consider this passage as representative of broader hermeneutical phenomena. The first and most conspicuous is the relation between the plain sense of a text and the symbolic sense. The absurd reading of the several rabbinic dicta does not, in my opinion, leave room for doubt that the metaphorical reading of the crucial elements of these dicta, and even the relationship between them, not only has been drastically transformed by the symbolic reading but also obliterates the possibility of approaching them seriously on the plain level. Both the disclosure of the incoherence and the decoding of the alleged hints in the rabbinic texts pointing to a metaphorical understanding seriously undermine the possibility that the plain sense retains the status of a significant statement after its symbolic explanation. The rabbinic texts as understood above do not function on the two levels but on one level alone. Before the understanding of the incoherence, they have a plain sense which is problematized when the symbolic one is imposed. Thus, the plain sense amounts to a misunderstanding, while the disclosure of the symbolic sense destroys the possibility of believing in the plain one. From this point of view the alleged critique of the anonymous philosophers dramatically affected the perception of rabbinic issues even among the "great" believers. Although a way of thought characteristic of the theosophical Kabbalah was adduced in order to safeguard the rabbinic material, it succeeded in some cases only at the price of sacrificing the plain sense. The assumption dominant in the scholarly understanding of the Kabbalistic symbols, that they do not weaken the plain sense of the interpreted material, should be modified.[23]

Even more important for the understanding of the manner in which Kabbalistic symbolism worked is R. Isaac's general strategy in this passage and many others. The quandary created by the philosopher can be solved only because there is an interpretive code that is deemed to be accepted by him and his readers: the symbolic code. The structure of the sefirotic realm is not described, but only the nature of the particular sefirot that are involved in the suggested "solution." In other words, at the beginning of the fourteenth century, when the above passage presumably was composed, the symbolic systems of Spanish Kabbalah were articulated enough from the systemic point of view, and known well enough, to allow resort to them without introducing the reader to their details. Or, to put it differently: in some parts—rather small ones, I assume—of the Jewish intelligentsia in Spain, Kabbalistic symbolism was known well enough to serve as a hermeneutical common denominator that could facilitate communication and rescue difficult aspects of Jewish tradition. However, such a function of the different Kabbalistic symbols as codes contradicts the role attributed to them by the dominant theory of Kabbalistic symbolism, which contends that symbols are the only available avenue for approaching the divinity.[24] The divine hypostatic system as composed of ten sefirot was already known by the Kabbalists from their studies of the available Kabbalistic literature. They subsequently resorted to their theosophical knowledge, and perhaps also their experiences, as was the case with R. Isaac, in order to elucidate problems provoked by classical Jewish texts, in the same manner in which I proposed to understand important parts of the Kabbalistic symbolism.[25] It is more what I called the impressive rather than the expressive aspect of the symbols that became more dominant with the later development of Kabbalah. In the writings of R. Isaac of Acre, the above passage in particular, and those of some of his contemporaries, most eminently the many books of R. David ben Yehudah he-Hasid, with whose Kabbalistic thought R. Isaac was presumably acquainted,[26] Kabbalistic theosophy made quantum jumps from the point of view of the multiplication of the divine powers and worlds. Not only were the four worlds introduced and referred to technically by the acronym 'ABYA', which also appears above,[27] but the move toward a theory allowing the existence of innumerable divine powers is already obvious, as the pun on *'eser* / *se'ar* in paragraph 2 evinces. This is not only a development concerning theosophy; it could also have implications for the nature of hermeneutics, since the different divine and non-divine realms of reality could invite corresponding exegetical approaches. The richer the supernal pole that serves as the map for the exegetical enterprises, the richer their results are. Indeed, the proliferation of the divine worlds should also be seen as relevant for the Kabbalistic exegetical projects described above as basically vertical,[28] although, as we have seen, at a certain stage in the development of Kabbalah the hypertrophy of divine powers diminished the symbolic function.[29]

Indeed, in R. Isaac of Acre's book from which we quoted above, a fourfold exegetical method has been put forward which, like pardes, is designated by an acronym: *nisa'n*. It is composed of three methods of interpretation: *nistar, sod*, and *'emmet*, to which a fourth method has been added as the highest one, the "correct true" sense, *ha-'emmet ha-nekhonah*, mentioned explicitly in paragraph 2. There it is explicitly related to the first world of 'ABYA', 'Atzilut, or Emanation.[30] Hence, an explicit correlation between the expanding theosophy and the developing exegetical methods is manifest.

What could have been the perception of R. Isaac as a commentator, according to the above passage? Did he believe, for example, that his symbolic interpretation is the one and only possible way of understanding the rabbinic dicta? Or did he allow, at least in principle, additional symbolic interpretations? In my opinion, the very mention of the highest way of interpretation allows the assumption that he would resort to the lower ones, too, were it necessary to do so. In a generation when several complex exegetical systems were already articulated, as we saw in

Chapter 12, it would be unnatural or implausible to return to monosemic types of interpretation.

Let me now turn to paragraph 5, which deals with the copying of the supernal, primordial Torah by Moses. As is the case in many Kabbalistic writings, Moses is conceived of here as symbolizing the sixth sefirah, which is also symbolized by the written Torah. R. Isaac accepts these symbolic commonplaces but interprets them as part of a supernal myth having to do with the descent of the primordial Torah to the level of Tiferet. Moses is not solely a human mortal; his name becomes, characteristically enough for the above passage, an acronym for the emanated Metatron, angel or prince of the divine presence,[31] which is now described as the copyist within the divine realm. Functioning as a copyist, Moses had an impact on the style of the Torah, which abounds in the letter *waw*, another classical symbol for Tiferet, in order to strengthen the linkage between the Torah and that sefirah.

R. Isaac addresses the issue of Moses the copyist because it is part of Nahmanides' introduction to his *Commentary on the Torah*, just as it occurs in some other rabbinic statements interpreted above.[32] Nahmanides insisted on copying from one book to another, in a manner reminiscent of the copying of the Qur'an from a preexisting book and in manifest opposition to Maimonides' insistence that Moses received a vocal revelation that he committed to writing.[33] In other words, what we find in the above passage is an attempt to offer symbolic valences for rabbinic statements that seemed to R. Isaac not sufficiently significant, even when brought together in Nahmanides' book. He had the feeling that without loading them with a detailed symbolic valence they might suffer the critique of the philosophers and lose their authority. He thereby arcanized not only some rabbinical statements but also a small segment of Nahmanides' classical book.[34] I would suggest seeing this arcanization of Nahmanides not as part of the much wider and better-known process of committing to writing the secrets Nahmanides hinted at in his *Commentary on the Torah* by some of his students' students, a process with which R. Isaac was well acquainted, but as an independent effort that does not claim a transmitted tradition but responds to some contemporary debates.[35] Indeed, at the end of the first third of the fourteenth century there are beginnings of a critique of Nahmanides in Catalan Halakhic circles which stem from his students, including somewhat later remarks that the great master had "immersed himself too much in Kabbalah."[36] Moreover, the general ambiance of early-fourteenth-century Catalonia was permeated by the second debate on Maimonides, one of the main protagonists in this debate being a Kabbalist, R. Shlomo ibn Adret. Jewish philosophy, we should recall, remained both a challenge and a trigger for Kabbalists long after it had articulated the theosophical-theurgical Kabbalistic systems at the beginning of the thirteenth century. In any case, in the immediate environment of R. Isaac in Spain, in R. Moses de Leon's *Sefer ha-Rimmon* Jewish philosophers were described as deriding the pious students of Torah and the dicta of the rabbis. What is pertinent for our discussion is the fact that de Leon describes the clash in terms of "sons of the books of the Greeks" who deride the students of the sacred books.[37]

Are R. Isaac's remarks responding to this nascent critique when they arcanized so many rabbinic statements occurring in Nahmanides' introduction? In any case, the analyzed passage demonstrates the strong urge of several Kabbalists, contemporaries of R. Isaac, to offer symbolic interpretations to parts of mystical or Kabbalistic books, which were not intended to be understood as symbols. This extreme symbolization is part of what I have proposed to designate as superarcanization.[38]

The question, however, is whether discovering symbols wherever a quandary appears does not testify to a certain strengthening of a mechanistic propensity that reduces the entirety of interpreted texts to a schematic, overdetermined code. This is especially evident in the case of the symbolization of Moses' copying the Torah. Yet it seems that the routinization of the massive resort to symbols does not automatically coincide with a literary activity devoid of experiential aspects. As we saw in Chapter 11 and Appendix 2, R. Isaac's description of Moses' experience is quite reminiscent of personal experiences of some contemporary mystics with whom he apparently was acquainted. Moreover, the juxtaposition of the idea that the Torah was copied by Moses and the view that it was written by two fires points, in my opinion, to a deep preoccupation with finding a more comprehensive meaning of Nahmanides' introduction. So, for example, we read: "I awoke from my sleep and suddenly I saw the secret of the saying of the rabbis concerning Moses our teacher's writing of the Torah, that he saw it written against the air of the sky, in black fire upon white fire."[39]

Let me emphasize that it is the textual quandary that provoked the exegetical discourse of R. Isaac of Acre, not his effort to understand the recondite secrets of the divine world. Indeed, another text, which plausibly predated R. Isaac's passage, may illustrate the impenetrability of the biblical text. R. Joseph of Hamadan wrote in his *Commentary on the Rationales of the Commandments*:

Woe to whoever believes that there is no more than the plain sense of the Torah,[40] because the Torah is the name of the Holy One, blessed be He, in its entirety . . . because the Torah in its entirety is the name of the Holy One,[41] and it consists in inner [namely spiritual] things . . . that any creature cannot comprehend the greatness of its rank, but God, blessed be He, the supreme and the wonderful that created it, and the Holy One, blessed be He, His Torah is within Him and in Him there is the Torah, and this is the reason why Kabbalists said that "He is in His name and the name is in Him,"[42] He is His Torah and the Torah is made out of the holy and pure chain, in [the image of the] supernal form, and it is the shadow of the Holy One, blessed be He.[43]

The depths of the Torah cannot be penetrated by mortals, and the Torah does not serve as a telescope to attain a vision of the divine. Rather, being identical to God, it is fraught with the divinity of the divine realm, designated as the pure and holy chain and the supernal form. Thus, the nontransparent nature of the Torah is emphasized, and I assume that any effort to achieve its spiritual essence consists in discovering the correspondence between the different aspects of the text and the divine structure, as we had already seen above.[44] The transparency achieved by theosophical-symbolic exegesis consists in the imposition of the theosophical scheme on the Torah, in a manner reminiscent of R. Isaac of Acre's enterprise. Thus, according to these two cases, in lieu of regarding the Kabbalistic theosophical symbols as tools for passing from the clear text to its symbolic but less clear meaning, which intimates the distant divinity, we may assert that in the theosophical-theurgical Kabbalistic literature there are instances where the divine secrets are the exegetical tools for making sense of a text whose recondite significance escapes otherwise human understanding.

It is worthwhile to point out the difference between the view that identifies the Torah with the divine realm and the contention that the Torah is the shadow of God. The term "shadow" should perhaps be understood not as diminishing the strong identification but as claiming that God is the image for or paradigm of the Torah. This seems to be the case in a book that was composed in the early 1280s in Castile, R. Shema'yah ben Isaac ha-Levi's *Sefer Tzeror ha-Hayyim*.[45] If this reading is accepted, the revealed Torah is to be understood as less transparent than the prevailing theory of symbolism would have it be. Rather than seeing the copy (the revealed Torah) as more understandable in comparison to the paradigm (the supernal Torah), we should better conceive the supernal paradigm as the clue to a better understanding of the lower copy. In other words, the understanding of supernal structures may be taken as a prerequisite for the understanding of the lower reverberations.

APPENDIX 4

THE EXILE OF THE TORAH
AND THE IMPRISONMENT OF SECRETS

I. CHRISTIAN KABBALAH AND JEWISH KABBALISTS

The centrality of the Torah as organizing a bibliocentric religiosity was generated by a variety of factors, one of them being the destruction of the Second Temple and the growing disintegration of the practical, ritualistic aspects of a topocentric religiosity. This means that the emergence of the centrality of the Torah and later the Talmud, and a geographically decentralized society, coincided to a great extent. Later, the more conspicuous the exilic existence was, the more central the book of the Torah became. This development is paralleled by the gradual arcanization of the canonical text. To a certain extent, the secrets imagined to be found in the Torah multiplied with the passage of the time in exile. This historical explanation of the development of the status of the text and its "secrets" has been seen in quite a different light by some Lurianic Kabbalists writing at the end of the sixteenth and early in the seventeenth centuries. The Torah and its secrets have been regarded as central issues before and beyond any historical development, and only a certain deterioration could be attributed to a historical event; with the destruction of the Second Temple, the Torah was described by Lurianic Kabbalists as burned and its secrets as imprisoned in the realm of evil. Before addressing the details of this specific theory, let me survey what seems to me to be the historical background of its emergence.

Since the late fifteenth century the emergence of the Christian Kabbalah attracted the attention of some Jews acquainted with the situation in northern Italy.[1] I assume that R. Elijah del Medigo criticized the Jewish Kabbalah as a result of his encounter with Pico della Mirandola's involvement with Kabbalah.[2] A few decades later, we learn from the writings of two Kabbalists about their acquaintance with Christians interested in Kabbalah. R. Elijah Menahem Halfan, a Kabbalist active in Venice in the first part of the sixteenth century, has left a remarkable description of what happened in his generation: "Especially after the rise of the sect of Luther,[3] many of the nobles and scholars of the land [namely the Christians] sought to have a thorough knowledge of this glorious science.[4] They have exhausted themselves in this search, because among our people there are but a small number of men expert in this wisdom, for after the great number of troubles and expulsions[5] but a few remain. So seven learned men[6] grasp a Jewish man by the hem of his garment and say: 'Be our master in this science.' "[7] R. Elijah Menahem Halfan was concerned with the emergence of Christian Kabbalah elsewhere too, in a Halakhic discussion dealing with the talmudic interdiction against revealing secrets of the Torah to gentiles.[8] The Venetian rabbi connected this development causally with the Christian openings as evinced in Italy and in Germany, in the case of Luther's early attitude toward Jews, which was positive.[9]

Much sterner is the attitude of Jewish Kabbalists active outside Christian Europe, in the Ottoman Empire. So, for example, we learn from R. Abraham ben Eliezer ha-Levi, a messianic Kabbalist who was asked to send his apocalyptic treatises to Italy:

In my opinion there is a danger sending to you this commentary, since it was said that our brethren, the sons of Esau, study Hebrew and these matters are ancient,[10] and whoever will write[11] anything there, it may, God forfend, fall into their hands. And despite the fact that those who study are faithful to us, nevertheless it is reasonable and compelling to conceal these matters from them, and there is also a severe ban concerning it.[12] In any case, I have refrained[13] from sending to you these treatises constituting the Epistle of the Secret of the Redemption and you, my masters, those who conceal the wisdom and the secret of the Lord are to the fearers of God,[14] the participants in the covenant will contemplate it, but this will not be accessible to every gentile.[15]

The sharpest reaction, however, to the study of Kabbalah in Italy was formulated by R. Moses Cordovero, in a treatise composed two decades after the passage by ha-Levi: "Just as foxes damaged the vineyard of God, the Lord of Hosts, nowadays in the land of Italy the priests studied the science of Kabbalah and they diverted it to heresy, because of our sins, and the ark of the covenant of the Lord, the very science [of Kabbalah] had hidden itself. But blessed is he who gave it to us, because neither they[16] nor the gentiles distinguish between right and left, but are similar to animals[17] because, ultimately, they did not fathom the inner [essence of the lore]."[18] Foxes in the divine vineyard is a well-known topos for heretics that caused damage to either the Torah or the people of Israel. In the Maimonidean controversy the topos had been applied to Jews from the other camp. Here, however, it stands for the gentiles, whose entry into the vineyard—*kerem*, a term related to pardes, the "mystical" orchard, which was understood, like the ark, as the wisdom of Kabbalah[19]—inflicted damage. The motif of the ark also hints at the theft of the ark by the Philistines, which is reminiscent of the Christians' taking over the Kabbalah in the present. Those damages were seen as the reason for the esoteric nature of the Kabbalah, a contention reminiscent of R. Elijah Menahem Halfan's claim that in his day the Kabbalists are few.

Another leading Kabbalist, R. Hayyim Vital, a former student of Cordovero's, was preoccupied with the transmission of secrets to Christians. In one of his dreams he reported that he arrived to Rome only to be arrested by the officials of the "Roman Caesar." After his detainment by soldiers he is brought into the presence of the "Caesar," who commands all persons to clear the hall, leaving the two men alone. Vital reports his dream as follows:

> We were left by ourselves. I said to him: "On what grounds do you want to kill me? All of you are lost in your religions like blind men. For there is no truth but the Torah of Moses, and with it alone can exist no other truth." He replied: "I already know all this and so I sent for you. I know that you are the wisest and most skilled of men in the wisdom of truth.[20] I most knowledgeable want you to reveal to me some of the secrets of the Torah and the Names of your blessed Lord, for I already recognized the truth" . . . Then I told him a little bit of the wisdom [of Kabbalah] and I awoke.[21]

The phrase "Roman Caesar" apparently points to the pope, with whom many messianic figures, Vital among them, looked for an audience. There is no doubt from the context, in which Vital portrays himself as dwelling in a cave with the paupers of Rome, that a messianic background informs the dream. The pope offers total recognition of the superiority of Vital over other Kabbalists, as well as the acceptance of the truth of Judaism over Christianity. The very resort to the phrase "Roman Caesar" must, however, have been associated by Vital with the destruction of the Temple. I assume that this interruption reflects an unconscious resistance, while dreaming, to teaching Kabbalistic secrets to a gentile.

R. Jacob Hayyim Tzemah, a younger contemporary of Vital, a Lurianic Kabbalist quoted earlier in this book,[22] wrote in his *Sefer Tiferet 'Adam:*

And also the gentile who wrote a book on occult philosophy, whose name is Enrico Cornelio Agrippa, wrote in it a little of every science, but no one [science] has successfully discussed it in its entirety; and he mixed profane and impure things which should not be accepted by Jews. He found some circles, tables, divine names, and figures from the Kabbalah, and he did not know that God had given the understanding of the truth to his people only, but not to him. And since he had seen himself empty and devoid of the essence of Kabbalah, he wrote another book and called it *The Vanity of Sciences*, that is, *De Vanitatis Scientiarum*, because he lacked the understanding of the truth.[23]

Elsewhere in the same work the Kabbalist wrote about the Christians that "since they do not know nor believe in the unity of God, we must not believe anything [of their teaching] even if it seems that part of it is correct. For there is no book dealing with the sciences of the gentiles in which profane and impure things are not mixed, and they direct their wisdom in the way of their faith and therefore, as regards the essence of any subject, they ultimately err."[24] There can be no doubt that Tzemah was well acquainted with Christianity, from his former period as a Christian in Portugal, and he knew much about Christian Kabbalah, but he insisted that there are impure things in those Kabbalistic treatises.

These quotes were taken from books written by major Kabbalists active in the land of Israel but aware of what was happening in Europe, especially in Italy. It is superfluous to adduce here quotes from the writings of Jewish Italian Kabbalists to this effect.[25] Those Kabbalists' awareness of developments taking place in some Christians circles is not only quite visible but, in my opinion, also influential on some developments in the politics of some Jewish Kabbalists. As I have pointed out elsewhere, it is plausible to discern certain affinities between the printing of books on Christian Kabbalah and the decision to print books on

Jewish Kabbalah, or to see the nexus between the Jewish critique of Jewish Kabbalah and the influence of the Christian Kabbalah on Jews, an influence that was
viewed as pernicious.[26] Here, however, I am concerned with the possibility of a
more subtle influence, one that pertains to certain details of a well-known ritual
cultivated by Kabbalists.

II. BEMOANING THE EXILE OF THE TORAH

As part of the widespread ritual of tiqqun hatzot, a rite performed at midnight,[27]
R. Hayyim Vital instructs the Kabbalist to touch the dust of the ground with his
face and so direct his thought to the ancient event of burning the Torah and
dispersing its secrets. This ritual includes an important component of the study
of the Torah in order to embellish the Shekhinah and repair the disharmony in
the divine world. In Sha'ar ha-Kavvanot Vital wrote: "The burning of the Torah,
which became ashes, and to what is miswritten in my Sha'ar Ruah ha-Qodesh[28]
that from the day the House was destroyed and the Torah was burned, Her secrets
and arcana were transmitted to the hitztzonim, and this is called the 'exile of the
Torah.' "[29] In addition to the two disasters, one concerning the Shekhinah and the
other concerning the city and the Temple, the Torah was also conceived of as
having been burned and as going in exile. Of utmost importance is the explicit
statement that the "secrets and arcana" have been dispersed within the impure,
external powers, the hitztzonim. This is reminiscent of the Lurianic view concerning the breaking of the vessels and the dispersing of the divine sparks in the realm
of the qelippot, as we shall see below. Unlike the ontological disaster, however, that
of the secrets is an amazing statement when formulated in a school dominated by
a particularistic attitude toward Kabbalah, as the Lurianic school was. It assumes
that the secrets of the Torah, which in my opinion are none other than the
Kabbalah, are now found in the realm of darkness, and that the linkage to the
destruction of the Temple makes plausible the view that the hitztzonim are the
nations in general, and perhaps the Christians in particular. As mentioned above,
Scholem has already pointed out the possible Christian context, and I propose to
qualify his assertion by emphasizing the importance of Christian Kabbalah as the
immediate trigger for the formulation of the Lurianic passage.

Following the line of the first generation of Lurianic Kabbalists, R. Jacob
Hayyim Tzemah composed a poem, to be recited according to his Siddur, as part of
the ritual. The poem opens with these two lines: "Let them cry over the beloved
after midnight—as well as on the Torah and Her secrets, / Because they have been
given over to the qelippot—in prison; and Her arcana have been obscured."[30] In
other words, the secrets of the Torah, presumably identical with the lore of Kabbalah, are known by the gentiles, and this event coincides with the destruction of

the Temple. The latter, just like the Torah and the divine configuration of the sefirot as vessels before their breaking, are in a state of total desolation because their content is now captured by the qelippot. What was the more historical picture as envisioned by Luria and Vital? According to a more elaborate discussion found in Sha'ar Ruah ha-Qodesh, to which Vital referred above, the pride of Israel, namely the secrets, designated as mistarim, have been taken by the nations, which are viewed expressly as qelippot, and this is the reason for the divine weeping and for the weeping of the Jews.[31] Therefore, according to those Kabbalists, even before the composition of the Zohar by R. Shim'on bar Yohay sometime in the second century, the gentiles were imagined to have had access to the secrets of the Torah.

The rather surprising aspect of the "exile of the Torah" is the view—expressed more powerfully in R. Jacob Hayyim Tzemah's poem, who claims that he follows the view of the rabbi, who is apparently Luria—that the secrets of the Torah are now obscure or sealed, nistemu. The captivity of the secrets within the realm of the shells, the qelippot, is apparently the ontological correspondent to the epistemological obscuration of the secrets. Although consonant with some main views of Luria dealing with the dispersion of the divine sparks in the realm of the demonic powers, the obscuration of the secrets is interesting when advocated by Lurianic Kabbalists. Formulated during one of the most creative periods of Kabbalah, one in which Luria was regarded as the ultimate revealer of the Kabbalistic secrets, the concept of the obscuration of secrets of the Torah demands elaboration. Some Kabbalists believed the revelation of the secrets to be part of the messianic scenario. In the ritual of tiqqun hatzot, however, one does not get the impression that the secrets have been revealed or that such a revelation is imminent. The secrets were already immersed in the demonic realm. If the acute messianism was one of the triggers of the ritual, as has sometimes been claimed,[32] it is not evident here, at least insofar as the concept of the secrets of the Torah in exile is concerned. Rather, I would see in Jewish Kabbalists' awareness of the adoption of Kabbalistic views by some Christian intellectuals a plausible reason for the theory of exiled secrets within the demonic realm.

This explanation may clarify a certain turn in Isaac Luria's politics of dissemination of his type of Kabbalah. According to one of the most important documents describing the study of Luria's secrets in his circle, he forbade the disclosure of those secrets to Kabbalists outside his small circle and their dissemination outside the land of Israel.[33] This is a sharp change which has not yet been explained. Is it connected with the danger of another "exile of the Torah"? I am not quite sure that the nexus between the claim related to tiqqun hatzot and the change in Luria's politics of esotericism can be demonstrated conclusively. In my opinion, however, such a nexus is possible.

III. HYDA': R. Hayyim Joseph David Azulai

Let me now enter on a more elaborate discussion of the theme of the exile of the Torah. In a late-eighteenth-century commentary on the Pentateuch a famous polymath, R. Hayyim Joseph David Azulai, known by the acronym HYDA', offers a striking example of an ergetic exegesis:

> It is incumbent on everyone to bring to light his part of the Torah that he received at Mount Sinai and which was immersed within the abysses of the qelippot because of the sin of the calf and our great sins. And it is necessary to toil very much in order to bring to light everything that he received in accordance with the root of his soul . . . Happy is the man who found wisdom, namely that he found that [special] wisdom that had been granted to him from heaven and has been lost within the qelippot; and man extracts sagacity, which means that he brings to light and understands one thing out of another, and he extracts it from the qelippot . . . the sparks of the Torah had fallen in the qelippot, behold this is the meaning of "you should not forsake my Torah,"[34] do not forsake my Torah there in the place of Sitra' 'Ahara', and toil in order to take it out.[35]

Unlike the ritual of mourning, which is more liturgical in nature and formulated in a more general manner, as it deals with the Torah and its secrets without any specification, HYDA' deals here with the particular spark that was granted to him *ab origine*. It is no longer the nocturnal crying that deplores the immersion of the secrets in exile but the diurnal and more mental activity of extracting the idiosyncratic revelation characteristic of the individual.

The Kabbalist resorts to three apparently distinct entities: the soul and its root; the spark; and the revealed entity or part of the Torah. Or, to put it in other terms, the soul in the above text stands for the soul of a person belonging to the people of Israel, the spark stands for the divine, and the interpretation stands for the Torah. The primordial unity between the three factors has been destroyed by sin, and the study of the Torah is intended to restore this unity. When the study of the Torah is neglected, it ceases to be a "tool and pipe to draw from it the influx of the holiness," but the "Torah goes to the Sitra' 'Ahara'."[36]

The identification of that part of the Torah that was delivered to someone at the Sinaitic revelation with a spark involves a reification of the Torah. It is not only the problem of dissemination of a certain type of instruction, shared by all Jews, but the immersion of one's own specific understanding. The part of the Torah destined to be his, which should be identified with something found elsewhere, and the study of the Torah, apparently following the Kabbalistic manner, is a rescue operation, both of the lost interpretation of the Torah and of part of one's own soul. In fact, following the Lurianic theory of *berur*, purification, one is required to extract the pure elements from impurity or the divine from the demonic. Study of the Torah, in fact exegesis, is therefore the search for part of one's lost soul. To resort to modern literary terminology, the reader is found in the book and is shaped by the author.

If the abstract assumption is that each of the souls present at the Sinaitic revelation was given a determined share in the collectively accepted Torah, the question may be asked how exactly one knows what this part is, when does one get it, or how precisely does one get it. According to the essentialistic vision of the Kabbalists, the encounter with one's alter ego will be self-evident. The Kabbalists, however, including HYDA', did not elaborate a set of instructions that would facilitate the recognition of the alter ego or the shaping of one's interpretation. I assume that it is much less the exploration of one's individuality, or even of one's redemption, that concerned those who formulated the theories similar to that expounded by HYDA', but the wish to urge Jews to study Torah. The extreme emphasis on individuality in fact served the goal of expanding the Torah by an intense preoccupation with the text. Since the borders between individuals had not been defined, despite the theoretical assumption of the existence of such borders, what happened in practice was a phenomenon reminiscent of C. S. Peirce's synechism, a continuity of activities based on the same text, which takes the earlier developments into consideration in its interpretation. This continuity is also shared by the metaphysical stand of the soul as an emanation from the divine realm, which is to be seen as a huge reservoir, where distinction is far from being clear. Or, to put it differently: the process of differentiation of the divine within the human bodies that incorporate the souls, and of the sparks of the Torah within the demonic realm, is to be undone by the study of the one, undivided entity, the text of the Torah. It is a unifying enterprise, which according to the Kabbalists is the manner of self-expression and self-redemption, while de facto it is much more a corporate activity serving to strengthen a corporate identity.

Let me now turn to a recurring theme in the passage from HYDA': the rescue of the spark is described three times as an act of bringing to light.[37] This theme presumably has something to do with the darkness of the shells and the imprisonment of the spark in that realm. But since this is a metaphor for bringing out a certain part or aspect or interpretation of the text, it is reminiscent also of the publication of a book, which has been designated in Hebrew as bringing to light, *hotza'ah la-'or.* HYDA', in addition to possessing stunning Halakhic and Kabbalistic knowledge, was a great bibliographer, perhaps the greatest among the traditional Jewish bibliographers. Thus, it is not an artificial claim to surmise that one's self-expression in the context of the Torah is also connected to the acts of writing and publishing.

HYDA"s emphasis on the individuality of a certain part of the Torah is reminiscent of the theory, thought to be characteristic of Polish Hasidism, that the tzaddiq is required to rescue those sparks that belong to his soul. Although HYDA' was indeed aware of Hasidism and its literature, I assume that there were earlier Lurianic and perhaps even pre-Lurianic sources that inspired his view.[38] This may also be the case insofar as the above passage is concerned. If we assume that the eighteenth-century author, who was acquainted with Polish Hasidism,[39] was nevertheless reflecting an earlier source, his discussion may serve as an indication of a development beginning with Lurianism and going in similar directions in Eastern Europe and somewhere in the Mediterranean basin, where HYDA' roamed for years. Given that the number of worlds from which the souls of the exegetes radiated is imagined to be infinite already in a Lurianic text, as we have seen above,[40] there is good reason to posit a Lurianic and perhaps even an earlier Kabbalistic source for the Hasidic views on the redemption of the sparks belonging to the soul of the tzaddiq.[41]

APPENDIX 5
On Oral Torah and Multiple Interpretations in Hasidism

I. The Besht and His Great-Grandson R. Nahman of Braslav

Orality can explode in and overcome even the most literate cultures. Centered as the varieties of Judaism up to the eighteenth century were on study and performance, a powerful phenomenon emphasizing orality took place beginning in the mid-eighteenth century in Eastern Europe and changed the spiritual physiognomy of many Jewish communities there. Hasidism is basically a move from literacy to orality, as we saw in an example in Chapter 6 dealing with the encounter between the Besht and the Great Maggid of Mezeritch. While the latest classical form of Kabbalah, Lurianism, accepted—more in principle than in practice—the concept of indeterminacy and infinity of the classical texts, whether the Bible or the Zohar, Lurianic Kabbalists restricted the plurality of interpretations one is able to offer.

As we saw in Chapter 3 and Appendix 4, each soul is almost identical to a certain interpretation, which is predetermined before birth and unique to this soul alone. The next major movement in Jewish mysticism, Beshtian Hasidism, represented a substantial departure. At least in one major case the claim is that the interpretive community, to use Stanley Fish's concept once again, is not that of the learned but often remote Kabbalists or of the entire Jewish people dispersed throughout the world, in the case of the ethical-Kabbalistic literature. Indeed, Kabbalah operated with the concept of an invisible audience insofar as the author is concerned, an audience regarded as cooperating in order to make manifest or to proclaim all the mystical and nonmystical dimensions of the divine text or of that of an ancient mystical authority, R. Shimeon bar Yohay—the tannaitic master who was believed to be the author of the *Zohar*.

The East European Hasidim, the followers of a living master who provides the religious text to be interpreted, are now the main audience of the new spiritual leaders. In other words, the Hasidic community as a text-consuming group is constituted less by acts of reading and interpreting canonical texts, as it was earlier in Jewish culture, than by the pneumatic Tzaddiq's "saying of the Torah," namely the homiletic exposition during the afternoon of the Sabbath, and its various interpretations offered afterward by adherents. This is a textual community before the text was committed to writing. According to this description of Beshtian Hasidism, the ensuing movement may be conceived of as the ascent of verbal teaching stemming initially from a secondary elite who emphasized some of the oral aspects of the Jewish tradition, as explicated by some forms of Kabbalah and as performed in the most accomplished manner by the perfect man, the polestar of the group, the Tzaddiq. This emphasis capitalized on the importance of orality in some developments in Kabbalistic thought, especially the talismanic accent on sonority, as expressed especially by R. Moses Cordovero.[1]

The Hasidic masters added, however, to the oral performative aspect of the objective Torah the interesting phenomenon of describing their oral, homiletic activity by resorting to the very term that refers to the divine instruction: Torah. In a moment I will try to trace the precise stages of the emergence of this influential terminological development, but here I would like to point out the affinity that might have been operative in this old/new situation. The Hasidic righteous was not only the charismatic leader, the pneumatic mystic, and the powerful magician, but also conceived of in divine and semidivine terms.[2] The apotheosis of the Tzaddiq to a new religious status is related to the apotheosis of the status of this figure. As such, the oral activity performed while in a state of union with the divine assumed the aura of a divine revelation. After all, the biblical God was a great speaker but not an accomplished writer.

In any case, the deep concern with the orality of the teaching that was referred to as Torah, apparently formulated in vernacular Yiddish, is evident in one of the legends attributed to the Besht:

There was a man who wrote down the torah of the Besht that he heard from him. Once the Besht saw a demon walking and holding a book in his hand. He said to him: "What is the book that you hold in your hand?" He answered him: "This is the book that you have written." The Besht then understood that there was a person who was writing down his torah. He gathered all his followers and asked them: "Who among you is writing down my torah?" The man admitted it and he brought the manuscript to the Besht. The Besht examined it and said: "There is not even a single word[3] here that is mine."[4]

Let me start with the alleged interlocutor of the Besht, the studious and curious demon. He is indeed a very curious guy, who attempts to keep himself up to date with any interesting spiritual development. It seems that Jewish culture was so imprinted with the concept of the importance of books that even its demons were imagined as avid readers.[5] In this particular instance, however, involving a story that in my opinion is emblematic of the nature of Hasidism, the very emergence of the book was regarded as questionable: the author, the Besht, was trying to preserve the oral form of his teachings as quintessential. Demons, so it seems, are especially fond of illicitly written books. In fact, in this case the demon focuses his attention on a composition that the author himself would take to be an extreme falsification of his thought. What went wrong is not a matter of bad intentions or sheer misunderstandings: it seems that, as in Plato's famous critique of writing, it is the very nature of the medium that is imagined as problematic, and not the faulty manner of its performance.

This legend, which portrays the Besht's adherence to the oral form of teaching, may be related significantly to R. Nahman of Braslav's description of the Tzaddiq as the oral Torah, in the explicit context of a discussion about his great-grandfather, the Besht. Concerning the Sabbateans, R. Nahman wrote that they

left the community and spoke deleteriously about the entire oral Torah, and this happened because hard gevurot[6] reached them and they did not sweeten them . . . and those utterances fell upon the paragon of the generation and the Besht was then the paragon of the generation and he departed because of it . . . because when there are deleterious utterances about the oral Torah or about the Tzaddiq of the generation, this is indeed the same thing because the quintessence of the oral Torah depends on the Tzaddiq of the generation, as it is said that the Shekhinah stands[7] between two Tzaddi-qim[8] which is the oral Torah . . . because the Tzaddiq makes from their [utterances][9] a Torah.[10]

In Bahiric and Zoharic symbolism, oral Torah stands for the last female sefi-rah, Malkhut, while the Tzaddiq is a distinct divine attribute possessing strong male features. These two attributes are quite distinct. There can be no doubt that R. Nahman did not extract his view from the only alleged proof text he explicitly mentions, the *Zohar*. The affinity between orality and the Tzaddiq does not stem from a reading of a Kabbalistic text, but rather it reflects an inference as to the impact of the Sabbatean disrespect of the rabbinic legislation on the righteous of the generation, who has to pay with his life for the sin of others. The identification of oral Torah with the Tzaddiq in general and with the Besht in particular seems to arise from a Hasidic tradition that is corroborated by the contemporary story about the Besht and his illicitly written book studied by the demon.

I assume that we witness a change of paradigm within the symbolism and the hierarchy of the two Torahs in the theosophical-theurgical Kabbalah: the elevation of the oral over the written Torah. In the rabbinic literature the status of the oral Torah has been elevated to that of *mystorin*,[11] the unique patrimony of the people of Israel, while the written one has already become the common property of the gentiles. In a text of R. Abraham bar Hiyya, the oral Torah was likened to the moon and the written Torah to the sun, a comparison that implies the elevation of the written over the oral.[12] This is also the case in the theosophical-theurgical Kab-balah; as we have already seen,[13] the oral Torah was identified with Malkhut and the written Torah with Tiferet. There can be no doubt that most of the Kabbalists belonging to a theosophical school, including those who were great Halakhic figures, conceived of the written Torah as higher, more sublime, and more important.[14]

The Hasidic axiology therefore represents a departure from the more general Kabbalistic-theosophical views, caused by the new type of direct and oral relations based not on the common study of written texts but on sermons and homilies. In a letter written by a student of the Gaon of Vilnius, addressed to R. Yehudah Leib de Botin, he accuses some unidentified Hasidim of speaking vanities and regard-ing them as "words of Torah."[15] This is, apparently, not his own formulation; from the context it appears that it was his addressee, a lesser-known rabbi who had some leanings to Hasidism, who had informed him about it in a previous and apparently no longer extant letter. In fact, it is a characteristically Hasidic view that the sermon delivered by the Hasidic rabbi at the end of the Sabbath is called Torah. This is quite a remarkable claim, to argue that the mystical sermons delivered each and every Sabbath in so many communities are part of, or even similar to, the sacrosanct Torah. In any case, it seems that this assumption is instrumental in the later printing of the greater part of Hasidic literature, which consists of homilies in Hebrew versions. Moreover, in several instances Hasidic masters contended that they could transform the ordinary speeches of the common people, and even of heretics, into Torah by elevating them or by changing the order of the letters of the words.[16]

How serious is this claim? Were those sermons, delivered in Yiddish,[17] indeed considered by the preacher or by his audience as Torah, according to the plain sense of the word? Although basically an explanation of the pericopes of the Torah, they were no more and no less than interpretations. Therefore we may ask whether this phenomenon represents an attempt, reminiscent of the modern debates in the fields of literature and hermeneutics, about the relationship between text and commentary. I would prefer not to offer an answer that may be held as pertinent for the whole range of Hasidic literature. There can be no doubt, however, that in some schools the teachings of the Hasidic leader became canonical, and this happened almost immediately. This is obviously the case with the teachings of the great-grandson of the Besht, R. Nahman of Braslav, each of which was designated as a Torah. According to his closest student, R. Nahman repeatedly recommended to his disciples that they transform his Torahs into prayers.[18] Thus, R. Nahman himself openly regarded his teachings as Torah. His student, R. Nathan Nemirov, however, went a little bit further; he describes his master's teachings as "containing, each and every one of them, the entire Torah, the whole people of Israel, and all the things in [all] the worlds."[19] Indeed, R. Nathan's whole introduction is a lengthy description of the manner in which the teachings are transformed into prayers. Unlike the story about the Besht, where the writing down of the teaching is conceived of as deleterious, in the case of his famous great-grandson the canonic status of the teaching of the Tzaddiq is much more pronounced, and his major book indeed attained the status of a classic within his group of disciples, who did not choose another leader but relied on the guidance found in his books.

Extremely relevant from this point of view is the rapid ascent of the practice and importance of saying Torah—lomar torah, another term for preaching[20]—which had already become a custom drawing upon some earlier source, perhaps certain practices in R. Moses Hayyim Luzzatto's circle.[21] Formulated near the beginning of the nineteenth century, the attempt to discredit the effort to commit to writing the Besht's teachings found in *In Praise of the Baal Shem Tov* only anticipated the flood of written descriptions of the oral teachings of the Hasidic masters and their lives. It was a desperate effort to maintain a culture of orality over the increasingly written transmission of Hasidic thought. Even among some of those early authors, like R. Shlomo of Lutzk, who wrote down their teacher's sayings, it is conspicuous that their enterprise needs explicit legitimation.[22] Unlike their opponents, the mitnaggedim, whose illustrious leader, a famous scholar named R. Elijah of Vilnius, was a recluse and hardly interacted with his students but assiduously studied and wrote, Hasidic leaders preferred orality over literacy. If the Gaon of Vilnius is the most accomplished paragon of Jewish literacy and writing, the Besht is the great oral teacher.

II. THE GREAT MAGGID AND HIS GREAT-GRANDSON R. ISRAEL OF RYZHIN

We have examined the views related to two members of the same family, the Besht and his great-grandson, R. Nahman. Let me move now to the second-most important family in the history of Hasidism, that of R. Dov Baer of Mezeritch, known as the Great Maggid, and his own great-grandson, R. Israel Friedmann, the famous Ryzhiner Rebbe. Friedmann once reported a

> great debate between the disciples of the Great Maggid concerning the Torah said by the Maggid, blessed be his memory. One argued that he said so, another otherwise. And the [Great] Maggid told them that both versions are the words of the living God, because the words I said include all of these [interpretations]. End of the words of the Maggid. And he [the Great Maggid], blessed be his memory, said that there are seventy facets to the Torah, and indeed it [the Torah] emerges from the place of true unity. Although in its source the Torah is one, only by its descent into these worlds does it become seventy facets. This is the reason why in the Torah of R. Meir it is written kuttonet 'or, spelled with 'aleph because R. Meir took over the Torah from its source, and this is why it was written with 'aleph, while with us it is written with 'ayin.[23]

As we saw earlier, the connection between the name of R. Meir and the version of the Torah in his possession was already adumbrated in a Lurianic passage.[24] The tannaitic figure is described here in terms that are reminiscent of Neoplatonic thinking: his name means "illumining," and that is why he is able to adhere to the source of light, and thus the version he had resorts to the letter 'aleph, with the value 1 which transforms the word 'or, "skin," into the word 'or, "light." The source of multiple interpretations is explained in rather Neoplatonic terms: one basic spiritual unit becomes diversified when descending into the lower worlds, where the 'aleph becomes 'ayin, namely 1 becomes 70, which stands for both multiplicity[25] and, in this specific context, skin. As indicated in the above passage, the Great Maggid regarded the divergences in the views expounded by his disciples as equally important, saying "both versions are the words of the living God," a recurrent phrase used in rabbinic literature to describe the status of the different stands concerning Halakhah that remained part of the talmudic heritage. Thus, those who debate about the Torah of the Great Maggid are conceived of as possessing a divine spirit—even more so, implicitly, the originator of the views under discussion.

Elsewhere, the same nineteenth-century master is said to have reported:

> When the [Great] Maggid said Torah at the table, the students repeated it afterward among themselves when going back to their houses; one said, "I heard it in such a way," another saying that he heard it in another way, because each of them heard it in a different way. I say that this is not a novelty, since there are seventy facets to the Torah, and each of them heard the Torah of the Maggid according to the [specific] facet he had in the Torah. And he [R. Israel] said: When I look attentively to the[ir] faces,[26] there is no need to say Torah, because "the show of their faces[27] witnessed against them."[28] And this suffices for one who understands.[29]

It is the living master, the Tzaddiq, who orally creates a new, polysemous text while his students should, much as the ancient Tannaites and Amoraites did, discuss the potential views inherent in his recently created oral discourse. The Hasidic master, the originator of the text, is surrounded by the disciples who presumably are understood to inhabit, at least spiritually, a lower religious level, where distinctions emerge as soon as the "Torah" is enunciated by the master in the vernacular, namely in Yiddish. Although the Lurianic view regarding the affinity between interpretation and the source of the soul in the Torah was absorbed at the level of the students of the Tzaddiq, it is the Tzaddiq's new status as the creator of a canonical text, emerging at the defining moment of the new community of mainly laymen, the tisch (the table of the third ritual meal on the Sabbath), that seems to be novel. This semi- or quasi-divine status of the Tzaddiq in many of the Hasidic ideologies is also well attested in a wide variety of other matters—his wonder making, for example. Whereas R. Isaac Luria, the greatest of all the historical Kabbalists, was thought to be able to be in contact solely with the souls of the departed ancient mystics in order to learn new interpretations, or with the manifestation of the rather popular figure of the prophet Elijah, the Hasidic masters were imagined as capable of being unified with the divine on its highest level.[30]

The case of R. Israel of Ryzhin, however, is particularly interesting because it reflects an awareness that the very act of generating a plurivocal text is dependent not so much on a pneumatic leader as on the spiritual configurations of its immediate consumers or recipients. Without the homilist's feeling that the semantic potential of the sermon will be understood and even explicated later by his listeners, the discourse itself will never emerge. At least in this case, the descent of the "Torah" is conditioned by the possibility of an adequate human appropriation. Without the visible propensity for multiple interpretations, the religiously authoritative text will never be promulgated. This testimony is especially relevant because R. Israel was certainly one of the most powerful leaders ever recorded in Hasidic history. Again, let me recall the invisible audience of the Kabbalists, who quite often did not meet the consumers of their books. Very rarely do we know about the impact of the audience on the Kabbalist as an author. In the Hasidic stories related to the Great Maggid and his great-grandson, the master needs first the mystical contact with the divine, namely the uttermost spiritual experience, but also the potential response of the simple audience, in order to perform.

Although the concept of accommodation of the divine revelation is visible here, it is far from being one that assumes an absolute power which takes into consideration the weakness of human nature. It is rather a weak master, despite the unprecedented power of R. Israel, which cannot cope with the even greater weakness of the recipients. Only the interpretive skills of the recipients are able to disclose the richness that elevates the sermon to the status of Torah. The more numerous the interpretations emerging in his audience are, the more authoritative the new, basically oral text may be. I would like to stress, however, that in the case of the Hasidic master, as in that of the text we adduced from *Yalqut Shim'oni* in a previous chapter,[31] it is the unwritten voice that suffices to create the diversity of interpretations. Hasidism is basically a textual community organized around an oral text that was imagined to attract interpretations, just as the Tzaddiq, the righteous, who is the core of the Hasidic community, attracts his Hasidim, the disciples. Hasidic communities depend not on the written text but on the charisma that compels attention. In this context let me draw attention to the relationship between the words and speeches arriving from above and interpretation, as formulated in a seminal passage from R. Nahman of Braslav translated and discussed in Chapter 6. It is the oral text that the Hasidim were listening for (to use Brian Stock's phrase) on the afternoon of the Sabbath, after the ritual reading of the written Torah. The above text should be compared to a homily of Saint Gregorius, a sixth-century pope, who professed, "I know that very often I understand many things in the sacred writings when I am with my brethren, which, when alone, I could not understand . . . Clearly, as this understanding is given me in their presence, it must be given me for their sake. Hence God grants that understanding increases and pride decreases, while I learn, on your behalf, that which I teach you. For, really, very often I hear what I am saying for the first time, just as you do."[32]

The dynamics of the group, which should be seen as one of the major triggers of any spiritual creativity, is well known in Jewish mysticism, where many important treatises were generated by mystics that were leaders of mystical groups. This seems to be the case for the most important book of Kabbalah, the Zohar, as Yehuda Liebes has proposed,[33] and the same dynamic seems to have inspired some of the main Kabbalists in sixteenth-century Safed.[34] If this factor is given a significant role, then the function of the interaction within a group, which was facilitated, probably by resorting to the vernacular, in the process of inducing a state of creativity in the leader, seems to be paramount.[35] It is also interesting to compare Gregorius' claim for an inspired homily to the contention of Hasidim that their sermons are divinely inspired, a point that recurs in many of the descriptions of early Hasidism.

Let me elaborate on the manner in which the possibility of finding seventy facets in a sermon delivered in Yiddish is understood. R. Israel of Ryzhin's assumption is that everyone has his own facet, or aspect, according to which he understands the written Torah, and consequently the Hasidic master stands on solid Kabbalistic grounds. This mode of idiosyncratic preunderstanding is expanded here, however, to his specific understanding of an oral Torah, generated not by God or Moses as part of the Sinaitic revelation, nor later on by ancient rabbis, but by the immediate speaker, the Tzaddiq. Again, a category stemming from the conceptualization of the written Torah was applied to the oral Hasidic Torah.

These traditions related to the Great Maggid deal, from the hermeneutical point of view, with the descent of the unified one of the orally innovated Torah into many of the seventy interpretations, or from the one central leader to his numerous disciples. This move is reminiscent of the Neoplatonic emanational scheme describing the processio, which had been loosely adopted in Hasidism. In another interesting discussion found in the work of an important Hasidic author related to the circle of the Great Maggid, R. Hayyim Tirer of Chernovitz, the relation between the 'aleph and the 'ayin is invoked again in the context of the Torah of R. Meir, but this time it concerns the Neoplatonic process of reversio. R. Hayyim describes the ascent of the source of the Torah implied by the change of the 'ayin into an 'aleph, which is achieved by intense study and the indwelling of the divine light within the student, a process that culminates in his own attainment of luminosity.[36] To a certain extent, this was the transformation undergone by the biblical Moses, whose facial skin was described as luminous.[37]

Let me close this discussion with a remark about the different garments of Adam and of the Torah. Garments of the Torah, whether material or spiritual—some of them even created by Torah study—are a topos in Kabbalistic literature.[38] In Hasidic literature they nevertheless play a particular role: from the time of the Besht, Hasidic teaching resorted to telling stories, which were conceived of as garments for the Torah, necessary for the dissemination of Hasidism in a simple manner that can be understood by all Jews.[39] The power of the spoken word is also obvious in the manner in which the Besht recites the book from the Heikhalot literature to his disciple, as demonstrated above.[40]

III. R. ISRAEL IN CONTEXT

R. Israel of Ryzhin's feeling of the need to speak, but also his awareness of the discrepancy between the ideal—perhaps also idealized—group that surrounded his great-grandfather and his own followers, is related to many issues. It is almost a ritual obligation to deliver a sermon on the eve of the feast of Shavuot, the kairos for the revelation of the Torah. The Tzaddiq is therefore requested to repeat the Sinaitic situation in nuce. Nevertheless, he is unable to do so: "Once, in the eve of feast of Shavuot, he was sitting at the table and did not say any Torah, neither did he speak one word; but he cried very much. The second night he did the same."[41] I assume that, historically speaking, this passage reflects the situation during the period of R. Israel's residence in Sadigura, near Chernovitz, after he had fled from Russia to the province of Bukovina, on the periphery of the Habsburg Empire. Far from the more vibrant centers of Hasidism and learning in Podolya and Galicia, he had to rebuild his hyparchy in an all-but-forgotten land. It seems that the Jewish entourage he was thrown amid by his escape from Russia did not meet his expectations.

Again, from the historical point of view R. Israel was right. Neither he nor any of his disciples and descendants contributed substantially to the development of Hasidism as a mystical movement, important as their status in the eyes of their many followers was. The feeling of intellectual inferiority, which stems not from his own inability to preach but from the absence of a learned audience, was probably coupled with the image of R. Israel, known in some Hasidic and non-Hasidic circles as an ignoramus. Nevertheless, he had the feeling that he had to speak, and I would say that many of the Hasidic masters had the feeling, expressed in a remarkable way by Emmanuel Levinas, that to be responsible is to speak.[42] R. Israel would, however, hesitate to attribute to the encounter with the faces of his disciples the same formative role that Levinas did. If the twentieth-century Jewish philosopher would envision such an encounter in general terms of the generic "other" that shapes the self, the nineteenth-century Hasidic master would say that such a move is a later development that must be preceded by an encounter with the transcendental, the divine, which may at the same time enrich and dissolve the personality of the mystic. The human faces of the Hasidim represent the descent of a personality that previously was illumined by a much higher plane of existence.

The plurality of the faces in the above text is also of some importance. Unlike Levinas's notion of the "other" or Ricoeur's concept of the "text" (both in the singular), Hasidic masters tended to be interested not in such generic abstractions but in individuals or communities. They were more concerned with what they were giving and whom they saved, religiously speaking, than with how their self was constituted by the encounters. Democratic elements are indeed to be found in Hasidism, but there are plenty of aristocratic approaches that sharply differentiate the spiritual leadership from the multitude. The Tzaddiq becomes the text, oral though it may be, that informs his followers, and if there is no pertinent audience the text-becoming enterprise of the leader is in vain. Plunging into leadership without a following is tantamount to producing a text that cannot be interpreted. This is why R. Israel is portrayed as crying: at the very moment of his (self-)revelation he had the feeling that his voice would be lost in a wilderness of ignorance.

Yet even this refusal to become a text for a moment, an oral one to be sure, became a written text, as the above passage testifies. Hasidic literature as it has reached us in its Hebrew garb, more concerned with specific individuals and situations than Kabbalah as a whole, underwent a deep process of textualization.

IV. CONCLUDING REMARKS

Let me conclude this appendix with a general observation regarding the nature of exegesis in Hasidic literature. Most of Hasidic exegesis is nonintercorporal and nonmetaphysical, in the manner in which I described these approaches in Chapters 8 and 9. No systematic metaphysical construct compelled them in a way that dictated a strong reference to a doctrine that should be introduced within and should force the direction of the interpretive process. The panoramic approach of the Hasidic masters, the relative dissolution of the dominance of Lurianism, and their flexible and often unsystematic attitude are evident when in comparison with those of almost all the Kabbalistic schools. Most of the theosophical symbols stemming from Lurianic systems were reinterpreted psychologically.[43] This deployment of psychological exegesis on Jewish canonical books, even on the theosophical-theurgical concepts, represents the most original of the Hasidic contributions to Jewish mystical hermeneutics. It seems, however, that in the oral Yiddish texts characteristic of the homiletic discourse of the Hasidic leaders there was one more element that is not represented in the written Hebrew and printed texts: the Hasidic rabbis were more concerned during their sermons with particular individuals and their specific concerns, as we learn from the fascinating testimony of Shlomo Maimon regarding the Great Maggid's sermons.[44] In fact, most of Hasidic literature as it has reached us in print represents not only a shift in language and style but also a tendency toward general instructions that is less related to the immediate audience listening to the original sermon.[45] To resort to the passage from R. Israel of Ryzhin, in the Hebrew texts of Hasidic homiletics the faces of the listeners were lost. Even in his own testimony no proper name is invoked. The uniqueness of the historical (non-)event was surpassed by its meaning.

APPENDIX 6
"Book of God"/"Book of Law"
in Late-Fifteenth-Century Florence

I. Medieval and Renaissance Syntheses

In scriptural religions a book means not only a reservoir of information but also the idea of a certain order that stems from the divine realm. Or, to put it in Blanchot's terms, "The book is in essence theological."[1] In the following I shall attempt to describe the relationship between two types of order, expressed by different understandings of the term "book," which developed in the Jewish elite during the Middle Ages and culminated in Renaissance Florence in the immediate circle of Marsilio Ficino.

The Renaissance may be described as the period when the relationship between the book of God and the book of nature started to shift in a new direction.

The earlier stages of the confrontation between the two had been decided in favor of the book of God, as the very resort to the metaphor of the book demonstrates. In the encounter between the Jewish sacred scriptures and the concepts of order shaped by Greek philosophical modes of thought, it seems that the former prevailed. This diagnosis is but another formulation of Harry A. Wolfson's theory of the history of Western religious philosophy from Philo to Spinoza, which assumes that philosophy has been a maidservant, *ancilla*.[2] But with the dramatic infusion of Greek speculative material in Western culture, a move to which Marsilio Ficino contributed so much, another type of balance started to become visible, one in which the book of nature became more dominant than the book of the law. The beginnings of modern science have been traced to the emergence of an occult philosophy, which Frances A. Yates described as follows: "This philosophy, or outlook, was compounded of hermeticism as revived by Marsilio Ficino, to which Pico della Mirandola added a Christianized version of Jewish Cabala. These two trends, associated together, form what I call 'the occult philosophy,' which was the title which Henry Cornelius Agrippa gave to his highly influential handbook on the subject."[3] This is but another version of a synthetic binarian approach opened by Wolfson, which now leads to secondary types of speculative corpora: no longer the classical Greek philosophies and the Jewish sacred scriptures but two forms of occultism: the hermetic and the Kabbalistic, both later bodies of writings.[4] If medieval religious thought, according to Wolfson, was the result of different amalgams between the older speculative corpora, Renaissance occult philosophy, which Yates says was destined to undermine medieval scholastic thought, stems from later layers of thought.

Although by and large I accept the two grand historiosophies of these two great scholars, the picture both in the Middle Ages and in the Renaissance is much more complex. Hermetic elements were also available in the Middle Ages, as has been asserted by Charles Trinkaus[5] insofar as the Latin Middle Ages are concerned, and, as I have attempted to show, in medieval Jewish sources hermetic themes were even more evident.[6] So as not to repeat findings I have presented elsewhere, I shall restrict the following discussion to the point that the trope of the book can serve as a good example of the complexity of medieval sources and of their impact on the entourage of two thinkers who flourished in the lifetime and the immediate vicinity of Marsilio Ficino in Florence: the famous Pico della Mirandola and his less renowned though extraordinarily gifted teacher, Rabbi Yohanan Alemanno. My claim will be that in Jewish sources, since the middle of the twelfth century, astrological understandings of religion slowly grew. I shall adduce several examples of this growth, culminating in some expressions offered by Alemanno as being reminiscent of the late-fifteenth-century formulation of the relationship between *liber legis* and *liber dei* as found in Pico. My point is that the entrance of astrology had a dramatic impact on the ways of conceptualizing religion no less than philosophy and contributed, at least in some cases, to the emergence of antinomian approaches.

II. The Cosmic Book and Astrology in Some Medieval Jewish Texts

In the Bible the existence of a supernal book, or books, where the fate of individuals is inscribed is assumed. This is the case in Exodus 32:32, in Psalms 69:29 and 139:16, and Daniel 7:10. The basic assumption is that being inscribed in a celestial book or some other book will determine the fate of an individual.[7] Such a vision reverberated in the Talmud, as we learn from BT, *Rosh ha-Shanah*, fol. 16b. I shall refer to these views as mythical books, which remained an integral part of Jewish culture in subsequent generations, although they were interpreted in various ways.

The image of the book was relatively widespread in the Middle Ages, as we learn from the very erudite treatment of Ernst R. Curtius.[8] As Curtius pointed out, there are few sources in the Greco-Roman literature that informed the medieval resort to book imaginary. Despite Curtius' encyclopedic knowledge of the topic, it seems that he left aside an issue that is important for understanding the development of medieval and Renaissance imageries of the book. This may have something to do with his orientation toward Latin culture.

One of the main contributors to the impact of astrology in the understanding of Judaism in the Middle Ages is R. Abraham ibn Ezra, who flourished in the middle of the twelfth century. Ibn Ezra was well aware of a great many classical astronomical and astrological books composed in Arabic, and he himself wrote some shorter though influential treatises on these topics. Moreover, he was acquainted with some hermetic books.[9] What is of particular consequence here is the far-reaching effort to correlate astronomy, astrology, and astromagic with some topics found in Jewish tradition, especially the Bible. Ibn Ezra's most significant achievement is an influential commentary on substantial parts of the Bible, where he alluded to the correspondence between biblical topics and astrological or astromagical concepts. Judaism thereby emerged as a more cosmic religion than it was in its rabbinic versions.[10]

So, for example, Ibn Ezra comments on Exodus 32:32, where Moses says to God: "Blot me, I pray Thee, out of Thy book which Thou hast written." Ibn Ezra writes: "I have already commented in [the commentary on] Daniel,[11] 'And the books were opened,' that all the decrees concerning the species and the individuals are found in the constellations of heaven."[12] When interpreting Psalms

69:29, where the term "the book of life" is mentioned, he writes: "I have already commented in 'my book'[13] that the book of life is heaven and all the future decrees are written there since the day of their creation." Thus, a more "scientific" understanding of the mythical books has been offered, one that integrates the archaic understanding of supernal books and the astronomical realm, which is understood to contain all the events in the sublunar world and thus the fate of all men.

On the other hand, in the commentary on Exodus 6:3, ibn Ezra avers that he discloses a secret:

> God created three worlds . . . and the mundane world receives power from the intermediary world,[14] each individual in accordance with the supernal constellation.[15] And because the intellectual soul is more exalted than the intermediary world, if she will be wise and will know the deeds of God—those done without any intermediary and those done by means of an intermediary—and [if] she will leave the desires of the world, and [if] she will isolate herself, in order to cleave to the exalted God. And if there is the constellation of the stars during pregnancy a bad time destined to come on a certain day, God who is cleaving to him will change the course of the causes in order to save him from evil . . . and this is the secret of the entire Torah . . . this is why Moses was able to change the course of the mundane world and perform miracles and wonders.[16]

I am especially interested in the statement regarding the "secret of the entire Torah." It contends that in order to decode the secret of the Torah one has to resort to astrological themes,[17] and indeed this is what happened in the large corpus of supercommentaries on ibn Ezra's commentary.[18] Astrology, and to a certain extent magic, therefore already play an exegetical role in some important instances in ibn Ezra's commentaries, although it is hardly a comprehensive approach to all the topics in the Bible.

In the next important commentary on the Pentateuch, written by Nahmanides a century after ibn Ezra, the latter's view on Exodus 32:32 is adduced in order to criticize it, just as Nahmanides criticizes R. Shlomo Yitzhaqi's (Rashi's) assumption that the book of God is none other than the Torah.[19] Though a Kabbalist, Nahmanides does not offer a Kabbalistic interpretation of the nature of the book. However, another important commentator, who can be described as a follower of Nahmanides' main follower, the late-thirteenth-century R. Bahya ben Asher ibn Hallewah, active in Barcelona, wrote on the same verse:

> According to the path of the intellect: "out of Thy book"—he called the constellation of the stars the book of the Holy One,[20] blessed be He, because

just as the book is the inscription and design of the letters concerning the sciences, so in the constellation of stars there is an inscription[21] and the designs of powers concerning the topics of man, and the number of his life in this world, as mentioned and inscribed there, as is the case of the thing inscribed and written in a book. And this is also the case in the verse "Thou hast seen the embryo[22] and on Thy book all is written"[23] . . . "that Thou hast written"—the meaning is "that Thou hast innovated" because the creature is a witness for its creator as the written is a witness for the writer. And Moses intended to say that since He, blessed be He, innovated these powers, He has the power to obliterate them.[24]

This is quite an extensive parallel between the celestial world and the structure of a book found in Jewish sources before the end of the thirteenth century. Despite Nahmanides' rejection of ibn Ezra, the Barcelonese Kabbalist accepted his view on the celestial book.

Being a Kabbalist, however, R. Bahya offers, immediately after the astrological interpretation, a theosophical one that relates the book to divine powers. Following an earlier Kabbalistic tradition, he contends that according to "the path of Kabbalah, [the meaning of] 'out of Thy book' is, from the sefirot, which means as if he said from the supernal extremities,[25] which are the six [lower] sefirot, because they are the beginning of everything done and they are called 'the work of heaven and earth' . . . the meaning of the saying of the sages of truth[26] is that the three books which are opened, one of the perfect righteous, one of the extreme wicked, and one of the mediocrities, are the [sefirot] Hesed [mercy], Din [judgment], and Rahamim [grace]."[27] In the vein of the Geronese Kabbalist, R. Bahya identifies the book with three supernal books where the deeds of all men are written and which should be understood as symbols for the three sefirot Hesed, Din, and Rahamim.

There can be no doubt that the path of Kabbalah is a higher way of interpretation than the astrological path. Both interpret the meaning of the book, but whereas the astrologers decode the Bible as pointing to the celestial bodies, the Kabbalists contend that it should be read as pointing to supernal attributes that are part of the divine structure, the sefirot. The three books, or sefirot, play a role that shares the nature of the mythical books in the Bible but also come closer to a more orderly structure, as dictated by the nature and dynamics of the sefirotic system. This system is not, however, as rigid as the astrological one.

The Barcelonese commentator does not make any attempt to establish a specific correspondence between the two exegetical systems, and I assume that he did not even intend to offer one. Kabbalah and astrology are, for the late-thirteenth-century Kabbalist, two distinct understandings of the Torah.

III. Cosmic Book and Astrology in Renaissance Florence

The conjugation of the astrological with the Kabbalistic reading of the books is found in two passages written in the second part of the fifteenth century in Florence by R. Yohanan Alemanno, one of the Jewish companions of Pico della Mirandola.[28] In one of his more interesting treatises Alemanno follows, in a more extreme manner, the avenue opened by ibn Ezra:

> Anyone who knows the science of the stars and constellations that emanate upon the creatures on earth may interpret the entire Torah according to the signs and rules of astrology. This is true of the masters of theoretical as well as practical astrology. Any man, either good or evil, who knows the work of the pure and impure angels who are superior to the stars may draw their fragrance upon our heads, for he has given a Kabbalistic interpretation to the entire Torah. This matter includes the masters of both the speculative and the practical sciences of the sefirot.[29]

The Torah may be read in two different ways, one astrological, the other Kabbalistic. Each has a speculative and a practical part.[30] It seems that through the practical interpretation of the Torah one "may draw their fragrance upon our heads." Unlike ibn Ezra, who exhibited a much more restrained attitude and did not embrace a comprehensive astrological interpretation of the Torah, Alemanno contends that such an interpretation is possible. In both the astrological and the Kabbalistic interpretations, the drawing down of the divine powers is related to the reading of the Torah. Unlike in R. Bahya, who did not offer a unified approach for the two levels of interpretation, in Alemanno such a unified vision is obvious: the Torah deals with the secret of the descent of supernal powers upon man. Alemanno, like some later Kabbalists, accentuated the astromagical aspects of the Torah. Although hierarchically different, astrology and Kabbalah coincide insofar as the type of activity involved in both cases: astrology, in fact astromagic, and Kabbalah, according to its practical implication, draw down powers upon the practitioner, who is portrayed as referring to the Torah, in fact as interpreting it in a magical manner. This passage, which deals explicitly with interpretation of the Torah, contends that the same structure informs the two lores, despite the fact that they activate different realms of reality. As in the case of R. Bahya ben Asher, Kabbalah is conceived of as higher than astrology, but with Alemanno the two lores are regarded as isomorphic from the point of view of their basic way of activity. In other words, we may describe Alemanno's understanding of Kabbalah as influenced by astromagic, for the center of gravity of this understanding of Kabbalah is the causing of the supernal powers to descend upon the mundane world.

The analogous structure of magic and a Kabbalistic reading of the Torah described in Ms. Paris BN 849 has an interesting partial parallel in Alemanno's *Collectanaea*:

> The astrologer studies every one of the creatures in relation to one of the seven planets. In the same manner, the Kabbalist studies every word of the Torah, as stated before in connection with the commandments of the Torah. That is, he studies the sefirah to which it is related. The astrologer studies the movements and governance of the stars. In the same way the Kabbalist knows what will happen to people in the future by reference to the influence and efflux of the sefirot. This is in accordance with the activities and movements of those who perform the commandments and divine service. This method is superior to that of the astrologer.[31]

Although the untitled treatise was composed toward the end of the fifteenth century, the last passage was set down at a very early date, perhaps before 1478 or even before 1470, but the proofs I have for this cannot be included here. This determination is significant in view of the similarity between Alemanno's statement and one of Pico's theses, as we shall see in the next section. The problematic relation of Kabbalah to astrology was discussed in Italy before Alemanno. In the opinion of R. Isaac Dieulosal, the systems of Kabbalah and astrology are compatible.[32]

For Alemanno, as he expressed himself early in his literary career, the astrologer's domain has nothing to do with the Torah, which is the patrimony of the Kabbalistic magical interpretation. Thus, we may assume that although later in his untitled treatise he offered a more harmonistic approach, earlier he did distinguish between the "books" addressed by the astrologer and the Kabbalist.

Thus a Kabbalistic study of the Torah is no longer seen as inspired by a preoccupation with the hidden processes of divinity, as is the case with many of the Spanish Kabbalists. According to the Italian author, the Kabbalist has become a "superastrologer" who utilizes his knowledge to foresee and perhaps also to foretell the future. Interestingly, already in this earlier text of Alemanno, the affinity, though certainly not the identity, between the astrological decoding and the Kabbalistic study of the Torah has been explicated rather clearly. This understanding of the two ways of envisaging "books" is not identical to the much more common terms *liber scripturae* and *liber naturae*.[33]

IV. THE MAGICAL INTERPRETATION OF KABBALAH AND PICO'S VIEW OF "BOOKS"

Late-fifteenth-century Florence, the cradle of the activity of two main intellectuals, Ficino and Pico, has also been the place where Alemanno lived for several years. He was in contact with Pico, teaching him an important philosophical-mystical treatise, *Hayy bin Yoqtan*.[34] Alemanno was acquainted with a broad range of medieval books, most prominently astromagical writings, which he considered the apex of an ideal curriculum he composed.[35] Thus, before the end of the 1480s, a thinker in Florence could have access to a variety of forms of thought previously not well known or even inaccessible to a Western intellectual.[36]

In addition to Alemanno, Pico was in close contact with a scholar who may be described as the closest parallel to Ficino during the Florentine Renaissance: Flavius Mithridates. He translated many Kabbalistic writings from Hebrew into Latin, in some cases inserting, as Chaim Wirszubski has demonstrated, observations that gave either a Christian or a magical flavor to the Kabbalistic text.[37]

The first person who could take advantage of this unique access to Jewish Kabbalah and Judeo-Arabic texts, and who was instrumental in encouraging Mithridates' translations, was the young count of Mirandola, Giovanni Pico. On good terms with both Ficino and Mithridates, he enjoyed their literary output but contributed his own views based on a variety of syntheses between ideas found in these two corpora.

While all the modern scholars dealing with the Florentine Renaissance had access to the entire opus of both Ficino and Pico, Pico's Kabbalistic sources remained in the dark. Frances Yates, who assigned a paramount importance to Pico's synthesis for a great variety of later developments in what she called the European "occult philosophy," composed all her books before the full exposition of Wirszubski's findings was made available to a Western scholar and had only a vague idea about what actually was before the eyes of the young count.

If my above analysis of Alemanno's view of the relation between Kabbalah and astrology is correct, then his understanding of practical Kabbalah is similar to Pico's. Both consider the practical Kabbalah to include the use of divine names.[38] Here, however, given our concern with the concept of the book, I would like to direct attention to the last of Pico's *Theses*, which deal with modes of reading two books. The young Pico claims that "as true Astrology teaches us to read in the book of God, so the Kabbalah teaches us to read in the book of law" (*sicut vera Astrologia docet nos legere in libro Dei, ita Cabbala docet nos legere in libro legis*).[39] There have been a few attempts to address the content of this thesis and its sources seriously. According to Henri de Lubac, Pico is conjugating two views found already in Bonaventure,[40] but obviously Kabbalah is never mentioned by the mid-thirteenth-century Christian mystic. And although Wirszubski refers to this thesis, he does not trace its precise sources.[41] Let me attempt to engage the problems hinted at in the short thesis.

Pico's statement about astrology's relation to the book of God and the Kabbalah's relation to the book of the law seems analogous to Alemanno's view. The practical side of astrology can be identified with *magia naturalis*, for it teaches the way to receive the influx of higher powers. Kabbalah is a higher form of magic because its speculative formation is, as Pico emphasized here, superior to that of astrology. Such a comparison between the writings of the two Renaissance authors who were in contact suggests what seems to be a very close similarity. If we assume that Alemanno's stand was known to the young Pico, we may offer a more specific interpretation of Pico's thesis, which refers to the purpose of reading. In the count's thesis it is not very clear what the ultimate gain is from such a reading. A better understanding of the celestial world and the Bible? Or are those understandings instrumental for an additional purpose? With the later Alemanno, in his *Untitled Treatise*, following ibn Ezra and R. Bahya, the answer is clear: the two readings of the Bible serve a quite practical purpose: to know the future. It is difficult to say whether this is the case with Pico. If the answer is yes, then in his understanding astrology differs from astronomy, and we should ask what the astrology is that is not identical to the *vera Astrologia*. If the answer is no, then true astrology should be understood as a more "scientific" approach, devoid of the practical implications. If this is the case, at least insofar as the topic under consideration is concerned, Pico is less "hermetic" than Alemanno.

I assume that it is possible to enhance the probability of a Jewish impact on Pico's understanding of the two books by an analysis of an important detail: Pico describes the book read by the astrologer as *libro Dei*. This is the closest Latin parallel to the Hebrew expression *sifro shel ha-qadosh barukh hu'* used by R. Bahya ben Asher in the text adduced above. The Kabbalist explicates the biblical expression *sifrekha*, "Thy book," in the third person. Also in his passage, this "book of God" stands not for the Bible but for the celestial world, just as in the case of Pico. Moreover, it is quite plausible that an additional topic related to the book and found in R. Bahya ben Asher had an impact on Pico, thus allowing a much greater probability of a Jewish source for Pico's thesis. As Wirszubski pointed out, the four ways of interpretation as adopted by R. Bahya alone had been mentioned explicitly by Pico.[42] Moreover, there is good reason to assume that another important topic of Pico might also have been influenced by R. Bahya.[43]

Let me return to Pico's thesis from another point of view. Pico, like Bahya, does not associate astrology and Kabbalah as operating according to the same principle, but sees them as two different modes of interpreting the Bible. Insofar as this thesis is concerned, Kabbalah is not by definition magical but merely exegetical. From this perspective Bahya and Pico are closer to each other than either of them is to Alemanno, who offered a conceptual, not only an exegetical, nexus between the two. Their texts use the same term, "book of God," one that is not found in Alemanno.

Assuming, as seems quite plausible, that Alemanno was influenced by Bahya's juxtaposition of Kabbalah and astrology, and that so was Pico, the most plausible assumption would be that Alemanno was instrumental in teaching Pico about Bahya's interpretations of the concepts related to "book." The young Alemanno, however, under the impact of additional sources, adopted a harmonistic attitude toward the two lores, which means the understanding of Kabbalah as an astro-magic lore. This type of understanding is also found in Pico.[44] If this were indeed the development that informed the Renaissance authors, we would see medieval sources and conceptualizations of knowledge as having had a deep impact. The contention that the book of law is higher than that of nature is certainly more medieval than Renaissance. Also, the ascent of the importance of magic among the Jewish elites in the Middle Ages is certainly not new.[45] This is especially obvious in Barcelona, where R. Bahya ben Asher studied and apparently also composed his commentary.[46] The description of the relationship between Kabbalah and astromagic, which Yates attributed to Pico as if emerging from his combination between Ficino's hermeticism and Christian Kabbalah, should therefore be substantially qualified. The concept of occult philosophy during the sixteenth century is indeed very much indebted to Pico. He developed, however, a pattern of understanding Kabbalah in its relationship to astrology, in fact more to astro-magic, that started its career much earlier in the Middle Ages, when the theo-sophical version of Kabbalah was conjugated to the astrological understanding of the Bible in Barcelona. This combination attracted the attention of Alemanno, and I assume that he, and to a certain extent also Mithridates, was instrumental in teaching or convincing Pico of the existence of two modes of reading: one appropriated for the Bible, the other for the celestial world or even perhaps nature.[47] Pico, like his medieval source, attributes to the inspection of the sacred book a status higher than the book of nature. Thus, Pico's treatment of the relationship between the two books represents nothing that is substantially novel in comparison to the attempts to offer a hierarchy of knowledge, a general approach that still awaits further interpretation, which integrated the astromagical within a greater scheme that puts Kabbalah on its peak.

It is therefore necessary to qualify Yates's description of the emergence of the occult philosophy as related to a twofold development, in which Ficino provided the hermetic material and Pico the Christian Kabbalah. In addition to the specific finding related to Pico's thesis on the two books from a perusal of Alemanno's manuscript treatises, it is obvious that a substantial quantity of astromagical material stemming from a variety of Arabic and Jewish treatises existed in Florence and influenced Alemanno, and could also have contributed to the process that generated the occult philosophy. By introducing astromagic of ultimately hermetic origins in Florence, Ficino was certainly not alone, nor was he the single or perhaps even the most important source for Pico's view on this topic.

NOTES

INTRODUCTION

1. See "Reification of Language" and my forthcoming *Powers of Language*. See below, chap. 14, note 1.

2. On rabbinic Judaism as a text-centered community see Halbertal, *People of the Book*. On textual communities in the Christian Western Middle Ages see Stock, *The Implications of Literacy*, pp. 88–240. On Judaism in general as a text-centered or text-obsessed religion see various discussions by Harold Bloom, e.g., *Agon*, pp. 318–329. See also Regis Debray, "The Book as a Symbolic Object," *The Future of the Book*, pp. 148–149.

3. By using the term *myth* I adopt the definition offered by Paul Ricoeur, *Symbolism of Evil* (Beacon Press, Boston, 1969), p. 5.

4. The oral components of Jewish mysticism, which are in my opinion an important

issue neglected by modern scholarship, will not preoccupy us here. See, e.g., Idel, *Kabbalah: New Perspectives*, pp. 20–22; Wolfson, *Circle in the Square*, pp. 161–163 and below, chap. 12, par. I. For the Christian contemporary milieux see Stock, *The Implications of Literacy*, pp. 12–87. On the need to resort to the concept of cultural "panorama" for a better understanding of Jewish mysticism, especially in its Hasidic version, see Idel, *Hasidism: Between Ecstasy and Magic*, pp. 9–15. My concept of panoramic landscape assumes a less unified series of worldviews than Gadamer's concept of horizon; see his *Truth and Method*, pp. 302–303.

5. For more on this issue see below chap. 1, par. I.

6. "Mysticism and Society," *Diogenes* 58 (1967), p. 16. See also his *Major Trends*, p. 11.

7. "Heresies artistiques," written in 1862. Cf. his *Oeuvres Complètes*, p. 257. See also Jabes, "Key," p. 356: "Sacred, Secret."

8. The reasons for my use of the term *arcanization*, in lieu of *mystère*, will be explained later on. See below, chap. 6, par. II. On crises and symbolism see below, chap. 10 par. II.

9. On this issue see more in par. II.

10. See Uriel Simon, "Interpreting the Interpreter: Supercommentaries on Ibn Ezra's Commentaries," in I. Twersky and J. M. Harris, eds., *Rabbi Abraham ibn Ezra: Studies in the Writings of a Twelfth-Century Jewish Polymath* (Harvard University Press, Cambridge, Mass., 1993), pp. 86–128.

11. See Idel, "Mystical Interpretations of Maimonides' *Guide of the Perplexed*" (forthcoming).

12. See Idel, "Nahmanides"; Abrams, "Orality." See also below, appendix 2.

13. See Tishby, *Wisdom of the Zohar*, 1:103–105; Idel, "Targumo"; Huss, "*Sefer ha-Zohar*."

14. For an example of such a superarcanization see below, appendix 2.

15. See Halbertal, *People of the Book*, pp. 6–10; Smith, *Imagining Religion*, pp. 36–52.

16. *Shimmushei Torah* and *Shimmushei Tehilim*. For more on these two books see below, chap. 4, par. I; chap. 8, pars. III-IV; chap. 11, par. III.

17. See above, note 4.

18. Tishby, *Path of Belief and Heresy*, pp. 16, 20, 22, the latest passage being quoted below, chap. 10, par. III.

19. See, e.g., Stephen Harvey's proposal to understand Maimonides' important parable of the castle in the *Guide of the Perplexed*, as reflecting an impact of the Heikhalot literature; "Maimonides in the Sultan's Palace," in Joel L. Kraemer, ed., *Perspectives on Maimonides, Philosophical and Historical Studies* (Littman Library, Oxford, 1991), pp. 47–75, esp. pp. 64–66. See also Wolfson, *Abraham Abulafia*, pp. 42–52.

20. See Idel, "Maimonides and Kabbalah."

21. See below, chap. 6, par. II.

22. See Harari, "Critical Factions/Critical Fictions," in Harari, *Textual Strategies*, pp. 69–70.

23. I adopted the term *world-absorbing* from Fodor, *Christian Hermeneutics*. On the absorbing nature of the sacred texts see the views of Hans Frei and George Lindbeck; cf. Van-

hoozer, *Biblical Narrative*, p. 162. On the "absorbing" aspects of later texts in relation to the earlier as part of an intertextual affinity see the well-known view of Julia Kristeva.

24. For the need of integrating magic much more into the study of Jewish mysticism see Idel, "On Judaism." For the relations between Jewish mysticism and philosophy see idem, "Abulafia's Secrets of the Guide," pp. 289–292.

25. See below, appendix 2, par. I.

26. See Idel, *Hasidism: Between Ecstasy and Magic*, pp. 21–22.

27. See below, chap. 11, par. IV.

28. For a much more detailed exposition of the three models see, for the time being, Idel, *Hasidism: Between Ecstasy and Magic*, chaps. 2–3; idem, *Messianic Mystics*, pp. 25, 248–256; idem, "Conceptualizations of Music."

29. On the relationship between symbolism and theurgy see Idel, *Kabbalah: New Perspectives*, pp. 260–264; Elkayam, "Between Referentialism and Performativism," Boaz Huss, *Sockets of Fine Gold: The Kabbalah of Rabbi Shim'on ibn Lavi* (Magnes Press, Jerusalem, 2000), pp. 77–87 (Hebrew); Giller, *The Enlightened*, and below, chap. 10, par. IV.

30. For this understanding of theurgy see Georg Luck, following E. R. Dodds, *Arcana Mundi: Magic and the Occult in the Greek and Roman Worlds* (Crucible, 1987), p. 21; See also more recently Georg Luck, "Theurgy and Forms of Worship in Neoplatonism," *Religion, Science, and Magic*, ed. J. Neusner et al. (Oxford University Press, New York, 1989), p. 186, and Ruth Majercik, *The Chaldean Oracles* (Brill, Leiden, 1989), p. 22, where she adduced also other similar definitions of theurgy. Again following some of these scholars, I draw a distinction between theurgy and magic; see Majercik, ibid., pp. 22–23; see also Lorberbaum, *Imago Dei*, pp. 87–95, and Mopsik, *Les grands textes*, passim.

31. See Idel, *Language, Torah and Hermeneutics*, pp. 6, 122–123, and below, chap. 11.

32. This talismanic magic has very little to do with the magic of language found in ancient Jewish sources. See, however, Idel, "Hermeticism and Judaism," pp. 61–62. On the talismanic magic in medieval Jewish texts, several important studies of Dov Schwartz have been printed in the recent years that clarify various aspects of the drawing-down operation in the writings of fourteenth- and fifteenth-century Jewish figures; Schwartz also has printed some important texts that deal with talismanic elements in non-Kabbalistic kinds of speculative Jewish literature. See, more recently, his "Different Forms of Magic in Jewish Thought of the Fourteenth Century," *PAAJR* 57 (1990/91), pp. 19–47 (Hebrew), and "Astrology and Astral Magic in Rabbi Shlomo Al-Qonstantini's Megalleh 'Amuqot," *Jerusalem Studies in Folklore* 15 (1993), pp. 37–82 (Hebrew); Norman E. Frimer and Dov Schwartz, *The Life and Thought of Shem Tov ibn Shaprut* (Ben-Zvi Institute, Jerusalem, 1992), pp. 156–163 (Hebrew), and his recent monograph *Astral Magic in Medieval Jewish Thought* (Bar-Ilan University Press, Ramat Gan, 1999) (Hebrew), and Y. Tzvi Langermann, "Some Astrological Themes in the Thought of Abraham ibn Ezra," in I. Twersky and J. M. Harris, eds., *Rabbi Abraham ibn Ezra: Studies in the Writings of a Twelfth-Century Jewish Polymath* (Harvard University Press, Cambridge, Mass., 1993), pp. 28–84, as well as Simon, "Interpreting the Interpreter,"

pp. 86–128, and Raphael Jospe, "The Torah and Astrology According to Ibn Ezra," *Daat* 32–33 (1994), pp. 31–51 (Hebrew). On the terms *talisman* and *amulet* see the literature mentioned in Roy Kotansky, "Incantations and Prayers for Salvation on Inscribed Greek Amulets," in Christopher A. Faraone and Dirk Obbink, eds., *Magika Hiera: Ancient Greek Magic and Religion* (Oxford University Press, New York, Oxford, 1911), p. 124n5.

33. I did not find a theoretical formulation of this observation in the writings of the talismanic Kabbalists. It occurs, rather, in the ecstatic Kabbalist Abraham Abulafia; see Scholem, "The Name of God," pp. 190–191; Idel, *Language, Torah and Hermeneutics*, pp. 20–22.

34. See Idel, *Messianic Mystics*, pp. 272–273.

35. See Idel, "On Judaism," pp. 195–202.

36. Ricoeur, *From Text to Action*, pp. 106–110; idem, *Hermeneutics of the Human Sciences*, pp. 146–148. Ricoeur accepts some of the points made already by Georg Gadamer related to the fusion of horizons. See Weinsheimer, *Gadamer's Hermeneutics*, pp. 221–222; Frank M. Kirkland, "Gadamer and Ricoeur: The Paradigm of the Text," *Graduate Faculty Philosophy Journal* 6 (1977), pp. 131–144. See also Michael Riffaterre, "The Self-Sufficient Text," *Diacritics* 3 (1973), pp. 39–45.

37. Ricoeur, *Hermeneutics and the Human Sciences*, p. 147. See especially Ricoeur's view of existence as "gift." Cf. Vanhoozer, *Biblical Narrative*, pp. 124, 126–128, 197–198.

38. "The 'Authority' of Scripture?" *Touchstone* 10 (1992), p. 6; see also Wilfred Cantwell Smith, *Religious Diversity* (Crossroad, New York, 1982), p. 46. For more on his view see Sandra Schneiders, "Biblical Spirituality, Life, Literature and Learning," in Steven Chase, ed., *Doors of Understanding: Conversations in Global Spirituality in Honor of Ewert Cousins* (Franciscan Press, Quincy, 1997), pp. 60, 74n24.

39. For a more articulated discussion of intercorporality see below, chap. 9, par. I.

40. On the importance of exegesis in Christian mysticism see McGinn, *The Presence of God*, 1:3–5.

41. See Idel, *Language, Torah, and Hermeneutics*; idem, *Kabbalah: New Perspectives*; Wolfson, *Abraham Abulafia*, pp. 52–93.

42. See Idel, "Unio Mystica," pp. 319–327; see also idem, *The Mystical Experience*, pp. 144–145, and Farber-Ginnat, "Inquiries in *Sefer Shi'ur Qomah*," p. 362n6. On the importance of the exegetical technique for the content of the interpretation see Smalley's short remark in *The Bible in the Middle Ages*, p. 356.

43. See below, chap. 10, pars. III, V.

44. See below, the studies mentioned in chap. 3, note 12.

45. See below, chap. 3.

46. See below chap. 3, par. IIa.

47. See, e.g., below, chap. 9, par. V; and chap. 11, par. VI.

48. On the concept of ergesis see Amos Funkenstein, *Theology and the Scientific Imagination from the Middle Ages to the Seventeenth Century* (Princeton University Press, Princeton,

1986), pp. 296–299; Idel, *Golem*, pp. xxvi–xxvii. See also Goldin, *Studies in Midrash*, p. 223.

49. On the triunity see Abraham J. Heschel, "God, Torah, and Israel," in *Theology and Church in Times of Change: Essays in Honor of John C. Bennett*, ed. E. LeRoy and A. Hundry (Westminster, 1970), pp. 81, 89n60; Tishby, *Studies in Kabbalah*, 3:941–960; see also the recurrent resort to this formula by R. Hayyim of Volozhin in his *Nefesh ha-Hayyim*. Meanwhile, more material that includes the triple identification surfaced: see Sack, *Be-Sha'arei ha-Qabbalah*, pp. 103–109, who pointed out several discussions, including Cordoverian evidence; and Moshe Idel, "Two Remarks on R. Yair ben Sabbatai's *Sefer Herev Piffiyot*," QS 53 (1979), pp. 213–214 (Hebrew). Heschel and Tishby in their longer discussions on this dictum are theologically orienting, leaving aside the far-reaching hermeneutical implications. For the identity between the Torah and the souls of the people of Israel see R. Abraham Hiyya', *Megilat ha-Megalleh*, pp. 72–76. See also below, chap. 3, note 89; chap. 4, par. III(1); chap. 6, par. VI; chap. 11, par. XI. Compare, however, Jabes, "Key," p. 357: "The Jew lives on intimate terms with God, and God with the Jew, within the same words: A divine page. A human page. And in both cases the author is God, in both cases the author is man." For the concept of belonging, which is a very weak form of affinity (in comparison to the Kabbalistic triunity) between the interpreter and the text see Gadamer, *Truth and Method*, pp. 259–264; Weinsheimer, *Gadamer's Hermeneutics*, pp. 251–254.

50. Cf. Ricoeur, *Conflict of Interpretations*, pp. 321–322; Hans Frei's distinction between the historical and the value-cargo status of the Bible in *The Eclipse of Biblical Narrative: A Study in Eighteenth and Nineteenth Century Hermeneutics* (Yale University Press, New Haven, 1974), pp. 1–9; Fodor, *Christian Hermeneutics*, pp. 262–263; Vanhoozer, *Biblical Narrative*, p. 162.

51. Cf. Rawidowicz, "On Interpretation," p. 117.

52. See Idel, *Kabbalah: New Perspectives*, p. 271; idem, in Arthur A. Cohen and Paul Mendes-Flohr, *Contemporary Jewish Religious Thought* (Scribners, New York, 1987), pp. 654–655. On Nietzsche's will-to-power over the interpreted text see also Bloom, *Kabbalah and Criticism*, p. 100; idem, *The Strong Light*, p. 7.

53. See Bloom, *Kabbalah and Criticism*, pp. 53ff; idem, *Agon*, p. 83. See also below, "Concluding Remarks," par. V.

54. *After Babel*, pp. 296, 303. See also Eco, *Foucault's Pendulum*, p. 565: "To manipulate the letters of the Book takes great piety, and we didn't have it."

55. See, e.g., Rawidowicz, "On Interpretation," p. 91.

56. See Erich Auerbach, *Mimesis: The Representation of Reality in Western Literature*, trans. W. R. Trask (Doubleday, New York, 1957).

57. See Halbertal, *People of the Book*, pp. 40–44.

58. See Victor Aptovitzer, "Derasha be-Shevah ha-Torah," *Sinai* 7 (1940/41), esp. pp. 186–188 (Hebrew).

59. *Derush 'al ha-Torah*. On his views on the Torah, which will concern us only tangentially

below, see Byron L. Sherwin, *Mystical Theology and Social Dissent: The Life and Works of Judah Loew of Prague* (Littman Library, London, 1982).

60. See their treatises printed in *'Amudei ha-Torah*.

61. See, respectively, *Sefer ha-Hokhmah* and *Sheva' Netivot ha-Torah*.

62. See, nevertheless, Bacher, *Die exegetische Terminologie*, who is helpful for rabbinic terms that had been adopted by Kabbalists; and Yehuda Liebes, "New Directions in the Study of Kabbalah," *Pe'amim* 50 (1992), p. 159 (Hebrew).

63. See Scholem, *The Messianic Idea*, pp. 282–303.

64. See, e.g., the comprehensive, though very technical, studies of Ezra Zion Melammed, *Bible Commentators* (Magnes Press, Jerusalem, 1975), 2 vols. (Hebrew), idem, *Biblical Studies in Texts: Translations and Commentators* (Magnes Press, Jerusalem, 1984) (Hebrew). Important collections of studies have been edited by Moshe Greenberg, *Jewish Biblical Exegesis: An Introduction* (Mossad Bialik, Jerusalem, 1983) (Hebrew), and Sara Japhet, *The Bible in the Light of Its Interpreters: Sarah Kamin Memorial Volume* (Magnes Press, Jerusalem, 1994) (Hebrew); see also the studies referred to below, chap. 8, note 2.

CHAPTER I: THE WORLD-ABSORBING TEXT

1. On this issue see Idel, "Maimonides and Kabbalah." On magical books that betray an effort to present themselves as a form of interpretation of biblical texts see the discussions about *Shimmushei Torah* and *Shimmushei Tehilim*, chap. 5, par. I; chap. 11, pars. III and IV, for their influence on thirteenth-century Kabbalah.

2. See Holdrege, *Veda and Torah*, pp. 175–176, etc., and note 17 below.

3. Idel, "The Concept of the Torah," pp. 41–42; Wolfson, *Circle in the Square*, pp. 1–29; Holdrege, *Veda and Torah*, pp. 145–146, 253, 256, 276–277, 302, 312, 338. See also below, note 29, and chaps. 6, par. VI, and 10, par. VIII.

4. See, e.g., Holdrege, *Veda and Torah*, pp. 276–278, 302–303, 372–373.

5. See Wolfson, *Along the Path*, pp. 1–61.

6. Idel, *Kabbalah: New Perspectives*, pp. 157–160; Mopsik, *Les Grands textes*, pp. 42–65.

7. See Idel, "The Concept of the Torah;" Holdrege, *Veda and Torah*.

8. See Peter Schaefer, *Rivalität zwischen Engeln und Menschen* (De Gruyter, Berlin, 1975).

9. See Idel, "The Concept of the Torah," pp. 27–33.

10. See below, chap. 5, par. I.

11. See more below, chap. 11, note 12.

12. Exodus 3:15.

13. Ibid.

14. *Midrash Konen*, printed in Y. Eisenstein, *'Otzar ha-Midrashim* (New York, 1927), p. 253; Idel, "The Concept of the Torah," p. 45. See also R. Dov Baer of Mezeritch, *'Or Torah*, p. 47, where these views are attributed to *Sefer Yetzirah*.

15. On intercorporality and intracorporality see below, chaps. 9, 11.

16. See Rorty's distinction as discussed in Eco, *The Limits of Interpretation*, pp. 57–58.

17. See *Genesis Rabba'* 1:1, p. 2. See Baer, *Studies*, 1:111–112. On the cosmological Torah, its

sources in earlier Jewish writings, and its identification with Hokhmah, cosmic wisdom, see Martin Hengel, *Judaism and Hellenism*, trans. John Bowden (Fortress Press, Philadelphia, 1981), 1:170–175; Greenberg, *Studies*, pp. 20–22; Faur, *Golden Doves*, p. 138. For the Kabbalistic reverberations of this identification see Wolfson, *Circle in the Square*, p. 54, and below, chap. 3, par. II-B, chap. 6, par. VI, and Appendix 2.

18. See BT, 'Avodah Zarah, fol. 3a; Idel, *Kabbalah: New Perspectives*, p. 171; and below, chap. 4, par. VI. See also below beside note 30.

19. BT, *Berakhot*, fol. 55a. See also Urbach, *The Sages*, p. 197.

20. Scholem, "The Name of God," p. 71.

21. See, e.g., the tradition mentioned by R. Jacob ben Sheshet, *Sefer ha-'Emunah ve-ha-Bittahon*, in C. D. Chavel, ed., *Kitvei ha-Ramban* (Mossad ha-Rav Kook, Jerusalem, 1964), 2:363; Urbach, *The Sages*, pp. 197–198. Compare also to R. Dov Baer of Mezeritch, *'Or Torah*, p. 47.

22. Urbach, *The Sages*, pp. 197–213.

23. See Idel, *Kabbalah: New Perspectives*, pp. 112–122, and below, chap. 8, pars. V–VI.

24. See note 6 above.

25. On this text see Scholem, *On the Kabbalah*, pp. 177–178.

26. For more on this text see Moshe Idel, *Golem*, trans. Azan M. Levi (Schocken, Jerusalem and Tel Aviv, 1996), pp. 271–275 (Hebrew). For more on this text see below, chap. 12, par. IV.

27. For the later reverberations of this view in Kabbalah, where all 231 combinations are designated expressly as Torah, see Idel, *Golem*, pp. 148–154.

28. Jeremy 16:11.

29. 'Eikhah Rabbati, Petiheta II; Pesiqta' de-Rabbi Kahana', 16:5. In this context see also the importance of the concept of God as student of the Torah, as described by Rawidowicz, "On Interpretation," pp. 93–94. See also the text referred to above, in note 3.

30. See 'Avot de-Rabbi Nathan, chap. 4; Numbers Rabba', 30:12; Tanna' de-Bei 'Eliyahu Rabba', 18:31 etc. On the three pillars on which the world stands see Judah Goldin, *Studies in Midrash and Related Literature*, ed. B. L. Eichler and J. F. Tigay (Jewish Publication Society, Philadelphia, 1988), pp. 27–37. See also note 18 above.

31. On this treatise see Pines, "Points of Similarity"; Scholem, *Kabbalah*, pp. 21–29. For the crucial role that *Sefer Yetzirah* played in medieval Jewish thought see, e.g., David Neumark, *Geschichte der jüdischen Philosophie des Mittelalters* (Berlin, 1907), 1:116–117, 131–132, 182–183; Gruenwald, "Jewish Mysticism"; and now Liebes, *Ars Poetica*.

32. Cf. Scholem, "The Name of God," pp. 72–74.

33. *Sefer Yetzirah*, 2:2; Cf. the edition of Ithamar Gruenwald, "A Preliminary Critical Edition of *Sefer Yezira*," Israel Oriental Studies 1 (1971), par. 19, p. 148; Wolfson, *Circle in the Square*, pp. 55–56 and 168, note 51.

34. *Sefer Yetzirah*, 3:5; Gruenwald (1971), par. 31, p. 154.

35. *Sefer Yetzirah*, 1:10 and 2:3; Gruenwald (1971), par. 12, p. 144 and par. 17, p. 147.

36. *Sefer Yetzirah*, 6:4; Gruenwald (1971), par. 61, p. 174. See also the imperative of

knowing, thinking, and formatting, *Sefer Yetzirah* [Tzur] 2:4, Gruenwald (1971), par. 4, p. 141; *Sefer Yetzirah*, 1:7, Gruenwald (1971), par. 6, p. 142. On the affinity between the beginning and the end of *Sefer Yetzirah* see Yehuda Liebes, *Het' o shel 'Elisha'*, pp. 102–103; idem, *Ars Poetica*, pp. 92, 96–104. Cf., however, Dan, *On Sanctity*, pp. 253–254.

37. Idel, *Golem*, pp. 12–13.

38. See BT, *Berakhot*, fol. 55a, and Scholem, "The Name of God," p. 71; Scholem, *Kabbalah*, p. 26; Gruenwald, "Jewish Mysticism," p. 28; Dan, "The Religious Meaning," p. 19; Holdrege, *Veda and Torah*, pp. 177, 185.

39. Compare, however, the different assessment of Dan, "The Religious Meaning."

40. This view emerged out of the early interpretations of Isaiah 28:4. See the numerous instances of using this verse, where a shorter form of the Tetragrammaton occurs, as pointed out in Nicholas Sed, *La mystique cosmologique juive* (Mouton, Paris, 1981), index, p. 331.

41. See Scholem, *Kabbalah*, pp. 23–26. For more on this issue see below, chap. 12.

42. Cf. Fodor, *Christian Hermeneutics*, pp. 258–330.

43. See below, Concluding Remarks and Appendix 6.

44. On this Kabbalist see, e.g., Scholem, *Kabbalah*, pp. 132–134, who offered a rather Neoplatonic interpretation of the Sarugian theory which is not corroborated by the authentic Sarugian texts; Alexander Altmann, "Lurianic Kabbalah in a Platonic Key: Abraham Cohen Herrera's Puerta del Cielo," *HUCA* 53 (1982), p. 340. I expressed doubts as to the innovative nature of the malbush theory in my "Differing Conceptions of Kabbalah," pp. 192–193, note 268, for reasons that differ from the point made here, which strengthens the possibility that the malbush theory was not entirely new with Sarug. Compare also the Kabbalistic tradition, quoted by R. Me'ir Poppers, that Vital was acquainted with the concepts related to the processes taking place on the plane higher than the supernal man, but he concealed them; cf. *Sefer Zohar ha-Raqi'a* (Siget, 1875), fol. 23d. On the malbush concept and its sources see especially Scholem, *On the Kabbalah*, pp. 73–74, and idem, "The Name of God," pp. 181–182; See also Idel, "The Concept of the Torah," p. 39, note 43; idem, *Golem*, pp. 148–154, Liebes, *Sod ha-'Emunah*, pp. 321–322, note 167; Wolfson, *Circle in the Square*, pp. 70–72; 182–183, note 129; 189–190, note 174. On sha'ashu'a see, e.g., Wolfson, *Circle in the Square*, pp. 69–71, and the bibliography mentioned there. On malbush in the late-eighteenth-century Kabbalist R. Elijah of Vilnius see Wolfson, "From Sealed Book"; R. Isaac Aizik Haver, *'Or Torah*, in *'Amudei ha-Torah*, p. 51; and R. Hayyim of Volozhin, *Nefesh ha-Hayyim*, pp. 222–223. On delight in the context of Torah study see below, chap. 6, note 32.

45. *Shever Yosef*, printed at the end of R. Hayyim Vital, *Sha'ar ha-Yihudim* (Koretz, 1783), fol. 20a. On fol. 20b the process of emanation within the *reshimu* is discussed in the framework of the white and black fires, to be addressed in the next chapter, note 60. On the concept of weaving see below, chap. 9, note 93. On garment and Torah see also below, chap. 12, par. I. The proliferation of this view in Kabbalah is so great that it deserves a detailed analysis in itself. Many later Kabbalists adopted the Sarugian

version of Lurianic Kabbalah and integrated the theory of malbush in their discussions of the Torah. See note 44 above.

46. See below, chap., 2, par. II, and chap. 12, par. VI; Idel, *Golem*, pp. 149–150, and in a more detailed form in "The Relationship of the Jerusalem Kabbalists and R. Israel Sarug," *Shalem* 6 (1992), pp. 165–174 (Hebrew). See also below, chap. 12.

47. *Sefer Sitrei Torah*, Ms. Paris, BN 774, fol. 162a. See also Scholem, *Major Trends*, p. 143, and Abulafia, *Hayyei ha-'Olam ha-Ba'*, p. 110. Abulafia's commentary on the *Guide* was translated into Latin by Flavius Mithridates and known by Pico della Mirandola. See Wirszubski, *Pico della Mirandola*, pp. 136–138; As Wirszubski has noticed, Pico's view of Kabbalah as comprising both the combinations of letters and the theosophical version of the merkavah owes to Abulafia's view only its first part. On the experience of a vision of Torah as a circle or sphere, see also Idel, *The Mystical Experience*, pp. 109–116, and below, chap. 3, note 41; chap. 11; and app. 2.

48. See also *Sefer Sitrei Torah*, Ms. Paris BN 774, fol. 148b. For more on this issue see below, chap. 12.

49. Chap. 9, fol. 27b. On the four worlds of 'ABYA' see below, app. 1 and 3.

50. This topic deserves a much more elaborate treatment than can be offered here. Compare, e.g., R. Moses Narboni, *Commentary on the Guide of the Perplexed*, ed. J. Goldenthal (Vienna, 1852), fol. 38b, and especially R. Abraham Shalom, *Sefer Never Shalom* (Venice, 1575), fol. 127a. On the issue of metaphorical tables see the discussion of the inner tables of law, found in the human spirit, as addressed in Islamic and Jewish thought, in Idel, *Language, Torah, and Hermeneutics*, pp. 46, 170–171.

51. See below, chap. 3, note 52. For a very interesting discussion of accommodation based on the concept of contractions, see R. Dov Baer of Mezeritch, *'Or Torah*, pp. 47–48.

52. See below, chap. 3, par. V, and notes 97–98.

53. I did not find this interpretation in the Talmud. See, however, BT, *Sanhedrin*, fol. 99b, and *Zohar*, I fol. 5a.

54. Isaiah 51:16, the second part of the verse.

55. Ibid., the first part of the verse.

56. *Degel Mahaneh 'Efrayyim*, p. 98. For the opposite view, which assumes that the Torah is restructured in accordance with human deeds, see below, chap. 12.

57. Ibid., p. 98.

58. See, e.g., *Nefesh ha-Hayyim*, pp. 229–230.

59. Cf. the whole chapter 5 of this treatise.

60. See also below, chap. 5, par. VI, Roland Barthes's theory of poetic language. On the question of constellation see discussions throughout the book, especially chap. 8.

61. See Idel, *Golem*.

62. See, e.g., the role of the letters in the visualizing processes. Cf. Idel, "On Talismanic Language," pp. 33–32.

63. There is no doubt, as has been shown in detail by A. P. Hayman, that the form of religiosity expressed in *Sefer Yetzirah* reflects a mode of thought that differs dramatically

from what we know from the Heikhalot literature. See Hayman, "*Sefer Yesira* and the Hekhalot Literature," JSJT 6 (1987), pp. 71–86.

64. See Scholem, "The Name of God," pp. 75–76; Gruenwald, "Jewish Mysticism," pp. 28–29; Idel, *Golem*, pp. 9–26; Yehuda Liebes, "The Seven Double Letters BGD KFRT: On the Double Reish and the Background of *Sefer Yezira*," Tarbiz 61 (1992), pp. 237–248 (Hebrew), where the astrological sources of some linguistic speculations *Sefer Yetzirah* have been pointed out. Compare, on the other hand, the view of Dan, *On Sanctity*, pp. 253–254, who does not accept the existence of magical elements in this book, as has been assumed by several scholars.

65. See, e.g., Zohar, II, fol. 161a; R. Hayyim of Volozhin, *Nefesh ha-Hayyim*, p. 223; R. Dov Baer of Mezeritch, *Maggid Devarav le-Ya'aqov*, p. 227; R. Benjamin of Zalitch, *Sefer Torei Zahav* (rpt., Brooklyn, 1983), fol. 3a; idem, *'Ahavat Dodim*, p. 116.

66. R. Isaac Aizik Haver, *'Or Torah*, in *'Amudei ha-Torah*, p. 23. See also ibid., pp. 26, 31. Compare also the much earlier view found in Gikatilla, *Ginnat 'Egoz*, p. 239.

67. Mallarmé, *Oeuvres Complètes*, p. 378. Compare also the fascinating discussion of R. Moses Cordovero, *Shi'ur Qomah*, fol. 9bc, on the preponderance of the Torah over the world.

68. Eco, *Foucault's Pendulum*, p. 565.

CHAPTER 2: THE GOD-ABSORBING TEXT

1. For more on the ten creative *logoi* see below, chap. 8, pars. V, VI.

2. See the various versions of *'Otiyyot de-Rabbi 'Aqivah*, in Shlomo A. Wertheimer and Avraham Wertheimer, eds., 2d ed., *Batei Midrashot* (Mossad ha-Rav Kook, Jerusalem, 1950), 2:203–466.

3. A more detailed discussion and bibliography on this issue is in Idel, "The Concept of the Torah," pp. 43–46.

4. Printed in *'Otzar ha-Midrashim*, ed. Yehudah Eisenstein (New York, 1927), p. 450.

5. Deuteronomy 4:24; 9:3. See also Idel, "The Concept of the Torah," pp. 44–45, note 62.

6. Song of Songs 5:11.

7. *Qevutzotav taltalim shehorot.*

8. *Qotz.*

9. *Tilei tilim.*

10. See Idel, "The Concept of the Torah," pp. 45–46.

11. For more on tittle see below, chap. 8., par. V.

12. See the standard edition printed at the end of BT, *'Avodah Zarah.*

13. Cf. Handelman, *The Slayers of Moses*, pp. 27–50.

14. Idel, *Kabbalah: New Perspectives*, pp. 157–158.

15. See below, chap. 10.

16. See below, chap. 10.

17. Cf. BT, *Sanhedrin*, fol. 21b; Idel, "The Concept of the Torah," pp. 43–44, note 59.

18. *Sefer Yetzirah*, ed. Ithamar Gruenwald, in "A Preliminary Critical Edition of Sefer Ye-zira," *Israel Oriental Studies* 1 (1971): 157, par. 38.

19. *Genesis Rabba'*, III:4, ed. J. Theodor and C. Albeck (Warmann Books, Jerusalem, 1965), p. 19. An analysis of this midrash is found in Altmann's study, mentioned below, note 26.

20. Psalms 104:2.

21. Daniel 2:22.

22. *The Rationales of the Letters*, first edited by Gershom Scholem, *Madda'ei ha-Yahadut* (Jeru-salem, 1927), 2:201–202; Scholem, *On the Kabbalah*, p. 50 and note 1.

23. Rojtman, *Black Fire on White Fire*, pp. 33–34, 45, 102, 131.

24. Ibid., pp. 7, 10.

25. See Idel, "Reification of Language."

26. See Alexander Altmann, "A Note on the Rabbinic Doctrine of Creation," *JJS* 6/7 (1955–1956): 195–206.

27. *'Ehad, yahid, u-meyuhad*. On this formula see Scholem, *Origins of the Kabbalah*, pp. 341–342.

28. On this phrase see below, chap. 4, par. IV.

29. See *Sefer Yetzirah*, 1:1.

30. Job 28:11.

31. On the secret of face and back at the beginning of Kabbalah see Scholem, *Origins of the Kabbalah*, pp. 218, 334.

32. This passage, stemming from an earlier, unidentified Kabbalistic book, was quoted later on in two untitled Kabbalistic books authored by R. Shem Tov. See the Hebrew original and the bibliographical details in Idel, "The Concept of Zimzum," pp. 69–70, and Lorberbaum, *Imago Dei*, pp. 321–322. Compare also the passage of the sixteenth-century Kabbalist R. Abraham Adrutiel, translated by Wolfson, *Circle in the Square*, pp. 58–59.

33. See Idel, "The Concept of Zimzum," pp. 79–80. The nexus between withdrawal and the emergence of the primordial Torah in later Kabbalah has already been discussed above, chap. 1, par. VII.

34. See the text printed and analyzed in Idel, "The Concept of Zimzum," pp. 79–80.

35. Ibid.

36. The rather hesitant attribution of this short treatise to the Provencal Kabbalist was repeated by J. Dan, who has even chosen a part of this text as representative of R. Isaac the Blind's thought! See *The Early Kabbalah*, pp. 71–79. Neither Scholem nor Dan, however, took the trouble to deal with the reasons behind their attribution of the commentary. See, e.g., Scholem, *Origins of the Kabbalah*, p. 260. As I have suggested elsewhere, this attribution is problematic for several reasons, and I propose that the time of the composition must be no earlier than the end of the thirteenth century. I cannot present here detailed proofs, but I would like to note that no evidence concern-ing the time of composition was adduced by Dan or Scholem that has to be analyzed

and rejected in order to postdate the commentary. See also Idel, *Golem*, p. 113; also below, note 38, and chap. 4, note 24.

37. *Bi-ymino.*

38. *Ketarim.* Scholem translated, correctly, *sefirot.* In my opinion, this specific use of the term "crown" to point to the sefirot represents a semantic development characteristic of late-thirteenth-century Kabbalah. In the earlier Kabbalistic writings the plural stands for the sefirot Hesed and Gevurah.

39. *Mahashevet torah kelulah.*

40. Ms. New York, JTS 1777, fol. 5a; for another translation and a different analysis see Scholem, *On the Kabbalah*, pp. 48–49; idem, *Origins of the Kabbalah*, pp. 287–289, 330, note 270; Dan, *The Early Kabbalah*, pp. 73–74. Scholem's discussions seem to be the source of Blanchot, *The Gaze of Orpheus*, p. 155, adduced also by Faur, *Golden Doves*, pp. 137–138. See also Blanchot, *The Infinite Conversation*, p. 430. I hope to deal with the impact of Scholem's thought on Blanchot in more detail elsewhere; see, e.g., *The Infinite Conversation*, pp. 110, 116–117, 446. See also Harold Bloom, "Breaking the Form," p. 7, and Handelman, *Fragments of Redemption*, p. 285.

41. See below, chap. 4, par. III,1.

42. See Idel, "Kabbalistic Material," pp. 174–175, 177.

43. Ibid., pp. 173–188; Idel, "The Image of Man."

44. See the fragment from the so-called "Circle of the Book of Contemplation" extant in Ms. New York, JTS 1887, fol. 7a, printed in Idel, "Kabbalistic Material," p. 175, note 19.

45. Derrida, *Dissemination*, p. 253.

46. Vajda, "Un chapître." For more on this Kabbalist see below, chap. 12. par. V.

47. *Meshekh.* Vajda, "Un chapître," p. 55, translates "trait."

48. *Halaq.*

49. See *Commentary on Bereshit Rabbah'*, ed. Hallamish, p. 44. This passage had been copied and printed in *Sefer Ma'or va-Shemesh*, ed. Yehudah Qoriat (Livorno, 1839), fol. 13a.

50. *Guide of the Perplexed* 2:4. See also Vajda, "Un chapître," pp. 49–56. For an additional rejection of the conventionality of the forms of the Hebrew letters see R. Moses Cordovero, *Pardes Rimmonim*, Gate 27, chaps. 1 and 2.

51. See Hallamish's note on p. 44 (note 78) and p. 230.

52. For more on this issue see below, chap. 10, beside note 37.

53. See Hallamish's introduction, p. 14.

54. See M. Idel, "R. David ben Yehudah he-Hasid's Commentaries on the Alphabet," *'Alei Sefer* 10 (1982), pp. 25–35 (Hebrew).

55. BT, *Menahot*, fol. 29a; See also below, app. 2, note 48.

56. *Magen David*, unpaged introduction. For God as the locus of the world see above, the quote from R. Isaac ha-Kohen. For more on the concepts found in this text see below, par. IV. See also his *Migdal David* (Lemberg, 1883), fol. 80b: "That *'illat ha-'illot* . . . is not limited by the number of portions [this refers to the four Torah portions, *parshiyyot*, that are in the phylacteries] and the first point that was emanated from Him

included the ten internal *tzahtzahot*." This stand indubitably reflects the opinion of R. David ben Yehudah he-Hasid.

57. See Scholem, *Origins of the Kabbalah*, pp. 437, 443.

58. See Scholem, *On the Kabbalah*, pp. 39–40.

59. *Sefer Shomer 'Emunim*, p. 82.

60. Ibid., p. 83. For another, earlier resort to the metaphor of white and black in Lurianic Kabbalah see the text preserved by R. Joseph Shlomo of Kandia, in Idel, "Differing Conceptions of Kabbalah," p. 186. See above, chap. 1, note 45.

61. For more on this issue see below, chap. 3, par. II.

62. See Idel, *Hasidism: Between Ecstasy and Magic*, pp. 172–185, and below, chap. 6.

63. Exodus 15:2.

64. See below, note 75.

65. *'Imrei Tzaddiqim* (Zhitomir, 1900), fol. 5b. Here a different translation of a larger portion of the discussion already analyzed by Scholem, *On the Kabbalah*, pp. 81–82, has been adduced. For the different ancient treatments of the new Torah see W. D. Davies, *The Setting of the Sermon on the Mount* (Cambridge, 1964), pp. 154–196; for medieval Kabbalistic discussion on the new Torah see Amos Goldreich, "Clarifications of the Self-Perception of the Author of *Tiqqunei Zohar*," *Massu'ot*, p. 476 (Hebrew).

66. Scholem, *On the Kabbalah*, p. 82; Derrida, *Dissemination*, pp. 344–345; Eco, *Semiotics*, pp. 155–156; Steiner, *After Babel*, p. 297.

67. *On the Kabbalah*, p. 81, says, "This notion [of the book of Temunah] of the invisible parts of the Torah which will one day be made manifest endured for centuries in a number of variants and was taken into the Hasidic tradition." For a somewhat more moderate exposition of the topic of the invisible letters in *Sefer ha-Temunah* see Scholem, *Origins of the Kabbalah*, pp. 466–467.

68. *Qedushat Levi*, p. 343.

69. *Behirut 'atzmiyyut*. See also this author's *'Or Torah*, p. 48, where the luminosity of the creator is mentioned, as well as the quote attributed to R. Barukh of Medzibezh, the grandson of the Besht, in *Botzina' di-Nehora'*, p. 111. See also below, note 72, and chap. 6, note 189.

70. *Behirut 'atzmiyyuto*.

71. *Me-'atzmiyuti*. This is an interpretation of *me-'itti*.

72. *Maggid Devarav le-Ya'aqov*, pp. 17–18. Compare also the discussion of the same author, ibid., on pp. 201–203. And see also R. Aharon of Zhitomir, *Toledot 'Aharon*, I, fol. 5c where an interesting passage on the forefathers is found. See also R. Dov Baer of Mezeritch, *'Or Torah*, p. 47, where the phrase *behirut ha-torah*, the luminosity of the Torah, occurs. On the revelations of the secrets of the Torah in messianic times, in the context of the two fires, see *Sefer ha-Meshiv*, in the passage quoted by Scholem, "The 'Maggid,'" p. 100.

73. See his *Qedushat Levi*, p. 183.

74. On the relation between letters, lights, and secrets in thirteenth-century Kabbalah in

the context of the contemplation of the Torah scroll see Wolfson, *Through a Speculum That Shines*, pp. 375–376, and the pertinent footnotes, and his "From Sealed Book," p. 153. See also below, note 108, and our discussion in chap. 12.

75. *Mekhilta'*, *Beshalah*, II. A list of mainly rabbinic sources dealing with this issue is found in Heschel, *Theology of Ancient Theology*, 1:283–284. See also above, note 64.

76. *Sovev*, namely the encompassing light.

77. *Qedushat Levi*, pp. 327–328. Interestingly enough, this passage is closest to the presentation of one of the most learned among the Kabbalists belonging to the camp of the Mitnaggedim, R. Isaac Aizik Haver, *'Or Torah*, in *'Amudei ha-Torah*, pp. 219–220.

78. *Toledot 'Aharon*, I, fol. 27a. See also a much earlier view found in *Sefer ha-Meshiv*, in a passage printed by Scholem, "The 'Maggid,'" p. 100. See also below, chap. 12, note 145.

79. As to the contention of antinomianism in this book, see Scholem, *Origins of the Kabbalah*, pp. 467–468, 472.

80. *On the Kabbalah*, p. 82.

81. Ibid., p. 82, note 2.

82. See his *The Messianic Idea in Judaism*, p. 35. Compare also Scholem's discussion of the lost keys to the understanding of the Torah in *On the Kabbalah*, pp. 12–13. For a Hasidic master, however, the assumption is that the "key of the Torah," *mafteah ha-torah*, is always available to one of the righteous of the generation. See the late collection of legends *Gedolim Ma'asei Tzaddiqim*, where R. Abraham Yehoshu'a Heschel of Apta reported that the Maggid of Zlotchov was that righteous. See also the quote from R. Nahman of Braslav below, chap. 6, par. IV, and beside note 195. On the study of Torah as a paradisiacal experience see R. Ze'ev Wolf of Zhitomir, *'Or ha-Me'ir*, fol. 3bc, 4b. On "inner and external keys" related to the divine names see the introduction to *Tiqqunei Zohar*, fol. 5a.

83. See Steiner, *After Babel*, p. 65.

84. See *On the Kabbalah*, pp. 12–13. The rhetoric of the "price" is one of the most fascinating examples of Scholem's axiology. Compare Scholem's claim that Hasidism paid a price when embracing, in his judgment, a nonapocalyptic approach to messianism: *The Messianic Idea in Judaism*, p. 35; see my critique of this approach in *Messianic Mystics*, pp. 276–277, 292.

85. See, e.g., *Qedushat Levi*, pp. 104–105, 145, 230; see also R. Dov Baer of Mezeritch, *'Or Torah*, pp. 8, 47.

86. *Qedushat Levi*, p. 350.

87. See, e.g., R. Dov Baer of Mezeritch, *'Or Torah*, pp. 47–48, and Idel, *Hasidism: Between Ecstasy and Magic*, pp. 117–120.

88. See Idel, *Messianic Mystics*, pp. 229–234.

89. *On the Kabbalah*, p. 12.

90. See Rachel Elior, *The Theory of Divinity in HaBaD Hasidism* (Magnes Press, Jerusalem, 1982), p. 34, note 44 (Hebrew); Green, *Devotion and Commandment*, pp. 62–64.

91. On this Hasidic concept see Scholem, *Devarim be-Go*, pp. 351–360. As in some of the

sources quoted by Scholem, so too in this book the primordial intellect is identified with the sefirah Hokhmah and the primordial Torah. See, e.g., *Toledot 'Aharon*, I, fols. 27a,cd.

92. *Toledot 'Aharon*, I, fol. 27cd. See also ibid., II, fol. 1a. On this theory and text see below, chap. 12.

93. Ibid., I fol. 27d.

94. Ibid., I fol. 18c.

95. *Hitlahavut*.

96. *Qedushat Levi*, p. 145. For other examples dealing with R. Levi Isaac's claim that the mystic is capable of contemplating divinity see Idel, *Hasidism: Between Ecstasy and Magic*, pp. 118–120.

97. Compare Scholem, *On the Kabbalah*, pp. 12–13.

98. *Qedushat Levi*, p. 345.

99. Ibid., p. 344. See also p. 346, where he mentions in this context his teacher, R. Dov Baer of Mezeritch. For another interesting example of the concept of the descent of the influx by means of letters see the quote adduced from R. Hayyim Tirer of Chernovitz below, chap. 4, note 80. The concept is much earlier, as we find a similar stand in R. Nathan Neta' Shapira of Cracow, *Megalleh 'Amuqot*, fol. 12d, no. 50 (quoted also in R. Elijah ha-Kohen 'Ithamari, *Midrash Talpiyyot*, fol. 18d), and ibid., fol. 18b no. 69.

100. *Qedushat Levi*, p. 348. See also R. Aharon of Zhitomir, *Toledot 'Aharon*, I, fol. 5c.

101. *Qedushat Levi*, p. 348.

102. See Idel, *Hasidism: Between Ecstasy and Magic*, pp. 111–145, esp. pp. 117–121, where the views of R. Levi Isaac reflecting this model are analyzed.

103. Contemplation of the 'ayin is a leitmotif of R. Levi Isaac of Berditchev's mysticism.

104. *Qedushat Levi*, p. 176; for another translation see Scholem, *Major Trends*, p. 5; see also W. T. Stace, *Mysticism and Philosophy* (Jeremy P. Tarcher, New York, 1960), pp. 106–107. According to other passages in *Qedushat Levi*, the contemplation of the divine luminosity causes the loss of the sense of identity and reality exactly like the contemplation of the Nought.

105. See also below, the next quote from the same book.

106. For Cordovero's view of *kavvanah* see Idel, *Hasidism: Between Ecstasy and Magic*, p. 160.

107. *Toledot 'Aharon*, I, fol. 6bc. See also II fol. 30a, where the luminosity is related explicitly to 'Ein Sof and the Torah as written on a white fire.

108. The presence of divine light within the letters of the Torah or prayer is recurrent in Hasidic literature. See above, note 74.

109. *Toledot 'Aharon*, I, fol. 40ab.

110. Ibid., II, fol. 47d. On the phenomenon of bringing down the influx by intense study see Idel, *Hasidism: Between Ecstasy and Magic*, pp. 182–185.

111. See *Toledot 'Aharon*, II, fol. 1a.

112. Or "contemplates."

113. *Toledot 'Aharon*, II, fol. 1a. See also ibid., II, fol. 36ab.

114. Ibid., I, fol. 27c.

115. See introduction, note 22.

116. See, e.g., *Toledot 'Aharon*, I, fol. 21cd.

117. See Buber, *The Origin and Meaning of Hasidism*, p. 124.

118. See below, chap. 6, par. III.

119. See Lorberbaum, *Imago Dei*, pp. 49–50.

120. See Scholem, *On the Kabbalah*, pp. 44–47; Idel, "The Concept of the Torah," pp. 49–52; Wolfson, *Through the Speculum That Shines*, pp. 247–251, 376.

121. Vol. II, fol. 60a.

122. I assume that the idea of perfection is related to the fact that the first and last letters were conceived of as near to each other. This idea is found, to a certain extent, in Nahmanides' introduction to his *Commentary on the Torah*, which also influenced the description of the visual aspect of the Torah in the following lines. See below, app. 3.

123. See *Tanna' de-Bei 'Eliyahu*, chap. 25.

124. *Sefer ha-Yihud*, Ms. Milano-Ambrosiana 62, fol. 113b, printed and discussed in Idel, "Concept of the Torah," pp. 62–64; See also Idel, *R. Menahem Recanati, the Kabbalist*, app. 2. See also Scholem, *On the Kabbalah*, pp. 43–44; Mopsik, *Les grands textes*, pp. 278–287, 560–565; Fishbane, *The Garments of Torah*, p. 43; Holdrege, *Veda and Torah*, p. 361. On the importance for modern hermeneutics of another quote from this book, and of its appropriation by R. Menahem Recanati, see below, chap. 4.

125. Alexander Altmann, "Concerning the Question of the Authorship of *Sefer Ta'amei ha-Mitzwot* Attributed to R. Isaac ibn Farhi," QS 40 (1964–1965), pp. 256–276, 405–412 (Hebrew); idem, "An Allegorical Midrash on Genesis 24 According to the 'Inner Kabbalah,'" in *Sefer ha-Yovel Tifereth Yisra'el likhevod Yisra'el Brodie*, eds. H. J. Zimmels, J. Rabbinowitz, and I. Finestein (London, 5727 [1968]), pp. 57–65 [Hebrew part]; Gottlieb, *Studies*, pp. 248–256; Shlomo Pines, "A Parallel between Two Iranian and Jewish Themes," *Irano-Judaica* 2 (1990), pp. 49–51; Liebes, *Studies in the Zohar*, pp. 103–126; Charles Mopsik, "Un manuscript inconnu du *Sefer Tashak* de R. Joseph de Hamadan suivi d'un fragment inedit," *Kabbalah* 2 (1997), pp. 167–205; idem, *Joseph de Hamadan, Fragment d'un commentaire sur la Genese* (Verdier, Lagrasse, 1998); idem, *Les grands textes*, pp. 211–234; M. Idel, "R. Joseph of Hamadan's Commentary on Ten Sefirot and Fragments of His Writings," *'Alei Sefer* 6–7 (1979), pp. 74–84 (Hebrew), idem, "Additional Fragments from the Writings of R. Joseph of Hamadan," *Daat* 21 (1988), pp. 47–55 (Hebrew).

126. *Morah*.

127. Exodus 13:17–17:16.

128. Exodus 15:1ff, which is included in the above-mentioned portion.

129. Deuteronomy 32:1–43.

130. Numbers 21:17.

131. *Berit*.

132. Ms. Jerusalem, JNUL 8° 3925, fol. 110b. For the affinities between this text and Geronese Kabbalists see the introduction to M. Meier, ed., "A Critical Edition of the *Sefer Ta'amei ha-Mitzwoth* Attributed to Isaac ibn Farhi" (Ph.D. diss., Brandeis Univer-

sity, 1974), pp. 32–33, and Idel, "The Concept of the Torah," pp. 49–56, and below, app. 3, for another quote from the *Commentary on the Rationales of the Commandments.* The identity between the Torah and the essence of God in quite explicit terms recurs in the late-fifteenth-century *Sefer ha-Meshiv,* cf. the passage printed by Scholem, "The 'Maggid,'" p. 100.

133. On *pereq* as chapter see Shmuel ha-Kohen Weingarten, "The Division of the Bible in Chapters," *Sinai* 42 (1958), pp. 281–293 (Hebrew).

134. Namely the sefirah of Gevurah, which is symbolized by the left hand.

135. *Sefer ha-Malkhut,* ed. J. Toledano (Casablanca, 1930), fol. 93ab. For establishing the authorship of this part of the book see Gottlieb, *Studies,* pp. 251–253.

136. Namely a human limb to a divine limb.

137. Deuteronomy 27:26. I have translated the verse in the literal way in which R. Joseph understood it.

138. Ms. Jerusalem JNUL 8° 3925, fol. 110b. See also Idel, "The Concept of the Torah," p. 65. For an additional analysis of aspects of this passage see below, chap. 10, par. V.

139. See Idel, *Kabbalah: New Perspectives,* pp. 184–190.

140. *Commentary on the Torah,* fol. 51b.

141. Idel, "The Magical and Theurgical Interpretations."

142. See *Sefer ha-Temunah,* fol. 6b, Idel, "The Concept of the Torah," pp. 72–73; Wolfson, *Circle in the Square,* p. 60.

143. *Kelal.*

144. Fol. 20c. See also Idel, "The Concept of the Torah," pp. 74–75. On this Kabbalist see Goetschel, *Meir Ibn Gabbai.*

145. See Idel, "The Concept of the Torah," p. 75,

146. *'Avodat ha-Qodesh,* fol. 36d.

147. Ibid.

148. Mallarmé, *Oeuvres Completes,* p. 378.

149. See Idel, "The Concept of the Torah," pp. 76–83.

150. Compare the theory of Iser, *The Act of Reading,* and chap. 11, beside note 21.

151. On these exegetical methods see below, app. 1.

152. On the hermeneutics of proclamation in the context of a phenomenology of manifestation see Ricoeur, *Figuring the Sacred,* pp. 48–67.

153. See Davies, *Torah,* pp. 91–94.

154. See Franz Dornseiff, *Das Alphabet in Mystik und Magie* (Leipzig and Berlin, 1922), p. 122; and more recently, W. Tucker, "Rebels and Gnostics: Al-Mughira ibn Sa'id and the Mughiriyya," *Arabica* 22 (1975), pp. 33–47; Pierre Lory, "Le Livre comme Corps de Dieu," *Magie du Livre, Livres de Magie, Aries* 15 (1993), pp. 67–69. See also Idel, "The Concept of the Torah," p. 67. For the view that the Qur'an is an organism that possesses limbs see F. Jadaane, *L'influence du stoïcisme sur la pensée musulmane* (Beirut, 1968), p. 170.

155. See Meir bar Ilan, "Magical Seals on the Body according to Jews in the First Centuries," *Tarbiz* 57 (1988), pp. 37–50 (Hebrew).

156. See A. D. Ewing, "Awareness of God," *Philosophy* 40 (1965), pp. 16–17; R. L. Patterson, *A Philosophy of Religion* (Duke University Press, Durham, N.C., 1970), p. 502, John Hick, *An Interpretation of Religion* (Yale University Press, New Haven, 1989).

157. See below, chap. 3, par. I. For more on this issue see Moshe Idel, "Torah: Between Presence and Representation of the Divine in Jewish Mysticism," in *Representation in Religion: Studies in Honor of Moshe Barasch*, ed. Jan Assmann and Albert I. Baumgarten (Brill, Leiden, 2001), pp. 197–236.

158. See Idel, "The Concept of the Torah," pp. 43–45; Wolfson, *Circle in the Square*, p. 56; idem, "The Anthropomorphic Imagery," pp. 147–148, and his more general claim in his *Through a Speculum That Shines*, esp. pp. 375–377.

159. See Idel, "On Talismanic Language," and below, chap. 5, par. V.

160. Cf. Jacques Scherer, *Le "Livre" de Mallarmé* (Gallimard, Paris, 1977), pp. 49–53.

161. See Derrida, *La dissémination*, pp. 245ff, 344–345.

162. See Eco, *Semiotics*, pp. 156–157; Handelman, *Fragments of Redemption*, p. 92.

163. See Blanchot, *The Gaze of Orpheus*, p. 153. For more on this issue see below, chap. 4.

164. See, e.g., Bertrand Marchal, *La religion de Mallarmé* (Jose Corti, Paris, 1988), pp. 482–483. See also below, chap. 3, note 45.

165. See ibid., pp. 445–493.

166. See ibid., p. 444.

167. Ibid., p. 483; cf. *Oeuvres complètes*, p. 375. See also ibid., p. 382, "Le mystère dans les lettres."

168. See above, introduction.

169. Derrida, *La dissémination*, p. 344. I would say that Derrida differs from Mallarmé on a crucial issue discussed here: whereas the poet introduces the category of mystery as very important for understanding a poetic text, Derrida strongly distances himself from such a move.

170. Eco, *Semiotics*, p. 156.

171. Blanchot, *The Gaze of Orpheus*, p. 152; idem, *The Infinite Conversation*, p. 428. See also Regis Debray, "The Book as a Symbolic Object," in *The Future of the Book*, pp. 141–142.

172. *Haqafatam*. This is an example of the influence of astronomical terminology, important for the structure of thought of this book. See also below, chap. 12, par. I.

173. *Sefer ha-Temunah*, fol. 30ab. This text reflects the influence of Nahmanides' introduction to the *Commentary on the Torah*. See Idel, "The Concept of the Torah," pp. 70–71, and the texts translated in par. V above.

174. Ibid., fol. 30b. On the bizarre shape of the letters in the Torah see Kasher, *Torah Shelemah*, vol. 29, pt. 2, pp. 100–136, esp. pp. 120–121; vol. 34, pp. 315–320.

Chapter 3: Text and Interpretation Infinities in Kabbalah

1. See above, chap. 1, note 1.

2. See below, chap. 10, par. III.

3. See below, chap. 9.

4. I would like to stress that for more than one reason Kabbalistic hermeneutics

follows earlier midrashic methods of exegesis: see, e.g., Joseph Dan's essay, "Midrash and the Dawn of Kabbalah," in *Midrash and Literature*. I am interested in concentrating here, however, on nonmidrashic, in my view sometimes even antimidrashic, trends in Kabbalistic hermeneutics without denying the existence of "conservative" Kabbalistic exegesis. For more on these issues see below, chaps. 7–9. On the split between "innovative" Kabbalah and "conservative" Kabbalah, which has in principle rejected the perceptions of Torah described herein, see Idel, "We Have No Kabbalistic Tradition," and below, note 106.

5. Cf. Scholem, "The Name of God."

6. See Idel, *Language, Torah, and Hermeneutics*; idem, "Reification of Language"; idem, *Golem*; idem, "A la recherche."

7. The single significant exception known to me is R. Yehudah ben Moses Romano, an early-fourteenth-century Italian writer whose doctrine was the subject of a series of studies by the late Prof. Joseph B. Sermoneta. See especially his important study " 'Thine Ointments Have a Goodly Fragrance': Rabbi Judah Romano and the Open Text Method," in M. Idel, Zeev W. Harvey, E. Schweid, and Shlomo Pines, eds., *Jubilee Volume on the Occasion of His Eightieth Birthday* (Jerusalem, 1990), 2:77–113 (Hebrew), and Caterina Rigo, "Human Substance and Eternal Life in the Philosophy of Rabbi Yehudah Romano," in Aviezer Ravitzky, ed., *Joseph Baruch Sermoneta Memorial Volume* (Jerusalem, 1998), pp. 181–222 (Hebrew). Compare, however, Dan, *On Sanctity*, pp. 121–122.

8. See Idel, "The Concept of the Torah," pp. 35–37, and below, chap. 6.

9. See above, chap. 2.

10. See, e.g., Scholem, *Kabbalah*, p. 88; idem, *Origins of the Kabbalah*, pp. 130–131, 265–289, 431–444; idem, *The Mystical Shape*, p. 38; Tishby, *The Wisdom of the Zohar*, 1:237.

11. A detailed study of the different interpretations of this term and its history in the Kabbalistic literature is a desideratum. Especially important from my point of view are several texts of R. Isaac of Acre, where the contemplation of the infinite and the cleaving to it are described as possible.

12. See, e.g., Idel, "The Sefirot above the Sefirot"; idem, "The Image of Man"; idem, "Jewish Kabbalah and Platonism in the Middle Ages and Renaissance," in Lenn E. Goodman, ed., *Neoplatonism and Jewish Thought* (SUNY Press, Albany, 1993), pp. 338–344; Elliot Wolfson, "Negative Theology and Positive Assertion in the Early Kabbalah," *Daat*, 32–33 (1994), pp. v–xxii. See also below, note 106; above, Introduction, par. V; and below, Concluding Remarks, par. V.

13. See chap. 2, par. III.

14. See Derrida, *Glas*. See also Caputo, *The Prayers and Tears of Derrida*, pp. 244–245. On the problem of the infinite and finite aspects in a work of art see also Eco, *The Open Work*, pp. 10, 21; Weinsheimer, *Gadamer's Hermeneutics*, pp. 252–253; and below, note 44. The following discussions, which engage texts dealing with the infinity of the Torah, reflect, in my opinion, the positive understandings of the infinite on the ontological level, in the sense that it is translated within the sacred book and interpretation. On

the issue of Hegel's understanding of Judaism and Jews, and its relation to Derrida see Caputo, *The Prayers and Tears*, pp. 234–243; Terence R. Wright, "'Behind the Curtain': Derrida and the Religious Imagination," in John C. Hawley, ed., *Through a Glass Darkly: Essays in the Religious Imagination* (Fordham University Press, New York, 1996), pp. 279–280. See also below, note 95, and Concluding Remarks, par. IV.

15. Cf. Scholem, *On the Kabbalah*, pp. 12–13, 50; idem, *On Jews and Judaism*, pp. 268–269. The rise of the notion that Torah has an infinite number of significances is a major development in Kabbalistic thought characteristic of the last third of the thirteenth century. See Idel, "We Have No Kabbalistic Tradition," p. 71.

16. On this issue see the important discussion in Scholem, *On the Kabbalah*, pp. 50–63, whose remarks deal in general with other facets of the subject. See also Handelman, *Fragments of Redemption*, pp. 87, 89–90.

17. See *The Book of Belief and Faith*, chap. 5. Cf. the edition of C. D. Chavel, *The Works of Nahmanides* (Mossad Harav Kook, Jerusalem, 1964), 2:370. On the issue of vocalization of the divine name and the requirement of *kavannah* in prayer in the circle from which R. Jacob emerged see Idel, "On R. Isaac Sagi Nahor," pp. 31–36. Compare R. Jacob's view in another Kabbalistic treatise, *The Book of Correct Answers*, ed. Georges Vajda (Israel National Academy of Sciences, Jerusalem, 1968), p. 107: "The scroll of the Torah may not be vocalized, in order to [enable us to] interpret each and every word according to every significance we can read [i.e., we can apply a certain vocalization to the words]." For additional material on the nonvocalized manner of writing the Torah scroll see Kasher, *Torah Shelemah*, 19:376. One of the Kabbalists who were quite interested in the implications of the nonvocalized text of the Bible, in the vein of the above passages, was R. Joseph of Hamadan. See, e.g., *Sefer Toledot 'Adam*, printed in *Sefer ha-Malkhut*, ed. J. Toledano (Casablanca, 1930), fol. 68c, found also in Ms. Paris BN 841, fols. 198b, 242b; Ms. Jerusalem, JUNL 8° 544, fol. 53a; etc. See also his Castilian contemporary R. Shema'yah ben Isaac ha-Levi, *Sefer Tzeror Hayyim*, Ms. Leiden-Warner 24, fol. 195b.

18. The very mention of innovation in connection with this view, which will generate an important aspect of the infinite Torah, is highly significant and constitutes a decisive departure from the previous conservative Kabbalistic view; see Idel, "We Have No Kabbalistic Tradition," p. 68, note 58.

19. This text is printed by Gershom Scholem, "The Authentic Commentary on *Sefer Yetzirah* of Nahmanides," QS 6 (1930), p. 414. On the infinite Torah in another passage of this text see below, note 28. This passage was copied by the important mid-sixteenth-century Halakhist and Kabbalist R. David ibn Avi Zimra, in his *Responsa*, vol. 2, no. 643, fol. 43c; Faur, *Golden Doves*, pp. 136–137, dealt with this text as if it were part of what he called the tradition of *ley mental*, related in this context to a philosophical stand without reference to its precise Kabbalistic sources. Also Blanchot's passage quoted there, p. 137, has Kabbalistic sources. See above, chap. 2, note 40.

20. Scholem, "Authentic Commentary," p. 414. Scholem's attribution of this text to Nahmanides was rightly questioned by Gottlieb, *Studies*, pp. 128–131, who brings impor-

tant evidence to prove the authorship of this short treatise. Notwithstanding this proof, the question of its authorship is still open, and the affinities between this text and those of R. Joseph of Hamadan are equally relevant, as are those between the anonymous text and Gikatilla's views.

21. *Beurei ha-Moreh* (Venice, 1574), fol. 20cd. See also, below, another passage illustrating this Kabbalist's dealing with vocalization. Compare also the issue of limitation of infinite meanings in Ricoeur, *The Conflicts of Interpretation*, p. 14.

22. *Commentary on the Pentateuch*, on Numbers 11:15, ed. C. D. Chavel, 3:62. Compare also the interpretations on Genesis 18:3 and Deuteronomy 7:2. This passage was quoted in R. Hayyim Joseph David Azulai, *Devash le-Fi*, fol. 40d. The term translated as "spark" is the Hebrew *nitzotzot*, which was used in contemporary Kabbalistic literature to refer to parcels of human soul; cf. the thirteenth-century text printed by Scholem in *Tarbiz* 16 (1965), p. 143 (Hebrew). Is there any affinity between the view that each word contains numerous sparks—i.e., meanings—and the view of the soul as containing several sparks? On the spark as a metaphor for the soul in its deepest aspect see Michel Tardieu's study in *Revue des Etudes Augustiniennes* 21 (1975), pp. 225–255; regarding Jewish discussions of this metaphor see Louis Jacobs, "The Doctrine of the 'Divine Spark' in Man in Jewish Sources," in *Rationalism, Judaism, Universalism: In Memory of Leon Roth* (New York, 1966), pp. 87–144. Interestingly enough, the vowels that fix the specific meaning of a given combination of consonants are described as their souls in a Kabbalistic passage dealing with vocalizations and meaning; see above, the text referred to in note 19; Idel, "R. Joseph of Hamadan's Commentary on Ten Sefirot," pp. 76–77. For the emphasis on the possibility of vocalizing the consonants of the scroll of the Torah in order to extract the desired homily see R. Moses Hayyim Ephrayyim of Sudylkov, *Degel Mahaneh 'Efrayyim*, p. 85. See also ibid., p. 96.

23. R. Menahem Recanati, *Commentary on the Torah* (Jerusalem, 1961), fol. 40b. See also Idel, *R. Menahem Recanati, the Kabbalist*, vol. 2 (forthcoming).

24. See Chaim Wirszubski, *Flavius Mithridates: Sermo de Passione Domini* (Magnes Press, Jerusalem, 1963), p. 61; Conclusio 70: "Per modum legendi sine puncti in lege, et modus scribendi res divinas . . . nobis ostenditur." On this thesis see also the comments of Wirszubski, *Pico della Mirandola*, pp. 181–182. En passant, Pico could have been acquainted also with the passage of R. Bahya ben Asher. See Wirszubski, ibid., pp. 262–263. For another plausible impact of this Kabbalist on modern hermeneutics see below, chap. 4, par. IV.

25. See Iser, *The Act of Reading*, pp. 163–179, Barthes, "From Work to Text," in *Textual Strategies*, pp. 74–75, 80; idem, *Le plaisir du texte* (Seuil, Paris, 1973), p. 82; See also Eco, *The Open Work*, p. 102–103, on the "field of possibilities." I am not sure that one may find in the classical midrashic literature an example of an explicit formulation of infinity of meaning, as assumed by Banon, *La lecture infinie*, pp. 137, 155, although a late midrash, *Bereshit Rabbati*, allows such a possibility. For the concept of divine infinity and infinite names, but not of infinity of meanings of the Torah, see R. Yehudah Barceloni, *Commentary on Sefer Yetzirah*, p. 128.

26. Cf. *Book of the Pomegranate*, Moses de Leon's *Sefer ha-Rimmon*, ed. E. R. Wolfson (Scholars Press, 1988), p. 326. See also R. Shem Tov ben Shem Tov, *Sefer ha-'Emunot* (Ferrara, 1556), fol. 105a. On other identifications of Torah with the sefirah Hokhmah (Wisdom) without paying attention, however, to the notion of infinity in this context, see Scholem, *On the Kabbalah*, pp. 41–42. and above, chap. 1, note 17.

27. Psalm 119:96. This verse is the classic *locus probans* for discussions of an infinite Torah. Compare Gikatilla's text printed in Gottlieb, *Studies*, p. 153.

28. Printed in Scholem, "Commentary on *Sefer Yetzirah*," p. 410. For a more philosophical formulation of the principle that the infinity of the author determines the infinity of the text see the rather unknown R. Zerahya's *Commentary on the Pentateuch*, Ms. Paris, Rabbinical Seminary 146, fol. 92a.

29. Compare the view quoted by de Lubac, "Mens divina liber grandis est," in *Exégèse medieval*, vol. 1, pt. 1, p. 326; and Annemarie Schimmel, "Sufism and the Islamic Tradition," in *Mysticism and Religious Traditions*, ed. S. T. Katz (Oxford University Press, Oxford, 1983), pp. 130–31. See also R. Moses Cordovero, *Shi'ur Qomah*, fol. 13b: "and the Torah is in the Wisdom, which is the wisdom of God, and as this Wisdom is infinite, so is our Torah infinite." See also Gikatilla's passage quoted below and R. Pinhas of Koretz's view, adduced by Scholem, *On the Kabbalah*, pp. 76–77.

30. *The Book of the Tradition of the Covenant*, ed. Gershom Scholem. in *Qovetz 'al Yad: Minora Manuscripta Hebraica*, n.s. 1, no. 11 (1936), p. 35 (Hebrew). On this work and its author see Gerhard G. Scholem, "David ben Abraham ha-labhan—ein unbekannter jüdischer Mystiker," *Occident and Orient . . . Gaster Anniversary Volume*, ed. B. Schindler and A. Marmorstein (Taylor's Foreign Press, London, 1936), pp. 505–508. See also R. Shem Tov ben Shem Tov, *Sefer ha-'Emunot*, fol. 105a, and the passage from *Sefer Ge'ulat Israel*, translated and discussed below, chap. 12; and R. Yehudah Leib of Yanov, *Qol Yehudah*, fol. 25a.

31. See Scholem, "Name of God," p. 189, n. 74; Eco, *The Limits of Interpretation*, pp. 51–52. The Kabbalistic view of the infinite potentialities of the Torah is significantly different from the midrashic assertion that there are seventy facets of the Torah. On the seventy facets see Wilhelm Bacher, "Seventy-two Modes of Expositions," *JQR* 4 (1892), p. 509; Kasher, *Torah Shelemah* 34, pp. 64–66; Scholem, *On the Kabbalah*, pp. 62–63; Idel, "Kabbalistic Materials," p. 199. The figure "seventy" stands for the totality of the aspects of a certain limited phenomenon, as we discover by comparing closely related phrases: "seventy facets," "seventy languages," "seventy nations," "seventy angels," etc. Though pointing to a comprehensive conception of the meanings inherent in the biblical text, the phrase "seventy facets" did not even hint at an infinity of significances. See also below, app. 4. For an interesting attempt to interpret the seventy facets as pointing to an infinity of meanings see the early-sixteenth-century R. Joseph Al-Ashqar's *Tzafnat Pa'aneah*, fol. 15a.

32. Although hardly any of Abulafia's combinatory techniques was his own innovation and he explicitly refers to the earlier books in which they were introduced, he seems to

be the first Kabbalist in Spain to present them as exegetical methods rather than mere sporadic ad hoc usages. See above, chaps. 9 and 11.

33. "In the beginning."

34. Cf. R. Isaiah Horowitz, Ha-Shelah, vol. 2, fol. 98ab: "you shall know and understand that even one letter has infinite permutations . . . man can comprehend that this thing [i.e., combinatory practices] has no end, and all this is because the Torah is the reflection of the Godhead which is infinite." See also ibid., vol. 3, fol. 87a, and the next footnote.

35. The Gate of Vowels, printed in 'Arzei ha-Levanon (Venice, 1601), fols. 39b–40a (Hebrew). On this text see also below, chap. 9, par. V. Cf. also R. Moses Cordovero's view in Pardes Rimmonim, introduction to Gate XXX (to be adduced below, chap. 9, par. V), and Gate VIII, chap. 4. Compare also to R. Abraham bar Hiyya's view that "every letter and every word in every section of the Torah has a deep root in wisdom and contains a mystery from among mysteries of [divine] understanding, the depths of which one cannot penetrate. God grant that we may know some little of his abundance." Cf. Scholem, On the Kabbalah, p. 63, and below, beside note 82, and app. 2. The impenetrability of the topics is the reason that I accept Scholem's approach to this text as dealing with mysteries rather than secrets. On "depth" and understanding of the Torah see below, chap. 7, note 24. Compare this view of contemplating the structure of the Torah by means of understanding the infinity of permutations to the contemplation of the fixed structure of the scroll of the Torah in theosophical Kabbalah, as discussed above, chap. 2.

36. See Idel, Language, Torah and Hermeneutics, pp. 97–101, and idem, Hasidism: Between Ecstasy and Magic, pp. 56–58, as well as below, chap. 12, par. VIII.

37. No wonder that Abulafia's exegetical methods were sharply criticized by a representative of the rabbinic authority, R. Shelomo ben Abraham ibn Adret. Abulafia, as ibn Adret remarked, interpreted in his peculiar way not only the Bible but also nonbiblical texts such as Maimonides' Guide of the Perplexed; see Idel, "Abulafia's Secrets of the Guide."

38. See below, chap. 12.

39. Cf. above, note 36.

40. Cf. Abulafia's recurrent motif of unknotting the knots of the soul as part of the mystical progress; see Idel, The Mystical Experience, pp. 134–137.

41. Abulafia uses the term galgal (circle or sphere) to refer to "path": nativ, i.e., way of interpretation. He starts with the smallest sphere and progresses toward the largest one. Compare Gregorius' interpretation of Ezekiel's 'ofan as referring to exegetical method, hinted at in de Lubac, L'écriture dans la tradition, p. 276. On galgal in Abulafia see also above, chap. 1, par. VII.

42. This is an interesting parallel to Origen's view: "extenditur anima nostra, quae prius fuerat contracta, ut possit capax esse sapientia Dei" (We enlarge our soul, which was previously contracted, in order to be capable of receiving the wisdom of God). See

Patrologia Latina, vol. 25, fol. 627c; de Lubac, L'écriture dans la tradition, p. 285; Eco, Semiotics, p. 150.

43. See Idel, "On the History," pp. 17–18, and below, chap. 9, note 86, and chap. 11, pars. V–VI.

44. Derrida, Dissemination, p. 344. Abulafia's text, discussed in detail in my study referred to in note 43 and below, chap. 9, par. VII, reached Derrida through the French version of Scholem's Major Trends: see Les grands courants de la mystique juive, trans. M. M. Davy (Payot, Paris, 1950), p. 390, n. 50, for the same verbatim statement as made by Derrida. See also Steiner, After Babel, pp. 60–61. For more on Derrida and Kabbalah see below, chap. 4, pars. IV–V, and Concluding Remarks, par. III.

45. See The Open Work, pp. 1–23. See also above, note 25. An intriguing and important subject is the probable influence, briefly discussed here, of Kabbalistic theories on the peculiar structure of Mallarmé's Le Livre. Mallarmé seems to be aware of Kabbalistic issues: see Thomas A. Williams, Mallarmé and the Language of Mysticism (University of Georgia Press, Athens, 1970), pp. 55–56. See above, chap. 2, notes 160, 164–167.

46. See Pico della Mirandola, Apologia, in Opera Omnia (1557), p. 180. On this text see Moshe Idel, "Ramon Lull and Ecstatic Kabbalah," Journal of the Warburg and Courtauld Institutes 51 (1988), pp. 170–174.

47. See Wirszubski, Pico della Mirandola, pp. 196–199.

48. See below, chap. 4, note 41. See also R. Joseph Ergas, Shomer 'Emunim, p. 16.

49. In Hebrew le-ma'alah u-lematah: compare Reuchlin's text referred to in note 38 above. See also above, chap. 1, note 45.

50. Jeremy 23:29; cf. BT, Sabbath, fol. 88b. See also below, note 80, and chap. 6, note 141.

51. In Hebrew gavvan commonly means "nuances" and "colors" but also "appearance," "example," and "form." See also below, note 81.

52. A similar anonymous passage, possibly by Gikatilla, is extant in two manuscripts: Ms. Paris BN 839, fol. 4ab, and Ms. Jerusalem, JNUL 8°, 488. fol. 45b; see also Swedenborg's passage analyzed in chap. 12 below. See also above, chap. 1, par. VII, the passage from R. Joseph Shlomo Rofe' of Candia, and also his view in Matzref le-Hokhmah, chap. 10, fol. 28b. See also R. Dov Baer of Mezeritch, Maggid Devarav le-Ya'aqov, pp. 234–235.

53. There may be an echo here of the Proclean view that everything receives the qualities of the world in which it exists.

54. Printed in Gottlieb, Studies, p. 154. See also Scholem, "Name of God," pp. 179–180. See also Liebes, "Zohar and Eros," p. 86, note 120. See also above, beside note 22, an additional text of Gikatilla's and below, chap. 12, for the theory of Neoplatonic accommodation.

55. On the nature of Kabbalistic symbols see Scholem, Major Trends, pp. 27–28; Tishby, Paths of Faith and Heresy, pp. 11–22; and our discussion below, chap. 10.

56. Although most Kabbalists share the symbolistic perception of Godhead and reality, this perception was not (as some scholars have maintained) universally accepted, as is evidenced, for example, by Abulafia's Kabbalah. See below, chap. 10.

57. In contrast to Abulafia's view of the Torah as allegorically referring to the processes within human consciousness, cf. chap. 11 below.

58. See Scholem, *Major Trends*, pp. 13–14.

59. On Zoharic symbolism in particular see Tishby, *The Wisdom of the Zohar*, 1:283–302. and Daniel C. Matt, *Zohar: The Book of Enlightenment* (Paulist Press, New York, 1983), pp. 32–38, and below, chap. 10.

60. Compare Barthes's description of "mot poetique," in *Le degré zero*, pp. 43–45.

61. See above, note 7.

62. See R. Hayyim Vital, *'Etz Hayyim*, I,I,5, fol. 15a.

63. Eco, *The Open World*, p. 13.

64. See texts printed and discussed in Idel, "The Image of Man," pp. 41–42, 51–52, and, apparently under the influence of these passages, in the fourteenth-century *Sefer ha-Temunah*, fol. 66a. See also above, Gikatilla's passage from *Sefer Sha'arei Tzedeq*, and above, chap. 2. On the theory of various worlds see Gershom Scholem, "The Development of the Theory of Worlds in Early Kabbalah," *Tarbiz* 3 (1932), pp. 59–63 (Hebrew). For more on this issue see below, app. 3.

65. *'Etz Hayyim*, I,I,3, fol. 13b. On infinite worlds see the early-fifteenth-century Jewish philosopher R. Hasdai Crescas, cf. Warren Zev Harvey, *Physics and Metaphysics in Hasdai Crescas* (Amsterdam Studies in Jewish Thought, 6, J. C. Gieben, Amsterdam, 1998), pp. 8–13.

66. *Sha'arei Qedushah*, pp. 102–103.

67. Job 11:9. For the use of this verse in order to aggrandize the Torah, which is not mentioned in the verse, see the text of the treatise *'Avot*, quoted and discussed in app. 2. below. Compare the inverse contention of Nietzsche, *The Gay Science*, par. 374, that the emergence of infinite interpretations may by a conduit to the world become infinite.

68. R. Jacob Hayyim Tzemah of Jerusalem, *Sefer Meqor Hayyim*, Ms. New York, JTS 2205, fol. 16b. On this Kabbalist see Gershom Scholem, "On the History of the Kabbalist R. Jacob Hayyim Zemah and His Literary Activity," *QS* 26 (1950), pp. 185–194, and 27 (1951), pp. 197–110 (Hebrew). For another discussion on R. Meir and biblical exegesis see below, app. 5. For more on the peculiar form of understanding the Torah granted to each person see below, app. 4, the discussion related to R. Hayyim Joseph David Azulai.

69. On this issue see Benin, *The Footprints of God*, pp. 169–176; idem, "The Mutability," and in Cordovero, cf. Joseph ben Shlomo, *The Mystical Theology of Moses Cordovero* (Bialik Institute, Jerusalem, 1965), pp. 42–43 (Hebrew); Sack, *Be-Sha'arei ha-Kabbalah*, p. 288.

70. See Idel, "Differing Conceptions of Kabbalah," pp. 197–198. On the impact of Kabbalah on Bruno see Karen Silva de Leon-Jones, *Giordano Bruno and the Kabbalah: Prophets, Magicians, and Rabbis* (Yale University Press, New Haven, 1997).

71. *Yiqonin*. See also Handelman, *The Slayers of Moses*, p. 61; Lorberbaum, *Imago Dei*, pp. 49–50, 167–177.

72. The first form is plural, while the second is singular, as in the Bible.

73. *Lefi koho.* This accommodationalist view had many repercussions which cannot be discussed here. See, e.g., R. Qalonimus Qalman Epstein, *Ma'or va-Shemesh,* 1:256.

74. On *Exodus,* par. 286, p. 172. On the portrayal of God as having many faces see also below, chap. 10, par. VI. On the different faces and the revelation of the Torah see also below, app. 4, and Hirshman, *A Rivalry of Genius,* pp. 90–93. On the idea that each of the embryos received the Sinaitic revelation and has seen the divine glory according to its capacity see *Zohar,* vol. 2, fol. 94a; Holdrege, *Veda and Torah,* p. 324. See also the important collection of texts in Heschel, *Theology of Ancient Judaism,* 2:267–271, and R. Moses Hayyim Luzzatto, *Tiqqunim Hadashim,* p. 7.

75. See Nahmanides's sermon "The Torah of God Is Perfect," *Nahmanides' Writings,* 1:162; R. Bahya ben Asher, *Commentary on Genesis* 46:27, 1:363; Alqabetz, *Sefer 'Ayelet 'Ahavim,* fol. 43a; Cordovero, *Derishot,* p. 70; Scholem, *On the Kabbalah,* pp. 13, 65; idem, *On Jews and Judaism,* pp. 269–270; idem, *The Messianic Idea,* pp. 295–303; Heschel, *Theology of Ancient Judaism,* pp. 259–261. Especially important for the development of the Safedian views on this topic is the existence of a quote from a lost treatise, cited from an "old manuscript" in R. Abraham Azulai, *Hesed le-'Avraham,* fol. 11b, where the nexus between the letters of the Torah and the number of Israelite souls is explicitly mentioned.

76. On this Kabbalist and his book see Yehuda Liebes, "To the Image, Writings and the Kabbalah of the Author of 'Emeq ha-Melekh," *JSJT* 11 (1993), pp. 101–137 (Hebrew).

77. *'Emeq ha-Melekh,* fol. 41d. See also R. Abraham Azulai, *Hesed le-'Avraham,* fol. 11ab; R. Ze'ev Wolf of Zhitomir, *'Or ha-Me'ir,* fol. 4a. On the duty to commit to writing the exegetical innovation one gains see the medieval texts adduced by Silman, *The Voice of the Torah,* pp. 136–137.

78. BT, *Menahot,* fol. 49a.

79. However, in another discussion, *'Emeq ha-Melekh,* fol. 42a, Moses is said to have comprised all six hundred thousand interpretations.

80. Jeremiah 29:23. See also above, note 50. On Torah as fire see Heschel, *Theology of Ancient Judaism,* 2:22–23, and Sack, *Be-Sha'arei ha-Kabbalah,* pp. 174–175, and note 131.

81. *Gavvan.* This term may also mean "color." See also above, note 50.

82. *Qelah Pithei Hokhmah* (Maqor, Jerusalem, 1961), fol. 2a. On the infinity of the individual letters see also above, note 35, and chap. 4, note 80.

83. See Moshe Hallamish, "On the Origin of a Dictum in the Kabbalistic Literature, 'Whoever Blows, Does So from His Inner Essence' " *Bar Ilan Annual* 13 (1976), pp. 211–223 (Hebrew).

84. See Vital's *Sha'ar ha-Gilgulim,* par. XVII. For more on pardes exegesis see below, app. 1.

85. *'Emeq ha-Melekh,* fol. 42a. Compare also an earlier Kabbalistic source, as represented by R. Abraham Azulai, *Hesed le-'Avraham,* fol. 11ab.

86. Ibid., fol. 42a. Scholem, *On the Kabbalah,* p. 65. note 1. Compare also the view of R. Hayyim Vital, *'Etz ha-Da'at Tov* (Jerusalem, 1982), vol. 2, fol. 91a, discussed in Idel, *Kabbalah: New Perspectives,* p. 241, and Vital's *Sha'ar Ruah ha-Qodesh,* introduction; R. Jacob Hayyim Tzemah, *Sefer Tiferet 'Adam,* pp. 177–178, 182–183; R. Isaiah Horo-

witz, *Ha-Shelah*, vol. 2, fol. 98ab, vol. 3, fol. 10a, etc.; R. Pinhas of Koretz, *Midrash Pinhas*, fol. 24a; R. Qalonimus Qalman Epstein, *Ma'or va-Shemesh*, 1:256. See also the view of R. Yehudah Arieh Leib of Gur, *Sefat 'Emmet*, vol. 3, fol. 85d, where the power of the Torah, which is implanted in the soul, enables one to innovate.

87. I owe this term for hermeneutics to Jean-Luc Nancy; see his "Sharing Voices," in G. L. Ormiston and A. D. Schrift, *Transforming the Hermeneutical Context: From Nietzsche to Nancy* (SUNY Press, Albany, 1991), p. 245.

88. See *'Emeq ha-Melekh*, fol. 42a. See also the very interesting development in R. Aharon of Zhitomir, *Toledot 'Aharon*, vol. 1, fol. 34b, where the assumption is that each of the Torah letters contains all the others, just as each soul of the Israelites contains all the others.

89. This seems to be another version of the identity found more explicitly in later sources between God—represented here by the roots of the souls, *'orayyta'*, namely Torah—and Israel. See also above, introduction, note 49. and below, beside note 95.

90. See Buber, *The Origin and Meaning of Hasidism*, p. 121, and the many myths described by Bruce Lincoln, *Myth, Cosmos and Society* (Harvard University Press, Cambridge, Mass., 1986).

91. *Sha'ar ha-Gilgulim*, par. XVI, p. 127.

92. See *Sha'ar ha-Gilgulim*, par. XVII, p. 129.

93. The Hebrew phrase is *Me-hamat ha-devequt shelkha*.

94. *Sefer Berit Abram*, by R. Joseph Moses of Zbarov (Brod, 1875), fol. 126d. Compare also R. Abraham of Turisck, *Magen 'Abraham*, part 3, fol. 26a; part 4 fol. 77c. See also Idel, *Kabbalah: New Perspectives*, pp. 245–246; idem, "Universalization and Integration: Two Conceptions of Mystical Union in Jewish Mysticism," in M. Idel and B. McGinn, eds., *Mystical Union and Monotheistic Faith: An Ecumenical Dialogue* (New York, London, 1989) p. 45.

95. See above, note 89. Compare, however, Scholem's view in *On Jews and Judaism*, p. 268, and see Handelman, *Fragments of Redemption*, p. 90. I would like to point out the positive aspects of all the factors involved in the experience. The Hasidic mystic does not meet the *Urgrund* or the divine darkness but a speaking divinity with which he can cleave.

96. Compare also the view of R. Menahem Mendel of Rimanov as presented by Scholem, *On the Kabbalah*, pp. 30–31.

97. For an elaborate description of the corpus of writings belonging to the *Zohar* see Scholem, *Major Trends*, pp. 156–243; Tishby, *The Wisdom of the Zohar*; Charles Mopsik, "Le corpus Zoharique, ses titres et ses amplifications," in Michel Tardieu, ed., *La formation des canons scriptuaires* (Le Cerf, Paris, 1993), pp. 75–105; and the innovative treatments of the composition of the *Zohar* by Liebes, *Studies in the Zohar*, pp. 85–138. On canonization see Huss, "*Sefer ha-Zohar*."

98. R. Hayyim Vital, *'Etz Hayyim*, I, I, 5, fol. 15a; quoted with few slight changes in R. Eliezer Tzevi Safrin of Komarno's preface to his father's comprehensive commentary on the *Zohar* named *Zohar Hai* (Lemberg, rpt. Israel, 1971), vol. 1, fol. 1b. Vital was

deeply interested in astronomy and even composed astronomical and astrological treatises; see his *Sefer ha-Tekhunah* (Jerusalem, 1866) and Bernard Goldstein, "The Hebrew Astronomical Tradition: New Sources," *Isis* 72 (1981), pp. 245, 248. On the daily renewal of the Torah see R. Isaac Aizik Haver, *'Or Torah*, in *'Amudei ha-Torah*, pp. 26–27.

99. *Zohar Hai*, vol. 1, fol. 3a.

100. Quoted in R. Moses Hayyim Ephrayyim of Sudylkov, *Degel Mahaneh 'Efrayyim*, p. 98; See above, chap. 1, par. VIII.

101. *Zohar Hai*, vol. 1, unnumbered, first folio. The title of the collection of Zoharic material printed at the end of the sixteenth century under the name *Zohar Hadash*—the new Zohar—may have influenced the emergence of the new interpretations of the Zohar as formulated by R. Isaac Yehudah Safrin. See also the tradition adduced in the name of R. Israel of Ryzhin, in Yiddish, that "the holy book of Zohar is studied in heaven each day according to another *peshat*." Cf. *Tiferet Israel* (Jerusalem, 1945), fol. 16a.

102. Abraham Stahl, "Ritual Reading of the Zohar," *Pe'amim* 5 (1980), pp. 77–86 (Hebrew); Harvey Goldberg, "The Zohar in Southern Morocco: A Study in Ethnography of Texts," *History of Religion* 29 (1990), pp. 249–251.

103. Compare, however, Scholem's claims that "the last and most radical step in the development of this principle of the infinite meanings of the Torah was taken by the Palestinian school of Kabbalists who flourished in sixteenth-century Safed." *On the Kabbalah*, pp. 64–65.

104. See Eco, *The Limits of Interpretation*, pp. 51, 57–62.

105. See Michael A. Sells, *Mystical Languages of the Unsaying* (University of Chicago Press, Chicago, 1994). On the other side see Idel, *Kabbalah: New Perspectives*, pp. xii–xiii; idem, "Reification of Language," p. 55; and Shira Wolosky, *Language and Mysticism: The Negative Way of Language in Eliot, Beckett, and Celan* (Stanford University Press, Stanford, 1995), especially pp. 228, 235–238, 260–261, 268–271.

106. Gershom Scholem asserted, "The Kabbalists do not start from the idea of communicable meaning." *On the Kabbalah*, p. 36, and the third of his ten nonhistorical theses on Kabbalah. This hypothesis has never been proven but was accepted and repeated recently by Dan, *On Sanctity*, pp. 43–58, esp. p. 58, where he adheres to the assumption of a signifier without a signified. I did not find in his exposition any addition to Scholem's hypothesis, nor a clear recognition that Scholem is the primary source of his view. Compare also my *Kabbalah: New Perspectives*, pp. 200–218, where I offered arguments against the vision of Kabbalistic symbols based on too strong a negative theological understanding of Kabbalistic theosophy, a stand influenced by Christian scholarship. See also above, note 12, and below, chaps. 10 and 12.

107. See M. Idel, "On Mobility, Individuals and Groups: Prolegomenon for a Sociological Approach to Sixteenth-Century Kabbalah," *Kabbalah* 3 (1998), pp. 145–173.

108. See notes 7, 35, above.

109. See Bori, *L'interpretazione infinita*; Rider, "Receiving Orpheus," p. 354; Talmage, "Apples of Gold," p. 319; and above, note 29.

110. See Dan, *On Sanctity*, pp. 87–130, esp. p. 122. Influenced by Scholem, Dan overemphasized the importance of the sanctity of language—a factor that is relevant for one period of Jewish mysticism—but he was not acquainted with any of the Christian material mentioned in the studies referred to in notes 42, 105, and 109, above, nor with the nonlinguistic Kabbalistic explanations of the infinity of the text discussed here. His opinion is based on a very limited number of texts and amount of scholarship. See also below, the end of this chapter.

111. See Idel, "A la recherche," pp. 415–422.

112. For more on experimental encounters with the Torah see below, chap. 6.

113. See Wirszubski, *Pico della Mirandola*.

114. See Idel, "We Have No Kabbalistic Tradition," pp. 71–73, and below, chap. 9, par. V, and app. 1.

115. See below, chap. 10, pars. IV–V.

116. See Idel, *Messianic Mystics*, pp. 274–275.

117. See Bori, *L'interpretazione infinita*.

118. Cf. note 94. above.

119. See note 110, above.

120. Book XII, 31. On this text and its impact on Ricoeur see the introduction to Patrick J. Gallacher and Helen Damico, eds., *Hermeneutics and Medieval Culture* (SUNY Press, Albany, 1989), pp. 1–2. See also Irvine, *The Making of the Textual Culture*, pp. 269–270.

121. Irvine, *The Making of the Textual Culture*, p. 271.

122. On pardes see below, app. 1. Compare also the view expressed by R. Gedalyah of Lunitz, *Teshu'ot Hen*, p. 93, about the reception of interpretations by each soul at Sinai, from the pardes!

123. Exodus 19:19. This verse became one of the proof texts for the claim of a continuous and evolving revelation. See, e.g., the texts adduced by Heschel, *Theology of Ancient Judaism*, 2:255–256. For one of the many Kabbalistic elaborations on this verse see R. Meir ibn Gabbai, 'Avodat ha-Qodesh, fol. 86a; cf. Scholem, *The Messianic Idea*, pp. 298–300; *Ha-Shelah*, vol. 1, fols. 39b–40a. For such an example in Hasidism see Schatz-Uffenheimer, *Hasidism as Mysticism*, pp. 130–131. See also below, the end of the Concluding Remarks.

124. 'Or ha-Me'ir, fol. 182b. Compare also ibid., fols. 4a, 202b.

125. Irvine, *The Making of the Textual Culture*, p. 266.

126. See also below, chap. 13, par. VI.

127. I took the term "fugitive truth" from Clifford Geertz, *Local Knowledge* (Basic Books, New York 1985), and see also Wlad Godzich, *The Culture of Literacy* (Harvard University Press, Cambridge, Mass., 1994), pp. 265–266.

128. *Midrash Pinhas*, fol. 23b.

129. Ibid.

CHAPTER 4: THE BOOK THAT CONTAINS AND MAINTAINS ALL

1. Cf. Ricoeur, *From Text to Action*, pp. 144–166, and below, chap. 13, par. V.

2. See Davies, *Torah*; Scholem, *The Messianic Idea*, pp. 55–56.

3. See Scholem, *On the Kabbalah*, pp. 66–71; idem, *The Messianic Idea*, pp. 75ff, 111–112, 163–164; Tishby, *The Wisdom of the Zohar*, 3:1101–1112; Gottlieb, *Studies*, pp. 545–550. On these concepts of Torah in Sabbateanism see Scholem, *Sabbatai Sevi*, pp. 322–323; Liebes, *Sod ha-'Emunah*, pp. 12, 15, 85, 96, 100, 164, 278–288. See more below, chap. 12, par. I.

4. Scholem, *On the Kabbalah*, p. 83.

5. See above, chaps. 2–3. For various visions of the book as a symbol in medieval Christian literature in Europe see the learned chapter of Ernst R. Curtius, *European Literature in the Latin Middle Ages*, trans. Williard R. Track, Bollingen Series, no. 36 (Princeton University Press, Princeton, 1990), pp. 302–347, which does not address, however, many of the issues presented below. For views of the book among Ashkenazi Jews in the Middle Ages see the collection of articles by C. Sirat, M. Dukan, C. Heymann, C. L. Wilke, and M. Zardoune, *La conception du livre chez les pietistes ashkenazes* (Droz, Geneva, 1996).

6. See Weiss-Ha-Livni, *Midrash*, p. 16, and above, chap. 3.

7. See *Midrash Devarim Rabba'*, VIII:6, ed. S. Liebermann (Wahrmann Books, Jerusalem, 1978), pp. 118–119.

8. See Ricoeur, *Hermeneutics and the Human Sciences*, pp. 146–147. See also below, app. 2. The single instance with which I am acquainted where Ricoeur addressed the referential value of sacred scripture as pointing to God is a rather short and far from clear statement in *Figuring the Sacred*, p. 221.

9. In the following, the distinction between the rabbinic and the mystical should not be seen as a neat differentiation between totally different aspects of a certain personality; in fact, some of the mystical aspects of the Torah have been exposed in writings of rabbinic figures. Modern scholarly attempts to offer too neat a distinction between mystical and rabbinic elites seem sometimes to be an exaggeration. See also below, app. 1.

10. See above, chap. 2, the various discussions about God as the substratum of the Torah.

11. See Idel, *Kabbalah: New Perspectives*, pp. 141–142. See also Wolfson, *Circle in the Square*, pp. 9–11; idem, *Along the Path*, pp. 239–240, note 99. For the identification of the two sefirot with the two types of Torah see Vajda, *Le commentaire*, pp. 370–380, and many other passages. See also Goetschel, *Meir ibn Gabbai*, pp. 97–99; R. Joseph al-Ashqar, *Tzafnat Pa'aneah*, fol. 15a; *Ha-Shelah*, vol. 3, fol. 1a.

12. *Torah 'Emmet*, cf. Malakhi 2:6. Is this nexus between the true Torat and Israel a polemic reference addressed to Christianity, which shares with Judaism the canonicity of the Hebrew Bible? On the *Book of Bahir* and Judeo-Christianity see Elliot Wolfson, "The Tree That Is All: Jewish-Christian Roots of a Kabbalistic Symbol in *Sefer ha-Bahir*," *Journal of Jewish Thought and Philosophy* 3 (1993), pp. 31–76.

13. Namely the attribute of supernal Israel.
14. *Bahir*, no. 94, ed. Abrams, pp. 179–181; on this passage see Scholem, *Origins of the Kabbalah*, pp. 126, 144–145: Mopsik, *Les grands textes*, pp. 111–114. For more on the Torah as a cosmic entity in the *Book of Bahir* see sections 8 and 15 and Scholem's analysis, *Origins of the Kabbalah*, pp. 132–133.
15. Scholem, *Origins of the Kabbalah*, p. 145.
16. Ibid., pp. 126–131.
17. Ibid., p. 145.
18. *'Avot de-Rabbi Nathan*, chap. 31, version A, pp. 90–91.
19. See Paul Kraus, "Hebräische und syrische Zitate in ismailitischen Schriften," *Der Islam* 19 (1930), p. 260; Salomon Pines, "Shi'ite Terms and Conceptions in Juda Halevi's Kuzari," *Jerusalem Studies in Arabic and Islam* 2 (1980), pp. 243–244.
20. *Midrash Tadsche'*, p. 145. For more on this passage see below, chap. 8, par. III.
21. See the bibliography referred to above, introduction, note 49; also see below, chap. 11, par. XI.
22. See H. A. Wolfson, "Extradeical and Intradeical Interpretations of Platonic Ideas," in *Religious Philosophy* (Harvard University Press, Cambridge, Mass., 1965), pp. 27–68; W. Norris Clarke, "The Problem of Reality and Multiplicity of Divine Ideas in Christian Neoplatonism," in Dominic J. O'Meara, ed., *Neoplatonism and Christian Thought* (Norfolk, Va., 1982), pp. 109–127.
23. Cf. *Genesis Rabba* 1:2. See also Idel, "The Sefirot above the Sefirot," p. 265, note 131, and below, in the discussion of a passage from R. Azriel of Gerona.
24. *Havvayot*; on this term see Scholem, *Origins of the Kabbalah*, p. 281, and Idel, "The Sefirot," pp. 240–249. Interestingly, this term, which is characteristic of R. Isaac the Blind and his school, does not occur in the *Commentary on Midrash Konen*, attributed, in my opinion spuriously, by Scholem to the Provençal master and discussed above, chap. 3, par. II.
25. Hokhmah, which is the second sefirah.
26. Namely Maimonides.
27. *Hilkhot Yesodei Torah* 2:10.
28. *Pamalia*.
29. *Sefer ha-'Emunah ve-ha-Bitahon*, chap. 18, ed. H. Chavel, *Kitvei ha-Ramban* (Jerusalem, 1964), 2:409, Idel, "The Sefirot," pp. 265–267. Compare the interpretation of R. Isaac ibn Latif to this Platonic stand as formulated by Maimonides, cf. S. O. Heller Wilensky, "Isaac ibn Latif: Philosopher or Kabbalist?" in A. Altmann, ed., *Jewish Medieval and Renaissance Studies* (Harvard University Press, Cambridge, Mass., 1967), pp. 188–189, esp. note 26.
30. Salomon Pines, "Some Distinctive Metaphysical Conceptions in Themistius' Commentary on the Book Lambda and Their Place in the History of Philosophy," *Aristoteles Werk und Wirkung, Paul Moraux gewidmet*, ed. J. Wiesner (Berlin, New York, 1987), pp. 177–204, esp. pp. 196–200. Compare also Gersonides' passage discussed below in this chapter.

31. The meaning of this term in *Sefer Yetzirah* itself is rather obscure. In our context it may point to "wondrous," a parallel to the term that occurs earlier.
32. Cf. *Sefer Yetzirah*, 1:1.
33. On this phrase see also below, note 49.
34. *Mahashavah*.
35. *Dibbur*.
36. *Ma'aseh*.
37. Compare also R. Azriel's *Commentary on the Talmudic 'Aggadot*, p. 110. where the beginning of the sefirot is posited in the divine will. See Scholem, *Origins of the Kabbalah*, pp. 438–439.
38. *Dimyonei*.
39. *Nitztayyru*.
40. *Commentary on the Talmudic 'Aggadot*, p. 82. On the division between *mahashavah*, *dibbur*, and *ma'aseh* as different ontological levels see ibid., p. 110. Earlier, on p. 108, the second sefirah is referred to as the "beginning of the Speechap." On the Torah and the thirty-two paths of wisdom see *Book of Bahir*, a work known to R. Azriel, section 43; cf., Scholem, *Origins of the Kabbalah*, pp. 168–169.
41. See below, note 48, and above, chap. 3, beside note 48.
42. *Ba'alei ha-Mehqar*, namely the philosophers.
43. *Sheneihem ke-'ahat*.
44. *Commentary on the Talmudic 'Aggadot*, p. 83.
45. See Ricoeur, *From Text to Action*, p. 152.
46. See his preface to the *Commentary on Pentateuch*, ed. H. D. Chavel (Mossad ha-Rav Kook, Jerusalem, 1959), 2:2, and below, app. 3.
47. See Moshe Idel, "R. Joseph of Hamadan's Commentary on Ten Sefirot and Fragments of His Writings," *'Alei Sefer* 6–7 (1979), pp. 81–84 (Hebrew).
48. See above, note 41.
49. Of the Torah. See also above, beside note 33.
50. See *Commentary on the Rationales for the Commandments*, ed. H. Liebermann (London, 1962), fol. 2ab; I checked the version in Ms. Paris, BN 825, fols. 1b–2a. On this quote see Scholem, *On the Kabbalah*, pp. 44, 124; Tishby, *The Wisdom of the Zohar*, 1:284. This quote had been copied in a widely read early-seventeenth-century classic, R. Isaiah Horowitz's *Ha-Shelah*, I, fol. 67a.
51. Scholem's study, printed in *Diogène* 14 (1955), pp. 1–16; 15 (1956), pp. 2–40. For an easily available reprint of the translation see Gershom Scholem, *Le nom et les symboles de Dieu dans la mystique juive*, trans. M. R. Hayoun and G. Vajda (Le Cerf, Paris, 1983), p. 111. For Derrida's resort in *Dissemination* to a passage found in Scholem's study see above, chap. 2, par. V.
52. For further references to this quote see Mopsik, *Les grands textes*, p. 279; Idel, "The Concept of the Torah," pp. 58–62, 68–70; idem, *Kabbalah: New Perspectives*, pp. 244–247; Holdrege, *Veda and Torah*, pp. 200–201, 334, 492, note 334.
53. See above, chaps. 2 and 3.

54. *De grammatologie* (Le Minuit, Paris, 1967), pp. 233, 227; *Of Grammatology*, trans. G. C. Spivak (Johns Hopkins University Press, Baltimore, 1976), pp. 163, 158. For another attempt to point out a similarity between Derrida and Jewish mystical thought, yet without claiming a real historical nexus, see Wolfson, *Circle in the Square*, p. 166, note 41. Compare also Eco's formulations in chapter 110 of *Foucault's Pendulum*, p. 565.

55. See Gershom Scholem, "New Remnants from the Writings of R. Azriel of Gerona," *Gulak and Klein Memorial Volume* (Jerusalem, 1942), p. 207: *'Ein davar hutz mimmenu*. This phrase is rather characteristic of R. Azriel's terminology, though it was rarely related to God but more often to the divine will. I assume that Derrida did not have access to the pertinent passage in its original Hebrew but could nevertheless read either the German version in Scholem's fuller description of the beginnings of Kabbalah, *Ursprung und Anfänge der Kabbala*, printed in Berlin in 1962, or in the French translation entitled *Les origines de la Kabbale*, trans. Jean Loewenson (Aubier-Montaigne, Paris, 1966), p. 447: "Rien n'existe hormis Lui." See also the English version published as *Origins of the Kabbalah*, pp. 423–424: "Nothing exists outside of Him."

56. See *Commentary on the Torah* (Venice, 1547), fol. 113bc; Compare also Faur's translation, *Golden Doves*, p. xxii. There are some affinities between this view and that of R. Jacob ben Sheshet, quoted above.

57. *Kabbalah: New Perspectives*, pp. 212–213.

58. On the need to resort to a panoramic approach to Jewish culture in Hasidism see Idel, *Hasidism: Between Ecstasy and Magic*, pp. 9–15.

59. This treatise has been ignored by modern scholarship. See the succinct remarks in Idel, "The Concept of the Torah," pp. 47–48.

60. Namely "righteous"; in the sentence that immediately precedes this passage, the author indicates the numerical relationship between the elliptical spelling of the term *gevurah* "the dynamic," namely 210, and *ve-tzaddiq*, "and the righteous."

61. Proverbs 10:25.

62. *Ha-meqareh*.

63. In Hebrew *'aliyotav*.

64. Psalm 104:3.

65. Ms. Berlin Or. 942, fol. 154a.

66. See Scholem, *On the Kabbalah*, pp. 44–46; Idel, "The Concept of the Torah," pp. 49–51.

67. The verb 'MD occurs in many of the texts quoted above, both in the midrashic literature and in the *Bahir*.

68. Isaiah 34:4.

69. Ms. Berlin Or. 942, fol. 149b. For more on the firmament in the context of the book see the Hasidic texts quoted and analyzed below.

70. Idel, "The Concept of the Torah," pp. 47–48.

71. See above, par. III, sec. 1, esp. note 11. Theurgical understandings of the study of the Torah are a leitmotif in the theosophical-theurgical Kabbalah. One of the most

influential Kabbalists who expressed theurgical views, most eminently in the context of ritualistic activities including the study of the Torah, was the early-sixteenth-century R. Meir ibn Gabbai. Cf. Mopsik, *Les grands textes*, pp. 364–383.

72. The angels, and this is the meaning of "they" below. For more on innovations while studying Torah see *Ha-Shelah*, II, fol. 98b.

73. *Ruhaniyyut ha-torah*. See above, chap. 4, note 63.

74. Cordovero, *Derishot*, p. 70; see also ibid., p. 72. See also, inter alia, R. Meir ibn Gabbai, *Tola'at Ya'aqov*, fol. 27b; Da Vidas, *Reshit Hokhmah*, cf. Lawrence Fine, *Safed Spirituality* (Paulist Press, New York, 1984), p. 109; R. Qalonimus Qalman Epstein, *Ma'or va-Shemesh*, 1:256.

75. See Idel, *Kabbalah: New Perspectives*, pp. 191–197; Green, *Keter*; Idel, *Hasidism: Between Ecstasy and Magic*, p. 378. note 35; Sack, *Be-Sha'arei ha-Kabbalah*, pp. 174–175, note 131; R. Hayyim of Volozhin, *Nefesh ha-Hayyim*, p. 343.

76. In fact, the core of the view is found already in *Shoher Tov*, a midrash on the Psalms, and recent Hasidic writers had to offer a pretext for adducing this view in the name of the Besht. See the special printing of *Sefer Tanya'* (Brooklyn, 1989), pp. 52–55.

77. Psalm 119:89.

78. *Ma'amarot*. See above, note 19.

79. See below, chap. 11, par. VIII, and chap. 12. On the Torah (here referred to implicitly as the 231 combinations) as the vitality of the worlds see R. Isaac Aizik Haver, *'Or Torah* in *'Amudei ha-Torah*, pp. 24–25.

80. See *Sefer Tanya'*, fols. 76b–77a, and the addition to *Keter Shem Tov*, fol. 84b. See also R. Yisrael, the Maggid of Kuznitz, *Sherit Yisrael* (Lublin, 1895), fol. 66a; *Ba'al Shem Tov*, 1:17, 55–57, for additional sources that mention the Besht's authorship on the above view. Compare also R. Qalonimus Qalman Epstein, *Ma'or va-Shemesh*, 1:147. See also Handelman, *The Slayers of Moses*, p. 73.

81. See *Maggid Devarav le-Ya'aqov*, pp. 66, 335.

82. *Sefer ha-Tanya'*, fol. 76b. Compare also his contemporary R. Ze'ev Wolf of Zhitomir, *'Or ha-Me'ir*, fols. 119c, 138b.

83. See the views of R. Joseph ben Shalom Ashkenazi, an influential late-thirteenth-century author apparently active in Barcelona.

84. See also *Be'er Mayyim Hayyim*, I, fol. 46c.

85. Psalms 119:89.

86. *Be'er Mayyim Hayyim*, I, fol. 8d. The idea reverberates in this book; see, e.g., ibid., fols. 8d–9a. See also below, chap. 5, note 103. On the view that vitality descends by means of letters see above, chap. 2, par. IV, in the quote in the name of R. Levi Isaac of Berditchev but already alluded to in his master, the Great Maggid. See also *Ha-Shelah*, II, fol. 98b.

87. *Le livre des questions* (Paris, 1963), pp. 32–33, translated and discussed by Shira Wolosky, "Derrida, Jabes, Levinas: Sign-Theory as Ethical Discourse," *Prooftexts* 2 (1982), p. 293.

88. See Scholem, *Major Trends*, pp. 7–8; see David Biale and Gershom Scholem, *Kabbalah*

and *Counter-History* (Harvard University Press, Cambridge, Mass., 1979), pp. 137, 202–203; Nathan Rotenstreich, *Judaism and Jewish Rights* (Hakibutz Hameuchad, 1959), pp. 119–120 (Hebrew); McGinn, *The Presence of God*, 1:334–336; Idel, *Studies in Ecstatic Kabbalah*, pp. 3–4.

89. See, e.g., *Tanhuma', Wa-Yiqra'*, pericope Tzav, chap. 14.

90. Cf. Baer, *Studies*, 1:111–112; Bloom, *The Strong Light*, pp. 30–31.

91. See, e.g., Davies, *Torah*, pp. 91–94; for the hermeneutical repercussions of this identification see Handelman, *The Slayers of Moses*, pp. 83–120.

92. On the different meanings of the term *torah* within the biblical texts see Greenberg, *Studies*, pp. 11–24; Alexander Rofe, "The Devotion to Torah-Study at the End of the Biblical Period: Joshua 1:8; Psalms 1:2; Isaiah 59:21," in Sara Japhet, ed., *The Bible in the Light of Its Interpreters: Sarah Kamin Memorial Volume* (Magnes Press, Jerusalem, 1994), pp. 622–628 (Hebrew); Kugel, in Kugel and Greer, *Early Biblical Interpretation*, pp. 20–24.

93. Davies, *Torah*, p. 94. note 11.

94. See above, chap. 2, passim.

95. Cf. Idel, *Messianic Mystics*, pp. 34, 58, 66, 116–119.

CHAPTER 5: MAGICAL AND MAGICAL-MYSTICAL ARCANIZATIONS OF CANONICAL BOOKS

1. See Trachtenberg, *Jewish Magic and Superstition*, pp. 104–113. For other magical aspects of the Torah scroll see Shalom Sabar, "Torah and Magic: The Scroll of the Torah and Its Appurtenances as Magical Artifacts in Jewish Culture in Europe and in Islamic Countries," *Pe'amim* 85 (2000), pp. 149–179 (Hebrew).

2. See Idel, "On Judaism."

3. On the rivalry between man and angels see above, chap. 1, par. III, and Alexander Altmann, "The Gnostic Background of the Rabbinic Adam Legends," *JQR* (n.s.) 36 (1944/45), pp. 371–391; J. P. Schultz, "Angelic Opposition to Ascension of Moses and the Revelation of the Law," *JQR* (n.s.) 61 (1970/71), pp. 282–307; Peter Schaefer, *Rivalität zwischen Engeln und Menschen* (De Gruyer, Berlin, 1975); Idel, "The Concept of the Torah," pp. 25–33. On Moses' ascent on high in earlier sources see Martha Himmelfarb, *Ascent to Heaven in Jewish and Christian Apocalypses* (Oxford University Press, New York, 1993); Swartz, *Scholastic Magic*, pp. 166–168. See also below, note 6, chap. 12, par. VI.

4. This expression is related to the assumption of the existence of a primordial magical structure of the Torah, now lost. See *Midrash Tehilim*, ed. S. Buber (Vilnius, rpt. Jerusalem, 1977), p. 35. The affinity between the two early medieval discussions has been noticed already by Scholem, *On the Kabbalah*, p. 37. Kabbalists adopted these views quite often. See, e.g., R. Bahya ben Asher, introduction to his *Commentary of the Torah*, p. 1; R. Solomon Molkho, *Sefer ha-Mefo'ar* (Jerusalem, 1962), fol. 6c.

5. This is a well-known midrashic view. See also below, the quote from *Sefer ha-Meshiv*.

6. *Ma'ayan Hokhmah*, printed by A. Jellinek, *Bet ha-Midrasch* (Wahrman, Jerusalem, 1967),

1:58–59; Idel, "The Concept of the Torah," pp. 27–28; Swartz, *Scholastic Magic*, pp. 166–167, 179–181, 191. On this passage see also chap. 1 above. On the presence of the prince of the Torah at the Sinaitic revelation see also the Heikhalot text translated and discussed in Swartz, *Scholastic Magic*, p. 112. It should be mentioned that Yefeifiah as the prince of the Torah is related to several instances when the angel Yuppi'el is described as *Sar ha-Torah*. See Cordovero, *Derishot*, p. 70. On the parallel to this passage found in a midrash, *Pesiqta' Rabbati*, see the bibliography referred to in note 3 above and K.-E. Groezinger, *Ich bin der Herr, dein Gott: Eine rabbinische Homilie zum ersten Gebot* (Pes. R. 20) (Frankfurt am Main, 1976), pp. 182–185.

7. For the antiquity of the concept of archangel to which has been attributed a great religious importance, whose vestiges are, in my opinion, still evident in Ashkenazi texts, see Larry W. Hurtado, *One God, One Lord: Early Christian Devotion and Ancient Jewish Monotheism* (Fortress Press, Philadelphia, 1988), pp. 45, 85–92; John J. Collins, "Messianism in the Maccabean Period," in J. Neusner, W. Green, and E. S. Frerichs, eds., *Judaisms and Their Messiahs at the Turn of the Christian Era* (Cambridge University Press, Cambridge, 1987), pp. 98–103; H. A. Wolfson, "The Pre-Existent Angel of the Magharians and al-Nahawandi," *JQR* (n.s.) 51 (1960–1961), pp. 89–106; Jarl E. Fossum, *The Name of God and the Angel of the Lord* (J. C. B. Mohr, Tübingen, 1985), pp. 18, 329–332, 337; idem, "The Magharians: A Pre-Christian Jewish Sect and Its Significance for the Study of Gnosticism and Christianity," *Henoch* 9 (1989), pp. 303–343; Ioan P. Couliano, *Experiences de l'extase* (Payot, Paris, 1984), pp. 70–71; idem, *The Tree of Gnosis* (Harper San Francisco, 1992), p. 54; Jean Danielou, *Theologie du Judeo-Christianisme* (Desclée/Cerf, Paris, 1991), pp. 205–207; Scholem, *Origins of the Kabbalah*, pp. 211–212; Idel, *Messianic Mystics*, pp. 342–343, note 52.

8. For magicians' inventions of pedigrees for their lore see Hans-Dieter Betz, "The Formation of Authoritative Tradition in the Greek Magical Papyri," in *Jewish and Christian Self-Definition*, ed. B. E. Meyer and E. P. Sanders (Fortress Press, Philadelphia, 1982), 3:161–170; Swartz, *Scholastic Magic*, pp. 178–186.

9. On Moses as a magician see John M. Gager, *Moses in Graeco-Roman Paganism* (Nashville, 1972), pp. 134–161; idem, "Moses the Magician: Hero of an Ancient Jewish Counter-Culture?" *Helios* 21 (1994), pp. 179–188; Hirshman, *A Rivalry of Genius*, pp. 140–141, note 15.

10. BT, *Sabbath*, fol. 88b–89a, and see also above, chap. 1, par. III. For a discussion of the talmudic and other types of materials see Idel, "The Concept of the Torah," pp. 25–32, where a richer bibliographical apparatus was supplied.

11. *Devarim Rabba'* XI:9.

12. See Fishbane, *Biblical Interpretation*, pp. 527–528; Israel Knohl, "The Revealed and Hidden Torah," *JQR* 85 (1994), pp. 103–108; Canah Werman (Nachliel) and Aharon Shemesh, "The Hidden Things and Their Revelation," *Tarbiz* 66 (1997), pp. 471–482 (Hebrew).

13. See Gruenwald, *Apocalyptic and Merkavah Mysticism*, pp. 23–24.

14. Ms. British Library 752, fol. 34b. On this book see Dan, *The Esoteric Theology*, pp. 220–224.

15. *Sefer ha-Hesheq*, ed. Y. M. Epstein (Lemberg, 1865), fol. 3b.

16. Ibid., fols. 5b, 9a.

17. Farber-Ginnat, "Inquiries in *Sefer Shi'ur Qomah*," p. 381, note 113.

18. See Idel, "Inquiries," p. 222.

19. See Israel Ta-Shma, "The Responsa of the Geonim Sha'arei Teshuvah, and 'Questions from Heaven,'" *Tarbiz* 58 (1989), pp. 21–48 (Hebrew).

20. The issue of strengthening the power of memory is a topos in Jewish magic, including in the rabbinic elite. See Idel, "Inquiries," pp. 239–240, note 287; Swartz, *Scholastic Magic*, pp. 33–48.

21. Namely the Name.

22. Isaiah 6:3.

23. *She'elot u-Teshuvot min ha-Shamayyim*, ed. R. Margolioth (Mossad ha-Rav Kook, Jerusalem, n.d.), par. IX, p. 17. For another discussion related to Metatron as an angel that was compelled to descend in order to solve a halakhic question, as an event that was discussed as having taken place in early-thirteenth-century Rouen by a certain R. Shmuel ha-Navi' see David Kaufmann, "La discussion sur les Philacteres," *REJ* 5 (1882), pp. 273–277; and in Gedaliah ibn Yahyya, *Shalshelet ha-Qabbalah* (Jerusalem, 1962), pp. 118–120; Nahum Golb, *History and Culture of the Jews of Rouen in the Middle Ages* (Devir, Tel Aviv, 1976), pp. 98, 99, 104 (Hebrew).

24. *Zohar*, II, fol. 206b. This view has been expressed in a somewhat more magical formulation by R. Meir ibn Gabbai, *Tola'at Ya'aqov*, fol. 26b. On the angel Yuppi'el as the angel of the Torah see a treatise contemporary to the *Zohar*: R. Joseph of Hamadan, *Sefer Toledot 'Adam*, in J. Toledano, ed., *Sefer ha-Malkhut* (Casablanca, 1930), fols. 69c, 70c.

25. Ms. Firenze-Laurenziana, II, 48, fol. 4a. On Metatron as *Sar ha-Torah* see also above, note 23.

26. Ibid., fol. 32b. On this passage see below, chap. 11, par. XI.

27. See Idel, *Language, Torah and Hermeneutics*, pp. 162–163, note 31.

28. *Sar Gan 'Eden*. The view that the Torah is the paradise or the way to it recurs in Hasidic literature. See, e.g., R. Yehudah Arieh Leib of Gur, *Sefat 'Emmet*, III, fol. 9d.

29. Ms. Firenze-Laurenziana, II, 48, fol. 22a.

30. Ibid., fol. 25b.

31. For the growing secondary literature on this book see Scholem, "'The Maggid,'"; idem, "On the Story of R. Joseph della Reina," *Hokhma Bina veDaat: Studies in Jewish History and Thought Presented to A. Altmann* (University of Alabama Press, University, Ala., 1979), pp. 100–108 (Hebrew), reprinted in *'Od Davar*, pp. 249–262; Georges Vajda, "Passages anti-chrétiens dans *Kaf Ha-Qetoret*," *Revue de l'histoire des religions* 117 (1980), pp. 45–58; Idel, "Inquiries"; idem, "The Attitude to Christianity in *Sefer ha-Meshiv*," *Zion* 46 (1981), pp. 77–91 (Hebrew), English version, *Immanuel* 12 (1981),

pp. 77–95; idem, "Neglected Writings"; idem, "Magic and Kabbalah in the *Book of the Responding Entity*," in M. I. Gruber, ed., *The Solomon Goldman Lectures* (Spertus College of Judaica Press, Chicago, 1993), 6:125–138.

32. These are the two famous "mystical" sages of ancient Judaism; the former is the principal hero of the *Zohar*, which was spuriously attributed to him. The second is the author of an Aramaic translation of the Bible. It is possible that the author of *Sefer ha-Meshiv* mentions them together because both of them "interpreted" the Torah, the *Zohar* being a homiletic commentary on the Bible and several scrolls.

33. With the exception of "our holy Rabbi," i.e., R. Yehudah ha-Nasi', the compiler of the Mishnah, all the names are those of ancient Tannaitic masters who were heroes of ancient Jewish mystical literature.

34. Fasting for forty days is mentioned in the Heikhalot literature in connection with the attempt to acquire mystical knowledge; interestingly, fasting was related to prophecy. See, e.g., Rudolf Arbesmann, "Fasting and Prophecy in Pagan and Christian Antiquity," *Traditio* 7 (1949), pp. 1–71. Prophecy is explicitly mentioned at the end of this quotation from *Sefer ha-Meshiv*.

35. This number recurs in similar contexts: see Idel, "Inquiries," pp. 213–215.

36. For a theory similar to *Sefer ha-Meshiv*, which incorporates the incarnation of the divine within the angel, including the *Sar ha-Torah* and Elijah, see Cordovero, *Derishot*, pp. 70–71. The impact of the theories about the Torah stemming from the circle of *Sefer ha-Meshiv* on Cordovero's view on Torah, especially that of the materialization or clothing of the Torah (see chap. 12 below), is a matter that requires further investigation. See, e.g., *Sefer Kaf ha-Qetoret*, Ms. Paris BN 846, fol. 2ab.

37. Literally, "his own head."

38. I.e., the knowledge of how to receive revelations.

39. Ms. Oxford, Bodleiana 1597, fols. 38a–39b; on this passage see Idel, "Inquiries," pp. 194–195, 240–241. For more details about part of this quote see below, chap. 6, par. IV. For another paramount description of the causing of the descent of sacred books see Idel, "Inquiries," p. 237, the quote from *Sefer Kaf ha-Qetoret*.

40. See Huss, "*Sefer ha-Zohar*," p. 276.

41. See R. J. Zwi Werblowsky, *Joseph Karo: Lawyer and Mystic* (Jewish Publication Society, Philadelphia, 1977), pp. 9–23; Lawrence Fine, "Recitation of Mishnah as a Vehicle for Mystical Inspiration: a Contemplative Technique Taught by Hayyim Vital," *REJ* 116 (1982), pp. 183–199. On the concept of maggid and its sources see also Shlomo Pines, "Le *Sefer ha-Tamar* et les maggidim des Kabbalistes," in *Hommages à Georges Vajda*, ed. Gerard Nahon and Charles Touati (Louvain, 1980), pp. 333–363; Assi Farber-Ginat, "Inquiries in *Sefer Shi'ur Qomah*," p. 381, note 113.

42. Ben-Amos-Mintz, *In Praise of the Baal Shem Tov*, p. 149. See also Rosman, *Founder of Hasidism*, p. 205.

43. Ibid., p. 18.

44. Ibid., p. 148.

45. Ben-Amos-Mintz, *In Praise of the Baal Shem Tov*, pp. 17–18. See also below, chap. 12, par. IX, the quote from R. Aharon of Zhitomir.

46. See chap. 6, par. III.

47. Ibid., p. 258.

48. See note 7 above.

49. See, e.g., Corbin, *Avicenne*, pp. 32, 88–89, 187; idem, *Alone with the Alone*, pp. 34–35, 223–224.

50. See above, introduction, note 32.

51. Traces of talismanic understanding of the ritual are discernible, however, in Gikatilla's introduction to *Sha'arei 'Orah*. See Idel, "The Magical and Neoplatonic Interpretations," p. 208.

52. See Idel, *Hasidism: Between Ecstasy and Magic*, pp. 215–216, as well as the passage of Luzzatto discussed above, chap. 3, par. III, sec. 3.

53. Ibid., pp. 216–218.

54. This is the case in the Provençal and Geronese Kabbalah, in many forms of Castilian Kabbalah, in Jewish Sufi mysticism in the Orient, and in Abraham Abulafia's ecstatic Kabbalah.

55. Exodus 19:15.

56. *Collectanaea*, Ms. Oxford 2234, fol. 164a. See also Simo Parpola, *Assyrian Prophecies* (Helsinki University Press, Helsinki, 1997), p. xcviii, note 147.

57. *Collectanaea*, ibid.

58. The view that the Jews worshiped Saturn is already evident in ancient texts. Cf. A. Bouché-Leclercq, *L'astrologie Greque* (Paris, 1899), pp. 318, 371, 478; Yohanan H. Levi, *Studies in Jewish Hellenism* (Mossad Bialik, Jerusalem, 1969), pp. 122, 143 (Hebrew); Martin Hengel, *Judaism and Hellenism*, trans. John Bowden (Fortress Press, Philadelphia, 1974), 2:176, note 47; Eric Zafran, "Saturn and the Jews," *Journal of the Warburg and Courtauld Institutes* 42 (1979), pp. 16–27; and the commentaries of ibn Ezra and R. David Qimhi on Amos 5:26 and the material collected by Ginzberg, *Legends of the Jews*, 5:135, note 6.

59. This angel was conceived of as presiding over the people of Israel. On the nexus between the angel and Saturn see Trachtenberg, *Jewish Magic and Superstition*, p. 251.

60. *Kishshuf*.

61. *Kishshufim*.

62. Ms. Paris BN 849, fols. 94b–95a; see also Idel, "The Magical and Neoplatonic Interpretations of Kabbalah in the Renaissance," p. 209.

63. On this phrase as pointing to astral magic see Shlomo Pines, "On the Term Ruhaniyyut and Its Sources and on Judah Halevi's Doctrine," *Tarbiz* 57 (1988), pp. 511–540 (Hebrew); idem, "Shi'ite Terms and Conceptions in Judah Halevi's Kuzari," *Jerusalem Studies in Arabic and Islam* 2 (1980), pp. 165–251, esp. 243–247; idem, "Le Sefer ha-Tamar."

64. *Peri 'Etz Hayyim* (Dobravorna, 1848), fol. 113bc. See also R. Ya'aqov Koppel Lipshitz,

Siddur Qol Ya'aqov (Lemberg, 1859), fols. 169b–171b, which was composed in the lifetime of Kaidanover, where very complex expositions almost identical to Vital's can be found.

65. Fol. 159a.

66. Ibid.

67. Ibid., fol. 159b. This phrase is found, in a similar context, in a quote from a much earlier Kabbalistic source adduced by R. Moses Cordovero in his *Pardes Rimmonim*, gate 30, chap. 1. See Idel, *Hasidism: Between Ecstasy and Magic*, p. 162, and below, chap. 12.

68. There may well be a correspondence between *mukhan* and *mekhavven*.

69. Fol. 100b. On *kavvanah* as intended to draw down the divine power or the celestial spirituality, see Idel, *Hasidism: Between Ecstasy and Magic*, pp. 152–154, 156–170.

70. See fol. 160a.

71. Fol. 159b.

72. See Cordovero, *Tefillah le-Moshe* (Premislani, 1892), fol. 344b. On a term very similar to *miqra'*, namely *maqra'*, which denotes the public reading of the Qur'an, see Graham, *Beyond the Written Word*, pp. 108, 112. On the Qur'an as talisman see recently Constant Hames, "L'usage talismanique du Coran," *Revue de l'histoire des religions* 218, no. 1 (2001), pp. 83–95.

73. See above, chap. 3, note 97.

74. *Tiqqunei Zohar* with *'Or Yaqar Commentary* (Jerusalem, 1975), 1:90; see also idem, *Shi'ur Qomah*, fol. 9c, where the attraction of parts of the supernal Torah is discussed. See Huss, "*Sefer ha-Zohar*," p. 289; Sack, *Be-Sha'arei ha-Qabbalah*, pp. 40–42, 122. On the "springs of wisdom" see below, chap. 6, note 24; Idel, *Messianic Mystics*, p. 216; and the Philonic material adduced by Maren R. Niehoff, "Philo's Mystical Philosophy of Language," *JSQ* 2 (1995), pp. 228–232.

75. See gate 32, chap. 1; part II, fol. 78ac.

76. See Sack, *Be-Sha'arei ha-Qabbalah*, pp. 40–41, where the term *hakhanah* occurs.

77. See especially the important discussion in Cordovero, *Derishot*, p. 70; Scholem, *On the Kabbalah*, p. 65; and Idel, *Hasidism: Between Ecstasy and Magic*, p. 158.

78. See R. Gedalyah ibn Yihyya, *Sefer Shashelet ha-Qabbalah*, p. 70.

79. See Zvia Rubin, *R. Moshe Hayyim Luzzatto and His Writings on the Zohar*, Ph. D. diss. (Hebrew University, Jerusalem, 1997) (Hebrew). See also Joseph Avivi, *Zohar Ramhal* (Jerusalem, 1997), passim (Hebrew).

80. Cf. Isaiah 11:9.

81. The Aramaic phrase *heila' dileih* literally means "his power," but I assume that my translation makes better sense.

82. *Zohar Tanniyana'*, p. 409. A detailed analysis of this passage is found in Zvia Rubin, "The Zoharic Treatises of Ramhal and the Messianic Concept of the Zohar in His Writings," in *The Age of the Zohar*, pp. 393–411 (Hebrew). Here I shall be emphasizing aspects other than those addressed by Rubin. See also below, chap. 12, par. VIII, the passage from *Qin'at ha-Shem Tzeva'ot*. For interesting parallels, which assume that in

the Messianic eon each and every person will have his own perception of God, see Scholem, *On the Kabbalah*, p. 65, and R. Israel of Ryzhin, *Tiferet Israel* (Jerusalem, 1945), fol. 17a.

83. Rubin, "The Zoharic Treatises," pp. 394–395, note 24.

84. *Zohar Tanyyana'*, p. 409.

85. Ibid.

86. Tishby, *Studies in Kabbalah*, 3:985. On drawing down according to other texts of this Kabbalist see Idel, *Messianic Mystics*, pp. 206–210.

87. Namely the Zohar composed by Luzzatto. The speaker is an angelic figure, the prophet Elijah.

88. Cf. Daniel 12:3.

89. *Zohar Tanyyana'*, p. 409.

90. See Idel, *Messianic Mystics*, pp. 161–162.

91. *Li-yqah*.

92. See Idel, "The Concept of the Torah," pp. 52–54, and below, chap. 11, par. III.

93. Ibid., pp. 49–52.

94. See Idel, *Hasidism: Between Ecstasy and Magic*, pp. 152–156.

95. Exodus 20:21.

96. Ibid.

97. *Degel Mahaneh 'Efrayyim*, p. 119.

98. Ibid., pp. 119–120. Compare the interpretation of this verse in *Shemu'ah Tovah*, p. 79. See also R. Shne'or Zalman of Liady, *Torah 'Or*, fol. 1c; R. Aharon Kohen of Apta, *Ner Mitzvah*, fol. 30b, and R. Isaac Aiziq Safrin of Komarno, *Heikhal ha-Berakhah*, vol. 5, fol. 41a. On the magical implication related to the study of the Torah for its own sake see R. Yehudah he-Hasid, *Sefer Gematria'ot*, pp. 28–29.

99. See Idel, "Reification of Language," pp. 62–63.

100. This view is found in several medieval and Renaissance sources; see Moshe Idel, Introduction to the facsimile edition of Rabbi Joseph Al-Ashqar's *Tzaphnat Pa'aneah*, pp. 43–46. See also Idel, *Hasidism: Between Ecstasy and Magic*, pp. 171–188.

101. R. Elimelekh of Lisansk, *Sefer No'am 'Elimelekh* (Jerusalem, 1960), fol. 8a. Compare also R. Menahem Nahum of Chernobyl, *Me'or 'Einayyim*, p. 208; R. Dov Baer of Mezeritch, *'Or Torah*, p. 113; R. Aharon ha-Levi of Zhitomir, *Toledot 'Aharon*, vol. 2, fol. 36b; R. Ze'ev Wolf of Zhitomir, *'Or ha-Me'ir*, fol. 201c. The pure utterances mentioned in this quote have something to do with the religious attitude mentioned in Elijah da Vidas's texts, under the influence of Cordovero's thought. See also Ramhal, *Tiqqunim Hadashim*, p. 78.

102. For more on this issue see Idel, *Hasidism: Between Ecstasy and Magic*, pp. 215–218.

103. This form of encounter with God within the vocal performance is not the only form of Hasidic mysticism. The separation from materiality or, as the Hasidim would put it, the divestment from corporeality is another avenue open to the Hasidic masters to encounter the less contracted modes of the divine. On the other hand, in Hasidic writings the linguistic immanentism frequently assumes the need to sustain the

letters that permeate the whole cosmos by performing the Jewish ritual. See, e.g., R. Hayyim Tirer of Chernovitz, *Sidduro shel Shabbat* (Jerusalem, 1960), fol. 146cd, and his passage from another book, translated and discussed above, chap. 4, par. VI, sec. 3. According to this text, each and every letter is conceived of as sustaining myriad worlds. Here we have an interesting example of devotion to the letter. Compare also R. Reuven ha-Levi Horowitz, *Diduim basode* (Lemberg, 1859), fols. 41b–42a, 131b, where the linguistic immanence serves as the starting point for his particular theory of restoration of the divine sparks, which are thought to be letters. See also the interesting treatment of R. Menahem Nahum of Chernobyl, *Me'or 'Einayyim*, pp. 266–267.

104. *She-hu' 'asur bi-shemo* means concretely that God is imprisoned in or bound by His name. The view that God is bound is reminiscent of a verse in the Song of Songs, 7:6, where the king, understood in many Jewish texts as an allegory for God, is described as having been caught or bound—the same verb, *'asur*, is used—in tresses. See also below, note 188. Compare, however, Scholem's view that light, sound, and "even the name of God are merely symbolic representations of an ultimate reality which is unformed, amorphous." *On the Kabbalah*, p. 8.

105. See Scholem, ibid., pp. 39–41; Idel, "The Concept of the Torah," pp. 49–52; Janowitz, *The Poetics of Ascent*, p. 88.

106. The verb *qore'* means both to read and to call. For the magical significance of this verb in the Heikhalot literature see Schaefer, *Hekhalot-Studien*, p. 259. In our context the role of the biblical phrase *qore' be-shem YHWH* (see Psalm 99 and Yoel 2:17) should be examined.

107. *'Or ha-'Emmet* (Zhitomir, rpt. Benei Beraq, 1967), fol. 14c. See also the text from the same collection quoted in Idel, *Hasidism: Between Ecstasy and Magic*, pp. 181–183, and the view of R. Menahem Nahum of Chernobyl discussed there. Compare also the text of R. Menahem Mendel of Vitebsk, translated and analyzed in Idel, "Reification of Language," pp. 62–63. On the concept that there is an identity between God and His name see the texts adduced in Idel, "The Concept of the Torah," p. 67. On the identity between Torah and God see ibid., as well as Wolfson, "Beautiful Maiden," pp. 167–168. On the identity between God, the Torah, and Israel, the latter hinted at in our passage by the word "us," see the detailed survey of Tishby, *Studies in Kabbalah*, 3:941–960, esp. 943, 945. Concerned as he was solely with the theological aspects of this identity, Tishby did not deal with this passage, nor with the magical and mystical implications of this intertwined triad.

108. In Hebrew *pe[rush]* means also the plain sense of the words.

109. Or emanation, *hamshakhah*. This author emphasizes that the source of the letters and of speech in general is higher than that of knowledge, because knowledge stems from the second sefirah, Hokhmah, while speech stems from the first, Keter. This stand is explicated in greater detail elsewhere in the same book; see *Liqqutei Torah*, *Huqqat*, IV, fol. 59a. This is a crucial passage, for it explicitly describes the source of speech as higher than that of knowledge, a position I am not acquainted with in

Kabbalah. See also ibid., Be-Huqqotai, II, fols. 45d–46b, another important and lengthy discussion on the "letters of thought" (ʾotiyyot ha-mahashavah), where the identity between thought and linguistic entities is conspicuous. In one of his more interesting statements he asserts that there is no manifestation of thought without letters. See also Idel, "Reification of Language," pp. 62–64.

110. Liqqutei Torah, Va-Yiqraʾ, II, fol. 5bc. On this passage see Wolfson, "Beautiful Maiden," p. 189, where a slightly different translation is offered. Wolfson adduced this text as part of his argument concerning the influence of the Zoharic positive evaluation of the plain sense of biblical text. In my opinion, here we have an example of the influence of the talismanic, rather than the symbolic, model. It should be noted that Wolfson was nevertheless aware of the magical implication of the drawing down, as he mentions it; see ibid., p. 202, note 193. On "callers" who cause the descent of the supernal pneuma by means of "enchanting songs" and "ineffable words" see Hans Lewy, Chaldaean Oracles and Theurgy, ed. M. Tardieu (Paris, 1978), p. 47.

111. Ibid., Va-Yiqraʾ, III, fol. 12c, adduced by Wolfson, "Beautiful Maiden," p. 190. See also note 113 below.

112. Ibid., Derushim le-Rosh ha-Shanah, V, fol. 59a.

113. See ibid., Derushim le-Rosh ha-Shanah, V, fol. 59b. See also ibid., Be-Huqqotai, III, fol. 45c, where the drawing down by means of the Torah is mentioned again. On the magical source of the view of the Torah as a continuum of divine names see Idel, "The Concept of the Torah," pp. 52–55, and below, chaps. 11–12. On the thaumaturgical view of the process of reading in general see Hartman, The Fate of Reading, p. 249.

114. Tzeror ha-Hayyim (Bielgoria, 1913), fol. 30a. For more on the view of letters as vessels —sometimes described as boxes, a pun on the noun teivah—see R. Menahem Nahum of Chernobyl, Meʾor ʿEinayyim, pp. 170–171; R. Jacob Joseph of Polonoy, Toledot Yaʿaqov Yosef, fol. 25ab; and R. Mordekhai of Chernobyl, Liqqutei Torah, fols. 5c, 10c, 19c, 25c, 29d, 30d.

115. Sippurei maʿasiyyot she-ba-Torah. See also below, app. 2.

116. Namely, how the reader is linked to God.

117. On the sympathetic approach to the ritual and study of the Torah, which is recurrent in the theosophical-theurgical Kabbalah and sometimes also in Hasidism, see Idel, Kabbalah: New Perspectives, pp. 173–181. Compare also R. Isaac Aizik Haver, ʾOr Torah, in ʿAmudei ha-Torah, p. 38.

118. Hirhur.

119. Indeed, in Zohar, III, fol. 105a, the view is expounded that ruminations do not affect anything in the supernal world because they do not ascend upward.

120. Zeʿir.

121. Tanyaʾ, Quntres Aharon, fol. 153ab. For another discussion of this passage see below, chap. 6, par. V.

122. R. Meir ha-Levi of Apta, ʾOr le-Shamayyim (Lublin, 1909), fol. 98d. On the context of this quote see Idel, Hasidism: Between Ecstasy and Magic, pp. 204–205. On the

importance of the "mouth" for drawing down divine influxes see *Torah 'Or*, a text from early Habad Hasidism; cf. ed. Brooklyn, 1985, fol. 52b.

123. See Graham, *Beyond the Written Word*, pp. 143–154, 161.

124. Compare Wolfson, "Beautiful Maiden," p. 190.

125. Barthes, *Le degré zero*, pp. 37–39.

126. Ibid., p. 38.

127. Ibid., p. 40.

128. Schatz-Uffenheimer, *Hasidism as Mysticism*, pp. 67–69, 242–243.

129. See Idel, "The Magical and Neoplatonic Interpretations," pp. 203–208, and above, par. II, the second quote from Alemanno.

130. For more on this issue see below, chap. 10.

131. See below, Concluding Remarks, par. 1.

132. Jacques Maritain, *Ransoming the Time*, trans. H. L. Binsse (Gordian Press, New York, 1972), pp. 248–249. In fact, this view is found, in a rather positive light, in many Jewish texts dealing with the extraordinary powers one acquires by study of the Torah, which allows one to change nature. See, e.g., R. Joseph Yavetz, *Commentary on 'Avot*, p. 68; R. Yehiel Nissim of Pisa, *Sefer Minhat Qena'ot*, ed. David Kaufmann (Mekize Nirdamim, Berlin, 1898), p. 108, or R. Joseph Shlomo of Candia, *Matzref la-Hokhmah*, chap. 10, fol. 28b. See also the recurring theme that nature is governed by the Torah in R. Yehudah Arieh Leib of Gur, *Sefat 'Emmet*, I, fols. 3b, 4b, and III, fols. 8d, 9cd.

133. Maritain, *Ransoming the Time*, pp. 248–249 and also 225–226. Maritain's distinction is reminiscent of a short discussion by Mary Douglas, *Natural Symbols: Explorations in Cosmology* (Pantheon Books, New York, 1982), p. 10, who distinguishes the inner efficacy of the sacraments from what she views as the external efficacy of magic.

134. Maritain, *Ransoming the Time*, p. 227. I take Maritain's use of the term "nocturnal" as a value judgment implying that Maritain prefers the sacramental, which is diurnal, over the nocturnal magic. I am attempting to escape such a unilateral, religion-fraught axiology.

135. Quoted in Raymond Bailey, *Thomas Merton on Mysticism* (Doubleday, New York, 1975), p. 118; see also Louis Dupré, "Unio Mystica: The State and the Experience," in Idel and McGinn, *Mystical Union*, pp. 14–16.

136. See Idel, *Hasidism: Between Ecstasy and Magic*, p. 6. Compare Buber, *The Origin and Meaning of Hasidism*, pp. 179–180.

CHAPTER 6: TORAH STUDY AND MYSTICAL EXPERIENCES IN JEWISH MYSTICISM

1. Bori, *L'interpretazione infinita*, p. 145.

2. Iser, *The Act of Reading*, p. 10; Barthes, "From Work to Text," in *Textual Strategies*, pp. 75–76; Eco, *The Open Work*, p. 27; Ricoeur, *From Text to Action*, p. 54. On experiential reading in the Middle Ages see Stock, *The Implications of Literacy*, p. 439, and Leclercq, *The Love of Learning*, esp. p. 73.

3. Fr. 15, analyzed by Walter Burkert, *Ancient Mystery Cults* (Harvard University Press,

Cambridge, Mass. 1987), pp. 69, 89–90. See also his "Der Geheime Reiz des Vergorgenen: Antike Mysterienkulte," in *Secrecy and Concealment*, pp. 79–100, and Angus, *The Mystery-Religions*, p. 93.

4. See below, chap. 7, note 8.

5. On these forms of arcanization see above, Introduction, par. III.

6. For "secret" and "mystery" as interchangeable terms see Kermode, *The Genesis of Secrecy*, p. 144.

7. See several cases where "mysterion" does stand for secret topics in early Christianity, in Marsh, "The Use of Mysterion."

8. Sermo 300, quoted from the translation in Hugo Rahner, "The Christian Mysteries and the Pagan Mysteries," in *Mysteries*, ed. J. Campbell (Pantheon Books, New York, 1955), p. 381. See also Guy Stroumsa, "From Esotericism to Mysticism in Early Christianity," in *Secrecy and Concealment*, pp. 302–309.

9. Rahner, "The Christian Mysteries," p. 378. For the nexus between mystery and symbol in Justin Martyr see Marsh, "The Use of Mysterion," pp. 66–67. See also below, chap. 8, par. V.

10. Rahner, "The Christian Mysteries," p. 371.

11. See Idel, *Messianic Mystics*, pp. 3, 34, 148.

12. See Urbach, *The Sages*, p. 305; Petuchowski, "Judaism as 'Mystery,'" pp. 150–151; Hirshman, *A Rivalry of Genius*, pp. 17–18.

13. Smith, *Clement of Alexandria*, p. 181; Petuchowski, "Judaism as 'Mystery,'" pp. 144–148.

14. See *Mekhilta' de-Rashbi* on Exodus 19:20, to be compared to the text from *Shimmushei Torah* discussed above, chap. 5, par. I.

15. Petuchowski, "Judaism as 'Mystery,'" pp. 148–150. Smith, *Clement of Alexandria*, pp. 181–183, points out the ritualistic aspect of the *mystorin* as related to circumcision and blurs the distinction between secrecy and mysteriousness; see also Liebes, "The Messiah of the Zohar," p. 140, note 205; Wolfson, *Circle in the Square*, pp. 30, 45, 141, note 3.

16. Compare, however, the use of *mystery* and *mysterium*, rather than *secret* or *Geheimnis*, sometimes in Scholem, *Jewish Gnosticism*, pp. 52, 55, and in a rather systematic manner in the German translations of the Heikhalot literature, and in the English translation of Schaefer's *The Hidden and Manifest God*, as well as in Swartz's *Scholastic Magic*.

17. Cf. Burkert, *Ancient Mystery Cults*, p. 90. On the idea of rebirth, which is crucial for the mystery mentality, see, e.g., ibid., pp. 91, 97–100; Angus, *The Mystery-Religions*, pp. 95–100, 140.

18. See Schaefer, *Synopse*, par. 279; Swartz, *Scholastic Magic*, pp. 33, 62–63.

19. See Burkert, *Ancient Mystery Cults*, pp. 80–81.

20. This does not mean that in the Middle Ages such allegorical or mystical interpretations of the earlier esoteric texts and concepts—a process I call arcanization of another arcanization—were not offered.

21. See Mircea Eliade, *Images and Symbols* (Sheed and Ward, New York, 1969), pp. 54–55.

Later on, such an instant religiosity will emerge under the influence of the Heikhalot literature, as well as in medieval ecstatic Kabbalah; see Idel, "Defining Kabbalah."

22. Angus, *The Mystery-Religions*, p. 169.

23. Proverbs 8:14.

24. Charles Taylor, ed., *Sayings of the Jewish Fathers* (Cambridge, 1897), p. 99. On this text see also David Flusser and Shmuel Safrai, "The Essene Doctrine of Hypostasis and Rabbi Meir," *Immanuel* 14 (1982), pp. 47–49; Fishbane, *The Garments of Torah*, pp. 77–78. On the metaphor of spring see also above, chap. 5, note 74.

25. Taylor, *Sayings of the Jewish Fathers*, chap. 5, p. 97.

26. On Binah see below, chap. 7, par. II.

27. *Seder 'Eliahu Zuta*, chap. 1. See also below, the quote from Heikhalot, par. 297, and Jacob Elbaum, "The Midrash *Tanna' De-vei 'Eliyahu* and Ancient Esoteric Literature," *Early Jewish Mysticism*, pp. 139–150 (Hebrew).

28. A similar phrase occurs also in another text, alluded to later in the chapter, beside note 85.

29. *Tzafita*.

30. *Ga'avah*. On this term, which recurs in the Heikhalot literature, see Idel, "The Concept of the Torah," p. 31, note 30.

31. On this term see Gruenwald, *Apocalyptic and Merkavah Mysticism*, p. 77, note 13, and chap. 7, note 43.

32. *Midrash Mishlei*, chap. 10, ed. B. Wisotzky (New York, Jewish Theological Seminary, 1990), pp. 84–85; Scholem, *Major Trends*, p. 71; Idel, "The Concept of the Torah," pp. 34–35 and accompanying notes. It is important to stress the huge impact of this passage on a variety of discussions in Jewish mystical literature, especially the contention that God delights in the study of the Torah here below. See, e.g., R. Isaac Aizik Haver, *'Or Torah*, in *'Amudei ha-Torah*, p. 38. See also chap. 1, note 44.

33. For more on this verb see below, chap. 7, par. IV.

34. See above, chap. 2.

35. See Idel, "The Concept of the Torah," pp. 41–42.

36. For more on the Sar ha-Torah in later Jewish mysticism see above, chap. 5, par. I.

37. For a general description of the Sar ha-Torah see Gruenwald, *Apocalyptic and Merkavah Mysticism*, pp. 169–173; Swartz, *Scholastic Magic*, passim.

38. *Tidreshuhu*.

39. *Tzofin*.

40. Schaefer, *Synopse*, p. 135, par. 298. The translation largely follows the rendition of Michael D. Swartz, "The Cultivation of the Prince of the Torah," in *Ascetic Behavior in Greco-Roman Antiquity: A Sourcebook*, ed. Vincent L. Wimbush (Fortress Press, Minneapolis, 1990), p. 230. See also below, chap. 7, par. IV.

41. One magical formula that is described as the great seal is preserved in Schaefer, *Synopse*, pp. 252–253, par. 689.

42. *Qol*. One manuscript has *kol*, which means "all."

43. Academies.

44. Malachi 3:20.
45. Schaefer, *Synopse*, pp. 128–129, par. 289.
46. Ibid., par. 288.
47. *Faces of the Chariot*, pp. 366–367, 385, 437.
48. *The Hidden and Manifest God*, pp. 158–166.
49. *Sod*. Other manuscripts have *sar*, namely "prince," or "archangel."
50. *Yidreshuhu*. On this verb see below, chap. 7, par. IV.
51. Schaefer, *Synopse*, pp. 132–133, par. 297. Idel, "The Concept of the Torah," pp. 36–37, note 39.
52. *Ga'avah*.
53. Schaefer, *Synopse*, pp. 136–137, par. 304; Swartz, "The Culmination," p. 232; idem, *Scholastic Magic*, p. 100.
54. *Sha'arei mizrah*.
55. *Galgalei 'eiynai*.
56. Schaefer, *Synopse*, pp. 250–251, par. 678; see also par. 279; idem, *The Hidden and Manifest God*, p. 115; Idel, "The Concept of the Torah," pp. 33–34; Halperin, *Faces of the Chariot*, pp. 376–377.
57. See also Schaefer, *Synopse*, pp. 142–143, par. 336, and pp. 214–215, par. 563; idem, *Hekhalot-Studien*, p. 294. See also the discussion below on *ha-tzenu'im*.
58. Compare also the phrase "paths of the Talmud" in Schaefer, *Synopse*, pp. 130–131, par. 292.
59. See the Hebrew book of Enoch, Schaefer, *Synopse*, pp. 10–11, par. 19. See also ibid., p. 49, par. 102. The encounter between the human look and the divine one has a mystical significance in the Heikhalot literature. The eye is definitively an organ of mystical contemplation, which is deemed to be transformed in crucial spiritual moments.
60. See Joseph Dan, "Hadrei Merkavah," *Tarbiz* 47 (1978), pp. 49–55 (Hebrew); Schaefer, *Synopse*, pp. 218–219, par. 569; Idel, "The Concept of the Torah," p. 38, note 41; Swartz, *Scholastic Magic*, p. 229.
61. Schaefer, *Synopse*, p. 210, par. 556.
62. See Origen's commentary on Psalm 1 and Scholem, *On the Kabbalah*, pp. 12–13. In general Origen should be considered one of the first and most explicit examples of the strong connection between the exegetical enterprise and the mystical experience in the Judeo-Christian tradition. See McGinn, *The Presence of God*, 1:110–116. See also Ambrosius' interpretation of the chambers, ibid., pp. 205–206.
63. See Loewe, "Apologetic Motifs in the Targum to the Songs of Songs," in *Biblical Motifs, Origins and Transformations*, ed. A. Altmann (Harvard University Press, Cambridge, Mass., 1966), p. 179.
64. On the similarity between the ascent on high of the Heikhalot literature and Sar ha-Torah see Halperin, *Faces of the Chariot*, pp. 434, 436–437.
65. See Schaefer, *The Hidden and the Manifest God*, pp. 165–166; Idel, "Enoch Is Metatron," *Immanuel* 24/25 (1990), p. 225, note 18, and the important study of Elliot R. Wolfson, "Yeridah la-Merkavah: Typology of Ecstasy and Enthronement in Ancient Jewish

Mysticism," in *Mystics of the Book: Themes, Topics, and Typologies*, ed. R. A. Herrera (Peter Lang, New York, 1993), pp. 13–44; Green, *Keter*, esp. pp. 49–68.

66. See Green, *Keter*, pp. 20–41.

67. Hints in that direction can be found in Meir Bar Ilan's study, "The Idea of Crowning God in Heikhalot Mysticism and the Karaitic Polemic," *Early Jewish Mysticism*, pp. 225–226 (Hebrew), who succinctly dealt also with the *Sar ha-Torah* passages, ibid., pp. 223–226.

68. The phrase *'orah shel torah* in a very similar context, but without mentioning the face, occurs in R. Yehudah Barceloni's *Commentary on Sefer Yetzirah*, p. 25, discussed in the context of other views of R. Eleazar by Wolfson, "The Mystical Significance," p. 65. See also below, chap. 12, esp. note 166, in the Cordoverian and Hasidic texts.

69. *'Ateret tzevi.*

70. Ecclesiastes 8:1.

71. Printed in R. Eleazar, *Perush ha-Torah*, I, pp. 31–32. See also Green, *Keter*, pp. 106–120.

72. See R. Eleazar, *Commentary on Liturgy*, Ms. Paris BN 772, fol. 84a, adduced by Wolfson, "The Mystical Significance," p. 61, note 70.

73. *Perush ha-Torah*, I, pp. 45–46; see also the text from Ms. Oxford Bodleiana 1567, fol. 71b, in the name of *Sefer ha-Kavod*, printed in Dan, *The Esoteric Theology*, p. 90; Idel, "Gazing at the Head," p. 285. The study and recitation of the Torah were conceived of as inducing experiences of light in other Ashkenazi texts as well. See, e.g., *Commentary on the Seventy Names of Metatron*, printed as *Sefer ha-Hesheq* (Lemberg, 1865), fol. 196b; Ignaz Goldziher, "La notion de la Sakina chez les Mahometans," *Revue de l'histoire des religions* 14 (1893), pp. 7–8, and Ayoub, *The Qur'an and Its Interpreters*, pp. 8–9; Idel, "The Concept of the Torah," pp. 36–37. For the descent of the Torah and the Shekhinah in the heart of the student see the anonymous late-thirteenth-century *Gates of the Eldry Man*, Ms. Oxford Bodleiana 2396, fol. 34b; R. Hayyim of Volozhin, *Nefesh ha-Hayyim*, pp. 250–251; R. Moshe Eliakum Beri'ah, *Da'at Moshe*, fol. 1c.

74. See Peter Schaefer, *Hekhalot-Studien* (Tübingen, 1988), pp. 118–153, 277–295. On magic and Heikhalot literature see more recently the important study of Shaul Shaked, " 'Peace Be Upon You, Exalted Angels': On Hekhalot, Liturgy and Incantation Bowls," *JQS* 2 (1995), pp. 197–219; Michael D. Swartz, " 'Like the Ministering Angels': Ritual and Purity in Early Jewish Mysticism and Magic," *AJS Review* 19/2 (1994), pp. 135–167; idem, *Scholastic Magic.*

75. See Farber-Ginnat, "Inquiries in Shi'ur Qomah," pp. 380–381.

76. See Idel, "The Concept of the Torah," pp. 37–38, note 39. Schaefer apparently was not sufficiently aware of this Hebrew article when offering, later on, his more radical magical reading of the goals of the Heikhalot literature. See, more recently, the important study of Farber-Ginat, "Inquiries in Shi'ur Qomah," pp. 361–394, esp. p. 380.

77. The Talmud is mentioned only in some of the manuscripts.

78. *Ha-tzenu'im.* On this term see the discussion below.

79. *Lehishtammesh bo*. This verb has, in both the rabbinic and Heikhalot literatures, a magical meaning.

80. Schaefer, *Synopse*, pp. 135–136, par. 303; Swartz, "The Cultivation," p. 231; Halperin, *Faces of the Chariot*, p. 433.

81. See Idel, "Defining Kabbalah," p. 115, note 14.

82. Fol. 30b.

83. *Tzanuʿa*.

84. Maimonides' version, as translated by Shlomo Pines, in *Guide of the Perplexed* (University of Chicago Press, Chicago, 1963), pp. 152–153.

85. See above, note 28.

86. Compare Schaefer, *The Hidden and Manifest God*, p. 115, note 124, and p. 166.

87. See beside note 60 above.

88. On this expression see Seder ʿOlam Rabba', ed. Neubauer, p. 67; Idel, "Sefirot above Sefirot," p. 243.

89. Schaefer, *Synopse*, pp. 70–71, par. 161.

90. For more on this issue see below, chap. 9.

91. See Idel, "Rabbinism versus Kabbalism," pp. 295–296, and below, Concluding Remarks.

92. See Schaefer, *Hekhalot-Studien*, pp. 293–294, and below, Concluding Remarks, par. I.

93. See the next paragraph as well as below, chap. 7, note 72.

94. *Pereq*. On this term see chap. 2, par. V.

95. Namely divine thought and divine will, which correspond to the two highest sefirot.

96. *Behinah*; this term is characteristic of Cordovero's writings, and it refers to the reflections of the features of the ten sefirot in each of them. See Bloom, *Kabbalah and Criticism*, pp. 64–71.

97. *Sefer 'Or Yaqar* (Jerusalem, 1983), vol. 12, p. 147. Compare the interesting parallel discussion in Cordovero, *Shiʿur Qomah*, fol. 18.

98. *Shaʿarei Qedushah*, III:3, p. 97.

99. See below, chap. 11, par. VI. The possibility of understanding the term *prophet* as applied to certain twelfth- and thirteenth-century Ashkenazic authors, as referring to "an ability to derive exegetically the esoteric divine will" was proposed by Ivan Marcus, *Piety and Society* (Brill, Leiden, 1981), p. 163, note 59.

100. The Besht. The speaker is the Great Maggid.

101. It is not clear whether this legend points to a text that contains Heikhalot treatises or to passages from this literature printed in *Sefer Raziel ha-Malakh*. See, e.g., the text from *Sefer Shiʿur Qomah*, in edition Amsterdam, 1701, fol. 35b.

102. Perhaps this is another description of the position of putting his head between his knees. See Idel, *Kabbalah: New Perspectives*, p. 78; Paul Fenton, "The Head Between the Knees," *Daat* 32–33 (1994), pp. 413–426 (Hebrew), and *Revue d'histoire et de philosophie religieuse* 4 (1992), pp. 413–426 [French].

103. Ben Amos-Mintz, *In Praise of the Baal Shem Tov*, p. 83. For the bibliography related to

this text see ibid., pp. 323–324; See also Naftali Loewenthal, *Communicating the Infinite* (University of Chicago Press, Chicago, 1990), pp. 18–19, 217–218; Emanuel Etkes, "Hasidism as Movement: The First Stage," in *Hasidism: Continuity or Innovation?* ed. B. Safran (Harvard University Press, Cambridge, Mass., 1988), p. 13; Joseph Dan, *The Hasidic Story* (Keter Printing House, Jerusalem, 1975), pp. 127–128 (Hebrew). For another hagiographical version of the Besht's study of *Ma'aseh Merkavah* with the Great Maggid, see Mondshein, *Shivhei*, p. 278; Avraham Rubinstein, *Shivhei ha-Besht* (Jerusalem, 1991), pp. 128–129, especially the content of note 44 in the name of Isaac Alfasi. See also R. Shlomo of Lutzk's preface to *Maggid Devarav le-Ya'aqov*, p. 2, where the divine names are also mentioned in this context.

104. See also the stories related to the enthusiastic recitations of the Song of Songs that were deemed to have induced phenomena similar to that produced by the Besht's recitation of the "Kabbalah" book above by his grandson, R. Barukh of Medzibezh; cf. Simon Dubnov, *Toledot ha-Hasidut* (Devir, Tel Aviv, 1967), pp. 208–209 (Hebrew).

105. For the mystical implication of this expression see above, par. III.

106. R. Meir Harif Margoliot of Ostrog, *Sod Yakhin u-Vo'az* (Jerusalem, 1990), pp. 41–42.

107. See chap. 2, par. IV.

108. *Liqqutei Torah*, fol. 29d.

109. On cleaving and Merkavah see below, chap. 11, par. IX.

110. *Yosher Divrei 'Emmet*, printed together with *Liqqutei Yeqarim* (Jerusalem, 1981), fol. 122a; R. Aharon Kohen of Apta, *Keter Shem Tov* (Brooklyn, 1987) vol. 1, fol. 31b; see Scholem, *The Messianic Idea*, p. 218; Idel, *Kabbalah: New Perspectives*, p. 58; idem, *Hasidism: Between Ecstasy and Magic*, p. 174.

111. *Sefer Ma'or va-Shemesh*, cf. the translation by Louis Jacobs, *Jewish Mystical Testimonies* (Schocken Books, New York, 1978), p. 220. See also R. Moses Eliakum Beri'ah, *Da'at Moshe*, fols. 2b, 127d, 130d.

112. See Ms. New York JTS 1805, fol. 6a; Boaz Huss, "*Sefer Poqeah Piqhim*: New Information on the History of Kabbalistic Literature," *Tarbiz* 61 (1992), pp. 489–504, esp. p. 492 (Hebrew).

113. On the significance of the term "prophetic holy intellect" or *intellectus acquisitus*, see the Avicennian theory of prophecy analyzed by Fazlur Rahman, *Prophecy in Islam* (London, 1958), pp. 14–20; Dov Schwartz, "The Quadripartite Division of the Intellect in Medieval Jewish Thought," *JQR* 84 (1994), pp. 227–236. See also the expression "holy intellect" in ancient Christianity, cf. de Lubac, *Histoire et esprit*, p. 295.

114. I.e., of their fast.

115. I.e., Elijah and the garment.

116. Literally, "his own head."

117. Namely how to receive revelations.

118. Ms. Oxford Bodleiana 1597, fols. 38a–39b; On this passage see Idel, "Inquiries," pp. 194–195, 240–241, and above, chap. 5, par. I. On causing the descent of the Torah in a less magical manner see the rabbinic texts adduced by Heschel, *Theology of Ancient Judaism*, 2:6–7.

119. See Elliot Wolfson, "The Secret of the Garment in Nahmanides," *Daat* 24 (1990), pp. xxv–xlix; Lorberbaum, *Imago Dei*, pp. 312–316. On the view of the Qur'an as brought down see Stefan Wild, " 'We Have Sent Down to Thee the Book With the Truth . . .': Spacial and Temporal Implications of the Qur'anic Concepts of Nuzul, Tanzil, and 'Inzal," in *The Qur'an as Text*, pp. 137–153.

120. See Idel, "Inquiries," pp. 261, notes 81. On Moses as copying the preexisting Torah see Nahmanides' introduction to his *Commentary on the Torah*, p. 2, and our discussion below, app. 2.

121. *Le-ha'atiq.*

122. In Hebrew *yoshev* means "to sit," but as Scholem pointed out in this corpus this verb can serve as an auxiliary. See Scholem, "The Maggid of Joseph Taitachek," p. 82.

123. This is an etymology of *hofniel.*

124. Ms. Oxford Bodleiana 1784, fol. 318a. On the importance of magical formulas for obtaining extraordinary capacities related to writing down Kabbalistic interpretations of the Torah see Amos Goldreich, "Clarifications of the Self-Perception of the Author of *Tiqqunei Zohar*," in *Massu'ot*, pp. 483–487 (Hebrew).

125. See Idel, "Neglected Writings," pp. 77, 88.

126. See idem, " 'Shlomo's Lost Writings': On the Attitude to Science in *Sefer ha-Meshiv*," *Daat* 32–33 (1934), pp. 235–246 (Hebrew).

127. See also below, app. 4, par. III.

128. The terms "academy" here and "Holy Academy" later in this passage stand for the celestial academy, the collectivity of the souls of the righteous, the angels, the Messiah, and God Himself, who study the Torah together in a supernal world. The phrase "celestial academy" in connection with revealing secrets from above occurs several times in the introduction to *Sefer ha-Qanah*, which influenced Molkho's visions. See A. Z. Aescoli, "Notes on the History of Messianic Movements," *Sinai* 12 (1943), pp. 84–89 (Hebrew), and see also Idel, "Inquiries," p. 237.

129. Thus the supernal academies are involved in both biblical and rabbinic studies.

130. Apparently statements related to rabbinic issues.

131. On instructions from heaven see Isadore Twersky, *Rabad of Posquieres* (Harvard University Press, Cambridge, Mass., 1962), pp. 296–297.

132. Idel, "Shlomo Molkho as Magician," pp. 204–205, where the following quotation was printed for the first time. The Hebrew version seems deficient in several instances, but its general meaning is nevertheless clear and corroborated, at least in part, by other texts connected to Molkho.

133. Ms. Moscow-Guenzburg, 302.

134. Cf. J. S. Preus, *From Shadow to Promise* (Harvard University Press, Cambridge, Mass., 1969), p. 148.

135. Compare a testimony in the same vein written by a Kabbalist at the end of the sixteenth century, who compares Molkho's ignorance and visionary experiences with those of Joan of Arc; printed in Idel, "Shlomo Molkho as Magician," pp. 202–203.

136. See chap. 5, par. IV.

137. See above, chap. 3, and below, app. 5.

138. No'am 'Elimelekh, per. Terumah, fol. 47d.

139. For the Safedian sources of this view, which is much earlier in Kabbalistic sources, see, e.g., R. Elijah de Vidas, Reshit Hokhmah, Gate of Holiness, chap. 10; II, p. 247, which was copied in Ha-Shelah, I, fol. 112b; R. Moses Cordovero, 'Elimah Rabbati (Jerusalem, 1966), fol. 132d; Idel, Hasidism: Between Ecstasy and Magic, pp. 215–218.

140. Salomon Maimon, An Autobiography, trans. J. Clark Murray (London, Montreal, Boston, 1888), pp. 164–165. See also Weiss, Studies, p. 80.

141. Jeremiah 23:29. On this verse see also above, chap. 3, notes 50, 80.

142. Liqqutei Moharan, par. 20, I, fol. 28ab. See Green, Tormented Master, pp. 200–201; Idel, Kabbalah: New Perspectives, pp. 242, 389, note 204. See also R. Nathan of Nemirov's introduction to Liqqutei Moharan, I, fol. 3a, where he describes R. Nahman as bringing down, lehorid, an accommodated version of the supernal secrets. Compare Cordovero's Derishot, p. 70. The existence of all the interpretations in one soul is to be compared to the view that there is one righteous in every generation that possesses the key to the Torah. See above, chap. 2, note 82.

143. See Idel, Kabbalah: New Perspectives, pp. 66–67. The term nishmat ha-kol, which means the universal soul, is found in Jewish writings since the twelfth century, and is already presents in R. Abraham ibn Ezra's writings. See Elliot R. Wolfson, "God, the Demiurge, and the Intellect: On the Usage of the Word Kol in Abraham ibn Ezra," REJ 119 (1990), pp. 89, 91, and esp. p. 107 on the soul of the tzaddiq.

144. See especially R. Nahman of Braslav's Liqqutei Tefillot, I, no. 14, p. 185, and no. 34, p. 501. See also the view that Moses' soul, which comprises all six hundred thousand souls of the Israelites, also contains all their interpretations, according to R. Isaac Luria, Sefer ha-Kavvanot (Venice, 1620), fol. 53b, and the widespread Sefer ha-Shelah, vol. 1, fol. 10a, of R. Isaiah Horovitz.

145. See Idel, Language, Torah, and Hermeneutics, pp. 170–171, note 87; Lory, Les commentaires esoteriques, pp. 26–27, 59.

146. Psalm 19:8. See also below, Concluding Remarks, par. IV.

147. See Idel, "Types of Redemptive Activity," pp. 264–265, note 46. See the interpretations of R. Bahya ben Asher, Introduction to the Commentary on the Torah, p. 8, and the Sermons of R. Joshua ibn Shu'aib, fol. 36c.

148. Psalm 19:8.

149. Meshiv.

150. R. Shema'yah ben Isaac ha-Levi, Sefer Tzeror ha-Hayyim, Ms. Leiden 24, fol. 190b. Compare also the famous mid-thirteenth-century R. Yonah Gerondi's interpretation of the verse from Psalms in Sefer Derashot u-Ferushei Rabbenu Yonah Gerondi, ed. S. Yerushalmi (Wagshel, Jerusalem, 1988), p. 19 (Hebrew), and Gikatilla's Ginnat 'Egoz, pp. 259, 263, 265.

151. Mordekhai Pachter, "The Concept of Devekut in the Homiletical Ethical Writings in Sixteenth-Century Safed," in Studies in Medieval Jewish History and Literature, ed. Isadore Twersky (Harvard University Press, Cambridge, Mass., 1984), 2:178, 189; Sack, Be-

Sha'arei ha-Kabbalah, pp. 104–105. See also his older contemporary R. Joseph Al-Ashqar, *Tzafnat Pa'aneah*, fols. 34a, 132b, and R. Abraham Azulai, *Hesed le-'Avraham*, fol. 1c.

152. See R. Hayyim Vital, *Sha'ar ha-Mitzvot*, per. Ve-ethanan, p. 78, and Luria, *Hanhagot*; cf. Laurence Fine, *Safed Spirituality*, p. 68; R. Jacob Hayyim Tzemah, *Naggid u-Metzavveh*, fols. 19b–20a; Idel, *Kabbalah: New Perspectives*, pp. 57 and 300, note 155.

153. Sixtus of Siena, *Biblioteca Sancta*, fol. 110v: "Est [autem Kabala] secretior divina legis expositio ex ore Dei a Moyse recepta, et ex ore Moysis per continuas successiones non quidem scripto, sed viva voce suscepta quen rursum nos ducat a terrenis ad coelestia." Kenneth Stow, "The Burning of the Talmud in 1553 in the Light of Sixteenth Century Catholic Attitude Toward the Talmud," *Bibliothèque d'humanisme et renaissance* 34 (1972), p. 457.

154. II Samuel 24:19. Interestingly enough, the words following the quoted phrase are two divine names, "Lord God." This may be an allusion to the transition from the Torah of man to a divine status, as implied by the peculiar interpretation of the verse in Psalm 19. See also the next note and below, chap. 13, par. V.

155. Psalm 19:8. For the interpretation of this verse as referring to the return of the soul to her source, back into Godhead, see above, note 148.

156. *Liqqutei Torah*, fol. 36a–b. Compare R. Leib Sarah's statement; cf. Buber, *Tales of the Hasidim: Early Masters*, p. 169. On the identification of the mystic with the Torah see more Idel, *Kabbalah: New Perspectives*, pp. 243–246, and idem, *Language, Torah, and Hermeneutics*, pp. 80 and 186, note 233. On the reception of the revelation of the Torah in accordance with one's preparation see R. Ze'ev Wolf of Zhitomir, *'Or ha-Me'ir*, fol. 165b.

157. *Perush*, literally "interpretation."

158. *Degel Mahaneh 'Efrayyim*, p. 103; Wolfson, *Circle in the Square*, pp. 24–25.

159. About the integration of the soul into Godhead see Idel, "Universalization and Integration," p. 200, note 49.

160. *Epistle on the Ascent of the Soul*, Shivhei ha-Besht, ed. Y. Mondshein (Jerusalem, 1982), pp. 235–236. See also R. Israel of Kuznitz, *'Avodat Israel* (Munkacz, 1928), fol. 97a. Compare Louis Jacobs, *The Hasidic Prayer* (Schocken Books, New York, 1978), pp. 75–77, 97, and R. Menahem Nahum of Chernobyl, *Me'or 'Einayyim*, p. 161; R. Abraham of Kalisk in *Peri ha-'Aretz*, Epistles, p. 81; R. Qalonimus Qalman Epstein, *Ma'or va-Shemesh*, I, fol. 21ab; R. 'Asher Tzevi of Ostraha, *Ma'ayan Hokhmah* (Podgorze, 1897), fol. 84c, R. Yehudah Arieh Leib of Gur, *Sefat 'Emmet*, IV, fol. 33d and fol. 33bc; R. Isaac Aiziq Safrin of Komarno, *Heikhal ha-Berakhah*, III, fol. 25c.

161. See above, chap. 4, par. V.

162. See above, chap. 2, par. IV.

163. Or "utters"; literally, "speaks."

164. The righteous.

165. *Toledot 'Aharon*, I, fol. 18c.

166. See, e.g., ibid., I, fol. 27a.

167. *Boletim u-mitztarefim*. These verses are reminiscent of the technique of *'urim ve-tummim*, which, as in the case of the text of R. Nahman, was characteristic of the *kohen* or priest. On the experiential nature of this technique in Kabbalah see also Idel, *The Mystical Experience*, pp. 105–108.

168. *Liqqutei Moharan*, I, fol. 47d.

169. See the bibliography on this topic below, chap. 13, note 67.

170. See *Liqqutei Moharan*, I, fol. 33b; Green, *Tormented Master*, pp. 319–320; Idel, "Universalization and Integration," p. 45; Fishbane, *The Exegetical Imagination*, p. 184. See also above, chap. 3, par. 4, the passage from R. Joseph Moses of Zbarov. Compare also R. Mordekhai of Chernobyl, R. Nahman's contemporary, who contends that "just as the Holy One, blessed be He, is infinite, so too is the Torah infinite, and the worship of Israel is infinite." Cf. *Liqqutei Torah*, fols. 14d–15a. On the affinity between the ontic and textual infinities see above, chap. 3. See also R. Nahman's identification of the *tzaddiqim* with the Torah, in *Liqqutei Moharan*, I, fol. 47c.

171. See already ecstatic Kabbalah and the Jewish mystical sources that might have been influenced by it, e.g., R. Nathan Neta' of Helm, *Neta' Sha'ashu'im*, fol. 19c, and Idel, *The Mystical Experience*, pp. 84–88, and below chap. 12, note 171.

172. See below, app. 5, par. I.

173. *Liqqutei Moharan*, I, fol. 98a. For the return of the combinations of letters to their supernal source in Braslav see Piekarz, *Studies*, pp. 116–117.

174. See Baer, *Studies*, 1:92–94. According to Urbach, *The Sages*, pp. 245–248, and the notes at pp. 796–797, the Platonic myth drew from an ancient Asian mythologoumenon, which was a common source for both the Platonic and the rabbinic theories.

175. On the expression *mevin davar mitokh davar* see below, chap. 7, pars. II–III.

176. See chap. 13, par. V.

177. On the correspondence between the theosophical and anthroposophical realms see Yehuda Liebes, " 'Two Young Roes of a Doe': The Secret Sermon of Isaac Luria Before His Death" and Mordekhai Pachter, "Katnut ('Smallness') and Gadlut ('Greatness') in Lurianic Kabbalah," in *Lurianic Kabbalah*, ed. Rachel Elior and Yehuda Liebes (Jerusalem, 1992), pp. 113–170 and 171–210, respectively (Hebrew).

178. See above, chap. 1, note 3. Compare the midrashic view quoted in chap. 1, note 29.

179. See below, chap. 11, par. VIII.

180. On Sabbatai Tzevi's marriage to the Torah see Scholem, *Sabbatai Sevi*, pp. 159–160, 400–401; Wolfson, *Circle in the Square*, pp. 1–28.

181. *Di-devequt*.

182. On the source of this passage see the story of R. Isaac of Acre, preserved in the sixteenth century by R. Elijah da Vidas, *Reshit Hokhmah*, *Sha'ar ha-'Ahavah*, chap. 4, translated and discussed in Idel, *Studies in Ecstatic Kabbalah*, pp. 115–119. See also R. Isaac Aiziq Safrin of Komarno, *Notzer Hesed*, p. 22.

183. *Hesheq 'ahavat nashim*.

184. *Toledot Ya'aqov Yosef*, fol. 45b.

185. See the discussion referenced in note 182 above and my forthcoming "The Transformations of an Idle Man's Story."

186. See *Reshit Hokhmah, Shaʿar ha-ʾAhavah*, chap. 4; vol. 1, p. 426. See Mordekhai Pachter, "Traces of the Influence of R. Elijah de Vidas's Reshit Hockhma Upon the Writings of R. Jacob Joseph of Polonnoye," *Studies in Jewish Mysticism, Philosophy and Ethical Literature Presented to Isaiah Tishby*, ed. J. Dan and J. Hacker (Jerusalem, 1986), pp. 569–592 (Hebrew).

187. *Toledot Yaʿaqov Yoseph*, fols. 71d–72a.

188. Cf. M. Idel, "The Beauty of Woman: Some Observations on the History of Jewish Mysticism," in *Within Hasidic Circles: Studies in Hasidism in Memory of Mordecai Wilensky*, ed. E. Etkes, D. Assaf, I. Bartal, and E. Reiner (Mossad Bialik, Jerusalem, 1999), pp. 317–334 (Hebrew).

189. *ʿEtzem me-ʿatzamav*. This phrase may point to the fact that the Torah is one with the essence of God. See above, chap. 2, note 69.

190. *Yosher Divrei ʾEmmet*, in *Liqqutim Yeqarim*, fols. 113b–114a. See also the comparison of the study of the Torah to the beautiful alien woman who is taken prisoner in war and is "converted" by several rites, in R. Qalonimus Qalman Epstein, *Maʾor va-Shemesh*, 2:604–605. On the experience of delight while studying the Torah see the quote in the name of R. Jacob Joseph of Polonnoye, adduced in R. Benjamin of Zalisch, *ʾAhavat Dodim*, pp. 20–21.

191. See Introduction, note 49.

192. See above, chap. 1, note 17.

193. Cf. Idel, *Kabbalah: New Perspectives*, pp. 62–67.

194. For Hasidic discussions influenced by the Zoharic parable of the maiden, or at least in its vein, see Wolfson, *Circle in the Square*, pp. 23–25. For more on Hasidic views of study of the Torah and sexuality see, e.g., R. Zeʾev Wolf of Zhitomir, *ʾOr ha-Meʾir*, fol. 3a.

195. On the matter of plenitude see above, chap. 2, note 82.

196. See *Qol Yehudah*, fol. 19c. For mystical death in Jewish mysticism see Michael Fishbane, *The Kiss of God: Spiritual and Mystical Death in Judaism* (University of Washington Press, Seattle, 1994); Idel, *R. Menahem Recanati, the Kabbalist*, pp. 142–150.

197. *Qinʾat ha-Shem Tzevaʾot*, p. 126. On the feeling of delight involved in the study of the Torah see the biblical antecedents discussed by Greenberg, *Studies*, p. 22.

Chapter 7: Secrecy, Binah, and Derishah

1. Cf. Assmann's paper "Semiosis and Interpretation in Ancient Egyptian Ritual."

2. See Moshe Weinfeld, "Divine Intervention in War in Ancient Israel and the Ancient Near East," in H. Tadmor and M. Weinfeld, eds., *History, Historiography and Interpretation: Studies in Biblical and Cuneiform Literatures* (Magnes Press, Jerusalem, 1983), pp. 142–143, note 119; Lieberman, "A Mesopotamian Background"; Parpola, "The Assyrian Tree of Life"; and claims regarding the origin of some forms of Jewish herme-

neutics, similar to those of Lieberman later on, already in Jeffrey H. Tigay, "An Early Technique of Aggadic Exegesis," in Tadmor and Weinfeld, *History, Historiography and Interpretation*, pp. 169–188; Fishbane, *Biblical Interpretation*, p. 464; and more recently in P. Kingsley's study, mentioned below, note 43. See also Fishbane, *The Exegetical Imagination*, pp. 41–55.

3. See Gruenwald, *From Apocalypticism to Gnosticism*, pp. 53–64.

4. On some aspects of esotericism in Qumran see my discussion of Binah, below, and the important remarks of Scholem, *Jewish Gnosticism*, pp. 3–4. Pertinent remarks on ancient Jewish esotericism can be found in G. A. Wewers, *Geheimnis und Geheimhaltung in rabbinischen Judentum* (De Gruyter, Berlin, 1975), and Smith, *Clement of Alexandria, s.v.* "secret, secrecy." Joseph Dan's attempt to point out the precise beginning of "Jewish mysticism" does not take into account the possible implications of the existence of esoteric topics in earlier Jewish, sometimes Hebrew, types of literature. See Dan, *The Revelation of the Secret of the World: The Beginning of Jewish Mysticism in Late Antiquity* (Providence, R.I., 1992).

5. See Michael Stone, "List of Revealed Things in the Apocalyptic Literature," in *Magnalia Dei: The Mighty Acts of God*, ed. F. M. Cross (New York, 1976), pp. 414–452. Gruenwald, *From Apocalypticism to Gnosticism*, pp. 74–76.

6. Gruenwald, *From Apocalypticism to Gnosticism*, pp. 59–61; Cecil Roth, "The Subject Matter of Qumran Exegesis," *Vetus Testamentus* 10 (1960), pp. 51–65; L. Schiffman, "Hekhalot Mysticism and Qumran Literature," in *Early Jewish Mysticism*, ed. J. Dan (Jerusalem, 1987), pp. 121–137 (Hebrew); C. A. Newsom, "Merkabah Exegesis in the Qumran Sabbath Shirot," *JJS* 38 (1987), pp. 11–30; J. M. Baumgarten, "The Qumran Sabbath Shirot and Rabbinic Merkabah Traditions," *Revue de Qumran (Memorial Jean Carmignac)* 13 (1988), pp. 199–213.

7. See Mowinckel, *He That Cometh*, pp. 385–393.

8. Goodenough, *By Light, Light*; David Winston, "Philo and the Contemplative Life," ed. Arthur Green, *Jewish Spirituality* (Crossroad, New York, 1986), 1:198–231, esp. pp. 223–236; idem, *Philo of Alexandria*, pp. 21–34. For more on Philo's interpretation see below, chap. 8, par. IV.

9. One of the major exceptions would be the magical text *Sar ha-Panim*. See Schaefer, *Hekhalot-Studien*, pp. 118–153.

10. See also the assumption that there are secrets in texts in Mesopotamian material, cf. Tigay, "An Early Technique," p. 171, note 4. For the claim that the later Kabbalistic symbolism, which is somehow related to esotericism, is based on the semantic reservoir of Jewish canonical writings see below, chap. 11.

11. See, respectively, the studies of Dan, Marcus, and Idel, mentioned below in notes 94, 95, and 97 and in chap. 11.

12. See studies by Lieberman, Tigay, and Parpola cited in note 2, above.

13. Verse 13. On Binah and interpretation in the Bible see Fishbane, *Biblical Interpretation*, pp. 108–109.

14. Verse 15.

15. See BT, 'Eruvin, fol. 100b; Rashi on Deuteronomy, 1:13.

16. See E. A. Finkelstein, "Tiqqunei Girsa'ot ba-Sifrei," Tarbiz 3 (1932), pp. 198–199. See also R. Abraham ibn Daud's view of R. Isaac al-Fassi, cf. Sefer ha-Qabbalah, The Book of Tradition, ed. Gerson D. Cohen (Jewish Publication Society, Philadelphia, 1967), p. 63 [Hebrew part], a reference kindly pointed out to me by Prof. Israel Ta-Shma.

17. See Sifrei, par. XIII, ed. L. Finkelstein (Jewish Theological Seminary, New York, 1969), p. 22.

18. Ibid., VIII:1.

19. On this verse see Mowinckel, He That Cometh, p. 175. Compare also Proverbs 2:4–5.

20. "Wisdom in Daniel and the Origin of Apocalyptic," Hebrew Annual Review 9 (1985), p. 377 = Biblical and Other Studies in Memory of S. D. Goitein, ed. R. Aharoni. See also Kugel in Kugel and Greer, Early Biblical Interpretation, pp. 58–59.

21. Daniel 8:15. Other interesting uses of this verb are found in the books of Ezra and Nehemiah, also of Babylonian background.

22. See Daniel, 9:2.

23. I wonder whether this Aramaic form corresponds to the Hebrew 'amuqot, which occurs in Job 12:22; in both cases the verb galleh occurs. See also Naftali Tur Sinai, Sefer 'Iyov (Jerusalem, 1972), pp. 131–132 (Hebrew), Bacher, Die exegetische Terminologie, 1:149–151, 2:28–35.

24. See especially the view that 'amiqata' was interpreted as dealing with either ma'aseh merkavah or 'omeq ha-merkavah, namely the depths of the divine chariot. See Seder 'Olam Rabba, ed. Ber Ratner (Vilnius, 1896), p. 150, and Yalqut Shim'oni on Daniel 2:22. Interestingly enough, two traditions that are related to Babylonian sources are equated: that of the book of Daniel and that of the book of Ezekiel. At the beginning of Kabbalah we found this equation also in a text of R. Ezra of Gerona, analyzed in Idel, "Sefirot above Sefirot," p. 243. On the view that there is a profound secret related to the seat of Glory see the text referring to R. Eleazar of Worms and printed by E. E. Urbach, 'Arugat ha-Bosem (Jerusalem, 1963), 4:83 (Hebrew), and the version brought out by and analyzed in Daniel Abrams, "The Literary Emergence of Esotericism in German Pietism," Shofar 12 (1994), pp. 72–73. Especially interesting from our point of view is the expression found in Abraham Abulafia's Sefer Shomer Mitzvah, Ms. Paris BN 853, fol. 39a, that ma'aseh merkavah is the depth of the science of divinity, 'omeq hokhmat ha-'Elohut, namely metaphysics. In the same context, this Kabbalist uses the phrase sitrei hokhmot [sic] ha-teva', the secrets of the sciences of nature; the depth corresponds to the secrets. See also R. Hayyim of Volozhin, Nefesh ha-Hayyim, p. 53: 'imqei matzpunei ha-torah. See also above, chap. 3, note 35, and below, notes 48 and 84.

25. Manual of Discipline, IV:22. Ed. Ya'aqov Licht, Megillat ha-Serakhim (Mossad Bialik, Jerusalem, 1965), p. 104; see Gruenwald, From Apocalypticism to Gnosticism, p. 78.

26. Such a use of the verb "haven" is found also much later, in the Middle Ages, in the context of the secret of the divine name. See R. Eleazar of Worms' preface to his Sefer ha-Shem, as printed in Dan, The Esoteric Theology, p. 75: Gillah lannu setarav, ve-havinenu leyda' shemo ha-gadol.

27. See David Flusser, *Judaism and the Origins of Christianity* (Magnes Press, Jerusalem, 1988), p. 201.

28. Emile Puech, "Fragment d'un apocryphe de Levi et le personnage eschatologique," in J. Trebolle Barrera and L. Vegas Montaner, eds., *The Madrid Qumran Congress* (Brill, Leiden, 1992), pp. 458, 461. Puech has pointed out the nexus to Daniel 2:22. On the affinity between the Qumran esoteric terminology and that of Daniel see also Devora Dimant, "New Light on the Jewish Pseudepigrapha," in ibid., p. 423. Thanks are due to Dr. Israel Knohl, who alerted me to the possible contribution of material printed in the Madrid conference volume.

29. Ibid., pp. 459, 461.

30. Ibid., p. 464.

31. *Binatekha*.

32. See *Megillat ha-Hoda'yyot*, ed. Ya'aqov Licht (Mossad Bialik, Jerusalem, 1957), pp. 42–43, 60–61, 188–189.

33. *From Tradition to Commentary: Tradition and Its Interpretation in the Midrash to Deuteronomy* (SUNY Press, Albany, 1991), p. 249, note 140; Moshe Weinfeld, "The Prayer for Knowledge, Repentance and Forgiveness in the Eighteen Benedictions: Qumran Parallels, Biblical Antecedents and Basic Characteristics," *Tarbiz* 47 (1979), p. 194 (Hebrew).

34. *Die Aggada der Tannaiten*, 2d ed. (1903), 1:70, note 42.

35. *The New Testament and Rabbinic Judaism* (Arno Press, New York, 1973), pp. 427, 431.

36. Ibid., p. 428.

37. Mishnah, *Hagigah*, II:1. On this passage see David Halperin, *The Merkabah in Rabbinic Literature* (American Oriental Society, New Haven, 1980), pp. 11–12, and the pertinent footnotes, as well as Bacher, *Die Aggada der Tannaiten*, and Daube, *The New Testament and Rabbinic Judaism*.

38. BT, *Hagigah*, fol. 13a.

39. See Scholem, *Jewish Gnosticism*, p. 58, and below, the quote from Hai Gaon.

40. *Hayah mevin*.

41. BT, *Hagigah*, fol. 13a. This incident, which occurs also in an Aramaic form and to which we shall return later, does not occur in the Heikhalot literature. See Scholem, *Jewish Gnosticism*, p. 19.

42. For more on this issue see below, par. V.

43. On the Hashmal as pointing to a much earlier tradition see Peter Kingsley, "Ezekiel by the Grand Canal: Between Jewish and Babylonian Tradition," *Journal of the Royal Asiatic Society*, 3d ser., vol. 2 (1992), pp. 339–346. See also Gruenwald, *Apocalyptic and Merkavah Mysticism*, pp. 77, 209.

44. See Halperin, *The Merkabah in Rabbinic Literature*, pp. 155–162.

45. Fol. 14b.

46. Ibid. On this issue and its possible sources and parallels see Urbach, *The World of the Sages*, pp. 486–492; Gruenwald, *Apocalyptic and Merkavah Mysticism*, pp. 75–76; Liebes, *Het'o shel 'Elisha'*, pp. 100–103.

47. See above, chap. 6, par. III, the story about the study of important texts by the Besht and the Great Maggid.

48. 'Imqei. Compare also another instance where the concept of the depths of the Torah is indicated in the Heikhalot literature. See Schaefer, *Synopse*, pp. 250–251, par. 678; see also par. 279; idem, *The Hidden and Manifest God*, p. 115; Idel, "The Concept of the Torah," pp. 33–34. Some of the conclusions drawn in the following have been presented in this study but explicated here on the basis of a greater amount of material. See also Halperin, *Faces of the Chariot*, pp. 376–377.

49. Hugo Odeberg, ed., *3 Enoch or the Hebrew Book of Enoch* (Cambridge, Cambridge University Press, 1928), p. 16, version C.

50. Silence as part of an ascetic path recurs in the Heikhalot literature. It should be mentioned that while in many other cases the recitation of hymns is quintessential, here a quite different approach is offered.

51. Schaefer, *Synopse*, pp. 142–143, par. 335.

52. See Rachel Elior, "The Concept of God in the Hekhalot Mysticism," in J. Dan, ed., *Early Jewish Mysticism* (Jerusalem, 1987), pp. 26–37 (Hebrew).

53. BT, *Megillah*, fol. 24b.

54. See Halperin, *Faces of the Chariot*, pp. 11–13, 318–319, 335.

55. Isaiah 29:14.

56. *Batei Midrashot*, ed. A. J. Wertheimer (Jerusalem, 1950), 2:358. See also ibid., p. 389, and Idel, "The Concept of the Torah," p. 38.

57. Psalms 12:7.

58. Psalms 8:8.

59. *Me'at*. It may well be that the letters *mem* and *tet*, which are part of the word *me'at*, are understood to be a hint at the number forty-nine. It seems also that the idea of the diminution of Adam, as mentioned in the rabbinic sources, might be relevant for the citation of this verse. See BT, *Hagigah*, fol. 12a, and note 101 below.

60. BT, *Rosh ha-Shanah*, fol. 21b, and Ginzberg, *The Legends of the Jews*, 6:284, note 25.

61. Rashi, ad loc.

62. Compare BT, *'Eruvin*, fol. 13b; JT, *Sanhedrin*, IV:2; *Midrash Shir ha-Shirim Rabba*, ed. S. Dunski (Devir, Jerusalem and Tel Aviv, 1980), p. 58, etc., where forty-nine ways of expounding the Torah are mentioned. The two talmudic texts have been already juxtaposed by Nahmanides in one of his sermons. See *Kitvei ha-Ramban*, ed. C. D. Chavel (Jerusalem, 1963), 1:134. and our discussion later below, par. IV.

63. BT, *Hagigah*, fol. 12a.

64. For a description of the content see Gruenwald, *Apocalyptic and Merkavah Mysticism*, pp. 225–234.

65. *Mevinim*.

66. *Mevonenim*.

67. *Sefer ha-Razim*, ed. Mordekai Margalioth (Yediyyot Aharonot, Jerusalem, 1967), p. 72 (Hebrew).

68. *Kevod ha-shamayim*.

69. For more on the verb *lidrosh* see below, par. 4.

70. Ms. Vatican 283, fol. 73a.

71. It may well be that the expounding mentioned here is that of the Merkavah: see the Heikhalot view that R. 'Aqivah "descended" in order "to expound the Merkavah." Cf. the text in Schaefer, *Synopse*, pp. 252–253, par. 685.

72. See also the view of R. Abbahu, one of the most mystical rabbinic figures in late antiquity, as adduced in the midrash on Psalms 16:10, which may be translated to the effect that "the Glory rejoiced in the moment the little (children) were pronouncing, in order to use it." Cf. *Midrash Tehillim*, ed. S. Buber (Vilnius; rpt. Jerusalem, 1977), p. 123. The text is not very clear, but nevertheless the nexus between *mishtammshim*, which points to a magical use, and Kavod seems to be rather plausible. In my opinion, this text is related, in a complex manner, to the quotes on the young boy adduced above and below from *Hagigah*. In the context of those quotes the name of R. Abbahu has also been mentioned. It should be stressed that the magical use of Kavod occurs in the Talmud, and probably in the above-quoted midrash, but not in the Heikhalot literature. In the closest parallel to the talmudic passage describing R. 'Aqivah as using the divine Glory, found in a Heikhalot text, *Heikhalot Zutarti* (Schaefer, *Synopse*, par. 346, pp. 146–147) the version is *histakkel bi-khevodi*, namely, R. 'Aqivah has contemplated the Glory. This is one of the examples that demonstrates that when a talmudic, as well as a midrashic, passage parallels one in the Heikhalot literature, it is quite possible that the more magical or theurgical stand will be found in the rabbinic versions, while the Heikhalot text may represent a more contemplative stand. See especially par. 335, where different attitudes toward the Glory are mentioned in order to warn the mystic, none of them being the theurgical use, as represented by the verb *mishtammesh*. See also Scholem, *Major Trends*, p. 46; idem, *Jewish Gnosticism*, p. 54; Liebes, *Het'o shel 'Elisha'*, pp. 90–91. Such a differing attitude may be explained by the different types of theology dominating the different types of literature. See Idel, *Kabbalah: New Perspectives*, pp. 157–158.

73. See Heschel, *The Theology of Ancient Judaism*, 1:3–23.

74. The transmission of secrets in a whisper is already mentioned in *Bereshit Rabba*, III:4, ed. J. Theodor and C. Albeck (Wahrman, Jerusalem, 1965), 1:19–20, and BT, *Hagigah*, fol. 13a. See also above, note 39.

75. *Kelalut*. This term is parallel to *rashei peraqim*, which is sometimes translated as rudiments, in the rabbinic sources. See also the text of R. Nathan, a student of Abulafia, the author of *Sefer Sha'arei Tzedeq*, p. 9, who mentions the *kelalim* as related to the rudiments.

76. *Mevin bahem*.

77. On this expression see Isadore Twersky, *Rabad of Posquieres: A Twelfth-Century Talmudist* (Harvard University Press, Cambridge, Mass., 1962), pp. 293–296. See also below, note 125, the quote from Todros Abulafia's *'Otzar ha-Kavod*.

78. Compare the requirement of having an anxious heart for receiving secrets, in BT, *Hagigah*, fol. 13a.

79. *'Otzar ha-Ge'onim*, ed. B. Levin, *Hagigah* (Jerusalem, 1932), p. 12; Scholem, *Jewish Gnosticism*, p. 58.

80. *Megillat Ahima'atz* (Jerusalem, 1964), pp. 1–3.

81. Namely of the Torah.

82. See Daniel Goldschmidt, *Mahzor le-Yamim Nora'im, According to the Ashkenazi Rite* (Jerusalem, 1970), 1:133.

83. Although scholars consider the following to be a relatively early text in the Ashkenazi literature, its similarity to Hasidei Ashkenaz thought invites, in my opinion, a somewhat later dating.

84. *Ma'amiqim.* On the relation between this verb and the concept of secret see Dan, *Studies*, p. 46, note 9; Marcus, *Piety and Society*, p. 85; and also below, note 133. As Israel Ta-Shma has pointed out, the verb recurs in medieval Ashkenazi nonmystical nomenclature in order to describe a certain kind of legalistic study. See his "An Abridgement of 'Hovot ha-Levavot,'" *'Alei Sefer* 10 (1982), p. 19 (Hebrew), and Soloveitchik's study mentioned below, note 100, p. 315, note 8. The term *'omeq* for secrets occurs also in ecstatic Kabbalah: see Idel, "Maimonides and Kabbalah," pp. 57, 62. See also an early-fourteenth-century Kabbalistic book whose influence on later Kabbalah was very great, *Berit Menuhah* (Amsterdam, 1648), fol. 2b, discussed in Daniel Abrams, "The Shekhinah Prays Before God," *Tarbiz* 63 (1994), pp. 509–533 (Hebrew). See also below, chap. 10, note 53.

85. The nexus between fathoming and understanding is found also in *Sefer Hasidim*, ed. J. Wistinetzki (Frankfurt am Main, 1924), p. 242, par. 983: *she-ma'amiq be-binah*, and in R. Eleazar of Worms' *Sefer Hokhmat ha-Nefesh* (Benei Beraq, 1987), p. 96: *'omeq ha-hokhmah ve-ha-binah*. On the other hand, in *Sefer Hasidim*, par. 984, understanding is presented as a condition for fathoming. On the latter paragraph see Peter Schaefer, "The Ideal of Piety of the Ashkenazi Hasidim and Its Roots in Jewish Tradition," *Jewish History* 4, no. 2 (1990), p. 17.

86. *Sefer ha-Pardes*, ed. H. Y. Ehrenreich (Budapest, 1924), p. 229, par. 174. On this text see E. E. Urbach, *Sefer 'Arugat Habosem, auctore R. Abraham b. R. Azriel* (Meqitzei Nirdamim, Jerusalem, 1963), 4:6, 73 (Hebrew).

87. *Sodekha.*

88. Namely the angels.

89. *Rubbei binatekha.*

90. Printed by Yehudah Leib Weinberger, "New Poems from the Byzantine Period," *HUCA* 43 (1972), p. 293 (Hebrew). For the date and place of this poet see more recently Ezra Fleisher, "'Azharot le-Rabbi Benjamin (ben Shmuel) the Poet," *Qovez al Yad*, n.s., vol. 11 (21) (1985), pp. 3–75 (Hebrew).

91. Compare also another part of this poem, printed in Fleisher, ibid., p. 74, where God is described as compelling men to deal with His secrets, *sodeikha*.

92. See Weinberger, "New Poems from the Byzantine Period," p. 296.

93. *Bereshit Rabbati*, p. 8.

94. On this composition see Dan, *Studies*, pp. 44–57, esp. p. 48, note 29.

95. Marcus, "Exegesis for the Few," pp. 1–24.

96. Numerically this word is equivalent to seventy-three, as is the form u-vinah.

97. Ibid., pp. 16–18. See also his *Piety and Society* (Brill, Leiden, 1980), pp. 69, 119.

98. Proverbs 2:4–5.

99. Namely Binah.

100. *Sefer Hasidim*, par. 1514, in the edition of J. Wistinetzki (Frankfurt am Main, 1924), p. 369, adduced and discussed by Marcus, "Exegesis for the Few," p. 22; Haym Soloveitchik, "Three Themes in Sefer Hasidim," AJSR 1 (1976), p. 314, note 7. See also Abrams, "The Literary Emergence," pp. 67–85.

101. For more on the esoteric aspects of the Torah in *Sefer Hasidim* see another important passage quoted and discussed by Marcus, ibid., p. 21. The nonexegetical nature of the fifty gates is corroborated by several discussions found in R. Eleazar's *Commentary on Prayer*, ed. M. Herschler and Y. A. Herschler (Jerusalem, 1992), p. 149, and in his *Sefer ha-Hokhmah*, in Y. Klugmann, ed., *Perushei Roqeah 'al ha-Torah* (Benei Berq, 1985), 1:48, and again in the milieu of R. Eleazar, in a writing of R. Abraham ben Azriel, who describes the fifty gates as granted to Adam. See Urbach, *Sefer 'Arugat ha-Bosem*, 3:53. Thus, it seems that they can be conceived of as a very high form of intellection, but totally unrelated to the contents of the Torah. In my opinion, the attribution of the gates to Adam, found in the sources mentioned above and in many others not adduced here, in lieu of the classical attribution to Moses, represents an earlier tradition that was later shifted to Moses. On this issue I hope to elaborate elsewhere. See, meanwhile, note 59 above. See also Abrams, "The Literary Emergence," p. 69.

102. *Sefer ha-'Emunah ve-ha-Bitahon*, chap. 23, in *Kitvei ha-Ramban*, ed. C. D. Chavel (Mossad ha-Rav Kook, Jerusalem, 1963), 2:435.

103. *Meshiv Devarim Nekhohim*, ed. Y. A. Vajda (Israeli Academy, Jerusalem, 1968), pp. 140–141.

104. See note 62 above.

105. *Commentary on the Pentateuch*, ed. C. D. Chavel (Jerusalem, 1959), 1:4; Halbertal, *People of the Book*, pp. 37–38.

106. Ibid.

107. Introduction to *Commentary on the Pentateuch*, 1:7. For the importance of this passage for the overall view of Kabbalah in Nahmanides' thought see Idel, "We Have No Kabbalistic Tradition," pp. 59–60.

108. Lo' itbonenu.

109. *Commentary on the Pentateuch*, 1:4. For more on this issue see below, chap. 13, par. I.

110. Ibid., 1:9.

111. Ibid., 1:14.

112. Compare Wolfson, "By Way of Truth."

113. Exodus 14:19–21. On this view of the alphabets and that found in an anonymous commentary on the liturgy from the school related to Abraham Abulafia, I hope to elaborate elsewhere.

114. Deuteronomy 34:10.

115. Preserved in Ms. Schocken Kabbalah 14, fol. 120b; see also Idel, *Language, Torah and Hermeneutics*, pp. 151–152. This book differs from that referred to above in chap. 2.

116. See *'Avot*, ed. Taylor, p. 43, and our discussion above.

117. See Moshe Idel, "To the History of the Interdiction to Study Kabbalah before the Age of Forty," *AJSR* 5 (1980), pp. 4–5 (Hebrew). See also R. Yehudah he-Hasid, *Sefer Gematria'ot*, p. 54.

118. See *Moreh ha-Moreh* (Pressburg, 1837), p. 6. For more on the background of this view see Idel, ibid., pp. 2–6.

119. According to the translation in Scholem, *Major Trends*, p. 139, Hebrew original p. 382, note 75. Compare also Idel, *Messianic Mystics*, pp. 299–300. See also another important text stemming from Abulafia's school, *Haqdamah*, in Ms. Paris, BN 851, fol. 29ab, printed in the appendix to Abrams, "The Shekhinah Prays Before God," where he adduced also a great variety of medieval sources dealing, inter alia, with secrets and understanding. On understanding and the divine name see also below, the quote from R. Todros ha-Levi Abulafia's book.

120. Scholem, ibid.

121. For more on this issue see Idel, "Defining Kabbalah," p. 111.

122. See also *'Otzar ha-Kavod*, fol. 19d.

123. This form of exclamation is characteristic of the Zoharic style. I assume that the whole passage, starting with "Happy," points to an awareness not only of the *Zohar* as a book but also of its ambiance. Indeed, this Kabbalist and his son were acquaintances of R. Moses de Leon. See especially Liebes, *Studies in the Zohar*, pp. 135–138.

124. *Tzenu'im*. On this term see Idel, "Defining Kabbalah," p. 115, note 14.

125. *Sefer 'Otzar ha-Kavod*, fol. 13d, also quoted by R. Meir ibn Gabbai, *Sefer 'Avodat ha-Qodesh*, fol. 16d. See, however, R. Todros's assault on Kabbalists who discuss divine names, below, appendix 2, note 20.

126. See the important passage of R. Hayyim Vital, *'Etz Hayyim*, gate Mohin de-Qatnut, chap. 3. The nexus between Binah and occult knowledge is still evident in the middle of the eighteenth century, when the Besht is described as someone who was graced by God with a bounty of Binah, *binah yeterah*, and he can understand things belonging to the upper world. *Epistle of the Ascent of the Soul*, printed in Joshua Mondshein, *Shivhei ha-Baal Shem Tov* (Jerusalem, 1982), p. 234. This term is found already in talmudic sources; see, e.g., BT, *Sotah*, fol. 35b. See also the importance of the *hit-bonenut*, a term that became current for contemplation, sometimes regarding textual issues, in later Hasidism, as for example R. Dov Baer of Lubavitch's *Quntres ha-Hitbonenut*. See also R. Hayyim of Volozhin, *Nefesh ha-Hayyim*, pp. 52–53. It should be mentioned that Binah was also understood by the Besht as pointing to the understanding of the meaning of words of prayer or a text that is studied, in a rather interesting manner. He is reported by R. Jacob Joseph of Polonnoye to have said that a person who prays or studies without understanding the meaning of the words

corresponds to the sefirah of Malkhut, while he who understands (mevin) the meaning, and intends it, links this sefirah to Binah. See *Ben Porat Yosef*, fol. 127b.

127. Fishbane, *Biblical Interpretation*, p. 245.

128. And PRSh, as pointed out by Fishbane, ibid.

129. For the relations between the two phenomena in later Jewish literature see Idel, *Kabbalah: New Perspectives*, pp. 234–249, and idem, *Language, Torah and Hermeneutics*, pp. 101–109; Elliot R. Wolfson, "Circumcision, Visionary Experience and Textual Interpretation: From Midrashic Trope to Mystical Symbol," *History of Religions* 27 (1987) pp. 189–215; idem, "The Hermeneutics of Visionary Experience: Revelation and Interpretation in the Zohar," *Religion* 18 (1988), pp. 311–345.

130. For attempts to separate between what could be called mystical literature and mystical experience—too radical a distinction, in my opinion—see, e.g., the views of Halperin, *The Merkabah in Rabbinic Literature*, passim; Schaefer, *Hekhalot-Studien*, pp. 294–295, and Joseph Dan, *The Revelation of the Secret of the World*, pp. 11–13.

131. I do not know the meaning of this verb. See, however, Moshe Z. Segal, *Sefer Ben Sira' ha-Shalem* (Mossad Bialik, Jerusalem, 1972), p. 53.

132. Ben Sira' 39:4, according to the reconstructed text of Segal, *Sefer Ben Sira' ha-Shalem*, p. 152, on the basis of a Syrian translation: *Nistarot mashal idrosh, uvehidot mashal itratash*. Compare Proverbs 1:6, and see also Kugel, in Kugel and Greer, *Early Biblical Interpretation*, pp. 62–63.

133. The term *'imqei* in Ben Sira' is reconstructed by Segal, *Sefer Ben Sira' ha-Shalem*, p. 152, on the basis of Syrian. On *'omeq* in contexts of secrets see above, notes 24, 47, 84, and Idel, "Defining Kabbalah," p. 102 and note 51, as well as below, in the context of the Hasidei Ashkenaz texts, where the notion of the depths of the Torah will be mentioned. In this context, the importance of the ten "depths" of the universe in *Sefer Yetzirah* should also be mentioned. See also Liebes, "The Messiah of the Zohar," p. 211, and Daniel Abrams, "The Book of Illumination of R. Jacob bem Jacob HaKohen" (Ph.D. diss., New York University, New York, 1993), p. 34 (Hebrew), where more Kabbalistic sources dealing with the depths of the Torah are adduced. The concept of depths of the sefirot and the depths of nothingness are important aspects of Kabbalistic theology, but those topics should be discussed separately.

134. Segal, *Sefer Ben Sira' ha-Shalem*, p. 16; See also Liebes, *Het' shel 'Elisha'*, p. 154.

135. *'Anavim*. See also verse 16.

136. Segal, *Ben Sira' ha-Shalem*, p. 16.

137. Ibid., pp. 17–18.

138. This is reminiscent of the idea found in the Greek Bible as to those who will inherit heaven.

139. Segal, *Ben Sira' ha-Shalem*, pp. 17–18.

140. See his "Interpretive Authority in Studying Community at Qumran," *JJS* 44 (1993), pp. 58–59, 62.

141. Mishnah, *Hagigah*, fol. 13a; Liebes, *Het'o shel 'Elisha'*, pp. 106–107, 131–141, 148.

142. *Hagigah*, fol. 13a.

143. Ibid.

144. Halperin, *Faces of the Chariot*, pp. 26–27.

145. See also the parallel pointed out by Halperin, ibid., p. 26, note 17, where the notion of the age is indicated in a talmudic text in connection with the study of the Merkavah topics.

146. Scholem, *Jewish Gnosticism*, p. 38, has merged these criteria in a way that presupposes one view that informed both Origen and the mishnaic material.

147. *The World of the Sages*, p. 522.

148. 'Avodah Zarah, chap. 2, Mishnah 8: *razei torah*. See also the parallel in *Midrash Rabba* on Song of Songs 1:2: *sitrei torah*.

149. BT, *Hagigah*, fols. 13a–14a. A different view of this legend is found in Liebes, *Het'o shel 'Elisha'*.

150. In my monograph on the *Four Sages Entered the Orchard*, in preparation.

151. Sod. Unlike many other studies which translate this word as "mystery," I prefer to translate it as "secret," for reasons I shall elaborate elsewhere. See, meanwhile, the different view of Alexander Altmann, "Maimonides's Attitude toward Jewish Mysticism," in Alfred Jospe, ed., *Studies in Jewish Thought* (Detroit, 1981), pp. 200–219, esp. pp. 201–202. According to other manuscripts, the version here is *sar*, namely "prince." On the prince of the Torah see also above, chap. 4, par. I.

152. Yidreshuhu.

153. Schaefer, *Synopse*, pp. 132–133, par. 297; Idel, "The Concept of the Torah," pp. 36–37, note 39. See also above, chap. 6, par. III.

154. See Gershom Scholem, ed., "Two Treatises of Moshe de Leon," in *Qovetz 'al Yad* 8 (18) (1976), p. 332 (Hebrew): "And by means of this secret is the Torah expounded." For another medieval use of the verb *darash* in the context of dealing with secrets see the text related to R. Eleazar of Worms mentioned above, note 24, and Abrams's discussion referred to there. On the history of *derash* in Jewish hermeneutics see David Weiss Halivni, *Peshat and Derash* (Oxford University Press, New York, 1991); Fishbane, *The Garments of Torah*, pp. 113–120; and Idel, *Language, Torah and Hermeneutics*, pp. 88–91.

155. See Sara O. Heller Wilensky, "The Dialectical Influence of Maimonides on Isaac ibn Latif and Early Spanish Kabbalah," in M. Idel, W. Z. Harvey, and E. Schweid, eds., *Shlomo Pines Jubilee Volume* (Jerusalem, 1988), 1:294 (Hebrew).

156. See Idel, *Language, Torah and Hermeneutics*, pp. 53–54, and the pertinent footnotes.

157. See note 2 above.

158. Cf. Palestinian Talmud, *Rosh ha-Shanah*, I:2.

159. See Scholem, *Major Trends*, pp. 41, 46, 84; Dan, *The Esoteric Theology*, pp. 18–20; Roberto Bonfil, "Tra Due Mondi: Prospettive di ricerca sulla storia culturale degli ebrei nell'Italia meridionale nell'Alto Medioevo," *Italia Judaica* 1 (1983), p. 149, note 54; Abrams, "The Literary Emergence," p. 68. The controversy between Israel Weinstock and Gershom Scholem concerning Weinstock's assumption that the secrets of Abu Aharon are still extant in a certain manuscript in the British Library is irrelevant

to the very possibility, which seems to be accepted by all scholars, including those mentioned above, that Abu Aharon apparently brought some secrets from Baghdad, whether they are still extant or not. It would be pointless to say that the possible Mesopotamian extraction of some of the topics related to Jewish ancient esoterics does not invalidate the possibility of other influences—Greek, Egyptian, Iranian, etc.

160. See Tishby, *The Wisdom of the Zohar*, 3:1077, and below, chap. 10.

CHAPTER 8: SEMANTICS, CONSTELLATION, AND INTERPRETATION

1. On hypertextuality see, e.g., the studies collected in *The Future of the Book* and in *Hyper/Text/Theory*, ed. George P. Landow (John Hopkins University Press, Baltimore, 1994).

2. Heinemann, *Darkhei ha-ʾAggadah*; Fishbane, *The Exegetical Imagination*; Fraenkel, *The Ways of ʾAggadah and Midrash*; Stern, *Midrash and Theory*, pp. 1–14; idem, *Parables in Midrash: Narrative and Exegesis in Rabbinic Literature* (Harvard University Press, Cambridge, Mass., 1991); Goldin, *Studies in Midrash*; Bruns, *Hermeneutics Ancient and Modern*, pp. 104–123; Weiss-Ha-Livni, *Midrash*; idem, "Aspects of Classical Jewish Hermeneutics," in Hendrik M. Vroom and Jerald D. Gort, eds. *Holy Scriptures in Judaism, Christianity, and Islam: Hermeneutics, Value and Society* (Rodopi, Amsterdam, Atlanta, 1997), pp. 77–97; Boyarin, *Intertextuality*; I. L. Seeligmann, *Studies in Biblical Literature*, ed. A. Hurvitz, S. Japhet, and E. Tov (Magnes Press, Jerusalem, 1996), pp. 429–474 (Hebrew); Jacob Neusner, *Midrash in Context: Exegesis in Formative Judaism* (Fortress Press, Philadelphia, 1983); Gary Porton, "Defining Midrash," in *The Study of Ancient Judaism*, ed. Jacob Neusner (New York, 1981), 1:55–92; Geza Vermes, "Bible and Midrash: Early Old Testament Exegesis," in *Post-Biblical Jewish Studies* (Brill, Leiden, 1975), pp. 59–91; Handelman, *The Slayers of Moses*, pp. 27–82; Herbert W. Baser, "Josephus as Exegete," *Journal of the American Oriental Society* 107, no. 1 (1987), pp. 21–30; Kugel, in Kugel and Reer, *Early Biblical Interpretation*, pp. 9–106. See also below, notes 8, 39. For a comprehensive bibliography on Midrash, see *Midrash and Literature*, pp. 369–395.

3. See Weiss-Ha-Livni, *Midrash*, p. 16.

4. See M. S. Cohen, *The Shiʿur Qomah: Liturgy and Theurgy in Pre-Kabbalistic Jewish Mysticism* (Lanham, New York, 1983), p. 93, where a phrase from the famous verse Psalms 147:5 is interpreted as pointing by its numerical equivalence to the size of the divine body.

5. See Stern, *Midrash and Theory*, pp. 73–93. According to Heinemann, *Darkhei ha-ʾAggadah*, it is the neglect of the logos that induced the linguovert attitude toward the text, which he designated by the term *creative philology*, a view that is consonant with the general approach of Handelman, *The Slayers of Moses*.

6. For more on this issue see below, chap. 9, par. III.

7. *Le degré zero*, pp. 45–47.

8. Compare Joseph Heinemann, "The Nature of the Aggadah," in *Midrash and Literature*, p. 53; Rawidowicz, "On Interpretation," p. 91; Mordechai Rotenberg, *Re-biographing and Deviance* (Praeger, New York, 1987).

9. On these practices see above, chaps. 5 and 6.

10. "*Poterion enheiri kyrion*: Philo and the Rabbis on the Powers of God and the Mixture in the Cup," *Scripta Classica Israelica* 16 (1997), pp. 91–101; see also Belkin, *Midrash Tadsche*', pp. 12–14. On the possible Greek source for the theology of two measures see Winston, *Logos*, pp. 18–20. On the possibility that the theology of the two attributes had been combined with the concept of ten sefirot as contributing to the emergence of Kabbalah see Buber, *The Origin and Meaning of Hasidism*, pp. 176–177.

11. Israel Knohl, *The Sanctuary of Silence: The Priestly Torah and the Holiness School* (Fortress Press, Minneapolis, 1994), pp. 124–148, 168–172, 227.

12. See above, chap. 3, par. III, and below, app. 5, par. II.

13. Isaiah 26:21. See below, note 24.

14. *Pesiqta' de-R. Kahana'*, ed. Jacob Mandelbaum (Jewish Theological Seminary, New York, 1962), 2:364; PT, *Ta'anit*, fol. 65b. See also the important discussion of A. Marmorstein, *The Old Rabbinic Doctrine of God* (Oxford University Press, London, 1927), 1:44 and note 14.

15. *Leviticus Rabba'*, 19:4. See also *Midrash Tanhuma' Huqat*, chap. 6; *Ecclesiastes Rabba'*, ad locum.

16. See BT, *Berakhot*, fol. 7a.

17. See Roland Barthes, "From Work to Text," in *Textual Strategies*, p. 78. It was Prof. Geoffrey Hartman, who drew my attention to the affinity between midrashic hermeneutics and the "disastered" view of Barthes. Somewhat along this line is the interesting study by Stern, *Midrash and Theory*, on earlier Jewish literature and Handelman's exposition of modern Jewish philosophers in *Fragments of Redemptions*, esp. p. 292. On hermeneutics and stars see Hartman, *The Fate of Reading*, pp. 114–123.

18. Printed in Epstein, *Mi-Qadmoniyyot ha-Yehudim*, p. 144. See also Raphael Patai, *The Hebrew Goddess* (New York, 1978), p. 82, who noted the affinity between Philo and *Midrash Tadsche*'; also pp. 76, 119–120, on Philo, Kabbalah, and divine attributes. For more on the possible affinities between this midrash and Philo see Belkin, *Midrash Tadsche*, esp. pp. 10–14.

19. *Be-yihud gamur*.

20. Cf. Exodus 36:13. The Tabernacle became a recurrent symbol in theosophical Kabbalah for the sefirotic realm, which should be unified.

21. This is a shorter form of the Tetragrammaton.

22. Genesis 19:24.

23. The Hebrew text was first printed by Gershom Scholem, *Reshit ha-Kabbalah* (Schocken, Jerusalem and Tel Aviv, 1948), p. 79 (Hebrew); see also idem, *Origins of the Kabbalah*, p. 217; Isadore Twersky, *Rabad of Posquieres: A Twelfth-Century Talmudist* (Harvard University Press, Cambridge, Mass., 1962), p. 291, note 20.

24. See Idel, *Kabbalah: New Perspectives*, pp. 128–129. The expression "the Tetragrammaton passed" has to do with Isaiah 26:21, where the Tetragrammaton occurs in an apocalyptic verse in which God is described as punishing, thus an operation that is not related to the attribute of mercy.

25. See Abrams, *R. Asher ben David*, pp. 61, 72.

26. See, e.g., R. Meir ibn Gabbai's discussions in his *Sefer 'Avodat ha-Qodesh*, fols. 88c, 97c, 98a, 104c.

27. See Dan, *Esoteric Theology*, p. 122.

28. 2 Samuel 2:6.

29. *Sodei Razaya*, ed. Israel Kamelhar (Bielgoria, 1936) p. 58. See also below, chap. 9, note 18.

30. See *Mekhilta' de-Rabbi Ishma'el*, ed. and trans. J. Z. Lauterbach, in Max Kadushin, *A Conceptual Approach to the Mekilta* (Jewish Theological Seminary, New York, 1969), part 2, p. 113; see also *Yalqut Shim'oni*, on Numbers 10:31, par. 730. On the *Mekhilta'* see Boyarin, *Intertextuality*, pp. 39–56, and the bibliography adduced on p. 130, note 3, and Hirshman, *A Rivalry of Genius*, pp. 55–66. For the background of the Exodus verse that is interpreted here see G. H. Skipwith, "The Lord of Heaven," *JQR* 19, o.s. (1902), p. 693.

31. Exodus 1:14.

32. Interestingly, the noun "sapphire" was also understood as hinting at slavery; in PT, *Sukkah*, IV:3, it is related to Ezekiel 1:26, "stone of sapphire," concluding that the Babylonian diaspora is harder than the Egyptian—stone in comparison to brick.

33. See Kadushin, *A Conceptual Approach to the Mekilta*, part 1, p. 186.

34. Printed by Abraham Epstein in *Ha-'Eshkol* 6 (1909), p. 207.

35. See Kadushin, *A Conceptual Approach to the Mekilta*, part 1, pp. 186–187.

36. Isaiah 63:10.

37. *Mekhilta' de-Rabbi Ishma'el, Masekhet de-Shirta'*, IV, ed. M. Friedmann (Vienna, 1870), fol. 37b.

38. See *Midrash Tanhuma'*, pericope Ha'azinu, 4, where a series of contradictory descriptions of God is adduced in relation to our verse.

39. See James L. Kugel, "Two Introduction to Midrash," in *Midrash and Literature*, pp. 91–100, for the concept of verse-centeredness, and Michael Fishbane, "Inner Biblical Exegesis: Types and Strategies of Interpretation in Ancient Israel," in ibid., pp. 19–37, and his *Biblical Interpretation* for the reinterpretation of some older traditions by the biblical authors themselves.

40. BT, *Menahot*, fol. 29b; Scholem, *The Messianic Idea*, pp. 282–283.

41. Idel, *Language, Torah and Hermeneutics*, pp. 87–91, 110–111.

42. See Joseph Dan, "Midrash and the Dawn of Kabbalah," in *Midrash and Literature*, pp. 127–139.

43. See Wolfson, "By Way of Truth."

44. Idel, *Kabbalah: New Perspectives*, pp. 217–218. See also, more recently, Magid, "From Theosophy to Midrash."

45. Or, as Charles Mopsik defined the *Zohar*, it is a midrash on Midrash; see *Le Zohar* (Verdier, Lagrasse, 1996), 4:16–23.

46. See Idel, *Kabbalah: New Perspectives*, pp. 156–199, 222–234; Mopsik, *Les grands texts*; Lorberbaum, *Imago Dei*.

47. Idel, *Kabbalah: New Perspectives*, pp. 230–232.

48. See Wolfson, "Letter Symbolism," pp. 195–236; idem, "Anthropomorphic Imagery and Letter Symbolism in the *Zohar*," in *The Age of the Zohar*, pp. 147–181 (Hebrew).

49. Idel, "The Concept of the Torah," pp. 70–74; see also above, chap. 3.

50. See Ithamar Gruenwald, "From Talmudic to Zoharic Homiletics," in Joseph Dan, ed., *The Age of the Zohar* (Jerusalem, 1989), p. 259 (Hebrew). Cf. also Stern, *Midrash and Theory*, pp. 31–32. See also above, Introduction, par. III, and below, chap. 10, par. II.

51. See Buber, *The Origin and Meaning of Hasidism*, pp. 117–119, 124, 133–137, 252–253.

52. See above, chap. 1, par. I, chap. 3, par. I, and also below, chap. 11, par. I. In this context the exegetical aspects of another ancient Jewish author drastically marginalized by the rabbinic tradition should be mentioned. See Baser, "Josephus as Exegete," esp. pp. 25–26, where esoteric topics are mentioned.

53. See Goodenough, *By Light, Light*, and *An Introduction to Philo Judaeus* (Yale University Press, New Haven, 1940); Winston, *Logos*; idem, *Philo of Alexandria*.

54. Bruns, *Hermeneutics Ancient and Modern*, pp. 83–103.

55. See, e.g., the critical review of Morton Smith, "Goodenough's Jewish Symbols in Retrospect," *Journal of Biblical Literature* 86 (1967), pp. 53–68, and Arnaldo Momigliano, *Essays on Ancient and Modern Judaism*, ed. Silvia Berti and trans. M. Masella-Gayley (University of Chicago Press, Chicago, 1994), pp. 48–57.

56. See R. J. Zwi Werblowsky, "Philo and the Zohar: A Note on the Method of the Scienzia Nuova in Jewish Studies," *JJS* 10 (1959), pp. 25–44, 113–135; Scholem, *On the Kabbalah*, p. 34, note 2. See the rejoinder of Joshua Finkel, "The Alexandrian Tradition and the *Midrash ha-Neʿelam*," in *The Leo Jung Jubilee Volume*, ed. M. M. Kasher, N. Lamm, and L. Rosenfeld (New York, 5722/1962), pp. 77–103, and Shmuel Belkin, "Philo's Symbolic Midrash in Comparison to the Rabbinic Midrash," *Wolfson Jubilee Volume* (Jerusalem, 1965), 1:25–32 (Hebrew). In this context the affinities between Philonic and Kabbalistic ideas that Yizhak F. Baer suggested should also be mentioned. See, e.g., Baer, *Studies*, 1:111–114, and Scholem's skeptical reaction, *On the Kabbalah*, p. 34, note 1. See now Liebes, *Ars Poetica*, passim.

57. See, e.g., *On the Kabbalah*, pp. 32, 40, 45–46, 53, note 1.

58. See Idel, *Kabbalah: New Perspectives*, pp. 131–132.

59. See Idel, "Be-'Or ha-Hayyim," p. 208.

60. On this topic see e.g., McGinn, *The Presence of God*, 1:35–41; Pinhas Carny, "Philo Alexandrinus' Theory of Allegory" (Ph.D. diss., Tel Aviv University, 1978) (Hebrew); David M. Hay, "Philo's View of Himself as an Exegete: Inspired, but Not Authoritative," *The Studia Philonica Annual, Studies in Hellenistic Judaism* 3 (1991), pp. 40–52; de Lubac, *Histoire et esprit*, pp. 150–166; Fraenkel, *The Ways of the 'Aggadah and Midrash*, pp. 473–475; Handelman, *The Slayers of Moses*, pp. 93–96, 100–104.

61. *De Cherubim*, par. 27–28; Winston, *Philo of Alexandria*, p. 89; Wolfson, *Philo*, 1:236–237; Belkin, *Midrash Tadsche*, pp. 10–14; Stroumsa, *Savoir et salut*, pp. 34–35. For the reverberation of the symbolic attitude toward the Bible after Philo see Francis T. Fallon, "The Law in Philo and Ptolemy: A Note on the Letter of Flora," *Vigiliae Christianae* 30 (1976), pp. 45–51.

62. According to Goodenough, *By Light, Light*, p. 25, Philo refers here to the Divine names Kyrios and Theos.

63. *Questiones et Solutiones in Exodus*, II:66, quoted in Goodenough, *By Light, Light*, pp. 25–26. See also Philo, *De Cherubin*, pars. 27–28, quoted above; *Quis Rerum Divinarum Heres Sit*, par. 166; cf. Winston, *Philo of Alexandria*, p. 89; Baer, *Studies*, 1:405–408; Belkin, *Midrash Tadsche*, pp. 10–14; Stroumsa, *Savoir et salut*, pp. 34–35; Idel, *Kabbalah: New Perspectives*, pp. 131–132; and Elliot R. Wolfson, "Woman—the Feminine as Other in Theosophic Kabbalah: Some Philosophical Observations on the Divine Androgyne," in L. J. Silberstein and R. L. Cohn, *The Other in Jewish Thought and History* (New York University Press, New York, 1994), pp. 173–175.

64. On the concept of the two powers in Philo's thought see Wolfson, *Philo*, 1:217–226; N. A. Dahl and A. F. Segal, "Philo and the Rabbis on the Names of God," *Journal of the Studies of Judaism* 9 (1978), pp. 1–28; Winston, *Logos*, pp. 21–22, 69–70, note 59.

65. *De Cherubim*, pars. 27, 42. See Bruns, *Hermeneutics Ancient and Modern*, p. 101.

66. For more on these issues see below, chap. 11.

67. See below, chap. 11.

68. *De Specialibus Legibus*, 3:178; cf. Winston, *Philo of Alexandria*, p. 79.

69. *De Migratione*, par. 89; Winston, *Philo of Alexandria*, p. 81.

70. See De Lubac, *Histoire et esprit*, p. 289.

71. Ibid., p. 288. For more on Origen's hermeneutics see Irvine, *The Making of Textual Culture*, pp. 252–257.

72. Colossians 1:15–17, 19. See S. J. Grasowski, "God 'Contains' the Universe: A Study in Patristic Theology," *Revue de l'Université de Ottawa* 26 (1950), pp. 90–113, 165–187. See also below, the discussion of the passage from *Midrash Tadsche'*.

73. *The Refutations of All Heresies*, VIII:6, pp. 318–319. I was unable to find any substantial discussion of Monoimos in the most important studies on Gnosticism, a fact that demonstrates that his views do not correspond to any of the main texts that constitute the Gnostic literature. On the tittle of iota in Monoimos and in Kabbalah see Carl G. Jung, *Mysterium Conjunctionis* (Princeton University Press, New Jersey, 1980), p. 44, note 26. In any case, it seems that the "inverted interpretation" of the biblical texts, representative of many of the Gnostic texts, is not corroborated by any of the passages attributed to Monoimos, which seem to be more representative of Jewish traditions. See below, notes 74–76.

74. The phrase "tittle of iota" seems to reflect the Jewish expression "tittle of yod"; see BT, *Menahot*, fol. 34a. The rabbinic authority who uses this phrase, Rav, adduces the following statement in another discussion in connection with R. 'Aqivah: "A man will come after several generations whose name is R. 'Aqivah ben Joseph, who is destined to comment upon each and every tittle [of the letters], heaps of halakhot." Cf. BT, *Menahot*, fol. 29b. For a later interpretation of the "heaps" as pointing to the infinity of the Torah see R. Moses ha-Darshan, *Bereshit Rabbati*, p. 20.

75. On the many faces of God see the rabbinic parable adduced above, chap. 3, par. III, from *Yalqut Shim'oni*.

76. The description of supernal beings, such as angels, as possessing innumerable eyes is known in Jewish sources; see BT, 'Avodah Zarah, fol. 2b.

77. *Refutation of All Heresies*, VIII:7, Anti-Nicene Christian Library (Edinburgh, 1968), 6:320. On this passage see Ginzberg, *Legends of the Jews*, 5:63, note 1. For two ontological decads related to biblical material see also the important discussions found in the Pseudo-Clementine *Recognitions of Clemet*, III, chap. 61, etc. I hope to elaborate elsewhere on the importance of this source for understanding the history of Kabbalah.

78. See Bruns, *Inventions*, pp. 37–38; see also the discussion by de Lubac, *Exégèse medieval*, 4:82–83.

79. The *Tripartite Tractate*, in James M. Robinson, ed., *The Nag Hammadi Library* (Harper & Row, San Francisco, 1981), p. 66. See also Irenaeus, *Against Heresies*, IV, 1, 1, in *Ante-Nicene Fathers* (Grand Rapids, Mich., 1977), 1:463.

80. Cf. the LXX translation of YHWH *tzeva'ot* as "the Lord of the powers."

81. *Apocalypse of Adam*, trans. G. Macrae, in James H. Charlesworth, ed., *The Old Testament Pseudepigrapha* (New York, 1983), 1:712.

82. Cf. Marc Philonenko, "Essenisme et Gnose chez le Pseudo-Philon," in *Le origine dello Gnosticismo* (Brill, Leiden, 1967), pp. 409–410.

83. See, e.g., George MacRae, "The Jewish Background of the Gnostic Sophia Myth," *Novum Testamentum* 12 (1970), pp. 86–101.

84. Such a view is found in Philo and occurs, though rarely, in rabbinic sources. See Yehoshua Amir, "The Decalogue According to the Teachings of Philo of Alexandria," in Ben-Zion Segal, ed., *The Ten Commandments* (Magnes Press, Jerusalem, 1985), pp. 95–126, esp. pp. 99–100 (Hebrew); Ephraim E. Urbach, "The Place of the Ten Commandments in Ritual and Prayer," in ibid., p. 135, idem, *The Sages*, pp. 360–365; Geza Vermes, "The Decalogue and the Minim," in *In Memoriam Paul Kahle* (Berlin, 1968), pp. 232–240; Wolfson, *Philo*, 2:201; for more general discussions on the Decalogue in Jewish culture see Greenberg, *Studies*, pp. 279–311; Heschel, *Ancient Theology of Judaism*, 2:75–79; Wolfson, *Through a Speculum That Shines*, pp. 354–355; Fishbane, *The Exegetical Imagination*, pp. 9–10. See also below, the discussion of the passage from the Zohar, and Ha-Shelah, I, fol. 172b, and the early-fourteenth-century *Sefer Yesod 'Olam*, by R. Abraham of Esquira, Ms. Moscow-Gunsburg 609, fol. 9a.

85. For other emanative theories in ancient Judaism see Shlomo Pines, "Points of Similarity between the Exposition of the Doctrine of the Sefirot in the *Sefer Yezira* and a Text of the Pseudo-Clementine Homilies," Israel Academy of Sciences and Humanities, *Proceedings* 7, no. 3 (1989), pp. 68–69, 104–106; idem, "God, the Divine Glory," and a Philonic text preserved in Armenian, translated in Ralph Marcus, *Philo: Supplement I, Questions on Genesis*, Loeb Series (Harvard University Press, Cambridge, Mass., 1953), p. 266, analyzed in Idel, "Be-'Or ha-Hayyim," p. 208, and the material adduced in idem, *Messianic Mystics*, p. 340, note 42.

86. See Idel, "The Concept of Torah," pp. 45–46; Moses Gaster, *The Tittled Bible* (London, 1929), pp. 15, 30–31.

87. See R. J. Zwi Werblowsky, "Some Psychological Aspects of Kabbalah," *Harvest* 3

(1956), pp. 77–96; cf. the opinion of F. C. Burkitt, *Church and Gnosis* (Cambridge, 1932), pp. 41–42, and E. R. Dodds, *Pagan and Christian in an Age of Anxiety* (New York, 1970), pp. 18–20, who regard the Gnostic mythologies as a hypostatization of the Gnostics' inner experiences.

88. *Dialogue with Trypho*, chap. 61, p. 170. See also Greer, in Kugeland Greer, *Early Biblical Interpretation*, pp. 146–147. The metaphor of the kindling of one candle or fire from another for the process of emanation is found also in Jewish rabbinic sources; see Tishby, *The Wisdom of the Zohar*, 1:303, note 21.

89. See especially chaps. 126 and 128.

90. See Pines, "God, the Divine Glory," pp. 5–7.

91. Kasher, *Torah Shelemah*, Va-'Era', 9:43. For later reverberations see Idel, "Sefirot above Sefirot," passim, and Wolfson, *Through a Speculum That Shines*, p. 139, note 53.

92. *Dibbur*, although the meaning is "word."

93. *Midrash Tadsche'*, p. 144. See the proposal of Belkin, *Midrash Tadsche'*, pp. 18–19, who sees in Philo's thought the source of the midrash. I believe that my suggestion is more pertinent. See also R. Moses ha-Darshan, *Bereshit Rabbati*, p. 55. On the ten commandments pronounced in one word see Baruch J. Schwartz, "'I Am the Lord' and 'You Shall Have No Other Gods' Were Heard from the Mouth of the Almighty: On the Evolution of an Interpretation," in Sara Japhet, ed., *The Bible in the Light of Its Interpreters: Sarah Kamin Memorial Volume* (Magnes Press, Jerusalem, 1994), pp. 172–173 (Hebrew).

94. *Midrash Tadsche'*, p. 145; see Hananel Mack, "*Midrash Ba-Midbbar Rabba*' and the Beginning of the Kabbalah in Provence," in *Myth in Judaism*, ed. Havivah Pedayah (Be'er Sheva', 1996), pp. 82–88 (Hebrew). Compare also the interesting version of a statement found in Tractate 'Avot but preserved in Hebrew only in an Isma'ili writing: "By means of ten *ma'amarot* the world was created, and by the Decalogue it stands." Cf. Paul Kraus, "Hebräische und syrische Zitate in ismäilitischen Schriften," *Der Islam* 19 (1930), p. 260; Salomon Pines, "Shi'ite Terms and Conceptions in Juda Halevi's Kuzari," *Jerusalem Studies in Arabic and Islam* 2 (1980), pp. 243–244.

95. See, e.g., the introduction of C. Albeck to *Bereshit Rabbati*, pp. 18, 64, and Martha Himmelfarb, "R. Moses the Preacher and the Testament of the Twelve Patriarchs," *AJSR* 9 (1984), pp. 55–78. See also below, note 97.

96. See *Commentary on 'Avot*, printed in R. Simhah, *Mahzor Vitri*, ed. Shim'on ha-Levi Hurvitz (Jerusalem, 1963), p. 536.

97. See R. Moses ha-Darshan, *Bereshit Rabbati*, p. 8, and note 16, and above, note 84.

98. *Zohar*, II, fol. 90b. See also Holdrege, *Veda and Torah*, pp. 200, 317–318, 323. On the view that the ten commandments comprise all the others see above, note 84, and in Spain the ethical treatise of R. Abraham bar Hiyya, *The Meditation of the Sad Soul*, pp. 131–132. See also Wolfson, *Along the Path*, pp. 74–75.

99. See Idel, "Sefirot above Sefirot," pp. 256–257. For '*amarin* in a context that points to *ma'amarot* see *Zohar*, II, fol. 34b. See also above, chap. 4, par. VI.

100. Cf. R. Abraham bar Hiyya, *The Meditation of the Sad Soul*, pp. 131–140, where the

expansion of revelation as articulated in writing is conceived of as representing greater involvement with materiality. See especially the view found in ibid., p. 131, that the nine commandments (all but the first commandment of the Decalogue) "are emanated from God." This is quite a Neoplatonic view, which presupposes a hierarchy within the different parts of the biblical text, a view that has been debated by many medieval thinkers.

101. The people of Israel.

102. This is a short mid-thirteenth-century ethico-mystical treatise attributed to various authors, one of them the twelfth-century R. Tam. The attributions, however, are spurious, and the identity of the author remains unknown.

103. See Sefat 'Emmet, 1:156. On combination of letters see also above, chap. 6, note 168, and below, chap. 12. The hierarchy that organizes the biblical material, starting with the divine name, then ten other names standing for the ten sefirot, and ultimately comprising the entire biblical text, is the core of R. Joseph Gikatilla's Sha'arei 'Orah, as we shall see in chapter 12, par. III. The Rabbi of Gur combines, however, Gikatilla's triangular attitude toward the text with the theory of letter combinations, which are two different models, as we shall see in chapter 12. Cf. also R. Abraham of Turisk, Magen 'Avraham, IV, fol. 77cd. For another triangular theory, similar to the one quoted above, see another Hasidic master, R. Samuel Aharon ha-Kohen of Ostrog, Sefer ve-Tziwah ha-Kohen (Jerusalem, n.d.), p. 57.

104. See Sha'arei Tzedeq, pp. 23–24.

105. Cf. R. Qalonimus Qalman Epstein, Ma'or va-Shemesh, 1:84.

106. Theologia aporrhetos.

107. Contra Celsum, I, 24. For a short discussion of this passage see John Dillon, "The Magical Power of the Names in Origen and Later Platonism," in Origeniana Tertia, ed. R. Hanson and H. Crousel (Rome, 1985), pp. 207–208. See also the interesting study by Naomi Janowitz, "Theories of the Divine Names in Origen and Pseudo-Dionysius," History of Religions 30 [1991], pp. 360–365. For another interesting tradition preserved by Irenaeus concerning the pronunciation of the divine names by Jews see Yehuda Liebes, "The Angels of the Shofar and Yeshua Sar ha-Panim," in Early Jewish Mysticism, p. 194, note 86 (Hebrew).

108. Dillon, "The Magical Power of the Names in Origen and Later Platonism," p. 208.

109. See Idel, Kabbalah: New Perspectives, pp. 123–127.

110. See John G. Gager, Moses in Greco-Roman Paganism (Abington Press, Nashville, 1972), pp. 142–143, 150, 152.

111. See BT, Qiddushin, fol. 71a. For the importance of the traditions related to divine names for the emergence of Kabbalah see Idel, "Defining Kabbalah."

112. Cf. Gikatilla's introduction to his Sha'arei 'Orah.

113. See Sefer Yetzirah, I:1.

114. On ten unerasable divine names see PT, Megilah, fol. 12b; Soferim 4:1; Mopsik, Le Sicle, pp. 278–289.

115. For more on the concept of code and symbolism see below, chap. 10, par. III.

116. See Vajda, *Le Commentaire*, pp. 47–49.

117. See the anonymous Kabbalistic text printed and analyzed by M. Idel, "Kavvana and Colors: A Forgotten Kabbalistic Responsum," in M. Idel, D. Diamant, and S. Rosenberg, *Tribute to Sara: Studies in Jewish Philosophy and Kabbala* (Magnes Press, Jerusalem, 1994), pp. 1–14 (Hebrew).

CHAPTER 9: RADICAL FORMS OF JEWISH HERMENEUTICS

1. See the studies mentioned below in notes 8, 11, 25.

2. It is only in the last two decades that the commentaries of R. Yehudah ben Shmuel he-Hasid and R. Eleazar of Worms have been printed. R. Abraham Abulafia's commentary on the Pentateuch, entitled *Sefer ha-Maftehot*, is extant only in manuscripts. The somewhat later commentaries, however, written in the same vein, those of R. Efrayyim ben Shimshon and of R. Jacob ben Asher, have been in print for centuries.

3. See John D. Caputo, *Radical Hermeneutics: Repetition, Deconstruction, and the Hermeneutic Project* (Indiana University Press, Bloomington, 1987). On "radical interpretation" see Bruns, *Hermeneutics Ancient and Modern*, pp. 83–103.

4. See Eco, *The Search*, p. 27. See also below, chap. 12.

5. See H. G. Enelow, *The Mishnah of Rabbi Eliezer or the Midrash of Thirty-Two Hermeneutic Rules* (Bloch, New York, 1933); Saul Lieberman, *Hellenism in Jewish Palestine* (Jewish Theological Seminary, New York, 1962), pp. 47–82; Lieberman, "A Mesopotamian Background"; Handelman, *The Slayers of Moses*, pp. 51–66, 225–227. See especially Stephen Lieberman's study, where additional pertinent bibliography is adduced. It should be mentioned, as Lieberman has pointed out, ibid., pp. 221–222, that systematic descriptions of exegetical rules are found neither in the Mesopotamian sources he investigated nor in early rabbinic discussions.

6. See the recent collection of articles on this figure edited by Isadore Twersky and J. M. Harris, *Rabbi Abraham ibn Ezra: Studies in the Writings of a Twelfth-Century Jewish Polymath* (Harvard University Press, Cambridge, Mass., 1993).

7. See Dan, "The Ashkenazi Hasidic"; idem, *On Sanctity*, pp. 87–107; Marcus, "Exegesis for the Few"; idem, "Judah the Pietist and Eleazar of Worms: From Charismatic to Conventional Leadership," in *Jewish Mystical Leaders*, pp. 97–126; Wolfson, "The Mystical Significance"; Daniel Abrams, "The Literary Emergence of Esotericism in German Pietism," *Shofar* 12 (1994), pp. 68–70.

8. For the pertinent bibliography on the Pardes exegesis see below, app. 1, notes 1–3.

9. Idel, *Language, Torah, and Hermeneutics*, pp. 82–124.

10. Scholem, *Kabbalah*, pp. 337–343; Heinemann, *Darkhei ha-'Aggadah*, pp. 106–107; Fraenkel, *The Ways of the 'Aggadah and Midrash*, pp. 132–137; Lieberman, "A Mesopotamian Background," pp. 167–176; Gruenwald, "Uses and Abuses"; Abrams, "From Germany to Spain." For the ancient rabbinic resort to gematria see Bacher, *Die exegetische Terminologie*, 1:127–128, 2:27–28. On the concept of *jafr* in Muslim sources see Nwyia, *Exégèse coranique*, pp. 164–168.

11. To be sure, I do not at all mean, by emphasizing the hermeneutical aspect, to minimize the importance of the material adduced by Gruenwald and Abrams as to the nexus between gematria and some mystical experiences. The relationship between interpretation and mystical experience has been dealt with in a number of studies. See, e.g., Idel, "The Concept of the Torah," pp. 34–38; idem, *Kabbalah: New Perspectives*, pp. 234–246; *Language, Torah, and Hermeneutics*, pp. 101–109. See also Elliot R. Wolfson, "Circumcision, Visionary Experience and Textual Interpretation: From Midrashic Trope to Mystical Symbol," *History of Religions* 27 (1987), pp. 189–215; idem, *Through a Speculum*, pp. 119–124, 326–377, 383–392.

12. See Martin Samuel Cohen, *The Shiʿur Qomah: Liturgy and Theurgy in Pre-Kabbalistic Jewish Mysticism* (University Press of America, Lanham, Md., 1983), pp. 104–105.

13. See especially Abrams, "From Germany to Spain."

14. *Remizaʿ.*

15. On derision in this context see also below, the quote from Nahmanides, and note 22. On parodies of gematria-like devices in ancient literature see Lieberman, "A Mesopotamian Background," p. 218.

16. *Perush Roqeah*, I, p. 17. For another description of the gematria technique in R. Eleazar that points to an ecstatic effect see Abrams, "From Germany to Spain," p. 93. A plausible source for R. Eleazar's "etymology" of gematria is R. Nathan of Rome's influential *Sefer ha-ʿArukh*, ed. Alexander Kohut, *Aruch Completum*, vol. 1, p. 309.

17. *ʾElohim* = 86 = *zeh dayyan*. The last phrase means "He is [functioning] as a judge."

18. The plain sense is chair, but in this context it stands for the divine throne. The same gematria occurs in R. Jacob ben Asher, in a famous commentary on the Torah known under the title *Baʿal ha-Turim*, ed. J. Reinitz (Benei Beraq, 1985), p. 3. See also the same gematria below, note 39. On the relation between a divine mode of action and the divine seat see below, R. Eleazar of Worms's passage adduced above, chap 8, par. II. The gematria *kisseʾ* = *ʾelohim* is quite widespread in Kabbalah, especially in the early writings of R. Joseph Gikatilla and in *Tiqqunei Zohar*. See, e.g., *Tiqqunei Zohar*, Introduction, fol. 4b, and below, note 39.

19. *Perush Roqeah*, p. 18.

20. See the texts and bibliography adduced by Wolfson, *Along the Path*, pp. 141–142, note 183; 158–159, note 234.

21. Evidently, ancient Jewish texts know about a throne of judgment, a view reiterated by R. Eleazar several times in his writings. See, e.g., Wolfson, *Along the Path*, pp. 50–51.

22. On this motif see above, the quote from R. Eleazar of Worms, note 15.

23. Compare again the fear of R. Eleazar that gematria is used by clowns.

24. *Gematriaʾot.*

25. See Ephrayim Kupfer, "The Concluding Portion of Nahmanides' *Torat ha-Shem Temimah*," *Tarbiz* 40 (1970), p. 74 (Hebrew). On Nahmanides and gematria see also Wolfson, "By Way of Truth," pp. 130–131, note 76. On ibn Ezra's even greater reticence to resort to gematria for commenting on the biblical texts see Lieberman, "A

Mesopotamian Background," p. 218, note 300. In a separate study I hope to show that ibn Ezra's reticence may point to the existence in his lifetime of individuals and techniques reminiscent of the somewhat later *Hasidei Ashkenaz*. See also below, chap. 13, par. I. For a much later warning against the perils of the gematria, formulated in the aftermath of Sabbateanism, see the passage from R. Jacob Emden printed and discussed by Liebes, *Sod ha-'Emunah*, p. 201.

26. Or divine attributes, *middot*.

27. *Ha-tzurot ha-tishboriyyot*.

28. *Ha-misppar*.

29. This is a medieval pronunciation of the classical Greek *geo*. Abulafia's etymology is found in earlier sources, and it is accepted by modern scholars; see Lieberman, "A Mesopotamian Background," pp. 173–174, 188.

30. *Medidah*.

31. *Heshbbon*. Gematria was designated as *heshbbon* also in other writings close to Abulafia. See R. Joseph Gikatilla, *Sefer Ginnat 'Egoz* (Jerusalem, 1989), pp. 408–410. See also below, note 66.

32. Apparently greater than the measuring thing.

33. *Ha-metziy'ut*. Compare also the view expressed by Abulafia in another book, written in the same year in Rome, *Sefer Hayyei ha-Nefesh*, Ms. München 408, fol. 65a, where the divine names are described as *malkhei ha-metziy'ut*, "kings of reality." From this point of view the divine names, as the quintessence of Torah, point to an absorptive quality.

34. Namely to the Kabbalists.

35. *Sefer Sitrei Torah*, Ms. Paris BN 774, fols. 162b–163a. For another, partial translation and additional analysis of this passage see Idel, *Language, Torah and Hermeneutics*, pp. 1–2.

36. See Idel, "Abulafia's Secrets of the Guide," pp. 300–306.

37. *'Elohiim*. Perhaps it is a mistake, in this unique and not very reliable manuscript, and the version was *'elohim*.

38. *Ha-teva'*.

39. *Ha-kisse'*. See above, note 18, in the quote from R. Eleazar. See also Idel, *Language, Torah, and Hermeneutics*, pp. 30–32, 41, 44.

40. Exodus 8:15.

41. *'Etzba' 'elohim*.

42. *Teva'*.

43. This is a common midrashic view; see, e.g., *Genesis Rabba*, XIV:1.

44. *Get ha-Shemot*, Ms. Oxford, Bodleiana 1682, fol. 101b. On this work by Abulafia see Idel, "Abraham Abulafia," pp. 4–5.

45. For more on the equation of nature and God in Abulafia see Idel, *Maimonides et la mystique juive*, pp. 110–114.

46. *Sefer ha-Hesheq*, Ms. New York Jewish Theological Seminary 1801, fol. 8b.

47. See Idel, *Language, Torah and Hermeneutics*, pp. 21, 24–25, 28, 30, 136, 138, 156, 158.

48. *Sefer Mafteah ha-Hokhmot*, Ms. Moscow-Guenzburg 133, fol. 25a. A similar though less radical claim is found in another contemporary Castilian Kabbalist, R. Todros ben Joseph ha-Levi Abulafia, *Sefer 'Otzar ha-Kavod* (Warsaw, 1879), fol. 6a: "See how the sages . . . commented on each and every word, by [resorting to] the inner and esoteric way." See also below, chap. 11, beside note 29.

49. See Marcus, "Exegesis for the Few," pp. 11, 13, 22–23.

50. See also above, note 7.

51. BT, *Rosh ha-Shanah*, fol. 21b.

52. On this issue I hope to elaborate in a separate study.

53. Marcus, "Exegesis for the Few," pp. 16–17.

54. See Marcus, *Piety and Society*, p. 69.

55. For a more elaborate description of these techniques see Idel, *Language, Torah, and Hermeneutics*, pp. 95–109.

56. Ibid., p. 99.

57. Ibid., p. 110; also pp. 96–97. On a specific gematria, related to a biblical term, described as a secret see Idel, "Maimonides and Kabbalah," pp. 62–63. On the esoteric nature of both gematria and temurah that will concern us below, see some explicit statements by Abulafia's student, R. Joseph Gikatilla, *Sefer Ginnat 'Egoz*, p. 13.

58. See above, note 5.

59. Lieberman, "A Mesopotamian Background," p. 217, and the claims regarding the origin of some forms of Jewish hermeneutics, similar to those of Lieberman later on, already in Jeffrey H. Tigay, "An Early Technique of Aggadic Exegesis," in H. Tadmor and M. Weinfeld, eds., *History, Historiography and Interpretation: Studies in Biblical and Cuneiform Literatures* (Magnes Press, Jerusalem, 1983), pp. 169–188; and above, chap. 7.

60. Lieberman, "A Mesopotamian Background," pp. 171–173.

61. Cf. the pioneering studies of Parpola, especially "The Assyrian Tree of Life." See also P. Kingsley, "Ezekiel by the Grand Canal: Between Jewish and Babylonian Tradition," *Journal of the Royal Asiatic Society*, 3d ser., vol. 2 (1992), pp. 339–346. On *ma'aseh merkavah*, a main topic of later Jewish esotericism, as represented by the first chapter of Ezekiel see Moshe Weinfeld, "Divine Intervention in War in Ancient Israel and the Ancient Near East," in Tadmor and Weinfeld, *History, Historiography and Interpretation*, pp. 142–143, note 119, and Moshe Greenberg, "Ezekiel's Vision: Literary and Iconographic Aspects," in ibid., pp. 159–168.

62. See Michael Sokoloff, *A Dictionary of Jewish Palestinian Aramaic of the Byzantine Period* (Bar Ilan University Press, Ramat Gan, 1990), p. 128; Gruenwald, "Uses and Abuses," p. 827, note 14. The use of Greek terms to point to an already existing technique is quite plausible. See Lieberman, "A Mesopotamian Background," p. 219, and notes 302–303.

63. On *temurah*, or *hillufei 'otiyyot*, see Lieberman, "A Mesopotamian Background," pp. 160–162, 164–166. My assumption is that although the technique of temurah has sometimes been included in the broader view of gematria (cf. ibid., p. 164, note 27),

that of *tzerufei 'otiyyot* should not be identified with gematria. See, e.g., Gikatilla, *Sefer Ginnat 'Egoz*, p. 410. Cf. Gruenwald, "Uses and Abuses," pp. 826–829. For a talmudic resort to temurah to explain the intriguing enigma found in Daniel 5:25 see BT, *Sanhedrin*, fol. 22a, and Idel, *Language, Torah, and Hermeneutics*, pp. 53–54 and 175–176, note 119.

64. *Tzerufei 'otiyyot*. See also below, notes 69 and 76. For more on this topic see below, chap. 12.

65. Of the category named *mishqal*. On the affinity between the two categories see the Kabbalistic treatise from Abulafia's school called *Sha'arei Tzedeq*, p. 37. In general this book was one of the major sources for the exposition of the techniques reproduced by R. Yehudah Albotini in his book *Sullam ha-'Aliyah*, which will be dealt with later in this chapter.

66. *Heshbbonot*. See also the discussion by his student, R. Joseph Gikatilla, *Ginnat 'Egoz*, pp. 408–409. See above, note 31, and below, note 78, and Lieberman, "A Mesopotamian Background," p. 189.

67. *Hokhmah mefo'arah*. See also below, note 71.

68. *Sefer Get ha-Shemot*, Ms. Oxford 1862, fol. 90ab. Interestingly, Abulafia does not introduce here the possibility of different vocalizations. Cf. above, chap. 3, par. II, where his former student, R. Joseph Gikatilla, mentions vocalizations in the context of using exactly the same word. See also his *Ginnat 'Egoz*, pp. 135, 401, 410, on the "science of combination." In general Abulafia was not so much concerned with permutations related to the vowels as part of an exegetical technique, although permutations of vowels are crucial in his mystical technique.

69. For an interesting discussion of this technique see Heinemann, *Darkhei ha-'Aggadah*, pp. 105; Nicolas Sed, "Le *Sefer ha-Razim* et la methode de 'combination des lettres,'" *REJ* 130 (1971), pp. 295–303; Idel, *The Mystical Experience*, pp. 20–24.

70. *Philosophie und Kabbala*, p. 4; Idel, *Language, Torah, and Hermeneutics*, p. 100. See also Abulafia's *Commentary on Genesis*, Ms. Moscow-Guenzburg 133, fol. 20ab.

71. *Hokhmah mefo'arah*. See also above, note 67.

72. In my opinion, here the significance of this term is mental concentration. See Idel, *Studies in Ecstatic Kabbalah*, pp. 122–123.

73. *Sefer Sullam ha-'Aliyah*, p. 19; Gruenwald, "Uses and Abuses," p. 827. On causing the descent of the divine power see above, chap. 5.

74. On this view see Idel, *Hasidism: Between Ecstasy and Magic*, pp. 155–162; idem, "On Talismatic Language."

75. See also Gruenwald, "Uses and Abuses," pp. 826–827. On the basis of Abulafian passages a more complex relationship between the initial introduction of the initiants to head chapters, *rashei peraqim*, then to gematria, *tzerufei 'otiyyot*, and mystical experience is in order. As Abulafia mentioned in an important passage, the study of the two techniques precedes the transmission of the divine names, the latter stage being the way to attain a mystical experience. See *Sefer Mafteah ha-Shemot*, Ms. New York, JTS 1897, fol. 60b. See also below, note 96. The sequence of the different techniques is

described in the autobiographical testimony of R. Nathan ben Saʿadyah in his Shaʿarei Tzedeq, pp. 22–23. I hope to deal with this issue in a separate study.

76. Tzerufei ha-ʾotiyyot. See also above, note 64.

77. Bahun u-menusseh bo. This phrase, which occurs elsewhere in Abulafia's writings in similar contexts, stems from magical terminology. See also Shevaʿ Netivot ha-Torah, p. 21.

78. Heshbbon ʾotiyyot. See also note 66 above.

79. Hilluqam. On the path of hilluq see Shaʿarei Tzedeq, pp. 33–35.

80. Hibburam. On the path of hibbur see Shaʿarei Tzedeq, p. 36.

81. Hippukham. On hippukh as close to gilgul see Abulafia, Hayyei ha-ʿOlam ha-Baʾ, pp. 104–105. For more on hippukh see below, app. 2.

82. Gilgulam. On gilgul as combination of letters see also the quote from the early Ashkenazi Sefer ha-Kavod, preserved in R. Abraham ben Azriel, Sefer ʿArugat ha-Bosem, ed. E. E. Urbach (Mekize Nirdamim, Jerusalem, 1939), 1:175–176; Wolfson, Circle in the Square, p. 169, note 62; see also below, note 90; chap. 12, note 57; and app. 2.

83. Temuratam. See note 63 above.

84. On this book as one of the major sources for Abulafia see Idel, "Maimonides and Kabbalah," pp. 67–68, and also below, note 111.

85. Sefer Sitrei Torah, Ms. Paris, BN 774, fol. 163a. This book had been translated into Latin by Flavius Mithridates; see Wirszubski, Pico della Mirandola, pp. 61–62.

86. Shevaʿ Netivot ha-Torah, pp. 14–15; L'Epître des sept voies, p. 72; Idel, Language, Torah, and Hermeneutics, p. xvi, and above, chap. 3, note 43. An issue of paramount historical importance, which cannot be dealt with here, is the apparent similarity between this view of Abulafia's and theories of combination of letters, described as a "superior etymology" in Arabic writings since 1000. See Henri Corbin, Histoire de la philosophie islamique (Paris, Gallimard, 1964), pp. 206–207. For the reverberation of this passage in the writings of a twentieth-century mystic, R. David ha-Kohen ha-Nazir, a figure who claimed prophetic experiences, see Dov Schwartz, Religious Zionism between Logic and Messianism (ʿAm ʿOved, Tel Aviv, 1999), pp. 305–306 (Hebrew).

87. Idel, Language, Torah, and Hermeneutics, pp. 97–101.

88. ʿOmeq; on depth as a hidden dimension of the Torah see also above, chap. 7, note 133. On R. Eleazar of Worms and Abulafia on depths see also Idel, The Mystical Experience, p. 17.

89. Gilgulam. See note 82 above.

90. Tzerufam. See also above, note 84. On another, much later nexus between prophecy and combinations of letters see R. Joseph Al-Qastiel in the text edited by Gershom Scholem, "For the Knowledge of Kabbalah in the Generation of the Expulsion," Tarbiz 24 (1954/55), p. 197 (Hebrew). Here, however, there is a synthesis between the combinatory and theosophical brands of Kabbalah.

91. Printed in ʾArzei Levanon, fol. 39b; See also above, chap. 3, note 35; Idel, Language, Torah, and Hermeneutics, p. 109. For the significance of the mystics referred to as prophets and visionaries see the next section of this chapter.

92. See my introduction to Gikatilla's *Sefer Sha'arei 'Orah*, in *Gates of Light*, p. 6. In this context it is worth mentioning a later development of the weaving theme in Kabbalah: the sixteenth-century concept of *malbush*, or the divine garment that is identical with both the primordial Torah and the combinations of the letters of the Hebrew alphabet; see Idel, *Golem*, pp. 148–154, and above, chap. 1, par. VII, and below, chap. 12. See also the Sarugian reverberations in R. Nathan Neta' Shapira of Cracow, *Megalleh 'Amuqot*, fol. 80bc.

93. See Baer, *Studies*, 1:114–118, who attempted to trace the theme of weaving from Plato to Philo to Gikatilla. For the image of weaving in connection with sacred scriptures see Rene Guenon, *Le symbolisme de la croix* (Vega, Paris, 1983), chap. 14. See also above, chap. 1, note 45.

94. See *The Gate of the Vowels*, fol. 39b.

95. *Pardes Rimmonim*, gate 30, Introduction, II, fol. 68c. See also above, chap. 3, note 35. There can be no doubt that Abulafia influenced Cordovero's reference to the exegetical technique concerning the head, middle, and end of words, designated by Abulafia by the acronym *seter*. See below, chap. 11, note 62, and more at the end of this chapter. For more on Cordovero's description of numerical and combinatory techniques see his *Shi'ur Qomah*, fols. 63d–64a, 92bc, and Sack, *Be-Sha'arei ha-Kabbalah*, p. 177. The combination of letters became a crucial issue in the Besht, and even more in R. Ze'ev Wolf of Zhitomir's 'Or ha-Me'ir. For more on this issue see chap. 12, par. VIII.

96. It should be noted that the logocentric nature of the supernal intellect was attenuated in Abulafia by its identification with linguistic concepts; see, e.g., Idel, *Language, Torah, and Hermeneutics*, pp. 22–23, 36, 40–41. Sometimes Abulafia described the Agent Intellect as primordial speech. On the direct nexus between the path of the divine names and mystical experience see above, note 75.

97. On the Nahmanidean source of this assertion and its interpretations in Abulafia see Idel, "Abulafia's *Secrets of the Guide*," pp. 306–311, and below chap. 11, pars. IV–VI, and chap. 12.

98. *Sefer Mafteah ha-Hokhmot*, Ms. Moscow-Guenzburg 133, fols. 7b–8a. See also a very similar discussion at fol. 12b. See also below, chap. 11, par. V.

99. See below, app. 1. On ontological and textual hierarchies see also above, chap. 8, par. VI.

100. See Idel, *Hasidism: Between Ecstasy and Magic*, pp. 56–57.

101. On this book see the succinct description by Francois Secret, *Les kabbalistes chrétiens de la Renaissance* (Dunod, Paris, 1964), pp. 198–199. I hope to elaborate on this interesting exposition of Kabbalistic hermeneutics in a separate study.

102. See esp. gates 19–21, 27, 30, and above, par. V, and R. Joseph Ergas, *Shomer 'Emunim*, pp. 17–19.

103. See Idel, *Hasidism: Between Ecstasy and Magic*, pp. 56–59, and below, chap. 12, par. VIII.

104. See R. Menahem Mendel's resort to allegory, gematria, and combination of letters in all of his printed Kabbalistic writings, and even more so in some of his manuscript writings. On this issue I shall elaborate elsewhere.

CHAPTER 10: THE SYMBOLIC MODE IN
THEOSOPHICAL-THEURGICAL KABBALAH

1. On the nonsymbolic nature of Judaism see A. Y. Heschel, "Symbolism and Jewish Faith," in F. E. Johnson, ed., *Religious Symbolism* (New York, 1954), pp. 53–79, esp. pp. 76–77, and Scholem's reaction in *On the Kabbalah*, p. 22, note 1.

2. See especially above, Introduction, par. III.

3. See Idel, *Kabbalah: New Perspectives*, pp. 210–218.

4. Eco, *Semiotics*, p. 153; idem, *The Limits of Interpretation*, pp. 14–15; idem, *The Aesthetics*, pp. 144–159. See also below, Concluding Remarks, par. I. See a somewhat similar approach to early Kabbalistic symbolism formulated by resorting to Eco's theory of codes—though following also some of the suggestions proposed in my *Kabbalah: New Perspectives*—in the pertinent observations of Mark B. Sendor, "The Emergency of Provencal Kabbalah: R. Isaac the Blind's Commentary on Sefer Yezirah" (Ph.D. diss., Harvard University, 1994), volume I, pp. 234–242.

5. See Idel, *Kabbalah: New Perspectives*, pp. 200–210. See also the important study by Liebes, "Myth vs. Symbol."

6. See, respectively, Huss, "Symbolism," and Rojtman, *Black Fire on White Fire*.

7. Tishby, *Paths of Faith and Heresy*, p. 13; idem, *The Wisdom of the Zohar*, 1:284. For the ancient and medieval sources of this approach see Eco, *Limits of Interpretation*, pp. 9–14.

8. Tishby, *Paths of Faith and Heresy*, p. 13.

9. Scholem, *On the Kabbalah*, p. 36; ibid., p. 22: "Symbols, by their very nature, are a means of expressing an experience that is in itself expressionless"; idem, *On Jews and Judaism*, p. 48; idem, *Major Trends*, p. 27: "the Kabbalist ... discovers ... a reflection of the true transcendence," or his view that the symbolized realm is "a hidden and inexpressible reality." See also ibid., p. 28. Cf. Goetschel, *Meir ibn Gabbai*, pp. 113–122. This view has been accepted by Dan, *The Early Kabbalah*, pp. 9–13, and again more recently in his collection of articles *On Sanctity*.

10. "The Name of God," p. 60. See also ibid., pp. 62, 165, 193; Scholem, *On the Kabbalah*, p. 36; idem, *On Jews and Judaism*, p. 48; Tishby, *Paths of Faith and Heresy*, pp. 11–22; Dan, *The Early Kabbalah*, p. 13. For more on Scholem's view of the Kabbalistic symbol see Handelman, *Fragments of Redemption*, pp. 82–84, 93–114, and Idel, *Kabbalah: New Perspectives*, pp. 200–234; idem, "The Function of Symbols," and my introduction to Reuchlin's *De Arte Cabalistica* in *On the Art of the Kabbalah*, pp. xv–xvi. It should be noted that both Scholem and Ernst Cassirer put a greater emphasis on the role of the symbolic than on the magical aspect of language, which in itself has been duly recognized elsewhere in their writings. Does their preference for the symbolic mode over the magical one reflect their Hegelian or Frazerian stance?

11. See a similar stand expressed in G. G. Coulton, *Medieval Panorama* (Meridian Books, New York, 1955), p. 519. Cf. also W. R. Inge, *Christian Mysticism* (Meridian Books, New York, 1956), pp. 249–332, who emphasizes the symbolic nature of Kabbalah, to a

great extent under the impact of Reuchlin's view mentioned above, note 10. See also H. P. Blavatsky, *Isis Unveiled* (Rpt., Pasadena, Calif., 1972), p. xxiv.

12. *Origins of the Kabbalah*, p. 408; when dealing with historical symbolism, Scholem again invokes the historical experiences of the Kabbalists as the source of their symbolic vision of reality. See also his *On Jews and Judaism*, p. 48.

13. Idel, "On Talismanic Language"; idem, *Hasidism: Between Ecstasy and Magic*, pp. 83–84.

14. See Elqayam, "Between Referentionalism and Performativism"; Idel, *Kabbalah: New Perspectives*, pp. 176, 204–206. Compare also Walter J. Ong's claim that words as sounds are hardly considered as symbols; *The Presence of the Word* (Simon & Schuster, New York, 1970), p. 323.

15. M. Idel, "Some Remarks on Ritual and Mysticism in Geronese Kabbalah," *Jewish Thought and Philosophy* 3 (1993), pp. 111–130.

16. Tishby, *Paths of Faith and Heresy*, p. 20.

17. Ibid., p. 22; Tishby, *The Wisdom of the Zohar*, 3:1077.

18. Tishby, *Paths of Faith and Heresy*, pp. 16, 22.

19. On Scholem's views of Gnosticism see M. Idel, "Subversive Catalysts: Gnosticism and Messianism in Gershom Scholem's View of Jewish Mysticism," in David N. Myers and David B. Ruderman, eds., *The Jewish Past Revisited: Reflections on Modern Jewish Historians* (Yale University Press, New Haven, 1998), pp. 46–56.

20. For the implicit mentioning of the Shoah see Tishby, *Paths of Faith and Heresy*, p. 22. For the existential background of Alexander Altmann's earlier studies on Gnosticism and Judaism see Paul Mendes-Flohr's introduction to Altmann, *The Meaning of Jewish Existence: Theological Essays, 1930–1939* (University Press of New England, Hanover, N.H., 1991], pp. xlv–xlvii. On the influence of the Shoah on Scholem's concept of history and symbol see Idel, "The Function of Symbols."

21. Scholem, *On the Kabbalah*, p. 2. See also idem, *On Jews and Judaism*, p. 48.

22. Ibid. See also another assertion to this effect: "The magnitude of the messianic idea corresponds to the endless powerlessness in Jewish history during all the centuries of exile." *The Messianic Idea in Israel*, p. 35; ibid., p. 7, as well as *Major Trends*, pp. 287–288.

23. Idel, "On the Concept of Zimzum"; idem, "An Anonymous Commentary on Shir ha-Yihud," in K.-E. Groezinger and Joseph Dan, eds., *Mysticism, Magic and Kabbalah in Ashkenazi Judaism* (Walter de Gruyter, Berlin, 1995), pp. 151–154.

24. *On the Kabbalah*, p. 2.

25. See Jonas, "Myth and Mysticism: A Study of Objectification and Interiorization in Religious Thought," *Journal of Religion* 49 (1969), pp. 328–329.

26. *On the Kabbalah*, p. 2.

27. See below, par. III. On a few philosophical terms that became Kabbalistic symbols see Idel, *Kabbalah: New Perspectives*, pp. 218–222.

28. Tishby, *Paths of Faith and Heresy*, p. 14; compare also his *The Wisdom of the Zohar*, 1:284. For the essential vision of Kabbalah as impressed by symbolism see Scholem, *Major Trends*, p. 26. See also Handelman, *Fragments of Redemption*, p. 109.

29. On the process of arcanization see above, Introduction, chaps. 2, 6, 7, and 9.

30. On philosophical allegoresis see below, chap. 11, note 1.

31. On Aristotelianism see Eco, *The Aesthetics*, pp. 140–141.

32. D. J. Silver, *Maimonidean Criticism and the Maimonidean Controversy* (Brill, Leiden, 1965); Joseph Sarachek, *Faith and Reason: The Conflict over the Rationalism of Maimonides* (New York, 1935); Bernard D. Septimus, *Hispano-Jewish Culture in Transition: The Career and Controversies of Ramah* (Harvard University Press, Cambridge, Mass., 1982); Charles Touati, *Prophetes, Talmudistes, Philosophes* (Le Cerf, Paris, 1990), pp. 201–218; idem, "Les deux conflits autour de Maimonide," *Juifs et Judaïsme de Languedoque,* ed. M. Vicaire and B. Blumenkranz (Toulouse, 1977), pp. 173–184; Sarah Stroumsa, "Twelfth Century Concepts of Soul and Body: The Maimonidean Controversy in Baghdad," in *Self, Soul and Body in Religious Experience,* ed. A. I. Baumgarten, J. Assmann, and G. G. Stroumsa (Brill, Leiden, 1998), pp. 313–334; on R. Jacob ben Sheshet's *Sefer Sha'ar ha-Shamayyim,* a polemic against the mental prayer, see Georges Vajda, *Recherches sur la philosophie et la Kabbale dans la Pensée Juive du Moyen Age* (Mouton, Paris, 1962), pp. 356–371.

33. On this theory of the emergence of the historical Kabbalah in general see Idel, "Maimonides and Kabbalah," pp. 32–50. See also above, chap. 1, par. I, and chap. 8, par. V. On the dialectical relationship between allegorization and remythologization see the important observations of Rider, "Receiving Orpheus."

34. See especially the important discussion of Zoharic hermeneutics by Scholem, *Major Trends,* p. 208, but compare his negation of the possible relevance of the Maimonidean controversy for the beginning of Kabbalah, ibid., p. 24, as well as his "Me-Hoqer li-Mequbbal," *Tarbiz* 6 (1935), pp. 91–92 (Hebrew), or "Maimonides dans l'oeuvre des Kabbalistes," *Cahiers Juifs* 3 (1935), pp. 104–105. Tishby, *Wisdom of the Zohar,* 3:1077–1078, did discuss the emergence of Kabbalistic symbolism as a reaction to philosophical allegorizations but assumed, like Heinrich Graetz before him, that there were no pertinent materials that contributed to the articulation of the symbolic alternative.

35. See Scholem, *Major Trends,* pp. 205–206.

36. On these two kinds of relation see Umberto Eco, *A Theory of Semiotics* (Indiana University Press, Bloomington, 1979), pp. 183ff, 217–260.

37. See Idel, *Language, Torah, and Hermeneutics,* pp. 11–12. See also the discussion above, chap. 2, par. III.

38. See Huss, "Symbolism." For more on Gikatilla's book see below, par. VI.

39. For an example of the relations between David the king and Malkhut see Idel, *Messianic Mystics,* pp. 110–114.

40. On Jerusalem as a symbol in thirteenth-century Kabbalah see Moshe Idel, "Jerusalem in Thirteenth-Century Jewish Thought," in J. Prawer and H. Ben Shammai, eds., *The History of Jerusalem: Crusaders and Ayyubids (1099–1250)* (Yad Izhak ben-Zvi Publications, Jerusalem, 1991), pp. 265–276 (Hebrew). On Jerusalem in medieval spirituality see, e.g., Leclercq, *The Love of Learning,* pp. 54–56.

41. See Idel, *Hasidism: Between Ecstasy and Magic,* pp. 215–218.

42. *Ma'arekhet ha-'Elohut,* fols. 104b–105a.

43. See the late sixteenth-century R. Abraham Azulai, *Hesed le-'Avraham*, fol. 21a.

44. The righteous, who is an everlasting foundation, namely the ninth sefirah.

45. Ms. Moscow-Ginsburg 90, fol. 41b. A short version of this passage appears in Ms. Cambridge, Add. 400.7, fol. 692a. A corresponding discussion, apparently preceding that in Ms. Moscow, appears in another anonymous *Commentary on Ten Sefirot* extant in Ms. Berlin Or. 122, fol. 91a, in which it is said about the sefirah of Yesod: "And it is called Mount Zion, for the heavenly Jerusalem is as the earthly Jerusalem, and the heavenly Zion corresponds to the earthly Zion; just as (from the border) [mi-gevul; the correct reading is *migdal*, the fortress] of Jerusalem and the fortress [*migdal*, instead of the faulty *mugdal*] guarding the city, so too does the supernal fortress [*mugdal*!], which is the righteous, guard the tenth [*sefirah*], i.e., Jerusalem, from the demonic powers." On this literary genre see below, note 64. For more on geographical symbolism see above, chap. 4, par. VII.

46. *The Limits of Interpretation*, p. 18.

47. For the importance of the myth of the Edomite kings in the Zoharic theosophy and other Kabbalists of his age see Liebes, *Studies in the Zohar*, pp. 66, 128. For an approach that strongly pleads for the priority of the religious, or typological interpretations of natural symbols in medieval Christian literature, see Ricoeur, *Conflict of Interpretations*, pp. 59–61.

48. See Idel, "A la recherche," pp. 417–420.

49. *Paths of Faith and Heresy*, p. 22.

50. *Kabbalah: New Perspectives*, pp. 112–122, 260–264, as well as above, chap. 8, par. V. See also Lorberbaum, *Imago Dei*.

51. *Kitvei ha-Ramban* (Mossad ha-Rav Kook, Jerusalem, 1964), 2:496. See also Tishby, *The Wisdom of the Zohar*, 3:1157–1157; Idel, "Maimonides and Kabbalah," pp. 42–45.

52. *Seder 'Amran Gaon*, ed. Fromkin (Jerusalem, 1912), p. 79; Idel, "Maimonides and Kabbalah," p. 44, note 39.

53. *'Al 'omeq diqduqam*. The term "depth" is related in many sources to the inner meaning of the Torah: see chap. 7, note 84.

54. Ms. Roma-Angelica 45.1, fol. 2b; Scholem, *Origins of the Kabbalah*, p. 38.

55. I hope to corroborate this analysis in a much more detailed discussion elsewhere. Meanwhile see Idel, "Maimonides and Kabbalah," pp. 42–50, and above, chap. 8, par. V.

56. See Idel, "Maimonides and Kabbalah," pp. 42–50.

57. See Eliade, "Methodological Remarks," p. 99; Ricoeur, *The Conflict of Interpretations*, pp. 58, 63–67; and the material referenced by Idel, *Messianic Mystics*, p. 426, note 63.

58. *Image and Pilgrimage in Christian Culture* (New York, 1978), p. 247; V. Turner, *The Forest of Symbols* (Cornell University Press, Ithaca, N.Y., 1967); for an interesting analysis of Turner's view of ritual see Mathieu Deflem, "Ritual, Anti-Structure, and Religion: A Discussion of Victor Turner's Processual Symbolic Analysis," *Journal for the Scientific Study of Religion* 30 (1991), pp. 1–25.

59. Mary Douglas, *Natural Symbols: Explorations in Cosmology* (Pantheon Books, New York, 1982), pp. 11–12; on the efficacy of the ritual see Marcel Mauss, *A General Theory of Magic* (Norton, New York, 1975), pp. 97–108. A very interesting treatment of the crucial role of the ritual is found also in the more recent approaches of Walter Burkert, *Homo Necans: The Anthropology of Ancient Greek Sacrificial Ritual and Myth*, trans. P. Bing (University of California Press, Berkeley and Los Angeles, 1983), pp. 29–34; Clifford Geertz, *The Interpretation of Cultures* (Basic Books, 1973), esp. pp. 112–118; the foreword by D. F. Pocock to Mauss, *A General Theory of Magic*, p. 4.

60. See, respectively, *Anthropologie structurale* (Plon, Paris, 1974), pp. 213–234; *Théologie symbolique* (Tequi, Paris, 1978), pp. 352–379. See also the important article by Elqa-yam, "Between Referentionalism and Performance," where he discusses the performative role of the symbol.

61. *On the Kabbalah*, p. 99.

62. See my discussion in *Kabbalah: New Perspectives*, pp. 14, 156–157.

63. See Scholem, *Major Trends*, pp. 205–207; Idel, *Kabbalah: New Perspectives*, pp. 234–248; Wolfson, *Through a Speculum That Shines*, pp. 383–392. See also above, chaps. 2, 3, and 6, and below, app. 2, as well as par. VI below.

64. See Gershom Scholem, "An Index to the Commentaries on Ten Sefirot," QS 10 (1932), pp. 498–515 (Hebrew); Idel, *Kabbalah: New Perspectives*, p. 213. See also note 45 above.

65. See the numerous articles by Wolfgang Kluxen, mentioned in his "Maimonides and Latin Scholasticism," in *Maimonides and Philosophy*, ed. Shlomo Pines and Yirmiyahu Yovel (Nijhoff Publishers, Dordrecht, Boston, Lancaster, 1986), pp. 224–323; Avital Wohlman, *Thomas d'Aquin et Maimonide: Un dialogue exemplaire* (Le Cerf, Paris, 1988); Jacob Haberman, *Maimonides and Aquinas* (KTAV, New York, 1979).

66. See Ferdinand Brunner, *Platonisme et aristotelisme: La critique d'Ibn Gabirol par Saint Thomas d'Aquin* (Louvain, 1965).

67. Scholem, *Major Trends*, p. 203; Idel, "Jewish Kabbalah and Platonism," pp. 319–352.

68. On the nexus between Platonism and symbolism see Eco, *Limits of Interpretation*, pp. 9–11; idem, *The Aesthetics*, pp. 139–140.

69. Namely the Kabbalists.

70. I.e., the same symbols refer to two or more sefirot, whereas the particular names refer to one sefirah alone.

71. I.e., of the sefirot.

72. *Nevokhim bahem me'od*. See *Ve-Zot Li-Yhudah*, p. 18, where Abulafia claims that "if the master of the sefirot thinks that he knows better than me the written or the oral Torah, according to their secrets, it will become clear to him that he errs and induces others in error." Therefore, according to Abulafia, the contest between the different forms of Kabbalah took place not only on the plane of theology but also on that of hermeneutics, that is to say, the main claim, as pointed out in this passage, is related to the esoteric understanding of canonic books. See also below, note 75.

73. Printed as an appendix by Adolph Jellinek in his *Philosophie und Kabbalah* (Leipzig,

1854), 1:37–38; Idel, *Kabbalah: New Perspectives*, p. 202; Elliot Wolfson, "The Doctrine of Sefirot in the Prophetic Kabbalah of Abraham Abulafia," JQS 2, no. 4 (1995), pp. 351–352.

74. See Jellinek, *Philosophie und Kabbalah*, p. 37. See also below, app. 2.

75. Abulafia sharply criticized some Kabbalists' view of the ten sefirot as the essence of God; see Idel, "Defining Kabbalah," pp. 109–110; Wolfson, "The Doctrine of Sefirot," pp. 342–343.

76. See Idel, *Language, Torah, and Hermeneutics*, pp. x–xi, 95–109.

77. See above, note 73.

78. See the lengthy discussion of a follower of ecstatic Kabbalah translated in Scholem, *Major Trends*, pp. 147–149.

79. See Scholem, *Major Trends*, p. 205.

80. See above, chap. 3, and below, app. 2.

81. See Idel, *Kabbalah: New Perspectives*, pp. 210–218; idem, "Kabbalah and Elites in Thirteenth-Century Spain," *Mediterranean Historical Review* 9 (1994), pp. 5–19; Moshe Idel, "The Kabbalah's Window of Opportunities, 1270–1290," in *Me'ah She'arim: Studies in Medieval Jewish Spiritual Life in Memory of Isadore Twersky*, ed. E. Fleisher, G. Blidstein, C. Horowitz, and B. Septimus (Magnes Press, Jerusalem, 2001), pp. 171–208; and app. 1 below.

82. See Idel, *Kabbalah: New Perspectives*, pp. 217–218.

83. See Daniel H. Matt, "New-Ancient Words: The Aura of Secrecy in the Zohar," in P. Schaefer and J. Dan, eds., *Gershom Scholem's Major Trends in Jewish Mysticism, 50 Years After* (J. C. B. Mohr, Tübingen, 1993), pp. 181–207; Liebes's study referenced above, note 5; for more on Zoharic hermeneutics as part of a general discussion of Kabbalistic hermeneutics see also Wolfson, "By Way of Truth"; idem, "Circumcision, Visionary Experience and Textual Interpretation: From Midrashic Trope to Mystical Symbol," *History of Religions* (1987), pp. 189–215; idem, "Left Contained in the Right: A Study in Zoharic Hermeneutics," AJSR 11, no. 1 (1986), pp. 27–52; idem, "The Hermeneutics of Visionary Experience: Revelation and Interpretation in the Zohar," *Religion* 18 (1988), pp. 311–345; Ithamar Gruenwald, "From Talmudic to Zoharic Homiletics," in Joseph Dan, ed., *The Age of the Zohar* (Jerusalem, 1989), pp. 255–298 (Hebrew), and Daniel C. Matt, "Matnita Dilan: A Technique of Innovation in the Zohar," in ibid., pp. 123–145 (Hebrew); Benin, "The Mutability"; Giller, *The Enlightened*; Eliezer Segal, "The Exegetical Craft of the Zohar: Toward an Appreciation," AJSR 17 (1992), pp. 31–49; and Fishbane, *The Exegetical Imagination*, pp. 105–122.

84. See Matt, *The Book of Mirrors*, pp. 13–17; Idel, "Targumo."

85. See chap. 8, par. V.

86. See Idel, "Sefirot above Sefirot," pp. 268–277; idem, *Kabbalah: New Perspectives*, pp. 113–118; Elliot Wolfson, "The Theosophy of Shabbetai Donnolo, with Special Emphasis on the Doctrine of the Sefirot in *Sefer Hakhmoni*," *Jewish History* 6 (1992) = *The Frank Talmage Memorial Volume II*, pp. 281–316; and Parpola, "The Assyrian Tree of Life."

87. See note 64 above.

88. For the contribution of this book to medieval Jewish speculations see e.g. David Neumark, *Geschichte der Jüdischen Philosophie des Mittelalters* (Berlin, 1907–1928), 1:116–117, 131–132, 182–183; Scholem, *Origins of the Kabbalah*, pp. 33–35; Gruenwald, "Jewish Mysticism's Transition from *Sefer Yesira* to the *Bahir*," in J. Dan, ed., *The Beginnings of Jewish Mysticism in Medieval Europe* (Jerusalem, 1987), pp. 15–54 (Hebrew); Liebes, *Ars Poetica*, passim. See also above, chap. 9, notes 84 and 111.

89. *Ta'amei ha-Mitzvot*, Ms. Jerusalem 8° 3925, fol. 110b; for details regarding this passage see above, chap. 2, par. V.

90. See Idel, "The Concept of the Torah," p. 67.

91. Genesis 2:10.

92. Proverbs 10:25.

93. It also means "because of."

94. Isaiah 27:5.

95. *Sod ha-Keruvim*, Ms. Parma, de Rossi 1230, fols. 108b–109b; Ms. Paris BN 823, fol. 54ab.

96. See Idel, *Kabbalah: New Perspectives*, pp. 191–197; Green, *Keter*, index, sub "ascent," esp. p. 149.

97. See Abulafia's epistle printed by Adolph Jellinek, *Auswahl Kabbalistischen Mystik* (Leipzig, 1853) 1:16–17.

98. Abulafia's basic assumption is that there are sefirot in man. See Idel, *Kabbalah: New Perspectives*, pp. 147–149; idem, *Hasidism: Between Ecstasy and Magic*, pp. 227–238.

99. Namely the attributes of man.

100. *Lehitboded*. In some texts this verb means mental concentration, though in many others it stands for isolating oneself. See Idel, *Studies in Ecstatic Kabbalah*, pp. 108–111.

101. The question of awareness of the source of revelation is crucial for Abulafia's experiential approach to mysticism. See the text from R. Nathan ben Sa'adyah's *Sha'arei Tzedeq* translated by Scholem, *Major Trends*, p. 140.

102. See note 100 above.

103. This is a metaphor for the union between the human and the divine intellect. See Idel, *The Mystical Experience*, pp. 180–184.

104. Namely the human intellect.

105. Namely the spiritual entities, the human and the divine intellect, which are united during the experience.

106. I assume that Abulafia alludes to the union between the corporeal and the spiritual, which is dissolved during the mystical experience.

107. The Kabbalist intends the inner, human reality, which is transformed by the mystical experience.

108. Exodus 26:6.

109. For Abulafia the divine name and its signified—God—are sometimes interchangeable.

110. Zechariah 14:9.

111. Ezekiel 37:17.

112. Ms. Sasson 56, fol. 56a.

113. Namely from the names.

114. *Sefer Gan Naʿul*, Ms. British Library Or. 13136, fol. 3a, printed also in *Sefer ha-Peliyʾah* (Premiszlany, 1883), I, fol. 73a.

115. See Idel, *The Mystical Experience*, pp. 24–41.

116. See his *Commentary on the Merkavah of Ezeqiel*, Ms. New York, JTS 1609, fol. 167b; R. Joseph Gikatilla's *Commentary on Ezekiel's Chariot*, ed. Asi Farber-Ginat (Cherub Press, Los Angeles, 1998), pp. 46–47, 51–52.

117. Deuteronomy 4:4.

118. *Shaʿar ha-Niqqud*, printed in *ʾArzei Levanon*, fol. 38a.

119. See *Shaʿarei ʾOrah*, pp. 7–8.

120. *Zohar*, II, fols. 99ab, which was analyzed in detail by several scholars: See Bacher, "L'exégèse biblique," pp. 36–38; Scholem, *On the Kabbalah*, pp. 55–56; Talmage, "Apples of Gold," pp. 316–317; Tishby, *The Wisdom of the Zohar*, 3:1084–1085; Idel, *Kabbalah: New Perspectives*, pp. 227–229; Wolfson, "Beautiful Maiden," passim; Matt, *Zohar*, pp. 121–126; Benin, *The Footprints of God*, pp. 168–169. See also above, chap. 6, par. VI.

121. See Idel, *Language, Torah and Hermeneutics*, p. xiv.

122. See Talmage, "Apples of God," p. 316 and note 21.

123. *Arcana Caelestia*, par. 1872, translated in *Internal Sense of the Word* (London, 1974), p. 41. See also above, chap. 3, par. II.

124. For more on this issue see below, app. 1.

125. See *Zohar*, I, fols. 25b–26a. For more on this passage see Moshe Idel, "Metatron: Remarks on Jewish Mythology," in Havivah Pedaya, ed., *Eshel Beer Sheva* (Beer Sheva, 1996), 4:29–44 (Hebrew). On this later layer see Giller, *The Enlightened*.

126. *Zohar*, I, fol. 26a.

127. Or, more precisely, dies.

128. BT, *Pesahim*, fol. 94b.

129. 1 Samuel 25:29.

130. Psalms 22:21.

131. Exodus 11:7.

132. First printed in Moshe Idel, "An Unknown Text from *Midrash ha-Neʿelam*," in J. Dan, ed., *The Age of the Zohar* (Jerusalem, 1989), pp. 73–87 (Hebrew).

133. Psalms 48:2.

134. *Zohar*, III, fol. 5a.

135. Idel, *Kabbalah: New Perspectives*, pp. 128–136. On the erotic and sexual symbolism in the Zohar see also Liebes, *Studies in the Zohar*, pp. 19–25, 37–43, 63–65, 67–74; idem, "Zohar and Eros," pp. 67–119. Compare the elaborate exposition of the view of Wolfson, *Circle in the Square*, pp. 95–110, adumbrated in earlier studies of this scholar, which assumes a tendency to obliterate the difference between the male and female divine powers, as part of the absorption of the female by and within the male. This

thesis, which is sometimes helpful in understanding texts of Zoharic Kabbalah and those influenced by it, does not hold, however, for numerous other Zoharic treatments of the nature of the sexual polarity.

136. Leviticus 1:2

137. On "ascending" versus "descending" symbolism, see Erich Kahler, "The Nature of the Symbol," in Rollo May, ed., *Symbolism in Religion and Literature* (George Braziller, New York, 1960), pp. 50–75; on a more general exposition of the two forms of sexual symbolism in Kabbalistic literature see Moshe Idel, "Sexual Metaphors and Praxis in the Kabbalah," in *The Jewish Family*, ed. D. Kraemer (Oxford University Press, New York, 1989), pp. 179–224.

138. See below, app. 3.

139. See Idel, *R. Menahem Recanati, the Kabbalist*, pp. 24–32. In this paragraph I draw on discussions in my *Kabbalah: New Perspectives*, pp. 210–218.

140. On this issue, see Idel, "Targumo," pp. 72–73.

141. Emile Mâle, *The Gothic Image* (Harper and Row, New York, 1958), p. 51.

142. Martin Buber, *Hasidism* (New York, 1948), pp. 69, 141, aptly describes the tendency of "the Kabbalah" to schematize the mystery; however, this evaluation is much more true of Safedian Kabbalah than earlier phases of Kabbalah; by and large, for Buber the Kabbalah is the Lurianic school. On the analogous phenomenon in Western Christian culture compare Johan Huizinga, *The Waning of the Middle Ages*, trans. F. Hopman (Penguin Books, 1968), pp. 193–205.

143. Quoted in W. P. Lehmann, "The Stony Idiom of the Brain," in Helmut Rehder, ed., *Literary Symbolism: A Symposium* (Austin, Texas, 1967), p. 15.

144. This understanding of the emergence of the Zoharic literature as the zenith of a certain process taking place over the two decades (1270–1290) is not, however, identical with the view that this work is the exclusive composition of R. Moses de Leon, as assumed by Scholem or Tishby. I believe that older elements, including theosophical views, symbols, and perhaps also shorter compositions, had merged into this vast Kabbalistic oeuvre, which heavily benefited from the nascent free symbolism. See now the important study by Liebes, *Studies in the Zohar*, pp. 85–138, and Idel, *Kabbalah: New Perspectives*, p. 380, note 66.

145. See Fine, *Safed Spirituality*, pp. 77–80.

146. On the place of symbolism in R. Nahman of Braslav see Joseph Dan, *The Hasidic Story: Its History and Development* (Keter, Jerusalem, 1975), pp. 132–188 (Hebrew); Yoav Elstein, *Ma'aseh Hoshev: Studies in Hasidic Tales* (Tel Aviv, 1983) (Hebrew); idem, *In the Footsteps of a Lost Princess* (Bar Ilan University, Ramat Gan, 1984) (Hebrew).

CHAPTER 11: ALLEGORIES, DIVINE NAMES, AND EXPERIENCES IN ECSTATIC KABBALAH

1. On Jewish medieval philosophical allegoresis in general and on that of Maimonides in particular see, among many others, Isaak Heinemann, "Die Wissenschaftliche Allegoristik des Jüdischen Mittelalters," *HUCA* 23, part 1 (1950–1951), pp. 611–644;

Talmage, "Apples of Gold," pp. 318–321, 338–340; Sara Klein-Braslavy, *Maimonides' Interpretation of the Adam Stories in Genesis* (Reuven Mass, Jerusalem, 1986) (Hebrew); Rawidowicz, "On Interpretation," pp. 97–100; Shalom Rosenberg, "Observations on the Interpretation of the Bible and Aggadah in the *Guide of the Perplexed*," in Shlomo Pines, ed., *Memorial Volume to Ya'aqov Friedman* (Hebrew University, Jerusalem, 1974), pp. 215–222 (Hebrew); Elqayam, "Between Referentionalism and Performativism," pp. 37–40; Jean Robelin, *Maïmonide et la langage religieux* (Presses Universitaires de France, Paris, 1991); Arthur Hyman, "Maimonides on Religious Language," in Joel Kraemer, ed., *Perspectives in Maimonides: Philosophical and Historical Studies* (Littman Library, Oxford University Press, 1991), pp. 175–191; Marc Saperstein, *Decoding the Rabbis* (Harvard University Press, Cambridge, Mass., 1980); Fraenkel, *The Ways of the 'Aggadah and Midrash*, pp. 501–531; Halbertal, *Concealment and Revelation*, passim.

2. For more on this issue see below, app. 1.

3. H. A. Wolfson, "Veracity of Scripture," in *Religious Philosophy* (Harvard University Press, Cambridge, Mass., 1961), p. 225.

4. Steven D. Fraade, *From Tradition to Commentary* (SUNY Press, Albany, 1991).

5. Recently important studies have helped to detect some of the resemblances between Greek and Jewish forms of hermeneutics stemming from common Babylonian sources; see above, chap. 9, as well as chap. 1, par. I, and chap. 3, par. I.

6. The first and secondary literatures on the divine names in Judaism are huge; I shall mention only a few of the pertinent bibliographical references: Abraham Marmorstein, *The Old Rabbinic Doctrine of God* (Oxford University Press, London, 1927), pp. 41–107; Samuel S. Cohon, "The Name of God, A Study in Rabbinic Theology," HUCA 23, part 1 (1950–1951), pp. 579–604; Idel, "Defining Kabbalah"; Dan, *On Sanctity*, pp. 123–130. For the topics to be discussed below see especially Idel, "The Concept of the Torah," pp. 26–30, and Wolfson, "The Mystical Significance," and the references to be adduced in notes 7–11 below.

7. See Idel, *The Mystical Experience*, pp. 14–41.

8. Idel, "On R. Isaac Sagi Nahor," pp. 31–42; Gruenwald, "The Writing, the Written and the Divine Name."

9. Gruenwald, "The Writing, the Written and the Divine Name"; Trachtenberg, *Jewish Magic and Superstition*, pp. 78–103.

10. See Idel, "Abraham Abulafia," pp. 133–137.

11. On this issue see below, pars. III–IV.

12. *Midrash Konen*, printed in Y. Eisenstein, *'Otzar ha-Midrashim* (New York, 1928), p. 253, *'Arzei Levanon*, fol. 2a, quoted above in chap. 1, and the discussion in Idel, "The Concept of Torah," p. 45.

13. See Dan, *The Esoteric Theology*, p. 124; Idel, "The Concept of Torah," p. 54; Wolfson, "The Mystical Significance."

14. See Idel, "The Concept of Torah," p. 54, note 102. See also the text quoted in the name of the tenth-century R. Hai Gaon in *'Otzar ha-Ge'onim*, *Massekhet Nedarim*, ed. B. M. Levin (Mossad ha-Rav Kook, Jerusalem, 1942), p. 11.

15. 'Aval. Compare, however, Scholem's assertion that this tradition of Nahmanides also stems from *Sefer Shimmushei Torah*: cf. "The Name of God," pp. 77–78.

16. Nahmanides, "Torat ha-Shem Temimah," in *Kitvei ha-Ramban*, ed. C. D. Chavel (Jerusalem, 1961), 2:167–168, Idel, "The Concept of Torah," p. 53, Holdrege, *Veda and Torah*, pp. 198–199.

17. Nahmanides, "Torat ha-Shem Temimah," p. 168.

18. *Commentary on the Torah*, p. 7; Halbertal, *People of the Book*, pp. 38–39.

19. Exodus 14:19–21.

20. See Ephrayim Kupfer, "The Concluding Portion of Nahmanides' *Torat ha-Shem Temimah*," *Tarbiz* 40 (1970), p. 74 (Hebrew), quoted above, chap. 9, par. III. On Nahmanides and gematria see also Wolfson, "By Way of Truth," pp. 130–131 and note 76.

21. Cf. Iser, *The Act of Reading*.

22. *Kitvei ha-Ramban*, ed. Chavel, 1:281.

23. See the interpretation of Ba'alei ha-Tosafot on BT, *Hagigah*, fol. 11b.

24. *Hayyei ha-'Olam ha-Ba'*, Ms. Paris BN 777, fol. 108a.

25. Scholem, *Origins of the Kabbalah*, pp. 387–388. For my understanding of radical interpreters see the beginning of chapter 9.

26. Exegetical techniques were expounded in great detail by the Ashkenazi Hasidim; see Dan, "The Ashkenazi Hasidic," and Marcus, "Exegesis for the Few." In Kabbalah they were adopted in Abraham Abulafia's hermeneutics; see Idel, *Language, Torah and Hermeneutics*, pp. 95–119; idem, "Abulafia's *Secrets of the Guide*"; and above, chap. 9.

27. See Idel, "Maimonides and Kabbalah," pp. 73–74.

28. *Mafteah ha-Hokhmot*, Ms. Moscow-Guenzburg 133, fols. 7b–8a. See also a very similar discussion, ibid., fol. 12b. On the expression "combination of holy names," which is implied in this quote, see below, chap. 12. For the theory that someone should combine the letters of the entire Torah see the text quoted in the name of the Besht in chap. 12, par. IX, from R. Gedalyah of Lunitz's *Teshu'ot Hen*.

29. *Mafteah ha-Hokhmot*, fol. 25a. For the passage referred to here see above, chap. 9, beside note 48 and below par. IX. On the particularistic approach in hermeneutics versus the universalistic one see Handelman, *The Slayers of Moses*, pp. 39, 56–57, 65, 225–227.

30. This term, though in another context, occurs in Daniel Matt, "The Old-New Words: The Aura of Secrecy in the Zohar," in P. Schaefer and J. Dan, eds., *Gershom Scholem's Major Trends in Jewish Mysticism, 50 Years After* (J. C. B. Mohr, Tübingen, 1993), pp. 200–202.

31. *Mafteah ha-Hokhmot*, fol. 20ab. See also his *Sheva' Netivot ha-Torah*, pp. 3–4, discussed in Idel, *Language, Torah and Hermeneutics*, pp. 100–101.

32. See above, chap. 3, par. III, 3.

33. On the interpretations of the forefathers' names in Abulafia see Idel, *The Mystical Experience*, pp. 127–128.

34. *Mafteah ha-Hokhmot*, fol. 23b; Idel, *Language, Torah and Hermeneutics*, p. 111.

35. *Mafteah ha-Hokhmot*, fol. 23b; Idel, *Language, Torah and Hermeneutics*, p. 111.

36. *Mafteah ha-Hokhmot*, fol. 23b.
37. Ibid.
38. Ibid.
39. *Mafteah ha-Hokhmot*, fols. 23b–24a. The phrase "according to nature" translates the Hebrew *lefi mishppat*, which means, regularly, "according to the judgment."
40. *The Bible in the Middle Ages*, p. 2. See also Handelman, *The Slayers of Moses*, pp. 110–111. This preoccupation with a definite truth more than with the textual details does not detract from the deep devotion to the study of the text. See especially the interesting remarks on the Christian attitude to the study of the text in André Vauchez, *La spiritualité du Moyen Age occidental, VIIIe–XIIIe* (Editions du Seuil, Paris, 1975), pp. 180–183; Leclercq, *The Love of Learning*, pp. 71–88; Stock, *The Implications of Literacy*, pp. 407–408.
41. This tradition is found in most of the versions at the very end of the book.
42. *Sha'arei Tzedeq*, p. 29; this passage should also be read in the context of another quote from this book discussed in Idel, *Language, Torah and Hermeneutics*, p. 17. On this passage see Georges Vajda, who has translated it into French in an appendix to his article "Deux chapîtres de l'histoire du conflit entre la Kabbale et la philosophie: la polemique anti-intellectualiste de Joseph b. Shalom Ashkenazi," AHDLMA 31 (1956), pp. 131–132. On part of this passage and its possible affinity to a view of Dante's see Eco, *The Search*, pp. 48–49. The possibility of contact between Abulafia's views on language and Dante's is strengthened by the fact that Abulafia's former teacher, R. Hillel of Verona, spent some years in Forli, a place where Dante was exiled. I hope to return to this issue in a separate study. See also below, chap. 12.
43. See *Sefer Hotam ha-Haftarah*, translated in Idel, *Language, Torah and Hermeneutics*, pp. 18, 52. See also below, chap. 12.
44. Ibid., p. 18.
45. See Idel, "The Concept of the Torah," pp. 55–56, note 107.
46. Ibid., pp. 55–56.
47. See *Sha'arei Tzedeq*, p. 17; Idel, *Language, Torah and Hermeneutics*, pp. 24–27.
48. *Sefer ha-'Edut*, Ms. Rome-Angelica 38, fols. 14b–15a; Ms. Munich 285, fol. 39b; see also Idel, *The Mystical Experience*, pp. 126–127, 199. The Hebrew original of the passage has been printed in the Hebrew version of this book (Magnes Press, Jerusalem, 1988), pp. 110–111, 154. See also idem, *Messianic Mystics*, pp. 82–83.
49. See Ms. München 285, fol. 39a.
50. Ibid., fol. 39b.
51. Idel, *The Mystical Experience*, pp. 127–128.
52. Written in a plene form by using *yod*.
53. Written in a defective form without *vav*.
54. For other similar expressions in Abulafia and his followers see Idel, *Studies in Ecstatic Kabbalah*, pp. 11–12; idem, "On Symbolic Self-Interpretations," and the next paragraph.
55. See above, chap. 9.

56. See above, chap. 10, note 32.
57. See Dov Schwartz, "Rationalism and Conservatism: The Speculative Thought of Rashba's Circle," *Daat* 32–33 (1994), pp. 143–180 (Hebrew); Halbertal, *People of the Book*, p. 174, note 54.
58. Chap. 3, par. II.
59. On this issue see below, app. 2.
60. See ibid.
61. *Sefer Gan Na'ul*, Ms. Munich 58, fols. 327b–328a.
62. Ms. Roma-Angelica 38, fol. 6a; Ms. Munich 285, fol. 10a; Idel, *Hasidism: Between Ecstasy and Magic*, p. 155, and above, chap. 9, note 95. See also Holdrege, *Veda and Torah*, p. 365.
63. For more on this technique see Idel, *Messianic Mystics*, pp. 298–302. See also R. Menahem Mendel of Shklow, *Menahem Tzion*, p. 22.
64. See ibid.
65. See Idel, *The Mystical Experience*, pp. 36–37.
66. On this issue see below, app. 2.
67. On this topic see also Idel, *The Mystical Experience*, pp. 96–98, 112, 113, 157–158, note 138.
68. Deuteronomy 12:23.
69. Leviticus 17:11.
70. *'Otzar 'Eden Ganuz*, Ms. Oxford, Bodeliana 1580, fols. 163b-164a. For the general context of this quote see Idel, *The Mystical Experience*, pp. 75–76.
71. Ibid., fol. 162a.
72. See *Sha'arei Tzedeq*, p. 24.
73. *Sefer ha-'Ot*, p. 82. 'Ot: a pun on the two senses of the word, "letter" and "sign." See also ibid., p. 81: "and the battle within the heart between the blood and the ink is very intense."
74. *Sefer ha-Hesheq*, Ms. New York JTS 1801, fol. 8a.
75. *Sikhliyyot u-muskkalot*.
76. *Ha-metzayyer 'inyano*.
77. *Hitztayyer meihem*.
78. *He-hakham ha-mamshil*.
79. *Melitzah ve-divrei hidah*.
80. *Sefer ha-Tzeruf*, Ms. Paris BN 770, fol. 168b. On this book and its various manuscripts see Idel, "Abraham Abulafia," pp. 69–72; Wirszubski, *Pico della Mirandola*, pp. 59–60, 63–64, 220–221, 258–260.
81. See *Genesis Rabba*, 82:7 etc. See Ira Chernus, *Mysticism in Rabbinic Judaism* (Walter de Gruyter, Berlin, 1982), pp. 19–21. On the mystical interpretations of this dictum see the learned studies of Vajda, *Le Commentaire*, pp. 339–351; Micheline Chaze, "De l'identification des patriarches au char divin: recherche du sens d'un enseignement rabbinique dans le midrash et dans la Kabbale prezoharique et ses sources," *REJ* 149

(1990), pp. 5–75; and Abrams, R. *Asher ben David*, pp. 196–197; Goldreich, *Me'irat 'Einayyim*, pp. 381–382, 393, 396.

82. Ecclesiastes 9:8.

83. On Torah as median see below, note 104, and app. 2, note 41.

84. Ms. Firenze-Laurenziana II, 48, fols. 25b–26a. See also above, chap. 5, par. I.

85. See R. Hayyim Vital, *'Etz Hayyim, Sha'ar ha-Kelalim*, chap. 1, where the goal of the creation of the world is to create creatures that will know God and become as a Chariot to Him in order to cleave to Him. However, I doubt if Vital refers here to *unio mystica*; rather, I assume that he implies that the divinity will dwell onto the mystic. See also Idel, *Messianic Mystics*, pp. 317–319. See also numerous instances where this view is found in R. Hayyim Joseph David Azulai, *Penei David*, fols. 11d, 92a, idem, *Tzavarei Shalal*, fol. 217c. As to Hasidism see, e.g., R. Aharon ha-Kohen of Apta, *Sefer 'Or ha-Ganuz le-Tzaddiqim*, col. 8, fol. 2b; col. 9, fol. 1b, fol. 4ab; col. 10, fol. 4b; R. Hayyim Haike of Amdur, *Sefer Hayyim va-Hesed* (Jerusalem, 1953), p. 210. On this passage see Schatz-Uffenheimer, *Hasidism As Mysticism*, p. 213, who interprets this text as pointing to *unio mystica*. However, provided that the divine attributes are explicitly involved here, I am inclined to doubt such a radical interpretation. See also ibid., p. 162. See also R. Abraham of Turisk, *Magen 'Avraham*, I, fol. 19c. Compare the Hasidic view of the Merkavah to the ecstatic description of this issue by R. Shem Tov ben Abraham ibn Gaon in his *Sefer Baddei 'Aron*, analyzed in Idel, *Studies in Ecstatic Kabbalah*, pp. 119–122. For another Hasidic source that uses the concept of becoming a Merkavah in order to point to mystical union see M. Idel, "Universalization and Integration: Two Concepts of Mystical Union in Jewish Mysticism," in Idel and McGinn, *Mystical Union*, p. 47; Naftali Loewenthal, *Communicating the Infinite: The Emergence of the Habad School* (University of Chicago Press, Chicago, 1990), pp. 59–60.

86. *Hitpatehut hiddush*. This awkward phrase is also found in Ms. British Library 757, fol. 41a.

87. *Sitrei Torah*, Ms. Paris BN 774, fol. 149ab.

88. Apparently "with the soul." However, these words are also missing in Ms. British Library 757, fol. 43a.

89. *Sitrei Torah*, Ms. Paris BN 774, fol. 151a.

90. Ibid., fol. 150a.

91. See ibid., fols. 5b–6a. This passage has Muslim mystical sources, and I hope to deal with them in a study which was originally planned to be written with the late Prof. Shlomo Pines. See also Lory, *Les Commentaires esoteriques*, p. 12.

92. See, e.g., Paul Fenton, ed. and trans., *The Treatise of the Pool, Al-Maqala al-Hwadiyya*, by Obadyah b. Abraham b. Moses Maimonides (Octagon Press, 1981), idem, *'Obadyah et David Maimonide: Deux traites de mystique juive* (Lagrasse, Paris Verdier, 1987); idem, "Some Judaeo-Arabic Fragments by Rabbi Abraham ha-Hasid, the Jewish Sufi," *Journal of Semitic Studies* 26 (1981), 47–72; idem, "The Literary Legacy of Maimonides' Descendants," in J. P. del Rosal, ed., *Sobre la vida y obra de Maimonides*, I Congreso internacional (Cordova, 1991), pp. 149–156, idem, "A Mystical Treatise on Perfection,

Providence and Prophecy from the Jewish Sufi Circle," in D. Frank, ed., *The Jews in Medieval Islam* (Brill, Leiden, 1995), pp. 301–334, and above, chap. 6, note 102, and below, Concluding Remarks, note 7. On mysticism and Maimonides' study see Ignaz Goldziher, "Ibn Hud, the Mahommedan Mystic, and the Jews of Damascus," *JQR*, o.s., 6 (1894), pp. 218–220.

93. See Idel, *Studies in Ecstatic Kabbalah*, passim; idem, *Language, Torah and Hermeneutics*, pp. 132, note 1, pp. 138–139, note 20.

94. See M. Idel, "Enoch Is Metatron," *Immanuel* 24/25 (1990), pp. 220–240.

95. See, more recently, Daniel Abrams, "The Boundaries of Divine Ontology: The Inclusion and Exclusion of Metatron in the Godhead," *Harvard Theological Review* 87 (1994), pp. 316–321; Moshe Idel, "Metatron: Observations on the Development of Myth in Judaism," in Haviva Pedaya, ed., *Myth in Judaism* (Beer Sheva', 1996), pp. 22–44 (Hebrew).

96. See Idel, *The Mystical Experience*, pp. 140–141, 200–201; idem, *Messianic Mystics*, pp. 73–74. See also above, chap. 4, par. I, where the material related to Metatron as the angel of the Torah in Abulafia has been adduced.

97. Cf. Idel, *Language, Torah and Hermeneutics*, pp. 29–41.

98. See Idel, *Studies in Ecstatic Kabbalah*, pp. 15–16; idem, *Messianic Mystics*, pp. 85–86.

99. Exodus 23:21.

100. See R. Abraham ibn Ezra, *Long Version on Exodus* 23:20–21.

101. Deuteronomy 30:19. See also the resort to this verse below, chap. 12, note 47.

102. Ms. Firenze-Laurentiana II, 48, fol. 32a. See a parallel stand in another text of Abulafia's, as translated in Idel, *Language, Torah and Hermeneutics*, p. 39.

103. On mystical potentials of this concept in medieval philosophy see Idel, *Messianic Mystics*, p. 349, notes 26, 27. For the mystical overtones of this concept in Islamic mysticism see the various studies of Corbin, especially *Alone with the Alone*, pp. 10–11, 17–18, 80; idem, *Cyclical Time and Ismaili Gnosis* (Kegan Paul International, London, 1983), p. 76.

104. Ha-'emtza'it. See below, app. 2, note 41.

105. See *Sitrei Torah*, Ms. Paris BN 774, fol. 155b, translated in Idel, *Language, Torah, and Hermeneutics*, p. 38. Compare also R. Dov Baer of Mezeritch, *'Or Torah*, pp. 58–59, and R. Menahem Mendel of Shklow, *Menahem Tzion*, p. 18, in a text that is reminiscent of Abraham Abulafia's thought. See also ibid., p. 21.

106. On *knesset yisra'el* as a metaphor for the supernal intellect, as well as for the human spiritual power, see also Idel, *The Mystical Experience*, pp. 211–212, note 36.

107. See above, Introduction, note 49, where the various discussions in this book are mentioned, and especially chap. 4, par. III.

108. Nissim Yosha, *Myth and Metaphor: Abraham Cohen Herrera's Philosophical Interpretation of Lurianic Kabbalah* (Ben-Zvi Institute, Magnes Press, Jerusalem, 1994) (Hebrew).

109. See also Idel, "Abulafia's *Secrets of the Guide*," and above, Introduction. On ibn Gabbai's critique of allegory see Goetschel, *Meir ibn Gabbai*, pp. 108–112.

110. See below, chap. 12, par. XI.

CHAPTER 12: *TZERUFEI 'OTIYYOT*

1. See, e.g., the sources collected by Heschel, *Theology of Ancient Judaism*, 2:360–367.
2. *Degel Mahaneh 'Efrayyim*, p. 89, also p. 87.
3. See, e.g., Scholem, *On the Kabbalah*, pp. 66–86; Heschel, *Theology of Ancient Judaism*, 3:70–74.
4. See Scholem, *Origins of the Kabbalah*, pp. 460–475; idem, *On the Kabbalah*, pp. 77–81, 83–84; idem, *Sabbatai Sevi*, pp. 313–314, 811–814; Liebes, *Sod ha-'Emunah*, pp. 47, 292–293 note 236.
5. On this term see Moshe Idel, "Some Concepts of Time and History in Kabbalah," in E. Carlebach, J. M. Efron, and D. N. Myers, eds., *Jewish History and Jewish Memory: Essays in Honor of Yosef Hayim Yerushalmi* (University Press of New England, Hanover, N.H., 1998), pp. 153–157.
6. See ibid.
7. See BT, *Sanhedrin*, fol. 97a; BT, *'Avodah Zarah*, fol. 9a; Urbach, *The Sages*, pp. 677–678; David Berger, "Three Typological Themes in Early Jewish Messianism: Messiah Son of Joseph, Rabbinic Calculations, and the Figure of Armilus," AJSR 10 (1980), pp. 149–150; Liebes, "The Messiah of the Zohar," pp. 170–171; Wolfson, "From Sealed Book," p. 174, note 66.
8. Cf. the numerous references found in Richard Landes, "Lest the Millennium Will Be Fulfilled: Apocalyptic Expectations and the Pattern of Western Chronography, 100–800 C.E.," in *The Use and Abuse of Eschatology in the Middle Ages*, ed. W. Verbeke, D. Verhelst, and A. Welkenhuysen (Leuven University Press, Leuven, 1988), pp. 137–211; Katharine R. Firth, *The Apocalyptic Tradition in Reformation Britain, 1530–1645* (Oxford University Press, Oxford, 1979), *sub voce* "Prophecy of Elijah"; Robin Bruce Barnes, *Prophecy and Gnosis: Apocalypticism in the Wake of the Lutheran Reformation* (Stanford University Press, Stanford, Calif., 1988), index, *sub voce* "Elijah, Prophecy of"; Yosef Hayim Yerushalmi, *From Spanish Court to Italian Ghetto, Isaac Cardoso, A Study in Seventeenth-Century Marranism and Jewish Apologetics* (University of Washington Press, Seattle, 1981), pp. 281–284.
9. On this concept see Liebes, *Studies in the Zohar*, pp. 48–49; idem, "The Messiah of the Zohar," pp. 165–174, 183; idem, *Sod ha-'Emunah*, p. 164. See also R. Nahman of Braslav, *Liqqutei Moharan*, I, fol. 47c.
10. See Isaiah Tishby, *Messianism in the Time of the Expulsion from Spain and Portugal* (Merkaz Zalman Shazar, Jerusalem, 1985), pp. 137–138 (Hebrew).
11. *Tiqqunim*, printed in Zohar, I, fol. 23ab, according to the translation in Tishby, *The Wisdom of the Zohar*, 3:1102.
12. See ibid., 3:1103–1104.
13. See the studies mentioned above, chap. 4, note 3, and Liebes, *Sod ha-'Emunah*, p. 164.
14. See the text printed and discussed by Liebes, *Sod ha-'Emunah*, p. 204.
15. See Liebes, "The Messiah of the Zohar," p. 166.
16. See passages found in chap. 1, par. VI; chap. 6, par. IV; chap. 5, par. I and note 36;

and app. 5, par. II. See especially the interesting passage from R. Dov Baer of Mezeritch, 'Or Torah, p. 47, where the separation or divestment from corporeality and the ascent to the higher worlds are related to the better understanding of the Torah. Cf. also ibid., pp. 41–42.

17. Metzuyyarot.

18. Ms. Paris BN 839, fol. 4ab; Ms. Jerusalem, JNUL 8° 488, fol. 45b. For a late-eighteenth-century reverberation of this view see R. Isaac Aizik Haver, 'Or Torah, in 'Amudei ha-Torah, pp. 23–24.

19. Emmanuel Swedenborg, The True Christian Religion (London, 1936), par. 6, pp. 6–7; cf., par. 212, p. 288; and Apocalypse Explained, par. 1074. See also above, chap. 5.

20. On the influence of another Kabbalistic view on Swedenborg see Idel, "The World of Angels in Human Form," Studies in Jewish Mysticism Presented to Isaiah Tishby (Jerusalem, 1984), p. 66, n. 251 (Hebrew), where I suggest that Swedenborg studied Kabbalah at Uppsala University. On Swedenborg's spiritual hermeneutics see Corbin, Face de Dieu, pp. 47–108.

21. See, e.g., R. Hayyim of Volozhin, Nefesh ha-Hayyim, pp. 274–275.

22. See chap. 1, pars. VI–VII; chap. 3, par. II,c; chap. 9, par. V; chap. 11.

23. See Scholem, On the Kabbalah, pp. 83–86.

24. See Ramhal, Tiqqunim Hadashim, p. 52.

25. Psalms 8:6.

26. This is the determinative particle, which is translated as "the."

27. Midrash Shmu'el, fol. 3a.

28. See Yarim Moshe, fol. 3cd.

29. See Notzer Hesed, p. 1.

30. On the question of the existence of the Torah on two planes see Heschel, Theology of Ancient Judaism, 1:238–241; Silman, The Voice Heard at Sinai, pp. 93–97.

31. This tension is, in my opinion, somehow different from what Scholem proposed to call absolute and relative; see On the Kabbalah, pp. 43, 73, 74, 77. As we shall see, what Scholem calls the absolute Torah consists in combinations of letters without ordinary semantic cargoes, whereas the relative Torah adopts semantic forms of expression.

32. See above, chap. 9, par. I.

33. See above, chap. 2, par. IV; chap. 4, par. VI.

34. On Gikatilla's views of the Torah in his later works see Scholem, On the Kabbalah, pp. 42–43; Idel, "The Concepts of the Torah," pp. 60–62.

35. On this view see also R. David ibn Avi Zimra, Magen David, fols. 1c, 50a; Cordovero, Pardes Rimmonim, gate 30, chap. 6; II, fol. 70d, and see Sack, Be-Sha'arei ha-Kabbalah, p. 116; Ha-Shelah, II, fol. 98a; R. Nahman of Braslav, Liqqutei Moharan, I, fol. 47c.

36. On weaving see above, chap. 9, notes 92, 93, and Sha'ar ha-Niqqud, in 'Arzei Levanon, fol. 36ab, and Asi Farber-Ginat, ed., R. Joseph Gikatilla's Commentary to Ezekiel's Chariot (Cherub Press, Los Angeles, 1998), pp. 45–46.

37. See especially Sha'arei 'Orah, gate 5, Gates of Light, pp. 244–245.

38. Qin'at ha-Shem Tzeva'ot, p. 115. See also Tiqqunim Hadashim, pp. 9, 14, 103. For this

specific technique of letter combination and its metamorphoses in later Kabbalah see Idel, *The Mystical Experience*, pp. 22–24, 44–45, notes 34–38.

39. *Tiqqunim Hadashim*, p. 7.

40. See R. Moses Hayyim Luzzatto, *'Adir ba-Marom*, fol. 6a.

41. See above, chap. 8, par. IX.

42. *Meshotetot*.

43. *Siyyimo*. Technically, it is possible to read this as either the world or *Sefer Yetzirah*, but I assume that the world when finished has been inserted within the already existing Torah.

44. Cf. several manuscripts dating from the end of the thirteenth century and the beginning of the fourteenth century; bibliographical references above, chap. 1, note 26.

45. *Commentary on Sefer 'Ish 'Adam*, Ms. Rome-Angelica 38, fol. 2a.

46. See also below, the passage from *Sha'arei Tzedeq*.

47. Deuteronomy 30:19. See also above, chap. 11, beside note 101.

48. Exodus 32:15.

49. *Sitrei Torah*, Ms. Paris BN 774, fol. 131a. For additional passages on the sphere or wheel of the Torah in Abulafia and one of his followers see Idel, *Language, Torah and Hermeneutics*, pp. 38–39, 41.

50. *Lefi kohakha*.

51. *Le-galgel ha-torah*.

52. *Sitrei Torah*, fol. 156a.

53. *Commentary on Hotam ha-Haftarah*, Ms. Rome-Angelica 38, fol. 45b.

54. The same view is found in Ms. Jerusalem JNUL 8° 1303 fol. 54a, in a passage written by Abraham Abulafia.

55. See *Sefer ha-Yihud*, Ms. Schocken-Jerusalem, Kabbalah 14, fol. 120b.

56. See below, apps. 1 and 3.

57. Or "combine it," *megalgelim bah*. On this verb as pointing to combination of letters see above, chap. 9, note 82.

58. *Sha'arei Tzedeq*, p. 29.

59. *Sha'arei Tzedeq*, p. 17; corrected according to Ms. Leiden, Warner 24, fol. 127a; Ms. Jerusalem 8° 148, fol. 47ab; the text in the second manuscript is missing in those lines.

60. See *Hayyei ha-'Olam ha-Ba'*, Ms. Paris BN 777, fol. 108a, and above, chap. 11, par. V, respectively.

61. See Nahmanides' introduction to his *Commentary on the Pentateuch*, p. 7: "The writing was continuous, without interruption between the words." On the writing of the inscriptions in ancient times without spaces between the words but with dots that give the impression of a continuous text, see the samples in Joseph Naveh, *Early History of the Alphabet* (Magnes Press, Jerusalem, 1989), pp. 55–57, 70–72 (Hebrew).

62. *On the Art of Kabbalah*, p. 293; *De Arte Cabalistica*, in J. Pistorius, *Ars Cabalistica* (Basel, 1587), p. 705.

63. Compare the way Abraham Abulafia described his stand in the quote from *Sefer Gan Na'ul*, cited above, chap. 11, par. IX.

64. *On the Art of Kabbalah*, p. 293. On the same page the Abulafian distinction between the Kabbalah of sefirot and the one concerning divine names is mentioned.

65. See also ibid., p. 337.

66. For the identification of the primordial Torah with the third sefirah see also the same Kabbalist's *Commentary on Bereshit Rabba'*, p. 138, as well as the writings of contemporary Kabbalists, e.g., *Zohar*, II, fols. 73b, 85a, *Tiqqunei Zohar*, Introduction.

67. *Tzeruf gashmi*.

68. *Sefer Yetzirah* (Jerusalem, 1961), fol. 18bc; cf. fol. 31a. On this Kabbalist see the important studies of Gershom Scholem, *Studies in Kabbalah*, ed. J. ben Shlomo (Am Oved, Tel Aviv, 1998), 1:112–136 (Hebrew); Vajda, "Un Chapître;" Hallamish's preface to *The Commentary on Genesis Rabba'*; see also Idel, *Golem*, pp. 119–128, 138–142. It is possible that R. Joseph's *Commentary* was known by Reuchlin.

69. See *Commentary on Sefer Yetzirah*, fols. 31a, 42d.

70. Ibid., fol. 33ab.

71. See Scholem, *On the Kabbalah*, pp. 39–41; Idel, "The Concept of the Torah," pp. 49–52, and below, app. 3, note 41.

72. Ms. Vatican 274, fol. 184a. On this text see M. Idel, "An Anonymous Kabbalistic Commentary on Shir ha-Yihud," in K. E. Groezinger and J. Dan, eds., *Mysticism, Magic and Kabbalah in Ashkenazi Judaism* (Walter de Gruyter, Berlin, 1995), pp. 139–154.

73. *Commentary on Bereshit Rabba'*, p. 102.

74. Gate 30, chap. 3: II, fol. 69b; the additions of R. Jacob Barukh, the editor of R. Yohanan Alemanno's introduction to his commentary on the Song of Songs, printed as *Sha'ar ha-Hesheq* (Halberstadt, 1860), fol. 32a; R. Ze'ev Wolf of Zhitomir, *'Or ha-Me'ir*, fol. 190ab.

75. See, e.g., the various discussions of Ramhal, and in R. Gedalyah of Lunitz, *Teshu'ot Hen*, pp. 33, 91, and the quote in the name of R. Yehiel Mikhal of Zlotchov, *Mayyim Rabbim*, fol. 21b, to be adduced below, par. VIII; Idel, *Hasidism: Between Ecstasy and Magic*, pp. 77–78.

76. Compare the same question in *Tiqqunei Zohar*, no. 67, fol. 98b.

77. *Sefer Tzeror ha-Hayyim*, Ms. London, Montefiore 318, fols. 84b–85a. See also ibid., fols. 28b–29a and 76a, where the primordial Torah, *torah qedumah*, is described as related to the 231 combinations. On this Kabbalist see the recent study by Yoni Garb, "The Kabbalah of R. Joseph ibn Tzayyah As a Source for the Understanding of Safedian Kabbalah," *Kabbalah* 4 (1999) (Hebrew). On issues related to the sources of ibn Tzayyah's view of combinations of letters and primordial Torah see Idel, *Golem*, pp. 151–152.

78. On this legend and the bibliography related to it see above, chap. 5, par. I and note 3.

79. *Tzerufei shemot ha-qodesh*. On this phrase see also below, the passage from HYDA' referenced in note 109, and in R. Ze'ev Wolf of Zhitomir, *'Or ha-Me'ir*, fol. 34b.

80. A term for divine names.

81. *Tzafnat Pa'aneah*, fol. 14b. See also my introduction to this book, pp. 39–41.

82. I.e., the angel's opposing the disclosure of the Torah to Moses.

83. *Sefer Metzudat David* (Zolkvoe, 1866), fol. 70b. The same text occurs also in his *Responsa*, III, no. 643.

84. See *Sefer 'Aqedat Yitzhaq* (rpt. Jerusalem, 1961), I, fols. 10b, 219a.

85. The most elaborate exposition of Cordovero's concept of the Torah is in Sack, *Be-Sha'arei ha-Kabbalah*, pp. 113–192; on some topics close to our following discussion see especially Scholem, *On the Kabbalah*, pp. 71–76. Some of the descriptions below are based on Cordovero's *Shi'ur Qomah*, fols. 63ad, 85cd.

86. See the text translated in Idel, *Studies in Ecstatic Kabbalah*, p. 127.

87. Ibid., fol. 63cd. Compare, above, the view of *Sha'arei Tzedeq* about the weakness of the back structure of the Torah.

88. Ibid.; see also fol. 85cd.

89. On the Torah as a seal see also Sack, *Be-Sha'arei ha-Kabbalah*, p. 114.

90. See also Cordovero's text printed in Sack, *Be-Sha'arei ha-Kabbalah*, p. 124 and note 26.

91. *Hesed le-'Avraham*, 2:27, fol. 12a; Scholem, *On the Kabbalah*, pp. 71–72; Sack, *Be-Sha'arei ha-Kabbalah*, pp. 113–114.

92. See the text printed in Sack, *Be-Sha'arei ha-Kabbalah*, p. 124.

93. Ibid., p. 125.

94. *Tzerufei shemoteiah*. This term also occurs in R. Moses Hayyim Luzzatto's writings.

95. On the view that the Torah can be read as a continuum of divine names see above, chap. 11, par. IV.

96. *Ha-Shelah*, III, fol. 177a; also II, fol. 112a.

97. See also R. Isaiah's commentary on liturgy, *Sha'ar ha-Shamayyim* (Amsterdam, 1698), fol. 31b.

98. Numbers 19:14.

99. *Midrash Talppiyyot*, fol. 35b.

100. Ibid.

101. See above, chap. 3, note 22.

102. Isaiah 51:4.

103. *Devash le-Fi*, fol. 40d. See the translation in Scholem, *On the Kabbalah*, pp. 74–75. Though taking into consideration Scholem's English version, I adopted a more literal rendition, which differs from his on some points.

104. I wonder if this view is not related to some of the interpretations of the three unconnected letters *'alif, lamid, mim*, in the Qur'an, which were conceived of as divine names. See Ayoub, *The Qur'an and Its Interpreters*, pp. 56–59.

105. BT, *Berakhot*, fol. 30a.

106. Scholem, *On the Kabbalah*, p. 75.

107. Ibid.

108. *Devash le-Fi*, fol. 41a.

109. See above, note 79.

110. For the midrashic sources of this dictum see Heschel, *Theology of Ancient Judaism*, 1:240 note 9.

111. *Sarsur.* This is a leitmotif in HYDA"s books. For one of its possible sources see Ha-Shelah, II, fol. 116ab. It is plausible that the mediator is Moses. See also an earlier discussion of Moses as *sarsur* in the anonymous Kabbalistic *Collectanaea*, Ms. Paris BN 974, fol. 147a. See also R. Abraham Azulai, *Hesed le-'Avraham*, fol. 12a, R. David ibn Avi Zimra, *Magen David*, fol. 39c; R. Mordekhai Ze'ev of Kalbiel, *Sefer Qol Ramaz* (Warsaw, 1904), fol. 27b.

112. *Tzavarei Shalal*, fol. 184ab.

113. *On the Kabbalah*, pp. 75–76, where Scholem adduces an additional passage from another of HYDA"s books.

114. *Qin'at ha-Shem Tzeva'ot*, pp. 131–133. The Hebrew passage in this book has been rewritten in Aramaic in *Tiqqunim Hadashim*, p. 9. Interestingly, the phrase *tzeruf ha-'avodah* occurs in Ramhal's *Mesillat Yesharim*, chap. 16, p. 275, where the meaning is different: the catharsis of worship.

115. Ibid., p. 133.

116. Ibid., p. 132. See also above, chap. 5, par. IV, on the view of Ramhal about the drawing down of the Zohar.

117. *'Adir ba-Marom*, fol. 96b.

118. See *Teshu'ot Hen*, pp. 32–33; also p. 96.

119. *Be-ta'arovot 'otiyyot*. Scholem translated it as "incoherent jumble of letters."

120. *Me'uravin be-ta'arovot.*

121. *Sefer Ge'ulat Yisrael* (Ostrog, 1821), fols. 1d–2a; for a slightly different translation see Scholem, *On the Kabbalah*, pp. 76–77. On the correspondence between the divine infinite wisdom and textual infinity mentioned at the end of this passage see above, chap. 3, note 30.

122. See chap. 3, par. II; chap. 9, par. V.

123. See Idel, *Hasidism: Between Ecstasy and Magic*, pp. 59, 278, note 73; cf. *Sha'ar ha-Niqqud*, printed in *'Arzei Levanon*, fol. 38a. First printed in Venice in 1601, this collection of early Kabbalistic texts was reprinted in Cracow in 1748.

124. See Sack, *Be-Sha'arei ha-Kabbalah*, p. 177.

125. See *Toledot Ya'aqov Yosef*, fol. 133ab.

126. *Teshu'ot Hen*, p. 82. For another very similar quote see ibid., p. 19. See also Heschel, *Theology of Ancient Judaism*, 3:72.

127. See especially the quote from Abulafia's *Mafteah ha-Hokhmot*, adduced above, chap. 11, par. V.

128. Ibid.

129. Ibid., pp. 18–19, 33, 96. For the possible sources of this explanation of the two kinds of Torah see HYDA', *Midbbar Qedeimot*, fol. 61a. See also R. Isaac of Komarno, *Notzer Hesed*, p. 1. This stand has something to do with the assumption that the primordial Torah is found in a state of union, higher than time, while the revealed Torah is characterized by separation. See, e.g., the Great Maggid of Mezeritch, *'Or Torah*,

p. 47, and cf. ibid., p. 79, where the separation is related to combination of letters. See also idem, *Maggid Devarav le-Ya'aqov*, pp. 227–228.

130. See Idel, *Language, Torah, and Hermeneutics*, p. 21.

131. See Gikatilla, *Commentary on Matters in The Guide of the Perplexed*.

132. *Ha-Shelah*, III, fol. 190b; *'Ahavat Dodim*, p. 237.

133. See Allen Tate, *The Man of Letters in the Modern World* (Meridian Books, New York, 1955), p. 39.

134. *Mayyim Rabbim*, fol. 21b. For more on this passage and its possible Abulafian sources in *Sefer ha-Peli'yah* see Idel, *Hasidism: Between Ecstasy and Magic*, pp. 56–58. See also the discussion in Weiss, *Studies*, pp. 129–135.

135. See above, chap. 2, par. IV.

136. Genesis 36:12.

137. *Sippurei ma'asiyyot*.

138. *Hishtalshelut*.

139. *Qedushat Levi*, p. 115.

140. Exodus 1:22.

141. On this term see above, chap. 2, note 91.

142. *Toledot 'Aharon*, I, fol. 27c. For more on changes of the Torah related to time see ibid., II, fol. 2ab.

143. On air as an important symbol for the highest divine hypostasis, Keter, see the various footnotes of Mopsik to *Le Sicle*, *s.v.* "Air," and especially his introduction, pp. 59–65.

144. Cf. *Toledot 'Aharon*, I, fols. 32c, 33a.

145. See below, note 161. Cf. also a similar discussion in *Ha-Shelah*, II, fol. 98a, and R. Isaac Aizik Haver, *'Or Torah*, in *'Amudei ha-Torah*, p. 219, and above, chap. 2, note 78.

146. For other examples of eccentric exegesis see *Ha-Shelah* II, fol. 24b.

147. See chap. 2, par. IV.

148. See, e.g., the Sabbatean epistle attributed to R. Abraham Peretz, *Magen 'Avraham*, printed by Gershom Scholem in *Qovetz 'al Yad*, n.s., 2 (12) (1937) pp. 145–146 (Hebrew).

149. *Ha-hester ha-gadol*.

150. BT, *Berakhot*, fol. 55a.

151. *Ha-hoshekh ha-gadol*.

152. *Qol Yehudah*, fol. 26a. The views of this Hasidic author require detailed analysis; I assume that an impact of ecstatic Kabbalah can be detected. See, e.g., fol. 21c.

153. *Mahashavah qedumah*, in *Qol Yehudah*, fol. 4c.

154. Ibid.

155. See also the text of Hasidei Ashkenaz, printed by Dan, *The Esoteric Theology*, p. 124, where the theory of the torah as the divine names is preceded by the assumption that the Torah is one unit.

156. *Qol Yehudah*, fol. 19c.

157. *'Or Yitzhaq*, p. 170.

158. Ibid., p. 171. On this figure see Schatz-Uffenheimer, *Hasidism as Mysticism*, pp. 129–136. Compare, however, in the printer's introduction, ibid., p. 2, where he claims that we do not know the nature of the future Torah.
159. Ibid., pp. 168–169.
160. Ibid., pp. 1–2, 6.
161. See more on this topic below, app. 3, and the beginning of the Kabbalistic text preserved anonymously in Ms. Paris BN 839, fol. 4ab, and Ms. Jerusalem, JNUL 488 8° fol. 45b, and note 145 above.
162. This theory occurs several times in R. Aharon of Zhitomir's *Toledot 'Aharon*; see note 144 above, to which I referred above. See also R. Gedalyah of Lunitz, *Teshu'ot Hen*, pp. 13, 110.
163. *Behirut*. On this term see above, chap. 2, par. IV.
164. The combination of the divine names.
165. The world.
166. *'Or ha-Torah*. This phrase is found already in ancient Jewish texts, as in Heikhalot literature, and at the beginning of Kabbalah; see R. Azriel of Gerona, *Commentary on the Talmudic 'Aggadot*, p. 77; see also Cordovero, *Shi'ur Qomah*, fol. 63c, and see also the passage from his *Sefer 'Elimah Rabbati*, printed in Sack, *Be-Sha'arei ha-Qabbalah*, p. 177. See also above, chap. 6, note 68.
167. The word that occurs twice and has been translated as "deficiency" is *qalut*, which literally means "light."
168. See above, note 78.
169. *Keli mukhan*. On this phrase see above, chap. 5, note 67.
170. *Shemu'ot Tovot ve-Razin de-'Orayita'*, ed. H. A. Rabinovitch (Chernovitz, 1885), fol. 20b–21b.
171. On this theme see above, chap. 6, note 171, and earlier in Hasidic literature in R. Dov Baer of Mezeritch, *'Or Torah*, pp. 158–159; R. Isaac of Radvil, *'Or Yitzhaq*, p. 167; R. Ze'ev Wolf of Zhitomir, *'Or ha-Me'ir*, fol. 191b; and in the camp of the Mitnaggedim, the contemporary R. Hayyim of Volozhin, *Nefesh ha-Hayyim*, pp. 186, 343.
172. See also above, chap. 2, note 74.
173. See, e.g., Cordovero, *Pardes Rimmonim*, gate 30, Introduction, II, fol. 88c; R. Yehudah Arieh Leib of Gur, *Sefat 'Emmet*, III, fol. 85d.
174. *On the Kabbalah*, p. 77.
175. See chap. 4, par. VI.
176. See below, end of app. 3 and note 44.
177. See, e.g., *Ha-Shelah*, I, vol. 9a; II, fol. 98ab, 112b; HYDA', *Penei David*, fol. 181b; R. Ze'ev Wolf of Zhitomir, *'Or ha-Me'ir*, fols. 165b, 239b.
178. *'Or ha-Me'ir*, fol. 190a.
179. Ibid., fol. 190b. Cf. also fols. 146a, 264a.
180. See also ibid., fol. 126cd. See also fols. 299d–300a, where this author refers to *Ha-Shelah* as a source for his view of combinations of letters.
181. See Green, *Devotion and Commandment*, esp. pp. 50–72.

182. See below, app. 2 and note 2.

183. According to this text, p. 164, this source is the sefirah of Hokhmah.

184. 'Or Torah, in 'Amudei ha-Torah, p. 219. See also ibid., p. 164.

185. The only significant exceptions are some of the writings of R. Menahem Mendel of Shklow, which absorbed some elements of the hermeneutical system that are characteristic of ecstatic Kabbalah, an issue that deserves a separate discussion. Many of the pertinent books are still in manuscript, and only their publication will demonstrate their relevance to the impact of ecstatic Kabbalah.

186. See also above, chap. 1, par. XI.

CHAPTER 13: TRADITION, TRANSMISSION, AND TECHNIQUES

1. For more on this issue see Idel, "Conceptualization of Music."

2. Chavel, ed., Commentary on the Torah, pp. 7–8. For more on Nahmanides' esotericism see Idel, "We Have No Kabbalistic Tradition," and above, chap. 7, par. III. See also the view of R. Shlomo ibn Adret, Nahmanides' main disciple, who was both a Halakhist and a Kabbalist, in his Responsa, no. 423, and R. Joseph Ergas, Shomer 'Emunim, p. 15. For esotericism in ibn Adret's student, R. Shem Tov ibn Ga'on, see Halbertal, Concealment and Revelation, pp. 69–75.

3. Compare the text quoted from a responsum of R. Hai Gaon and analyzed in Idel, "Defining Kabbalah," pp. 101–102.

4. The Commentary on Job, in Kitvei ha-Ramban, ed. C. D. Chavel, 1:23.

5. Traditions related to the cosmic cycles, shemittah and yovel, topics that can be understood by their relationship to the theosophical system. See below, note 18.

6. Mi-da'at 'atzmo.

7. Compare the responsum of R. Hai Gaon, discussed in more detail in Idel, "Defining Kabbalah," pp. 101–102.

8. Nahmanides, Kitvei ha-Ramban, ed. C. D. Chavel (Jerusalem 1964), 1:190.

9. Cf. Wolfson, "By Way of Truth"; Halbertal, Concealment and Revelation, pp. 53–57, 63–69.

10. This assumption has some antecedents in earlier periods in the rabbinic texts. See G. A. Wewers, Geheimnis und Geheimhaltung in rabbinischen Judentum (de Gruyter, Berlin, 1975); Smith, Clement of Alexandria, s.v. "secret, secrecy"; Scholem, Jewish Gnosticism, p. 58.

11. Kitvei ha-Ramban, 1:163.

12. See Idel, "On the History," pp. 6–9.

13. See BT, Hagigah, fol. 13a.

14. See also the passage of Nahmanides quoted above, chap. 9, note 25.

15. See his "Interpreting the Variorum," Critical Inquiry 2 (1976), pp. 473–485.

16. See Stock, The Implications of Literacy, p. 74. On tradition in a more dynamic manner see also Banon, La lecture infinie, pp. 71–84.

17. See Idel, "Nahmanides."

18. See his On the Mystical Shape, pp. 207–209. See also above, note 5.

19. *Sefer Hayyei ha-'Olam ha-Ba'*, Ms. Oxford 1582, fol. 45b. See also Idel, *Language, Torah, and Hermeneutics*, pp. 3–11. On the influence of this quote on R. Mordekhai Dato's description of R. Moses Cordovero's Kabbalistic activity see Idel, *Studies in Ecstatic Kabbalah*, p. 137.

20. See the discussions of this acronym in R. Barukh Togarmi and Joseph Gikatilla's early *Sefer Ginnat 'Egoz*.

21. *Sefer 'Otzar 'Eden Ganuz*, Ms. Oxford 1580, fol. 55a.

22. See Idel, *Language, Torah, and Hermeneutics*, pp. 51–53.

23. *Sefer 'Imrei Shefer*, Ms. München 285, fol. 90a; Scholem, *Major Trends*, pp. 139–140.

24. See the three volumes of studies published by Oxford University Press and edited by Steven T. Katz, *Mysticism and Religious Traditions* (1983), *Mysticism and Philosophical Analysis* (1978), and *Mysticism and Language* (1992), as well as the opposite stand as presented in the studies edited by Robert K. C. Forman, *The Problem of Pure Consciousness: Mysticism and Philosophy* (1990).

25. *Rashei peraqim*.

26. *Sefer Sha'arei Tzedeq*, p. 9.

27. Namely the path of Kabbalah.

28. *Sha'arei Tzedeq*, p. 23. For another view of Jewish esotericism in terms of an experiential event, the union with God see the view of the mid-eighteenth-century Hasidic master R. Menahem Mendel of Premiszlany, above, chap. 6, par. III.

29. *Sheva' Netivot ha-Torah*, p. 21.

30. A list of ancient mystical books appears in a similar context in his epistle *Sheva' Netivot ha-Torah*, p. 21.

31. The manuscript has MHTY; it is possible that this is one of the many errors of the copyist of this unfortunately unique manuscript. If so, we should read the sentence as follows: "which came to me in the form of Bat Qol." However, it is possible that Abulafia alluded to the Greek form THY, namely God, and then MTHY would mean "from God." Abulafia used the form THYV to point to God in his earlier *Sefer Get ha-Shemot*; see Idel, *Language, Torah, and Hermeneutics*, p. 24.

32. Bat Qol. See the mention, at the beginning of this text, of *qolot*, voices. It is also possible that the similarity between the sounds and the written forms of *qolot* and *qabbalot* is implied in the idea that traditions coming from above are voices.

33. Compare his epistle *Sheva' Netivot ha-Torah*, p. 21, where he counts the revelation from the Agent Intellect as higher than the secrets he learned from various esoteric books. Cf. Idel, "Maimonides and Kabbalah," pp. 57–58.

34. See Idel, "Maimonides and Kabbalah," pp. 58–59 and note 90; p. 69. On the superiority of oral transmission to written documents, see Abraham Abulafia's view as discussed in Idel, *Language, Torah and Hermeneutics*, pp. 46–55. For the Renaissance misunderstanding of the identity of Abulafia's master as Maimonides himself see Wirszubski, *Pico della Mirandola*, pp. 87–88, 91–98.

35. See also Idel, *The Mystical Experience*, pp. 180–184.

36. Scholem, *Major Trends*, p. 140.

37. *Studies in Ecstatic Kabbalah*, pp. 50–51.

38. See above, chap. 7, par. III.

39. See Idel, *The Mystical Experience*, pp. 24–37.

40. Ibid., pp. 20–21.

41. See Idel, "Maimonides and Kabbalah," p. 69, note 128.

42. See Scholem, *Major Trends*, p. 137.

43. *Shomer Mitzvah*, Ms. Paris BN 853, fol. 48b. On this view of Kabbalah, which assumes both mystical and magical aspects, see my discussion of the mystico-magical model in *Hasidism: Between Ecstasy and Magic*, pp. 103–145.

44. This issue deserves a separate treatment.

45. *Qabbalah sikhlit*. This view, characteristic of some of the innovative Kabbalists, was reiterated by several Kabbalists, especially in the period of the Renaissance and later.

46. Ms. Paris BN 770, fol. 175b.

47. *Sheva' Netivot ha-Torah*, p. 12. On this issue see also Wolfson, *Abraham Abulafia*, pp. 55–58.

48. *Sefer Shomer Mitzvah*, Ms. Paris BN 853, fol. 74ab. See also Wolfson, *Abraham Abulafia*, pp. 81–82.

49. See Idel, "On the History," pp. 6–9.

50. PT, *'Avodah Zarah*, II:8.

51. *Shomer Mitzvah*, Ms. Paris BN 853, fol. 48b.

52. On this term see above, chap. 7, notes 24, 48.

53. *Sefer Shomer Mitzvah*, Ms. Paris BN 853, fol. 78a.

54. See, e.g., Marsilio Ficino's description, drawn explicitly from Jewish sources, that the science of the divine names was already revealed to the patriarchs, adduced in Francois Secret, *Les Kabbalistes chrétiens de la Renaissance* (Paris, 1964), p. 77, and Athanasius Kircher's view of the Adamic language, cf. L. Deikman, *Hieroglyphics: The History of a Literary Symbol* (St. Louis, 1970), pp. 97–99. It should be mentioned that a book quoted by Abulafia in the context of books he has studied, *Sefer Raziel*, is attributed in some sources to Adam, to whom it, like *Sefer ha-Razim*, was revealed by an angel. This book was known in various European translations at the end of the fifteenth century. See also Scholem, *Origins of the Kabbalah*, p. 106. On the Adamic source of Kabbalah see Mopsik, *Le Sicle*, pp. 109–110. Another issue that cannot be addressed here is the difference between the normative rabbinic tradition that attributes to Moses the reception of fifty gates of understanding and the tradition that attributes this divine gift to Adam. The latter view, which seems to reflect a much earlier mythologoumenon, is still extant in Ashkenazi mystical literature. See above, chap. 7, notes 59, 101.

55. *Sefer ha-Hezyonot*, p. 49. See also above, chap. 6, note 154.

56. See Lory, *Les Commentaires esoteriques*, pp. 79–82, and above, chap. 11, notes 92, 93.

57. See Idel, *The Mystical Experience*, pp. 86–95.

58. On the contention of easiness in Abulafia's thought see Idel, "Defining Kabbalah," pp. 112–113.

59. Ricoeur, *Hermeneutics and the Human Sciences*, pp. 141–144; idem, *The Conflicts of Interpretations*, p. 331; idem, *From Text to Action*, pp. 99–101. Compare this view with the much more static approach of a mid-eighteenth-century Hasidic master, R. Pinhas of Koretz, who claims that everyone finds himself in the Torah, just as he does. Cf. *Midrash Pinhas*, fol. 23a.

60. Cf. Paul Ricoeur, "Philosophical Hermeneutics and Theological Hermeneutics," *Studies in Religion/Sciences Religieuses* 5, no. 1 (1976), p. 30; idem, *From Text to Action*, pp. 100–101; Vanhoozer, *Biblical Narrative*, pp. 132–141.

61. See above, chap. 11, par. IX.

62. See above, chap. 3, par. II, and chap. 4, note 41.

63. BT, *Babba' Batra'*, fol. 12a. See also Heschel, *Theology of Ancient Judaism*, 2:314–316.

64. *Tiqqun ve-hashlamah 'el ha-torah.*

65. *Tiferet Israel*, chap. 69 (Benei Beraq, 1980), p. 216. On the souls of the people of Israel as the perfection of the Torah see R. Barukh of Medzibezh, *Botzina' di-Nehora'*, p. 77, and Heschel, *Theology of Ancient Judaism*, p. 29.

66. Eco, *The Open Work*, pp. 15, 19.

67. On the reader as author in a hypertextual context see Luca Toschi, "Hypertext and Authorship," in *The Future of the Book*, pp. 169–207; Michael Joyce, "(Re)Placing the Author: 'A Book in Ruins,' " in ibid., pp. 273–293; Eco, "Afterword," in ibid., p. 303. See also above, chap. 6, note 169.

CHAPTER 14: CONCLUDING REMARKS

1. See, e.g., Idel, *The Mystical Experience*, pp. 83–95; idem, *Language, Torah, and Hermeneutics*, pp. 101–109; and below, note 2. On Gadamer see Weinsheimer, *Gadamer's Hermeneutics*, pp. 247, 249–251. See also above, Introduction, note 1, and Joseph Dan, "Prayer as a Text, and the Prayer as Mystical Experience," in Ruth Link-Salinger, ed., *Torah and Wisdom: Essays in Honor of Arthur Hyman* (Shengold Publishers, New York, 1992), pp. 33–47.

2. See also above, chap. 5, par. VI. On linguocentric spirituality see Idel, "On Talismanic Language" and "The Voiced Text of the Torah," *Deutsche Vierteljahrsschrift für Literaturwissenschaft und Geistgeschichte* 68 (1994), pp. 145–146. On some cases of emphasizing experiential dimension of the loud lectio for meditation and of encountering God in the twelfth-century Christian mystic St. Bernard of Clairvaux see Stock, *The Implications of Literacy*, pp. 408–409.

3. Schaefer, *Hekhalot-Studien*, pp. 293–294. Interestingly, the term "mysteries" is used to describe what I believe it would better to translate as "secrets." On casuistic elements in Kabbalistic literature see Scholem and Werblowsky, the passages adduced in Idel, "Defining Kabbalah," p. 98.

4. See above, chap. 6, par. II.

5. Cf. the translation of Smalley, *The Bible in the Middle Ages*, pp. 170–171.

6. For the two different treatments of translation see Bruns, *Inventions*, pp. 23–24,

41–42; idem, *Hermeneutics Ancient and Modern*, pp. 88–89; compare the positive attitude to the event of translation of the Septuagint in Greek sources to the negative reactions found in some Hebrew sources.

7. See the survey of Paul Fenton, "Abraham Maimonides (1186–1237)," in *Jewish Mystical Leaders*, pp. 127–154, and above, chap. 11, notes 92, 93.

8. Cf. Handelman, *The Slayers of Moses*, Faur, *Golden Doves*, and Shira Wolosky, *Language and Mysticism: The Negative Way of Language in Eliot, Beckett, and Celan* (Stanford University Press, Stanford, Calif., 1995). See also Caputo, *The Prayers and Tears*, pp. 335–336; Wolfson, *Through the Speculum That Shines*, pp. 13–16.

9. Cf. Baer, *Studies*, 1:111–112, Bloom, *The Strong Light*, pp. 30–31, 69.

10. Hans Jonas, *Philosophical Essays: From Ancient Creed to Technological Man* (Englewood Cliffs, N.J., Prentice-Hall, 1973), p. 29, adduced and discussed by Handelman, *The Slayers of Moses*, pp. 27–28. Compare also Steiner, *After Babel*, pp. 59–63.

11. See, e.g., chap. 2 and chap. 11, par. VI.

12. Cf. Scholem, *On the Kabbalah*, p. 59.

13. Frank Talmage, "The Term 'Haggada' in the Parable of the Beloved in the Palace in the Zohar," *JSJT* 4 (1984/85), pp. 271–274 (Hebrew).

14. See, e.g., Wolfson's *Philo*.

15. Moshe Idel, "Ramon Lull and Ecstatic Kabbalah," *Journal of the Warburg and Courtauld Institutes* 51 (1988), pp. 170–174; Eco, *The Search*, pp. 53–69.

16. See Wirszubski, *Pico della Mirandola*, pp. 63, 73–74, 81.

17. Eco, *The Search*, pp. 132–139.

18. On Leibniz and Kabbalah see Allison Coudert, *Leibniz and the Kabbalah* (Kluwer, Dordrecht, 1995).

19. The relatively significant divergences between the main concepts that informed the different corpora mentioned above should not minimize the fact that earlier contacts between them, in Europe or in the East, preceded the medieval episodes and even facilitated them by "allowing" some later figures, like Pico della Mirandola and Johann Reuchlin, to claim that there were basic concordances between these corpora. See also above, chap. 9, par. I, and below, app. 6.

20. Derrida, *Dissemination*, p. 344; See also the French edition, Jacques Derrida, *La Dissémination* (Le Seuil, Paris, 1972), p. 382, copied from Abulafia's *Sheva' Netivot ha-Torah*, pp. 14–15. See above, chap. 3, note 44, and chap. 9, par. VII.

21. See Derrida, *L'écriture et la différence*, pp. 117–228; see also Shira Wolosky, "Derrida, Jabes, Levinas: Sign-Theory as Ethical Discourse," *Prooftexts* 2 (1982), pp. 283–302.

22. See *Dissemination*, pp. 342–345. Derrida resorted to at least two additional forms of Jewish mystical thinking: Lurianism and Hasidism. On the latter see above, chap. 2. On Mallarmé's emphasis on the importance of the blank space and that of some texts in Kabbalah and Hasidism see ibid., p. 345, and above, chaps. 2 and 3.

23. See, e.g., Harold Bloom's theory of misprision.

24. See above, chap. 9, par. III.

25. Compare also the emphasis found in Ricoeur on stability, completeness, and intact-

ness of text. Cf. *Hermeneutics and the Human Sciences*, p. 147, and see also p. 139. On Derrida's view of textuality and its possible sources see Howard Felperin, *Beyond Deconstruction: The Uses and Abuses of Literary Theory* (Clarendon Press, Oxford, 1985), pp. 36–37.

26. See Idel, *The Mystical Experience*, pp. 22–23.

27. *Hermeneutics and the Human Sciences*, p. 146.

28. See Derrida, *L'écriture et la différence*, pp. 117–227, especially the last page, where he refers to James Joyce's expressions "Jewishgreek" and "Greekjewish."

29. See Idel, *Language, Torah, and Hermeneutics*, pp. 11, 100–101, 103.

30. Ibid., pp. 101–109.

31. See also above, notes 1–2.

32. See also above, chap. 9, note 84.

33. Ms. Leipzig 39, fol. 5b. On the Latin, glossed version of this statement see C. Wirszubski, *Between the Lines, Kabbalah, Christian Kabbalah and Sabbatianism*, ed. M. Idel (Magnes Press, Jerusalem, 1990), p. 42 (Hebrew). See also below, app. 2, note 32.

34. On Abulafia's exegetical strategies in his three commentaries on the *Guide* see Idel, "Abulafia's Secrets of the *Guide*."

35. See the various interpretations of this thesis in David Biale, "Gershom Scholem's Ten Unhistorical Aphorisms on Kabbalah," in Harold Bloom, ed., *Gershom Scholem* (Chelsea House, New York, 1987), pp. 120–123, and Joseph Dan, "Beyond the Kabbalistic Symbol," *JSJT* 5 (1986), pp. 383–385 (Hebrew). None of these authors, however, addressed the issues to be discussed below. See, however, Bloom, *The Strong Light and Ruin the Sacred Truths* (Harvard University Press, Cambridge, Mass., 1989), p. 192, who repeatedly resorts to terms found in this thesis.

36. See chap. 6, par. V.

37. Bloom, *The Strong Light*, p. 55. For Scholem's negativity see ibid., pp. 7, 13, 61–67; idem, *Agon*, p. 83, idem, *Kabbalah and Criticism*, pp. 53ff. See also above, chap. 2, par. IV, and chap. 12.

38. See Scholem, *On the Kabbalah*, pp. 48–50.

39. Bloom, *The Strong Light*, pp. 60–61.

40. See Bloom's description of Scholem as being in "an obsession with the imagery of catastrophe." Cf. his "Scholem: Unhistorical or Jewish Gnosticism," in Harold Bloom, ed., *Gershom Scholem* (Chelsea House, New York, 1987), p. 217.

41. Cf. Bloom's introduction to Scholem's *From Berlin to Jerusalem* (Schocken Books, New York, 1988), p. xx. See also ibid., p. xxi: "He [Scholem] longed for a wholly Gnostic Kabbalah, and indeed for a Gnostic Judaism, though he was wary of expressing this desire too overtly." To believe another expert on Scholem, he has been alienated, in exile even while in Israel; See Irving Wohlfarth, " 'Haarscharf an der Grenze zwischen Religion und Nihilismus': Zum Motiv des Zimzum bei Gershom Scholem," *Gershom Scholem zwischen den Disziplinen*, ed. Peter Schaefer and Gary Smith (Suhrkamp, Frankfurt am Main, 1995), pp. 176–256.

42. See above, chap. 3, note 12, and Handelman, *Fragments of Redemption*, pp. 82–92. See

also Scholem's interpretation of a Hasidic story that in its Hasidic original version is much more positive but has been interpreted in a rather weak, not to say negative, manner in Scholem, *Major Trends*, pp. 349–350; Hartman, *The Fate of Reading*, pp. 273–274, and compare Idel, *Kabbalah: New Perspectives*, pp. 270–271; Idel, *Hasidism: Between Ecstasy and Magic*, pp. 185–186.

43. Cf. Scholem, *The Messianic Idea*, p. 35; Idel, *Messianic Mystics*, pp. 233, 283–289.

44. See Jacques Riviere, "La crise du concept de littérature," *Nouvelle Revue Française*, February 1, 1924.

45. See the view of Jacques Maritain, *Creative Intuition in Art and Poetry* (New American Library, New York, 1953), p. 150.

46. Cf. Riviere, "La crise du concept de littérature."

47. On Kafka see also above, chap. 5, par. VI, and Introduction, note 52. On Celan see Stephane Moses, "Patterns of Negativity in Paul Celan's 'The Trumpet Place,'" in S. Budick and W. Iser, eds., *Languages of the Unsayable: The Play of Negativity in Literature and Literary Theory* (Columbia University Press, New York, 1989), pp. 209–224. On Kafka and Scholem on negativity see ibid., pp. 222–223.

48. Idel, *Kabbalah: New Perspectives*, p. 271.

49. Cordovero, *Derishot*, p. 70. See also above, chap. 3, note 75. Compare the similar imagery found in earlier Kabbalistic texts treated in Idel, *Hasidism: Between Ecstasy and Magic*, pp. 158–159. See also the important passage of Cordovero's disciple, R. Elijah da Vidas, *Reshit Hokhmah, Sha'ar ha-Qedushah*, chap. IV, vol. 2, p. 59, where the contention is that the intensive study of the Torah creates an experience of divestment of spirituality, and man becomes an angel.

50. Namely the angels.

51. Cordovero, *Derishot*, p. 70; see also ibid., p. 76. See also R. Barukh of Medzibezh, *Botzina' di-Nehora'*, p. 111.

52. The Israelites at the Sinaitic revelation.

53. *Botzina' di-Nehora'*, pp. 109–110.

54. *'Or ha-Me'ir*, fol. 4a; the Hebrew is *mamtzi'im ta'am hadash*. On this very page the verb *mamtzi'* occurs several times; see also ibid., fol. 38cd.

55. Ibid. See also ibid, fols. 216d–217a; *Ha-Shelah*, II, 108b. See also the earlier texts adduced and discussed by Weiss-Halivni, *Revelation Restored*, pp. 87–89, and the Kabbalistic passages quoted in Silman, *The Voice Heard at Sinai*, pp. 98–100.

56. *Sefat 'Emmet*, III, fol. 85d. The concept of the implantation of the Torah, which has much earlier sources, occurs also at ibid., I, fol. 89b, III, fol. 85. On continuous revelation see above, chap. 3, note 123. On combination of Torah letters see above, chap. 12.

57. See Smith, *Imagining Religion*, pp. 36–52; Gadamer, *Truth and Method*, pp. 329–30. See also Weiss-Halivni, *Revelation Restored*, pp. 47–74.

58. Jacques Derrida, *Margins of Philosophy*, trans. Alan Bass (University of Chicago Press, Chicago, 1982), p. 173; Simon Critchley, *The Ethics of Deconstruction: Derrida and Levinas* (Blackwell, Oxford, 1992), pp. 59–106.

APPENDIX 1: PARDES

1. See Scholem, *On the Kabbalah*, pp. 5–32.

2. "L'exégèse biblique," pp. 33–46, esp. pp. 37–40. See also idem, "Das Merkwort PRDS in der Jüdischen Bibelexegese," *Zeitschrift für die alttestamentliche Wissenschaft* 13 (1893), pp. 294–305.

3. "On the Question of Pardes and the Fourfold Method," *Sefer Eliahu Auerbach* (Jerusalem, 1955), pp. 222–235 (Hebrew). See also van der Heide, "Pardes"; Banon, *La lecture infinie*, pp. 204–216; Fishbane, *The Garments of the Torah*, pp. 112–120.

4. *On the Kabbalah*, p. 61: "I am inclined to agree with Bacher." Several years earlier, however, Scholem's opinion was much more clear-cut in favor of the Christian influence: "I have no doubt that this method *(pardes)* was taken from the Christian medieval exegesis." Scholem, *Devarim be-Go*, p. 249.

5. Talmage, "Apples of Gold," p. 320; van der Heide, "Pardes," pp. 154–155.

6. See Talmage, "Apples of Gold," p. 349, note 48; Idel, *Language, Torah and Hermeneutics*, p. 93 and p. 191, note 52. See also the proposal of Amos Funkenstein "Nahmanides' Symbolical Reading of History," in J. Dan and F. Talmage, eds., *Studies in Jewish Mysticism* (Cambridge, Mass., 1982), pp. 129–150, that Nahmanides adopted the Christian typological interpretation. For more on this type of interpretation see Marc Saperstein, "Jewish Typological Exegesis after Nahmanides," JSQ 1 (1993), esp. pp. 167–168; Idel, *Messianic Mystics*, p. 62.

7. See Isadore Twersky, *Studies in Jewish Law and Philosophy* (KTAV, New York, 1982), p. 208.

8. Van der Heide, "Pardes," p. 149.

9. See e.g. the tension between the plain sense and the esoteric one in Isma'ili hermeneutics, where the plain sense was regarded as Satanic! For Kabbalistic examples of a similar tension see Idel, *Kabbalah: New Perspectives*, pp. 207–208.

10. Idel, *Language, Torah and Hermeneutics*, pp. 82–124.

11. See Bacher, "L'exégèse biblique," passim.

12. See e. g. one of the most important discussions of Zoharic hermeneutics, the maiden parable, which has been analyzed in detail by several scholars: see Bacher, "L'exégèse biblique," pp. 36–38; Scholem, *On the Kabbalah*, pp. 55–56; Talmage, "Apples of Gold," pp. 316–317; and above, chap. 10, par. VIII.

13. Idel, *Language, Torah and Hermeneutics*, pp. 83–87.

14. *Midbbar Qedeimot*, par. Peh, section Peshat, fol. 49a, quoted in the name of R. Isaac Luria. For more on this paragon of Jewish learning see above, chap. 12, and below, app. 4, par. III. See also the discussion of R. Moses Eliyakum Beri'ah, *Da'at Moshe*, fol. IIId, where he describes the study of the first three senses of the Bible as intended solely for that of Sod.

15. On Bahya's version of the fourfold method see Scholem, *On the Kabbalah*, pp. 59, 62.

16. See e.g. *Tiqqunei Zohar*, printed in *Zohar*, I, fol. 26b.

17. BT, *Hagigah* fol. 15a. On the whole issue see Scholem, *Jewish Gnosticism*, pp. 14–19.

18. See *Sha'ar ha-Yihudim* (Qoretz, n.d.), fol. 33d; *Shulhan 'Arukh le-ha-Ari* (Krakow, n.d.), fol. 26a, par. *Qeriah be-Hokhmat ha-Kabbalah*. See also the text from *Sha'ar ha-Gilgulim*, discussed by Scholem, *On the Mystical Shape*, p. 239.

19. In the domain of the theosophical-theurgical Kabbalah a relevant example is the maiden parable mentioned above, note 12. See also Idel, *Kabbalah: New Perspectives*, pp. 223–224.

20. As to the experiential implication of a mystical interpretation of the Bible in ecstatic Kabbalah see Idel, *Language, Torah and Hermeneutics*, pp. xi, 101–109, 121–124.

21. See Iser, *The Act of Reading*, p. 10, and above, chap. 6.

22. On this Kabbalistic type, in opposition to the conservative Kabbalah, see Idel, "We Have No Kabbalistic Tradition," 63–73; idem, *Kabbalah: New Perspectives*, pp. 212–213, and idem, "Nahmanides."

23. See Idel, "Nahmanides."

24. On the last quarter of the thirteenth century as one of the most creative periods of Kabbalah see Idel, *Kabbalah: New Perspectives*, pp. 211–212.

25. Kabbalistic hermeneutics, especially the Zoharic type, was treated recently by Wolfson, "By Way of Truth"; idem, "Circumcision, Visionary Experience and Textual Interpretation: From Midrashic Trope to Mystical Symbol," *History of Religions* 27 (1987), pp. 189–215; idem, "Left Contained in the Right: A Study in Zoharic Hermeneutics," *AJSR* 11, no. 1 (1986), pp. 27–52; idem, "The Hermeneutics of Visionary Experience: Revelation and Interpretation in the Zohar," *Religion* 18 (1988), pp. 311–345. See also Ithamar Gruenwald, "From Talmudic to Zoharic Homiletics," in *The Age of the Zohar*, pp. 255–298 (Hebrew), and Daniel C. Matt, "Matnita Dilan: A Technique of Innovation in the Zohar," in *The Age of the Zohar*, pp. 123–145 (Hebrew).

26. I propose to distinguish between the narrative symbolic interpretation, namely those cases—very common in theosophical Kabbalah—where the biblical story was decoded as pointing to another supernal story, and the static symbolism, when the external structure of the text functions as an iconic symbol of another supernal entity. For more on this issue see above, chap. 8.

27. On this issue see Idel, *Hasidism: Between Ecstasy and Magic*, pp. 154–156; idem, "Reification of Language." On the Kabbalistic theory of language see Scholem, "The Name of God."

28. For an example of such a view see above, chap. 3, par. I. On indeterminacy in ancient Jewish exegesis see Stern, *Midrash and Theory*. For more on the function of the ideogrammic attitude toward the biblical text as it was exposed by Nahmanides and those influenced by him see Haviva Pedayah, "Tziyyur and Temunah in Nahmanides' Commentary on the Pentateuch," *Mahanayyim*, n.s., 6 (1994), pp. 114–123 (Hebrew).

29. Those techniques were exposed in detail by the Ashkenazi Hasidim; see Dan, "The Ashkenazi Hasidic," and Marcus, "Exegesis for the Few," pp. 1–24. In Kabbalah they were adopted in Abraham Abulafia's hermeneutics; see Idel, *Language, Torah and Hermeneutics*, pp. 95–119.

30. Cf. Idel, *Kabbalah: New Perspectives*, pp. 247–249, and above, chap. 3.

31. That is obviously the case in Abraham Abulafia's hermeneutics, which explicitly includes three major types of Kabbalistic exegesis; cf. Idel, *Language, Torah and Hermeneutics*, pp. 95–117, and above, chap. 11. See also the sevenfold exegetical method of the anonymous author of *Sefer Tiqqunei Zohar*, cf. Tishby, *The Wisdom of the Zohar*, 3:1083–1084.

32. Benin, "The Mutability," and above, chap. 12.

33. See Idel, *Hasidism: Between Ecstasy and Magic*, pp. 157–179, and above, chap. 2, par. IV.

34. *'Or ha-Ganuz* (Jerusalem, 1981), fol. 3b.

35. On some medieval examples of applying the exegetical devices employed for biblical interpretation to writings of the mystics see Idel, "On Symbolic Self-Interpretations."

36. See Idel, *Kabbalah: New Perspectives*, pp. 238–239, and above, chap. 6, par. IV.

37. See ibid., pp. 150–153.

38. See R. Abraham of Turisk, *Magen 'Avraham*, I, fol. 28a.

APPENDIX 2: ABRAHAM ABULAFIA'S TORAH OF BLOOD AND INK

1. See the seventh article in *Thirteen Articles of Faith*.

2. On the whole issue see Tishby, *The Wisdom of the Zohar*, 3:1082–1089. For later treatments of this issue see R. Joseph Ergas, *Shomer 'Emunim*, pp. 16–18, and in Polish Hasidism see Piekarz, *Studies*, pp. 87, 117–127. For more on the emergence of the biblical stories see the various texts adduced above, chap. 12.

3. Chap. 5:26–27. On the peculiar version of *'Avot* used by Abulafia see Charles Taylor, *Sayings of the Jewish Fathers* (Cambridge, 1897), pp. 60, 69. See also *Ethics of the Fathers*, trans. Hyman Goldin (Hebrew Publishing Company, New York, 1962), pp. 89–90.

4. *Middah*. See the occurrence of the word in Job 11:9. See also above, chap. 3, note 67.

5. See Maimonides' *Commentary on 'Avot*, ad locum.

6. *Genesis Rabba'* 9:11, p. 73.

7. The numerical value of the consonants Bag Bag He' He' amount to 22, which is the number of the Hebrew letters and Tovah.

8. Exodus 19:9.

9. Twice in the text.

10. On this image see above, chap. 2.

11. Psalms 119:18.

12. In our versions, however, the word here is *dibbur*, "saying," not "letter."

13. Here I have translated *hokhmah* in a different manner than earlier, where I preferred the term *science*.

14. Job 11:9. This verse had often been adduced in relation to the concept of infinity. See, e.g., above, chap. 3, note 67.

15. In the Bible *middah*, "measure." This is apparently the earliest instance where *middah* and Torah are explicitly related.

16. *Sefer Sitrei Torah*, Ms. Paris BN 774, fols. 169b–170a. In his *Migdal 'Oz*, a commentary on Maimonides' *Hilkhot Yesodei Torah*, chap. 1, he writes that in Sefarad, on a very old parchment, *qelaf yashan meyushan*, he saw an epistle that starts with the following

sentence: "I, Moses, the son of Maimon, when I had descended to the chambers of the Merkavah, understood the issue of the end etc., and his words were similar to the words of true Kabbalists, which were alluded to by our great Rabbi, Ramban, blessed be his memory, at the beginning of [his] commentary on the Torah." For more on this passage and its background see Idel, "Abulafia's Secrets of the Guide," pp. 316–317.

17. See above, chap. 6, par. II.

18. See Idel, *Messianic Mystics*, p. 296.

19. See above, chap. 9, note 82.

20. See R. Todros ha-Levi Abulafia's critique of a Kabbalah that is reminiscent of Abraham Abulafia's: "There is no need for the words of those who allude to the seventy-two names in connection with 'Av 'Anan, despite the fact that it is known to the masters of Kabbalah that seventy-two names surround the seat of glory. This issue is distant from our intention concerning the hints which we have hinted, as West is distant from East. The Kabbalah of the sages of the divinity [hakhmei ha-'elohut] regarding the secrets of the Torah is separated from the Kabbalah of the knowers of the names, except those that are not to be erased." *'Otzar ha-Kavod*, fol. 11c. See also above, chap. 7, note 125.

21. See above, chap. 9, note 81.

22. Ms. Paris BN 768, fol. 11a: *ve-ha-dam bo ha-satan ve-ha-satan bo ha-dam*. See Idel, *Studies in Ecstatic Kabbalah*, pp. 35–36.

23. The Hebrew consonants of the words *'Adam ve-Havah*, AVY *ve-'Immy*, *Dam ve-Dyo*, YHWH *Yod He' WaW He'* amount to seventy. For an elaboration of the similarity between the blood and ink on the one hand and the semen of mother and father on the other see Abulafia's *'Otzar 'Eden Ganuz*, Ms. Oxford Bodleiana 1580, fol. 31b.

24. Hebrew *ve-dyo* ("and ink") amounts to 26, like the Tetragrammaton.

25. See Ezekiel 9:4. See also BT, *Sabbath*, fol. 55a: "The Holy One, blessed be He, said to Gabriel: Go and record upon the forehead of the righteous a line of ink, that the angels of destruction may not rule over them; and upon the foreheads of the wicked a line of blood, so that the angels of destruction may rule over them."

26. *She-muledet*, compounded of the consonants of *tav shel dam*.

27. *Demut* = *tav dam*.

28. *Yoledet* = *tav dyo*.

29. *Sefer Sitrei Torah*, Ms. Paris BN 774, fol. 166a. For another discussion of blood and ink see below, the quote from Abulafia's *Sefer Gan Na'ul* and R. Isaac of Acre's *Sefer 'Otzar Hayyim*.

30. On this affinity see Idel, *The Mystical Experience*, p. 97.

31. See Idel, *Language, Torah and Hermeneutics*, p. 102.

32. *Sefer ha-Ge'ulah*, Ms. Leipzig 39, fol. 5b. On the Latin, glossed version of this statement, see Wirszubski, *Between the Lines*, p. 143. See also above, chap. 9, note 112.

33. See chap. 11, pars. III, IV.

34. See *Sefer Mafteah ha-Re'ayon*, Ms. Vatican 291, fol. 49b.

35. See also the very similar distinction found in a fragment of R. Isaac of Acre, "Blood is the secret of the Unique Name in plene reading, as follows: Yod He Waw He, and its literal meaning is without the plene spelling . . . is 'and ink.' Therefore, the secret of the Ineffable Name is blood and ink. The blood alludes to the secret of the sacrifices and the prayers, while ink is like the writing of the Torah in ink upon a book." Cf. Ms. Sasson 919, p. 209. The affinity between the passage of R. Isaac of Acre and Abulafia is one of the most convincing philological arguments for the relations between texts found in the writings of the two ecstatic Kabbalists.

36. This is one of the main topics in *Sefer Sha'arei 'Orah*. See above, chap. 12, par. III.

37. Ms. Roma-Angelica 38, fol. 37a. For more on this quote and its possible implications see Idel, *Messianic Mystics*, pp. 306–307.

38. See also *Sefer ha-Melammed*, Ms. Paris BN 680, fol. 298a.

39. *Metzuyyar*.

40. Compare, e.g., to the Zohar statement in I, fol. 134b.

41. *'Emtza'it*. Abulafia is fond of the gematria *'emtza'it* = *torah* = 611. See, e.g., above, chap. 11, note 83, and Idel, *Language, Torah and Hermeneutics*, pp. 37–38, 165, note 47.

42. BT, *Megillah*, fol. 13b.

43. *Mafteah ha-Sefirot*, Ms. Milano-Ambrosiana 53, fols. 164b–165a. See also Scholem, *Major Trends*, p. 141.

44. Ms. Munich 58, fol. 328a. For the fuller context of this quote see above, chap. 11, par. IX. See also an important discussion of blood and ink in relation to the different forms of the divine name in Abulafia's *Sefer ha-Melammed*, Ms. Paris BN 680, fols. 291b–298a. This is the correct order of the folios, unlike that found today in the unique manuscript.

45. See above, chap. 11, par. IX.

46. Ibid.

47. For more on this issue see app. 3.

48. For this halakhic requirement see also above, chap. 2, note 55.

49. *Sefer 'Otzar Hayyim*, Ms. Moscow-Guenzburg 775, fols. 105b–106a; see also Gottlieb, *Studies*, p. 244. On the combinations of letters stemming from the primordial Torah see above, chap. 12.

50. Barceloni, *Commentary on Sefer Yetzirah*, p. 107.

51. Namely a scroll.

52. *Sefer Quppat ha-Rokhelin*, Ms. Oxford Bodeliana 1618, fol. 10a. See also the fifteenth-century North African author R. Simeon ben Tzemah Duran, *Magen 'Avot* (Livorno, 1785), fol. 29b.

53. See above, chap. 12, pars. IV–V.

54. Cf. Scholem, *Peraqim be-Sifrut ha-Qabbalah* (Jerusalem, 1931), p. 102. See already R. Moses ha-Darshan, *Bereshit Rabbati*, p. 46, and note to line 8, and above, chap. 12.

55. See above, chap. 12, note 61.

56. Chap. 4, par. IV.

APPENDIX 3: R. ISAAC OF ACRE'S EXEGETICAL QUANDARY

1. This is the opening of the acronym '[A]HYD[A]' which recurs in his writings. The term "youth" should be understood as an epithet pointing to modesty, not as an indication of the Kabbalist's actual age. On R. Isaac's resort to various acronyms for his name see Amos Goldreich's observations in *Me'irat 'Einayyim*, pp. 2, 371; Idel, *Studies in Ecstatic Kabbalah*, p. 81.

2. See Nahmanides, *Introduction to the Commentary on the Torah*, p. 2. A Kabbalistic interpretation of this rabbinic dictum can be found already in the Geronese school, in R. Azriel's *Commentary on the Talmudic Aggadot*, pp. 3–4; see also Tishby's footnote, p. 3, note 21. R. Isaac of Acre apparently did not know this text.

3. Genesis 1:14.

4. Namely the divine world of emanation, which is the first of the four worlds designated by the acronym 'ABYA'.

5. *'Al derekh ha-'emmet ha-nekhonah*.

6. See R. Moses ha-Darshan, *Bereshit Rabbati*, p. 47, and the note to line 8; R. Yehudah Barceloni, *Commentary on Sefer Yetzirah*, p. 270.

7. BT, *Berakhot*, fol. 8a.

8. *Le-'olam*.

9. *Peshitut 'elyonah*. Compare this phrase, and two others below, to the similar description of the highest ontological level in the theosophical scheme according to the *Collectanaea* of R. Nathan the Sage, which I have proposed to identify with a student of Abraham Abulafia and as one of R. Isaac of Acre's teachers. Cf. Idel, *Studies in Ecstatic Kabbalah*, p. 81.

10. *Heikhalah*, namely its body. This is a common way of designating the body in his writings. See, e.g., *'Otzar Hayyim*, Ms. Moscow-Ginsburg 775, fol. 216a.

11. Proverbs 8:22.

12. Namely the second sefirah.

13. BT, *Hagigah*, fol. 14b.

14. The numerical value of each of the three words, *mahashavah*, *shannah*, and *sefirah*, is 355.

15. The formulation in Hebrew is rather clumsy.

16. This is the sixth letter of the Hebrew alphabet; its numerical value is six.

17. *Genesis Rabba'*, I:1, p. 2. See also above, chap. 1, note 17.

18. *Sefer 'Otzar Hayyim*, Ms. Moscow-Ginsburg 775, fol. 129a. There are some structural similarities between R. Isaac's understanding of the Aggadic statement and that of R. Moses Cordovero in his *Shi'ur Qomah*, fol. 13b, but I am not sure that we can assume a direct influence of R. Isaac's solution on the Safedian Kabbalist. See also a book by another Kabbalist close to Abulafia's thought, R. Reuven Tzarfati's treatise found in Ms. Moscow-Gunsburg, 134, fol. 110ab, R. Joseph ben Shalom Ashkenazi, *Commentary on Bereshit Rabba'*, p. 138; and *Ha-Shelah*, I, fol. 10a; II, fol. 97b.

19. On this title for Nahmanides' *Commentary on the Pentateuch* see Abrams, "Orality," p. 90.

20. See, e.g., Me'irat 'Einayyim, pp. 88, 90, 92. See also Gottlieb, Studies, pp. 231–247; Idel, The Mystical Experience, pp. 140–141.

21. See Me'irat 'Einayyim, pp. 38–40.

22. Ibid., pp. 87–88, 218, quoting R. Todros ben Joseph ha-Levi Abulafia's 'Otzar ha-Kavod, fol. 5b. See also in the Kabbalistic traditions found in Ms. Paris BN 680, fol. 271a, Ms. Jerusalem, JNUL 8° 1073, fol. 23a, and in the Nahmanidean additions to R. Moses de Leon's Sefer ha-Nefesh ha-Hakhamah (Basel, 1608), col. G, fols. Id–IIa.

23. Cf. Tishby, The Wisdom of the Zohar, 1:285–286. I would say that the Zoharic approach had been adopted by the scholars, who generalize as if its stand is characteristic of the entire Kabbalistic literature. This is part of what I call the monochromatic approach that is characteristic of most of the modern academic approaches to Kabbalah.

24. See above, chap. 10, par. II.

25. See above, chap. 10, par. IV.

26. See Matt, The Book of the Mirrors, p. 3.

27. On the possibility that this acronym was already found in R. Nathan's Collectanaea see Idel, Studies in Ecstatic Kabbalah, pp. 82, 88, note 47. See also Goldreich's remark in Me'irat 'Einayyim, pp. 401–402.

28. Chap. 6, pars. IV, V; chap. 10, par. VII.

29. See chap. 10, par. X.

30. I cannot enter here into a detailed analysis of R. Isaac's exegetical system. The above passage seems, however, to demand a qualification of the opinion expressed by Goldreich, Me'irat 'Einayyim, p. 401, and Gottlieb, Studies, p. 239, note 16, that this higher exegetical method is related to the role played by the 'Ein Sof. Moreover, in one of the cases, in Sefer 'Otzar Hayyim, Ms. Moscow-Ginsburg 775, fol. 148b, the highest means of interpretation is connected to the divine name and to the attainment of prophecy, in a manner quite reminiscent of Abraham Abulafia's seventh exegetical method. See Idel, Language, Torah and Hermeneutics, pp. 101–109. For more on nisa'n see Boaz Huss, "NISAN—The Wife of the Infinite: The Mystical Hermeneutics of R. Isaac of Acre," Kabbalah 5 (2000), pp. 155–181. See also above, app. 1.

31. For more on this acronym see Idel, Messianic Mystics, pp. 303–304.

32. Introduction, p. 2. See Wolfson, Circle in a Square, p. 164, note 36, and also above, chap. 4, note 46, and app. 2, as well as Heschel, The Theology of Ancient Judaism, 2:346–347.

33. See the seventh of Maimonides' Thirteen Articles of Faith.

34. See Abrams, "Orality," p. 97. Indeed, the resort to the term "secret" in the text is evident: fifteen times in a rather short passage. It fits the fondness with this term in the late-thirteenth-century innovative Kabbalah.

35. For a discussion between a philosopher and R. Shem Tov ibn Gaon, a student of a student of Nahmanides who also interpreted Nahmanides' secrets, see Idel, R. Menahem Recanati, the Kabbalist, chap. 15. Moreover, R. Isaac apparently overlooked a passage from R. Shem Tov ibn Gaon, Sefer Keter Shem Tov, Ms. Paris BN 774, fol. 75a, where the same rabbinic dictum has been adduced and succinctly interpreted. See especially the text of R. Isaac that criticized the extreme arcane interpretations of

Nahmanides' *Commentary on the Pentateuch* by his followers. Cf. Scholem, *Origins of the Kabbalah*, pp. 384–385. Scholem's view, that Nahmanides was in possession of a variety of Kabbalistic traditions that reached him from various sources, is as yet unfounded.

36. See Moshe Idel, "The Vicissitudes of Kabbalah in Catalonia," in Moshe Lazar and Stephen Haliczer, eds., *The Jews of Spain and the Expulsion of 1492* (Labyrinthos, Lancaster, Calif., 1997), pp. 35–36.

37. See Scholem, *Major Trends*, pp. 203, 397–398.

38. See Introduction, par. IV.

39. *Sefer 'Otzar Hayyim*, Ms. Moscow-Ginsburg 775, fol. 105b.

40. See also above, app. 2, note 2.

41. See above, chap. 12, note 71.

42. On this dictum and its sources in *Sefer Shi'ur Qomah* and early Kabbalah see Idel, "The Concept of the Torah," p. 52.

43. Ms. Jerusalem, 8° 3925, fol. 116b; *Commentary on the Commandments*, Ms. Vatican 177, fol. 24a. See also Idel, "The Concept of the Torah," pp. 66–67.

44. See chap. 2, par. V.

45. See Ms. Leiden 24, fols. 197bc, 198a. For the view of the divine logos as shadow see Philo, *Leggum Allegoriae*, 3:96, a passage dealt with by Charles Mopsik, though in the context of the relation between man and God. Cf. *Les grands textes*, p. 376.

APPENDIX 4: THE EXILE OF THE TORAH AND THE IMPRISONMENT OF SECRETS

1. For the earlier phases of Christian Kabbalah see, e.g., Gershom Scholem, "The Beginnings of the Christian Kabbalah," in Joseph Dan, ed., *The Christian Kabbalah* (Harvard College Library, Cambridge, Mass., 1997), pp. 17–51; Wirszubski, *Pico della Mirandola*; M. Idel, "Jewish Kabbalah in Christian Garb: Some Phenomenological Remarks," in Michael Terry, ed., *The Hebrew Renaissance* (Newberry Library, Chicago, 1997), pp. 10–16. See also above, chap. 9, the end of par. VI.

2. See Idel, "The Magical and Neoplatonic Interpretations," p. 201.

3. *Kat Luther.*

4. *Ha-hokhmah ha-mefo'arah.*

5. In Hebrew *galuyyot*, meaning literally "exiles." It seems, however, that there is no reason to doubt that he refers to the expulsions from Spain and Portugal, perhaps as well as the expulsion of the Jews from Sicily.

6. Namely Christians.

7. See Idel, "The Magical and Neoplatonic Interpretations," pp. 186–187.

8. See the text printed, translated, and discussed by David Kaufmann, "Elia Menachem Chalfan on Jews Teaching Hebrew to Non-Jews," JQR, o.s., 9 (1896/1897), pp. 500–508.

9. For other positive reactions to the first stage of Luther's activity, which was positive in relation to Judaism, see Hayyim Hillel Ben-Sasson, "The Reformation in Contempo-

rary Jewish Opinion," *Proceedings of the Israel Academy of Sciences and Humanities* 4 (1970), pp. 239–326.

10. A phrase pointing to an esoteric topic.

11. Namely "send."

12. I.e., the disclosure.

13. The version is not so clear here. Abraham David, "A Jerusalemite Epistle from the Beginning of the Ottoman Rule in the Land of Israel," in *Chapters in the History of Jerusalem at the Beginning of the Ottoman Period* (Yad Ben Zvi, Jerusalem, 1979), p. 59 (Hebrew), reads the manuscript text as *hita'aqti*, which makes no sense, and he proposed to correct it for *hitama'tzti*, "I made efforts to," but this reading and analysis of the context (see ibid., p. 43) contradicts the stand expressed in the preceding sentence. I have therefore proposed to amend the version to *hitappaqti*, "I refrained."

14. Psalms 25:14.

15. See R. Abraham ben Eliezer ha-Levi, *Commentary on the Prophecies of the Child*, Ms. Firenze-Laurentiana, Plut. 44, 7, printed in David, "A Jerusalemite Epistle," p. 59.

16. Apparently the priests.

17. Cf. Psalms 49:13.

18. See his *Commentary on the Tiqqunei Zohar* (Jerusalem, 1975), 3:204; Sack, *Be-Sha'arei ha-Qabbalah*, p. 37, note 22.

19. See especially the expression *pardes ha-torah*, in *Tiqqunei Zohar*, cf. *Zohar Hadash*, fol. 102d.

20. Namely Kabbalah.

21. *Sefer ha-Hezyonot*, ed. A. Aescoli (Mossad ha-Rav Kook, Jerusalem, 1954), p. 68; Abraham Berger, "Captive at the Gate of Rome: The Story of a Messianic Motif," *PAAJR* 44 (1977), pp. 16–17.

22. See chap. 3, note 68.

23. *Sefer Tiferet 'Adam*, p. 110.

24. Ibid., p. 101.

25. See Robert Bonfil, *Rabbis and Jewish Communities in Renaissance Italy* (Littmann Library, London, Washington, 1993), pp. 295–296. On this Kabbalist see Yoram Jacobson, *Along the Path of Exile and Redemption: The Doctrine of Redemption of Rabbi Mordecai Dato* (Mossad Bialik, Jerusalem, 1996) (Hebrew).

26. See Idel, "Differing Conceptions of Kabbalah," pp. 166–168, 174–178.

27. For more on this ritual see Shaul Maggid, "Conjugal Union, Mourning and Talmud Torah in R. Isaac Luria's *Tikkun Hatzot*," *Daat* 36 (1996), pp. xvii–xlv; Scholem, *Sabbatai Sevi*, pp. 51–52; Idel, *Messianic Mystics*, pp. 308–320. On the ritual study of the Torah at midnight see R. Elijah da Vidas, *Reshit Hokhmah*, in Fine, *Safed Spirituality*, pp. 103–107.

28. *Sha'ar Ruah ha-Qodesh* (Jerusalem, 1912), fol. 17ab.

29. Vital, *Sha'ar ha-Kavvanot* (Hotza'at Meqor Hayyim, Jerusalem, 1963), fol. 58b; idem, *Peri 'Etz Hayyim*, p. 348; see also R. Ya'aqov Hayyim Tzemah, *Siddur*, p. 78; idem, *Naggid u-Metzavveh*, p. 23. See the important remark by Scholem, *Sabbatai Sevi*, pp. 51–52, who

already pointed out the possible nexus between this view and "Christian exegesis of the Bible." My claim is that it is more precisely the Christian Kabbalah than general Christian exegesis that is involved here.

30. *Siddur*, p. 79.

31. See Peter Kuhn, *Gottes Trauer und Klage in der rabbinischen Überlieferung (Talmud und Midrasch)* (Brill, Leiden, 1978), pp. 254–257. On the myth of *mistarim* see already in BT, *Berakhot*, fol. 3a, which has been exploited but interpreted in a quite different manner from the original myth. On the sparks found in the shells see Scholem, *On the Mystical Shape*, pp. 75–77.

32. See Scholem, *On the Kabbalah*, pp. 146, 152.

33. See idem, *Major Trends*, pp. 256–257; idem, "Shetar ha-hitqasherut shel Talmidei ha-'Ari," *Zion* 5 (1940), pp. 133–160.

34. *Proverbs* 4:2.

35. *Penei David*, fol. 175cd. See also Ramhal, *Qin'at ha-Shem Tzeva'ot*, p. 119.

36. *Tzavarei Shalal*, fol. 217c. This characterization of the Torah is presumably drawn from earlier, apparently Cordoverian sources, and they are paralleled by Hasidic views, which often resort to the concepts of instrument and pipe.

37. See also above, chap. 3, note 23.

38. See Idel, *Hasidism: Between Ecstasy and Magic*, p. 375, note 130. Compare especially the view found in a pseudo–Midrash '*Orah Hayyim*, apparently forged by R. Moses de Leon, printed in Eisenstein, '*Otzar ha-Midrashim*, p. 29–30.

39. On this topic see Meir Benayahu, *Rabbi Hayyim Yosef David Azulai* (Mossad ha-Rav Kook, Jerusalem, 1959), pp. 145–146 (Hebrew).

40. See chap. 3, par. III.

41. Not only has the rite of *tiqqun hatzot* been known and sometimes performed by Hasidim, but also the view of the Torah in exile has been mentioned by Hasidic authors. See, e.g., R. Ze'ev Wolf of Zhitomir, '*Or ha-Me'ir*, fols. 184c, 190c, who discusses the combinations of letters of the Torah that have fallen within the *qelippot*; and R. Qalonimus Qalman Epstein, *Ma'or va-Shemesh*, 2:605.

APPENDIX 5: ON ORAL TORAH AND
MULTIPLE INTERPRETATIONS IN HASIDISM

1. See Idel, *Hasidism: Between Ecstasy and Magic*, p. 178, and also my forthcoming "The Voiced Torah and Sonorous Community in Jewish Mysticism." On orality and religion see Graham, *Beyond the Written Word*, esp. p. 143, where he discusses Calvin's view of the importance of orality as a main form of divine revelation.

2. Rapoport-Albert, "God and the Zaddik."

3. *Dibber* or *dibbur*.

4. Ben-Amos and Mintz, *In Praise of the Baal Shem Tov*, p. 179. The distinction in spelling between "Torah" versus "torah" is that of the translators. See also the important parallel adduced by Scholem, *Devarim be-Go*, pp. 307–308, and discussed again by Rosman, *Founder of Hasidism*, pp. 146–147.

5. Compare also above, app. 4, the Lurianic discussion about the sparks of the Torah that are found within the realm of evil.

6. Namely the negative powers stemming from the stern aspect of the divine system.

7. *Yatva'*.

8. Cf. *Zohar*, I, fol. 153b.

9. The words of the stupid.

10. *Liqqutei Moharan*, no. 207, fol. 112d. See Liebes, *Sod ha-'Emunah*, pp. 249–251.

11. See above, chap. 6, note 12.

12. See his *Sefer Megillat ha-Megalleh*, p. 27. This passage has been copied in R. Bahya ben Asher's *Commentary on the Pentateuch*, on Genesis 2:4, p. 55. For more on this issue see above, chap. 13, par. VI.

13. See chap. 4, III.

14. It seems that only in the ecstatic Kabbalah is there a discussion of the oral Torah as the Torah that is in actu, *be-fo'al*, a description that implies its superiority over the written one. See Idel, *Language, Torah and Hermeneutics*, pp. 48–49, and above, chap. 13, par. VI.

15. See Wilensky, *Hasidim and Mitnaggedim*, 1:317. This letter was written in 1805.

16. See, e.g., the continuation of R. Nahman of Braslav's quote mentioned above, note 10, and Liebes, *Sod ha-'Emunah*, pp. 249–250.

17. On the question of the language of these sermons there can be no dispute that, although printed in Hebrew, they were delivered in the vernacular, Yiddish.

18. See the first statement of R. Nathan of Nemirov's introduction to *Liqqutei Tefillot*, and above, chap. 6, par. V.

19. Compare the sources of this view in Idel, *Hasidism: Between Ecstasy and Magic*, p. 334, note 22.

20. See, e.g., R. Yisrael Loebel, in Mordecai Wilensky, *Hasidism and Mitnageddim* (Mossad Bialik, Jerusalem, 1970), 2:317, *No'am 'Elimelekh*, fol. 67c.

21. See Tishby, *Studies in Kabbalah*, 3:988–994. See also Weiss, *Studies*, pp. 80–81.

22. See his introduction to *Maggid Devarav le-Ya'aqov*.

23. *'Irin Qaddishin* (rpt. Jerusalem, 1983), fol. 49d. On this Hasidic master see David Assaf, *The Regal Way: The Life and Times of R. Israel of Ruzhin* (Zalman Shazar Center, Jerusalem, 1997) [Hebrew], and above, chap. 12. See already the Great Maggid of Mezeritch, *'Or Torah*, p. 11. For another discussion of this topic in Hasidism, where R. Meir is presented as repairing the 'ayin to 'aleph thus as a theurgist, see *Tiferet Shlomo, Tisa'*. R. Meir is described as repairing the letter that is particular to him in the Torah. See also Piekarz, *Studies*, p. 127. For more on the topics discussed in paragraphs III and IV below see also Idel, *Hasidism: Between Ecstasy and Magic*, pp. 239–244.

24. See chap. 3, note 68.

25. On seventy facets of the Torah see above, chap. 3, note 31. On the possible source for the shift from 'aleph to 'ayin see Cordovero, *Pardes Rimmonim*, gate 21, chap. 1; I, fol. 105a.

26. In Hebrew the term *panim* means both face and facets. See also the Braslav stand discussed by Piekarz, *Studies*, p. 120.

27. On metoposcopy in Jewish mysticism see Gershom Scholem, "Ein Fragment zur Physiognomik und Chiromantik aus der Tradition des spätantiken jüdischen Esoterik," in *Liber Amicorum: Studies in Honour of Professor Dr. C. J. Bleeker* (Brill, Leiden, 1969), pp. 175–193; Ithamar Gruenwald, "New Fragments from the Literature on *Hakarat Panim* and *Sidrei Sirtutim*," *Tarbiz* 40 (1970), pp. 301–319 [Hebrew]; Schaefer, *Hekhalot-Studien*, pp. 84–95.

28. Isaiah 3:9.

29. '*Irin Qaddishin Tanyana*' (Barfeld, 1887), fol. 24c. My assumption is that the author had in mind a Sabbath afternoon sermon. On the relation between Sabbath and seventy facets of the Torah see already R. Pinhas of Koretz, *Midrash Pinhas*, fol. 22b. On the Hasidic practice of repeating the sermon on the way home, it is plausible that the above text reflects a mnemonic technique that was intended not to offer new interpretations but to help memorize the content of the sermon because it could not have been written down during the Sabbath. To a certain extent, the oral performance of the sermon is a continuation of the written Torah in another medium, which allows and compels reflection on its exposition without resorting to the written text because of the unusual authority of the homilist.

30. See, e.g., Ada Rapoport-Albert, "God and the Zaddik as the Two Focal Points of Hasidic Worship," *History of Religions* 18 (1979), pp. 296–325. For more on the union with the divine in Hasidism as part of the process of understanding the Torah see above, chap. 2, par. IV.

31. Chap. 3, note 74.

32. Homily on Ezekiel, translated in Smalley, *The Bible in the Middle Ages*, p. 32.

33. *Studies in the Zohar*, pp. 85–138.

34. See Moshe Idel, "On Mobility, Individuals and Groups: Prolegomenon for a Sociological Approach to Sixteenth Century Kabbalah," *Kabbalah* 3 (1998), pp. 145–173.

35. See above, chap. 3, note 110.

36. See *Be'er Mayyim Hayyim*, I, fols. 45c–47b.

37. Ibid., I, fol. 46b. See also the thirteenth-century ecstatic text discussed in Idel, *The Mystical Experience*, p. 148, note 38.

38. See Scholem, *On the Mystical Shape*, pp. 251–273; idem, "The Paradise Garb of Souls and the Origin of the Concept of *Haluqa' de-Rabbanan*," *Tarbiz* 24 (1955), pp. 297–306 [Hebrew].

39. See Piekarz, *Studies*, pp. 88–89.

40. See above, chap. 6, par. III.

41. See note 29 above.

42. "Le moi et la totalité" and some subsequent expositions discussed in Etienne Feron, *De l'idée de transcendance à la question du language* (Millon, Grenoble, 1992), pp. 87–88.

43. See above, chap. 6, par. V, in the discussion of the quote from R. Nahman of Braslav.

44. See Maimon's description of the Great Maggid during his sermons as analyzed by Weiss, *Studies*, pp. 70–78.

45. On the discrepancy between the written literature and Hasidic life see the caveats of Abraham Y. Heschel, *Kotzk: The Struggle for Integrity* (Tel Aviv, 1973), 1:7–10 [Yiddish], part of it translated in Samuel Dresner's introduction to Heschel, *Circle of the Ba'al Shem Tov: Studies in Hasidism*, ed. S. H. Dresner (University of Chicago Press, Chicago, 1985), p. xxiii; Heschel, "Hasidism," *Jewish Heritage*, vol. 14 (1972), pp. 14–16; and Ze'ev Gries, *The Book in Early Hasidism* (Hakkibutz Hameuchad, 1992), p. 92 [Hebrew].

APPENDIX 6: "BOOK OF GOD"/"BOOK OF LAW"

1. See above, chap. 2, note 171.

2. Wolfson, *Philo*.

3. Henry Cornelius Agrippa, *The Occult Philosophy in the Elizabethan Age* (Routledge and Kegan Paul, London, 1979), p. 1.

4. For more on binary syntheses in explaining the emergence of major intellectual systems see M. Idel, "On Binary 'Beginnings' in Kabbalah-Scholarship," *Aporematha: Kritische Studien zur Philologiegeschichte*, Band 5 (2001), pp. 313–337.

5. Charles Trinkaus, "In Our Image and Likeness" (University of Chicago Press, Chicago, 1970), 2:730–740.

6. See Idel, "Hermeticism and Judaism."

7. The belief in heavenly books is widespread in Assyrian and Babylonian literatures, an issue that does not concern us here.

8. *European Literature in the Latin Middle Ages*, trans. Williard R. Track, Bollingen Series, 36 (Princeton University Press, Princeton, 1990), pp. 302–347.

9. See Idel, "Hermeticism and Judaism," pp. 62–64; Shlomo Sela, "Scientific Data in the Exegetical-Theological Work of Abraham ibn Ezra: Historical Time and Geographical Space Conception" (Ph.D. diss., Tel Aviv University, 1997), pp. 367–375 (Hebrew).

10. See the recent collection of articles on this figure edited by I. Twersky and J. M. Harris, *Rabbi Abraham ibn Ezra: Studies in the Writings of a Twelfth-Century Jewish Polymath* (Harvard University Press, Cambridge, Mass., 1993); Sela, *Scientific Data*.

11. Daniel 7:10.

12. Ma'arakhot ha-shamayyim.

13. Namely in Exodus 32:32.

14. Namely the celestial world, constituted by planets and stars.

15. Ha-ma'arakhah ha-'elyonah.

16. *Commentary on the Pentateuch*, ed. A. Weiser (Mossad ha-Rav Kook, Jerusalem, 1977), 2:47 (Hebrew).

17. See especially Y. Tzvi Langermann, "Some Astrological Themes in the Thought of R. Abraham ibn Ezra," in *Rabbi Abraham ibn Ezra*, pp. 33–49.

18. On this literature see Uriel Simon, "Interpreting the Interpreter," ibid., pp. 86–128.

19. Nahmanides, *Commentary on the Pentateuch*, ed. C. D. Chavel (Mossad ha-Rav Kook, Jerusalem, 1959), 1:514.

20. *Sifro shel ha-qadosh barukh hu'*.

21. Apparently, R. Bahya was acquainted with a famous Jewish book of magic entitled *The Alphabet of Metatron*, which establishes some forms of affinity between an alphabet, described as the alphabet of stars, and magic. See the edition by Israel Weinstock, "'Alpha Beta shel Metatron," *Temirin* 2 (1982), pp. 51–76 (Hebrew).

22. *Golmi*.

23. Psalms 139:16. For interpretations of this verse see Idel, *Golem*, pp. 298, 300.

24. *Commentary on Exodus* 32:32, ed. C. D. Chavel (Mossad ha-Rav Kook, Jerusalem, 1967), 2:338 (Hebrew).

25. Namely the six lower sefirot, which according to many Kabbalistic traditions surround the sefirah of Tiferet.

26. BT, *Rosh ha-Shanah*, fol. 16b.

27. *Commentary on Exodus*, 2:339. The source for this theosophical interpretation is, as Efrayyim Gottlieb pointed out, R. Ezra of Gerona's *Commentary on the Talmudic Legends*. See Gottlieb, *The Kabbalah in the Writings of Rabbi Bahya ben Asher* (Qiriat Sefer, Jerusalem, 1970), p. 50 (Hebrew). See also R. Bahya's contemporary Castilian Kabbalist R. Todros ha-Levi Abulafia, *'Otzar ha-Kavod*, fol. 16c.

28. Fabrizio Lelli, "Retorica, poetica e linguistica nel *Hay ha-'Olamim* di Yohanan Alemanno" (Ph.D. diss., Universitá degli Studi di Torino, 1990/1991); Fabrizio Lelli, *Yohanan Alemanno: Hay Ha-'Olamim (L'Immortale)* (Leo S. Olschki, Florence, 1995); B. C. Novak, "Giovanni Pico della Mirandola and Jochanan Alemanno," *Journal of the Warburg and Courtauld Institutes* 45 (1982), pp. 125–147; M. Idel, "The Anthropology of Yohanan Alemanno: Sources and Influences," *Annali di storia dell'esegesi* 7 (1990), pp. 93–112.

29. Untitled treatise, Ms. Paris BN 849, fol. 7b. On Alemanno's authorship of this book see Gershom Scholem, "An Unknown Treatise of R. Yohanan Alemanno," *Qiriat Sefer* 5 (1928/1929), pp. 286–302 (Hebrew).

30. See M. Idel, "The Study Program of R. Yohanan Alemanno," *Tarbiz* 48 (1979), pp. 310–312, 316, 320 (Hebrew).

31. Ms. Oxford Bodleiana 2234, fol. 2b.

32. See Joseph Hacker, "The Connections of Spanish Jewry with Eretz Israel between 1391 and 1492," *Shalem* 1 (1974), p. 145, note 64, and p. 147 (Hebrew).

33. See, more recently, Amos Funkenstein, *Theology and the Scientific Imagination from the Middle Ages to the Seventeenth Century* (Princeton University Press, Princeton, 1986), pp. 13, note 3, and p. 49, note 28. See also Leroy E. Loemker, *Struggle for Synthesis: The Seventeenth Century Background of Leibniz's Synthesis of Order and Freedom* (Harvard University Press, Cambridge, Mass., 1972), pp. 89–95.

34. Cf. Idel, "The Study Program," p. 307, note 36, and p. 313.

35. Idel, "The Study Program."

36. Another form of thought, medieval Arabic and Jewish philosophy, was also influential on Christian intellectuals. See, e.g., Shlomo Pines, "Medieval Doctrines in Renaissance Garb? Some Jewish and Arabic Sources of Leone Ebreo's Doctrines," in B. D.

Cooperman, ed., *Jewish Thought in the Sixteenth Century* (Harvard University Press, Cambridge, Mass. 1983), pp. 390–391; M. Idel, "Magical Temples and Cities in the Middle Ages and the Renaissance," *Jerusalem Studies in Arabic and Islam* 3 (1981/1982), pp. 185–189; Kalman Bland, "Elijah del Medigo's Averroistic Response to the Kabbalahs of the Fifteenth-Century Jewry and Pico della Mirandola," *Jewish Thought and Philosophy* 1 (1991), pp. 23–53; Bohdan Kieszkowski, "Les rapports entre Elie del Medigo et Pic de la Mirandole," *Rinascimento* 4 (1964), pp. 58–61; Stephane Toussaint, "Ficino's Orphic Magic or Jewish Astrology and Oriental Philosophy? A Note on *spiritus*, the Three Books on Life, Ibn Tufayl and Ibn Zarza," *Accademia* 2 (2000), pp. 19–33.

37. See Wirszubski's magisterial *Pico della Mirandola*, pp. 80, 106–112, 150–151.

38. On this issue see more above, chap. 4.

39. *Opera Omnia* (Basel, 1557), p. 113. See also Eugenio Garin, *Astrology in the Renaissance: The Zodiac of Life* (Arkana, London, 1990), pp. 85, 92; Ernst Cassirer, "Giovanni Pico della Mirandola," *Journal of History of Ideas* 3, no. 3 (1942), pp. 341–342. On the relationship between Kabbalah and astrology in Christian Kabbalah see F. Secret, "L'Astrologie et les Kabbalistes Chrétiens et la Renaissance," *Le Tour Saint-Jacques* 4 (1956), pp. 45–49.

40. Henri de Lubac, *Pic de la Mirandole* (Aubier Montaigne, Paris, 1974), pp. 317–318.

41. Wirszubski, *Pico della Mirandola*, p. 175. His reference in note 13 to Isaiah 34:4 does not solve the conceptual question of the thesis.

42. Ibid., pp. 262–263. See Scholem, *On the Kabbalah*, p. 62, note 1.

43. Wirszubski, *Pico della Mirandola*, pp. 248–250.

44. See above, note 38.

45. See Idel, "On Judaism."

46. See R. Bahya ben Asher's commentary on Deuteronomy 18:11; cf. Idel, "The Magical and Neoplatonic Interpretations," p. 233, note 68; idem, "Abulafia's Secrets of the Guide," pp. 313–319.

47. See also R. Abraham Abulafia, *Sheva' Netivot ha-Torah*, pp. 14–15, a Kabbalist who started his Kabbalistic career in Barcelona, like Bahya ben Asher. This epistle has been translated into French as *L'Epître des sept voies*, trans. J.-C. Attias (Editions de l'Eclats, 1985), p. 72. Abulafia contrasts the Kabbalistic interpretation of the Bible by means of combinations of letters, a method understood as an inner, more sublime logic, and the Aristotelian logic, which is appropriate to the knowledge of nature.

BIBLIOGRAPHY

JOURNALS

AJSR   Association of Jewish Studies Review
HUCA   Hebrew Union College Annual
JJS   Journal of Jewish Studies
JQR   Jewish Quarterly Review
JSJT   Jerusalem Studies in Jewish Thought
JSQ   Jewish Studies Quarterly
MGWJ   Monatschrift für Geschichte und Wissenschaft
                des Judentums
PAAJR   Proceedings of the American Academy of Jewish
                Research

QS	*Qiriat Sefer*
REJ	*Revue des Etudes Juives*

EDITIONS OF PRINTED TEXTS

'Adir ba-Marom
: R. Moses Hayyim Luzzatto, *Sefer 'Adir ba-Marom* (Benei Beraq, 1968).

'Ahavat Dodim
: R. Benjamin of Zalisch, *Sefer 'Ahavat Dodim* (rpt., Brooklyn, 1978).

'Amudei Torah
: R. Shmuel Mayevski, ed., *Sefer 'Amudei Torah* (Jerusalem, 1971), which includes R. Abraham ben Shlomo of Vilnius (the Gra's brother), *Sefer Ma'alot ha-Torah*, and R. Isaac Aizik Haver, *'Or Torah*.

'Arzei Levanon
: *'Arzei Levanon* (Venice 1601).

'Avodat ha-Qodesh
: R. Meir ibn Gabbai, *Sefer 'Avodat ha-Qodesh* (Jerusalem, 1963).

Be'er Mayyim Hayyim
: R. Hayyim Turer of Chernovitz, *Be'er Mayyim Hayyim*, 2 vols. (Israel, n.d.).

Bereshit Rabbati
: R. Moses ha-Darshan, *Midrash Bereshit Rabbati*, ed. C. Albek (Mekize Nirdamim, Jerusalem, 1967).

Botzina' di-Nehora'
: R. Barukh of Medziebuz, *Sefer Botzina' di-Nehora' ha-Shalem* (n.p., 1985).

Commentary on Bereshit Rabba'
: R. Joseph ben Shalom Ashkenazi, *Commentary on Bereshit Rabba'*, ed. Moshe Hallamish (Magnes Press, Jerusalem, 1985).

Commentary on Sefer Yetzirah
: R. Yehudah Barzilai Barceloni, *Commentary on Sefer Yetzirah*, ed. S. Z. H. Halberstam (Mekize Nirdamim, Berlin, 1885).

Commentary on the Talmudic Aggadot
: R. Azriel of Gerona, *Commentary on the Talmudic Aggadot*, ed. Isaiah Tishby (Magnes Press, Jerusalem, 1989).

Da'at Moshe
: R. Moses Elyakum Beri'ah, *Sefer Da'at Moshe 'al ha-Torah* (rpt., Jerusalem, 1987).

Degel Mahaneh 'Efrayyim
: R. Moses Hayyim Ephrayyim of Sudylkov, *Degel Mahaneh 'Efrayyim* (Jerusalem, 1963).

Derishot	R. Moses Cordovero, *Derishot be-'Inianei Mal'akhim*, printed as an appendix to Reuven Margaliot, *Mal'akhei 'Elyon* (Mossad ha-Rav Kook, Jerusalem, 1945).
Devash le-Fi	R. Hayyim Joseph David Azulai, *Devash le-Fi* (Jerusalem, 1962).
'Etz Hayyim	R. Hayyim Vital, *Sefer 'Etz Hayyim* (Warsaw, 1891).
Ginnat 'Egoz	R. Joseph Gikatilla, *Sefer Ginnat 'Egoz* (Hoatza'at ha-Hayyim ve-ha-Shalom, 1989).
Ha-Shelah	R. Isaiah Horowitz, *Shenei Luhot ha-Berit*, 3 vols. (Jerusalem, 1960).
Heikhal ha-Berakhah	R. Isaac Aiziq Yehudah Safrin of Komarno, *Sefer Heikhal ha-Berakhah*, 5 vols. (Lemberg, 1869).
Hesed le-'Avraham	R. Abraham Azulai, *Hesed le-'Avraham* (Lemberg, 1863).
Liqqutei Torah, 1860	R. Mordekhai of Chernobyl, *Liqqutei Torah* (1860; rpt. Benei Beraq, 1983).
Liqqutei Torah, 1979	R. Shne'or Zalman of Liady, *Liqqutei Torah* (Brookline, Mass., 1979).
Liqqutei Moharan	R. Nahman of Braslav, *Liqqutei Moharan* (Benei Beraq, 1972).
Ma'arekhet ha-'Elohut	*Sefer Ma'arekhet ha-'Elohut*, attributed to R. Peretz (Mantua, 1558).
Magen 'Avraham	R. Abraham of Turisk, *Sefer Magen 'Avraham* (Lublin, rpt., Brooklyn, 1985).
Magen David	R. David ibn Avi Zimra, *Sefer Magen David* (Munkacz, 1912).
Maggid Devarav le-Ya'aqov	R. Dov Baer, Maggid of Mezeritch, *Maggid Devarav le-Ya'aqov*, ed. R. Schatz-Uffenheimer (Magnes Press, Jerusalem, 1976).
Ma'or va-Shemesh	R. Qalonimus Qalman Epstein, *Ma'or va-Shemesh*, 2 vols. (Jerusalem, 1992).
Mayyim Rabbim	R. Yehiel Mikhal of Zlotchov, *Sefer Mayyim Rabbim* (Brooklyn, 1979).
The Meditation of the Soul	R. Abraham bar Hiyya, *The Meditation of the Sad Soul*, trans. Geoffrey Wigoder

	(Routledge and Kegan Paul, London, 1969).
Megalleh ʿAmuqot	R. Nathan Neta' Shapira of Cracow, Sefer Megalleh ʿAmuqot (Jerusalem, 1981).
Megillat ha-Megalleh	R. Abraham bar Hiyya, Sefer Megillat ha-Megalleh, ed. Adolf Poznanski (Mekize Nirdamim, Berlin, 1924).
Meʾirat ʿEinayyim	R. Isaac of Acre, Meʾirat ʿEinayyim, ed. Amos Goldreich, critical edition with preface and commentary (Jerusalem, 1984).
Menahem Tzion	R. Menahem Mendel of Shklow, Sefer Menahem Tzion (Jerusalem, 1987).
Midbbar Qedeimot	HYDA', Midbbar Qedeimot (Jerusalem, 1962).
Midrash Pinhas	R. Pinhas Shapira of Koretz, Midrash Pinhas (Warsaw, 1910).
Midrash Tadsche'	Mi-Qadmoniot ha-Yehudim, ed. Abraham Epstein (Mossad ha-Rav Kook, Jerusalem, 1957), pp. 144–171.
Midrash Talppiyyot	R. Elijah ha-Kohen 'Ithamari of Smyrna, Midrash Talppiyyot (Jerusalem, 1963).
Naggid u-Metzavveh	R. Jacob Hayyim Tzemah, Naggid u-Metzavveh (Lemberg, 1863).
Nefesh ha-Hayyim	R. Hayyim of Volozhin, Sefer Nefesh ha-Hayyim, ed. Y. D. Rubin (Benei Beraq, 1989).
Notzer Hesed	R. Isaac Aizik Yehudah Safrin of Komarno, Sefer Notzer Hesed (Jerusalem, 1982).
On the Art of Kabbalah	Johann Reuchlin, On the Art of Kabbalah/De Arte Cabalistica, Latin text and English translation by Martin and Sarah Goodman (University of Nebraska Press, Lincoln, 1993).
'Or ha-Ganuz le-Tzaddiqim	R. Aharon Kohen of Apta, 'Or ha-Ganuz le-Tzaddiqim (Zolkiew, 1800).
'Or ha-Meʾir	R. Ze'ev Wolf of Zhitomir, 'Or ha-Meʾir (Perizek, 1815).
'Or Torah	'Or Torah ve-Rimzei Torah, traditions and teachings of R. Dov Baer of Mezeritch (Jerusalem, 1968).

'Or Yitzhaq R. Isaac of Radvil, *Sefer 'Or Yitzhaq* (Jerusalem, 1961).

'Otzar ha-Kavod R. Todros ben Joseph ha-Levi Abulafia, *Sefer 'Otzar ha-Kavod* (Warsaw, 1879).

Pardes Rimmonim R. Moses Cordovero, *Sefer Pardes Rimmonim*, ed. Munkacz, 2 parts (rpt., Jerusalem, 1962).

Penei David ve-Tzavarei Shalal HYDA', *Penei David ve-Tzavarei Shalal* (Jerusalem, 1965).

Perush Roqeah R. Eleazar of Worms, *Perush Roqeah*, ed. Yoel Klugmann, 3 vols. (Benei Beraq, 1986).

Qedushat Levi R. Levi Isaac of Berditchev, *Qedushat Levi* (Jerusalem, 1993).

Qin'at ha-Shem Tzeva'ot R. Moses Hayyim Luzzatto, *Qin'at ha-Shem Tzeva'ot*, printed in *Ginzei ha-Ramhal* 2 (Benei Beraq, 1980).

Qol Yehudah R. Yehudah Leib of Yanov, *Sefer Qol Yehudah* (1906).

Reshit Hokhmah R. Elijah da Vidas, *Sefer Reshit Hokhmah*, ed. H. Y. Waldman, 3 vols. (Jerusalem, 1984).

Sefer ha-Temunah Anonymous, *Sefer ha-Temunah* (Lemberg, 1892).

Sefat 'Emmet R. Yehudah Arieh Leib of Gur, *Sefat 'Emmet 'im Liqqutim*, 5 vols. (Jerusalem, n.d.).

Sha'arei 'Orah *Sefer Sha'arei 'Orah*, translated as *Gates of Light*, trans. Avi Weinstein (Harper-Collins, San Francisco, 1994).

Sha'arei Qedushah R. Hayyim Vital, *Sefer Sha'arei Qedushah* (Benei Beraq, 1973).

Sha'arei Tzedeq R. Nathan ben Sa'adyah, *Sefer Sha'arei Tzedeq*, ed. Y. E. Porush (Jerusalem, 1989).

Sheva' Netivot ha-Torah Abraham Abulafia, *Sheva' Netivot ha-Torah*, ed. Adolph Jellinek, in *Philosophie und Kabbala, erstes Heft* (Leipzig, 1854). This epistle has been translated into French by J.-C. Attias as *L'Epître des sept voies* (Editions de l'Eclats, 1985).

Shi'ur Qomah — R. Moses Cordovero, *Sefer Shi'ur Qomah* (Ahuzat Israel, Israel, 1966).

Shomer 'Emunim — R. Joseph Ergas, *Sefer Shomer 'Emunim* (Jerusalem, 1965).

Siddur — R. Jacob Hayyim Tzemah, *Siddur Kavvanot ha-Tefillot bi-Qetzarah* (Jerusalem, 1986).

Sullam ha-'Aliyah — R. Yehudah Albotini, *Sefer Sullam ha-'Aliyah*, ed. J. E. Porush (Jerusalem, 1989).

Teshu'ot Hen — R. Gedalyah of Lunitz, *Sefer Teshu'ot Hen* (Brooklyn, 1982).

Tiferet 'Adam — R. Jacob Hayyim Tzemah, *Sefer Tiferet 'Adam* (Benei Beraq, 1982).

Tiqqunim Hadashim — R. Moses Hayyim Luzzatto, *Tiqqunim Hadashim* (Jerusalem, 1997).

Tola'at Ya'aqov — R. Meir ibn Gabbai, *Sefer Tola'at Ya'aqov* (Jerusalem, 1967).

Toledot 'Aharon — R. Aharon of Zhitomir, *Sefer Toledot 'Aharon*, 2 parts (Lemberg, 1865).

Toledot Ya'aqov Yosef — R. Jacob Joseph of Polonoy, *Toledot Ya'aqov Yosef* (Koretz, 1780).

Tzafnat Pa'aneah — R. Joseph al-Ashqar, *Sefer Tzafnat Pa'aneah*, ed. M. Idel (Misgav Yerushalayyim, Jerusalem, 1991).

Zohar — *The Book of the Zohar*, ed. Reuven Margalioth, 5 vols. (Mossad ha-Rav Kook, Jerusalem, 1978).

Zohar Tanniyana' — R. Moses Hayyim Luzzatto, *Sefer Zohar Tanniyana'*, printed by Simeon Ginsburg, Rabbi Moshe Hayyim Luzzatto u-vnei Doro, *'Ossef 'Iggrot u-Te'udot* 2 (Mossad Bialik, Jerusalem, 1937).

STUDIES

Abrams, "From Germany to Spain" — Daniel Abrams, "From Germany to Spain: Numerology as a Mystical Technique," JJS 47 (1996), pp. 85–101.

Abrams, "Orality" — Daniel Abrams, "Orality in the Kabbalistic School of Nahmanides: Preserving and Interpreting Esoteric

Traditions and Texts," JSQ 3 (1996), no. 1, pp. 85–102.

Abrams, R. Asher ben David — Daniel Abrams, R. Asher ben David: His Complete Works and Studies in His Kabbalistic Thought (Cherub Press, Los Angeles, 1996).

The Age of the Zohar — The Age of the Zohar, ed. Joseph Dan (Jerusalem, 1989) (Hebrew).

Angus, The Mystery-Religions — S. Angus, The Mystery-Religions: A Study in the Religious Background of Early Christianity (Dover Publications, New York, 1975).

Ayoub, The Qur'an and Its Interpreters — Mahmoud M. Ayoub, The Qur'an and Its Interpreters, vol. 1 (SUNY Press, Albany 1984).

Bacher, "L'exégèse biblique" — Wilhelm Bacher, "L'exégèse biblique dans le Zohar," REJ 22 (1891), pp. 33–46, 219–229.

Bacher, Die Exegetische Terminologie — Wilhelm Bacher, Die Exegetische Terminologie der Jüdischen Traditionsliteratur, 2 parts (rpt., Olms, Hildesheim, 1965).

Baer, Studies — Yizhak F. Baer, Studies in the History of the Jewish People, 2 vols. (Historical Society of Israel, Jerusalem, 1985) (Hebrew).

Banon, La lecture infinie — David Banon, La lecture infinie (Seuil, Paris, 1987).

Barthes, Le degré zero — Roland Barthes, Le degré zero de l'écriture (Editions Gonthier, Paris, 1964).

Belkin, "Midrash Tadsche'" — Shmuel Belkin, "Midrash Tadsche' or the Midrash of R. Pinhas ben Yair, an Ancient Hellenistic Midrash," Horev 11, no. 21–22 (1951), pp. 1–52 (Hebrew).

Ben-Amos and Mintz, In Praise of the Baal Shem Tov — In Praise of the Baal Shem Tov, trans. D. Ben-Amos and J. R. Mintz (Aronson, Northvale, London, 1993).

Benin, The Footprints of God — Stephen D. Benin, The Footprints of God: Divine Accommodation in Jewish and Christian Thought (SUNY Press, Albany, 1993).

Benin, "The Mutability" — Stephen Benin, "The Mutability of an Immutable God: Exegesis and Individual Capacity in the Zohar and Several Christian Sources," in *The Age of the Zohar*, pp. 67–86 (Hebrew).

Blanchot, *The Gaze of Orpheus*
Maurice Blanchot, *The Gaze of Orpheus*, trans. Lydia Davis (Stantion Hill Press, New York, 1981).

Bloom, *Agon*
Harold Bloom, *Agon: Toward a Theory of Revisionism* (Oxford University Press, Oxford, 1983).

Bloom, *Kabbalah and Criticism*
Harold Bloom, *Kabbalah and Criticism* (Continuum, New York, 1984).

Bloom, *The Strong Light*
Harold Bloom, *The Strong Light of the Canonical: Kafka, Freud and Scholem as Revisionists of Jewish Culture and Thought* (City College Paper, New York, 1978).

Bori, *L'interpretazione infinita*
Pier Cesare Bori, *L'interpretazione infinita: L'ermeneutica cristiana antica e le sue transformazioni* (Il Mulino, Bologna, 1987).

Boyarin, *Intertextuality*
Daniel Boyarin, *Intertextuality and the Reading of the Midrash* (Indiana University Press, Bloomington, 1990).

Bruns, *Hermeneutics Ancient and Modern*
Gerald L. Bruns, *Hermeneutics Ancient and Modern* (Yale University Press, New Haven, 1992).

Bruns, *Inventions*
Gerald L. Bruns, *Inventions, Writing, Textuality, and Understanding in Literary History* (Yale University Press, New Haven, 1982).

Buber, *Hasidism and Modern Man*
Martin Buber, *Hasidism and Modern Man*, ed. Maurice Friedman (New York, 1966).

Buber, *The Origin and Meaning of Hasidism*
Martin Buber, *The Origin and Meaning of Hasidism*, ed. and trans. Maurice Freedman, intro. David B. Burrell (Atlantic Highlands, N. J., 1988).

Buber, *Tales of the Hasidim*
Martin Buber, *Tales of the Hasidim: The Early Masters*, trans. Olga Marx (Schocken Books, New York, 1964).

Caputo, *The Prayers*
John D. Caputo, *The Prayers and Tears of Jacques Derrida: Religion Without Religion* (Indiana University Press, Bloomington, 1997).

Chittick, The Sufi Path of Knowledge | William C. Chittick, Ibn 'Arabi's Meta-physics of Imagination: The Sufi Path of Knowledge (SUNY Press, Albany, 1989).

Corbin, Alone with the Alone | Henry Corbin, Alone with the Alone (Princeton University Press, Princeton, 1998).

Corbin, Face de Dieu | Henry Corbin, Face de Dieu, Face de l'homme: Hermeneutique et soufisme (Flammarion, Paris, 1983).

Couliano, Eros and Magic | Ioan P. Couliano, Eros and Magic in the Re-naissance (University of Chicago Press, Chicago, 1987).

Dan, "Ashkenazi Hasidic" | Joseph Dan, "The Ashkenazi Hasidic 'Gates of Wisdom,'" in G. Nahon and C. Touati, eds., Hommages à Georges Va-jda (Louvain, 1980), pp. 183–189.

Dan, The Early Kabbalah | Joseph Dan, ed., The Early Kabbalah (Paul-ist Press, New York, 1986).

Dan, The Esoteric Theology | Joseph Dan, The Esoteric Theology of Ash-kenazi Hasidism (Jerusalem, 1968) (He-brew).

Dan, On Sanctity | Joseph Dan, On Sanctity (Magnes Press, Jerusalem, 1997) (Hebrew).

Dan, Studies | Joseph Dan, Studies in Ashkenazi-Hasidic Literature (Massadah, Ramat Gan, 1975) (Hebrew).

Davies, Torah | W. B. Davies, Torah in the Messianic Age and/or the Age to Come (Society of Bibli-cal Literature, Philadelphia, 1952).

De Lubac, L'écriture dans la tradition | Henri de Lubac, L'écriture dans la tradition (Aubier-Montaigne, Paris, 1966).

De Lubac, Exégèse medieval | Henri de Lubac, Exégèse medieval: Les quatre sens de l'écriture, 4 vols. (Aubier-Montaigne, Paris, 1959).

De Lubac, Histoire et esprit | Henri de Lubac, Histoire et esprit: L'intel-ligence de l'écriture d'après Origène (Aubier-Montaigne, Paris, 1950).

Derrida, Dissemination | Jacques Derrida, Dissemination, trans. Barbara Johnson (University of Chi-cago Press, Chicago, 1981).

Derrida, L'écriture et la différence | Jacques Derrida, L'écriture et la différence (Editions du Seuil, Paris, 1967).

Eco, *The Aesthetics*   Umberto Eco, *The Aesthetics of Thomas Aquinas*, trans. Hughes Bredin (Harvard University Press, Cambridge, Mass., 1988).

Eco, *Foucault's Pendulum*   Umberto Eco, *Foucault's Pendulum*, trans. W. Weaver (Harcourt Brace Jovanovich, San Diego, 1988).

Eco, *The Limits of Interpretation*   Umberto Eco, *The Limits of Interpretation* (Indiana University Press, Bloomington, 1990).

Eco, *The Open Work*   Umberto Eco, *The Open Work*, trans. Anna Cancogni (Harvard University Press, Cambridge, Mass., 1989).

Eco, *The Search*   Umberto Eco, *The Search for the Perfect Language*, trans. James Fentress (Blackwell, Oxford, 1995).

Eco, *Semiotics*   Umberto Eco, *Semiotics and the Philosophy of Language* (Indiana University Press, Bloomington, 1984).

Eliade, "Methodological Remarks"   Mircea Eliade, "Methodological Remarks on the Study of Religious Symbolism," in *The History of Religions: Essays in Methodology*, eds. M. Eliade and J. M. Kitagawa (University of Chicago Press, Chicago, 1959), pp. 86–107.

Elqayam, "Between Referentionalism   Avraham Elqayam, "Between Referentionalism and Performativism: Two
and Performativism"   Approaches to the Understanding of the Symbol in *Sefer Ma'arekhet ha-'Elohut*," *Da'at* 24 (1990), pp. 29–37 (Hebrew).

Farber-Ginnat, "Inquiries in *Sefer Shi'ur*   Assi Farber-Ginnat, "Inquiries in *Sefer*
Qomah,"   *Shi'ur Qomah*," in *Massu'ot*, pp. 361–394 (Hebrew).

Faur, *Golden Doves*   Jose Faur, *Golden Doves with Silver Dots* (Indiana University Press, Bloomington, 1986).

Fine, *Safed Spirituality*   Lawrence Fine, *Safed Spirituality* (Paulist Press, New York, 1984).

Fishbane, *Biblical Interpretation*   Michael Fishbane, *Biblical Interpretation* in

	Ancient Israel (Clarendon Press, Oxford, 1985).
Fishbane, *The Exegetical Imagination*	Michael Fishbane, *The Exegetical Imagination: On Jewish Thought and Theology* (Harvard University Press, Cambridge, Mass., 1998).
Fishbane, *The Garments of the Torah*	Michael Fishbane, *The Garments of the Torah: Essays in Biblical Hermeneutics* (Indiana University Press, Bloomington, 1989).
Fodor, *Christian Hermeneutics*	James Fodor, *Christian Hermeneutics: Paul Ricoeur and the Refiguring of Theology* (Clarendon Press, Oxford, 1995).
Fraenkel, *The Ways of the 'Aggadah and Midrash*	Yonah Fraenkel, *The Ways of the 'Aggadah and Midrash*, 2 vols. (Massada, Ramat Gan, 1991) (Hebrew).
The Future of the Book	*The Future of the Book*, ed. Geoffrey Nunberg (University of California Press, Berkeley and Los Angeles, 1996).
Gadamer, *Truth and Method*	Hans-Georg Gadamer, *Truth and Method*, 2nd rev. ed., translation revised by J. Weinsheimer and D. G. Marshall (Crossroad, New York, 1989).
Giller, *The Enlightened*	Pinchas Giller, *The Enlightened Will Shine: Symbolization and Theurgy in the Later Strata of the Zohar* (SUNY Press, Albany, 1993).
Ginzberg, *The Legends of the Jews*	Louis Ginzberg, *The Legends of the Jews*, 7 vols. (Jewish Publication Society, Philadelphia, 5728/1968).
Goetschel, *Meir ibn Gabbaï*	Roland Goetschel, *Meir ibn Gabbaï: Le discours de la Kabbale espagnole* (Peeters, Leuven, 1981).
Goldin, *Studies in Midrash*	Judah Goldin, *Studies in Midrash and Related Literature*, ed. Barry L. Eichler and Jeffrey H. Tigay (Jewish Publication Society, Philadelphia, 5748/1988).
Goodenough, *By Light, Light*	Erwin Goodenough, *By Light, Light* (Yale University Press, New Haven, 1935).
Gottlieb, *Studies*	Efraim Gottlieb, *Studies in the Kabbalah Literature*, ed. J. Hacker (Tel Aviv University, Tel Aviv, 1976) (Hebrew).

Graham, *Beyond the Written Word*

William A. Graham, *Beyond the Written Word: Oral Aspects of Scripture in the History of Religion* (Cambridge University Press, Cambridge, 1993).

Green, *Devotion and Commandment*

Arthur Green, *Devotion and Commandment: The Faith of Abraham in the Hasidic Imagination* (Hebrew Union College Press, Cincinnati, 1989).

Green, *Jewish Spirituality*

Arthur Green, ed., *Jewish Spirituality*, 2 vols. (Crossroad, New York, 1986–1987).

Green, *Keter*

Arthur Green, *Keter: The Crown of God in Early Jewish Mysticism* (Princeton University Press, Princeton, 1997).

Green, *Tormented Master*

Arthur Green, *Tormented Master: A Life of Rabbi Nahman of Bratslav* (University of Alabama Press, University, 1979).

Green, "Zaddiq as Axis Mundi"

Arthur Green, "The Zaddiq as Axis Mundi in Later Judaism," *Journal of the American Academy of Religion* 45, no. 3 (1977), pp. 327–347.

Greenberg, *Studies*

Moshe Greenberg, *Studies in the Bible and Jewish Thought* (Jewish Publication Society, Philadelphia, Jerusalem, 1995).

Gruenwald, *From Apocalypticism to Gnosticism*

Ithamar Gruenwald, *From Apocalypticism to Gnosticism* (Peter Lang, Frankfurt am Main, 1988).

Gruenwald, "Jewish Mysticism"

Ithamar Gruenwald, "Jewish Mysticism's Transition from *Sefer Yesira* to the *Bahir*," in *The Beginnings of the Jewish Mysticism in Medieval Europe*, ed. J. Dan (Jerusalem, 1987), pp. 15–54 (Hebrew).

Gruenwald, "On Writing and Written and the Divine Name"

Ithamar Gruenwald, "On Writing and Written and the Divine Name: Magic, Spirituality and Mysticism," in *Massu'ot*, pp. 75–98 (Hebrew).

Gruenwald, "Uses and Abuses"

Ithamar Gruenwald, "Uses and Abuses of Gimatria," in M. Bar-Asher, ed., *Rabbi Mordechai Breuer Festschrift: Collected Papers in Jewish Studies* (Akademon Press, Jerusalem, 1992), 2:773–782 (Hebrew).

Halbertal, Concealment and Revelation   Moshe Halbertal, *Concealment and Revelation: The Secret and Its Boundaries in Medieval Jewish Tradition* (Yeriot, Jerusalem, 2001) (Hebrew).

Halbertal, Interpretative Revolutions   Moshe Halbertal, *Interpretative Revolutions in the Making* (Magnes Press, Jerusalem, 1997) (Hebrew).

Halbertal, People of the Book   Moshe Halbertal, *People of the Book: Canon, Meaning, and Authority* (Harvard University Press, Cambridge, Mass., 1997).

Halperin, Faces of the Chariot   David Halperin, *Faces of the Chariot* (J. C. B. Mohr, Tübingen, 1988).

Handelman, Fragments of Redemption   Susan A. Handelman, *Fragments of Redemption: Jewish Thought and Literary Theory in Benjamin, Scholem, and Levinas* (Indiana University Press, Bloomington, 1991).

Handelman, The Slayers of Moses   Susan A. Handelman, *The Slayers of Moses* (SUNY Press, Albany, 1982).

Hartman, The Fate of Reading   Geoffrey H. Hartman, *The Fate of Reading and Other Essays* (University of Chicago Press, Chicago, London, 1975).

Heinemann, Darkhei ha-'Aggadah   Yitzhaq Heinemann, *Darkhei ha-'Aggadah* (Magnes Press, Jerusalem, 1974).

Heschel, The Theology of Ancient Judaism   A. Y. Heschel, *The Theology of Ancient Judaism*, 3 vols. (Soncino Press, London, 1962–1990) (Hebrew).

Hirshman, A Rivalry of Genius   Marc Hirshman, *A Rivalry of Genius: Jewish and Christian Biblical Interpretation in Late Antiquity* (SUNY Press, Albany, 1996).

Holdrege, Veda and Torah   Barbara A. Holdrege, *Veda and Torah: Transcending the Textuality of Scripture* (SUNY Press, Albany, 1996).

Huss, "Sefer ha-Zohar"   Boaz Huss, "Sefer ha-Zohar as a Canonical, Sacred and Holy Text: Changing Perspectives in the *Book of Splendor* between the Thirteenth and Eighteenth Centuries," *Journal of Jewish Thought and Philosophy* 7 (1998), pp. 257–307.

Huss, "Symbolism"   Boaz Huss, "Rabbi Joseph Gikatilia's Definition of Symbolism and Its Influ-

	ence on Kabbalistic Literature," *JSJT,* 12 (1996), pp. 157–176 (Hebrew).
Idel, "A la recherche"	M. Idel, "A la recherche de la langue originelle: Le témoignage du nourisson," *Revue d'histoires des religions* 213–214 (1996), pp. 417–420.
Idel, "Abraham Abulafia"	Moshe Idel, "Abraham Abulafia's Works and Doctrines" (Ph.D. diss., Hebrew University, Jerusalem, 1976) (Hebrew).
Idel, "Abulafia's Secrets of the *Guide*"	Moshe Idel, "Abulafia's Secrets of the *Guide*: A Linguistic Turn," in A. Ivri, E. R. Wolfson, and A. Arkush, *Perspectives on Jewish Thought and Mysticism* (Harwood Academic Publishers, Amsterdam, 1998), pp. 289–329.
Idel, "Be-'Or ha-Hayyim"	Moshe Idel, "*Be-'Or ha-Hayyim*: An Observation on Kabbalistic Eschatology," in I. M. Gafni and A. Ravitsky, eds., *Sanctity of Life and Martyrdom: Studies in Memory of Amir Yekutiel* (Merkaz Zalman Shazar, Jerusalem, 1992), pp. 191–212 (Hebrew).
Idel, "The Concept of the Torah"	M. Idel, "The Concept of the Torah in Heikhalot Literature and Its Metamorphoses in Kabbalah," *JSJT* 1 (1981) pp. 23–84 (Hebrew).
Idel, "The Concept of Zimzum"	M. Idel, "On the Concept of Zimzum in Kabbalah and Its Research," in R. Elior and Y. Liebes, eds., *Lurianic Kabbalah* (Jerusalem, 1992), pp. 59–112 (Hebrew).
Idel, "Conceptualizations of Music"	Moshe Idel, "Conceptualizations of Music in Jewish Mysticism," in Lawrence Sullivan, ed., *Enchanting Powers: Music in the World's Religions* (Harvard University Press, Cambridge, Mass., 1997), pp. 159–188.
Idel, "Defining Kabbalah"	Moshe Idel, "Defining Kabbalah: The Kabbalah of the Divine Names," in *Mystics of the Book: Themes, Topics and Typology,* ed. R. A. Herrera (Peter Lang, New York, 1992), pp. 97–122.

Idel, "Differing Conceptions of Kabbalah"

M. Idel, "Differing Conceptions of Kabbalah in the Early Seventeenth Century," in *Jewish Thought in the Seventeenth
  Century*, ed. Isadore Twersky and Bernard D. Septimus (Harvard University
  Press, Cambridge, Mass., 1987),
  pp. 137–200.

Idel, "The Function of Symbols"

M. Idel, "The Function of Symbols in G.
  G. Scholem," *Jewish Studies* 38 (1998),
  pp. 43–72 (Hebrew).

Idel, "Gazing at the Head"

M. Idel, "Gazing at the Head in Ashkenazi Hasidism," *Journal of Jewish
  Thought and Philosophy* 6 (1997),
  pp. 265–300.

Idel, *Hasidism: Between Ecstasy and Magic*

Moshe Idel, *Hasidism: Between Ecstasy and
  Magic* (SUNY Press, Albany, 1995).

Idel, "Hermeticism and Judaism"

Moshe Idel, "Hermeticism and Judaism," in I. Merkel and A. Debus, eds.,
  Hermeticism and the Renaissance (Folger
  Shakespeare Library, Washington,
  1988), pp. 59–76.

Idel, "The Image of Man"

Idel, "The Image of Man above the
  Sefirot: R. David ben Yehudah he-
  Hasid's Doctrine of the Supernal
  Sefirot (Tzahtzahot) and Its Evolu-
  tion," *Da'at* 4 (1980), pp. 41–55
  (Hebrew).

Idel, "Inquiries"

M. Idel, "Inquiries in the Doctrine of
  Sefer Ha-Meshiv," *Sefunot* 17, ed.
  J. Hacker (Jerusalem, 1983), pp. 185–
  266 (Hebrew).

Idel, "Jewish Magic"

Moshe Idel, "Jewish Magic from the Renaissance Period to Early Hasidism,"
  in Jacob Neusner Ernest S. Frerichs,
  and Paul Virgil McCracken Flesher,
  eds., *Religion, Science, and Magic* (Oxford University Press, Oxford, 1989),
  pp. 82–117.

Idel, *Kabbalah: New Perspectives*

M. Idel, *Kabbalah: New Perspectives* (Yale
  University Press, New Haven, 1988).

Idel, "Kabbalistic Material"

Moshe Idel, "Kabbalistic Material from
  the Circle of R. David ben Yehudah he-

Hasid," JSJT, 2, no. 2 (1983), pp. 169–207 (Hebrew).

Idel, *Language, Torah and Hermeneutics* — Moshe Idel, *Language, Torah and Hermeneutics in Abraham Abulafia*, trans. Menahem Kalus (SUNY Press, New York, 1989).

Idel, "The Magical and Neoplatonic Interpretations" — M. Idel, "The Magical and Neoplatonic Interpretations of Kabbalah in the Renaissance," in B. D. Cooperman, ed., *Jewish Thought in the Sixteenth Century* (Harvard University Press, Cambridge, Mass., 1983), pp. 186–242.

Idel, "The Magical and Theurgical Interpretation" — M. Idel, "The Magical and Theurgical Interpretation of Music in Jewish Texts: Renaissance to Hasidism," *Yuval* 4 (1982) pp. 33–63 (Hebrew).

Idel, *Maïmonide et la mystique juive* — M. Idel, *Maïmonides et la mystique juive*, trans. Charles Mopsik (Le Cerf, Paris, 1991).

Idel, "Maimonides and Kabbalah" — M. Idel, "Maimonides and Kabbalah," in *Studies in Maimonides*, ed. I. Twersky (Cambridge, Mass. 1990), pp. 31–82.

Idel, *Messianic Mystics* — Moshe Idel, *Messianic Mystics* (Yale University Press, New Haven, 1998).

Idel, *The Mystical Experience* — M. Idel, *The Mystical Experience in Abraham Abulafia*, trans. J. Chipman (SUNY Press, Albany, 1987).

Idel, "Nahmanides" — Moshe Idel, "Nahmanides: Kabbalah, Halakhah and Spiritual Leadership," in *Jewish Mystical Leaders and Leadership*, ed. M. Idel and M. Ostow (Jason Aronson, Northvale, N.J., 1998), pp. 15–96.

Idel, "Neglected Writings" — M. Idel, "Neglected Writings of the Author of *Sefer Kaf ha-Qetoret*," *Peʿamim* 53 (1993), pp. 75–89 (Hebrew).

Idel, "On Judaism" — Moshe Idel, "On Judaism, Jewish Mysticism and Magic," in P. Schaefer and Hans G. Kippenberg, eds., *Envisioning Magic* (Brill, Leiden, 1997), pp. 195–214.

Idel, "On R. Isaac Sagi Nahor"

M. Idel, "On R. Isaac Sagi Nahor's Mystical Intention of the Eighteen Benedictions," in *Massu'ot*, pp. 25–52 (Hebrew).

Idel, "On Symbolic Self-Interpretations"

M. Idel, "On Symbolic Self-Interpretations in Thirteenth-Century Jewish Writings," *Hebrew University Studies in Literature and the Arts* 16 (1988), pp. 90–96.

Idel, "On Talismatic Language"

M. Idel, "On Talismatic Language in Jewish Mysticism," *Diogenes* 43, no. 2 (1995), pp. 23–41.

Idel, "On the History"

M. Idel, "On the History of the Interdiction against the Study of Kabbalah before the Age of Forty," AJSR 5 (1980), pp. 1–20 (Hebrew).

Idel, *R. Menahem Recanati*

M. Idel, *R. Menahem Recanati, the Kabbalist*, 2 vols. (Schocken Books, Jerusalem, 1998) (Hebrew).

Idel, "Reification of Language"

Moshe Idel, "Reification of Language in Jewish Mysticism," in S. Katz, ed., *Mysticism and Language* (New York, 1992), pp. 42–79.

Idel, "Sefirot above Sefirot"

M. Idel, "Sefirot above the Sefirot," *Tarbiz* 51 (1982), pp. 239–280 (Hebrew).

Idel, "Sexual Metaphors"

M. Idel, "Sexual Metaphors and Praxis in the Kabbalah," in *The Jewish Family*, ed. D. Kraemer (Oxford University Press, New York, 1989), pp. 179–224.

Idel, *Studies in Ecstatic Kabbalah*

M. Idel, *Studies in Ecstatic Kabbalah* (SUNY Press, Albany, 1988).

Idel, "Targumo"

M. Idel, "Targumo shel R. David ben Yehudah he-Hasid le-Sefer ha-Zohar," '*Alei Sefer* 8 (1980), pp. 60–73; 9 (1981), pp. 84–98 (Hebrew).

Idel, "Types of Redemptive Activities"

M. Idel, "Types of Redemptive Activities in Middle Ages," in Z. Baras, ed., *Messianism and Eschatology* (Merkaz Zalman Shazar, Jerusalem, 1984), pp. 253–279 (Hebrew).

Idel, " 'Unio Mystica' "

Moshe Idel, " 'Unio Mystica' as a Criterion: 'Hegelian' Phenomenologies of

Jewish Mysticism," in Steven Chase, ed., *Doors of Understanding: Conversations in Global Spirituality in Honor of Ewert Cousins* (Franciscan Press, Quincy, Ill., 1997), pp. 305–333.

Idel, "We Have No Kabbalistic Tradition" — M. Idel, "We Have No Kabbalistic Tradition on This," in Isadore Twersky, ed., *Rabbi Moses Nahmanides (Ramban): Explorations in His Religious and Literary Virtuosity* (Harvard University Press, Cambridge, Mass., 1983), pp. 63–73.

Idel and McGinn, *Mystical Union* — M. Idel and B. McGinn, eds., *Mystical Union and Monotheistic Faith: An Ecumenical Dialogue* (New York, 1989).

Irvine, *The Making of Textual Culture* — Martin Irvine, *The Making of Textual Culture: "Grammatica" and Literary Theory, 350–1100* (Cambridge University Press, Cambridge, 1994).

Iser, *The Act of Reading* — Wolfgang Iser, *The Act of Reading* (John Hopkins, Baltimore, 1979).

Jabes, "Key" — Edmond Jabes, "Key," translated by Rosmarie Waldorf, in *Midrash and Literature*, pp. 349–360.

Jacobs, *Hasidic Prayer* — Louis Jacobs, *Hasidic Prayer* (Schocken Books, New York, 1978).

Jacobs, *Jewish Mystical Testimonies* — Louis Jacobs, *Jewish Mystical Testimonies* (Schocken Books, New York, 1987).

Jewish Mystical Leaders — *Jewish Mystical Leaders and Leadership in the Thirteenth Century*, eds. M. Idel and M. Ostow (Jason Aronson, Northvale, N.J., 1998).

Kasher, *Torah Shelemah* — Menahem Kasher, ed., *Torah Shelemah*, 45 vols. (rpt. Jerusalem, 1992).

Kermode, *The Genesis of Secrecy* — Frank Kermode, *The Genesis of Secrecy: On the Interpretation of Narrative* (Harvard University Press, Cambridge, Mass., 1979).

Kugel-Greer, *Early Biblical Interpretation* — J. L. Kugel and Rowan A. Greer, eds., *Early Biblical Interpretation* (Westminster Press, Philadelphia, 1988).

Leclercq, *The Love of Learning* — Jean Leclercq, *The Love of Learning and the Desire for God: A Study in Monastic Culture,* trans. Catharine Misrahi (Fordham University Press, New York, 1982).

Lieberman, "A Mesopotamian Background"   Stephen Lieberman, "A Mesopotamian Background for the So-Called Aggadic 'Measures' of Biblical Hermeneutics?" HUCA 58 (1987), pp. 157–225.

Liebes, Ars Poetica   Yehuda Liebes, Ars Poetica, in Sefer Yetzirah (Schocken, Tel Aviv, 2000) (Hebrew).

Liebes, Het' o shel 'Elisha'   Yehuda Liebes Het' o shel 'Elisha' (Akademon, Jerusalem, 1990).

Liebes, "The Messiah of the Zohar"   Yehuda Liebes, "The Messiah of the Zohar," in The Messianic Idea in Israel (Israel Academy of Sciences and Humanities, Jerusalem, 1982), pp. 87–234 (Hebrew).

Liebes, "Myth vs. Symbol"   Yehuda Liebes, "Myth vs. Symbol in the Zohar and Lurianic Kabbalah," in Lawrence Fine, ed., Essential Papers on Kabbalah (New York University Press, New York, 1995), pp. 212–242.

Liebes, "New Directions"   Yehuda Liebes, "New Directions in the Study of Kabbalah," Pe'amim 50 (1992) pp. 150–170 (Hebrew).

Liebes, Sod ha-'Emunah   Yehuda Liebes, On Sabbateanism and Its Kabbalah: Collected Essays (Mossad Bialik, Jerusalem, 1995) (Hebrew).

Liebes, Studies in the Zohar   Yehuda Liebes, Studies in the Zohar, trans. A. Schwartz, S. Nakache, and P. Peli (SUNY Press, Albany, 1993).

Liebes, "Zohar and Eros"   Yehuda Liebes, "Zohar and Eros," 'Alp-payyim 9 (1994), pp. 67–119 (Hebrew).

Lorberbaum, "Imago Dei"   Yair Lorberbaum, "Imago Dei: Rabbinic Literature, Maimonides and Nahmanides" (Ph.D. diss., Hebrew University, Jerusalem, 1997) (Hebrew).

Lory, Les commentaires ésoteriques   Pierre Lory, Les commentaires ésoteriques du Coran d'après 'Abd ar-Razzaq al-Qashani (Les Deux Oceans, Paris, 1980).

Magid, "From Theosophy to Midrash"   Shaul Magid, "From Theosophy to Midrash: Lurianic Exegesis and the Garden of Eden," AJSR 27 (1997), pp. 37–75.

Mallarmé, *Oeuvres complètes*   Stéphane Mallarmé, *Oeuvres complètes*
                                       (Gallimard, Paris, 1970).

Marcus, "Exegesis for the Few"   Ivan G. Marcus, "Exegesis for the Few
                                       and for the Many: Judah he-Hasid's
                                       Biblical Commentary," in *The Age of the
                                       Zohar*, pp. 1–24.

Marsh, "The Use of Mysterion"   H. G. Marsh, "The Use of Mysterion in
                                       the Writings of Clement of Alexandria
                                       with Special Reference to His Sacra-
                                       mental Doctrines," *Journal of Theologi-
                                       cal Studies* 37 (1936), pp. 64–80.

Massu'ot   *Massu'ot: Studies in Kabbalistic Literature and
                                       Jewish Philosophy in Memory of Prof.
                                       Ephraim Gottlieb*, ed. Michal Oron and
                                       Amos Goldreich (Mossad Bialik,
                                       Jerusalem, 1994) (Hebrew).

Matt, "Ayin"   Daniel Matt, "Ayin: The Concept of
                                       Nothingness in Jewish Mysticism," in
                                       Robert K. C. Forman, ed., *The Problem
                                       of Pure Consciousness: Mysticism and Phi-
                                       losophy* (Oxford University Press, New
                                       York, 1990), pp. 121–159.

Matt, *The Book of Mirrors*   Daniel Matt, *The Book of Mirrors: Sefer
                                       Mar'ot ha-Zove'ot by R. David ben Yehudah
                                       he-Hasid* (Brown Judaic Studies,
                                       Scholars Press, 1982).

Matt, *Zohar*   Daniel Matt, trans. and intro., *Zohar: The
                                       Book of the Enlightenment* (Paulist Press,
                                       New York, Ramsey, Toronto, 1983).

McGinn, *The Presence of God*   Bernard McGinn, *The Presence of God: A
                                       History of Western Christian Mysticism*, 3
                                       vols. (Crossroad, New York, 1991–98).

Midrash and Literature   *Midrash and Literature*, ed. Geoffrey Hart-
                                       man and Sandford Budick (Yale Uni-
                                       versity Press, New Haven, 1986).

Mopsik, *Les grands textes*   Charles Mopsik, *Les grands textes de la Kab-
                                       bale* (Verdier, Lagrasse, 1993).

Mopsik, *Le sicle*   Charles Mopsik, trans., Moise de Leon,
                                       Le sicle du sanctuaire (Verdier, Lagrasse,
                                       1996).

Mowinckel, *He That Cometh*   Sigmund Mowinckel, *He That Cometh*,
                                       trans. G. W. Anderson (Oxford, 1959).

Neumann, "Mystical Man"

Erich Neumann, "Mystical Man," in J. Campbell, ed., and R. Manheim, trans., *The Mystic Vision: Papers from the Eranos Yearbooks* (Princeton University Press, Princeton, 1982), pp. 375–415.

Nwyia, *Exégèse coranique*

Paul Nwyia, *Exégèse coranique et langage mystique* (Dar al-Machreq, Beyruth, 1970).

Parpola, "The Assyrian Tree of Life"

Simo Parpola, "The Assyrian Tree of Life: Tracing the Origins of Jewish Monotheism and Greek Philosophy," *Journal of Near Eastern Studies* 52 (1993), pp. 161–208.

Petuchowski, "Judaism as 'Mystery' "

Jakob J. Petuchowski, "Judaism as 'Mystery': The Hidden Agenda?" *HUCA* (1981), pp. 141–152.

Piekarz, *Studies*

Mendel Piekarz, *Studies in Braslav Hasidism* (Mossad Bialik, Jerusalem, 1972) (Hebrew).

Pines, "God, the Divine Glory"

Shlomo Pines, "God, the Divine Glory, and the Angels according to a Second Century Theology," in J. Dan, ed., *The Beginnings of Jewish Mysticism in Medieval Europe* (Jerusalem, 1987), pp. 1–14 (Hebrew).

Pines, "Points of Similarity"

Shlomo Pines, "Points of Similarity between the Doctrine of the Sefirot in the *Sefer Yetzirah* and a text from the Pseudo-Clementine Homilies: The Implications of This Resemblance," *Proceedings of the Israel Academy of Sciences and Humanities* 7, no. 3 (1989), pp. 63–142.

Rapoport-Albert, "God and the Zaddik"

Ada Rapoport-Albert, "God and the Zaddik as the Two Focal Points of Hasidic Worship," *History of Religions* 18 (1979), pp. 296–325.

Rawidowicz, "On Interpretation"

Simon Rawidowicz, "On Interpretation," *PAAJR* 26 (1957), pp. 83–126.

Les règles de interpretation

Les règles de interpretation, ed. Michel Tardieu (Le Cerf, Paris, 1987).

Ricoeur, *The Conflict of Interpretations* Paul Ricoeur, *The Conflict of Interpretations: Essays in Hermeneutics* (Northwestern University Press, Evanston, 1974).

Ricoeur, *Figuring the Sacred* Paul Ricoeur, *Figuring the Sacred: Religion, Narrative, and Imagination*, ed. Mark I. Wallace and trans. David Pellauer (Fortress Press, Minneapolis, 1995).

Ricoeur, *From Text to Action* Paul Ricoeur, *From Text to Action: Essays in Hermeneutics*, vol. 2, trans. K. Blamey and J. B. Thompson (Northwestern University Press, Evanston, Ill., 1991).

Ricoeur, *Hermeneutics and the Human Sciences* Paul Ricoeur, *Hermeneutics and the Human Sciences*, ed. and trans. John B. Thompson (Cambridge University Press, Cambridge, 1982).

Rider, "Receiving Orpheus" Jeff Rider, "Receiving Orpheus in the Middle Ages: Allegorization, Re-mythification and Sir Orfeo," *Papers on Language and Literature* 24, no. 4 (1988), pp. 343–366.

Rojtman, *Black Fire on White Fire* Betty Rojtman, *Black Fire on White Fire: An Essay on Jewish Hermeneutics, from Midrash to Kabbalah*, trans. S. Randall (University of California Press, Berkeley and Los Angeles, 1998).

Rosman, *Founder of Hasidism* Moshe Rosman, *Founder of Hasidism: A Quest for the Historical Ba'al Shem Tov* (University of California Press, Berkeley and Los Angeles, 1996).

Ruderman, *Kabbalah, Magic, and Science* David Ruderman, *Kabbalah, Magic, and Science: The Cultural Universe of a Sixteenth-Century Jewish Physician* (Harvard University Press, Cambridge, Mass., 1988).

Sack, *Be-Sha'arei ha-Qabbalah* Bracha Sack, *Be-Sha'arei ha-Qabbalah shel Rabbi Moshe Qordovero* (Ben-Gurion University, Beer Sheva, 1995) (Hebrew).

Schaefer, *Hekhalot-Studien* Peter Schaefer, *Hekhalot Studien* (J. C. B. Mohr, Tübingen, 1988).

Schaefer, *Synopse* Peter Schaefer, *Synopse zur Hekhalot-*

	Literatur (J. C. B. Mohr, Tübingen, 1981).
Schatz Uffenheimer, *Hasidism as Mysticism*	Rivka Schatz Uffenheimer, *Hasidism as Mysticism: Quietistic Elements in Eighteenth Century Hasidic Thought*, trans. Jonathan Chipman (Princeton University Press, Princeton, 1993).
Scholem, *Devarim be-Go*	Gershom Scholem, *Devarim be-Go* ('Am 'Oved, Tel Aviv, 1976) (Hebrew).
Scholem, *Jewish Gnosticism*	Gershom Scholem, *Jewish Gnosticism: Merkabah Mysticism and Talmudic Tradition* (Jewish Theological Seminary of America, New York, 1960).
Scholem, *Kabbalah*	Gershom Scholem, *Kabbalah* (Keter Printing House, Jerusalem, 1974).
Scholem, " 'The Maggid' "	Gershom Scholem, " 'The Maggid' of Joseph Taitachek and the Revelations Attributed to Him," *Sefunot* 11 (1971–1978), pp. 69–112 (Hebrew).
Scholem, *Major Trends*	Gershom Scholem, *Major Trends in Jewish Mysticism* (Schocken Books, New York, 1967).
Scholem, *The Messianic Idea*	Gershom Scholem, *The Messianic Idea in Judaism* (Schocken Books, New York, 1972).
Scholem, *The Mystical Shape*	Gershom Scholem, *The Mystical Shape of the Godhead* (Schocken Books, New York, 1991).
Scholem, "The Name of God"	Gershom Scholem, "The Name of God and the Linguistic of the Kabbala," *Diogenes* 79 (1972), pp. 59–80, 164–194.
Scholem, *On Jews and Judaism*	Gershom Scholem, *On Jews and Judaism in Crisis*, Werner J. Dannhauser, ed. (Schocken Books, New York, 1976).
Scholem, *On the Kabbalah*	Gershom Scholem, *On the Kabbalah and Its Symbolism* (Schocken Books, New York, 1969).
Scholem, *Origins of the Kabbalah*	Gershom Scholem, *Origins of the Kabbalah*, ed. R. J. Zwi Werblowski and trans. Allan Arkush (Jewish Publica-

tion Society, Philadelphia, and Princeton University Press, Princeton, 1987).

Scholem, *Researches in Sabbateanism* — Gershom Scholem, *Researches in Sabbateanism*, ed. Yehuda Liebes (Mossad Bialik, Tel Aviv, 1991) (Hebrew).

Scholem, *Sabbatai Sevi* — Gershom Scholem, *Sabbatai Sevi, the Mystical Messiah*, trans. R. J. Z. Werblowsky (Princeton University Press, Princeton, 1973).

Secrecy and Concealment — *Secrecy and Concealment: Studies in the History of Mediterranean and Near Eastern Religions*, eds. Hans G. Kippenberg and Guy Stroumsa (Brill, Leiden, 1995).

Silman, *The Voice Heard at Sinai* — Yochanan David Silman, *The Voice Heard at Sinai: Once or Ongoing?* (Magnes Press, Jerusalem, 1999) (Hebrew).

Smalley, *The Bible in the Middle Ages* — Beryl Smalley, *The Study of the Bible in the Middle Ages*, 3rd ed. (Blackwell, Oxford, 1984).

Smith, *Imagining Religion* — Jonathan Smith, *Imagining Religion* (University of Chicago Press, Chicago, 1982).

Smith, *Clement of Alexandria* — Morton Smith, *Clement of Alexandria and a Secret Gospel of Mark* (Harvard University Press, Cambridge, Mass., 1973).

Steiner, *After Babel* — George Steiner, *After Babel: Aspects of Language and Translation* (Oxford University Press, London, Oxford, New York, 1975).

Stern, *Midrash and Theory* — David Stern, *Midrash and Theory: Ancient Jewish Exegesis and Contemporary Literary Studies* (Northwestern University Press, Evanston, Ill., 1996).

Stock, *The Implications of Literacy* — Brian Stock, *The Implications of Literacy: Written Language and Models of Interpretation in the Eleventh and Twelfth Centuries* (Princeton University Press, Princeton, 1983).

Stroumsa, *Savoir et Salut* — Gedaliahu Guy Stroumsa, *Savoir et Salut* (Le Cerf, Paris, 1992).

Swartz, *Scholastic Magic* — Michael Swartz, *Scholastic Magic: Ritual and Revelation in Early Jewish Mysticism*

	(Princeton University Press, Princeton, 1996).
Talmage, "Apples of Gold,"	Frank Talmage, "Apples of Gold: The Inner Meaning of Sacred Texts in Medieval Judaism," in Arthur Green, ed., *Jewish Spirituality* (Crossroad, New York, 1986), 1:313–355.
Textual Strategies	*Textual Strategies: Perspectives in Post-Structuralist Criticism*, ed. Josue V. Harari (Cornell University Press, Ithaca, N.Y., 1979).
Tishby, *Paths of Faith and Heresy*	Isaiah Tishby, *Paths of Faith and Heresy* (Massada, Ramat Gan, 1964) (Hebrew).
Tishby, *Studies in Kabbalah*	Isaiah Tishby, *Studies in Kabbalah and Its Branches*, 3 vols. (Magnes Press, Jerusalem, 1982–1992) (Hebrew).
Tishby, *The Wisdom of the Zohar*	Isaiah Tishby, *The Wisdom of the Zohar: An Anthology of Texts*, trans. D. Goldstein, 3 vols. (Littman Library, London, Washington, 1991).
Trachtenberg, *Jewish Magic and Superstition*	Joshua Trachtenberg, *Jewish Magic and Superstition: A Study in Folk Religion* (Atheneum, New York, 1970).
Urbach, *The Sages*	Ephraim E. Urbach, *The Sages: Their Concepts and Beliefs*, trans. I. Abrahams, 2 vols. (Magnes Press, Jerusalem, 1979).
Vajda, "Un chapître"	Georges Vajda, "Un chapître de l'histoire du conflit entre la Kabbalah et la philosophie: La polemique anti-intellectualiste de Joseph ben Shalom Ashkenazi de Catalogne," *Archives d'histoire doctrinale et littéraire du Moyen Age* 23 (1956), pp. 45–127.
Vajda, *Le commentaire*	Georges Vajda, *Le commentaire d'Ezra de Gerone sur le Cantique des Cantiques* (Aubier, Montaigne, Paris, 1969).
van der Heide, "Pardes"	A. van der Heide, "Pardes: Methodological Reflections on the Theory of Four Senses," *JJS* 34 (1983), pp. 147–159.

Vanhoozer, Biblical Narrative — Kevin J. Vanhoozer, Biblical Narrative in the Philosophy of Paul Ricoeur: A Study in Hermeneutics and Theology (Cambridge University Press, Cambridge, 1990).

Vickers, "Analogy versus Identity" — Brian Vickers, "Analogy versus Identity: The Rejection of Occult Symbolism, 1580–1680," in B. Vickers, ed., Occult and Scientific Mentalities in the Renaissance (Cambridge University Press, Cambridge, 1986), pp. 95–163.

Weinsheimer, Gadamer's Hermeneutics — Joel C. Weinsheimer, Gadamer's Hermeneutics: A Reading of Truth and Method (Yale University Press, New Haven, 1985).

Weiss, Studies — Joseph Weiss, Studies in Eastern European Jewish Mysticism, ed. David Goldstein (Oxford University Press, Oxford, 1985).

Weiss, Studies in Braslav Hassidism — Joseph Weiss, Studies in Braslav Hassidism, ed. Mendel Piekarz (Jerusalem, 1974) (Hebrew).

Weiss Halivni, Midrash — D. Weiss Halivni, Midrash, Mishnah and Gemara (Harvard University Press, Cambridge, Mass., 1986).

Weiss Halivni, Revelation Restored — David Weiss Halivni, Revelation Restored: Divine Writ and Critical Response (Westview Press, Boulder, Colo., 1997).

Winston, Logos — David Winston, Logos and Mystical Theology in Philo of Alexandria (Hebrew Union College Press, Cincinnati, 1985).

Winston, Philo of Alexandria — David Winston, trans., Philo of Alexandria (Paulist Press, New York, 1981).

Wirszubski, Pico della Mirandola — Chaim Wirszubski, Pico della Mirandola's Encounter with Jewish Mysticism (Harvard University Press, Cambridge, Mass., and Israel Academy of Sciences and Humanities, Jerusalem, 1987).

Wolfson, Abraham Abulafia — Elliot R. Wolfson, Abraham Abulafia—Kabbalist and Prophet: Hermeneutics, Theosophy, and Theurgy (Cherub Press, Los Angeles, 2000).

Wolfson, *Along the Path*

Elliot R. Wolfson, *Along the Path* (SUNY Press, Albany, 1995).

Wolfson, "Beautiful Maiden,"

Elliot R. Wolfson, "Beautiful Maiden without Eyes: Peshat and Sod in Zoharic Hermeneutics," in Michael Fishbane, ed., *Midrashic Imagination* (SUNY Press, Albany, 1993), pp. 155–203.

Wolfson, "By Way of Truth"

Elliot R. Wolfson, "By Way of Truth: Aspects of Nahmanides' Kabbalistic Hermeneutic," AJSR 14 no. 2 (1989), pp. 103–178.

Wolfson, "From Sealed Book"

Elliot R. Wolfson, "From Sealed Book to Open Text: Time, Memory, and Narrativity in Kabbalistic Hermeneutics," in Steven Kepnes, ed., *Interpreting Judaism in a Postmodern Age* (New York University Press, New York, 1996), pp. 145–178.

Wolfson, "Letter Symbolism"

Elliot R. Wolfson, "Letter Symbolism and Merkavah Imagery in the Zohar," in M. Hallamish, ed. ʿAlei Shefer, pp. 195–236.

Wolfson, "The Mystical Significance"

Elliot R. Wolfson, "The Mystical Significance of Torah Study in German Pietism," JQR 84 (1993), pp. 43–78.

Wolfson, *Through a Speculum That Shines*

Elliot R. Wolfson, *Through a Speculum That Shines: Vision and Imagination in Medieval Jewish Mysticism* (Princeton University Press, Princeton, 1994).

Wolfson, *Philo*

Harry A. Wolfson, *Philo: Foundation of Religious Philosophy* (Harvard University Press, Cambridge, Mass., 1982).

INDEX